Cakewalk© SONAR™
User's Guide

Information in this document is subject to change without notice and does not represent a commitment on the part of Twelve Tone Systems, Inc. The software described in this document is furnished under a license agreement or nondisclosure agreement. The software may be used or copied only in accordance of the terms of the agreement. It is against the law to copy this software on any medium except as specifically allowed in the agreement. No part of this document may be reproduced or transmitted in any form or by any means, electronic or mechanical, including photocopying and recording, for any purpose without the express written permission of Twelve Tone Systems, Inc.

Copyright © 2004 Twelve Tone Systems, Inc. All rights reserved.

Program Copyright © 2004 Twelve Tone Systems, Inc. All rights reserved.

ACID is a trademark of Sonic Foundry, Inc.

Cakewalk is a registered trademark of Twelve Tone Systems, Inc. SONAR and the Cakewalk logo are trademarks of Twelve Tone Systems, Inc. Other company and product names are trademarks of their respective owners.

Visit Cakewalk on the World Wide Web at www.cakewalk.com.

Table of Contents

Preface xix
   About This Book xix
   Registering SONAR Today xix
   Conventions Used in this Book xx
   Getting Help xx

1 Introduction 21
   About SONAR 22
      Music Composition and Exploration 22
      Remixing 22
      Game Sound Development 22
      Sound Production and Engineering 22
      Web Authoring 23
      Film and Video Scoring and Production 23
      Flexibility 23
   Computers, Sound, and Music 23
      MIDI 23
      Digital Audio 24
   Installation and Setup 25
      Installing SONAR 26
   Starting SONAR 27
   SONAR Basics 31
      SONAR File Types 32
      Opening a File 33
      Views 33
      Working on a Project 44
   Windows Taskbar Indicators 45
   Screen Colors and Wallpaper 45
   Starting to Use SONAR 46

2 Tutorials 47

Tutorial 1—The Basics 48
Opening a Project File 48
Setting Outputs 48
Playing the Project 50
Restarting the Project Automatically 52
Changing the Tempo 54
Muting and Soloing Tracks 56
Changing a Track's Instrument 58
Playing Music on a Keyboard 59

Tutorial 2—Recording MIDI 61
Creating a New Project 61
Recording a MIDI Track 61
Saving Your Work 64
Loop Recording 65
Punch-In Recording 66

Tutorial 3—Recording Digital Audio 68
Setting the Sampling Rate 69
Setting the Audio Driver Bit Depth 69
Setting the File Bit Depth 70
Open a New Project 70
Setting Up an Audio Track 70
Checking the Input Levels 70
Recording Digital Audio 71
Listening to the Recording 72
Recording Another Take 72
Input Monitoring 72
Loop and Punch-In Recording 73
Recording Multiple Channels 73

Tutorial 4—Editing MIDI 74
Transposing 74
Copying Clips with Drag and Drop 75
Editing Notes in the Piano Roll View 75
Slip Editing 77
Drawing MIDI Envelopes 78
Converting MIDI to Audio 79

Tutorial 5—Editing Audio 81
Opening the Project 81
Importing a Wave File 81
Moving and Looping the Clips 82
Slip Editing a Clip 83
Automatic Crossfades 83
Bouncing Tracks 84

Tutorial 6—Using Groove Clips 85
    Adding Groove Clips to a Project 86
    Looping Groove Clips 87
    Changing the Pitch of Groove Clips 89
    Changing the Tempo of Your Project 90
    Creating Your Own Groove Clips 91

Tutorial 7—Mixing 95
    Adding Real-time Audio Effects 95
    Automating an Individual Effect's Settings 96
    Grouping Controls 97
    Automating Your Mix 97
    Exporting an MP3 File 98

Tutorial 8—Using Soft Synths 100
    Inserting Cakewalk TTS-1 into a Project 101
    Playing MIDI Tracks through a DXi 102
    Converting Your DXi Tracks to Audio 102

Tutorial 9—Drum Maps 104
    Create a New Project 104
    Creating a Drum Map 104
    Create a Drum Track 105
    Map Drum Notes to Different Outputs 106

Tutorial 10—Cyclone DXi 108
    Cyclone Overview 108
    Adding Files to a Pad Group 108
    Setting a Pad's Volume and Pan 109
    Playing Cyclone 110
    Editing Loops in the Loop Editor 111

3 Controlling Playback 113

The Now Time and How to Use It 114
    The Now Time Marker 116
    Displaying the Now Time in Large Print 117
    Other Ways to Set the Now Time 118
    The Time Ruler 119

Controlling Playback 120
    Handling Stuck Notes 121
    Looping 122

Track-by-Track Playback 124
    The Playback State Toolbar 125
    Silencing Tracks 125
    Soloing Tracks 126
    Inverting the Phase of a Track 126
    Changing Tracks' Mono/Stereo Status 127

v

Changing Track Settings 127
    Setting Up Output Devices 134
    Assigning Tracks to Outputs 136
    Choosing the Instrument Sound (Bank and Patch) 136
    Adding Effects 139
    Adjusting Volume and Pan 139
    Configurable Panning Laws 140
    Adjusting Volume Trim 140
    Assigning a MIDI Channel (Chn) 141
    Adjusting the Key/Transposing a Track (Key+) 141
    Adjusting the Note Velocity (Vel+) 142
    Adjusting the Time Alignment of a MIDI Track (Time+) 143
    Other MIDI Playback Settings 144
Controlling Live MIDI Playback—MIDI Echo 144
Local Control 147
Playing Files in Batch Mode 148
    The Play List View 148
Video Playback, Import, and Export 150
    Inserting and Playing Back Videos 151
    Exporting Video 153
    Optimizing Video Performance 154
    Using the Video Thumbnails Pane 154
Locating Missing Audio 157
    The Find Missing Audio File Dialog 157
    Restoring Missing Audio Files 157
    Managing Shared and External Files 158

4 Recording 161

Creating a New Project 162
    Using Per-Project Audio Folders 162
    Creating a New Project File 162
    Setting the Meter and Key Signatures 163
    Setting the Metronome and Tempo Settings 165
    Setting the Audio Sampling Rate and Bit Depth 168
    Setting the MIDI Timing Resolution 169
Preparing to Record 170
    Recording Modes 170
    Choosing an Input 171
    Arming Tracks for Recording 174
    Auto Arming 174
Recording Music from a MIDI Instrument 175
Recording Audio 175
    Tuning an Instrument 177

Confidence Recording	179
Input Monitoring	180
The Audio Engine Button	183
Loop Recording	184
Punch Recording	185
Step Recording	188
Step Pattern Recording	191
Recording Specific Ports and Channels	192
Input Filtering	194
Importing Music and Sound	195
Importing Audio Files	195
Importing Material from Another SONAR Project	196
Importing MIDI Files	197
Saving Your Work	198
Labeling Your Projects	199
File Statistics	201

5 Arranging 203

Arranging Tracks	204
Changing the Order of Tracks	205
Configuring the Display of Tracks in the Track View	207
Copying Tracks	208
Erasing Tracks	208
Arranging Clips	209
Displaying Clips	209
Using the Navigator View	213
Double-clicking Clips	213
Selecting Clips	214
Moving and Copying Clips	214
Nudge	218
Nudge Settings	218
Working with Partial Clips	220
Markers and the Snap Grid	221
Showing Gridlines	222
Defining and Using the Snap Grid	222
Snap Offsets	224
Creating and Using Markers	224
Working with Linked Clips	228
Splitting and Combining Clips	230
Take Management and Comping Takes	232

Clip Muting and Isolating (Clip Soloing) 234
    Clip Muting with the Default Style 235
    Clip Muting with the Alternate Style 236
    Audition (Selection Playback) 237
    Isolating (Clip Soloing) 237
Track Folders 238
Adding Effects in the Track View 240
Changing Tempos 241
    Using the Tempo Toolbar 242
    Using the Tempo Commands 244
    Using the Tempo View 246
Undo, Redo, and the Undo History 249

6 Using Loops 251

The Loop Construction View 252
    Loop Construction Controls 252
The Loop Explorer View 256
    Folders Pane 257
    Contents List Pane 258
Working with Loops 259
Working with Groove Clips 260
    How Groove Clips Work in SONAR 260
    Using Groove Clips 261
    Creating and Editing Groove Clips 262
    Editing Slices 265
    Saving Groove Clips as Wave Files/ACIDized Wave Files 266
    Using Pitch Markers in the Track View 266
MIDI Groove Clips 267
    Exporting, and Importing MIDI Groove Clips 269
Importing Project5 Patterns 271

7 Editing MIDI Events and Controllers 273

Event Inspector Toolbar 274
The Piano Roll View 275
    Note Map Pane 275
    Drum Grid Pane 276
    Note Pane 276
    Controllers Pane 276
    Track List Pane 276
    Opening the View 276
    Selecting and Editing Notes 277
    Working with Multiple Tracks in the Piano Roll View 282
    Note Names 283

Selecting and Editing Events 283
    Transposing 284
    Shifting Events in Time 285
    Inserting Time or Measures into a Project 285
    Stretching and Shrinking Events 288
    Reversing Notes in a Clip 290
    Adding Crescendos and Decrescendos 290
  Slip Editing MIDI (Non-destructive Editing) 291
    Slip Editing Modes 291
    Using Slip Editing for MIDI Clips 292
    Slip-editing Multiple MIDI Clips 293
  Changing the Timing of a Recording 294
    Quantizing 294
    Fit Improvisation 304
  Searching for Events 305
    Event Filters 306
  Controllers, RPNs, NRPNs, and Automation Data 311
    Using the Controllers Pane 313
  The Event List View 318
    Event List Buttons and Overview 319
    Selecting Events in the Event List View 321
    Event List Display Filter 322
    Editing Events and Event Parameters 322
    Additional Event Information 324
  MIDI Effects (MIDI Plug-ins) 325
    Presets 326
    Quantizing 327
    Adding Echo/Delay 328
    Filtering Events 329
    Adding Arpeggio 329
    Analyzing Chords 330
    Changing Velocities 331
    Transposing MIDI Notes 332

8 Drum Maps and the Drum Grid Pane 335

The Basics 336
Creating and Editing a Drum Map 336
  The Drum Map Manager 336
  Working in the Drum Map Manager 338
  The Map Properties Dialog 339
  Saving a Drum Map 339

Using Drum Maps 340
    Assigning a MIDI Track to a Drum Map 340
    Opening a Drum Map 340
    Displaying Tracks in the Drum Grid Pane 340
    Velocity Tails 341
    Editing Note Velocities 341
    Previewing a Mapped Sound 342
The Note Map Pane 342
    Changing Mapped-note Settings 343
The Drum Grid Pane 344
    Grid Lines 344
The Pattern Brush Tool 345
    How the Pattern Brush Tool Works 345
    Creating Custom Patterns 347

9 Editing Audio 349

Digital Audio Fundamentals 350
    Basic Acoustics 350
    Example—A Guitar String 350
    Waveforms 352
    Recording a Sound 354
    The Decibel Scale 355
    Audio Clips 356
    Managing Audio Data 356
Basic Audio Editing 357
    Editing Clip Properties 358
    Moving, Copying, Pasting and Deleting Audio Clips 359
    Audio Scaling 359
    Splitting Audio Clips 363
    Bouncing to Clips 364
    Scrubbing 365
Basic Audio Processing 365
    Increasing or Decreasing Volume 366
    Reversing Audio Data 368
    Equalizing Audio Data 368
Advanced Audio Processing 369
    Removing Silence 369
    Extracting Timing 371
    Parametric Equalization 374
Slip-editing Audio (Non-destructive Editing) 375
    Slip-editing Modes 376
    Using Slip-editing 376
    Slip-editing Multiple Audio Clips 379

Fades and Crossfades 380
    Using Fades and Crossfades in Real Time 380
    Applying Fades and Crossfades Offline 384
Audio Effects (Audio Plug-ins) 386
    Applying Audio Effects 387
    Mixing Audio Effects 388
    Adding Parametric Equalization 389
    Adding Chorus 390
    Applying Delay 391
    Adding Flanging 393
    Applying Reverb 394
    Shifting Pitch 395
    Stretching Time and Pitch 395

10 Working with Software Synthesizer 399

Kinds of Soft Synths 400
Synth Rack View 400
DX Instruments (DXi's) 401
    Multi-port DXi's 402
    Inserting a DXi 402
    Opening a DXi's Property Page 404
    Playing a DXi 405
    Muting and Soloing DXi Tracks 407
    Converting Your DXi Tracks to Audio 407
    Automating a DXi's Controls 408
ReWire Instruments 410
    Inserting a ReWire Instrument 412
    Mixing Down ReWire Instruments 414
    Automating ReWire Instruments 414
    ReWire Troubleshooting Guide 414
Stand-alone Synths 415
    Playing a Stand-alone Synth 415
    Recording a Stand-alone Synth 416
Using VST Synths and Plug-ins 417

11 Mixing and Effects Patching 419

Preparing to Mix 420
    Configuring the Console and Track Views 424
Mixing MIDI 428
    Mixing a MIDI Track 428
    Converting MIDI to Audio 429

xi

Routing and Mixing Digital Audio 430
    Audio Tracks 432
    Stereo Buses 434
    Surround Buses (Producer Edition Only) 435
    Main Outs 436
Metering 436
    What the Meters Measure 437
    Hiding and Showing Meters 437
    Changing the Meters' Display 438
    Changing the Meters' Performance 440
Freeze Tracks and Synths 441
Using Real-Time Effects 444
    Effects Parameters 445
    How to Use Real-Time Effects 445
    Using the Per-track EQ (Producer Edition Only) 446
    Applying Audio Effects 447
    Applying MIDI Effects 448
Using Control Groups 449
Using Remote Control 454
    Using the Learn Option 456
Bouncing Tracks 456
    Preparing to Create an Audio CD 459
Preparing Audio for Distribution 459
    Dithering 468

12 Surround Mixing 471

Surround Basics 472
Configuring SONAR for Surround Mixing 473
    Using Surround Format Templates 473
    Choosing a Surround Format 475
    Surround Buses 476
    Routing in Surround 477
    Downmixing 478
Panning in Surround 479
    Controlling Surround Panning 480
    Automating Surround Panning 485
Joystick Support 485
Surround Metering 486
Bass Management 487

Surround Effects 488
    The SurroundBridge 488
    Effect Property Pages 488
    Effect Presets 489
    How to Patch and Configure Surround Effects 489
Importing Surround Mixes 491
Exporting Surround Mixes 492

13 Using Automation 493

Quick Automation Guide 494
The Automation Toolbar 495
Automation Methods 495
    Recording Individual Fader or Knob Movements 496
    Drawing Audio Envelopes in the Track View 497
    Drawing MIDI Envelopes in the Track View 499
    Dotted Lines 501
    Drawing Envelopes on Clips 501
    Showing or Hiding Envelopes 502
    Deleting Envelopes 502
    Copying and Pasting Envelopes 503
    Resetting Envelopes and Nodes to Current or Neutral Values ... 504
    Envelope Mode and Offset Mode 504
    Snapshots 506
Automating Effects 507
    Automating Individual Effects Parameters 508
    Recording Groups of Faders and/or Knobs 509
    Recording Automation Data from an External Controller 510
Reassigning Envelopes 510
The Envelope Editing and Node Editing Menus 511
    Automated Muting 512

14 Layouts, Templates and Key Bindings 513

Layouts 514
    Floating Views and Dual Monitor Support 517
Templates 517
    Template Example: Three MIDI Instruments 519
Key Bindings 520
    Importing Key Bindings 523
    Exporting Key Bindings 523

15 Working with Notation and Lyrics 525

The Staff View 526
- Opening the Staff View 527
- Staff Pane Layout 527
- The Staff Pane Right-Click Menu 528
- The Fretboard 529
- Fretboard Popup Menu 530

Basic Musical Editing 531
- Inserting Notes on the Staff 531
- Inserting Notes with the Fretboard 532
- Selecting Notes 533
- Moving, Copying, and Deleting Notes on the Staff 533
- Moving Notes from within the Fretboard 534
- Auditioning 535
- Changing Note Properties 536
- Deglitch Dialog 537
- Working with Triplets 538
- Beaming of Rests 538
- Changing the Way Notes Are Displayed 539
- Using Enharmonic Spellings 541
- MIDI Channels and the Fretboard 542

Chords and Marks 543
- Adding Chord Symbols 543
- Adding Expression Marks 547
- Adding Hairpin Symbols 548
- Adding Pedal Marks 549

Tablature 550
- Tablature Settings 550
- Changing Fretboard Texture and Orientation .552
- Quick TAB 552
- Regenerate TAB 553
- Entering Notes from the TAB Staff 553
- Single Note Editing from the TAB Staff 554
- Editing Chords or Groups of Notes from the TAB Staff 554
- Editing Notes and Chords from the Fretboard .555

Working with Percussion 556
- Setting Up a Percussion Track 556
- Setting Up a Percussion Staff or Line 557
- Ghost Strokes 559

Printing 559

The Meter/Key View 560
- What Is Meter? 560
- What Is Key? 561

Opening the Meter/Key View	561
Adding and Editing Meter/Key Changes	562
Music Notation for Non-concert-key Instruments	563
Working with Lyrics	565
Adding and Editing Lyrics in the Staff View	565
Opening the Lyrics View	566
Adding and Editing Lyrics in the Lyrics View	567

16 Using Instrument Definitions ... 569

Assigning Instruments	570
Importing Instrument Definitions	572
Creating Instrument Definitions	573
Creating and Editing Patch Name and Other Lists	576
Copying Name Lists	577
Assigning the Bank Select Method	577
Assigning Patch Names	578
Assigning Note Names	580
Assigning Controller, RPN, and NRPN Names	581
Instrument Definition Tutorial	582
Why Use Instrument Definitions?	583
What Can They Do and Not Do?	583
Where Do Instrument Definitions Come From?	583
Start of Tutorial	583

17 Using System Exclusive Data ... 587

What Is System Exclusive?	588
Sysx Events	588
Using the System Exclusive View	588
Sending Sysx Banks at Startup	589
Importing, Creating, and Dumping Sysx Banks	590
More about Dump Request Macros	592
Editing Sysx Banks	593
Sysx View Buttons	593
Send	593
Send All	593
Receive	593
Clear Bank	594
Name	594
Auto	594
Output	594
Edit Bytes	594
Load Bank and Save Bank	594

Transmitting Banks During Playback 595
Real-time Recording of System Exclusive Messages 596
Sysx Echo 596
Sysx .INI File Settings 597
Troubleshooting 598

18 Synchronizing Your Gear 601

Synchronization Overview 602
Choosing Clock Sources When SONAR is the Master 603
MIDI Synchronization 604
    SONAR as the Slave 605
    SONAR as the Master 606
    Using MIDI Sync with Drum Machines 607
    Troubleshooting MIDI Sync 608
SMPTE/MIDI Time Code Synchronization 608
    Playing Digital Audio under SMPTE/MTC Sync 612
    SMPTE/MTC Sync and Full Chase Lock 613
    Troubleshooting SMPTE/MTC Sync 614
MIDI Machine Control (MMC) 615

19 Audio File Management 617

The Project Files Dialog 618
Project Files and Bundle Files 619
Audio Folders 620
    Global Audio Folders 620
    Per-project Audio Folders 621
    Imported Audio Files 623
Backing Up Projects with Digital Audio 624
Deleting Unused Audio Files 625

20 Improving Audio Performance 627

System Configuration 628
    The Wave Profiler 628
    Enabling and Disabling Audio Devices 630
    Configuring SONAR for 18 bit-, 20-bit, and 24-bit Operation 630
    Converting Sample Rates and Bit Depths 632

Improving Performance with Digital Audio 634
    Getting the Most Out of Your PC 635
    Mixing Latency 637
    WDM vs. MME Drivers 638
    ASIO Drivers 638
    Queue Buffers 638
    Status Bar/CPU Meter/Disk Meter 639

Appendix A: Troubleshooting 641

When I Play a File, I Don't Hear Anything 641
I Can't Record from My MIDI Instrument 643
When I Play a File Containing Audio, the Audio Portion Doesn't
Play 644
I Can't Record Any Audio 645
My Track or Bus Fader is Maximized, But There's No
Sound or Level 645
The Music Is Playing Back with the Wrong Instrument Sounds 646
How Do I Use SONAR to Access All the Sounds on My
MIDI Instrument? 646
My Keyboard Doubles Every Note I Play 647
I Don't See the Clips Pane in the Track View 647
Why Can't SONAR Find My Audio Files? 648
I Get an a Error Message When I Change a Project to 24-bit Audio . . 648
Bouncing Tracks Takes a Long Time 648
Why Do I Get Errors from the Wave Profiler? 649
I Hear an Echo When I Record 649
Audio Distorts at Greater than 16 Bits 650
No Sound from My DXi 650
My Pro Audio 9 Files Sound Louder/Softer When I Open
Them in SONAR 651
I Can't Open My Project 651
SONAR Can't Find the Wavetable Synth or MPU401 652

Appendix B: Hardware Setup 653

Connect Your MIDI Equipment 653
Set Up to Record Digital Audio 656

Appendix C: Cyclone 661

Overview 661
    Cyclone DXi Toolbar 662
    Pad Groups 662
    Pad Inspector 663
    Loop Bin 665
    Loop View and Key Map View 665
    Pad Editor 666
    Slice Inspector 666
Using Cyclone DXi 667
    Controlling Individual Pads—Volume, Pan, Mute, Solo, Sync,
    Looping, and Content 670
    Mixing Down Cyclone DXi 671
    Loop Editing 671
    Keyboard Shortcuts in Cyclone DXi 672
    Undo and Redo 672

Appendix D: New Features in SONAR 4 673

Surround Mixing 673
SurroundBridge (Surround Effects Linker) 673
Track Folders 673
Slip-editing Multiple Clips 673
Freeze Synths or Tracks 674
Loop Construction View Enhancements 674
Audio Metronome 674
Clip Muting and Isolating (Clip Soloing) 674
Video Thumbnails 674
Enhanced Key Bindings 674
Enhanced Import/Export/Bounce Features 675
Navigator Pane in the Track View 675
Take Management and Comping Takes 675
Audition (Selection Playback) 675
Nudge 675
Configurable Panning Laws 675
Joystick Support 676
PoW-r Dither 676
Meter Ballistics 676
Surround Plug-ins 676
Cakewalk TTS-1 676

Preface

The *SONAR User's Guide* is designed to help you learn and use SONAR. This *Guide* explains how SONAR works and how to use it to create, edit, produce, and perform. The *SONAR User's Guide* is task-oriented, with lots of cross-references, so that you can find the information you need. The *User's Guide* also includes a comprehensive index that you can use to find information on any specific topic.

About This Book

The SONAR *User's Guide* is organized as follows:

Chapter 1, *Introduction,* provides an overview of SONAR, installation instructions and basic equipment setup options.

Chapter 2, *Getting Started,* contains tutorials that cover many of the features of SONAR.

The remaining chapters cover all the basic and advanced skills you need to use SONAR to play, record, edit, arrange, and mix your projects.

The appendices contain additional information you can use for troubleshooting, setting up SONAR for use with audio hardware, and SONAR's new features.

Registering SONAR Today

Please be sure to register your product on our Web site (**www.cakewalk.com**). If you do not register, we cannot provide you with technical support, or inform you when free updates and upgrades become available. By registering with Cakewalk, you also become eligible for discounts on other great software products.

You can also register by phone. Call toll-free at **888-Cakewalk** (617-423-9004 outside the U.S.).

Conventions Used in this Book

The following table describes the text conventions in this book:

Convention...	Meaning...
Bold Italics	Text that appears in bold italics is a command in SONAR.
hyphen (***File-Open***)	A hyphen represents a level in the menu hierarchy. For example, ***File-Open*** means to click on the File menu and select the Open command.
SMALL CAPS	Small caps are used for file extensions (.MID) and file names (AUD.INI).

Getting Help

In addition to this *User's Guide*, SONAR includes online help that can provide you with quick reference information whenever you need it. Simply press F1 or click the Help button in any dialog box to find the information you need. If you are new to recording and editing music on your PC, see the online help topic "Beginner's Guide to Cakewalk Software" for an introduction.

If you need more information than you can find in the *User's Guide* or the online help, here are two great places to look:

- Check the Support page of our Web site (www.cakewalk.com) for updated technical information and answers to frequently asked questions.

- Post messages to the SONAR user community using one of the Cakewalk newsgroups. For more information about the newsgroups, visit www.cakewalk.com.

You can also get technical support directly from Cakewalk. In order to obtain technical support, you must register your product. You can obtain technical support for this product in the following ways:

- Visit http://www.cakewalk.com/Support/SONAR/SR4.asp.

- Call Cakewalk Technical Support at (617) 423-9021 on weekdays, 10:00 AM to 6:00 PM, Eastern time. Be sure to have your serial number ready when you call.

Technical support hours, policies, and procedures are subject to change at any time. Check our Web site for the latest support information.

Introduction

SONAR is a professional tool for authoring sound and music on your personal computer. It's designed for musicians, composers, arrangers, audio and production engineers, multimedia and game developers, and recording engineers. SONAR supports Wave, MP3, ACIDized waves, WMA, AIFF and other popular formats, providing all the tools you need to do professional-quality work rapidly and efficiently.

SONAR is more than an integrated MIDI and digital audio authoring software package—it's an expandable platform that can function as the central nervous system of your recording studio. With drivers for common high-end audio hardware, full support for DirectX and VST audio plug-ins, DXi software synthesizers, MFX MIDI plug-ins, and MIDI Machine Control (MMC) of external MIDI gear, SONAR can handle your most demanding projects.

In This Chapter

About SONAR *22*
Computers, Sound, and Music. *23*
Installation and Setup *25*
Starting SONAR. *27*
SONAR Basics. *31*
Windows Taskbar Indicators *45*
Screen Colors and Wallpaper *45*
Starting to Use SONAR *46*

About SONAR

SONAR is the flagship product of the Cakewalk line of integrated MIDI and digital audio sequencers for the Windows platform. SONAR has a comprehensive feature set that makes it the single most productive tool for sound and music authoring. Here are some of the ways you can use SONAR.

Music Composition and Exploration

SONAR is a powerful music-composition application, providing tools to record your own musical performances; enhance or improve the quality of those performances; and edit, arrange, and experiment with the music. With a few simple clicks of the mouse, you can arrange, orchestrate, and audition your composition. Fully integrated sequencing allows you to combine the convenience and flexibility of MIDI composition with the high-quality sound and subtlety of digital audio sound recording and reproduction. Change the feel of a piece by locking it to a musical groove, or add delicate delays, anticipations, or echoes that add richness to the music.

SONAR displays and lets you edit your music using standard musical notation and guitar tablature, so you can adjust individual notes, add performance markings, and print individual parts or full scores. You can graphically draw tempo and volume changes, or add lyrics to display on-screen or to include with printed scores.

Remixing

SONAR's Groove clips allow you to import, create, export and edit loops, making it possible to quickly change tempos and keys for an entire project. The Loop Explorer view lets you preview loops in the project's tempo and key before dragging and dropping them onto a track.

Game Sound Development

There's no better tool than SONAR for composing music for electronic games. Clip-based sequencing lets you create and reuse musical themes freely, so you can associate musical sections with game characters, locations, objects, and actions. Your creations can be saved and replayed using the compact MIDI file format, which adapts its sound automatically to the target hardware for the best possible sound reproduction.

Sound Production and Engineering

If you want to produce music CDs or master tapes, SONAR has virtually everything you need from recording to mixing and mastering. Multichannel recording lets you capture studio or live performances track by track. Reconfigurable buses provide full control over your mix. Real-time stereo effects like chorus, flange, reverb, parametric EQ, and delay/echo can be applied as track inserts, in effects loops, or to the master mix. SONAR supports 44.1 KHz sampling for CD-quality sound and lets you choose from lower or higher sample rates as well. All audio effects are 32-bit floating point for faster processing and high-quality sound reproduction.

Web Authoring
SONAR is the ideal tool for developing and producing music and sound for the World Wide Web, because it lets you save your work in the formats that are most commonly used on web sites: MIDI, RealAudio, MP3, and Windows Media Advanced Streaming Format. Any SONAR project—musical composition, audio clip, commercial spot, jingle with voice-over—can be stored in a web-compatible format with a few simple mouse clicks.

Film and Video Scoring and Production
SONAR has many of the tools you need to execute audio post-production projects quickly and efficiently. SONAR provides chase lock sync to time code for frame-by-frame accuracy when synchronizing audio or MIDI to film or video. Or, you can turn chase lock off to conserve CPU power. SONAR provides high-quality time stretching and sample-accurate editing with zero-crossing detection so you can make the fine adjustments you need in record time. In addition, SONAR's support for video files gives you convenient synchronized access to digitized video, making film and video scoring easier than ever.

Flexibility
SONAR works the way you want to work—you can customize screen layouts, toolbars, and audio and MIDI system configurations to make your work more efficient. SONAR integrates with other sound editing tools so you can access them in an instant without leaving SONAR.

Computers, Sound, and Music

This section provides some background on the different ways that computers store and play sound and music. Computers work with sound and music in two different forms: **MIDI** and **digital audio**.

MIDI
MIDI (short for Musical Instrument Digital Interface) is the way computers communicate with most sound cards, keyboards, and other electronic instruments. MIDI refers to both the type of cables and plugs used to connect the computers and instruments, and to the language those computers and instruments use to talk to each other. The MIDI standard is accepted and used worldwide. Almost any electronic instrument you buy today will have MIDI connectors and can be used with other MIDI instruments and with your computer's MIDI interface.

The MIDI language conveys information and instructions, both from the computer to the instrument and from the instrument to the computer. For example, if your computer wants your keyboard to play a note, it sends a MIDI "Note On" message and tells the keyboard which note to play. When your computer wants the keyboard to stop playing that note, it sends another message that stops the note from playing.

The MIDI language has many other instructions, such as messages to change the sound that is used to play the notes (the bank and patch), messages used to work the sustain pedal and the pitch-bend wheel, and others. By sending the right messages at the right times, your computer can control your electronic instrument and make it play music.

MIDI information can be sent on 16 different channels. You can set up your MIDI equipment to listen for messages on all channels or on only a few.

MIDI files contain all the MIDI messages and timing information that are needed to play a song. MIDI files can be read and played by many different programs, including SONAR, and can even be played by programs on other types of computers. MIDI files have the extension .MID.

There are several important advantages of the MIDI format:

- Large amounts of music can be stored in a very compact form
- Different parts of a piece can easily be assigned to any instrument you can imagine
- The music contains information on notes, tempos, and key signatures that makes it possible to display and edit the piece using standard musical notation

The primary disadvantage of MIDI is that the quality of the music a listener hears will vary depending on the MIDI equipment the listener is using. For example, MIDI usually sounds much better on an expensive synthesizer than it does on an inexpensive sound card.

Digital Audio

Digital audio is a simple way to record and play sounds of any type. It works like a tape recorder—you record something, then later play it back. Digital audio stores the sound as a long series of numbers.

Sound Waves

Sound waves are vibrations in the air. Sound waves are generated by anything that vibrates; a vibrating object causes the air next to it to vibrate, and the vibration is passed through the air in all directions. When the vibrating air enters your ear, it makes your eardrum vibrate, and you hear a sound. Likewise, if the vibrating air hits a microphone, it causes the microphone to vibrate and send electrical signals to whatever it's connected to.

These vibrations are very fast. The slowest vibration frequency you can hear is about 20 vibrations per second, and the fastest is around 16,000 to 20,000 vibrations per second.

Recording Digital Audio

To record digital audio, your computer monitors the electrical signal generated by a microphone, an electric guitar, or another source. At equal intervals of time (for CD-quality sound, this means 44,100 times a second), the computer measures and saves the strength of the electrical signal from the microphone, on a scale from 0 to 65,535.

That's it. Digital audio data is just a long series of numbers. The computer sends these numbers, in the form of electrical signals, to a speaker. The speaker then vibrates and generates the same sound that was recorded.

The primary advantage of digital audio is the quality of the sound. Unlike MIDI, a digital audio recording is very rich, capturing all the nuances, overtones, and other characteristics of the sound exactly as performed. The main drawback of digital audio is that it takes up a lot of disk space. To record a 1-minute segment of stereo, CD-quality digital audio, you need about 10 megabytes of disk space.

On the PC, digital audio is usually stored in Wave files (extension .wav). There are many programs available that let you create, play, and edit these files. SONAR reads, writes, and lets you edit Wave files.

More information about digital audio can be found in Chapter 9, *Editing Audio*.

Installation and Setup

You can install SONAR on any computer that runs Windows 2000 or XP and has a sound card or built-in sound module. If you want to hook up other devices, like a MIDI keyboard, an electric guitar, or a microphone, you need the right cables, and you need to find the right connectors on your computer.

Before you install SONAR, take a minute to register the software so we can let you know when updates become available and provide you with technical support. To register your copy of SONAR, fill in the registration card in your product package and mail it back to us. Or, register at our Web site: www.cakewalk.com.

To connect a MIDI keyboard to your computer, you need standard MIDI cables or a MIDI adapter cable, such as the one available in Cakewalk's *PC Music Pack*. One end of the adapter cable should have two 5-pin DIN connectors that connect to your keyboard or other MIDI device. At the other end, you need a 15-pin connector to connect to a sound card through its MIDI/joystick port.

If you have a dedicated MIDI interface, lots of electronic music gear, or work with many different music software packages, see *Appendix B: Hardware Setup*.

Before you attach or detach any cables from your computer, you should shut down your computer and turn off the power to all your equipment. This greatly reduces the chance of electrical damage to your equipment while plugging and unplugging cables.

To Connect a MIDI Keyboard to Your Computer

1. One of the 5-pin connectors on the MIDI cable is labeled Out. Plug this connector into the MIDI In jack on your electronic keyboard.

2. The other 5-pin connector on the MIDI cable is labeled In. Plug this connector into the MIDI Out jack on your electronic keyboard.

3. If you are using a MIDI adaptor cable, plug the 15-pin connector on the MIDI cable into the MIDI/joystick port on your sound card. If you have a joystick, unplug it, plug in the MIDI cable, and plug the joystick into the pass-through connector on the MIDI cable.

   Or

   If you are using standard MIDI cables, plug the cable connected to the MIDI Out on your MIDI instrument into the MIDI In of your sound card or MIDI interface. Plug the cable connected to the MIDI In on your MIDI instrument into the MIDI Out of your sound card or MIDI interface.

To Connect an Electric Guitar to Your Computer

1. Plug your 1/4" mono guitar cable into a 1/8" stereo adapter.

2. Plug the 1/8" adapter into the microphone input or line input jack on your computer sound card.

To Connect a Microphone to Your Computer

1. If your microphone does not have a 1/8" mono or stereo plug, plug the microphone into a 1/8" adapter.

2. Plug the 1/8" adapter into the microphone input jack on your computer sound card.

That's it! Now that your instruments are all set to go, you can restart your computer and turn on your keyboard, guitar, and microphone.

Installing SONAR

SONAR is easy to install. All you need to do is choose the folder where the program and sample project files should be stored. Before you start, make sure you have your serial number handy. Your serial number is located on the back of your CD case.

Installation note: If you choose to not install the Sample files, you will not have the necessary content to use the tutorials in Chapter 2.

To Install SONAR

1. Start your computer.
2. Close any open programs you have running.
3. Place the SONAR CD-ROM in your CD-ROM drive.

    If you have autorun enabled, the SONAR AutoRun menu opens automatically, showing you a dialog box with several buttons. If autorun is not enabled, you can open the SONAR AutoRun menu by selecting **Start-Run** and entering d:\AutoRun.exe (where d:\ is your CD-ROM drive).

4. Click the Install SONAR button.

Note:

If you exit Setup without completing the installation, choose **Start-Run**, type D:\AutoRun.exe (where D:\ is your CD-ROM drive), and click OK. This will reopen the AutoRun window, and you can click Install SONAR to start installation again.

5. Follow the installation instructions on the screen.

    You can also install SONAR by choosing **Start-Run** and running the application named SETUP.EXE from the CD.

Uninstalling SONAR 4

When you installed SONAR, the setup program placed an Uninstall icon in the Start menu. To uninstall SONAR, click the Start button and choose *Programs-Cakewalk-SONAR 4 (Studio Edition* or *Producer Edition)-Uninstall SONAR 4 (Studio Edition* or *Producer Edition)*.

Starting SONAR

There are many different ways to start SONAR. Here are a few:

- Click on the SONAR icon on your desktop.

- Click on the Start button, and choose *Programs-Cakewalk-SONAR 4 (Studio Edition* or *Producer Edition)-SONAR 4 (Studio Edition* or *Producer Edition)*.

- Click the Start button, point to Documents, and choose a SONAR project from the menu.

- Double-click the SONAR program or any SONAR document from the Windows Explorer or the Find menu.

When you start SONAR, you see the Quick Start dialog box.

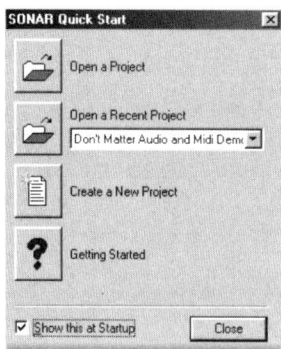

The Quick Start dialog box has several options:

Option...	How to use it...
Open a Project	Choose a project from the Open File dialog box to open it
Open a Recent Project	Select a project from the list, and click this button to open it
Create a New Project	Click here to create a new project.
Getting Started	Click here to view the Getting Started topic in the help file. This topic has links to a glossary of terms, as well as some basic procedures.

If you don't want to see the Quick Start dialog box in the future, uncheck the box at the bottom of the dialog box, and click Close. You can see the Quick Start dialog box later by choosing ***Help-Quick Start***.

Migrating Preferences

If you have a previous version of Cakewalk installed, SONAR will detect it and give you the option of migrating certain preferences from a single earlier version.

When you choose to migrate preferences, SONAR migrates the following settings from an earlier Cakewalk version:

Setting...	Description
Global Options	Settings in the Global Options dialog. Open by selecting **Options-Global**.
Key Bindings	Your customized key bindings for controlling SONAR using your MIDI keyboard or computer keyboard.
Instrument Definitions	Files used to control specific MIDI instruments. See Chapter 16, *Using Instrument Definitions*.
Audio data directory (WaveData folder) and Picture Cache directory locations	SONAR uses the Data directory and Picture Cache directories from the previous Cakewalk version for storing project wave files and their waveform image files.

Running Wave Profiler

The first time you start SONAR, it automatically runs the Wave Profiler utility. Wave Profiler determines the proper MIDI and Audio timings for your sound card and writes them to a file that SONAR refers to when using the card. Wave Profiler does not change the sound card's DMA, IRQ, or port address settings.

Wave Profiler detects the make and model of your sound card, which determine the card's audio characteristics. If Wave Profiler finds a card that has a WDM driver, it only profiles that card. If you want to use more than one sound card at a time, and they don't both have WDM drivers, you must force the one with the WDM driver to use that driver as an older, MME driver. It is not necessary to run the Wave Profiler for a sound card using an ASIO driver. For more information about Wave Profiler, WDM, and MME, see "The Wave Profiler" on page 628. When Wave Profiler determines the kind of card you have, always accept the default settings.

Note:

You can run the Wave Profiler again at a later time (for example, if you install a new sound card or driver) by choosing the **Options-Audio** General tab command and clicking Wave Profiler.

Setting Up the MIDI In and MIDI Out Devices

When you start SONAR for the first time, it checks your computer to find all the MIDI input and output devices you have installed (such as sound cards and MIDI interfaces). However, sometimes you need to tell SONAR exactly which devices you want it to use. If you're not getting sound from your sound card or MIDI keyboard, or if you just want to change the MIDI outputs and devices that you are using, follow the steps in this section.

Choose **Options-MIDI Devices** to open a dialog box in which you select the MIDI In and MIDI Out devices that SONAR will use. Each item in the list is a MIDI Input or MIDI Output from drivers installed using the Windows Control Panel.

1. Select **Options-MIDI Devices**. You will see the MIDI Devices dialog box, which lets you choose instruments on MIDI inputs and outputs.

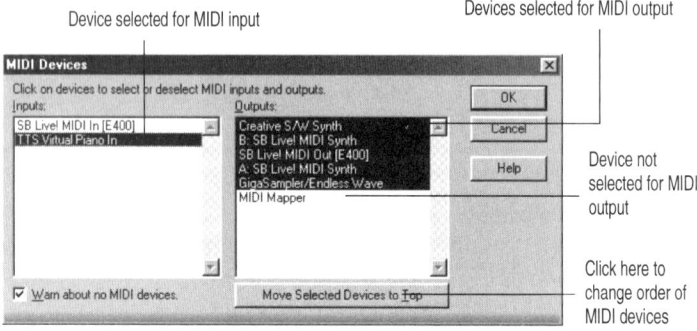

2. Look at the left window. Notice that it shows devices on MIDI Inputs; make sure that all devices in this window are highlighted. If a device isn't highlighted, click on it once to select it for MIDI Input.

3. Look at the window on the right. Notice that it shows devices on MIDI Outputs. SONAR numbers its MIDI Outputs by the order of the devices in this window. The device on top is on Output 1, the one below it is on Output 2, and so on.

4. Highlight one device at a time in the Outputs window and click Move Selected Devices to Top to change its order. Then highlight all the devices that appear in the window to select them for output.

Tip!

Be sure to choose MIDI output devices from **Options-MIDI Devices**. If you don't do this, you won't hear any of your MIDI instruments when you play songs in SONAR.

Using MIDI Devices After Making Driver Changes

If you later add or remove drivers using the Drivers icon of the Windows Control Panel, SONAR reacts in the following way:

- If you remove a Control Panel driver, SONAR will not use the device it belongs to the next time you run the program. Any other devices you had selected using the ***Options-MIDI Devices*** command will remain selected.

- If you add a driver through the Control Panel, SONAR does *not* automatically use it. You must use the ***Options-MIDI Devices*** command to enable the new driver in SONAR's list.

Note:

After you add or remove a driver with the Drivers icon in the Windows Control Panel, you must restart Windows for the change to take effect.

Defining Your MIDI Instrument or Sound Card

Once you have selected your MIDI Input and Output devices, SONAR, by default, plays back MIDI sequences using a General MIDI instrument definition. If you are using a synthesizer or sound card that does not adhere to the General MIDI standard, you may want to define that instrument. For information about instrument definitions, see Chapter 16, *Using Instrument Definitions*.

SONAR Basics

SONAR's **menus** and **toolbars** give you quick access to all the features of SONAR. Some menu choices and tools display **dialog boxes** that let you choose among various options, or type in the values you want. If you click in most views, in time rulers, or on certain other items with the right mouse button, you see a popup menu that provides quick access to many common operations.

The **project** is the center of your work in SONAR. If you're a musician, a project might contain a song, a jingle, or a movement of a symphony. If you're a post-production engineer, a project might contain a 30-second radio commercial or a lengthy soundtrack for a film or videotape production. By default, every project is stored in a file (known as a **project file**). The normal file extension for a SONAR work file is .CWP.

SONAR organizes the sound and music in your project into tracks, clips, and events.

Tracks are used to store the sound or music made by each instrument or voice in a project. For example, a song that is arranged for four instruments and one vocalist may have 5 tracks—one for each instrument and one for the vocals. Each project can have an unlimited number of tracks. Some of these tracks may be used in your finished project, while others can hold alternate takes, backup tracks, and variations that you might want to keep for future use. Each track can be made up of one or many clips.

Clips are the pieces of sound and music that make up your tracks. A clip might contain a horn solo, a drum break, a bass or guitar riff, a voice-over, a sound effect like the hoot of an owl, or an entire keyboard performance. A track can contain a single clip or dozens of different clips, and you can easily move clips from one track to another.

Groove clips are audio clips which have tempo and pitch information embedded within them, allowing them to follow changes to the project tempo or project pitch. You can click on either edge of a Groove clip and drag out repetitions in the track.

Events are MIDI data (in MIDI tracks) or automation data.

SONAR File Types

Projects in SONAR can be saved as a project file with the extension .CWP or as a Bundle file with the extension .CWB.

For a complete description of the differences between project files and bundle files, see "Project Files and Bundle Files" on page 619.

Other Types of Files

SONAR lets you create and work with several other types of files, in addition to project (.CWP) and bundle (.CWB) files that store your projects:

File type...	Description...
MIDI files (extension .MID)	Standard MIDI files.
Template files (extension .TPL)	Templates for new files you create
StudioWare (extension .CAKEWALKSTUDIOWARE)	To control external MIDI devices from SONAR
OMF (extension .OMF)	Open Media Framework format files.

Opening a File

Use the following procedure to open a file.

To Open a File in SONAR

1. If you haven't already done so, start SONAR.

2. Choose *File-Open*.

3. In the Open dialog box, navigate to the directory where the project you want to open is located and select it.

4. Click the Open button.

5. If you are opening an OMF file, the Unpack OMF dialog appears. Set the initial tempo and specify the directory where you want to save the file and its audio. For more information about opening OMF files, see Unpack OMF dialog in the online help.

SONAR loads the project.

Views

SONAR displays your project in windows on the screen that are known as views. You can have many views open at once, all showing the same project. When you edit a project in one view, the other related views are updated automatically.

The Track View

The **Track view** is the main window that you use to create, display, and work with a project. When you open a project file, SONAR displays the Track view for the project. When you close the Track view for a project, SONAR closes the file.

The Track view is divided into several sections: toolbars (at the top), the **Navigator pane**, the **Video Thumbnails pane** (Producer Edition only), the **Track pane,** the **Track/Bus Inspector,** the **Clips pane,** and the **Bus pane**. You can change the size of the panes by dragging the vertical or horizontal splitter bars that separate them.

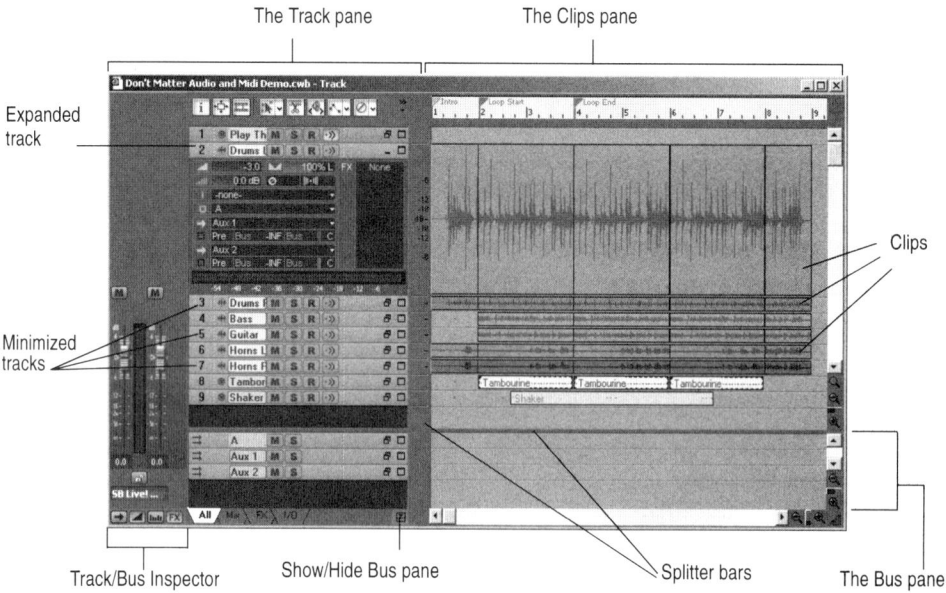

All of the current track's controls, plus a few that are only available in the Console view, are contained in the **Track/Bus Inspector** which is an expanded version of the current track's controls located on the far left side of the Track view. You can hide or show the Track/Bus Inspector by pressing *i* on your keyboard (see "Track/Bus Inspector" on page 35, for more information).

The Track pane lets you see and change the initial settings for each track. By default, the current track is displayed in gold. To change the current track, move the highlight using the mouse or the keyboard as follows:

Key...	What it does...
Left/Right Arrow	Moves the highlight to the next or previous control.
Up/Down Arrow	Moves to the same control in the adjacent track, or the next track of the same type if the control only applies to a specific track type (for example, the Patch control only applies to MIDI tracks).
Page Down	Displays the next page of tracks.

Page Up	Displays the previous page of tracks.
Home	Moves the focus to the first track.
End	Moves the focus to the last track.

The current track's controls are contained in the **Track/Bus Inspector**.

The Clips pane shows the clips in your project on a horizontal timeline called the Time Ruler that helps you visualize how your project is organized. Clips contain markings that indicate their contents. The Clips pane lets you select, move, cut and copy clips from place to place to change the arrangement of music and sound in your project.

The Bus pane shows the buses in the project. The Show/Hide Bus pane button 🗔 allows you to show or hide the Bus pane at the bottom of the Track view.

The Navigator pane displays a large part of your project so you can see an overview of your song. The Navigator pane displays all of your project's tracks.

The Track view makes it easy to select tracks, clips, and ranges of time in a project. These are the most common selection methods:

To...	Do this...
Select tracks	Click on the track number, or drag over several track numbers
Select clips	Click on the clip, or drag a rectangle around several clips
Select time ranges	Drag in the Time Ruler, or click between two markers
Select partial clips	Hold down the Alt key while dragging over a clip

As with most other Windows programs, you can also use the Shift-click and Ctrl-click combinations when selecting tracks and clips. Holding the Shift key while you click adds tracks or clips to the current selection. Holding the Ctrl key while you click lets you toggle the selection status of tracks or clips.

Track/Bus Inspector
The Track/Bus Inspector makes it easy to adjust the current track's (or bus's) controls, because it's a greatly expanded version of the current track's controls that is located on the left side of the Track pane. You can hide or show any one or all of the controls in the Track/Bus Inspector by clicking the four buttons at the bottom of the Track/Bus Inspector.

The following graphic shows most of the Track/Bus Inspector's controls (there may not be room to display all of a track's controls on the Track/Bus Inspector, depending on the resolution of your monitor):

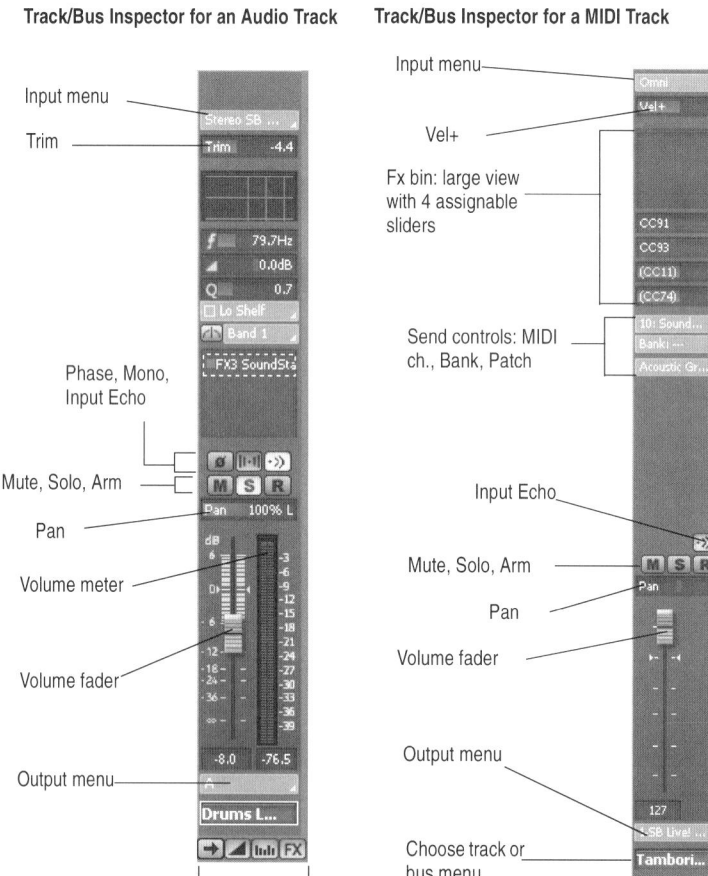

You can hide or show any of the Track/Bus Inspector's controls, and use it to display the controls from any track or bus. The following table shows you how:

To do this...	Do this...
Hide or show the Track/Bus Inspector	Press *i* on your keyboard.
Display a certain track's or bus's controls in the Track/Bus Inspector	Click the track or bus to make it current, or choose the track or bus in the track/bus dropdown menu that's at the bottom of the Track/Bus Inspector.
Hide or show any of the Track/Bus Inspector's controls	Click any of the four buttons at the bottom of the Track Inspector (these are 3-position buttons, except for the Volume button): • Send button ➡—when yellow, displays send controls for audio tracks and busses; and channel, bank, and patch controls for MIDI tracks. When blue, shows as many sends as possible. • Volume button ▲—hides or shows the volume fader in MIDI tracks, audio tracks, and busses. • EQ button —in audio tracks and busses shows the built-in EQ controls. When yellow, shows band 1; when blue, shows all 4 bands. In MIDI tracks it has no function. • FX button FX—when yellow, shows the FX bin in audio tracks and busses. When blue, also shows the first 4 parameters of the selected effect (if it's an automatable effect). In MIDI tracks, shows the FX bin when yellow. When blue, shows sliders for 4 assignable MIDI continuous controllers. **Note**: you can not display a MIDI track's Time + or Key + controls in the Track/Bus Inspector.
Reassign MIDI controller sliders in a MIDI Track's Fx bin	Right-click the slider you want to reassign and choose **Reassign Control** from the popup menu, choose the new parameter, and click OK.
Display the parameters of a different automatable effect	Click the name of the effect you want to select.
Assign a control to a group, arm it for automation, take an automation snapshot, or set up remote control	Right-click the control and choose options from the popup menu.

Narrow the Track Inspector	Right-click a blank area and choose **Narrow Strip** from the popup menu.
Bypass the FX bin	Right-click the FX bin and choose **Bypass Bin** from the popup menu.

The Console View

The **Console view** is where you can mix the sounds on all the different tracks to create the final mix of your project. While the Track view provides most of the same controls, you may want to use the more familiar interface of the Console view for mixing.

You use the Console view to adjust the levels of sound for the different tracks in your project, to change the stereo panning, and to apply real-time effects to an individual track, combinations of tracks, or the final mix.

The Console view contains several groups of controls. There is one module for each track in your project, and one module for each bus. You can use bus sends to direct certain tracks to special modules that are known as **buses**.

The Console View:

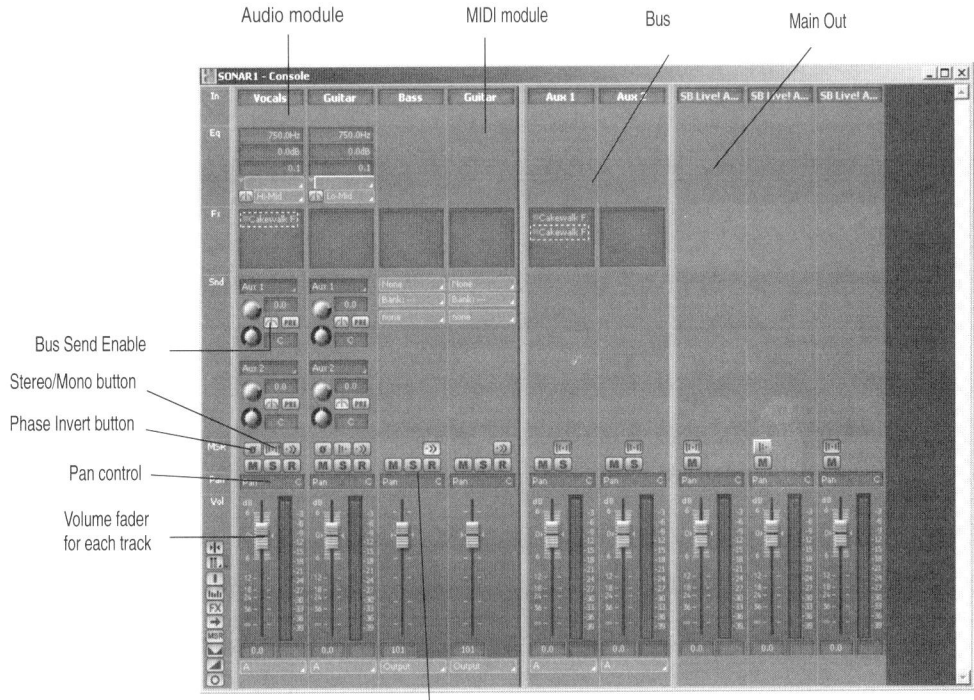

As in the Track view, you can change track settings or record new music or sound in the Console view. You may choose to use one view or the other, or the choice you make may depend on which project you are working on.

Other Views

SONAR has a number of other views you can use to display and work on your project. To display these views, select one or more tracks, by Ctrl-clicking their track numbers and:

- Click the icon for the view in the Views toolbar

    OR

- Choose the view you want from the *View* menu

The **Piano Roll view** : shows the notes from a MIDI track or tracks as they would appear on a player-piano roll. You can move the notes around, make them longer or shorter, and change their pitches by just dragging them with the mouse.

You can also use the Piano Roll view to display and edit MIDI velocity, controllers, and other types of information. The Piano Roll view also contains the Drum Editor, which allows you to "paint" drum patterns using the Pattern Brush tool and play different drum modules from a single track.

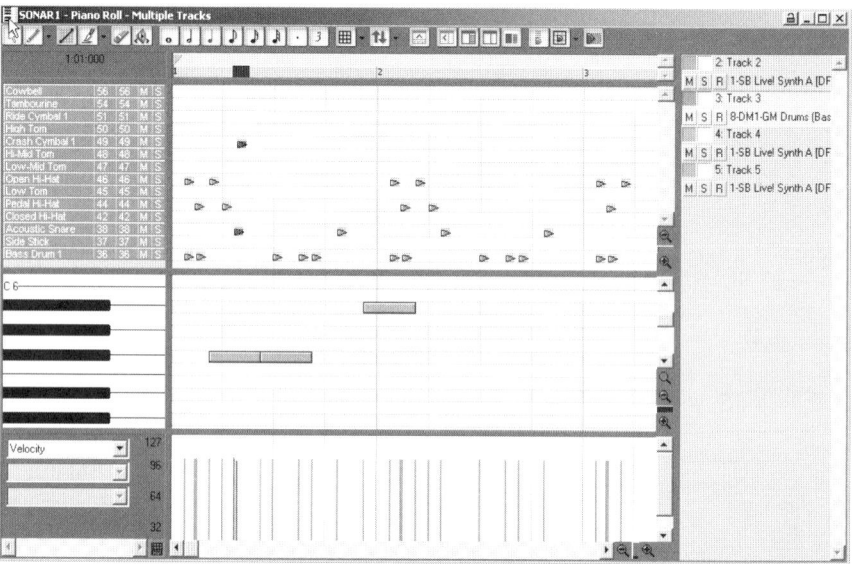

The **Staff view** 🗉: displays the notes from one or more MIDI tracks using standard music notation, similar to the way the notation would appear on a printed page. You can add, edit, or delete notes; create percussion parts; add guitar chords and other notation markings; display guitar tablature; display the Fretboard pane; and print whole scores or individual parts to share with other musicians.

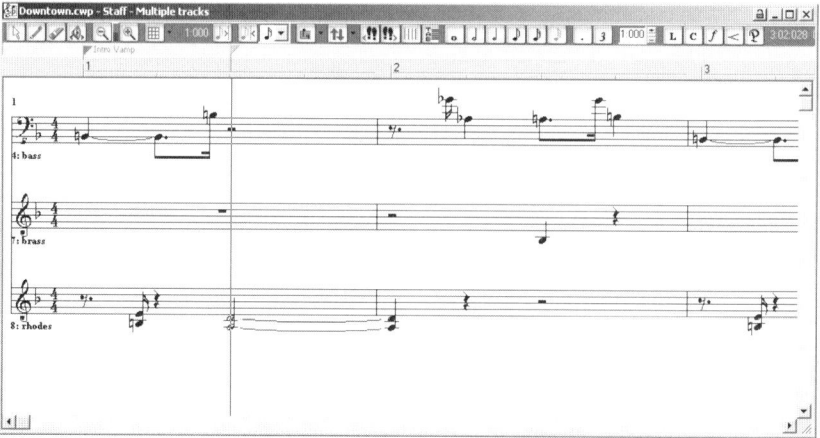

The **Loop Construction view** 🔧: allows you to create and edit Groove clips (SONAR loops that "know" the tempo and key in which they were recorded), and export these clips as ACIDized files.

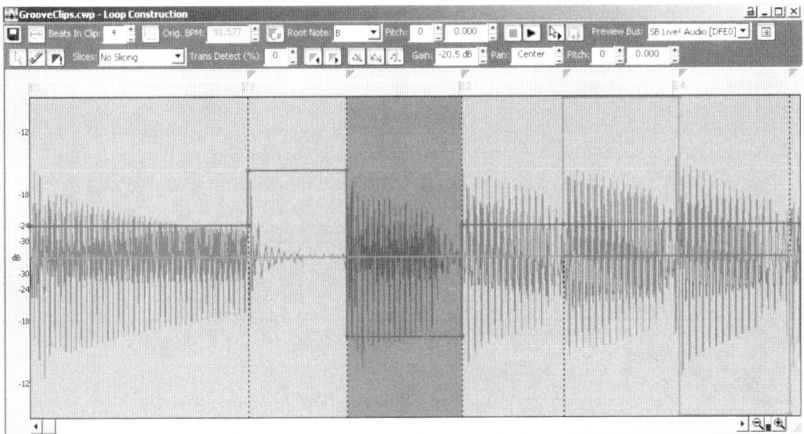

The **Loop Explorer view** 🔍: allows you to preview ACIDized files and other Wave files; and drag and drop them into your project.

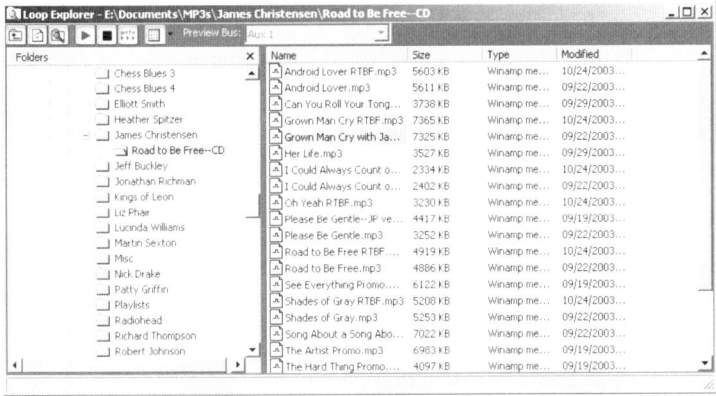

The **Event List view** 📋: displays the events in a project individually, so that you can make changes at a very detailed level.

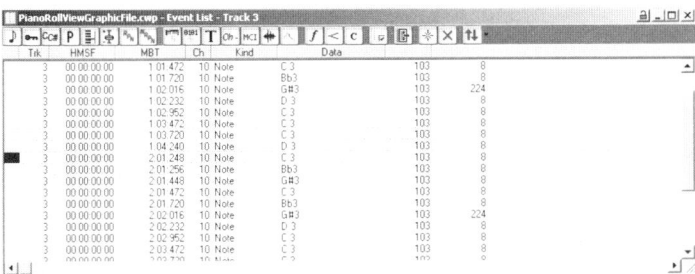

41

SONAR has several other views that are used for very specific purposes:

View...	How you use it...
Meter/Key	To change the meter (time signature) or key signature, or to insert changes in the meter or key signature at specific times in a project.
Big Time	To display the Now time in a large, resizable font that you can read more easily.
Markers	To add, move, rename, or delete labels for parts of your project that make it easier to move from one point to another.
Lyrics	To add and display lyrics for a track.
Video	To display a loaded video file.
Sysx	To create, display, store, and edit System Exclusive MIDI messages used to control instruments and other gear that are MIDI capable.
Tempo	To view and edit the project's tempo changes.

Zoom Controls

Many of the views contain Zoom tools that let you change the horizontal and vertical scale of the view:

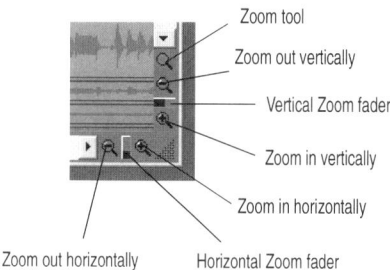

The zoom tools are used as described in the following table:

Tool...	How you use it...
Zoom out	Click to zoom out incrementally, or press Shift and click to zoom all the way out

Zoom in	Click to zoom in incrementally, or press Shift and click to zoom all the way in
Zoom fader	Click and drag to zoom continuously
Zoom tool	Click to arm, then click and drag in the view to select the zoom area

The Zoom tool is automatically disarmed after use. Double-click the Zoom tool to make the selection stick. You can also zoom with the keyboard:

Key...	What it does...
Ctrl+up arrow	Zoom out vertically
Ctrl+down arrow	Zoom in vertically
Ctrl+right arrow	Zoom in horizontally
Ctrl+left arrow	Zoom out horizontally
G	Go to (center) the Now time, without zooming
Z	Arm the Zoom tool
U	Undo the current zoom
F	Fit tracks to window
A	Show all tracks
Shift+F	Fit project to window
Shift+Double Click a clip	Maximize track height

Locking Views

By default SONAR allows only one instance of each view, but you can lock the contents of most views, preserving the current view by forcing a new instance of the view to appear if necessary. Locking views is the only way you can have multiple instances of the same view open. Only the Track and Console views cannot be locked.

To lock a view, just click the lock button at the top right of the view. An unlocked view looks like this, and a locked view looks like this. A view can be locked automatically by pressing the Ctrl key when opening the view.

43

Floating Views

When a view is float enabled, you can move it outside of the confines of SONAR. This is particularly useful if you take advantage of SONAR's dual monitor support. Using **dual monitor support**, you can keep the Track or Console view on one monitor and "float" other views to the other monitor by dragging them to the second screen.

For more information, see "Floating Views and Dual Monitor Support" on page 517.

Layouts

You may spend a lot of time making sure that all the views are laid out on the screen just the way you want. When you save your work, you can save the screen layout along with it. You can also save the layout by itself and then use the layout with other projects. See "Layouts" on page 514

Working on a Project

Much of your time in SONAR is spent recording and listening to your project as it develops. The Transport toolbar, shown below, contains the most important tools and other pieces of information you'll need to record and play back your project.

Every project has a current time, known as the **Now time**. As you record or play back a project, the Now time shows your current location in the project. When you create a project, the Now time is set to the beginning of the project. The current Now time is saved with your project.

You control recording and playback using tools on the Transport toolbar, which work a lot like the ones on your tape deck or CD player:

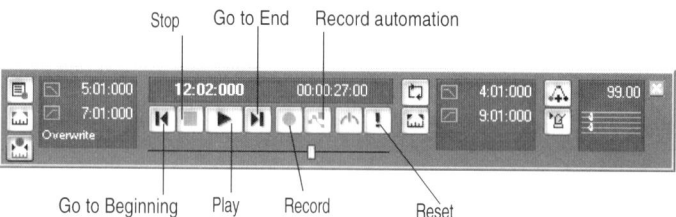

As you work with a project, you can use SONAR's mute and solo features to choose which tracks are played, or you can create loops to play a particular section over and over again. You can also create **markers**, which are named time points you add to your project to make it easy to jump to a particular location.

Windows Taskbar Indicators

When SONAR is running, you'll normally see two indicators in your Windows Taskbar, right next to the clock.

The MIDI activity monitor contains two lights that indicate MIDI input and output. When you play your MIDI keyboard, the first light flashes when each note is pressed, and it flashes again when each note is released. When you play back a project that contains MIDI, the second indicator lights up.

The volume control is used to control the playback and record volumes on your sound card. Double-click on this indicator to open a dialog box that lets you control the levels for audio, MIDI, CD playback, and record.

The volume control is available only if your sound card is using a native Windows driver. If your sound card does not use a native Windows driver, no volume control will be displayed in the taskbar. In this case, your sound card probably came with a separate program to control input and output levels. See your sound card documentation for more information.

Screen Colors and Wallpaper

SONAR lets you customize the colors that are used for virtually all parts of the program using the ***Options-Colors*** command. This command also lets you change the background bitmap that is displayed in the SONAR window.

For any SONAR screen element, you can assign a color in two ways:

- Choose one of the colors that is part of your Windows color scheme.
- Assign a custom color.

To Assign Custom Colors
1. Choose ***Options-Colors*** to display the Colors dialog box.
2. Choose the screen element whose color you want to change from the Screen Element list.
3. Assign a color to the screen element in one of two ways:
    - To use a color from the Windows color scheme, choose one of the options in the Follow System Color list
    - To use a custom color, check Use Specific Color, click the Choose Color button, and select the color you want
4. To save these changes from session to session, check the Save Changes for Next Session box.
5. Click OK when you are done.

SONAR uses the colors you have chosen.

To Restore the Default Colors

1. Choose *Options-Colors* to display the Colors dialog box.

2. Click the Defaults button.

3. Click OK.

SONAR uses the default colors for all screen elements.

To Change the Wallpaper

1. Choose *Options-Colors* to display the Colors dialog box.

2. Choose the desired wallpaper according to the table:

To do this...	Do this...
Use the default wallpaper	Check Default in the Wallpaper list
Not use any wallpaper	Check None in the Wallpaper list
Use a custom bitmap	Check Custom, choose a bitmap, and click Open

3. Click OK when you are done.

Starting to Use SONAR

This chapter has provided you with an overview of SONAR and basic information on how to install the software and configure your system. To get started with SONAR, you can try the tutorials in Chapter 2. When you're finished with the tutorials, move on to Chapter 3 to learn the details of how you can use SONAR to create your projects.

2 Tutorials

Now that you've learned some of the basics, it's time to put that knowledge to work. These tutorials will give you some hands-on practice in playing, recording, and mixing your projects. If you want to learn more about any topic, you'll find references to the appropriate part of the *User's Guide*.

Note:
If, during installation, you chose in the Select Components dialog not to install the Tutorials folder (part of the Sample files), you will not have access to the sample tutorial files needed to follow the tutorials in Chapter 2, *Tutorials*. If you didn't install these files, insert your product CD and copy the files to your hard drive.

In This Chapter

Tutorial 1—The Basics	48
Tutorial 2—Recording MIDI	61
Tutorial 3—Recording Digital Audio	68
Tutorial 4—Editing MIDI	74
Tutorial 5—Editing Audio	81
Tutorial 6—Using Groove Clips	85
Tutorial 7—Mixing	95
Tutorial 8—Using Soft Synths	100
Tutorial 9—Drum Maps	104
Tutorial 10—Cyclone DXi	108

Tutorial 1—The Basics

The first tutorial teaches you the basics of SONAR. You'll learn how to:

- Open and play a project file
- Make the project repeat automatically
- Use markers
- Speed or slow the tempo
- Mute a track and play a track solo
- Change a track's instrument
- Play a track on a MIDI instrument

If you have not already done so, please read Chapter 1, *Introduction,* for basic background information about projects, tracks, clips, the Track view, and the Console view.

Opening a Project File

As you learned in Chapter 1, SONAR stores MIDI and digital audio data in **project files**. The first thing you need to do is load a project file.

To Open a Project File

1. If you haven't already done so, start SONAR.
2. Choose *File-Open*.
3. In the Open dialog box, navigate to the directory in which you installed SONAR, double-click the Tutorials folder to open it and select the file TUTORIAL1.CWP.
4. Click the Open button.

SONAR loads the project and opens the Track view. Feel free to move and resize the Track view to better fit your screen.

Setting Outputs

Before you can play a project, you must set the outputs for both MIDI sounds and audio sounds. By setting the outputs, you are telling SONAR from which outputs you want to hear the sounds. You may have a sound card with just one output or several sound cards, each with several outputs. These sound cards may contain their own synthesizers, which SONAR sees as MIDI outputs. Also, if you have a separate MIDI interface connected to your computer, it has one or more MIDI outputs.

Before we assign a track to an output, let's make sure the outputs we want to use are available.

To Enable MIDI Outputs

1. Select *Options-MIDI Devices* from the menu to open the MIDI Devices dialog box.

2. In the MIDI Devices dialog in the Outputs field, arrange the outputs by doing the following:

To do this...	Do this...
Enable or disable a device	Click on it—an enabled device appears highlighted; a disabled device does not appear highlighted.
Move a device to the top of the list	Highlight it, temporarily deselect all other highlighted devices, and click the Move Selected Devices to Top button.

3. Click OK.

Note: If you have a large number of MIDI outputs enabled, you may occasionally get MIDI transmission errors or an out-of-memory message. You can try either deselecting some outputs, or lowering the number of Sysx buffers by using the *Options-Global* command to open the Global Options dialog box: on the MIDI tab, lower the value in the Number of Buffers field to 16.

To Enable Audio Outputs

1. Select *Options-Audio* from the menu.

   The Audio Options dialog box appears.

2. Click on the Drivers tab in the Audio Options dialog box.

3. In the Output Drivers field, select the drivers you want enabled. All enabled drivers appear highlighted.

4. Click OK.

To Set MIDI Outputs for Your Project's Tracks

1. In the Track view, click the Output dropdown menu in a track. You may need to enlarge the track to show the Output control: In Track 1, click the Restore Strip Size button to expand the track. Also, you may have to click the All tab control that's at the bottom of the Track pane to display all the controls in the track.

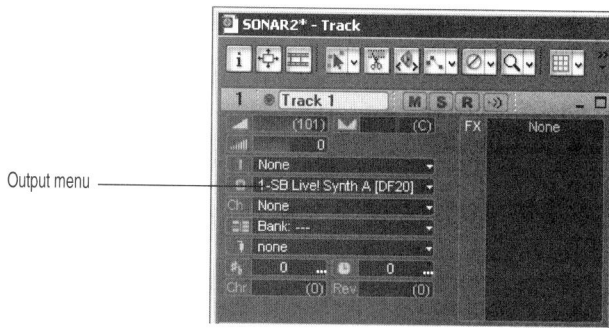

Output menu

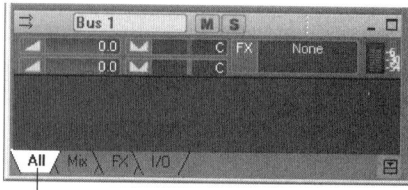

All tab control—click this to display all the track controls. Click the other tabs to display smaller groups of controls.

A popup menu appears, containing a list of enabled MIDI outputs.

2. Select the output you want to use for that track.

3. Press the down arrow on your computer keyboard to move to the Output field for the next track and choose an output.

4. Repeat step 3 for each track.

Let's play the project!

Playing the Project

Buttons in the Large Transport toolbar, shown in the following picture, can control most of SONAR's basic playback functions.

If you don't see the Large Transport toolbar, then choose **View-Toolbars** and check **Transport (Large)**.

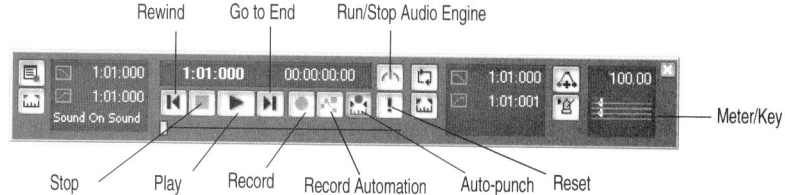

To Start Playback
- To play the project, click the Play button ▶, or press the Spacebar.

Do you hear music? If you don't hear anything, see the online help topic called Troubleshooting for some troubleshooting tips.

To Restart the Project
When SONAR gets to the end of the project, it stops. To play the project again, do the following:

1. Click the Rewind button ⏮, or press *w* to go back to the first measure.
2. Click the Play button, or press the Spacebar.

To Pause Playback
- To temporarily pause playback, click the Play button ▶ or the Stop button ■, or press the Spacebar. Click the Play button ▶ again to resume playback.

Certain SONAR functions can only be used when the project is paused. If a function or command does not seem to work, try pausing the project.

The Now Time
The **Now time** is the current time in the project. In the Clips pane of the Track view, the Now time is indicated by a vertical line. The Now time is also shown in the Transport toolbar, both in MBT (measure/beat/tick) format and in time code format (hour/minute/second/frame). During playback, the Now time increases in accordance with the progress of the project.

You can set the Now time of the project by clicking in the Time Ruler in the Clips pane, or (when playback is paused) by dragging the Now time slider in the Large Transport toolbar.

While you are playing the project, you may want to keep an eye on the Now time. The Big Time view displays the Now time in a large font so you can more easily see it from a distance. To open this view, choose ***View-Big Time***. You can change the time format displayed in the Big Time window by clicking on it. You can change its font by right-clicking on it.

Starting from a Marker
Markers make it easier to find certain points within the project. You may want to set markers at the beginning of each section of your project or at times with which some event must be synchronized. The Markers toolbar lets you move the Now time to a marker, add a new marker at the Now time, and edit the marker list. If

you don't see the Markers toolbar, then choose **View-Toolbars** and check **Markers**.

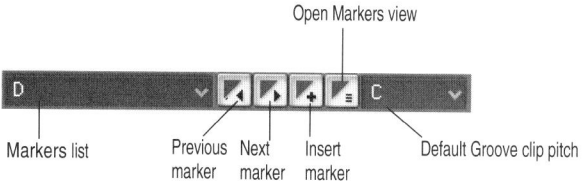

The current project contains several markers. Let's try starting playback from the marker labeled C:

1. If the project is playing, pause playback by clicking the Stop button ■.

2. In the Current Marker dropdown menu in the Markers toolbar (the larger dropdown menu, on the left), select the marker labeled C. The Now time moves to the start of measure 17.

3. Click the Play button ▶.

You can jump to the next or previous marker by pressing Ctrl+Shift+ Page Down or Ctrl+Shift+Page Up.

For more information on markers, see "Creating and Using Markers" on page 224.

Restarting the Project Automatically

Wouldn't it be easier to practice your solo if you didn't have to rewind and restart the project each time it ended? Rather than manually rewinding and restarting the project, you can make SONAR automatically jump back to the beginning and keep playing.

Looping Over the Entire Project

To control looping, use the tools in the Loop/Auto Shuttle toolbar. If you don't see this toolbar, choose **View-Toolbars** and check **Loop**.

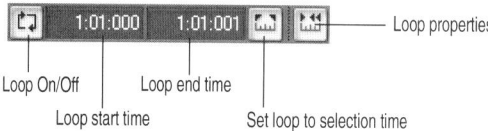

To loop over the entire project, do the following:

1. In the Loop toolbar, click the Loop Start time. The time display changes to an edit box with spin controls.
2. To loop over the entire project, the loop must start at 1:01:000. If the Loop Start time is not already set to 1:01:000, use the keyboard or spin controls to enter this value. To set it to 1:01:000, click the Loop Start time, enter 1 and press Enter.
3. In the Loop toolbar, click the Loop End time.
4. Press F5 to open the Markers dialog box.
5. Select the marker named <End> and click OK. The Loop End time is set to the end of the project.
6. Click the Loop On/Off button to enable looping.
7. Click Play.

When looping is enabled, the Time Ruler displays special flag markers that indicate the loop start and end times. You can drag these markers to change the loop start and end times.

To turn looping off, click the Loop button again.

Looping Over a Section of the Project

Maybe you would like to practice one section of the project over and over. Or, maybe you'd like one section played repeatedly so you can practice an extended solo. In either case, you need to set the start and end times of the loop section. Let's have SONAR loop over the section between markers C and D:

1. In the Loop toolbar, click on the Loop Start time.
2. Press F5 to open the Markers dialog box.
3. In the Markers dialog box, select marker C and click OK. The loop start time is set to the marker time.
4. In the Loop toolbar, click on the Loop End time.

5. Press F5 to open the Markers dialog box.

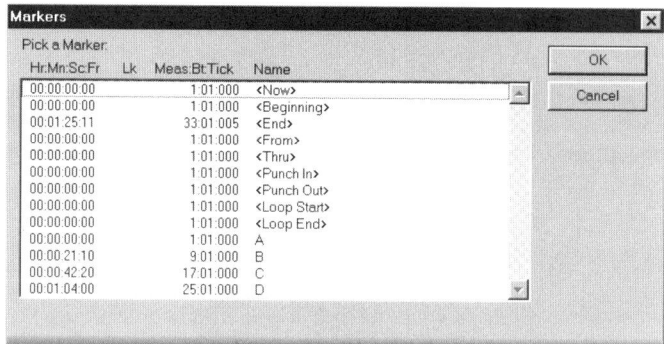

6. In the Markers dialog box, select marker D and click OK.
7. Click the Loop On/Off button 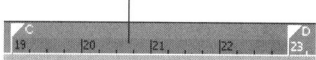 to enable looping.
8. Click Rewind. The project rewinds to the Loop Start time.
9. Click Play.

A quicker way of selecting the loop times in the preceding example would be to simply click in the area between the markers at the top of the Clips pane, then click [⟷] to copy the selection start and end times to the Loop/Auto Shuttle toolbar.

Click here to select the portion of the project between markers C and D

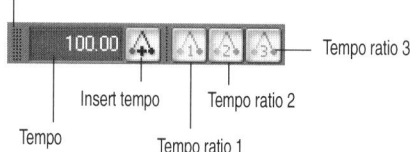

Changing the Tempo

If the project is having trouble keeping up with you (or if you're having trouble keeping up with the project!), you can easily speed up or slow down the project, since it contains only MIDI data. There are two ways to do this: you can change the tempo, or you can change the tempo ratio, which determines the tempo by multiplying it by a user-defined amount. The controls for either method are found on the Tempo toolbar. If you don't see this toolbar, choose **View-Toolbars** and check Tempo.

Setting the Tempo

Let's pick up the pace a little. Do the following:

1. With the project playing, click on the tempo value in the Tempo toolbar. The tempo will be highlighted and spin controls will appear.
2. Use the spin controls to increase the tempo to 100 beats per minute.
3. Press Enter. The project will play a little faster.

Changing the Tempo with the Tempo Ratio Buttons

By default, the Tempo Ratio buttons let you play the project at half or double tempo. Try this:

1. Click Button 1 . The project slows to half its normal tempo. Note that the displayed project tempo has not changed.
2. Click Button 3 . The project speeds to twice its normal tempo.
3. Click Button 2 . The project returns to its normal tempo.

Note: The Tempo Ratio buttons do not function in projects containing audio clips. Also, the clock source setting on the Clock tab of the Project Options dialog (***Options-Project*** command) must be set to Internal.

Setting the Tempo Ratios

Tempo ratios can be changed by Shift-clicking on them in the Tempo toolbar and entering a new number in the dialog box. By default, tempo ratios are set to 0.50, 1.00, and 2.00, respectively.

Advanced Tempo Control

This project is a special case in that it has only one tempo for the entire project. If you need to vary the project's tempo, SONAR lets you insert tempo changes. Tempo changes can be inserted individually so that different sections can be played at different tempos, or they can be inserted graphically in the Tempo view. For more information, see "Changing Tempos" on page 241.

Tempo ratios affect the entire project, even if there are tempo changes. SONAR always multiplies the current tempo in the project by the tempo ratio to determine the playback tempo.

Muting and Soloing Tracks

Muting a track causes it not to sound when you play your project. Soloing a track mutes all the tracks except the ones that are soloed.

You can change a track's mute or solo status while your project is playing.

Muting a Track

Frequently you will want to temporarily turn off one or more instruments in your ensemble. SONAR makes it easy to mute the parts you don't want to hear.

For example, suppose that you are practicing the piano part for this project and want to hear only the other instruments. Let's mute the piano part. With the project playing, do the following:

1. In the Track pane, click the Mute button [M] in the Piano track (track 1). The button turns yellow, and the piano part drops out of the project.
2. To turn the piano back on, click the Mute button again.

Note that the yellow MUTE indicator lights up in the Status bar whenever a track is muted (the Status bar is located at the bottom of the SONAR window). This can be very helpful if there are muted tracks that aren't visible.

Let's try using a different method to mute two tracks simultaneously:

1. In the Track pane, click the track number (the left-most column) of the Piano track. The track is selected.
2. While pressing Ctrl, click the track number in the Sax track. The Piano and Sax tracks are selected.
3. Choose **Track-Mute**. Both tracks are muted.

You can also mute or unmute tracks by using the popup menu:

1. In the Track pane, click the track number of the Piano track.
2. While pressing Ctrl, click the track number of the Sax track. The piano and sax tracks are selected.
3. Right-click on either track to bring up the popup menu.
4. Choose **Mute** (which should have a check mark beside it).

SONAR unmutes the tracks. You can also unmute all tracks by clicking the Mute indicator on the Status bar.

Playing a Track Solo

If you want to hear one track by itself, you could mute all other tracks. But there's a quicker way to do it—the Solo button. For example, to play the drum part by itself, do the following:

1. Click the Solo button [S] in the Drum track (track 5). Voila, a percussion solo!
2. To let the other instruments back into the project, click the Drum track's Solo button again.

Solo is not exclusive—you can let as many instruments as you like into the solo. Note that the green SOLO indicator lights up in the Status bar whenever a track is soloed.

Let's use a different method to solo all three percussion tracks:

1. In the Track pane, click the track number in the Drums track. The track is selected.
2. While pressing Shift, click the track numbers in the Shaker and Triangle tracks. All three percussion tracks are selected.
3. Choose **Track-Solo**.

When you want to let the entire ensemble back into the project, click the Solo indicator on the Status bar to unsolo all the tracks, or select all soloed tracks and choose **Track-Solo**. As a third option, right-click, bring up the popup menu, and turn off the solo from there.

Note that Mute takes priority over Solo. If both buttons are selected in a track, the track does not play.

Mute and Solo in the Console View

The Console view contains Mute and Solo buttons identical to those in the Track view. The two sets of buttons are synchronized. To see this, do the following:

1. In the Console view, mute the Bass, Sax, and Drums tracks.
2. Solo the Piano track.
3. In the Track view, check that the first track is soloed and that tracks 2, 3, and 5 are muted. Click the selected Solo and Mute buttons to return the tracks to normal.

Changing a Track's Instrument

If your sound card is like most, its internal synthesizer is capable of producing at least 128 different instrument sounds, plus several dozen percussion sounds. Now you'll find out how to get some of those other instruments into the act. Let's try changing the instrument playing the piano line.

Changing the Patch in the Track View

With the project playing, do the following:

1. Solo the Piano track so you can hear the piano part more clearly. To do this, click the Solo button **S** in the Piano track (track 1).

2. Loop the project, or a part of the project and click Play.

3. In the Piano track in the Track pane, find the Patch control (it's the field just after the Bank control). Click the down arrow that is at the end of the patch name (the patch name should be something like Acoustic Grand Piano).

4. To change the patch, select a new patch from the menu that appears. SONAR closes the menu and immediately starts playing the piano part with that new instrument.

5. Have fun trying all the different patches!

6. Click the Solo button in track 1 again to unsolo the Piano track.

You can change the patch at other times in the project besides the beginning by using the ***Insert-Bank/Patch Change*** command:

1. Stop playback.

2. Select the track in which you want to insert a patch change by clicking on its track number.

3. Move the Now time to the place where you want to insert the patch change.

4. Use the ***Insert-Bank/Patch Change*** command.

    The Bank/Patch Change dialog box appears.

5. Choose a patch from the Patch field and click OK.

    SONAR inserts the patch change that you selected at the Now time.

6. Move the Now time to a place before the patch change and play the project so that the Now time moves through the place where you put the patch change. You may want to solo the track to hear it clearly.

7. Listen to the sound change when the Now time reaches the patch change.

You may want to experiment with changing all the instruments used by the project. One thing you should know: Changing the instrument on a percussion track (such as the Drum, Shaker, and Triangle tracks in this project) may have no effect. Percussion instruments are played on MIDI channel 10, which in General

MIDI is dedicated to percussion. The note determines the instrument, and the patch is irrelevant.

Changing the Patch in the Track/Bus Inspector

You can also change a track's patch in the Track/Bus Inspector, which is a vertically expanded version of the *current track's* controls at the far left side of the Track view. The current track is the one with the gold title bar. Whichever track's controls that you click becomes the current track. For example, to change the Piano track's patch, click the Patch button in the Piano track's Track/Bus Inspector and choose a new patch from the menu. The Patch button is just below the Bank button. You can hide or show the Track/Bus Inspector by pressing *i* on your computer keyboard.

Playing Music on a Keyboard

If you've connected a MIDI keyboard (or another instrument) to your external MIDI interface or the MIDI interface of your sound card, you can play one or more parts of the project on the keyboard instead of the sound card's internal synthesizer. For instructions on connecting a keyboard to your computer, see "To Connect a MIDI Keyboard to Your Computer" on page 26. For this section, we assume that you want to connect the keyboard to the MIDI In and MIDI Out of your sound card.

Checking Your MIDI Device Settings

First, let's make sure that SONAR is set up to send MIDI output to your keyboard.

1. Choose **Options-MIDI Devices** to open the MIDI Devices dialog box.

2. In the Outputs field, two devices should be selected. The first should be your sound card synthesizer device; the second should be the MIDI output your MIDI device is connected to (it should say something like "SB Live MIDI Out"). The uppermost selected device will correspond to Output 1, the second device to Output 2, and so on. For help with these settings, see "Setting Up Output Devices" on page 134.

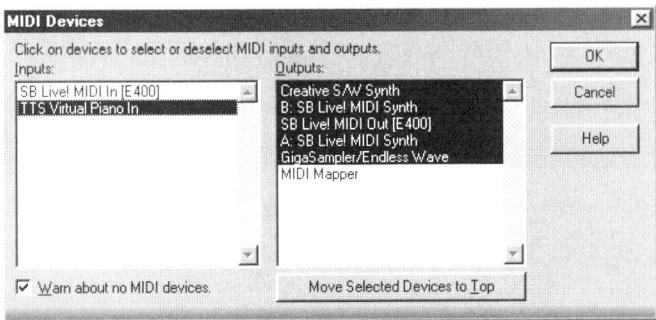

3. Click OK.

59

Routing MIDI Data to the Keyboard

Let's play back the Piano track through your MIDI keyboard. First, turn your keyboard on and make sure it is set up to receive MIDI input on channel one. Then, do the following:

1. In the Track view, in the Piano track (track 1), click the Output field to open the menu of outputs.
2. Select the output that your keyboard is attached to.
3. Click the Play button or press the Spacebar to play your project.

SONAR plays the piano part through your keyboard.

Or, if you prefer, the procedure is similar in the Console view:

1. In the Console view (to display, use the **View-Console** command), click the Output button in the Piano module to open the menu of outputs. The Output button is just below the volume fader.
2. Select the output that your keyboard is attached to.
3. Play your project. If you don't hear anything from your keyboard, see *Appendix A: Troubleshooting* for some hints on troubleshooting.

Tutorial 2—Recording MIDI

This tutorial teaches you how to record MIDI data with SONAR. You'll learn how to:

- Set up the metronome
- Record MIDI tracks
- Use loop recording
- Use punch recording

Creating a New Project

If you haven't already done so, the first thing you need to do is create a project file:

1. Start SONAR.
2. Choose *File-New*.
3. In the New Project File dialog box, select the MIDI tracks template.
4. Click OK.

SONAR opens a new project, containing only MIDI tracks.

Recording a MIDI Track

Let's record a new MIDI track in the project.

Setting Up the Metronome

Musicians often use a metronome to keep track of the beat. SONAR's metronome is more versatile than most real metronomes. You can configure it to sound on playback or recording; it can count off any number of lead-in measures or beats; it can use audio clips or MIDI notes to produce sounds; and it can accent the first beat of each measure. It also quickly and accurately follows any tempo changes that happen in the project.

You can set up the metronome with the Metronome toolbar. If you don't see the Metronome toolbar, choose *View-Toolbars* and select Metronome.

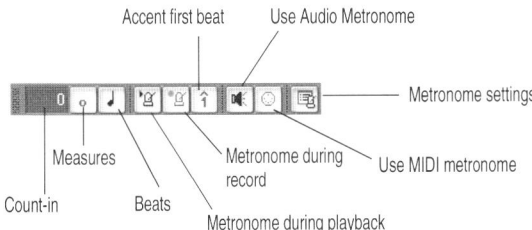

Let's set up the metronome to play audio for two count-in measures when recording. Here's what to do:

1. In the Metronome toolbar, click in the Count-in box.
2. Use the + or - buttons to set the count-in value to 2.
3. Click the Count-in Measures option to select it.
4. Deselect the Metronome During Record option.
5. Select the Use Audio Metronome option.
6. Deselect the Use MIDI Metronome option.

By disabling the Metronome During Record option, you cause the metronome to turn off after the count-in measures. If you would prefer to hear the metronome during the entire project while recording, enable this option instead.

In this example, the metronome counts in for recording, not for playback.

Setting MIDI Inputs

Let's make sure that SONAR is set up to receive MIDI data from your instrument.

1. Choose **Options-MIDI Devices** to open the MIDI Devices dialog box.
2. In the Inputs column, select your sound card's MIDI In device or the MIDI In for your external MIDI interface. For help with these settings, see "Setting Up the MIDI In and MIDI Out Devices" on page 30.

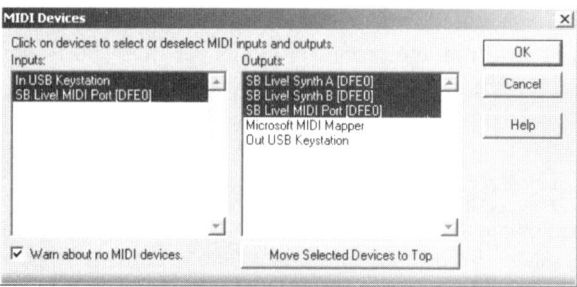

3. Click OK.

Setting Up Playback

During recording, SONAR will play the rest of a project as usual. Depending on what instrumental part of the project you are going to record, you may want to mute one or more tracks, or solo certain tracks. For example, if you are going to record a new piano part, you might want to mute the old piano part so that you're not competing with it while recording (you can also record over the old piano part—arm the piano track and make sure Overwrite is the selected mode in the

Record Options dialog box, which you open with the ***Transport-Record Options*** command). To mute any track, click the track's Mute button [M].

Since this is a new project, there is no need to mute or solo any track.

You can also set other playback options, such as the tempo ratio, to make your recording session easier.

Recording MIDI
Now you'll record a track in the project. Do the following:

1. Make sure your instrument is turned on and set up to transmit MIDI data.
2. If you don't have an unused MIDI track in the project, create a new MIDI track by right-clicking in the Track pane and selecting ***Insert MIDI Track*** from the menu that appears.
3. In a MIDI track, click the Arm button [R] (arming a track automatically sets the Input field to MIDI Omni, meaning that this track will record incoming MIDI data from any channel).
4. On the Transport toolbar, click Record [●], or press ***r***.

    The metronome counts off two measures, then SONAR starts recording.
5. Play your MIDI instrument.
6. When you finish recording, click the Stop button [■], or press the Spacebar.

If you've played any notes, a new clip appears in the Clips pane in the track you recorded on. If no new clip appears, see "I Can't Record from My MIDI Instrument" on page 643 for some troubleshooting hints.

Listening to the Recording
Let's play back your performance on your sound card. For an added dimension, we'll open a few other views in the process. Do the following:

1. Display the controls of the track you recorded by clicking its Restore Strip Size button [⊡], or by dragging the Vertical Zoom control that's located at the lower right corner of the Clips pane. You may need to click the All tab at the bottom of the Track pane to display all the controls.
2. Click the Output dropdown arrow to display the menu of available outputs.
3. Select your sound card's MIDI synthesizer (if you don't see the outputs you expect to see, use the ***Options-MIDI Devices*** command and enable the correct outputs—see "Setting Outputs" on page 48).
4. In the Ch field, click the dropdown arrow to select a MIDI channel, and select an unused channel.
5. In the Patch field, select any patch.
6. Choose ***View-Piano Roll*** to open the Piano Roll view.

7. Choose **View-Staff** to open the Staff view.

8. Choose **View-Event List** to open the Event List view.

9. Choose **Window-Tile in Rows** to tile the views.

10. To return to the start of the project, click the Rewind button, or press *w*.

11. Click Play ▶ or press the Spacebar.

It's almost as easy to listen to your performance on your MIDI instrument. For instructions on how to play a track on a MIDI keyboard, refer to Tutorial 1.

The Piano Roll, Staff, and Event List views all show the same basic information—the notes that you recorded. The Piano Roll view displays the track as a player-piano roll. The Staff view shows notes in traditional music notation. The Event List view lists all MIDI events for the track. When you need to edit a track, you can work in any of these views. On different occasions you may have reason to use different views. More information about the Piano Roll, Staff, and Event List views can be found in later chapters of this *User's Guide*.

When you're ready to continue, close the Piano Roll, Staff, and Event List views.

Recording Another Take

Maybe your first attempt at recording resulted in a perfect performance, but maybe not. If you'd like to remove your first take and try again, do the following:

1. Choose **Edit-Undo Recording** or press Ctrl+Z to undo your recording.

2. Click Rewind ⏮, or press *w*. The track is still armed for recording, so you don't need to re-arm it.

3. Click Record ⏺, or press *r*.

4. When you finish recording, click the Stop button in the Transport toolbar or press the Spacebar.

Alternatively, you could record your next attempt on a new track. That way you can keep all the takes and select the best one later (or combine the best parts of each!). If you record on a new track, be sure to arm the new track for recording and to disarm the previous track. See "Loop Recording" on page 65 for a convenient way to record multiple takes.

Saving Your Work

When you have something you'd like to keep, you can save the project by doing the following:

1. Choose **File-Save As**.

2. In the File Name box, type a new file name, such as *my project*.

3. Click OK.

SONAR saves the project under the new name. From now on, you can click the Save button ![] to save this project.

Loop Recording

If you'd like to record several takes successively, you can set up SONAR to loop over the entire project, or just some section of it. SONAR will record a new take during each loop, storing that take in a new clip. You can set SONAR to place each clip in a new track or to pile all clips in one track.

Let's try recording a few takes of the first four measures of a project, placing each take in a new track.

Setting Up Looping

First, let's set up SONAR to loop over the first four measures:

1. Click the down arrow in the Snap to Grid combo button ![] to open the Snap to Grid dialog box.

2. In the Snap to Grid dialog box, click the Musical Time button and select Measure from the list of durations. In the Mode field, select Move To, and click OK to close the dialog box.

   Now you can only select exact one-measure blocks of time in the Time Ruler, which is located at the top of the Clips pane.

3. In the Time Ruler, drag through the first four measures to select them.

4. In the Loop/Auto Shuttle toolbar, click the Set Loop to Selection button ![] to set the Loop Start and Loop End times.

Clicking ![] enables looping automatically.

Setting Up the Tracks

Now let's set up the first of the tracks where the takes will be stored:

1. Arm a MIDI track by making sure its Arm button ![R] is red.

2. Click the track's Output field to set its output to your sound card's MIDI synthesizer.

3. Use the track's Ch field to set its Channel to an unused channel.

4. Use the track's Patch field to select any patch.

As usual, you could set the tracks to play back on your MIDI keyboard instead by specifying the appropriate output and channel.

Loop Recording

Finally, let's record our takes:

1. Choose **Transport-Record Options** to display the Record Options dialog box.

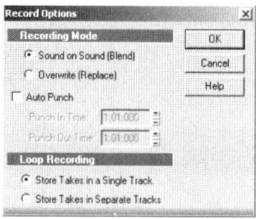

2. Choose the Store Takes in Separate Tracks option to store each new take in a separate track. Each time a new take starts, the settings from the first track will be copied to the new track.

3. Click OK.

4. Click Rewind .

5. Click Record .

   SONAR loops over the designated section and records your takes to successive tracks. If you want to erase the most recent take during loop recording, choose **Transport-Reject Loop Take**.

6. To stop recording, click Stop , or press the Spacebar.

Now you can listen to each take individually by muting the other ones.

Punch-In Recording

Imagine that one of your takes was close to ideal, except for one or two notes in one measure. Rather than recording another full take, you'd prefer to keep the take but replace that measure.

Punch-in recording lets you replace a section of a track. The way it works is this: First, you set the start and end times of the punch to the section you want to replace, and turn on punch recording. Then, you arm the track and start recording. You can play along with the original take to get the rhythm and feeling. However, nothing will be recorded until the Now time reaches the punch start time. During the punch, the material already in the track will be replaced with what you record. When the punch ends, the project will continue to play, but recording will stop.

Let's try it. Suppose you want to replace several measures in the recording you made earlier in this tutorial.

1. Display the Record toolbar by choosing *View-Toolbars-Record.*

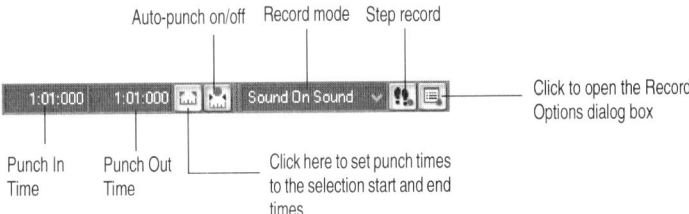

2. In the Record toolbar, click the Punch In Time.
3. Type the number of the measure at which you want to begin punch recording and press Enter.
4. Click the Punch Out Time.
5. Type the number of the measure at which you want to end punch recording and press Enter.
6. Click the Auto-Punch On/Off button to enable punch recording.
7. Select Overwrite from the Record Mode dropdown menu.
8. Arm the track in which you want to punch record.
9. If looping is still on, click the Loop button to turn it off.
10. Click Rewind.
11. Click Record.

Play along until you are past the punch end time, then click Stop. Replay your take to hear the difference. If it's still not right, try again!

An alternative method is to select measures by dragging in the Time Ruler. Then right-click the Time Ruler and choose *Set Punch Points*. This automatically enables punch recording.

You can combine loop recording with punch recording; see "Punch Recording" on page 185 for details.

When Auto Punch is enabled, the Time Ruler displays special markers that indicate the punch in and punch out times. You can drag these markers to change the punch in and punch out times.

Punch In   Punch Out

Tutorial 3—Recording Digital Audio

To record digital audio, you need some sort of device hooked up to your sound card's line or mic input—an electric guitar, a preamp, or a mixer, for example. If nothing else, try playing or singing into a microphone!

If you have never connected an instrument to your sound card, see "To Connect an Electric Guitar to Your Computer" on page 26.

This tutorial covers these procedures:

- Setting the sampling rate
- Setting the audio driver bit depth
- Setting the file bit depth
- Opening a new project
- Setting up an audio track
- Checking the input levels
- Recording digital audio
- Listening to the recording
- Recording another take
- Input monitoring
- Loop and punch-in recording
- Recording multiple channels

Setting the Sampling Rate

Each SONAR project has a parameter that specifies the sampling resolution for all digital audio data in the project. You should set this rate before recording any digital audio.

To set the sampling rate:

1. Choose **Options-Audio** to open the Audio Options dialog box.
2. Click the General tab.
3. Under Default Settings for New Projects, select a Sampling Rate. For CD-quality sound, use 44100 Hz.
4. Click OK.

Lower sampling rates will save disk space but will result in lower-quality audio. Before embarking on any major project, try sampling at different rates to determine which one best suits your needs.

Setting the Audio Driver Bit Depth

The drivers for most sound cards use anywhere from 16 to 24 bits to handle the data and calculations for audio processing. CD's use 16 bits. You can possibly get better sound quality by recording at a higher bit depth and converting to 16 bits when it's time to master your project, but keep in mind that 24 bit audio takes 50% more memory than 16 bit audio, possibly straining your computer's storage capability and speed of operation.

Your sound card's documentation could have some advice on choosing an audio driver bit depth.

To set the audio driver bit depth:

1. Use the **Options-Audio** command to open the Audio Options dialog box.
2. On the General tab, find the Audio Driver Bit Depth field and select one of the options.
3. Click OK.

For more information about audio driver bit depth, see "Configuring SONAR for 18 bit-, 20-bit, and 24-bit Operation" on page 630.

Setting the File Bit Depth

The file bit depth is the size of the blocks of memory that SONAR allocates to store your project's audio data. SONAR allocates memory in 8-bit bytes. If you are using an audio driver bit depth of 16, choose a file bit depth of 16. If you are using an audio driver bit depth that's greater than 16, use a file bit depth of 24.

To set the file bit depth:

1. Use the *Options-Audio* command to open the Audio Options dialog box.
2. On the General tab, find the File Bit Depth field and select either 16 or 24.
3. Click OK.

Open a New Project

Let's open a new project for this tutorial.

1. Select *File-New* from the menu.
2. Select the Normal template and click OK.

Setting Up an Audio Track

Let's set up a track for digital audio:

1. Insert a new track by doing the following: in the Track pane, right-click below the last track, or wherever you want to insert a track, and choose *Insert Audio Track* from the popup menu.

   SONAR inserts a new audio track.

2. In the track's Output field, click the dropdown arrow and select an audio output from the menu.

3. In the track's Input field, choose an audio input. Usually you select the left channel of one of your sound card's inputs to record a mono track, or the stereo input to record a stereo track.

The Normal template has several audio tracks in it already, which you could use to record with. You don't have to insert a new audio track to record with if your project already has one or more empty audio tracks.

Checking the Input Levels

Before trying to record, you need to check and adjust the audio input levels. If your audio input is too low, it will be lost in the background noise. If it is too high, it will overload the input channel and be distorted/clipped. Before you check input levels, make sure that the Record Meters are set to be displayed in the Track view. Click the right arrow next to the Show/Hide Meters button and in the menu that appears, select the Record Meters command if it is not already checked.

You may need to drag the splitter bar that separates the Track pane from the Clips pane to the right to see all the buttons in the Track view toolbar.

Note: SONAR has a button called the Audio Engine button [icon] in the Transport toolbar, which you click to stop any feedback you may experience if there is a loop somewhere in your mixer setup. Whenever you play a project, SONAR automatically enables the audio engine, which you can tell by watching the Status bar—whenever the audio engine is running, the Audio Running indicator in the Status bar lights up. The Status bar is located at the bottom of the SONAR window.

To check the audio input levels:

1. Click the Arm button [R] in your new audio track. The track's meter becomes a record meter. You may need to use the Vertical Zoom Control in the lower right corner of the Clips pane to see the track's meter.

2. Perform as you would during recording. Watch the meter respond to the sounds you produce. If the meter does not respond, you may need to raise the volume of your plugged-in instrument. Also, make sure that the Audio Engine button [icon] in the Transport toolbar is depressed.

   If you still don't see any movement of the audio meters, you may have an audio input problem. Refer to "I Can't Record Any Audio" on page 645 for troubleshooting hints.

3. If the meter never comes even close to the maximum, increase the input level by using the Windows mixer or your sound card's software mixer (or if you are recording your instrument through an amplifier or mic preamp, turn up the amp or preamp).

4. If the meters even occasionally reach the maximum, decrease the input level.

The idea is to try to get the input level to rise as high as possible, but without ever reaching the maximum. That way, you get the strongest possible signal without distortion.

SONAR's meters are extremely adjustable for the kind and range of data they display. For more information, see "Metering" on page 436.

Recording Digital Audio

It's time to record!

1. If you haven't already set up the metronome, follow the directions in "Setting Up the Metronome" on page 61 to set the metronome for a two-measure count-in.

2. The track is already armed for recording.

3. In the Transport toolbar, click Record [●], or press *r* on your computer keyboard.

   You'll hear two measures counted in by the metronome, then playback and recording begin.

4. Go ahead and perform!

5. When you finish recording, click the Stop button ■, or press the Spacebar.

A new clip appears in the Clips pane. If no new clip appears, see "I Can't Record Any Audio" on page 645 for some troubleshooting hints. Also, right-click in the Clips pane and choose **View-Options** to open the Track View Options dialog box—make sure Display Clip Names and Display Clip Contents are checked.

Listening to the Recording

Let's play back your performance. Do the following:

1. In the track's Output field, click the dropdown arrow to display the menu of available outputs, and select a pair of your sound card's stereo outputs (if your sound card only has two outputs, just select the name of your sound card).

2. To return to the start of the project, click the Rewind button.

3. Disarm your audio track by clicking its Arm button again—this changes the track's meter to a playback meter. The track is disarmed when its Arm button is not red.

4. Click Play ▶.

5. Watch the track's meter. If the level is not what you want, record your track again.

Recording Another Take

If you'd like to delete your performance and try again, do the following:

1. Choose **Edit-Undo Recording** to undo your recording, or press Ctrl+Z (Undo).

2. Click Rewind ◄ or press *w*.

3. Make sure the track is still armed for recording.

4. Click Record ●.

5. When you finish recording, click the Stop button ■, or press the Spacebar.

Alternatively, you could record your next attempt on a new track.

Input Monitoring

SONAR has a feature called **input monitoring**, which allows you to hear any instrument that is plugged into your sound card whether you are currently recording the instrument or not. You can hear your instrument, including any plug-in effects, whenever input monitoring is enabled and the Audio Engine button in the Transport toolbar is depressed. You can enable or disable input monitoring on an individual track by clicking the track's Input Echo button, and you can enable or disable input monitoring on all tracks at once by clicking the

Input Echo button that's on the Playback State toolbar (to display, use the *View-Toolbars-Playback State* command).

Caution: If you have any kind of a loop in your mixer setup that causes the output of your sound card to be fed back into the input, you can get feedback, and input monitoring can make it very intense because both the direct signal and the processed signal are coming out of your sound card. Turn your speakers off whenever you enable input monitoring, and then try turning them up very gradually to try it out. **If you hear feedback, click the Audio Engine button in the Transport toolbar to turn input monitoring off.**

For more information on Input Monitoring, see "Input Monitoring" on page 180.

Loop and Punch-In Recording

Loop and Punch-in work the same for digital audio recording as they did for MIDI recording. For more information, refer to the relevant sections preceding, or to "Loop Recording" on page 184 or "Punch Recording" on page 185.

Recording Multiple Channels

If you can gather the entire band around your computer, and if you have the proper equipment, you can record a full multiple-instrument performance all at once. If you have several MIDI instruments, you can route their input into your sound card through a MIDI merger—data that arrives on different MIDI channels can be routed to different tracks (see "Recording Specific Ports and Channels" on page 192). Likewise, a typical sound card can record audio on both right and left channels—each can be recorded on a different track by choosing the right channel as an input for one track, and the left channel as an input for another. Multiple sound cards and multi-I/O sound cards can expand the number of possible inputs. For more information, see "System Configuration" on page 628.

That completes the audio recording tutorial. Now you've learned the basics of playing and recording material for your projects. In the following tutorials you'll learn about basic editing techniques for both MIDI and audio.

Tutorial 4—Editing MIDI

SONAR has too many powerful MIDI features to look at in one tutorial, so let's look at some of the most basic features and also cover some exciting new ones, such as slip editing and MIDI envelopes.

In this tutorial, start by opening the file TUTORIAL4.CWP in the Tutorials folder where SONAR is installed. We will be doing the following tasks:

- Transposing
- Copying Clips with Drag and Drop
- Editing Notes in the Piano Roll View
- Slip Editing
- Drawing MIDI Envelopes
- Converting MIDI to Audio

Transposing

Here are two ways to transpose MIDI data in SONAR:

- You can apply the *Transpose* command to selected data (see the procedure below).
- You can use the Key+ control for a specific track—the Key+ control is located with the other track parameter controls in the Track pane. This method causes a track to play higher or lower by the number of half steps you enter in the Key+ control. This is a non-destructive form of editing that leaves the pitch of the original data unchanged, but adds an "offset" when the track plays back.

To Transpose our Tutorial File

1. Select all the notes in the bass track by clicking the bass track's track number. The track number should appear highlighted when it is selected.
2. Select all the notes in the organ track by Ctrl-clicking (holding down the Ctrl key while you click) the organ track's track number. Ctrl-clicking allows you to make multiple selections.
3. Use the *Process-Transpose* command to open the Transpose dialog box.
4. Enter -2 (negative 2) in the Amount field and click OK.
5. Ctrl-click both track numbers again to deselect them.

SONAR transposes the selected data down a whole step (2 half steps). Choose MIDI outputs for your tracks and play the project. You can undo the transposition by pressing Ctrl+z, and redo the transposition by pressing Ctrl+Shift+z.

Copying Clips with Drag and Drop

The first clip in the bass track is two measures long; we can easily drag-copy it to make it eight measures long. When we drag-copy some of the clips, we can make them into **linked clips**. When you edit a linked clip, SONAR performs the exact same edits on all other clips that the clip is linked to.

To Copy Clips Using Drag and Drop

1. In the Track view toolbar, click the Snap to Grid button's down arrow to open the Snap to Grid dialog box.
2. Make sure that the Musical Time radio button is selected, and in the list to the right of it, select Measure.
3. In the Mode field, select Move By and click OK. Now we can only move clips in the Clips pane by distances of an exact measure or measures.
4. While holding down the Ctrl key, drag the first clip in the bass track to the right and release the mouse when the start of the clip is at measure three. The Drag and Drop Options dialog box appears. Click OK—SONAR places a copy of the clip in measures three through four. Ctrl-dragging a clip copies and moves it, while dragging without holding down any extra keys moves a clip without making a copy of it.
5. Now let's make a linked clip copy of the new clip in measure three: Ctrl-drag the clip from measure three to measure five. When the Drag and Drop Options dialog box appears, click the Copy Entire Clips as Linked Clips checkbox and click OK. SONAR places a linked clip copy into measures five and six. The two linked clips have dotted outlines to show they are linked.
6. Make another linked copy of one of the linked clips and place it in measures seven and eight. Because this copy overlaps the clip that's in measure 9, make sure that the Blend Old and New option is checked in the Drag and Drop dialog box. Because none of the notes in the two clips overlap, blending the two clips does not change any of their data.

Now you have linked clip copies in measures three through eight: when you edit any of these three clips, SONAR performs the exact same edits on the other two.

Editing Notes in the Piano Roll View

SONAR's Piano Roll view gives you complete control of individual note properties. Let's edit a couple of notes.

To Edit Notes in the Piano Roll View

1. Open the Piano Roll view of the first bass clip by double-clicking the clip. In the Piano Roll view, you may have to use the Up Arrow and Down Arrow keys on your computer keyboard to display the note data (the Right and Left Arrow keys scroll the display in the horizontal direction).
2. Drag the Piano Roll's Horizontal Zoom control that's at the lower right corner of the Notes pane to make the note data large enough for easy editing.

3. In the Piano Roll toolbar, right-click the Snap to Grid button to open the Snap to Grid dialog box (Snap to Grid settings in each view are independent of each other).

4. Make sure the Musical Time radio button is selected, and in the window to the right of it, select Eighth.

5. In the Mode field, make sure that the Move By radio button is selected and click OK. Now we can only move data in the Piano Roll view by exact distances of one or more eighth notes.

6. In the Piano Roll toolbar, click the Draw tool to activate it.

7. Find the note that starts at the beginning of measure three and move the cursor over the beginning of the note so that the cursor becomes a cross. Drag the beginning of the note to the left by a half beat, and release the mouse.

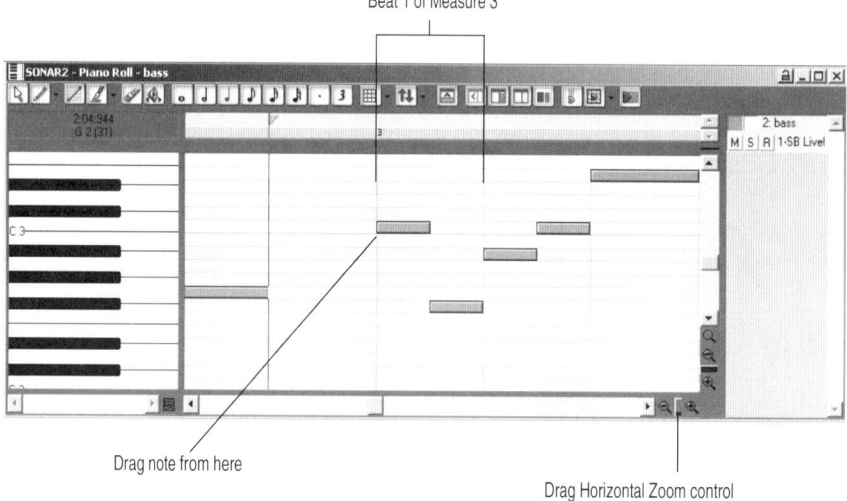

SONAR moves the note to the left by a half beat and lengthens the note by a half beat, and also performs the same edits on the identical notes that are at the beginnings of the other two linked clips.

8. Close the Piano Roll view when you finish editing.

If you want to **unlink clips** when you're through editing them, select the clips you want to unlink (in the Track view), right-click one of them, and choose *Unlink* from the Clips pane popup menu. Select Independent, Not Linked At All in the Unlink Clips dialog box and click OK.

When you move the Draw tool over a note, it changes into one of 3 different editing tools, depending on what part of the note you move it over:

- If you move the Draw tool over the beginning or end of a note, the Draw tool changes into a cross. When you drag one end of a note with the cross icon, the other end of the note stays put, thereby changing the duration of the note as you move the opposite end.

- If you move the Draw tool just inside the beginning of a note, the Draw tool changes into a horizontal, double-ended arrow. When you drag the beginning of a note with this icon, the other end of the note moves with the beginning of the note, thereby keeping the duration of the note constant.

- If you move the Draw tool over the middle of a note, the Draw tool changes into vertical, double-ended arrow. Use this tool to drag the note up or down in pitch.

Slip Editing

Now let's take advantage of one of the most convenient new features of SONAR: slip editing. Slip editing lets you drag the beginning or ending borders of a clip to hide the notes or other MIDI data that are in the area that you drag through (slip editing also works on audio clips). SONAR does not delete these notes or data, but does not play them either. As soon as you drag the clip borders to display the data again, SONAR plays them again. Slip editing is a very fast and convenient way to try out different sounds, without destroying any data. You can also leave the clip borders unchanged and only drag the data that's within the clip, which is called scroll-trimming. Scroll-trimming changes the rhythmic placement of data without changing the clip's borders.

To Slip Edit TUTORIAL4.CWP

1. Drag the horizontal zoom controls in the Clips pane so that a space of about 2 measures fills up the Clips pane.

2. Click the down arrow in the Snap to Grid combo button to open the Snap to Grid dialog box, change the Musical Time resolution to Eighth, make sure Move By is selected in the Mode field, and click OK. Now we can only drag the borders of clips by units of eighth notes.

3. In the organ track in the Clips pane, move the cursor over the right end of the first clip until the cursor changes to a square. Drag the right border to the left until the MIDI data at the end of the clip is hidden.

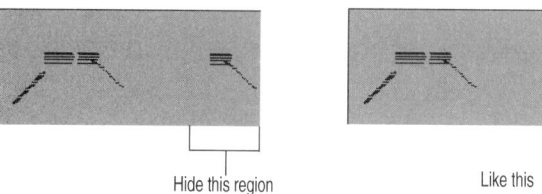

Hide this region   Like this

Now you can't hear those notes.

4. Drag the end of the second clip to the left until just the "tail" or glissando of the data is hidden.

Hide this region   Like this

5. In the third clip, hold down both the Alt and Shift keys and drag only the data inside the clip to the left by about one eighth note.

You can experiment as much as you want with slip editing, all without destroying any data! For more information about Slip Editing, see "Slip-editing Audio (Non-destructive Editing)" on page 375.

Drawing MIDI Envelopes

MIDI envelopes are lines and curves you can draw on MIDI data in the Clips pane. Each envelope produces continuous control over one of the following track parameters: volume, pan, chorus, reverb, automated mute, or a MIDI controller. You can show or hide any envelope you create, but the envelope still functions when it is hidden. For our tutorial, let's create a MIDI volume envelope.

To Draw and Edit a MIDI Volume Envelope

1. In the Clips pane in the organ track, right-click and choose **Envelopes-Create Track Envelope-Volume (default Ch. 1)** from the Clips pane popup menu.

   SONAR creates a blue line through the organ track, with a small square dot (a **node**) at the beginning of the line. The line shows the initial volume of the track, if it has an initial volume. Otherwise, it shows a default value.

2. Scroll the Now Time to the next marker by pressing Ctrl+Shift+Page Down; the marker is called Verse, and is located just before measure nine. Drag the

Horizontal zoom control so that the beat markers are visible in the Time Ruler.

3. At the fourth beat of measure eight, add a node to the envelope by moving the cursor over it until a double-ended, vertical arrow appears under it, right-clicking to open the Envelope Editing menu, and choosing **Add Node** from the menu. A shortcut to add a node is to double-click the line.

4. At the start of measure nine, add another node.

5. Move the cursor over the newest node until a cross appears under it, and drag the node downwards until it's just below the MIDI data that's at the start of the clip.

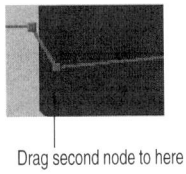

Drag second node to here

6. At the fourth beat of measure twelve, add another node and drag it up to the top of the track. Now you have a gradual volume increase in the organ track for almost four measures.

7. At the start of measure thirteen, add another node and drag it downward just below the MIDI data at the start of the measure.

8. Right-click the line that's between the last two nodes, and choose **Slow Curve** from the Envelope Editing menu. SONAR changes the line to a curve. Now the drop in volume is a little more gradual.

Now you have some interesting dynamics in your track. You can add a lot more to your envelope, and add more envelopes if you wish. You can also copy and paste envelopes. For more information, see "Automation Methods" on page 495.

Converting MIDI to Audio

When you finally get your MIDI project into the shape you want. You can convert the MIDI tracks to audio for export as Wave, MP3, or other file formats. If you are using external MIDI modules, just record the outputs of your modules into your sound card. If you are using DXi soft synths, use the **File-Export-Audio** command, or the **Edit-Bounce to Track(s)** command. If you are using the built-in synthesizer in your sound card to produce MIDI sounds, you can use your sound card's "what you hear" or wave capture function to convert the MIDI tracks, if your sound card can function this way. See the following procedure:

To Convert MIDI to Audio

1. Pick a destination audio track (or create a new one) and set the Input field to *Stereo (name of your sound card)*.

   Note: If you have more than one sound card installed, select the one that has the built-in synth that your MIDI tracks use.

2. Arm the destination track. Make sure its Input Echo button is off, so you won't hear an echo when you're recording.

3. Mute or archive any tracks that you don't want to record to the destination track.

4. If SONAR's metronome is set to use any software synth to produce a click, disable the metronome during recording option in the Project Options dialog box. To do this, select ***Options-Project*** to open the Project Options dialog box, select the Metronome tab and uncheck Recording in the General section. Alternatively, you could set the metronome to use the audio metronome and not use a MIDI note.

5. Open your sound card's mixer device. This is normally done by double-clicking the speaker icon on your Windows taskbar, or by choosing ***Start-Programs-Accessories-Entertainment-Volume Control-Options-Properties***.

   Note: Some sound cards have their own proprietary mixer. If yours has one, please use it instead.

6. If you're using the Windows mixer, use its ***Options-Properties*** command to open the Properties dialog box, click Recording (in the Adjust Volume For field), and make sure all boxes in the Show the Following Volume Controls field are checked.

7. Click OK, and locate the slider marked MIDI, Synth, Mixed Input, or What You Hear. Check the Select box at the bottom, then close the window.

8. In SONAR, rewind to the beginning of your project, click the Record button, and click the Stop button when you're done recording.

SONAR records all the MIDI tracks that are assigned to your sound card synth as a stereo audio track.

After you finish recording, mute the MIDI tracks that you just recorded so you don't hear them and the new audio track at the same time.

Tutorial 5—Editing Audio

In this tutorial we will be editing a bundle file with drums, bass, guitar and organ. We will add some additional percussion, and edit some of the existing tracks. This tutorial covers the following:

- Importing wave files
- Dragging and looping clips
- Slip editing
- Using automatic crossfades
- Bouncing tracks

Opening the Project

1. In SONAR select *File-Open* from the menu.
2. In the Open dialog, select TUTORIAL5.CWB and click OK.

   The audio data is loaded into SONAR and TUTORIAL5.CWB opens.

Importing a Wave File

Now that you have the file open, click the Play button to hear the project. The project contains drums, bass, and two guitar tracks. Let's import an organ track:

To Import a Wave File

1. Click the down arrow in the Snap to Grid combo button located in the Track view toolbar.

   The Snap to Grid dialog appears.

2. In the Snap to Grid dialog, click the Musical Time radio button, select Measure from the list of durations and click OK.

3. Make sure the Snap to Grid button is depressed (on).

4. In the Track pane, right-click below the bottom track and select *Insert Audio Track* from the menu that appears.

5. Click the track number of the new track to select it.

6. We want to insert the new part at measure 18, so click in the Time Ruler at measure 18. The Time Ruler is at the top of the Clips pane above the drum track.

7. Select *File-Import-Audio* from the File menu.

   The Open dialog appears.

8. Open the Tutorials folder located in the directory where SONAR is installed.

9. Select ORGAN.WAV and click Open.

   A new clip appears in the selected track at the specified Now Time—measure 18.

10. Double-click the track name, and type in a new name: "Organ," and press Enter.

11. Move the Now time to the beginning, insert another audio track, import the file MARACAS.WAV, and name the track.

    After you import MARACAS.WAV, notice that the clip has beveled or rounded corners instead of sharp ones. That means it's a Groove clip, and contains tempo and pitch information. We'll learn more about Groove clips in the next tutorial.

12. Insert another audio track, import the file CONGAS.WAV (which is also a Groove clip) and name the track.

Moving and Looping the Clips

When you drag and drop clips in the Clips pane, the Snap to Grid setting determines the resolution to which the clips "snap to." If your Snap to Grid setting is Measures and you drop a clip between two measures, the clip appears aligned to the closest measure.

We have just dropped two percussion clips into our project, and we could have dropped them where we wanted, but then we wouldn't get a lesson on how to move clips in SONAR.

Let's move both clips to the 18th measure of the project.

1. Click and drag the maracas clip to measure 18 (the Snap Grid is still set to Measure).

2. The Drag and Drop Options dialog appears. The Drag and Drop Options dialog box has options for how the clip you are dragging affects existing clips. Since the clip we are dragging is not being moved onto an existing clip, we can just accept the default setting. Click OK to accept the default settings.

   The clip now appears at the 18th measure.

3. Now move the congas clip to the 18th measure by using the same method.

Now let's loop the two percussion clips to make copies of them by using their Groove clip characteristics:

1. Move the cursor over the end of the maracas clip until the cursor looks like this ⬚.

2. When the cursor changes, click the end of the clip and drag it to the right until you have created repetitions of the clip through the end of measure 28.

3. Copy the congas clip the same way until it reaches the end of measure 28.

Slip Editing a Clip

Solo the two guitar tracks and listen to the project. We are going to combine these two tracks and create an automatic crossfade between them. Before we do, we have to hide the beginning of the second guitar part so it doesn't affect the crossfade. We'll do this using slip editing.

1. Click the Snap to Grid button to turn off Snap to Grid. The Snap to Grid settings control slip editing as well as drag and drop.

2. Move the cursor over the beginning of the second guitar clip.

3. When the cursor turns into a rectangle, click and drag the beginning of the clip until you have reached the beginning of the waveform.

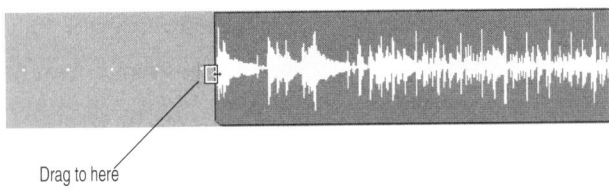

Drag to here

The beginning of the clip is now hidden. The data is not lost, as you will see if you drag the beginning to where it was originally. Slip-edited data is still in the project, but it is not seen or heard.

Automatic Crossfades

Let's combine these two tracks and create a crossfade.

1. Enable automatic crossfades by clicking (depressing) the Enable/Disable Automatic Crossfades combo button located next to the Snap to Grid button on the Track view toolbar.

2. Click the down arrow on the Enable/Disable Automatic Crossfades combo button, select **Default Crossfade Curves** and select a crossfade curve.

3. Make sure no clips are currently selected by clicking in the Clips pane outside of any clips.

4. Hold down the Shift key and drag the second guitar clip on top of the first guitar track and drop it there; make sure that Blend Old and New is selected in the Drag and Drop dialog box before you click OK. Shift-dragging ensures that a clip can only move vertically and not horizontally, so you don't need to enable the Snap to Grid button to keep the same exact rhythmic placement of a dragged clip.

The two clips appear on the same track with a crossfade marker on the overlapping data. The first guitar track fades out as the second guitar fades in. For more information about crossfades, see "Using Fades and Crossfades in Real Time" on page 380.

Bouncing Tracks

When you finish editing a certain number of audio tracks, you can conserve memory and simplify your mix by bouncing (combining) some tracks down to one or two tracks. You can choose to include any effects and automation in the new track that are on the tracks that you want to combine, greatly reducing the load on your CPU.

Let's bounce, or combine our two percussion tracks together:

1. Make sure no time range is selected by clicking in the Clips pane outside of any clips.

2. Select the tracks that you want to combine: in this case, Maracas and Congas. To select multiple tracks, hold down the Ctrl key while you click each track's track number. You can also solo tracks instead of selecting them.

3. Click the Snap to Grid button to turn it on (the Snap to Grid setting is still set to Measure).

4. In the Time Ruler, select measures 18 through 28.

5. Use the **Edit-Bounce to Track(s)** command to open the Bounce to Track(s) dialog box.

6. In the Destination field, choose <8> New Track.

7. In the Source Category field, choose Entire Mix.

8. In the Channel Format field, since our two original percussion tracks are in stereo, choose Stereo. This way we preserve their stereo quality.

9. In the Source Bus(es) field, make sure the name of the sound card that the relevant tracks use to play back on is highlighted.

10. In the Mix Enables field, make sure everything is checked. By checking the Track Mute/Solo option, you make sure that SONAR only mixes down the unmuted tracks. If any tracks are soloed, this option causes SONAR to mix down only the soloed tracks.

11. Click OK.

SONAR creates a new, stereo track that combines both percussion tracks. Now you can archive the old percussion tracks so that they don't consume memory. Do this by right-clicking each track number and choosing **Archive** from the popup menu.

Tutorial 6—Using Groove Clips

Groove clips are audio clips that "know" their tempo and root note pitch. SONAR uses this information to stretch the clips to match changes in tempo and to transpose the root note pitch to match the project's pitch and pitch changes. SONAR also has MIDI Groove clips (see "MIDI Groove Clips" on page 267 for more information) that work much the same as audio Groove clips.

You can create repetitions, or loops of Groove clips simply by dragging their ends in the Track view, creating as many repetitions as you want.

You can change the pitch of your Groove clips by inserting pitch markers in the Time Ruler. The default project pitch for Groove clips in a new project is C. The root note of your Groove clips is transposed to the default for any part of the Groove clips that come before the first pitch marker, or if you do not have pitch markers in your project. You can change the default pitch of the current project in the Markers toolbar.

You can create and edit Groove clips in the Loop Construction view.

This tutorial covers the following:

- Adding Groove clips to a project
- Looping Groove clips
- Changing the pitch of Groove clips
- Making Groove clips follow the project tempo

Adding Groove Clips to a Project

There are two ways to add a Groove clip to your project. Let's use both.

To Import a Groove Clip

1. Select *File-New* to create a new project.

2. Set the default pitch to E by clicking the dropdown arrow in the Markers toolbar and choosing E (if you don't see the Markers toolbar, use the *View-Toolbars* command and check Markers).

 Click here

3. Click the Rewind button in the Transport toolbar to move the Now Time to the beginning of the project.

4. Select track 1 by clicking its track number.

5. Select *File-Import-Audio* from the menu.

   The Open dialog appears.

6. Navigate to the Tutorials folder in the directory where you installed SONAR.

7. Select 100FX.WAV and click Open.

The clip appears on the track at the beginning of your project—the clip's corners are beveled instead of sharp, indicating that it is a Groove clip.

Before we import another loop, let's give this track a name. In the track titlebar, double-click on the track name and enter the name Sound Effect and press Enter.

Let's add some more Groove clips:

To Drag and Drop a Groove Clip into a Project

1. Click the down arrow in the Snap to Grid combo button located in the Track view toolbar.

   The Snap to Grid dialog appears.

2. In the Snap to Grid dialog, select the Musical Time radio button and the duration Measure.

3. In the mode section, select the Move To radio button.

4. Click OK to close the Snap to Grid dialog.

5. Make sure Snap to Grid is on. When Snap to Grid is on, the buttons depressed.

6. Open the Loop Explorer view by clicking the Loop Explorer icon in the Views toolbar .

7. Navigate to the Tutorials folder in the directory where you installed SONAR.

8. Select 100ONETWO.WAV and drag it into the Clips pane below the Sound Effect track at measure 3.

Repeat step 8 by dragging 100BEAT2.WAV below Track 2 at measure 7 and 100ORGAN.WAV below Track 3 at measure 1, and close the Loop Explorer view. SONAR automatically creates any necessary audio tracks when you import audio data.

You now have a four track project. If you haven't done so yet, click the play button to take a listen to your project before we begin to arrange the clips.

Your project should look something like this:

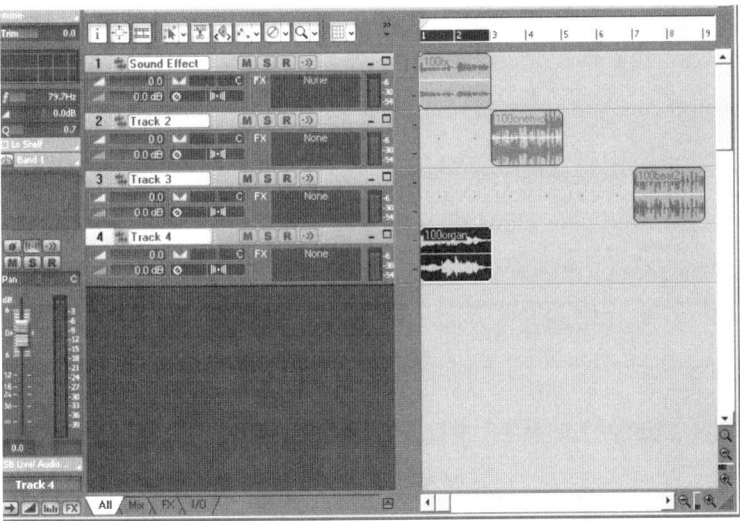

Looping Groove Clips

Here's where Groove clips get real fun. You need only drag the beginning or end of a Groove clip to create repetitions or loops.

First, though, lets copy the Groove clip in Track 2.

To Copy a Groove Clip

1. Press the Ctrl key and click and drag the clip until the beginning is at measure 8 and release.

   The Drag and Drop Options dialog appears.

2. Make sure the Copy Entire Clips as Linked Clips option is not checked and click OK.

A copy of the Groove clip now appears on the same track at measure 8.

To Loop a Groove Clip

1. Move the cursor over the end of the first Groove clip in Track 2 until the cursor looks like this ⊡.

2. When the cursor changes, click the end of the clip and drag it to the right until you have created one repetition of the clip (through the end of measure 6).

You can also create a partial loop of a Groove clip if the Snap to Grid setting is set to less than one measure. You can create a partial loop as small as the Snap to Grid setting allows. For example, if your Snap to Grid setting is set to quarter notes, you can create partial repetitions as small as a quarter of a measure.

Now lets edit the clip we copied on Track 2.

To Crop a Groove Clip

1. Click the dropdown arrow on the Snap to Grid button to open its dialog box, set the Musical Time duration to Quarter, and click OK to close the dialog box.

2. Move your cursor over the beginning of the second clip in Track 2 until it looks like this ⊡.

3. "Crop" the beginning of the clip one and a quarter measure (you may want to expand the Clips pane a little by dragging the Horizontal Zoom slider that's in the lower right corner).

   Like this:

   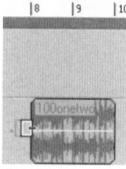 

4. Crop the end of the clip by one quarter measure.

   Like this:

   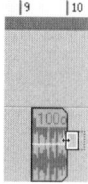 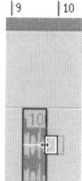

5. Click on the clip and drag it one measure to the left.

   Like this:

   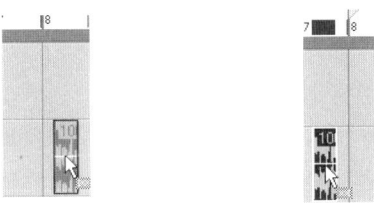

   The Drag and Drop Options dialog appears.

6. In the Drag and Drop Options dialog, click Blend Old and New and click OK.

You have added Groove clips and edited them. Your project should look like this:

Let's take a listen to what we have. Click the Play button in the Transport toolbar.

Changing the Pitch of Groove Clips

Now that you have heard what your project sounds like, let's change some pitch settings.

To Set a Groove Clip to Not Follow the Project Pitch

1. Double-click on the Groove clip in Track 4.

   The Loop Construction view appears.

2. Deselect the Follow Project Pitch button.

3. Close the Loop Construction view and listen to your project again.

89

It sounds different because the Groove clip on Track 4 is no longer following the default project pitch of E, instead it follows its own root note of C.

Next, let's add some pitch markers.

To Add Pitch Markers

1. Click the Solo button [S] in Track 4 to solo the track.

2. Right-click in the Time Ruler at the beginning of measure 1 and select Insert Marker from the menu.

   The Marker dialog appears.

3. In the Groove Clip Pitch dropdown, select C and click OK.

4. Create another pitch marker at the beginning of measure 2, this time selecting F from the Groove Clip Pitch Change dropdown.

5. Double-click on the clip in track 4 to open the Loop Construction view.

6. In the Loop Construction view, click the Follow Project Pitch button to enable it.

   Listen to the project. Because the default pitch of the project is now C at measure 1, the clip in track 4 sounds at its original pitch, because its original root note is C. When the Now time reaches measure 2, the project pitch changes to F, which forces the clip to transpose all of its data up a perfect 4th, from a root note of C to a root note of F.

Now let's change the tempo of the project.

Changing the Tempo of Your Project

Groove clips follow the project's tempo, so we can change the tempo, either for the entire project or just one part, and still have all our clips playing in time with each other.

To Change the Project Tempo

1. Select *Insert-Tempo* Change from the menu.

2. In the Tempo field, enter 110 and click OK.

   The project's tempo is now 110.

Play your project. Do you hear the difference? Try other tempos.

Now that we have created a project that uses existing Groove clips, let's take the next step and learn how to create our own Groove clips.

Creating Your Own Groove Clips

Any audio clip (of a reasonable size) can be a Groove clip.

We are going to take a clip, slip-edit it so that it contains just the parts we want, and open it in the Loop Construction view to add tempo and pitch information to it.

To Create a Groove Clip (example 1)

In this example we will import a short clip of a bass guitar, slip-edit it and convert it to a Groove clip.

1. Select *File-New* to create a new project.

2. Right-click the Snap to Grid button to open its dialog box, set the Musical Time duration to Measure, and click OK to close the dialog box.

3. Click [icon] in the Views toolbar to open the Loop Explorer view.

4. In the Explorer view, navigate to the Tutorials folder in the directory where you installed SONAR.

5. Drag and drop the BASS.WAV file into the new project at measure 1.

6. Double-click the clip.

    The Loop Construction view appears. You see that there is silence at both the beginning and end of the clip. We are going to slip-edit the clip so that the clip begins with the attack of the first note and ends as the last note tails off.

7. Move you cursor to the beginning of the clip.

8. When the cursor changes to look like this [icon], drag the beginning of the clip until you reach the edge of the first rise in the waveform.

9. Slip-edit the end of the clip until you reach the end of the last notes decay.

    Note: You can not slip edit a clip that has its Groove clip characteristics enabled. You can turn a clip's Groove clip characteristics on or off either in the Loop Construction view, or in the Clips pane. In the Clips pane, right-click the clip and choose *Groove-Clip Looping* from the popup menu.

Your clip should look something like this:

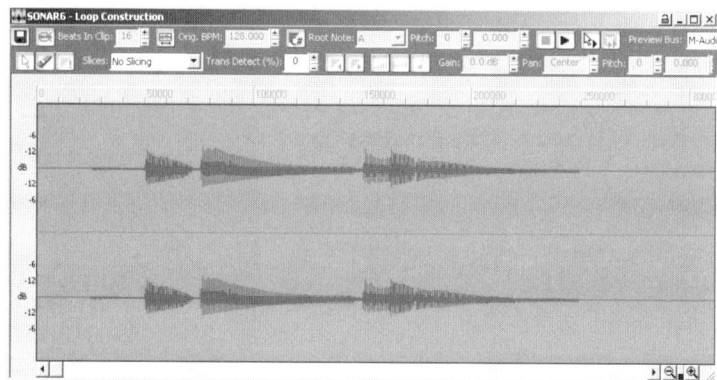

10. Click the Enable Looping button ⌘ on the Loop Construction view toolbar to enable the clip's Groove clip characteristics.

    SONAR automatically slices the clip and assigns in a number of beats. Notice that SONAR has sliced this clip at eighth note intervals. This is a clip with a waveform that does not have dramatic transients (sharp rises in volume). For clips like this, markers at beat intervals work best.

    The clip is now a Groove clip, and it looks like this:

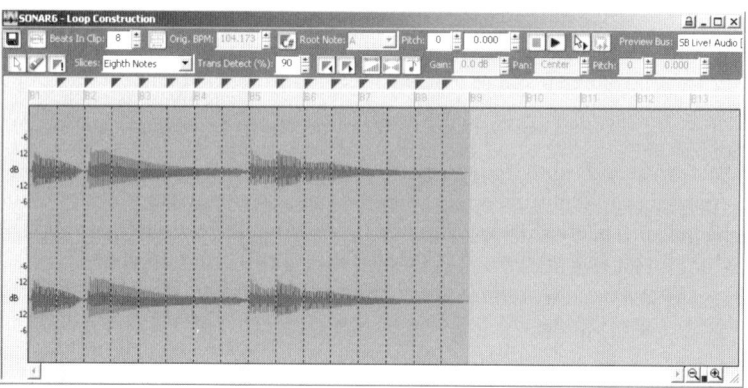

The bass track is now a Groove clip, so you can move it where you want and create repetitions by dragging it out.

Let's create another Groove clip.

To Create a Groove Clip (example 2)

For this example we are going to use a clip that does not need to be slip-edited.

1. In the Explorer view, navigate to the Tutorials folder in the directory where you installed SONAR.

2. Drag and drop the DRUMS.WAV file into the new project below your bass track at measure 1.

3. Double-click the clip.

4. Click the Enable Looping button [icon].

   SONAR automatically slices the clip and assigns in a number of beats. Notice that SONAR has sliced this clip at eighth notes and at the beginning of some transients. This has dramatic transients. For clips like this, transient markers work best.

   The clip is now a Groove clip, and it looks like the following picture. You can click the zoom buttons in the lower right corner to get a better view.

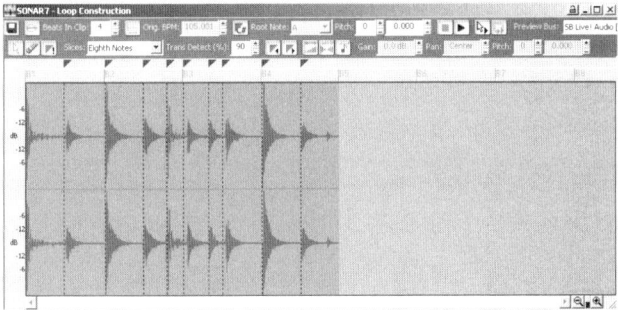

The markers in the Loop Construction view are used to tell SONAR where to preserve timing. The idea is to preserve the clip while being able to change the tempo. When a clip has a lot of transients, as this one does, it is a good idea to make sure that the slicing markers fall at the beginning of the transients, thus preserving their timing. This clip has several markers which can be fine tuned to give better results. Let's move some markers to better preserve the timing of this clip.

To Fine Tune the Slicing Markers in a Groove Clip

1. Identify the markers which are close to the beginning of a transient.

   An example of transients that should be moved:

   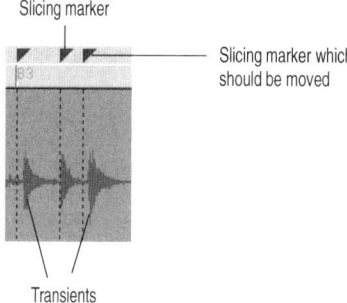

2. Click the Select tool.

3. Click and drag the slicing markers that need to be fine tuned so that they are at the very beginning of the transient.

   Like this:

   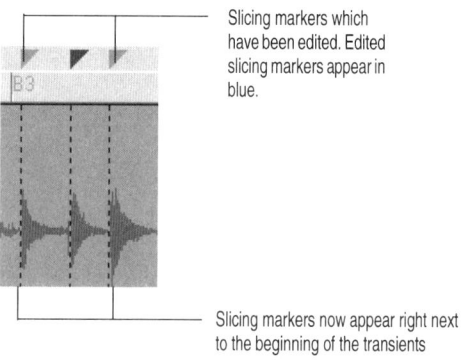

Use the two projects you have created to experiment with Groove clips further. Try new loops, change tempos, add pitch markers, record clips and use them to create your own loops. For more information about Groove clips, see Chapter 6, *Using Loops*.

Tutorial 7—Mixing

SONAR has an almost unlimited number of tools to help you mix down. You can automate almost any knob, fader, or button by using any of several methods. You can even automate the internal settings of some effects—not just the bus controls but the controls on some individual effects. When your project sounds the way you want, you can save it and export it in Wave, MP3, Real Audio, or Windows Media Advanced Streaming format.

Let's do some more work on TUTORIAL5.CWB, and explore the following tasks:

- Adding real-time audio effects
- Automating an individual effect's settings
- Grouping controls
- Automating your mix
- Exporting an MP3 file

Adding Real-time Audio Effects

Let's add some flanging to the first guitar track in TUTORIAL5.CWB:

1. Add the flange effect to a guitar track by right-clicking its Fx field, and choosing **Audio Effects-Cakewalk-FxFlange** from the popup menu.

    The effect's dialog box appears.

2. Choose a preset flange setting from the Presets field.

3. Play the project to hear what it sounds like. You can continue to adjust the effect while the project plays; there is a slight delay before your adjustments are audible.

Close the dialog box. You can add effects to buses with the same method (right-click the Fx field in a bus, and choose an effect from the popup menu).

You can delete an effect from an FX field by right-clicking the effect's name and choosing **Delete** from the popup menu. Instead of moving the controls manually, let's automate them by drawing an envelope in the Clips pane.

Automating an Individual Effect's Settings

Let's draw an envelope to automate one of the flanger's controls:

1. In the Clips pane, right-click in the first guitar track (the track you added the FxFlange effect to) and choose ***Envelopes-Create Track Envelope-FxFlange 1*** from the popup menu.

   The FxFlange1 dialog box appears.

2. Let's create only one envelope, even though we could create many: in the Envelope Exists field, check the Voice 1 Feedback option to create an envelope that controls the level of feedback on voice 1 of the FxFlange effect.

3. Click OK (you could choose a color for the envelope before you click OK by clicking the Choose Color button).

   A dotted line with a **node** (rectangular dot) at the beginning appears on top of the guitar clip. A dotted line means there is no automation data in that area of a track—only nodes and solid lines represent actual values.

4. Let's add a node at measure 17 of the guitar track: move the cursor over the dotted line at measure 17 until a vertical, double-ended arrow appears under it, and right-click the dotted line.

   The Envelope Editing menu appears.

5. Choose ***Add Node*** from the menu.

   A new node appears on the envelope at measure 17.

6. Move the cursor over the node until a cross appears under it, and drag the node up to the top of the track. Now you have a gradual increase in the level of Voice 1 Feedback. Notice that the line between the two nodes is solid, indicating that there is automation data everywhere between the two nodes.

7. Change the straight line between the two nodes, which is called a **Linear shape**, into a **Slow Curve** shape, by moving the cursor over the straight line until the vertical, double-ended arrow appears, then right-clicking the dotted line, and choosing ***Slow Curve*** from the Envelope Editing menu.

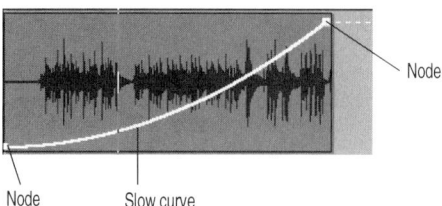

Now you have a gradual, but not linear increase in the Voice 1 Feedback level of your flange effect. You can drag linear and curve shapes vertically, but not horizontally. To change their horizontal positions, drag the node at either end of a shape. You can drag a node in any direction.

Grouping Controls

To assist in manipulating the controls, you can tie faders to one another. For example, if you want to increase the volume level on several tracks at the same time, you can assign them to a group. Then, when you move one volume fader, you move them all. You can even have the controls move in opposite directions. For example, you can fade one track in and another out.

To group faders:

1. In the Track view (you can use the Console view if you want), right-click the volume fader for track 2 (bass).

2. In the popup menu, choose **Group** and select **A** from the dropdown list. This assigns the fader to group A. A red marker appears next to the volume fader, indicating that it belongs to group A, whose color is red.

3. Repeat steps 1 and 2 for tracks 3 and 4.

Now you've grouped the volume faders of three tracks. When you move one fader, all of the others follow. If you want to move a single fader independently of the others, hold the Ctrl key while moving the fader. To ungroup a fader, right-click it and choose **Ungroup** from the popup menu. For more information, see "Using Control Groups" on page 449.

Automating Your Mix

You can record the fader movements of the mix, which is called **automating** them. To do so:

1. Rewind to the beginning of the project.

2. Move the faders, pans, and any other controls to the initial settings you desire. You should set up a good balance between the tracks.

3. Arm the volume fader for track 4 by right-clicking it and choosing **Arm for Automation** from the popup menu. A highlighted rectangle appears around the armed fader.

4. Display the Automation toolbar by using the ***View-Toolbars-Automation*** command.

5. Make sure that the Enable Automation Playback button in the Automation toolbar is in the depressed position.

6. To start recording the automation, click the Record Automation button in the Transport toolbar, and move the armed fader as needed so that the balance between the guitar and other instruments is optimized throughout the project.

7. Stop recording by clicking the Stop button or by pressing the Spacebar.

You've now automated the volume fader of track 4 of your project—SONAR draws a graph (an envelope) of the automation in the Clips pane of track 4. You can hide or show envelopes by using the dropdown arrow that's on the side of the Envelope tool button in the Track view toolbar, or by using the Clips pane popup menu, or the Envelope Editing menu. Now let's listen to the project again and watch the fader move automatically:

1. Rewind to the beginning.
2. Press the Spacebar to start playing the project.

You'll see the fader move just the way it moved when you recorded its movements. You can compare this mix to a mix with no automation by clicking the Enable Automation Playback button and playing your project again. Clicking the Enable Automation Playback button toggles the automation off and on.

When you're done tweaking the mix, to make sure you don't accidentally erase any automation data, you can disarm any armed controls by clicking the Disarm all automation controls button that's in the Automation toolbar, or the red Aut indicator that's in the Status bar.

For more information, see Chapter 13, *Using Automation*.

Exporting an MP3 File

When your project finally sounds the way you want, you can export it in any or all of several file formats, including:

- Wave (CD format)
- MP3
- Real Audio
- Windows Media Advanced Streaming Format

When you export a file from SONAR, you can choose to include any or all of the effects, automation, and mute and solo settings that your project contains.

Let's export our project as an MP3:

1. Make sure all the tracks you want to export are unmuted and unarchived. If you only want to export one or two tracks, it's easier to solo these tracks instead of muting all the others.
2. Make a time selection, if necessary. If any tracks use real-time effects such as reverb or delay, select your whole project plus an extra measure or two at the end so you won't cut off the reverb "tail."
3. Choose **File-Export-Audio** to display the Export Audio dialog box.
4. Select a destination folder using the Look In field.
5. Enter a file name.
6. Choose MP3 from the Files of type dropdown list.

7. In the Format field, select one of the following options:
   - Export to Stereo File(s)—All exported tracks are mixed down to a single stereo file.
   - Export to Separate Left and Right Files—All exported tracks are mixed down to two mono files, left and right.
   - Export to Mono File(s)—All exported tracks are mixed down to a single mono file.
8. In the Bit Depth field, select the bit depth that you want your exported file to use. For MP3s use 16.
9. In the Source Bus(es) field, select a sound card or sound cards from the list. If you select more than one, you can select the Each Source to Separate Submix checkbox to create separate files for each device selected in the Source Bus(es) field.
10. If the Outputs of the tracks you are combining are the same (if they have the same thing listed in their Output fields—they should in this tutorial example), you can ignore this step. Otherwise, in the Separation field, choose from these options:
    - Each Bus to Separate Submix—if the tracks you are combining use different buses in their Output fields, choose this option if you want to create separate files for each different output that the tracks use.
    - Each Main Out to Separate Submix—if the Outputs of the tracks you are combining go to different Main Outs, choose this option to create separate files for each different Main Out that the tracks use.
    - All Main Outs to Single Mix—if the Outputs of the tracks you are combining go to different Main Outs, choose this option to create a single new file that combines the output data from all the Main Outs.
11. In the Mix Enables field, select the effects you want to include in your new file—usually, you select all the listed options.

    Note: Selecting the Track Mute/Solo option causes muted tracks to be left out of the exported mix, and soloed tracks to be the only tracks exported.
12. Click Export.

    The Cakewalk MP3 Encoder (Trial Version) dialog box appears.

To use the Cakewalk MP3 Encoder:

1. You don't need an unlock code until the trial period is up, so for now click Continue.

   A new dialog box appears.
2. Choose the options you want for your new MP3 file—for help choosing options click the Help button in the dialog box.
3. When you finish choosing options, click the Encode button.

SONAR compresses and mixes your project to a file with the extension .MP3 that is located in the folder you chose in the Look In field of the Export Audio dialog box.

That's the end of the mixing tutorial. For more information, see "Mixing and Effects Patching" on page 419 and "Using Automation" on page 493.

Tutorial 8—Using Soft Synths

A software synthesizer is a software program that produces various sounds through your audio interface when the soft synth program receives MIDI data from a MIDI controller or sequencer program. SONAR supports all major varieties of software synthesizers, including DX instruments, or DXi's for short, and VST Instruments (you can use VST instruments by running SONAR's included VST Adapter to configure the VST instruments). SONAR has a Synth Rack view to make inserting a DXi, VSTi, or ReWire instrument a one-step process.

Cakewalk TTS-1 is a great example of a DXi, so let's use it for our tutorial. Because this DXi supports the DXi 2.0 format, it has multiple outputs (4), and you can record the movement of some of its controls as automation. You probably installed Cakewalk TTS-1 when you installed SONAR. To make sure, open a project that has at least one audio track, right-click the FX field of an audio track to open the plug-in popup menu, and look under ***DXi Synth*** (if you've installed and adapted any VST instruments, you'll see a ***VST*** option on the DXi Synth menu). You should see Cakewalk TTS-1 listed. If you don't, insert your SONAR CD into your CD drive, copy the software synthesizers including Cakewalk TTS-1 to your hard drive, and restart SONAR.

This tutorial covers the following:

- Inserting Cakewalk TTS-1 into a project
- Playing MIDI tracks through a DXi
- Adding effects to a DXi
- Playing a DXi in real time
- Converting DXi tracks to audio

Inserting Cakewalk TTS-1 into a Project

Inserting a DXi into a project means that the name of the DXi appears in the dropdown menus of MIDI track Output fields and audio track Input fields.

To Insert Cakewalk TTS-1 into a Project

1. Open a MIDI project—for this tutorial use TUTORIAL8.CWP.

2. Use the ***Insert-DXi Synth*** command and click Cakewalk TTS-1 on the popup menu.

   The Insert DXi Synth Options dialog appears.

3. In the Create These Tracks fields, deselect MIDI Source Track, because we want to patch some pre-existing tracks into Cakewalk TTS-1.

4. Select All Synth Outputs (Audio) because we're going to use a different audio track for each of Cakewalk TTS-1's 4 outputs. The new audio tracks have Cakewalk TTS-1 already patched to them as audio inputs.

5. In the Open These Windows fields, select both Synth Property Page and Synth Rack view. These two options open Cakewalk TTS-1's property page (interface), and the Synth Rack view, respectively.

6. Click OK.

SONAR inserts 4 audio tracks that each have one of Cakewalk TTS-1's outputs as an input (notice that these tracks have the DXi label next to their track numbers), opens the Synth Rack view with Cakewalk TTS-1 displayed in the first row, and opens Cakewalk TTS-1's property page.

Notice that the Output field of the MIDI track is labeled Cakewalk TTS-1 1. The "1" means that this is the first instance of Cakewalk TTS-1 that you have inserted into this project. If you use the ***Insert-DXi Synth*** command to insert another instance or copy of Cakewalk TTS-1 into this project, its label will be Cakewalk TTS-1 2, and it will function as a totally separate synth. MIDI data in tracks that use Cakewalk TTS-1 1 as an output will have no effect on MIDI tracks that have Cakewalk TTS-1 2 as an output.

Playing MIDI Tracks through a DXi

Now that you have verified that Cakewalk TTS-1 is installed, let's try some of its sounds on some pre-recorded MIDI data.

To Play MIDI Tracks through Cakewalk TTS-1

1. Drag Cakewalk TTS-1 property page out of the way for now, and in the first MIDI track (Guitar 1), click the dropdown arrow in the track's Output field, and choose Cakewalk TTS-1 as an output.

   Notice that when you choose Cakewalk TTS-1 as a track's output, the patch for that track's MIDI channel in Cakewalk TTS-1 interface changes to the same one that the track displays.

2. Set the Output fields in all the other MIDI tracks to Cakewalk TTS-1. **Note**: When the cursor is in the Output field of one track, pressing the Up or Down arrow key moves the cursor to the same field in the next track.

3. Let's insert a patch change in track 1: click the track number of the Guitar 1 track to select it, and move the Now time to the Verse 1 marker by clicking the Next Marker button once (the Next Marker button is in the Markers toolbar; if you don't see it, use the ***View-Toolbars*** command and check Markers).

4. Use the ***Insert-Patch/Bank Change*** command to open the Bank/Patch Change dialog box.

5. In the Bank field, select 15488-Preset Normal 0, and in the Patch field, select Overdrive Gt, and click OK.

Now you've routed your MIDI tracks through Cakewalk TTS-1, and inserted a patch change. Rewind the project and play it to hear the project through Cakewalk TTS-1.

Converting Your DXi Tracks to Audio

Once your project sounds the way you want it, it's extremely easy to convert your DXi MIDI tracks to either new audio tracks, or Wave, MP3, or other exportable files.

To Convert Your DXi Tracks to New Audio Tracks

1. Mute all tracks that you don't want to convert; make sure you don't mute the audio track(s) that the DXi is patched into, or the MIDI track(s) that you are using as a source.

2. Let's set our MIDI tracks to use different outputs on the TTS-1: in the TTS-1 interface, click the System button to open the System Settings panel, and click the Option button in System Settings to open the Options dialog.

3. On the Output Assign tab look in the Tone Name column, and click one of the four Output buttons next to each name in the Tone Name column. This assigns your individual MIDI instruments to different audio outputs from the TTS-1. Click the Close button.

4. Use the ***Edit-Bounce to Track(s)*** command.

   The Bounce to Track(s) dialog box appears.

5. In the Source Category field, choose Tracks.

6. In the Channel Format field, choose mono if you want mono tracks, and stereo if you want stereo tracks.

7. In the Source/Buses field, make sure all 4 outputs are selected. This will create a separate audio track for each selected output. If you wanted to combine your MIDI tracks into just one audio tracks, send all the MIDI tracks through just one output (Step 3), and select only that output in the Source/Buses field.

8. In the Mix Enables field, make sure all choices are selected.

9. Click OK.

SONAR creates new audio tracks from the outputs you selected. When you're through converting, don't forget to mute your MIDI tracks so you won't hear them and the new audio track(s) at the same time.

To Export Your DXi Tracks as Wave, MP3, or Other Type Files

1. Mute all tracks that you don't want to export; make sure you don't mute the audio track(s) that the DXi is patched into, or the MIDI track(s) that you are using as a source.

2. Use the ***File-Export-Audio*** command.

   The Export Audio dialog box appears.

3. In the Look in field, choose the location where you want the exported file to be.

4. Type a file name in the File name field.

5. In the Files of Type field, choose the kind or file you want to create.

6. In the Source Category field, choose Tracks if you want to create separate files for each MIDI track, or choose Entire Mix if you want to create one file.

7. Choose a channel format, sample rate, and bit depth that are appropriate for the new file(s) you are creating. Don't choose Split Mono in the Channel Format field if you want to export a single file.

8. In the Source/Buses field, select all outputs if you chose Tracks in Step 6, or accept the default if you chose Entire Mix.

9. In the Mix Enables field, make sure all choices are selected.

10. Click OK.

SONAR creates a new audio file or files of the type you specified. Find the file(s) in the folder you specified, and double-click each file to listen to it.

Tutorial 9—Drum Maps

In SONAR drum maps allow you to assign a single MIDI track to multiple outputs. MIDI drum tracks appear in the Piano Roll view's Drum Grid pane. In the Note Map pane you can map pitches to notes in any number of software or hardware outputs.

In this tutorial we are going to create a drum map, create a MIDI drum track using the Pattern Brush, and use the drum map to map drum notes to several different outputs.

Create a New Project

First, we need to create a new project.

1. Select **File-New** from the menu.

    The New Project dialog appears.

2. Select the Normal template and click OK.

Creating a Drum Map

Drum maps allow you to map note pitches from the same track to different output devices, either hardware or software.

Note: Before you begin, make sure you have some MIDI devices selected. To check, select **Options-MIDI Devices**. For more information about selecting MIDI devices, see "To Choose MIDI Devices" on page 136.

To Create a New Drum Map

1. In a MIDI track, click the Output dropdown menu and choose **Drum Map Manager** from the menu that appears.

    The Drum Map Manager dialog appears.

2. Click the Create New Drum Map button ![New].

    A new drum map appears in the Drum Maps Used in Current Project field.

3. Click the Presets dropdown arrow and select GM Drums (Complete Kit).

4. In the Out Port column, click one of the down arrows, hold down the Ctrl and Shift keys, and click the name of the port or instrument that you want to hear drums on.

    All the Out Port entries change to the port or instrument you selected. Later, we'll start sending individual notes to different outputs.

5. In the Chn column, make sure all entries are set to 10, or whatever MIDI channel your drum sounds are on.

6. Close the Drum Map Manager.

Create a Drum Track

You can use any blank MIDI track for your drums. If you don't have a MIDI track, create using the *Insert-MIDI Track* command.

To Assign a MIDI Track to a Drum Map

1. Display the Track view if it is minimized.

2. In the track you want to assign to a drum map, click the Output dropdown and select *DM1GM Drums (Complete Kit)* from the options in the menu that appears.

To Create a Drum Track Using the Pattern Brush

1. Select the track you have assigned to a drum map and select *View-Piano Roll*.

   The blank drum track appears in the Drum Grid pane of the Piano Roll view.

2. In the Piano Roll view, click on the down arrow to the right of the Pattern Brush tool and select *Kick+Snare Patterns (R-T)-Stacy 7*.

3. Click the down arrow again and select *Use Pattern Polyphony*. This option tells SONAR to use the original pitch values when "painting" notes in the Drum Grid pane.

4. Click on the Pattern Brush to select it.

5. Starting at the beginning of your track, click and drag the Pattern Brush tool for a few measures in the Drum Grid pane.

   A series of notes, at different pitch values appears in the Drum Grid pane. If you don't see any notes, scroll down in the Drum Grid to see the notes.

6. Click the Pattern Brush down arrow again and select *Cymbal Patterns (C-F)-Fill 4*.

7. Repeat step 5.

8. Listen to your drum track. Make a mental note of the drum sounds your hear, because they are about to change.

Now it is time to mix things up a bit. Lets send some of your drum sounds to a different output.

Map Drum Notes to Different Outputs

First, we need to create an output to use, so lets open Cakewalk TTS-1 and use that soft synth for this part of the tutorial.

To Open Cakewalk TSS-1

1. Select *View-Synth Rack* from the menu.

2. Click the Insert Synth button [+] in the Synth Rack toolbar and select *DXi Synth-Cakewalk TTS-1* from the menu that appears.

   The Insert DXi Synth Options dialog appears.

3. Make sure that the MIDI Source Track option in the Create These Tracks section is unchecked.

4. In the Create These Tracks section, check the First Synth Output (Audio) option. This option creates a single audio output track.

5. In the Open These Windows section, check the Synth Property Page option. This option opens Cakewalk TTS-1 when we close the Insert DXi Synth Options dialog.

6. Click OK.

7. An audio output track for the Cakewalk TTS-1 appears in the Track view and the Cakewalk TTS-1 appears. If you don't see the track, scroll down in the Track pane to find it.

Now, we can map notes to different outputs.

To Map a Note to a New Output

1. Select your drum track and open the Piano Roll view by selecting *View-Piano Roll* from the menu.

2. Right-click in the Note Map pane (the list of drum names on the far left of the Piano Roll view) and select *Drum Map Manager* from the right-click menu.

   The Drum Map Manager appears.

3. In the Drum Map Manager, change the Out Port for the In Note 46 (Bb3) to Cakewalk TTS-1.

   The new Port/Channel pair Cakewalk TTS-1 1 / 10 appears in the Port and Channels field at the bottom of the Drum Map Manager.

4. In the Bank column for the Port/Channel pair Cakewalk TTS-1 1 / 1 select 15360-Preset Rhythm.

5. In the Patch column for the Port/Channel pair Cakewalk TTS-1 1 / 1 select Standard Set.

6. In the Drum Map Manager, change the Out Port setting for In Note 38 (D3) to Cakewalk TTS-1.

7. Close the Drum Map Manager and play your project to listen to the different drum sounds.

To Change Other Drum Map Settings

You can open the Drum Map Manager from either a MIDI track's Output menu, or with the ***Options-Drum Map Manager*** command.

Change map settings in the Drum Map Manager as described in the following table:

To do this...	Do this...
Add a row (a mapped pitch)	Click the Add New Drum Map Entry button ![New].
Change In Note value	Double-click in the appropriate cell and enter a new value, or click on the right side of the cell, and when the cursor changes to an up and down arrow, drag it up to increase the value or down to lower the value.
Change the Name setting	Double click on the appropriate cell and enter a new name.
Change the Channel setting	Click the appropriate channel cell's down arrow and select a channel from the menu that appears.
Change the Out Port setting	Click the appropriate Out Port cell's down arrow and select an output port from the menu that appears.
Change the Vel+ setting	Double-click in the appropriate cell and enter a new value, or click on the right side of the cell, and when the cursor changes to an up and down arrow, drag it up to increase the value or down to lower the value.
Change the V Scale setting	Double-click in the appropriate cell and enter a new value, or click on the right side of the cell, and when the cursor changes to an up and down arrow, drag it up to increase the value or down to lower the value.

When you are happy with the drum sounds you have mapped, you can mixdown to an audio file. For more information, see "Converting MIDI to Audio" on page 429.

For more information about drum maps and editing drum tracks in the Piano Roll view, see Chapter 8, *Drum Maps and the Drum Grid Pane*.

That's the end of Tutorial 9. For more information, see "Working with Software Synthesizer" on page 399.

Tutorial 10—Cyclone DXi

This tutorial explains how to use Cyclone DXi. You will learn how to open, play and edit loops as you create a short song.

Cyclone Overview

Cyclone DXi allows you to trigger individual parts or "slices" of Riff Wave files and ACIDized files. There are 16 pads, and you can assign a file to each pad. You can trigger pads with a MIDI file, your mouse or a MIDI keyboard. You can edit the content and length of each file all while syncing to SONAR's tempo changes and pitch markers.

Let's start by opening Cyclone.

To Open Cyclone DXi
1. Open a new project by selecting **File-New** and selecting the Normal template.
2. Select **View-Synth Rack**.

    The Synth Rack appears.

3. In the Synth Rack click the Insert DXi Instrument button and select Cyclone from the menu that appears.

    The Insert DXi Synth Options dialog appears.

4. For the purposes of this tutorial, select First Synth Output (Audio) in the Create These Tracks section, and Synth Property Page in the Open These Windows section.

5. Click OK.

    Cyclone DXi and the Cyclone DXi's audio output track appear.

Now let's add some files.

Adding Files to a Pad Group

There are several ways to assign a file to a Pad Group.

To Import Files to a Pad Group
1. Click the Load Files button in pad group 1.

    The Open dialog appears.

2. Open the Tutorials folder located in the directory where you installed SONAR.

3. In the Tutorials folder select 100BEAT2.WAV and click Open.

The loop 100BEAT2.WAV appears in the Loop bin and Loop view.

To Import Files to the Loop Bin
1. Click the Load Files button in the Loop Bin.

   The Open dialog appears.

2. Open the Tutorials folder located in the directory where you installed SONAR.

3. In the Tutorials folder select 100FX.WAV and click Open.

The loop 100FX.WAV appears in the Loop bin and the Loop view.

To Drag Files from the Loop Bin to a Pad Group
- Click on 100FX in the Loop bin and drag it onto pad 2.

To Drag Files from Loop Explorer to the Loop Bin
1. Select *View-Loop Explorer*.

2. In the Loop Explorer, navigate to the Tutorials folder located in the directory where you installed SONAR.

3. Click and drag the loop 100ONETWO.WAV onto pad 3.

4. Click and drag the loop 100ORGAN.WAV onto pad 4.

Click the Preview button to listen to the song so far.

Now let's make some changes.

Setting a Pad's Volume and Pan
Now let's tweak some of the pad groups' controls.

To Change the Volume and Pan in a Pad Group
1. In pad group two, click on the Volume knob and drag your mouse down to lower the volume until the volume level indicator is vertical.

2. Repeat step 1 for the Volume knob in pad group 3.

3. In pad group two click the Pan knob and drag the mouse up until it is panned hard left.

4. In pad group four, click the Pan knob and drag the mouse down until it is panned hard right.

Click Play to hear all the pad groups together.

Now let's explore the different ways you can use Cyclone.

Playing Cyclone

Now that we have added loops and adjusted some of the pad group controls, let's use Cyclone as a real-time instrument and as a synth device.

To Play an Existing MIDI Track Through Cyclone

First, we'll create a MIDI track which will trigger the pads in Cyclone.

1. In the Track view, select an empty MIDI track. If you don't have a blank MIDI track, select **Insert-MIDI Track**.
2. In the MIDI track's Output field, select Cyclone 1.
3. Select the MIDI track and open the Piano Roll view.
4. In the Piano Roll view, right-click on the Snap to Grid button to open the Snap to Grid dialog.
5. In the Snap to Grid dialog, click the Musical Time radio button and select Measure.
6. In the Mode section of the Snap to Grid dialog, select the Move To radio button and click OK.
7. Click the Draw tool button.
8. Use your mouse to move the Draw tool over the Notes pane in the Piano Roll view.
9. Enter a C5 note at the beginning.
10. Enter a D5 note at the fifth measure.
11. Enter a E5 note at the beginning.
12. Enter a F5 note at the beginning and fifth measure.
13. Drag the ends of the notes on C5 and E5 until their duration is eight measures. (If you have Auto Erase enabled, you have to disable it to drag out the duration of the note. Disable Auto Erase by clicking on the black arrow to the right of the Draw tool and clicking the Auto Erase command. The command appears unchecked when disabled.)
14. Drag the end of the D5 note until its duration is four measures (through measure eight).
15. Drag the ends of the F5 notes until their duration is two measures (through measures two and six, respectively).
16. Rewind the project and play it back.
17. Experiment by changing the note start times and durations.

You can "play" Cyclone either using your mouse to trigger pads and clicking them once again to shut them off, or by using an external controller. Let's try both.

To Play Cyclone with Your Mouse
As soon as you click on a pad in Cyclone the first loop begins to play. Simply click pads to turn them on and click on them again to turn them off.

To Play Cyclone with a MIDI Keyboard or Controller
For the purposes of this part of the tutorial we assume you have an external MIDI controller like a keyboard. If you don't, just move on to the next part of the tutorial, "Editing Loops in the Loop Editor" on page 111. There's plenty more to know about Cyclone!

1. Make sure your MIDI device is hooked up properly.
2. Select the MIDI track that is assigned to Cyclone DXi.
3. On your MIDI keyboard press and hold C5, D5, E5 or F5 (the C, D, E or F keys in the center of your keyboard.

   The appropriate loop plays through Cyclone DXi.

Now let's create new loops by substituting slices.

Editing Loops in the Loop Editor
Each beat of a loop, as it appears in the Loop view or the Pad Editor can be replaced with a beat from another loop.

To Replace Slices
1. Click the Load Files button in pad 5 and select MARACAS.WAV from the Tutorials folder.
2. In the Cyclone DXi toolbar, click the Auto Preview button.
3. Select the maracas loop in the Loop Bin.

   The maracas loop appears in the Loop view.
4. Click the first slice of the maracas loop in the Loop view. We are going to use this slice as a substitute for some of the slices in pad 1.
5. Click and drag the first slice of the maracas loop into the Pad Editor over the slices in the pad 1.
6. Drop the loop on the third slice, a cymbal hit that's located half-way through beat 1 of the 100BEAT2.WAV loop.
7. Listen to the other slices in pad 1, and substitute the slice of the maracas loop for parts of the 100BEAT2.WAV loop.
8. Click Play in Cyclone DXi to hear the changes.

There is much more to the Cyclone DXi. For more information, see "Appendix C: Cyclone" on page 661.

3 Controlling Playback

When you play your SONAR project, you have full control over the tempo or speed of playback, which tracks are played, which sound cards or other devices are used to produce the sound, and what the tracks sound like.

SONAR's multi-MIDI enhancements give you the ability to play multiple synths or tracks from a single keyboard or controller, or let multiple performers play the same or different tracks. You have total control over MIDI echo (MIDI echo refers to where MIDI input signals are sent once SONAR receives them).

Note: SONAR has a button called the Audio Engine button in the Transport toolbar which you click to stop any feedback you may experience if there is a loop somewhere in your mixer setup. Whenever you play a project, SONAR automatically enables the audio engine, which you can tell by watching the Status bar—whenever the audio engine is running, the Audio Running indicator in the Status bar lights up.

In This Chapter

The Now Time and How to Use It	114
Controlling Playback	120
Track-by-Track Playback	124
Changing Track Settings	127
Controlling Live MIDI Playback—MIDI Echo	144
Local Control	147
Video Playback, Import, and Export	150
Locating Missing Audio	157

The Now Time and How to Use It

Every project has a current time, known as the **Now time**, which keeps track of where you are in a project. The Now time appears as a vertical line in the Track view and is displayed in both the Large Transport toolbar and the Position toolbar, in two formats:

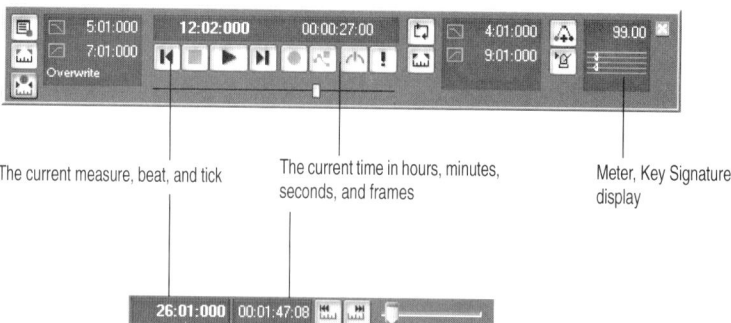

The measure, beat, and tick number (MBT) identifies the Now time in musical time units. Ticks are subdivisions of quarter notes and indicate the timebase of the project. For more information about the timebase, see "Setting the MIDI Timing Resolution" on page 169. The other time format is the SMPTE format, expressed in hours, minutes, seconds, and frames.

Here are some examples of times expressed in measure, beat, and tick (MBT) format:

Time...	What it means...
1:01:000	First beat of the first measure
9:04:000	Fourth beat of the ninth measure
4:02:060	The 60th tick of the second beat of the fourth measure

The hours-minutes-seconds-frames format is commonly referred to as the SMPTE time. SMPTE is the acronym for the Society of Motion Picture and Television Engineers. In this format, time is measured in hours, minutes, seconds, and frames. It's not necessary for a project to begin at time zero in this format—any time can be used to represent the start of a project. If you are synchronizing SONAR with an external device whose start time is not 0, you must offset SONAR to match the external device's start time. For more information, see Chapter 18, *Synchronizing Your Gear*.

Here are some examples of times expressed in this format (assuming that zero is the start time):

Time...	What it means...
00:00:00:00	The beginning of the project
00:05:10:00	Five minutes and ten seconds from the beginning of the project
01:30:00:00	One hour and thirty minutes into the project
00:00:00:05	Five frames into the project

SONAR provides many ways to set the Now time. Here are just a few:

To Change the Now Time

- Click the desired time on the Time Ruler in the Track view, Piano Roll view, or Staff view

- In the Navigator pane, click anywhere in the view while holding down the Ctrl key to change the Now Time to that location

- Click on the Now time in the Large Transport toolbar, enter the desired time, and press Enter

- Choose **Go-Time** or press F5, enter the desired time, and click OK

- Click on an event in the Event List view

You can also set the Now time by right-clicking in the Clips pane if you enable the Right Click Sets Now option in the Track View Properties dialog. Right-click a clip and select **View Options** from the menu that appears to open the Track View Properties dialog.

When entering a time in MBT format, the beat and tick values are optional. You can use a colon, space, decimal point, or vertical bar to separate the parts of the Now time:

You enter...	The Now time is set to...
2	2:01:000
4 2 0	4:02:000
9	9:01:000
5|1:30	5:01:030

115

When entering a time in SMPTE format, you can enter a single number (hour), two numbers (hour and minutes), three numbers (hour, minutes, and seconds), or all four numbers.

If you click in the Time Ruler while the snap grid is enabled, the Now time will be snapped to the nearest point in the grid. By setting the grid size to a whole note or quarter note, you can easily set the Now time to a measure or beat boundary.

You can also use the buttons and the scroll bar in either the Transport toolbar or Large Transport toolbar (shown below) to adjust the time.

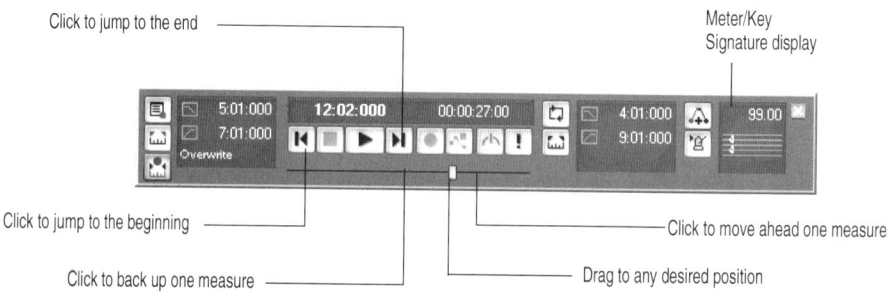

The Large Transport toolbar differs from the Transport toolbar because it displays the Now time (which you can set by entering numbers into the display fields in either MBT or SMPTE time) and the Meter/Key Signature display. The Meter/Key Signature display shows the current meter, key signature, and tempo. You can edit the meter and key signature by clicking the display to open the Meter/Key Signature dialog box. You can display the Large Transport toolbar by selecting the *View-Toolbars* command to open the Toolbars dialog box, and checking Transport (Large).

When playback or recording is stopped, the Now Time either remains at the point where the project stopped or snaps back to the Now Time Marker. This behavior is controlled in the General tab of the Global Options dialog.

The Now Time Marker

In the Track view, the Now time appears as a black vertical line. When you set the Now time in the Track view a white triangle called the Now time marker appears in the Time Ruler. This marker represents the point at which the Now time will snap back to after you stop playback or recording. You can change the Now time marker behavior so that the marker moves to the current Now time when playback or recording is topped.

To Change the Now Time Marker Behavior

1. Select *Options-Global* from the SONAR menu.

   The Global Options dialog appears.

2. Click the General tab.

3. Uncheck the On Stop, Rewind to Now Marker option to have the Now time marker move to follow the current Now time when you stop playback.

   Or

   Check the On Stop, Rewind to Now Marker option to have the Now time snap back to the Now time marker when you stop playback.

4. Click OK.

Displaying the Now Time in Large Print

SONAR can display the Now time in large print so that it's easier to see when you are far from your monitor (for example, when you're at your keyboard or another instrument) or when several people need to read the Now time from a distance. Here's how:

To Display the Big Time View

1. Choose *View-Big Time* to display the Big Time view.

2. Change the settings according to the table:

To do this...	Do this...
Switch time format	Click on the view to toggle between MBT and SMPTE time
Change font or color	Right-click on the view, choose the font and color you want, and click OK
Change the size of the view	Drag any corner of the view to change its size

Note that SONAR ignores font styles and effects such as strikeout and underline.

Other Ways to Set the Now Time

There are a variety of commands and keyboard shortcuts you can use to set the Now time:

Command...	Shortcut...	What it does...
Go-Time	F5	Lets you enter the Now time in the Position toolbar or in a dialog box
Go-From	F7	Sets the Now time to the From time (the start time of the current time selection)
Go-Thru	F8	Sets the Now time to the Thru time (the end time of the current time selection)
Go-Beginning	Ctrl+Home	Sets the Now time to the beginning of the project
Go-End	Ctrl+End	Sets the Now time to the end of the project
Go-Previous Measure	Ctrl+PgUp	Sets the Now time to the start of the current measure if the Now time is not on a barline, or to the start of the previous measure if the Now time is on a barline.
Go-Next Measure	Ctrl+PgDn	Sets the Now time to the start of the next measure

If your project has markers, you can use the Marker toolbar to set the Now time:

To do this...	Do this...
Skip to the next marker	Click on the Markers toolbar (or press Ctrl+Shift+PgDn).
Skip to the previous marker	Click on the Markers toolbar (or press Ctrl+Shift+PgUp).
Jump to any marker	Click on the Markers toolbar to open the Markers view. Click on the marker you want to jump to in the Markers view.

For more information about markers, see "Creating and Using Markers" on page 224.

The Time Ruler

The Time Ruler appears in the Track view, Tempo view, Staff view and Piano Roll view. It has several functions, including:

- Making a Time Selection

    The Time Ruler follows the Snap to Grid settings, if enabled. For more information about using the Snap to Grid, see "Defining and Using the Snap Grid" on page 222.

- Changing the Now time

    For more information about the Now time, see "The Now Time and How to Use It" on page 114.

- Adding loop, punch, and pitch markers

    You can right-click in the Time Ruler to add markers. For more information, see "Creating and Using Markers" on page 224 and "Using Pitch Markers in the Track View" on page 266.

In the Track view, the Time Ruler has the following time display options or formats:

- Measures, Beats and Ticks (M:B:T)
- Hours, Minutes, Seconds and Frames (H:M:S:F—also called SMPTE)
- Samples

The M:B:T setting follows your settings in the Meter/Key view. If you project is set to 4/4 time, you have four beats in the Time Ruler for each measure. If your project is set to 6/8 time, you have six beats in the Time Ruler for each measure.

To Set the Time Ruler Format to M:B:T
1. Right-click in the Track view Time Ruler.
2. In the menu that appears, select *Time Ruler Format-M:B:T*.

To Set the Time Ruler Format to H:M:S:F (SMPTE)
1. Right-click in the Track view Time Ruler.
2. In the menu that appears, select *Time Ruler Format-H:M:S:F*.

To Set the Time Ruler Format to Samples

1. Right-click in the Track view Time Ruler.

2. In the menu that appears, select *Time Ruler Format-Samples*.

Note:

The Display All Times as SMPTE checkbox in the General tab of the Global Options dialog forces all times in the project to be displayed in SMPTE time, regardless of your setting in the Time Ruler.

Controlling Playback

To control playback, you have your choice of tools, menu commands, and shortcut keys for most common operations.

When you start playback, the Now time updates continuously to show the current time. When you stop playback, the Now time stops at the time you stopped. When you start playback again, it continues from the same point.

If the Now time is advancing but you don't hear any sound, see *Appendix A: Troubleshooting*. If you are using MIDI sync or syncing to MIDI time code, SONAR waits to receive external timing data before it begins playing. If the various views are not updating during playback, make sure the Scroll Lock key on your computer keyboard is not enabled. For more information, see Chapter 18, *Synchronizing Your Gear*.

Note: If your Windows setup uses any system sounds that are associated with any typical activity, such as minimizing a window, etc., you should disable these sounds. They can sound extremely loud through your monitors, and also interrupt playback and recording, if you open any dialog boxes or do anything that has a system sound attached to it while a project plays. The quickest way to disable all system sounds is to open the Control Panel (*Start-Settings-Control Panel*), double-click the Sounds icon to open the Sounds Properties dialog box, and in the Schemes field select No Sounds. Click Apply, and then click OK.

To Start and Stop Playback

To do this...	Do this...
Start playback	Press the Spacebar, click ▶, or choose **Transport-Play**
Stop playback	Press the Spacebar, click ■, or choose **Transport-Stop**
Rewind to the start of the project	Click ⏮, press the *w* key, or choose **Transport-Rewind**
Skip to the end of the project	Click ⏭

Note:

The default behavior for the Now time when you click the Stop button is for it to return to the Now time marker where playback began. If you want the Now time to remain where it is when you stop playback, you can use the keyboard shortcut Ctrl+Spacebar. If you want to change the default behavior, select ***Options-Global*** and click the General tab. In the General tab, uncheck the On Stop, Rewind to Now Marker option.

Handling Stuck Notes

Under MIDI, the events that turn notes on are separate from the events that stop notes from playing. Normally, when you stop playback, SONAR attempts to turn off all notes that are still playing. Depending on how your equipment is configured, it's possible for notes to get stuck in the "on" position. The ***Transport-Reset*** command is used to stop all notes from playing. The ***Transport-Reset*** command also stops feedback from input monitoring.

Note:

You can control the MIDI messages that are sent by the ***Transport-Reset*** command by changing the Panic Strength variable in the CAKEWALK.INI file.

To Clear Stuck Notes

- Choose ***Transport-Reset***, or click ! on the Large Transport toolbar.

Looping

Sometimes you want to listen to one portion of a project over and over, either so you can play along and rehearse or because you want to edit that section of the project while it is playing and hear the results as you make changes. SONAR has a playback looping feature that makes this simple.

Looping is defined in the Loop/Auto Shuttle toolbar, as shown here:

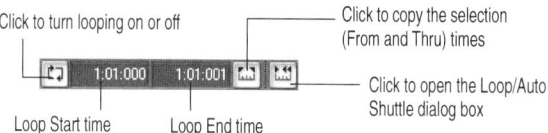

To set up a loop, you do three things:

- Set the start time of the loop
- Set the end time of the loop
- Enable looping

From then on, SONAR will automatically jump back to the start of the loop when it reaches the end.

When looping is enabled, the loop times are indicated by special markers in the Time Ruler.

The Loop/Auto Shuttle dialog box, which appears when you use the ***Transport-Loop and Auto Shuttle*** command or click the Loop and Auto Shuttle button in the Loop toolbar, contains two additional settings that affect the details of how looping operates:

Option...	How it works...
Stop at the end time	Playback does not proceed beyond the end of the loop
Loop continuously	When playback reaches the end of the loop and rewinds to the start, playback continues automatically (this option is on by default)

With the default option settings, SONAR will play the loop over and over again, continuously.

If you start playback before the loop start time, SONAR will play until the loop end time is reached, then jump back to the loop start time.

Note: If you stop playback while looping is enabled, the Now time jumps to the Now time marker. If you disable the On Stop Rewind to Now Marker option in the General tab of the Global Options dialog, the Now time stays wherever you stopped playback.

The Rewind command operates slightly differently when looping is in effect. The first time you rewind, the Now time is set to the start of the loop. If the Now time is already at the start of the loop, Rewind takes you to the beginning of the project. From then on, Rewind switches back and forth between the loop start time and the start of measure 1.

To Set Up a Playback Loop

1. Set the loop start and end times in one of the following ways:

    - Drag the mouse between two points in the Time Ruler of the Track view, Staff, or Piano Roll view to select a range of times, then click 🔲 in the Loop/Auto Shuttle toolbar to copy the selection time to the loop time.

    - Click between two markers in the Track, Staff, or Piano Roll view to select a range of times, then click 🔲 in the Loop/Auto Shuttle toolbar to copy the selection time to the loop time.

    - Type the loop start and end times directly into the toolbar.

    - Select a range of times, then right-click in the Time Ruler and choose **Set Loop Points** (this method makes the second option unnecessary).

Looping is automatically turned on when you use the Set Loop to Selection command.

To Change the Loop Settings

1. Click 🔲, or choose **Transport-Loop and Auto Shuttle** to display the Loop/Auto Shuttle dialog box.

2. Check the options you want to use.

3. Click OK.

To Cancel a Playback Loop

- Click 🔲 on the toolbar to disable looping.

Track-by-Track Playback

SONAR lets you play back any combination of tracks at one time by changing each track's **status**. You can control the status of each track with the individual controls that are on every track, or with the global controls on the Playback State toolbar or the Status bar that's at the bottom of the SONAR window. For more information on the Status bar, see "Status Bar/CPU Meter/Disk Meter" on page 639. For more information on the Playback State toolbar, see "The Playback State Toolbar" on page 125.

There are several different status settings for each track:

Status...	What it means...
Normal	The track plays unless one or more of your other tracks is soloed.
Muted	The track is not played, but you can turn it on while playback is in progress.
Archived	The track is not played, and you must stop playback to re-enable it. Archived tracks do not tax your CPU during playback so they can be used to store alternate takes.
Soloed	Only those tracks that are designated as solo tracks are played; all others are muted.
Armed	The track is armed for recording.
Mono/Stereo	The track plays back in either mono or stereo, depending on what the individual track setting is, and whether the Play in Mono button in the Playback State toolbar is depressed.
Phase normal or inverted	If a track was accidentally recorded out of phase with another track, the Phase button lets you reverse the phase of a track.

While playback is in progress, you can mute and unmute tracks in any combination, which means you can hear only the tracks that you want. You can change the status of a track in the Track view, the Console view, the Track menu, the Playback State toolbar, or the Status bar.

If a track is both muted and soloed, it does not play. Mute has precedence.

The track status is saved with the SONAR project file. If you save a SONAR project as a Standard MIDI File, however, all tracks are saved without mute, solo, or archive indicators.

The Playback State Toolbar

To display the Playback State toolbar, use the ***View-Toolbars*** command to open the Toolbars dialog box, and make sure Playback State is checked. The Playback State toolbar is a global control that allows you to mute or unmute, solo or unsolo, arm or disarm, and toggle the input echo status of all tracks.

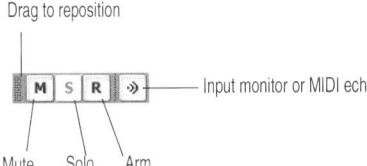

Silencing Tracks

When a track is muted, SONAR processes the track while playback is in progress so that you can unmute the track without stopping playback. If you have lots of muted tracks, this can place a heavy load on your computer. Archived tracks, on the other hand, don't place any load on your computer. Therefore, if there are tracks you want to keep but don't need to play, you should archive them instead. Archived tracks are indicated by the letter A in the Mute button that is displayed in the Track and Console views.

When you mute or unmute a track while playback is in progress, there may be a slight delay before you hear the effect of the change. This is to be expected and does not indicate a hardware or software problem.

To Mute or Unmute Individual Tracks
- To mute or unmute a track, click its M button in the Track or Console view.
- To mute or unmute several tracks at once, select the tracks and choose ***Track-Mute***, or select the tracks, right-click, and choose ***Mute*** from the popup menu.

To Unmute All Tracks
- Click the M button in the Playback State toolbar or the Mute label in the Status bar.

To Mute All Tracks
- If no tracks are currently muted, click the M button in the Playback State toolbar.

To Archive or Unarchive Tracks
1. Select one or more tracks in the Track view.

2. Choose **Track-Archive**, or right-click and choose **Archive** from the menu to toggle the archive status of the selected tracks.

Soloing Tracks

Sometimes you want to hear a single track, or a few tracks at once, without having to mute all the other tracks. You can do this by soloing the tracks you want to hear.

As soon as any track is marked as a solo track, SONAR ignores all mute settings (unless a soloed track is also muted—mute takes precedence over solo) and plays *only* the track or tracks that are set to solo. Any number of tracks at one time can be marked as solo. All these tracks will play together. As soon as the solo status of the final solo track is turned off, SONAR once again plays back tracks based on their mute settings.

To Solo or Unsolo Individual Tracks
- To solo or unsolo a track, click the Solo button in the Track or Console view

- To solo or unsolo several tracks at once, select the tracks and choose **Track-Solo**, or right-click, and choose **Solo** from the popup menu.

To Unsolo All Tracks
- Click the S button in the Playback State toolbar or the Solo label in the Status bar.

To Solo All Tracks
- If no tracks are currently soloed, click the S button in the Playback State toolbar.

Inverting the Phase of a Track

A waveform's exact opposite is called an inversion. It is a shift of 180 degrees. A waveform and its inversion cancel each other out completely, so it is usually not desirable to have two track recordings of the same source if one is phase inverted. It can lead to reduced volume, lowered or distorted response in certain frequencies, or even silence in the case of two tracks which are exactly identical (i.e. cloned tracks).

Occasionally, for example when recording a source using two microphones, one of the microphones may be recording an inversion of the other, the resulting tracks may, to some degree, be cancelling each other out. SONAR allows you to invert the phase of a track to match another.

To Invert the Phase of a Track
1. Open the Track view or Console view.

2. In the track you want to invert the phase, click the phase inversion button .

Changing Tracks' Mono/Stereo Status

SONAR has a mono/stereo button in each track module in the Track and Console views. The buttons in the track modules force each track to play in either stereo or mono, but preserve the tracks' pan positions in the stereo mix.

The Mono/Stereo button in each track forces the track's audio signal to enter any patched plug-ins as either mono or stereo, whether or not the tracks are mono or stereo. This allows you to use either mono effects on a stereo track or stereo effects on a mono track.

Note: You may lose important stereo data by using mono effects with stereo tracks because your stereo tracks are summed to mono in order to pass through the effect. If you never want your stereo data to be summed to mono, select stereo.

To Use a Track's Stereo/Mono Button
1. Display the Track view or Console view.
2. In the track you want to force to either mono or stereo for processing effects, click the Stereo/Mono button ▭ to the desired position:

   - Speaker icon pointing left—This choice means that you manually selected mono for this track.
   - Speaker icon pointing left and right (as pictured above)—This choice means that you manually selected stereo for this track.

Changing Track Settings

Each track in a project contains MIDI or audio information and has a variety of settings that determine how the track sounds. By changing these settings, you can change the sound of your project. For audio tracks, you control the volume, the stereo panning, and the output device that is used to produce the sound. For MIDI tracks, you control many additional settings, including the type of instrument sound that is used to play the notes stored in the track.

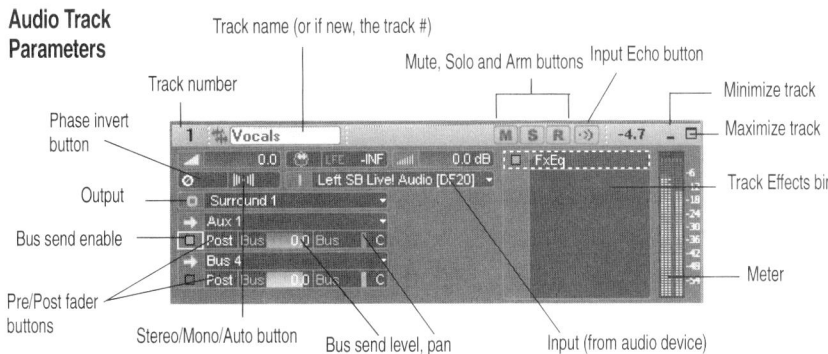

127

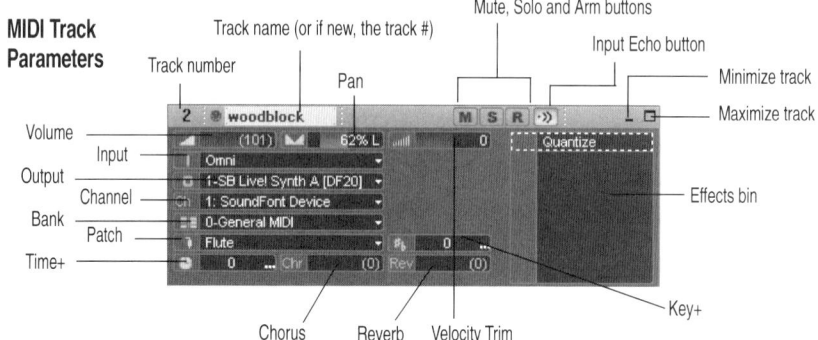

Here is a summary table of the different track parameters and how they are used.

Audio Track Parameters

The following parameters apply to audio tracks:

Setting...	What it means...
Number	A sequential track number used only for reference
Name	A name that you assign the track for easy reference. **Note that if you do not assign a name to a track, the default name is the track number. This track number will change if you change the order of your tracks.**
Input	The input source for the track, used in recording
Output	The output bus through which the track is played
Vol (volume)	The starting volume level for the track, ranging from -INF (silent) to +6 dB (maximum volume).
Pan	The stereo distribution of the output, ranging from 100% left (hard left) to 100% right (hard right); a value of "C" indicates sound that is centered left-to-right. On stereo tracks, pan acts as balance.

Trim (volume trim)	Volume Trim is a pre-fader control which allows the fine tuning of a single track's volume. For example, let's say you have four tracks, three tracks have their volume fader set to 0 dB while the fourth track's fader is set to +10 dB. You want to group the faders and do a slow fade out, but the slightly higher level of the fourth track causes its volume to be higher in relation to the other tracks towards the end of the fade out. To balance the fader levels, reduce the fader level for the fourth track to 0 dB and raise the Volume Trim value for that track to +10 dB. The resulting volume levels for the project are the same, but now you can group the faders and perform a fade out with no track standing out disproportionately at the end of the fade out.
Bus Enable	Allows the track to be sent to the bus.
Bus Send Level	Each track has a Bus Send Level for each Bus in the project. The default number of Buses for a new project is 2.
Bus Send Pan	Each track has a Bus Send Pan for each Bus in the project. The Bus Send Pan adjusts the send pan setting.
Bus Pre/Post	Each track has a Bus Send Pre/Post for each Bus in the project. Pre (pre-fader) means that the signal goes to the bus prior to the track's volume fader.
Mono/Stereo	A switch that determines whether a track's signal enters an effect or chain of effects as mono or stereo, regardless of the nature of the track.
Phase In/Out	A switch that inverts the phase of the track.
Effects bin	The patch point for a track's DirectX plug-ins or DXi soft synths.
Meters	The recording and playback levels are displayed in the Playback and Record meters.

MIDI Track Parameters

The following parameters apply to MIDI tracks:

Setting...	What it means...
Number	A sequential track number used only for reference
Name	A name that you assign the track for easy reference. **Note that if you do not assign a name to a track, the default name is the track number. This track number will change if you change the order of your tracks.**
Input	The input source for the track, used in recording
Output	The output device through which the track is played
Vol (volume)	The starting volume level for the track, ranging from 0 (silent) to 127 (maximum volume).
Pan	The stereo distribution of the output, ranging from 100% left (hard left) to 100% right (hard right); a value of "C" indicates sound that is centered left-to-right.
Ch (channel)	The MIDI channel through which the notes will be played
Bnk (bank)	The set of patch names available for the track
Pch (patch)	The instrument sound that will be used for playback.
Vel+	The change in velocity (volume) that will be applied to notes in this track on playback; ranges from −127 to +127
Key+	The number of steps by which the notes in the track are transposed on playback (e.g., 12 to transpose up one octave)
Time+	An offset applied to the start time of the events in the track

To Change a Track Name

1. Double-click on the current track name.
2. Enter the new track name.
3. Click Enter.

The default track names (Track 1, Track 2, etc.) are not actually names, but placeholders until you name a track. If you reorder the tracks these placeholders change.

You can rearrange and resize the panes in the Track view as shown in the following table:

To do this...	Do this...
Change the size of the Track pane	Drag to the left or right the divider that separates the Track and Clips panes
Change the Size of the Mains/Buses pane	Drag up or down the divider that separates the Track and Clip panes from the Bus pane

You can customize which tracks are displayed or not displayed, and enlarge or maximize individual tracks while other tracks remain minimized. You can also manually set the exact size of a track's display. The following table shows how to customize the appearance of tracks in the Track pane:

To do this...	Do this...
Maximize a track	Click the Maximize button in the track
Restore a track to its default size	Click the Restore button in the track
Minimize a track	Click the Minimize button in the track
Change the default size of a track using splitter bars	Move the cursor over the gap below a track until the cursor looks like this ⯭. Click and drag until the track is the size you want.

You can display subsets of the Track pane's controls by selecting one of the tabs located at the bottom of the Track view. The following table lists the controls displayed when each tab is selected:

Tab	Controls displayed when selected
All	• All controls are displayed
Mix	• Volume
	• Pan
	• Volume Trim
	• Phase (audio tracks only)
	• Key+ (MIDI tracks only)
	• Time+ (MIDI tracks only)

FX	- FX
- Bus enable/disable (audio tracks only)
- Bus Output Level (audio tracks only)
- Bus Output Pan (audio tracks only)
- Bus Pre/Post Fader (audio tracks only)
- Mono/Stereo (audio tracks only)
- Chorus (MIDI tracks only)
- Reverb (MIDI tracks only)
I/O	- In
- Output
- Channel (MIDI tracks only)
- Bank (MIDI tracks only)
- Patch (MIDI tracks only)

Changing Audio Track Settings in the Track Pane

You can change the values in the Track pane in a number of ways:

Control	How to change the setting
Volume, Pan, Volume Trim, Bus Output Level, and Bus Output Pan	Click on the control and move your cursor left or right to adjust values, or press Enter and type a value.
Input and Output	Click on the black arrow on the right of the control and select a driver from the menu that appears, or double-click on the control and select a driver from the menu.

Changing MIDI Track Settings in the Track Pane

Control	How to change the value
Channel	Click on the black arrow on the right of the control and select a channel from the menu that appears, or double-click on the control and enter a value.
Bank	Click on the black arrow on the right of the control and select a bank from the menu that appears, or double-click on the control and enter a value.
Patch	Click on the black arrow on the right of the control and select a patch from the menu that appears, or double-click on the control and enter a value.
Volume, Pan, Volume Trim, Chorus and Reverb	Click on control and move your cursor left or right to adjust values, or double-click on the control and enter a value.
Key+ and Time+	Double-click the control or click on the black arrow on the right of the control and enter a new value, or double-click on the control and enter a value.
Input	Click on the black arrow on the right of the control and select a MIDI channel from the menu that appears, or double-click on the control and select a driver from the menu.
Output	Click on the black arrow on the right of the control and select a driver from the menu that appears, or double-click on the control and select a driver from the menu.

You can change numeric values in MIDI tracks as shown in the following table:

To do this...	Do this...
Change the value by 1	Press the - or + key on your numeric keypad, or click on the spinner control
Change the value by 10 (for Key+, by 12)	Press the [or] key, or right-click on the spinner control
Enter a new value	Press Enter and type the new value using the keyboard, and press Enter

For numeric fields, you can press and hold both mouse buttons to change the value by increments of 10 (12, a full octave, for Key+).

You can also edit Track properties in the Track Properties dialog box. To open this dialog box, right-click on the Track bar and select **Track Properties**.

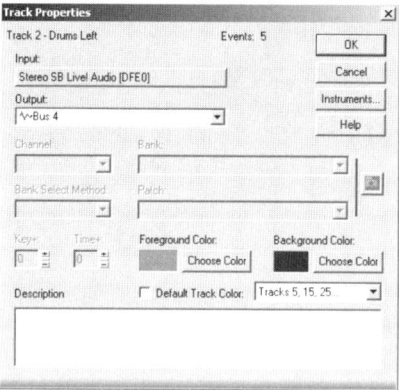

You can change the value of a track parameter for several tracks at once using commands on the **Track-Property** menu. For example, to assign a group of tracks to the same output, select the tracks you want to assign, then choose **Track-Property-Output**. These menu commands can also be used to change the settings for individual tracks.

All track parameters are saved with a SONAR project. However, if you export a project to a Standard MIDI File, several of the parameters (Key+, Vel+, Time+, and Chan) are applied to the MIDI data as the file is being exported. Other parameters, including Input, Output, Mute, Solo, and Archive, are lost when you export the project to a MIDI file.

The following sections contain more information about many of the parameters in the Track view. For more information on the track inputs and the track Arm button, see "Preparing to Record" on page 170.

Setting Up Output Devices

The output setting for a track determines which piece of hardware will be used to produce the sound stored in your project. In a very simple equipment setup, you might have only a computer equipped with a basic sound card. In this case, you want to play all MIDI and audio output through the sound card on your computer.

If your equipment setup also includes a MIDI keyboard attached to the MIDI port on your sound card, you can choose to route MIDI data directly to the sound card or through the sound card MIDI port to the keyboard. If you choose the former, the music will play from your computer speakers. If you choose the latter, the sound will play from the speaker attached to your keyboard. You can even choose to send some MIDI information to each of these devices so that they both play at once.

You can purchase MIDI interfaces that plug into your parallel, serial, or USB port to add MIDI ports to your computer. For more information on complex system configurations, see *Appendix B: Hardware Setup*.

If your computer has several MIDI outs, choose the ones you want to use and put them in a particular order using the **Options-MIDI Devices** command. The order in which your MIDI devices appear in the Output menus in the Track and Console views is based solely on the order in which the selected outs appear in the MIDI Devices dialog box. As a result, the order in which your devices appear in a track's output control may not match the port numbers that appear on your external multiport MIDI device.

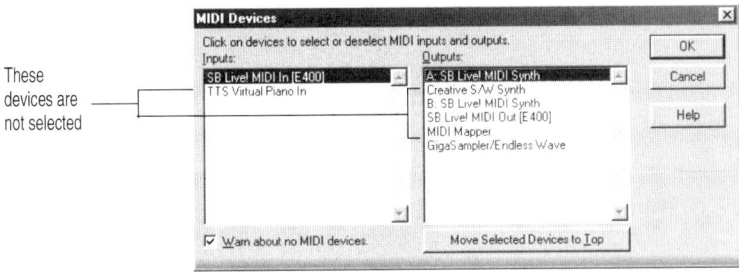

These devices are not selected

When you first run SONAR it asks you to select MIDI devices. You may want to change these selections in the future. You can do so by selecting different devices in the MIDI Devices dialog box.

Your computer is usually equipped with at least one audio device—your computer sound card. Your setup may have several different audio output devices, or you may have a multichannel sound card that presents itself to your computer as though it were several different devices, one for each stereo pair. In SONAR, audio tracks are assigned to main outs or buses. Each main out represents a hardware device. You use the Output control to assign a track in a project to the main or bus you want to use.

While you need to choose the MIDI output devices you want to use before you assign them to tracks, all of your audio devices can be assigned to tracks freely. You do not need to configure them the way you do MIDI devices. If you have a voice modem or speakerphone in your computer, however, you might want to set up SONAR so that it won't use those devices. Also, note that some dedicated audio equipment has specific setup requirements. For more information, see Chapter 20, *Improving Audio Performance*.

135

To Choose MIDI Devices

1. Choose ***Options-MIDI Devices*** to display the MIDI Devices dialog box.
2. Click on any MIDI device in the Outputs list.
3. To move any device to the top of the list, deselect all other devices and click Move to Top to move the selected device to the top of the list.
4. When all devices are selected in the order you want, click OK.

Assigning Tracks to Outputs

You assign each track to a MIDI or an audio output using the Output dropdown in the Track view. From then on, material on that track will be sent to the appropriate output device.

Note:

If you rearrange your MIDI output devices after making output assignments, you may find MIDI information being sent to different instruments than you expect. Also, SONAR allows you to define instruments that are associated with certain outputs and channels. If you use this feature, the name of the output will change to reflect the instrument you have chosen. For more information about instrument definitions, see Chapter 16, *Using Instrument Definitions*.

To Assign a Track to an Output

1. Click the Output dropdown of the track you want to assign.
2. Select the output you want to use.

To change the output setting for more than one track at a time, select the tracks you want to change and choose ***Track-Property-Output***.

Choosing the Instrument Sound (Bank and Patch)

Electronic keyboards and synthesizers often contain hundreds or thousands of different sounds. Each sound is known as a **patch**. The name comes from the early days of synthesizers, for which you physically rewired (using patch cords) the oscillators and modulators to produce different sounds. Patches are normally organized into groups of 128, called **banks**. Most instruments have between 1 and 8 banks, but MIDI supports up to 16,384 banks of 128 patches each (that's over 2 million patches).

The bank and patch settings in the Track view control the initial bank and patch of a track during playback. Every time SONAR starts playback at the beginning of a project, the bank and patch settings for the track are set to these initial values.

Many instruments have descriptive names for their banks and patches. SONAR stores these names in an instrument definition. For more information about instrument definitions, see Chapter 16, *Using Instrument Definitions*. If you are using an instrument that supports General MIDI, your patch list will contain the 128 sounds that are defined by the General MIDI specification.

Note to Experts:
Different MIDI instruments use different types of commands to change banks. SONAR supports four common methods for changing banks. For information about the bank selection method you should use with your MIDI gear, see your MIDI equipment's documentation.

Tip:
If your bank name is too long to fit in the bank field, hold your cursor over the bank name. A tooltip appears with the complete bank name.

Note that a single MIDI channel can only play one patch at a time on each instrument assigned to that channel. Therefore, if two or more MIDI tracks are set to the same output and channel but have different bank and patch settings, the patch of the highest-numbered track will be used for all the tracks.

In some projects you want the sound played by a track to change while playback is in progress. You can accomplish this using the **Insert-Bank/Patch Change** command. When you start playback in the middle of a project, SONAR searches back through the track to find the correct patch to use—either the initial bank and patch or the most recent bank/patch change. Note that the Track view only shows the initial bank and patch, even while a different bank and patch are being played back. The only way to see and edit a bank/patch change is in the Event List view. For more information, see "The Event List View" on page 318.

To Assign an Initial Bank and Patch to a Track
1. Right-click on the Track titlebar (the top of the track which contains the track name) and select **Track Properties**.

    The Track Properties dialog box appears.

2. In the Track Properties dialog box, choose the desired bank and patch from the dropdown lists.

3. To search for a patch containing specific text, click the Patch Browser button to the right of the dropdown lists. You can also open the Patch Browser by right-clicking a bank or patch control in the Track or Console views.

4. Click OK.

Another Way to Assign a Patch to a Track
1. Select the patch you want from the Patch dropdown.

To change the bank and patch settings for more than one track at a time, select the tracks you want to change and choose **Track-Property-Bank** or **Track-Property-Patch.**

To Insert a Bank/Patch Change
1. Highlight the track whose bank and patch you want to change by clicking on the track number.
2. Set the Now time to the time at which you want the change to occur.
3. Choose **Insert-Bank/Patch Change** to display the Bank/Patch Change dialog box.
4. Choose a bank and patch from the lists.
5. Click OK.

SONAR inserts a change in bank and patch. When you play back the project, the initial bank and patch shown in the Track view will be used to the point at which the bank/patch change takes place. You can remove a bank/patch change in the Event List view.

To Choose Patches with the Patch Browser
1. In the Track view or Console view, right-click the patch name in the track module you want to change patches in.

   The Patch browser dialog box appears, displaying a list of all the Instrument patch names that have been installed.

2. Search for a patch name, if desired, by filling in text in the search field at the top of the dialog box.

3. When you find the right patch, click its name and click OK.

   SONAR changes the patch of the track you selected.

Adding Effects

You can add both MIDI and audio effects directly from the Track view. SONAR adds these effects in real-time, preserving your track's original data.

To Add an Audio Effect in the Track Pane

1. In an audio track, right-click in the FX field, choose **Audio Effects-Cakewalk**, and select an effect from the menu that appears.

Adjusting Volume and Pan

The Volume and Pan settings control the initial volume and pan of a track during playback. Every time SONAR starts playback, the Volume and Pan settings for the track are set to these initial levels. SONAR allows you to choose different panning laws if you want (see"Configurable Panning Laws" on page 140).

In some projects you want the volume or panning of a track to change while playback is in progress. You can accomplish this by drawing a volume or pan envelope in the Track view, or by recording automation. For more information, see Chapter 13, *Using Automation*, Chapter 11, *Mixing and Effects Patching*, and Chapter 7, *Editing MIDI Events and Controllers*.

Note to Experts:

SONAR processes the volume and pan settings by transmitting MIDI volume and pan events (controllers 7 and 10, respectively) when playback starts. If two or more MIDI tracks are set to the same output and channel but have different volume or pan settings, the settings for the highest-numbered track will prevail.

Note also that not all keyboards and synthesizers respond to these events. Check your instrument's manual for more information.

To Set the Initial Volume Setting

1. Move your cursor to the Volume control of the track you want to change.
2. Click and drag to the left to lower the volume or the right to raise the volume.

You can also change the volume settings in a variety of other ways, as described on page 132. To change the volume settings for more than one track at a time, select the tracks you want to change and choose **Track-Property-Volume**.

To Set the Initial Pan Setting

1. Move your cursor to the Pan control of the track you want to change.
2. Click and drag to the left to adjust the pan to the left or to the right to adjust the pan to the right.

   Hard left is 100% left. Hard right is 100% right. Pan is centered at C.

You can also change the pan and volume settings in a variety of other ways, as described on page 132. To change the pan settings for more than one track at a time, select the tracks you want to change and choose ***Track-Property-Pan***.

Configurable Panning Laws

You can choose from six different panning laws, if you want. A panning law is the mathematical formula that a sequencer or mixer uses to control panning.

To Change Panning Laws

1. Use the ***Options-Audio*** command to open the Audio Options dialog.

2. On the General tab, in the Stereo Panning Law field, choose one of these options:

    - (Default) 0 dB center, sin/cos taper, constant power—this choice causes a 3 dB boost in a signal that's panned hard left or right, and no dip in output level in either channel when the signal is center panned.

    - -3dB center, sin/cos taper, constant power——this choice causes no boost in a signal that's panned hard left or right, and 3dB dip in output level in either channel when the signal is center panned.

    - 0dB center, square-root taper, constant power—this choice causes a 3 dB boost in a signal that's panned hard left or right, and no dip in output level in either channel when the signal is center panned.

    - -3dB center, square root taper, constant power——this choice causes no boost in a signal that's panned hard left or right, and 3dB dip in output level in either channel when the signal is center panned.

    - -6dB center, linear taper——this choice causes no boost in a signal that's panned hard left or right, and 6dB dip in output level in either channel when the signal is center panned.

    - 0 dB center, balance control——this choice causes no boost in a signal that's panned hard left or right, and no dip in output level in either channel when the signal is center panned.

3. Click OK.

Adjusting Volume Trim

Volume Trim acts like the trim control on a mixer, raising or lower the level prior to the volume fader. Volume Trim is useful for calibrating your faders to match a dB reference level or for aligning your faders for grouping. The Volume Trim control has a range of -18dB to +18dB. Raising or lowering the Volume Trim raises or lowers the apparent volume of the track by that amount without affecting the actual fader level.

To Set the Volume Trim Level
1. Move your cursor to the Volume Trim control of the track you want to change.
2. Click and drag to the left to lower Volume Trim level or to the right to raise Volume Trim level.

Assigning a MIDI Channel (Chn)

MIDI transmits information on 16 channels, numbered 1 through 16. Every MIDI event is assigned to a particular channel. Some MIDI equipment can accept MIDI information on only a single channel. This channel may be preassigned, or you may be able to change it. Other MIDI equipment, including many electronic keyboards and synthesizers, can accept information on several different MIDI channels at once. Usually, these devices use a different instrument sound for each channel.

On playback, the channel number is used to direct the MIDI information to a particular piece of equipment.

The Chn parameter in the Track view redirects all events in the track to the specified channel, ignoring the channel number stored with each event. If this parameter is left blank, all events in the track are sent to their original channels.

This parameter does not affect the channel information that is stored with each MIDI event. When the track is displayed in other views, like the Piano Roll or Event List view, you will see the original channel that is stored in the file. You can edit the channel values in those views or use the ***Process-Interpolate*** command.

To Set the Channel for a Track
1. In the track you want to change, click on the black arrow to the right of the Chn field and select the channel you want to use.

You can also change the channel setting in a variety of other ways, as described on page 132. To change the channel assignment for more than one track at a time, select the tracks you want to change and choose ***Track-Property-Channel***.

Adjusting the Key/Transposing a Track (Key+)

Each MIDI note event has a key number, or pitch. On playback, the **key offset** (Key+) parameter transposes all notes in the track by the designated number of half-steps. The value can range from -127 to +127. A value of 12 indicates that notes will be played back one octave higher than they are written.

This parameter does not affect the note number that is stored for each note event. When the clip is displayed in other views, like the Piano Roll, Staff, or Event List view, you will see the original notes as they are stored in the file. To permanently change the pitches, you can edit them individually or use the ***Process-Transpose*** command.

If the key offset value transposes the key number (MIDI note) outside the allowable MIDI range (0–127), the key number will be transposed to the lowest or highest octave within that range.

You can use the Key+ parameter to assist in preparing scores for instruments whose music is written in something other than "concert" key (such as Bb trumpet). For more information, see "Music Notation for Non-concert-key Instruments" on page 563.

When you edit the Key+ parameter, pressing [or] changes the value by 12 instead of by 10. This makes it easy to transpose by octaves.

To Set the Key Offset for a Track

1. In the track you want to change, click on the Key+ control.

2. Enter a value (1 = a semitone), or press the + or – key to change the key by a single semitone. Use the [or] key to change the key by 12 semitones (one octave).

You can also change the key offset in a variety of other ways, as described on page 132. To change the key offset for more than one track at a time, select the tracks you want to change and choose *Track-Property-Key+*.

Adjusting the Note Velocity (Vel+)

Each MIDI note event has a velocity, which represents how fast the key was struck when the track was recorded. On playback, the **velocity offset** parameter adjusts the velocity data for all notes in the track by the designated amount. The value can range from -127 to +127. The effect of changing velocities depends on the synthesizer. Some synthesizers do not respond to velocity information. For others, the effect varies depending on the sound or patch you have chosen. Normally, higher velocities result in louder and/or brighter-sounding notes.

This parameter does not affect the velocity that is stored for each note event. When the clip is displayed in other views, like the Piano Roll view, Staff view, or Event List view, you will see the original velocities as they are stored in the file. You can edit the velocity values in those views, or use the *Process-Scale Velocity* or *Process-Interpolate* command.

Velocity is different from volume in that it is an attribute of each event, rather than a controller that affects an entire MIDI channel. Here's an example of where this distinction might be important. Suppose you have several tracks containing different drum parts. All of these parts would probably be assigned to MIDI channel 10 (that's the default channel for percussion in General MIDI). If you change the volume setting for any track that uses channel 10, all the different drum parts—regardless of what track they're in—would be affected. If you change the note velocity for one drum track, it will be the only one whose volume is affected.

To Set the Velocity Offset for a Track

- In the track you want to change, click and drag the Vel+ control to the desired setting.

You can also change the velocity offset in a variety of other ways, as described on page 132. To change the velocity offset for more than one track at a time, select the tracks you want to change and choose ***Track-Property-Vel+***.

Adjusting the Time Alignment of a MIDI Track (Time+)

Each event takes place at a known point in the project. On playback, the **time offset** (Time+) parameter adjusts the times for MIDI events in the track by the designated amount. The value can be as small as a single clock tick or as large as you want.

This parameter can be used to make a part play behind the beat or in front of it or to compensate for tracks that sound rushed or late. The time shift can be used to create a chorus or slap-back echo effect by making a copy of a track and then applying a small offset to the copy. You can use larger time offsets to shift a track earlier or later by several beats or measures.

Note that you cannot shift any event earlier than 1:01:000. For example, if the first event in the track starts at 2:01:000, you cannot shift its start time earlier by more than one measure.

This parameter does not affect the time that is stored for each note event. When the clip is displayed in other views, like the Piano Roll, Staff, or Event List view, you will see the original times as they are stored in the file.

To Set the Time Offset for a Track

1. In the track you want to change, click on the Time+ control.
2. Enter a value, or press the + or – key until you reach the value you want.

You can also change the time offset in a variety of other ways, as described on page 132. To change the time offset for more than one track at a time, select the tracks you want to change and choose ***Track-Property-Time+***.

Other MIDI Playback Settings

Two other MIDI settings can affect what happens when you play back your project, as described in the following table:

Option...	How it works...
Zero Controllers When Play Stops	If this option is enabled, SONAR zeroes (resets) the pitch wheel, the pedal Controller, and the modulation wheel Controller on all 16 MIDI channels whenever playback is stopped. It also sends a "Zero All Continuous Controllers" MIDI message, which turns off other continuous Controllers on newer synthesizers. If you experience frequent stuck notes when playback stops, try checking this option.
Patch/Controller Searchback Before Play Starts	If this option is enabled, SONAR searches for and sends the most recent patch change, wheel, and pedal events on each output and MIDI channel before starting playback. This ensures that all these settings are correct, even if you start playback at an arbitrary point in your project.

To set these options, choose **Options-Project** and click the MIDI Out tab. If you have set up a playback loop, enabling either of these options can cause an audible delay when the loop is restarted.

Controlling Live MIDI Playback—MIDI Echo

When you play your MIDI keyboard or controller, the sound that SONAR produces is determined by what hardware or software synth SONAR sends the incoming MIDI data to after SONAR receives the data. This is called MIDI echo. By default, SONAR sends the data to the MIDI output or software synth listed in the Output field of the *current track*. The current track is the one whose titlebar has the golden color—press the up and down arrows on your computer keyboard and watch each track turn golden in succession as you change different tracks into the current track (you can also click any of a track's controls to make it current).

However, you can echo MIDI data to much more than just the current track, or turn echoing off on the current track if you want. With a single keyboard or controller, you can echo MIDI data to as many MIDI tracks as you want, meaning that you can simultaneously play as many hardware and software synths as you can hook up to your MIDI interface or run on your computer. You can also have multiple performers on different controllers sending MIDI data to either the same synth or multiple synths. Each SONAR track allows you to select what MIDI input ports and channels the track will respond to. The Output field of the track determines what instrument will sound when the track receives the data. Each track's Input Echo button determines whether the track echoes MIDI data.

The Input Echo Button

Each MIDI track has an Input Echo button, which controls whether the track will echo MIDI data or not. The button has three states: on , dimmed , and off . When the button is on, the track echoes MIDI data. When the button is dimmed, the track echoes MIDI data because the track is the current track. When the button is off, the track does not echo any data, even if it is the current track. The off position on a current MIDI track is only available if you disable the Always Echo Current MIDI Track option in the General tab of the Global Options dialog (***Options-Global*** command). The dimmed position becomes unavailable with this setting.

There are several ways to turn Input Echoing on:

- Click a track's Input Echo button so that it is on.

- Click a track to make the track the current track (if the Always Echo Current MIDI Track option on the General tab of the Global Options dialog is enabled). In this situation (which is the default), if the track's Input Echo button is not on, it appears dimmed, to show that this track echoes data because it is the current track.

- If the Always Echo Current MIDI Track option on the General tab of the Global Options dialog is disabled, make a track the current track, and use the ***Track-Input Monitor/Echo*** command (or click the track's Input Echo button).

Storing Favorite Configurations

If you want a track to respond to more than one port or channel, you must create a preset input configuration. If you create some favorite configurations of MIDI input options, not only will they be stored with the project you created them in, but you can save each one as a preset to load in any MIDI track in any project you want. Clicking the dropdown arrow in a track's Input field displays the Inputs dropdown menu, which has the ***Manage Presets*** choice that allows you to create and store your favorite combinations of MIDI input choices.

To Play One Synth at a Time from One or More MIDI Keyboards

- Since this is SONAR's default behavior, simply use the Up or Down arrow keys on your computer keyboard to choose the current track (the current track has a gold titlebar), and choose the synth you want to play by using the track's Output, Bank, Patch, and Channel fields. With the default behavior, all MIDI input from all ports and channels is merged and sent through the current track. Notice that the track's Input field says Omni.

- If you've disabled the default behavior (see next procedure), you must make sure that the current track's Input Echo button is lit up (on) before you can play the synth that the track is patched to.

To Disable the Default MIDI Echo Setting

- If you want to turn off the automatic MIDI echoing of the current track, disable the Always Echo Current MIDI Track option in the General tab of the Global Options dialog (***Options-Global*** command). If you then turn off the current track's Input Echo button and play your keyboard, SONAR will not produce sound.

To Play Multiple Synths from a MIDI Keyboard

1. Choose a synth for each track that you want to play by using each track's Output, Channel, Bank, and Patch fields.

2. In the Input field of each track that you want to play, click the dropdown arrow and choose the MIDI input port and channel that you want the track to respond to from the following options:

    - ***None***—this option actually sets the Input field to Omni: with this setting the track will respond to any MIDI input coming in on any port (MIDI interface input driver) on any channel.

    - (***name of MIDI input driver***)-***MIDI Omni***—choosing this option causes the track to respond to any MIDI channel coming from the named MIDI interface input driver.

    - (***name of MIDI input driver***)-***MIDI ch 1-16***—choosing this option causes the track to respond ONLY to whatever MIDI channel you choose coming from the named MIDI interface input driver.

    - ***Preset***—if you've created any preset collections of input ports and channels, you can select one here.

    - ***Manage Presets***—if you want to create or edit any preset collections of input ports and channels, you can select this option (see following procedure).

3. Make sure that the Input Echo button on each track that you want to play is turned on.

To Create or Edit a Preset Input Configuration

1. In the Input field of a track that you want to select inputs for, click the dropdown arrow and choose ***Manage Presets*** from the dropdown menu.

    The MIDI Input Presets dialog appears.

2. In the Input Port column, find the input port that you want to use for this track (if you only use a single-port MIDI interface, you'll only see one choice).

3. To the right of the input port, select the MIDI channels that you want this track to respond to on this MIDI port.

4. Select channels for any other MIDI port that's listed, if you want to use channels on that port also.

5. If you want to save this configuration, type a name for it in the window at the top of the dialog, and click the disk icon to save it.

Now, when you choose inputs for other tracks, you can choose the preset you saved by clicking the **Presets** option in the track's Input dropdown menu. If you want to edit a preset, select it in the top window of the MIDI Input Presets dialog, edit it, and click the disk icon. If you want to delete a preset, select it in the same dialog and click the X button to delete it.

To Use Multiple Performers on Multiple Tracks

1. For performer number 1, click the Input dropdown menu(s) of the track(s) you want that performer to play, and choose the port and MIDI channel that performer 1's keyboard is sending data to SONAR on.

2. Repeat step 1 for all other performers.

3. If there is any track that you want more than one performer to play, create a preset of the input ports and channels that you want that track to respond to (see previous procedure).

4. Make sure the Input Echo button is on for each track you want to play.

To Turn MIDI Echo (and Input Monitoring) On or Off for All Tracks

- In the Playback State toolbar (to display, use the **View-Toolbars-Playback State** command), click the Input Monitor button (last one on the right).

Local Control

You should normally disable the Local Control setting on your master keyboard to prevent notes from being doubled when you play your keyboard. If you disable Local Control, your keyboard sends notes that you play to SONAR, which echoes them to the synthesizer, which plays them only once.

When SONAR starts, you can have it send a special MIDI message that attempts to disable Local Control automatically. Most modern synthesizers respond to this message. If yours does not, you will need to disable Local Control every time you turn it on for use with SONAR.

If your synthesizer does not let you disable Local Control (this is rare), you can use the Local On Port setting in the Input tab of the Project Options dialog box to indicate the number of the output port connected to your synthesizer. SONAR will then refrain from sending MIDI echo data to that port. In this configuration, you may need to turn your synthesizer's volume control up and down from time to time to avoid hearing it play along with your other modules. If this situation doesn't apply to you, the Local On Port should be set to 0.

To Automatically Disable All Local Control Whenever You Launch SONAR

1. In the directory where SONAR is installed, double-click on the TTSEQ.INI file to open it.
2. In the Options section, add the line:

   SendLocalOff=1

3. Save the file and close it.
4. When you launch SONAR, it automatically sends a Local Off message to your keyboard.

Note: Not all keyboards respond to this message.

Playing Files in Batch Mode

SONAR allows you to play several files in sequence automatically using the Play List view. You can use this feature in live performance applications or just for fun.

SONAR's Play List view lets you create and work with a series of project, MIDI, and bundle files. As each file plays, SONAR loads it and displays it in the Track view and other views like any other project file.

The Play List View

The Play List view lets you create, edit, and save a **play list** (or **set**) of up to 999 SONAR projects. Once you've created the list, you can play back the entire sequence automatically. You can even program the list to pause between songs for a fixed amount of time or to wait for a keystroke before proceeding.

The Play List view looks like this:

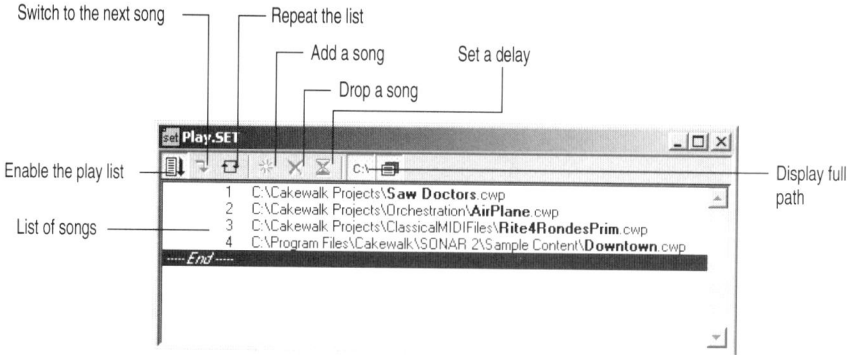

Play lists can be saved for future use. Play list files have the extension .SET.

To Create and Edit a Play List

- To create and edit a play list in the Play List view, follow the instructions in the table:

To do this...	Do this...
Open an existing play list	Choose **File-Open**, choose Play List from the Files of Type list, choose the file you want and click Open
Create a new play list	Choose **File-New**, choose Play List Set from the list, and click OK
Add songs to the play list	Click or press Insert, choose a file from the Add Song to Play List dialog box, and click Open
Set the delay after a song	Click on the song in the play list, click , enter the delay you want, and click OK
Change the order of songs	Drag the file to a new location in the play list
Copy a song to another location in the play list	Ctrl-drag the file to a new location in the play list
Remove a song from the play list	Select the song and click or press the Delete key
Save the play list	Choose **File-Save**; or choose **File-Save As**, enter a file name, and click Save

To Play Files from the Play List View

- To play back files from the Play List view, follow the instructions in the table.

To do this...	Do this...
Activate the play list	Click in the Play List view toolbar so that the button is pressed. If this button is not pressed, only a single file will play when you start playback.
Choose the starting song	Double-click the file you want to start with. The project is opened and displayed as usual.
Start playback	Click , choose **Transport-Play**, or press the Spacebar.
Stop playback	Choose **Transport-Stop**, or press the Spacebar.

149

Skip to the next file	Click [icon] in the Play List view toolbar.
Loop continuously over the play list	Click the [icon] button in the Play List view toolbar.
Show or hide file name extensions and folder names (path)	Click the [icon] button to enable or disable the display of folders.

Video Playback, Import, and Export

Video files play in the Video view in real time as your project plays.

The ***File-Import-Video*** command lets you include the following video file types in your project:

- AVI (also called Video for Windows)
- MPEG
- Windows Media Video
- QuickTime (.MOV files only)

Note: some .MOV and .AVI files contain no video. You can't import these files with the ***File-Import-Video*** command. You must use the ***File-Import-Audio*** command instead, and set the Files of Type field to All Files.

The ***File-Export-Video*** command lets you export your audio tracks and your imported video as the following file types:

- AVI (also called Video for Windows)
- Windows Media Video
- QuickTime

SONAR Producer also has a Video Thumbnails pane at the top of the Track view, which shows individual frames of your video at different places in your project (See below for more information).

You open the Video view by using the ***View-Video*** command. The Video view displays the Now time (as in the Big Time view) and the video itself. The display in the Video view is synchronized with the Now time, giving you convenient random access to the video stream. This makes it easy to align music and digitized sound to the video.

Commands in the Video view's right-click popup menu let you set the time display format, the size and stretch options for the video display, the video start and trim times, and other options.

Inserting and Playing Back Videos

Here are step-by-step procedures for inserting and playing back videos:

To Load a Video File Into a Project

1. Choose **File-Import-Video**, or choose **Insert** from the Video view's popup menu.

   The Import Video dialog appears.

2. In the Files of Type field, select the kind of video file you're looking for.

3. Select a file.

4. Check the Show File Info option to display information about the file in the File Info section of the dialog.

5. Check the Import Audio Stream option if you want to load the file's audio data.

6. Check the Import As Mono Tracks option if you want to import the file's audio data as one or more mono tracks.

7. Click Open.

SONAR loads the video file and displays it in the Video view. If you choose to import audio data, SONAR inserts a new track above the currently selected track, and puts the audio data in a clip or clips on the new track.

Note: when you save a project that contains video, SONAR saves the project's video file by reference only; the actual video data remains in the original file. Video data is not saved in bundle files, so it must be backed up on its own.

To Play a Video File

1. Open the Video view by choosing **View-Video.**

2. Press the Spacebar to play or stop video playback.

3. To change the display size of the video, right-click in the Video view and choose **Stretch Options-[desired size]** from the popup menu.

Note: When you play a video file that has high temporal compression, such as movies optimized for web delivery, playback may not be smooth unless you disable video thumbnails (found in SONAR Producer only), (see "Using the Video Thumbnails Pane" on page 154 for more information).

To Delete the Video From the Project

1. Open the Video view by choosing **View-Video.**

2. Right-click in the Video view and choose **Delete**.

SONAR removes the video from the project. Note that imported audio data is not deleted.

To Enable or Disable Video Playback

1. Open the Video view by choosing *View-Video.*

2. Right-click in the Video view and choose *Animate*.

If your computer is not fast enough to play back video efficiently, you can get better performance by temporarily disabling video animation during playback.

To Set the Time Display Format

- Click the time display to cycle between MBT, SMPTE, Frames and None

  Or

- Right-click in the Video view and choose an option from the *Time Display Format* menu:

To do this...	Do this...
Select a time format	Choose *MBT*, *SMPTE*, *Frames* or *None*
Change font or font color	Choose *Font* and select new font characteristics
Turn off the time display	Choose *None*

To Set the Video Display Format

Right-click in the Video view and choose an option from the *Stretch Options* menu:

To do this...	Do this...
Display the video in its original size	Choose *Original Size*
Stretch the video to fill the Video view	Choose *Stretch to Window*
Stretch the video as much as possible while preserving the original aspect ratio	Choose *Preserve Aspect Ratio*
Make the video display as large as possible, but only enlarge by integral multiples	Choose *Integral Stretch*
Display the video in full screen mode	Choose *Full Screen*

SONAR adjusts the video display according to the selected option. The stretch option is used to recalculate the video display size whenever you resize the Video view.

To Set the Background Color
- Right-click in the Video view and choose a color option from the ***Background Color*** menu.

To Set the Start and Trim Times
1. Right-click in the Video view and choose Video Properties.
2. Set options as described in the table:

Option...	What it means...
Start Time	The time in your SONAR project at which you want the video file to start playing
Trim-in Time	The time in the video file at which you want video playback to start
Trim-out Time	The time in the video file at which you want video playback to stop

SONAR synchronizes the video to the project according to the specified Start and Trim times.

Exporting Video

After you've mixed your audio tracks the way you want them, you can export the inserted video file together with your audio tracks to create a new video file.

When you export a video, any changes you've made to the Start, Trim-In, or Trim-Out times determine how long your new exported video is compared to the original video that you inserted into your SONAR project.

To Export a Video
1. Make sure your audio tracks are completely mixed, and your video Start time, Trim-In time, and Trim-Out time are set the way you want them.
2. Use the ***File-Export Video*** command.

   The Export Video dialog appears.
3. In the File Name field, type a name for your new video.
4. In the Files of Type field, choose the kind of video file you want the exported file to be.
5. Click the Encoding Options button to open a dialog of encoding options for the kind of file you're creating. Click the Help button in the dialog for help choosing options.

6. Click the Audio Mixdown Options button to open a dialog of audio mixdown options. Click the Help button in the dialog for help choosing options.

7. Click Save to export your video.

Optimizing Video Performance

Here are a few tips to optimize video performance:

- If you intend to do a lot of seeking around or looping and editing while a video file is loaded, make sure that your video file has sufficient keyframes. Since each frame has to be computed from the last keyframe encountered, if you have very few keyframes in the video, performance may be slow. To change the number of keyframes, you may recompress the file using the ***File-Export Video*** command and specify more frequent keyframes. Choose a suitable video compressor such as Cinepak and change the KeyFrame Rate parameter to a number between 1-5. A value of 1 makes every frame a keyframe, and higher numbers insert a keyframe after that many frames.

- Changing the video properties of an AVI file, such as Trim and Start time, can make realtime performance slightly slower. You can make these changes permanent (and thereby reduce the load on your CPU) by using the ***File-Export Video*** command.

- Playing videos at a resolution (video size) of 320x240 is usually a high enough resolution to monitor the video while you're composing a soundtrack. You can still choose to stretch the video to full screen at this resolution. You set the video size on the Render Quality tab of the Video Properties dialog. Using a higher resolution can bog down your computer if you're processing audio tracks at the same time.

Using the Video Thumbnails Pane

At the top of the Track view in SONAR Producer is the Video Thumbnails pane, which displays individual frames of your video at certain time intervals of your project. The time interval between displayed frames is determined by the zoom level you choose. If you zoom in far enough, you can view each individual frame of your video.

Note 1: if you're playing back a highly compressed movie (not many keyframes in the file), it can take about a minute to redraw video thumbnails when you're playing the movie or resizing a window.

Note 2: some Windows Media videos do not report their frame rate to SONAR. SONAR can play these files, but cannot create thumbnails from them, so no thumbnails appear in the thumbnail pane.

Video Thumbnails pane

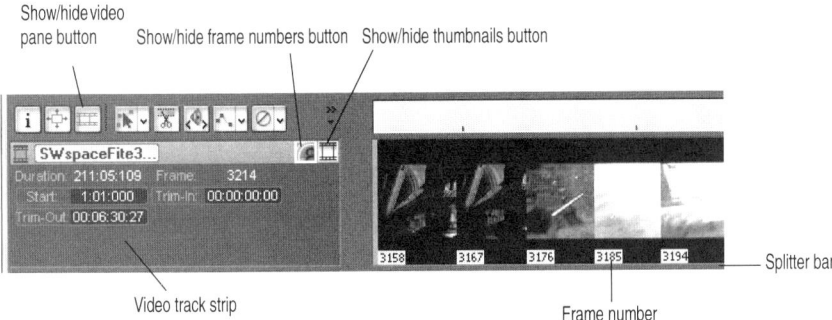

Here are the various commands and functions of the Video Thumbnails pane:

- You can show or hide the pane.
- You can show or hide the video thumbnails.
- You can display absolute frame numbers.
- You can resize the thumbnails while preserving the aspect ratio by dragging the splitter bar.
- The video track strip at the top of the Track pane has display fields for Video File Name, Start Time, Trim-In Time, Trim-Out Time, Duration, and Current Frame, as well as a toggle buttons to show/hide the thumbnails (without hiding the Video Thumbnails pane), and to show/hide frame numbers on individual frames. You can edit the Start Time, Trim-in Time, and Trim-Out time fields.
- SONAR saves the size and state of the Video Thumbnails pane on a per/project basis.
- The Video Thumbnails pane zooms horizontally when you use the standard Track view commands for horizontal zooming. You control the height of the Video Thumbnails pane by dragging the splitter bar up or down that's at the bottom of the Video Thumbnails pane.

For step-by-step instructions, see the following procedures:

To Hide or Show the Video Thumbnails Pane
- Drag the splitter bar that separates the Video Thumbnails pane from the Clips pane.

Or

- Use the ***View-Video Thumbnails*** menu command.

Or

- Click the Show/Hide Video Pane button in the Track view toolbar.

To Turn Video Thumbnails On or Off
1. Right-click the Video Thumbnails pane or the Video Thumbnails track strip.
2. Choose ***Show/Hide Thumbnails*** from the popup menu that appears.

Or

- Click the Show/Hide Thumbnails button in the Track view toolbar.

To Hide or Show Frame Numbers on Frames
- In the video track strip, click the Show/Hide Frame Numbers button.

To Open the Video Properties Dialog
- Double-click the video track strip.

To Open the Video View
- Double-click the Video Thumbnails pane.

To Move the Now Time to a Thumbnail
- Click the thumbnail.

To Change the Start Time
- In the video track strip, click the Start field, type a new number in Measure/Beat/Tick format, and press Enter. The start time is the time in your SONAR project at which your video starts to play.

To Change the Trim-In Time
- In the video track strip, click the Trim-In field, type a new number in SMPTE format, and press Enter (you can press the Spacebar instead of typing colons, if you want, and you can type single zeros instead of double zeros). The trim-in time is the time in your video file at which you want to start video playback.

To Change the Trim-Out Time
- In the video track strip, click the Trim-Out field, type a new number in SMPTE format, and press Enter (you can press the Spacebar instead of typing colons, if you want, and you can type single zeros instead of double zeros). The trim-out time is the time in your video file at which you want to stop video playback.

To Use the Video Thumbnails Context Menu
1. Right click the Video Thumbnails pane or the Video Thumbnails track strip.
2. Choose any of these options from the popup menu that appears:
   - Show/Hide Thumbnails
   - Display Absolute Frames
   - Open Video View
   - Insert Video
   - Delete Video
   - Export Video
   - Video Properties

Locating Missing Audio

If you try to open a project and SONAR is unable to locate all the audio files that the project references, the Find Missing Audio dialog appears. The Find Missing Audio dialog helps you find any missing audio in your project.

The Find Missing Audio File Dialog
Use the Locate Missing Audio File dialog to find missing audio in your project. The following is a brief description of the options you have in this dialog:

- **Open**—Click this button once you have searched for and found the missing audio file.

- **Skip**—Click this button to move to the next missing file. When you skip and audio file your project opens without that piece of missing audio.

- **Skip All**—Click this button to skip all missing audio files. When you skip all missing audio files, you project opens without those pieces of missing audio

- **Search**—Click this button to begin a search of all available hard drives for your missing audio file.

- **After locating the file Options**—You can choose to either move an audio file to the project's audio data folder, copy an audio file to the project's audio data folder, or leave an audio file in its current folder.

Restoring Missing Audio Files
When you open a project file that references audio files which SONAR can not find, the Locate Missing Audio dialog appears. Use the following procedure to restore the missing audio files to your project.

To Restore Missing Audio Files

1. In the Locate Missing Audio dialog, click the Search button.

   The Search for Missing Audio dialog appears and SONAR begins searching all available hard drives for the missing file or files.

2. When SONAR is finished searching, the files that it has found appear in the dialog.

3. Select the file or files that SONAR has found and click OK.

   The Locate Missing Audio dialog appears.

4. Select one of the following options:

   - **Move file to Project Audio Folder**—Use this option if you are sure that no other projects are referencing this file in its present location.

   - **Copy file to Project Audio Folder**—Use this option if the missing file is shared with another project and you want to keep all of your project's audio files together.

   - **Reference file from present location**—Use this option if you want to leave the missing file in its current location now that SONAR knows where it is.

5. Click Open.

SONAR moves, copies or references the missing file or files as you instructed.

Managing Shared and External Files

You may want to share files between projects. The files you want to share may be frequently used sound effects or drum loops. SONAR allows you to choose whether to copy imported audio files to your project's audio data directory or to link to them in their current (external) location.

Note: External files are defined as any file not in the project's audio data folder (or a subfolder within the project's audio data folder).

To Configure SONAR to Always Copy Files to the Project Audio Data Folder

Use this procedure if you want to keep all of your project's audio in one folder (your project's audio data directory).

1. Select *Options-Global* and click on the Audio Data tab.

2. In the All Projects section, click the Always Copy Imported Audio Files option.

To Configure SONAR to Share External Files

SONAR allows you to share external files (files not in the project's audio data directory). There are some exceptions, however. Files that have a different sampling rate or bit depth are always copied to the project's audio data directory. Also, if the Always Copy Imported Audio Files option in the Audio Data tab of the Global Options dialog is checked, imported audio is always copied to your project's audio data directory.

Do the following to ensure that you are sharing files:

1. Uncheck the Always Copy Imported Audio Files option in the Global Options dialog.
2. In the Open dialog, when importing audio, make sure the Copy Audio to Project Folder option is unchecked.

4 Recording

You can add sound or music to a SONAR™ project in many different ways. You can record your own material using a MIDI-equipped instrument, use a microphone or another audio input to record digital audio information, or import sound or music data from an existing digital data file. With the **input monitoring** feature, you can hear your audio instruments exactly the way SONAR records them, including any plug-in effects. When you record audio or MIDI tracks, SONAR displays a wave preview of your recorded data as you record it.

You can also input new material using your computer keyboard or mouse using the Piano Roll view, the Staff view, or the Event List view. For more information on entering music using these views, see Chapter 15, *Working with Notation and Lyrics*, "The Piano Roll View" on page 275, and "The Event List View" on page 318.

In This Chapter

Creating a New Project	*162*
Preparing to Record	*170*
Recording Music from a MIDI Instrument	*175*
Recording Audio	*175*
Confidence Recording	*179*
Input Monitoring	*180*
The Audio Engine Button	*183*
Loop Recording	*184*
Punch Recording	*185*
Step Recording	*188*
Recording Specific Ports and Channels	*192*
Importing Music and Sound	*195*
Saving Your Work	*198*

Creating a New Project

You can add music and sound to an existing project or to a new project. Just as in any Windows program, you open an existing project file using the **File-Open** command, and create a new project file using the **File-New** command.

When you create a new SONAR project, there are some additional parameters you can set to make it easier to work on your project. These include:

- Meter and key signature
- Metronome and tempo settings
- Audio sampling rate
- MIDI timing resolution

Using Per-Project Audio Folders

For ease of backing up your audio files in a project, SONAR allows you to use a separate audio folder for each project. This feature is off by default.

To Enable Per-Project Audio
1. Select **Options-Global**.

    The Global Options dialog appears.

2. Click the Audio Data tab.
3. In the Audio Data tab, click the Use Per-Project Audio Folders option.
4. Click OK.

Note: If you use the default project that is created when you open SONAR, you are not using per-project audio. You must use the Copy All Audio with Project option in the Save As dialog to create a per-project audio folder. For more information, see "To Save an Existing Project Using Per-project Audio" on page 622.

Creating a New Project File

When you create a new project you are asked to choose a template to use for your new file. If you have per-project audio folders enabled (for more information, see the online help topic Using Per-Project Audio Folders), you are also asked to specify a file name, the folder where you want to store the file, and the folder where you want to store the file's audio. You can override per-project audio by unchecking the Store Project Audio in its Own Folder option.

SONAR includes a set of templates you can use to create a new project. These templates include common types of ensembles, such as rock quartets, jazz trios, and classical full orchestras. When you create a new project using one of these templates, SONAR creates a project that has MIDI settings predefined so that one track is set up for each of the instruments in the ensemble. SONAR also includes a template with two MIDI and two audio tracks (called the Normal template). If you are creating a new project that will contain only audio material, use the Audio Only template. If you are creating a new project that will contain only MIDI material, use the MIDI Only template.

You can create your own template files and use them as the basis for other new projects. For more information, see "Templates" on page 517.

To Create a New Project File
1. Choose *File-New* to display the New Project File dialog box.

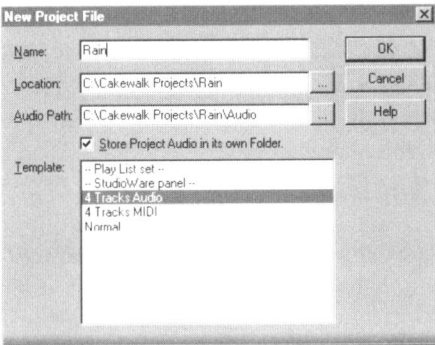

2. If you have the per-project audio folders option enabled, enter a file name, set the folder where you want to store the new file, and set the folder where you want to store the new file's audio.
3. Choose a template from the list.
4. Click OK.

SONAR creates the new project file and displays it with the Track view open.

Setting the Meter and Key Signatures
By default, a new SONAR project is in 4/4 time and the key of C major. You can change these settings to any desired **meter** or key. These settings apply to all the tracks in a project. You cannot set different meter or key signatures for different tracks.

The meter or key signature of a project can change at any measure boundary. To insert changes in the meter or key signature, use the *View-Meter/Key* command to display the Meter/Key view, or use the *Insert-Meter/Key Change* command.

If you are creating a new project that will contain only audio material (no MIDI material), you do not need to set the meter and key signature.

Note:

Groove clips do not follow your project's key. Groove clips follow the project pitch in the Markers toolbar and pitch markers in the Time Ruler. For more information, see "Working with Groove Clips" on page 260.

The key signature controls how SONAR displays notes in the Staff view, the Event List view, and elsewhere. The meter tells SONAR the number of beats per measure and the note value of each beat. Common meters include:

- 2/4 (two beats per measure, each quarter note gets a beat)
- 4/4 (four beats per measure, each quarter note gets a beat)
- 3/4 (three beats per measure, each quarter note gets a beat)
- 6/8 (six beats per measure, each eighth note gets a beat)

The top number of a meter, the number of beats per measure, can be from 1 through 99. The bottom number of a meter is the value of each beat. You can pick from a list of values ranging from a whole note to a thirty-second note.

The meter determines the following:

- Where the metronome accents are placed
- How the Now time is displayed
- How the Staff view is drawn
- How grid lines are displayed in the Piano Roll view

To Set the Meter and Key Signature

1. Display the Views toolbar by choosing **View-Toolbars-Views.**
2. Select **Insert-Meter/Key Change**.
3. Click ![icon] on the View toolbar to open the Meter/Key view.
4. Select the first (and only) meter/key change in the list.
5. Click ![icon] to open the Meter/Key Signature dialog box.

The Meter/Key Signature dialog appears.

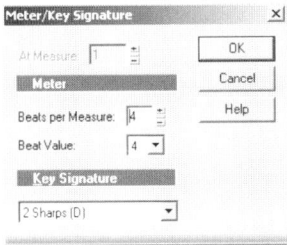

6. Enter the top and bottom meter values in the Beats per Measure and Beat Value fields.
7. Choose the key signature from the Key Signature list.
8. Click OK.

You can also set the meter and key signature in the Large Transport toolbar display.

Setting the Metronome and Tempo Settings

The metronome counts off each beat in a measure, so you can hear the tempo of your project. You can choose to have the metronome sound during recording, during playback, or both. When you start recording, SONAR can play any number of beats or measures of metronome clicks before recording begins. This can help you "get in the groove" before you start performing. These beats or measures are called the **count-in**.

When you create a new project, you should set the metronome to play during the count-in and while recording. If you are adding material to an existing project, you might only need the metronome for the count-in.

You can customize the metronome sound to use audio or any note on a MIDI instrument. By default, SONAR uses a hi-hat cymbal sound from a General MIDI drum kit for the MIDI metronome, but you can change this setting to anything you like by changing the MIDI output, MIDI channel, and duration. You can also choose the note and velocity (volume) to use for the first beat of each measure and for all other beats. The metronome settings are stored separately with each project, so you can use different settings for each one.

Most metronome options can be set in the Metronome toolbar:

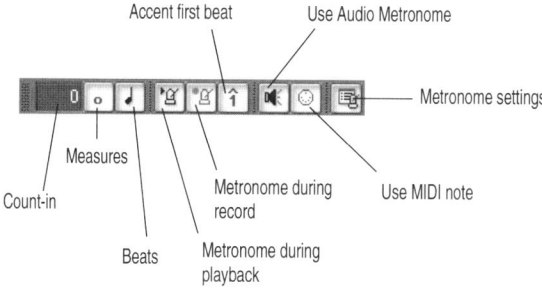

If you don't see the Metronome toolbar, use the **View-Toolbars** command to open the Toolbars dialog box, and check the Metronome checkbox. The metronome MIDI note parameters must be set in the Metronome Settings dialog box.

Note:

If you are synchronized to an external clock source, you cannot use the count-in feature. For more information, see "Synchronizing Your Gear" on page 601.

To Set the Tempo and Metronome for a New Project

1. In the Metronome toolbar, select the Metronome during Recording and Metronome during Playback options.

2. If you want to hear a count-in before recording begins, set the count-in to 1 or more. Select Count-in Measures or Count-in Beats .

3. Select Use Audio Metronome and/or Use MIDI Metronome .

4. Arm at least one track.

5. Press *r* or click to start recording. The count-in will play, and the Now time will start to advance.

6. If necessary, stop playback and adjust the tempo using the tempo controls in the toolbar and restart playback. Repeat until the metronome plays the tempo you want.

7. Press the Spacebar or click to stop recording.

8. Press *w*, or click to rewind to the beginning of the piece.

Your tempo and metronome settings are now ready. When you save the project file, the metronome and tempo settings will be saved as well.

To Change Your Metronome Settings

1. Open the Metronome Settings dialog box in one of the following ways:

   - Click Metronome Settings 🖼 in the Metronome toolbar.

   - Choose *Options-Project* and click the Metronome tab.

2. Change the metronome settings as indicated in the following table:

To do this...	Do this...
Enable the metronome during playback	Check Playback
Enable the metronome during recording	Check Recording
Enable the count-in	Enter the number of clicks for the count-in in the Count-in box, and select Measures or Beats
Accent the first beat of each measure	Check Accent First Beat
Use the audio	Check Use Audio Metronome
Use a MIDI note as the sound	Check Use MIDI Note and choose the output, channel, and other settings

3. Click OK.

Your metronome settings will be saved with the project file.

To Set the MIDI Metronome Sounds from your MIDI Instrument

1. Select a track in the Track view that is assigned to the MIDI device you want to use for the metronome sound.

2. Click Metronome Settings 🖼 in the Metronome toolbar to open the Project Options dialog box.

3. Make sure that the settings in the Output and Channel fields match those for the track in the Track view.

4. Click on the Key box in the First Beat or the Other Beats section.

5. Play a note on your MIDI instrument. The note number is entered automatically. The velocity is not updated.

6. Click OK.

Your metronome settings will be saved with the project file.

Setting the Audio Sampling Rate and Bit Depth

Each SONAR project has an audio **sampling rate** and an audio driver **bit depth** that indicate the level of accuracy with which audio data are sampled and processed. The same parameters are used for all the digital audio in a project. When you create a new project, if you do not want to use the default setting, you must choose a sampling rate before you start recording audio.

SONAR lets you choose from several different sampling rates: 11025 Hz, 22050 Hz, 44100 Hz, 48000 Hz, 88200 Hz, 96000 Hz, 176400Hz, and 192000 Hz. The default used by SONAR is 44100 Hz, the same rate as audio CDs. However, you may choose a higher rate and later mixdown to 44100. You can also enter any hardware-supported value in the Sampling Rate field. Consult your hardware documentation for supported sampling rates.

Note: For most sound cards, all digital audio in the same song must be at the same sampling rate. Some dedicated audio systems let you mix different sampling rates in the same song; SONAR only lets you do this if the audio system supports it. This feature is meant primarily for sound cards that use different Windows drivers for input and output; SONAR treats such cards as two different programs.

A higher sampling rate produces better quality sound. However, a higher sampling rate also means that each audio clip takes up more memory and disk space and requires more intensive processing by your computer. If you have an older computer, or a slow hard drive, you might be better off with a lower sampling rate. For more information, see "Improving Performance with Digital Audio" on page 634.

By default, the audio driver bit depth of audio data is 16 bits. If your sound card supports 18, 20, 22, or 24 bit audio, you can choose to take advantage of these higher resolutions.

If you are creating a new project that will contain only MIDI material (no audio), you do not need to set the audio sampling rate or bit depth. If you import audio from a Wave file or another digital audio file, the sampling rate and audio driver bit depth of the wave file are converted to your default setting, if necessary.

Note:
If you are planning to move your project to a Digital Audio Tape (DAT) or to some other media via a digital transfer, set your sampling rate and bit depth to match the target unit. For example, use 44100Hz/16 bit for a project that will be mastered to a CD, so that no sample rate conversion is required.

To Set the Sampling Rate and Audio Driver Bit Depth for New Projects

1. Choose *Options-Audio* to display the Audio Options dialog box.

2. On the General tab of the dialog, select a value in the Sampling Rate dropdown menu, and a value from the Audio Driver Bit Depth dropdown menu.

3. If you choose an audio driver bit depth of 16, also choose 16 in the File Bit Depth field. If you choose an audio driver bit depth higher than 16, choose a File Bit Depth of 24.

4. Click OK.

The sampling rate and audio driver bit depth are saved with the project file.

Setting the MIDI Timing Resolution

Each SONAR project has a setting for the timing resolution, or **timebase**, that indicates the resolution of MIDI data. This resolution is measured in ticks or pulses per quarter note and is often abbreviated as PPQ. The default resolution is 960PPQ, which is accurate enough for most applications. In this timebase, each quarter note is represented by 960 ticks, each eighth note by 480 ticks, each eighth-note triplet by 320 ticks, and so on.

In some projects you may need a different timebase. For example, if you wanted to use eighth-note septuplets (7 eighth notes per quarter note) and represent them accurately, you would need to have a timebase that is divisible by 7, such as 168PPQ. SONAR uses the timebase you choose for a project to determine the range of tick values in the Now time.

To Set the Timebase for a Project

1. Choose *Options-Project* and click the Clock tab.

2. Choose the timebase you want from the Ticks per Quarter Note list.

3. Click OK.

The timebase will be saved with the project file.

Preparing to Record

To prepare for recording, you need to do the following:

- Set the recording mode.
- Choose your input(s).
- Arm one or more tracks for recording.
- Check your recording levels (audio only).
- Tune your instrument if necessary (audio only).
- Set the Now time to the point where recording should start.
- Start recording.

After you record, you can use the **Edit-Undo** command to erase the most recently recorded material. You can use the **Edit-Redo** command to restore the recording and toggle between **Undo** and **Redo** as many times as you like.

If you are using MIDI Sync or time code sync for the clock source, SONAR waits to receive external timing data before it begins recording. For more information see Chapter 18, *Synchronizing Your Gear*.

Recording Modes

Any material you record is stored in a new clip. If you record into several tracks at once, one clip is created in each track. If you record into a track that already contains clips, you can choose one of three **recording modes** to determine what happens to those clips. When you save your project, you also save whatever recording mode you choose together with that project:

Recording mode...	How it works...
Sound on Sound	The new material is merged with any existing material. This means that any existing clips on the track are left unchanged and all newly recorded material is stored in new clips. While recording, you will be able to hear material from existing clips.
Overwrite	The new material replaces (overwrites) any existing material. This means that portions of existing clips may be "wiped clean" to make room for newly recorded material. While recording, you will not be able to hear material from existing clips.
Auto Punch	Recording only takes place between the punch-in and punch-out times. You can use Auto Punch in either Sound on Sound or Overwrite mode.

To Choose a Recording Mode

- Select a mode from the dropdown list in the Record toolbar.

    Or

- Choose **Transport-Record Options** or click 🔲 to display the Record Options dialog box, then select the desired mode.

SONAR saves your recording options with each project, so you can save a different recording mode with each of your projects.

Choosing an Input

To record into a track, you must choose an input for the music or sound to be recorded. Usually, you choose All Inputs - Omni to record material from a MIDI instrument, or the left or right channel of a digital audio device (such as a sound card) to record audio material, or stereo if you want to record stereo audio in a single track. The input for each track is displayed in the track's Input field and at the top of each module in the Console view.

When you choose All Inputs - Omni as the input for a track, SONAR merges material from all MIDI inputs and instruments. This means you don't have to worry about input, channel, or other MIDI settings. Sometimes, you may want to record different MIDI channels into different tracks. To learn how to do this, see "Recording Specific Ports and Channels" on page 192.

While each track can have a different input, it is also possible for several tracks to have the same input.

To Choose a MIDI Input in the Track View

1. Click the dropdown arrow of an Input field of a MIDI track (an Input field has this icon to the left of it: 🔲).

    A dropdown menu of MIDI inputs appears.

2. Choose an input from the following:

    - **None**—this option actually sets the Input field to Omni: with this setting the track will record any MIDI input coming in on any enabled port (MIDI interface input driver) on any channel.

    - **All Inputs-(MIDI Omni or MIDI ch 1-16)**—with this setting the track will record any MIDI input coming in on any enabled port (MIDI interface input driver) on any channel, unless you choose a particular MIDI channel instead of MIDI Omni. Then the track will only record input that's on the MIDI channel you chose.

    - **(name of MIDI input driver)-(MIDI Omni or MIDI ch 1-16)**— choosing this option causes the track to record any MIDI channel coming from the named MIDI interface input driver, unless you choose a particular MIDI channel instead of MIDI Omni. Then the track will only record input that's on the MIDI channel you chose, from the named input driver.

- **Preset**—if you want to record multiple data from multiple ports and/or channels, you need to select a preset collection of those ports and channels. You can select one here (to create presets, see next line).

- **Manage Presets**—if you want to create or edit any preset collections of input ports and channels, you can select this option (see "To Create or Edit a Preset Input Configuration" on page 194).

To Choose an Audio Input in the Track View

1. Click the dropdown arrow of the Input field of an audio track (an Input field has this icon to the left of it: ▮).

   A dropdown menu of audio drivers appears.

2. Select the audio driver for the sound card you want to record with from these options:

   - None—This choice ensures that you do not record to the track in question.

   - Left (name of your sound card)—Choose this if you want to record a mono signal on the left channel of your sound card.

   - Right (name of your sound card)—Choose this if you want to record a mono signal on the right channel of your sound card.

   - Stereo (name of your sound card)—Choose this if you want to record a stereo signal.

If your sound card has more than one pair of inputs, a pair of numbers appears after the name of each audio driver to indicate which pair of inputs the driver is attached to.

To Choose an Audio Input in the Console View

1. At the top of an audio track module, click the Input button.

   A popup menu of audio drivers appears.

2. Select the audio driver for the sound card you want to record with from these options:

   - None—This choice ensures that you do not record to the track in question. It also turns off input monitoring for this track.
   - Left (name of your sound card)—Choose this if you want to record a mono signal on the left channel of your sound card.
   - Right (name of your sound card)—Choose this if you want to record a mono signal on the right channel of your sound card.
   - Stereo (name of your sound card)—Choose this if you want to record a stereo signal.

If your sound card has more than one pair of inputs, a pair of numbers appears after the name of each audio driver to indicate which pair of inputs the driver is attached to.

To Choose a MIDI Input in the Console View

1. At the top of a MIDI track module, click the Input button.

   A popup menu of MIDI channels appears.

2. Choose an input from the following:

   - *None*—this option actually sets the Input field to Omni: with this setting the track will record any MIDI input coming in on any enabled port (MIDI interface input driver) on any channel.
   - *All Inputs-(MIDI Omni or MIDI ch 1-16)*—with this setting the track will record any MIDI input coming in on any enabled port (MIDI interface input driver) on any channel, unless you choose a particular MIDI channel instead of MIDI Omni. Then the track will only record input that's on the MIDI channel you chose.
   - *(name of MIDI input driver)-(MIDI Omni or MIDI ch 1-16)*— choosing this option causes the track to record any MIDI channel coming from the named MIDI interface input driver, unless you choose a particular MIDI channel instead of MIDI Omni. Then the track will only record input that's on the MIDI channel you chose, from the named input driver.
   - *Preset*—if you want to record multiple data from multiple ports and/or channels, you need to select a preset collection of those ports and channels. You can select one here (to create presets, see next line).
   - *Manage Presets*—if you want to create or edit any preset collections of input ports and channels, you can select this option (see "To Create or Edit a Preset Input Configuration" on page 194).

Arming Tracks for Recording

SONAR lets you record any number of tracks at one time. You indicate the tracks you want to record by **arming** the tracks. You can arm a single track or several tracks at one time. Each track records material received though its selected input. Whenever a track is armed, not only does the track's R button turn red, but the Clips pane that's to the right of that track's controls turns a reddish hue.

To Arm One or More Tracks for Recording

- To arm a track in the Track view, click [R].

  Or

- To arm a track in the Console view, click [R] (to see the Arm button in the Console view, the MSR button on the left side of the Console view must be depressed).

  Or

- To arm several tracks at the same time, select one or more tracks in the Track view, then right-click and choose **Arm** from the popup menu.

A track's Arm button turns red to indicate that the track is armed for recording.

To Disarm All Tracks at Once

- Click the red Arm label that's located in the Status bar at the bottom of the SONAR window.

  Or

- Click the red Arm button in the Playback State toolbar, which you can display by using the **View-Toolbars** command and checking Playback State in the Toolbars dialog box.

Auto Arming

You must arm tracks in order to record. To safeguard your data, there is no automatic arming of any tracks.

If you want to record MIDI tracks without arming a track, choose **Options-Global**, and select the General tab. Click the Allow MIDI Recording without an Armed Track checkbox.

This feature lets you start recording a new track simply by making it the current track and pressing R or clicking the Record button in the toolbar. Auto-arming makes it possible to inadvertently record over existing material in the current track, however.

Recording Music from a MIDI Instrument

Once you have set your tempo and metronome, and armed one or more tracks, you are ready to start recording.

To Record MIDI
1. Set the Now time to the point in the project where you want to start recording.

2. Click ●, press *r*, or choose ***Transport-Record***. If your metronome count-in is turned on, it will play the count-in.

3. Play or perform the material you want to record. As you record, SONAR displays a clip containing the new material in the Clips pane (unless you've turned off this option on the General tab of the Global Options dialog—***Options-Global*** command).

4. Click ■, press the Spacebar, or choose ***Transport-Stop*** to stop recording.

To listen to the new material, set the Now time to the start of the clip and press the Spacebar or click ▶. If you're not happy with the recording, use ***Edit-Undo*** or press Ctrl+Z to erase the new material.

When you stop recording, if you do not see a new clip in the Clips pane, you may have a problem with MIDI input. See *Appendix A: Troubleshooting* for more information.

Recording Audio

Before you record audio, you should check your input levels. If the levels are too low, you may end up with too much hiss and background noise in your recording. If the levels are too high, your recording will be inaccurate or distorted. To check your audio levels, use the audio meters in the either the Track view or Console view. To adjust the input levels, you must use your sound card's software mixer program (or the Windows 2000 or XP mixer) or an external hardware mixer for certain sound cards.

The audio meters indicate the volume at which the audio will be recorded, in units called decibels (dB). The meter values range from -INF (silent) to 0dB (maximum volume). You can change many options in the way SONAR's meters display data:

see "Metering" on page 436. To maximize the dynamic range of your recording, you want to set the levels as high as possible without clipping.

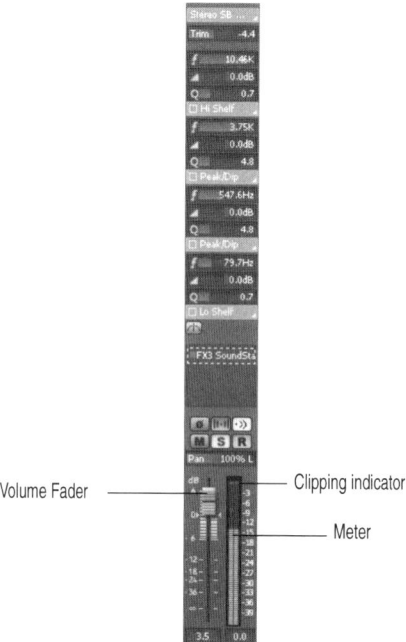

When the audio level exceeds 0dB, some of the audio information is lost. This is known as **overload**. Many sound cards use clipping to deal with an overloaded signal, but clipping can distort the audio signal. As a result, you should avoid letting the meter level exceed 0dB.

Note to Experts:

Because SONAR is a digital recorder, a level of 0dB indicates digital zero. Digital distortion will occur at 0dB. You will not get analog compression or warmth from pushing the input levels. If you are transferring data from a DAT or another device, you may want to calibrate the input levels of your sound card with the output levels of other devices in your studio. This will ensure that 0dB on one unit will appear as 0dB in SONAR.

To Check the Input Levels

1. In the Track view, choose the inputs for the tracks you want to record, and arm the tracks for recording. Make sure that the Show/Hide All Meters button at the top of the Track view is enabled.

2. The default meter range is from 0 dB to -60 dB. To change the range, right-click on the meter and choose a new range from the menu.

3. Perform at the loudest level at which you plan to record.

   Watch the meters respond. Increase the input volume as high as possible without ever letting the meters move all the way to 0dB, even for an instant, or letting the Clipping indicator turn red. If either of these things happen, reduce the input volume just enough to avoid them during the entire performance. Note that some kinds of audio, such as percussive or plucked musical instruments, can produce very short, high-level "transients" when struck or plucked aggressively, which can lead to clipping if the input volume is set too high. Consider the possibility of these transients when examining the meters and setting your record level.

   Note: If the Clipping indicator is illuminated, click on it to reset.

Once you have set your sampling rate and input levels, you are ready to start recording. If the meters do not move, check your sound card software's mixer program and make sure that you have the proper input enabled for recording.

When you record audio, SONAR stores each audio clip in a separate file. These files have the same format as a Wave (.WAV) file, but they have special names and are stored in a separate directory on your hard disk. SONAR automatically manages these audio files for you, making it easier for you to manage your projects. If you want to work with these files directly, or to learn more about how SONAR stores audio data, see "System Configuration" on page 628.

Tuning an Instrument

SONAR Chromatic Tuner analyzes any input signal from the sound card and displays the intonation (in cents) on the meter. The tuner automatically determines which string/pitch you are trying to tune, so that you can keep both hands on the instrument while tuning. The VU Meter shows how loud your input signal is–a strong signal is essential for accurate tuning.

The Tuner works just like an effect and each track can have its own instance.

With a microphone, you can also tune acoustic instruments.

To Tune an Instrument
1. In the track you want to record your instrument on, right-click in the Effects bin.
2. From the menu that appears, select ***Audio Effects-Cakewalk-Tuner***.
3. **Click the track's Input Monitor button**. If you don't click the Input Monitor button on the track the Tuner is patched into, you will not be able to use the tuner.
4. With your instrument plugged into your sound card and turned up, play a note.

   The Tuner displays the intonation reading on the cents meter and the name of the note you played between the three arrows. One of the three arrows lights up, indicating one of the following:

   - Up arrow indicates the note is in tune.
   - Right arrow indicates the note is sharp.
   - Left arrow indicates the note is flat.

5. Adjust the pitch if necessary and repeat for the rest of the pitches you need to tune.

To Record Audio
1. Choose the audio inputs for the track(s) you want to record.
2. Arm the tracks for recording. The Clips pane next to each armed track turns a reddish hue when the track is armed.
3. Set the Now time to the point in the project where you want to start recording.
4. Click ●, press *r*, or choose ***Transport-Record***. If your metronome count-in is turned on, it will play the count-in measures or beats.
5. Play or perform the material you want to record.

   As you record, SONAR displays a waveform preview of the new material in the Clips pane, unless you've turned off the Display Waveform Preview option on the General tab of the Global Options dialog (***Options-Global*** command). If you've turned off the option, SONAR displays a red swath along the area of the Clips pane where you're recording.

6. Click ■, press the Spacebar, or choose ***Transport-Stop*** to stop recording.

SONAR displays a clip containing the new material in the Track window. To listen to the new material, set the Now time to the start of the clip and press the Spacebar or click ▶. If you're not happy with the recording, use ***Edit-Undo*** to erase the new material.

If you do not see a new clip in the Clips pane, you may have a problem with audio input. See *Appendix A: Troubleshooting* for more information.

Important: Make sure you have enough space on your hard disk when recording digital audio. Running out of hard disk space when recording can lead to unpredictable results.

Confidence Recording

When you're recording audio or MIDI data, SONAR gives you many visual cues that tracks are armed and that SONAR is recording data.

When one or more tracks are armed:

- The R button in each armed track turns red.
- The Clips pane next to each armed track gets a reddish hue.
- The R button in the Playback State toolbar is depressed (to display the toolbar, use the ***View-Toolbars-Playback State*** command).
- The Status bar displays the red Arm message.

While you're recording, SONAR displays these cues:

- Audio tracks display a waveform preview in the area in the Clips pane where you're recording. This is actually a visual record of the record meter's progress. When you stop recording, SONAR displays the actual waveform, which is slightly different from the preview. The preview is a snapshot taken at certain time intervals, while the actual waveform represents all the data that is recorded.
- MIDI tracks display the actual data that they record, both in the Clips pane and the Piano Roll view (not the Staff view).
- Automation data appears as a red block. When you finish recording, the actual envelopes are shown.

If you want to turn off the real-time display of audio clips, see the following procedure.

To Turn Off Waveform Preview for Audio Recording

1. Use the ***Options-Global*** command to open the Global Options dialog.
2. On the General tab, uncheck the Display Waveform Preview While Recording option, and click OK.

Now when you record audio tracks, a red swath appears in the Clips pane in the area you're recording.

Input Monitoring

Being able to hear plug-in audio effects applied to a live signal is an exciting feature of SONAR. However, there are two issues that users commonly stumble upon when using the **input monitoring** feature. The first is that the monitored signal seems to have an echo associated with it. The second is that live input monitoring can lead to nasty feedback problems, particularly if you have an outboard audio mixer, or you record from a different sound card from the one you are playing back with.

SONAR has several buttons to control input monitoring:

- Per-track Input Echo button —each audio track has an Input Echo button that turn's that track's input monitoring on or off.

- Global Input Monitor button—the Playback State toolbar (to display, use the *View-Toolbars-Playback State* command) has the Input Monitor button on the right end, which turns input monitoring on or off on all audio tracks with one click.

- Audio Engine button —clicking this button so that it's in its up position turns all audio activity in SONAR off, which includes input monitoring.

Note: When you use input monitoring, make sure that the track you're playing through uses the same audio interface (sound card) for both input and output. Using different audio interfaces for a track's input and output can produce distortion during input monitoring.

To understand the echo and feedback problems, let's look at how audio signals travel through your sound card, the drivers, and SONAR. The following diagram depicts a simplified version of this signal flow.

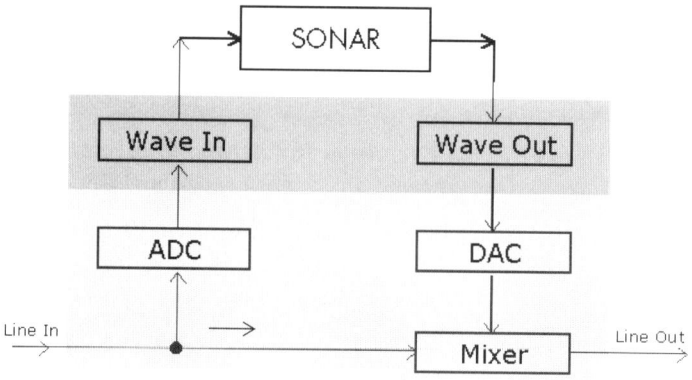

The bottom block of the picture represents the sound card. The shaded area above it represents the audio drivers. The unshaded area at the top represents the main environment of the operating system.

As the diagram shows, analog audio flows into the card's line input (on the left), and is immediately split in two. One branch goes up through the analog-to-digital converter (ADC), where the audio is digitized, buffered and fed to the driver (labeled Wave In in the diagram).

The digital audio data buffers are read by SONAR from the Wave In driver, processed, and then sent out to the Wave Out driver. The driver passes the digital audio buffers through a digital-to-analog converter (DAC), where the audio data is converted back to an analog signal.

Finally, this analog output signal is mixed with the original branch of the input analog signal, and the summed result is presented to the sound card's line output.

With this information in hand, let's follow a simple audio signal through the system to understand how echoes get introduced into the input monitor path.

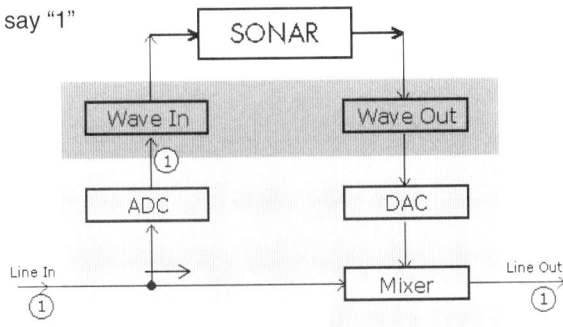

Suppose you are counting "1, 2, 3" into your sound card very quickly. When you say the first "1," this sound immediately appears in all the places indicated in the illustration above. In other words, the analog audio signal is pure electrical signal traveling at the speed of light, so it is immediately present across all analog audio paths inside the sound card.

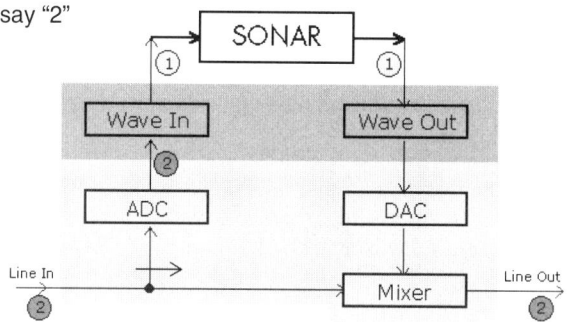

Next, you say "2." In the time it takes you do that, the ADC has converted the "1" to digital form and the Wave In driver has fed it to SONAR for processing. SONAR processes the buffer right away and passes the processed data right back to the Wave Out driver.

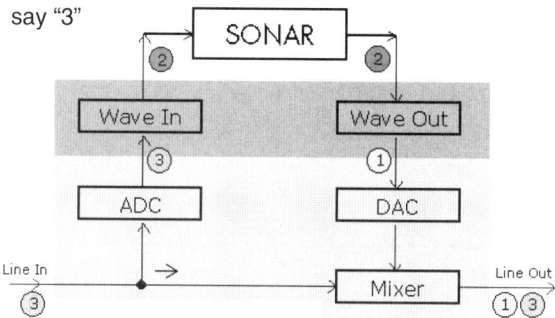

Finally, you say "3." By this time the original "1" has been converted back to analog audio by the DAC, and that analog signal is mixed in with the "3" you have just said. The ultimate result is that you hear a "1" and "3" mixed together at the line output of card—seemingly sounding like an echo, but actually just an artifact of the signal flow through the system.

You can eliminate the echo by muting the line-in from playing back (see "To Eliminate the Echo from Input Monitoring" on page 183); you'll send only the processed signal to the sound card outputs. This technique introduces a little extra latency to what you hear coming out of your sound card, but if you use WDM or ASIO drivers with your sound cards, the latency is negligible.

The feedback problem results whenever you have a loop in your mixer path: the output of your mixer is patched into the input of your sound card. Feedback can happen with or without input monitoring, but since input monitoring can add several levels of gain to the signal flow, it's of greater concern when you have input monitoring enabled. Input monitoring is disabled by default when you install SONAR, and you enable it with the following procedure.

To Enable Input Monitoring

- Turn your speakers down, and on an audio track that you want to monitor, click the Input Echo button so that it's lit up (on) . **To disable monitoring** for this track, click the button off.

    Or

- Turn your speakers down, and on the Playback State toolbar (to display, use the ***View-Toolbars-Playback State*** command), click the Input Monitor button so that it's lit up—this enables input monitoring on all tracks. To disable monitoring for all tracks, click the button off.

Now you can hear your instrument in real time with any plug-in effects that you want to patch into the current track. You might also hear an echo, because the dry signal is coming out of your sound card slightly ahead of the processed signal. To eliminate the dry signal, see the next procedure.

To Eliminate the Echo from Input Monitoring

1. Open the software mixer that controls your sound card. If your sound card uses the Windows mixer, open the mixer by using the ***Start-Programs-Accessories-Entertainment-Volume Control*** command, or double-clicking the speaker icon on the Windows taskbar.

2. In the Play Control window of the mixer, check the Mute checkbox in the Line-In column, or in the column of whatever jack your instrument is plugged into, and close the mixer window.

Now you can hear only the processed sound when you use input monitoring. Using WDM or ASIO drivers for your sound card keeps latency to a negligible amount.

Note: This procedure does not eliminate feedback from you system, only the echo. If you experience feedback, you have a feedback loop somewhere in your mixer setup.

The Audio Engine Button

SONAR has a button in the Transport toolbar called the Audio Engine button . This button lets you turn SONAR's audio engine off if you're getting distortion or feedback and want to cut the sound off. When playback or recording are in progress, SONAR enables the button automatically—however, the button appears greyed-out during playback or recording because you can't control the button at that time. Whenever the button is enabled, the Audio Running message lights up on the Status bar that's at the bottom of the SONAR window.

If you experience feedback during input monitoring, you can click the Audio Engine button to turn off the audio engine. However, if playback or recording are in progress, the button is unavailable, and you should click the Reset button that's just to the right of it instead, or else stop recording or playback first and then click the Audio Engine button.

You may experience slightly better playback and recording performance by turning the Audio Engine button off before you press the Play or Record buttons. This happens if your computer's resources are already stretched to the limit. When you start recording or playback with the audio engine already functioning, there is still some processing that SONAR has to do that's left over when you start the transport. This places an extra load on your system that can cause dropouts if your system is already stretched thin. A more effective solution than disabling the audio engine before starting the transport is to reduce the load on your system by hiding some meters, increasing latency slightly, reducing the number of plug-ins and/or tracks, etc.

Loop Recording

When recording a vocal or an instrumental section, you might want to record several different takes so that you can choose the one you like best. You might even want to record several takes to double a part or merge the best parts of each.

Normally, to record each take you would have to arm a track, start recording, perform the take, and then stop recording. You can record multiple takes more easily using a feature called **loop recording**. Loop recording lets you start recording and record as many takes as you like, all in a single step.

SONAR loops between the loop start and loop end time, allowing you to record one take on each pass. SONAR creates a clip for each take. You have three choices for where these clips are stored:

- All clips can be recorded in Sound on Sound mode and stored in a single track, where they are stacked on top of one another.

- All clips can be recorded in Overwrite mode in a single track, where each take overwrites the previous one.

- Each clip can be recorded to a different track. SONAR automatically places each take into a new, empty track. No existing tracks are changed in any way.

When you stack takes, using the **Sound on Sound** record mode, you hear all the previous takes as you record each new take. When you store takes in different tracks, each take is automatically muted as you record the next one. You choose the option you want from the Record Options dialog.

When you finish recording, you can use the ***Edit-Undo*** command to erase all your takes in a single step.

To Use Loop Recording

1. Choose the input for the track(s) you want to record, and arm the track(s) for recording.

2. Set the loop start and end times in either the Loop/Auto Shuttle dialog box or in the Loop toolbar.

3. Choose *Transport-Record Options*, or click 🗐 on the Record toolbar, to display the Record Options dialog box.

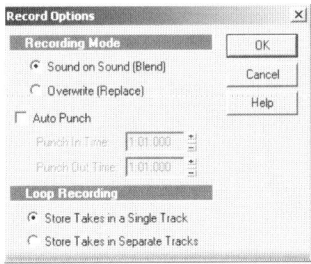

4. Choose to stack all takes in a single track or to store them in separate tracks.

5. If you choose to stack all takes in a single track, choose either Sound on Sound or Overwrite mode.

6. Click OK to close the Record Options dialog, and set the Now time to the point in the project where you want to start recording.

7. Click ⦿, or press *r*, or choose *Transport-Record*. If your metronome count-in is turned on, it will play the count-in measure.

8. Play or perform the material you want to record. At the end of the loop, SONAR will return to the start of the loop and you can record the next take.

9. If you want to erase the most recent take while loop recording is underway, choose *Transport-Reject Loop Take* or press Ctrl+Spacebar.

10. Click ■, or press the Spacebar, or choose *Transport-Stop* when you want to stop recording.

The takes are stored in the manner you requested.

Punch Recording

Suppose you are happy with most of a track but want to replace one small section—perhaps as small as a couple of notes. This is where punch recording comes in handy, because it lets you record new material only within a specified range of times.

For example, suppose you recorded a 32-bar keyboard solo but made some mistakes in the 24th and 25th bars. With punch recording, you can play the entire solo again, so you make sure you can get the feel you want. However, only the bars you want to correct are actually recorded. That way, you don't have to worry about introducing new mistakes elsewhere in the recording.

To use punch recording, follow these steps:

- Enable punch recording.
- Set the start and end times of the punch.
- Start recording by pressing *r* or clicking the ⏺ button on the Transport toolbar.

The Record toolbar shows the punch settings, as shown here:

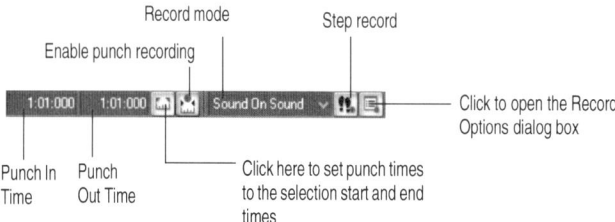

When punch recording is enabled, the punch times are indicated by special markers in the Time Ruler, which is at the top of the Clips pane:

After you punch record, choosing **Edit-Undo** both discards any new material you recorded and restores the original material that had been deleted.

You can also combine loop and punch recording to record several takes of a punch. Say you are working on that perfect take of a guitar solo and you need to hear a couple of bars of the project as "pre-roll" before you punch in. By combining looping with punch, you can have each take begin before you start to play and still have the solo cut in at the appropriate instant.

In the example mentioned previously, you could loop from bar 17 to bar 26 but record only bars 24 and 25. Here's what this looks like:

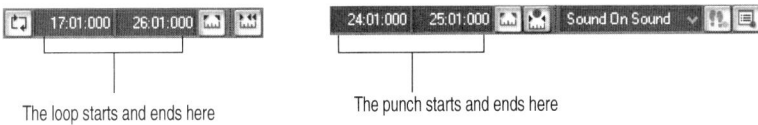

The loop starts and ends here   The punch starts and ends here

To Punch Record
1. Choose the input(s) for the track(s) you want to record, and arm the track(s) for recording.

2. Enable the Auto Punch button in the Record toolbar (the button is red when enabled).

3. Set the start and end times in one of the following ways:

    - Enter the times directly on the toolbar

    - Select a range of time and click [icon] on the Record toolbar

    - Select a range of time, then right-click in the Time Ruler and choose *Set Punch Points*

4. Choose either Sound on Sound or Overwrite from the Record toolbar.

5. Set the Now time to a point where you want to start playback.

6. Click [icon], or press *r*, or choose *Transport-Record*. If your metronome count-in is turned on, it will play the count-in measures or beats.

7. Play or perform the material you want to record.

8. Click [icon], or press the Spacebar, or choose *Transport-Stop* to stop recording.

The material you play during the punch time is recorded in the chosen track, either replacing any existing material (Overwrite mode) or blending with it (Sound on Sound mode).

To Use Punch While Looping
1. Choose the input for the track(s) you want to record, and arm the track(s) for recording.

2. Set the loop start and end times.

3. Set the punch start and end times, as described previously.

4. Choose *Transport-Record Options*, or click [icon] on the Record toolbar, to display the Record Options dialog box.

5. Choose to stack all takes in a single track or to store them in separate tracks.

6. Set the Now time to the beginning of the loop.

7. Click ●, or press *r*, or choose ***Transport-Record***. If your metronome count-in is turned on, it will play the count-in measures.

8. Play or perform the material you want to record. At the end of the loop, SONAR will return to the start of the loop and you can record the next take.

9. If you want to erase the most recent take while loop recording is underway, choose ***Transport-Reject Loop Take*** or press Ctrl+Spacebar.

10. Click ■, or press the Spacebar, or choose ***Transport-Stop*** when you want to stop recording.

The takes are stored in the manner you requested.

Step Recording

Sometimes you may want to record MIDI material that is too difficult to play. One way to make this easier is to slow the tempo of the project while you are recording until it is slow enough to play. Step recording is another method that lets you record from a MIDI instrument without having to worry at all about your timing.

To use step recording, you set a step size, such as a quarter note. Then, you simply record one step at a time, taking as much time as you need to play each step. You can also set a note duration that is independent of the step size. If the duration is shorter than the step size, rests will be inserted between each note and the next step. If the duration is longer than the step size, the notes will overlap with the notes recorded at the next step.

MIDI data is recorded using Step Record even if the track is not armed, loop markers are ignored, and **Step Record always uses the Sound on Sound (blend) record mode**, regardless of the current record mode.

You use the Step Record dialog box to perform step recording:

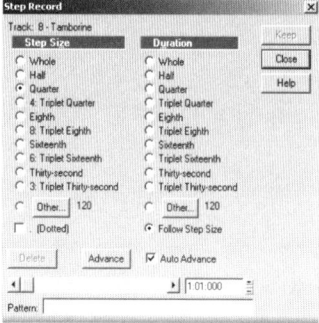

The step size and the duration can each be set to one of three things:

Setting...	How to use it...
A particular note value	Simply choose the note value from the list
A dotted note value	Choose the note value and check the Dotted option
A number of MIDI ticks	Click Other, enter the number of MIDI ticks, and click OK

The Auto Advance option automatically advances recording to the next step when all MIDI input stops. For example, if you press the three keys that make up a C major chord, as soon as you release all three keys, SONAR automatically advances to the next step. This makes it very easy to record a series of chords that are spaced at regular intervals.

With Auto Advance disabled, you must click Advance each time you want to advance to the next step. While this requires more effort, it also provides you with more flexibility. For example, with Auto Advance disabled, you do not even need to play the notes at a single step at the same time! You can play any number of notes one at a time, and they will all be recorded at the same step until you click the Advance button. You can even record notes of different durations at the same step – simply record the notes of one duration, change the duration, and play more notes, without clicking Advance.

You can click Delete to erase the notes you recorded in a single step. If Auto Advance is enabled, the Delete button deletes the notes played at the prior step, and it also backs up a step so you can rerecord the notes at that step. With Auto Advance disabled, the Delete button erases any notes you have recorded at the current step.

To Use Step Recording

1. Choose the input for the track you want to record.

2. Click in the Track pane in the track you want to record. You can only step record in the current track—the track that has the focus.

3. Set the Now time to the point in the project where you want to start recording.

4. Choose ***Transport-Step Record***, or click 🎛 in the Record toolbar to display the Step Record dialog box.

5. Follow the instructions in the following table:

To do this...	Do this...
Record the next step	Play the note(s) you want on your MIDI instrument
Erase the most recent step	Click Delete
Skip a step (add rests)	Click Advance without playing any notes
Move forward or backward one step	Click the scroll arrows in the scroll bar
Move forward or backward one measure	Drag the indicator in the scroll bar
Jump to a particular Now time	Enter the measure, beat, and tick number next to the scroll bar
Change the step size	Pick the step size you want from the Step Size list
Change the note duration	Pick the duration you want from the Duration list
Stop recording and save your work	Click Keep or press Enter
Stop recording and discard your work	Click Close or press Esc
Advance to the next step	With Auto Advance disabled, click the Advance button

6. Click OK.

As always, you can use the *Edit-Undo* and *Edit-Redo* commands after you have finished recording. Note that these commands erase or restore all the material you recorded while in step record mode. Remember that **Step Record always uses the Sound on Sound (blend) record mode**, regardless of the current record mode.

Step Pattern Recording

The Pattern option lets you define a repeating rhythmic pattern of notes and rests so that you can use step recording more efficiently. For example, suppose your project is in 4/4 time, and one track has a pattern that is two measures long: quarter notes in the first measure and on the first two beats of the second measure, followed by a half-note rest on the last two beats. This pattern has six quarter notes followed by two quarter-note rests.

When you use step recording with Auto Advance, you can play the six quarter notes and SONAR will automatically advance to the next step. However, to skip over the rests, you need to click the Advance button two times.

With pattern recording, you define a pattern that indicates where the rests appear in the pattern. SONAR will then skip over the rests automatically, so you don't need to click the Advance button at all.

SONAR displays patterns as a combination of digits (which represent beats that contain notes) and dots (which represent beats that contain rests). The pattern described previously looks like this:

1 2 3 4 5 6 . .

Here is another example:

1 2 . 4

This pattern automatically skips over every third beat; SONAR interprets this pattern as "one, two, rest, four."

Here is one final example based on 4/4 time, with a step size of eighth-note triplets (twelve steps per measure):

1 2 3 4 . 6 7 . 9 0 . 2

No matter how you enter a pattern, SONAR displays the digits in sequence, with periods replacing digits at each step where a rest would occur. You can create patterns with up to 64 steps.

To Use Pattern-Based Step Recording

1. Choose the input for the track(s) you want to record.
2. Set the Now time to the point in the project where you want to start recording.
3. Choose **Transport-Step Record** to display the Step Record dialog box.
4. Click in the Pattern box.
5. Press any number key to indicate a beat at which notes will be played.

6. Press the Spacebar, period, or the letter *r* to indicate a beat on which there is a rest.
7. When the pattern is complete, click elsewhere in the dialog box.
8. Step record as before.

From now on, after you record each step, SONAR automatically advances past all rests to the next step on which notes will be played. To stop pattern-based step recording, simply delete the pattern from the Pattern box.

Recording Specific Ports and Channels

Most MIDI instruments are capable of sending information on several different channels at once. By default, SONAR merges all incoming MIDI data and records it on whatever MIDI tracks are armed. However, SONAR also allows you to control which MIDI input ports and channels each track will record. Here are some examples of when this feature might be useful:

- There are several performers, each playing a different MIDI instrument. By setting each instrument to transmit MIDI on a different channel and/or port, you can record each player's performance into a separate track, even though they are all playing at the same time.

- You are using a MIDI guitar controller and want to record the notes played on each string on a separate track.

- Your electronic keyboard has a built-in auto accompaniment feature that plays a drum part and an accompaniment while you play lead. You want to record each of these three parts into a different track in a SONAR project.

- You have a MIDI sequence stored on your synthesizer's built-in sequencer, and you want to record each channel onto a different track. **Note**: You can use external MIDI synchronization to automate the process of loading multichannel sequences from other MIDI devices. For more information, see Synchronizing Your Gear.

You can choose MIDI inputs for a track by using either the Inputs field on each individual track, or by using the ***Track-Property-Inputs*** command to display the Track Inputs dialog box.

SONAR allows you to filter MIDI input so that you can record only certain kinds of MIDI data (see "Input Filtering" on page 194), and also allows you to automatically turn off the Local On setting of your master keyboard.

To Assign Input Ports and Channels to MIDI Tracks

1. Click the dropdown arrow on an individual track's Input field to display the Input dropdown menu (jump to step 4, below).

   Or

1. Use the *Track-Property-Inputs* command to display the Track Inputs dialog box.

2. In the Track column, select a MIDI track or tracks that you want to choose inputs for.

3. Click the MIDI Inputs button that's at the bottom of the dialog to open the MIDI inputs dropdown menu.

4. Choose track inputs from these choices:

   - *None*—this option actually sets the Input field to Omni: with this setting the track will record any MIDI input coming in on any enabled port (MIDI interface input driver) on any channel.

   - *All Inputs-(MIDI Omni or MIDI ch 1-16)*—with this setting the track will record any MIDI input coming in on any enabled port (MIDI interface input driver) on any channel, unless you choose a particular MIDI channel instead of MIDI Omni. Then the track will only record input that's on the MIDI channel you chose.

   - *(name of MIDI input driver)-(MIDI Omni or MIDI ch 1-16)*— choosing this option causes the track to record any MIDI channel coming from the named MIDI interface input driver, unless you choose a particular MIDI channel instead of MIDI Omni. Then the track will only record input that's on the MIDI channel you chose, from the named input driver.

   - *Preset*—if you've created any preset collections of input ports and channels, you can select one here.

   - *Manage Presets*—if you want to create or edit any preset collections of input ports and channels, you can select this option (see following procedure).

5. Click OK.

SONAR shows new track inputs in the Input fields in the Track pane.

Note:

You can use external MIDI synchronization to automate the process of loading multichannel sequences from other MIDI devices. For more information, see "Synchronizing Your Gear" on page 601.

To Create or Edit a Preset Input Configuration

1. In the Input field of a track that you want to select inputs for, click the dropdown arrow and choose **Manage Presets** from the dropdown menu (this menu is also available from the MIDI Inputs button in the Track Inputs dialog).

   The MIDI Input Presets dialog appears.

2. In the Input Port column, find the input port that you want to use for this track (if you only use a single-port MIDI interface, you'll only see one choice).

3. To the right of the input port, select the MIDI channels that you want this track to respond to on this MIDI port. Clicking the OMNI button in this row of MIDI channels clears or fills all the checkboxes in this row.

4. Select channels for any other MIDI port that's listed, if you want to use channels on that port also.

5. If you want to save this configuration, type a name for it in the window at the top of the dialog, and click the disk icon to save it.

Now, when you choose inputs for other tracks, you can choose the preset you saved by clicking the **Presets** option in the track's Input dropdown menu. If you want to edit a preset, select it in the top window of the MIDI Input Presets dialog, edit it, and click the disk icon. If you want to delete a preset, select it in the same dialog and click the X button to delete it.

Input Filtering

SONAR lets you filter out specific types of MIDI messages or filter the MIDI input stream channel by channel. Any MIDI information that is filtered out is neither recorded nor echoed to any other MIDI devices.

You can use the message type filter to screen out resource-intensive MIDI messages like key and channel aftertouch. By default, SONAR records all types of events except these two.

You can use message-type filtering to record short System Exclusive (Sysx) messages in real-time. These will end up in the track as Sysx data events, which can hold System Exclusive messages up to 255 bytes. Leave the Buffers setting at 128 unless you experience data not being recorded. For more information about Sysx, see Chapter 17, *Using System Exclusive Data*.

To Filter Event Types

1. Choose **Options-Global** and click the MIDI tab.

2. Check the message types you want recorded.

3. Click OK.

From now on, SONAR records only the types of events you have chosen.

Importing Music and Sound

While recording is perhaps the most common way of adding material to a SONAR project, there are several other methods you can also use. SONAR lets you import music into a project from several different types of digital data files, including MIDI files; audio files in Wave, MP3, AIFF, and other formats; and other SONAR project files.

Importing Audio Files

SONAR lets you insert digital audio information into any track of a project. If the audio file you are importing is in stereo, then it can be imported into a single stereo track, a pair of mono tracks or a single mono track.

The *File-Import-Audio* command supports the following digital audio file types:

- Wave (extension .wav)
- MPEG (extensions .MPEG, .MPG, .MP2, and .MP3)
- Apple AIFF (extensions .AIF and .AIFF)
- Active Streaming (extension .ASF)
- Next/Sun (extensions .AU and .SND)

The sampling rate and bit depth for a project is set based on your default settings in the Audio Options dialog. If the sampling rate from the Wave file does not match the sampling rate in your project, then it will be converted to the current project's sampling rate and bit depth.

To Import an Audio File

1. Set the Now time and current track to indicate where the audio should be placed.
2. Choose *File-Import-Audio* to display the Open dialog box.
3. Choose the audio file you want to import. SONAR displays information about the file at the bottom of the dialog box.
4. Click Play to listen to the audio file before importing.
5. If the new file is stereo, check the Stereo Split option if you want to insert the file into two separate tracks.
6. Click Open.

SONAR loads the audio data from the audio file and places it in the selected track at the Now time.

Broadcast Wave Files

Broadcast Wave files are wave files with some additional information stored in them. Broadcast Wave files have the following information:

- Description—A brief description of the contents of the Broadcast wave. Limited to 256 characters.

- Originator—The author of the Broadcast wave. This information is taken from the Author field in the File Info dialog.

- Originator Reference—A unique reference identifier created by SONAR.

- Origination Date—The date the file was created.

- Origination Time—The time the file was created.

- Time Reference—The SMPTE time stamp for the beginning of broadcast wave.

To import a Broadcast Wave file:

1. If you want SONAR to import Broadcast Wave files always at their timestamped location, select **Options-Global**, click the Audio Data tab and check the Always Import Broadcast Waves At Their Timestamp option. Otherwise, set the Now Time and current track to indicate where the audio should be placed.

2. Choose **File-Import-Audio** to display the Open dialog box.

3. Choose the audio file you want to import. SONAR displays information about the file at the bottom of the dialog box.

4. Click Play to listen to the audio file before importing.

5. If the new file is stereo, check the Stereo Split option if you want to insert the file into two separate tracks.

6. Click Open.

If the Always Import Broadcast Waves At Their Timestamp option is selected in the Global Options dialog, the imported Broadcast Wave file appears at its timestamp on the selected track. Otherwise, the file appears at the Now Time on the selected track.

Importing Material from Another SONAR Project

You use the **Edit-Copy** and **Edit-Paste** commands to import material from one project to another using the Windows clipboard. The project that contains the material you want to import is the **source project**. The project into which the material is imported is the **target project**.

Normally, if you copy material from several different tracks to the Windows clipboard, the information will be pasted back into separate tracks. You can choose to paste all the material from the clipboard into a single destination track in the target project.

You can also copy material from one project to another by displaying the Track view for both projects side by side, then using drag-and-drop editing.

To Import Material from Another Project
1. Open the source project, or click in the Track view for that project.
2. In the Track view, select the material you want to import.
3. Choose ***Edit-Copy*** to display the Copy dialog box.
4. Make sure that Events in Tracks is checked. If you don't want to import tempo changes, meter/key changes, or markers, uncheck those options. Click OK.
5. Open the target project, or click in the Track view for that project.
6. Set the Now time and current track to indicate where the material should be placed.
7. Choose ***Edit-Paste*** to display the Paste dialog box.
8. Check Paste to One Track if you want all material imported into the current track (not recommended if you're importing both MIDI and audio data).
9. Click OK.

SONAR imports the material and displays it in the Track view.

Importing MIDI Files

You can create a new SONAR project from a MIDI file simply by opening the file. SONAR takes material from the file and places it into one or more tracks in the Track view.

To Import Data from a MIDI File into a Project
1. Open the MIDI file as a new, separate project.
2. Choose ***Edit-Select-All***.
3. Choose ***Edit-Copy*** to display the Copy dialog box.
4. Make sure that Events in Tracks is checked. If you don't want to import tempo changes, meter/key changes, or markers, uncheck those options. Click OK.
5. Open the target project, or click in the Track view for that project.
6. Set the Now time and current track to indicate where the material should be placed.
7. Choose ***Edit-Paste*** to display the Paste dialog box.
8. Check Paste to One Track if you want all material imported into the current track.
9. Click OK.

SONAR imports the material and displays it in the Track view.

Saving Your Work

Like most Windows programs, SONAR has a ***File-Save*** command and a ***File-Save As*** command to save your work. Normally, you save your projects in the standard project file format, with a file extension of .CWP. This file contains all your MIDI data and all your project settings. Any digital audio that is part of your project is stored in a separate file, as described in "System Configuration" on page 628.

SONAR also lets you save files in several other formats, as described in the table:

File type...	Format...	Explanation...
Standard MIDI	.MID	Used to transfer MIDI-only projects to other software products that support Standard MIDI files.
Bundle	.CWB	A single file that includes all the material in your project: MIDI data, project settings, and audio data. This format is used for projects that contain digital audio, when you want to back up your work or transfer a project to a different computer. See "Backing Up Projects with Digital Audio" on page 624 for more information. **Note: Bundle files do not save video data.**
Template	.CWT	A file that is used as a pattern to create another. Templates make it easy to create and configure new projects. See Chapter 14, *Layouts, Templates and Key Bindings* for more information.

If you have made changes to a project and then attempt to close the project, either by closing the Track view or by choosing ***File-Close***, SONAR asks if you want to save the changes you have made. This prevents you from accidentally losing your work. You can tell whether changes have been made to a project by looking for an asterisk (*) after the project name in the SONAR title bar.

SONAR has an Auto Save feature that periodically saves your work into a special backup file. You can request automatic backups at fixed time intervals or every time a certain number of changes have been made to the file. When the limit is reached, the file is saved automatically. If your original project is called MYPROJECT.CWP, the Auto Save version is called AUTO SAVE VERSION OF MYPROJECT.CWP.

If there is a power failure or if you make a significant mistake, you can recover the last-saved version of your project by opening this file. You should then save your project under a different name by using the ***File-Save As*** command.

To Save a Project
1. Choose ***File-Save As*** to display the Save As dialog box.
2. Choose the type of file you want to save from the Save as Type list.
3. Enter a file name and click Save.

SONAR saves the file.

To Change the Auto Save Settings
1. Choose ***Options-Global*** and click the General tab.
2. To enable Auto Save, set either the number of minutes or the number of changes between saves.
3. To disable Auto Save, set both values to zero.
4. Click OK.

From now on, your projects are saved automatically according to the settings you entered.

Labeling Your Projects

SONAR lets you attach subtitles, composer credits, copyright, and other information to your projects, as shown in the following table:

Title	The title for your project; prints automatically at the top of a Staff view printout.
Subtitle	For a subtitle or dedication; prints directly below the title in a Staff view printout.
Instructions	Use for performance instructions; prints flush left in a Staff view printout.
Author	Put your name here if you are the composer. Prints flush right in a Staff view printout.
Copyright	Copyright information prints flush right, under the author name, in a Staff view printout.
Keywords	Put keywords describing the project here for future reference.
Comments	Free text comments. Type as much as you like. You can enter approximately the same amount of text as you can in Windows *Notepad*.

This information is shown in the File Info dialog box, which is displayed using the ***File-Info*** command. If the File Info window is open when you save a file, then this window is displayed automatically the next time the file is opened. This is useful if you:

- Share files with others and want them to see special instructions when they open the file
- Want your copyright information to be displayed automatically

If the File Info window is closed when you save the file, it will not be automatically displayed the next time the file is opened.

Although you cannot use ***Edit*** menu commands while working in the File Info window, standard Windows hot keys like Ctrl+X, Ctrl+C, and Ctrl+V can be used to cut, copy, and paste text.

To Display and Edit Project Information

1. Choose ***File-Info*** to display the File Info window.
2. Edit the information as desired.

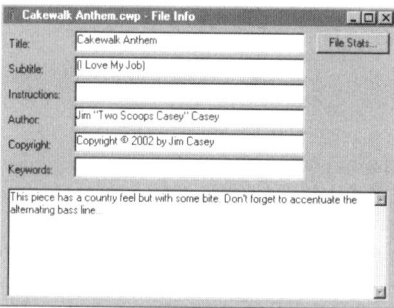

3. If you want the File Info window to display automatically, save the file.
4. Click Stats to see statistics about the contents of the file.
5. Choose ***File-Print Preview*** if you want to print the project information
6. Close the File Info window.

File Statistics

To open the File Statistics dialog, select ***File-Info*** and click the Stats button in the File Info dialog. The File Statistics dialog box displays the following information about the contents of the project file:

Statistic...	What it means...
Created	The date the project was first saved.
Editing time	The total time you've had the project open, from the time it was created to the last time it was saved. This does not include time spent editing the project since you last saved it. If you want to update this value, save the project.
Revision	Each time you save a file that has been changed, this number is incremented. If you open a project, make no changes, then save it, the revision number is not changed.
Events	The total number of events in the project.
Sample rate	The sample rate for digital audio.
Bit depth	The audio driver bit depth of digital audio.
File version	The SONAR version number.

5 Arranging

The Track view makes it easy to arrange and mix your projects from a single view. From one location, you can select, copy, move, mix, and rearrange the parts of your project, using menu commands or drag-and-drop tools. You can add real-time audio and MIDI effects from the Effects bin and buses. Markers provide easy-to-use reference points and labels for the different parts of your project, and the Snap Grid makes it easy to align your clips to the desired time points. Slip Editing allows you to non-destructively change the start and/or end time of a clip, just by dragging its borders. With Slip Editing, you can easily create repetitions of your clips using your mouse. Both the Track view and Console view have a full set of record and playback meters, which you can configure in several ways. SONAR™ also has a variety of tools and commands for changing the tempo of your project. Composite tracks allow you to keep all your takes in one track if you want, and selectively mute and solo the various clips in the track. Track folders let you edit multiple tracks at once and conserve screen space.

In This Chapter

Arranging Tracks 204
Arranging Clips 209
Nudge 218
Working with Partial Clips 220
Markers and the Snap Grid 221
Working with Linked Clips 228
Splitting and Combining Clips 230
Take Management and Comping Takes 232
Clip Muting and Isolating (Clip Soloing) 234
Track Folders 238
Adding Effects in the Track View 240
Changing Tempos 241
Undo, Redo, and the Undo History 249

Arranging Tracks

SONAR provides a variety of commands that let you work with the tracks in your project. Here are some of the things you can do:

You can...	Here's why...
Rearrange the tracks in the Track view so that they appear in a different order	This makes it easier to see and work with a subset of tracks, like the rhythm section, or the vocals and vocal backing tracks, or all muted tracks.
Hide individual tracks	This makes it easier to work in a large project. You can display only the tracks you want to see at a given time.
Move tracks into a track folder	Lets you group tracks by function, edit several tracks at once, hide groups of tracks easily, and mute, solo, archive, arm, or input monitor a group or tracks with one click. See "Track Folders" on page 238 for more information.
Make copies of a track	Copying a track and then adding a time offset or changing the patch is an easy way to double a part. You can also copy and then transpose a track to add harmony.
Erase or delete a track	Tracks and clips that you are no longer using in your project are distracting and take up space in your project file.

All the commands you use to arrange tracks work on selected tracks. The current track (the one with the gold titlebar) is always selected. You can select additional tracks as shown in the table:

To do this...	Do this...
Select a track	Click the track number in the Track view. The track is selected, and all other tracks—except the current track—are deselected.
Select several adjacent tracks	Click the track number for the first track in the group, drag the mouse to the last track in the group, and release the mouse button.
Select/deselect all tracks	Double-click a track number.
Add or remove a single track from the selection	Hold the Shift key and click the track number to add it to the selection; hold the Ctrl key and click the track number to toggle its selection status.

Changing the Order of Tracks

There are several ways you can change the order of tracks in the Track view:

- Drag a track to a new position in the Track view.

- Use the *Track-Sort* command to rearrange the tracks in order based on the track name, status, or other setting.

- Insert new, blank tracks between existing tracks.

To Drag a Track to a New Position
1. Position the mouse just to the right of the track number, over the track icon of the track you want to move.

   The cursor changes to an up/down arrow.

2. Drag the track to its new location, and release the mouse button.

SONAR rearranges and renumbers the tracks.

You can sort the tracks in a project based on several parameters, in either ascending or descending order:

Sort by...	What happens...
Name	Ascending puts track in alphabetic order, descending puts them in reverse order
Size, output, or channel	Ascending puts them in increasing numeric order, descending puts them in decreasing numeric order
Muted, archived, selected	Ascending puts qualifying tracks at the end, descending puts them at the beginning

No matter how you sort, blank tracks always go to the end of the list.

Note that track numbers are used for reference only. When you re-arrange the order of tracks, they are automatically assigned sequential numbers based on the order in which they are displayed in the Track view.

To Sort the Tracks

1. Choose **Track-Sort** to display the Sort Tracks dialog box.

2. Choose the attribute by which to sort from the Sort By list:

Attribute...	How it works...
Name	If you choose this attribute, SONAR puts the tracks into alphabetical order, either ascending or descending, depending on what you choose in the Order list.
Muted	If you choose this attribute, SONAR puts all the muted tracks at either the top or bottom of the Tracks window, depending on whether you choose descending (top) or ascending (bottom) in the Order list.
Archived	If you choose this attribute, SONAR puts all the archived tracks at either the top or bottom of the Tracks window, depending on whether you choose descending (top) or ascending (bottom) in the Order list.
Selected	If you choose this attribute, SONAR puts all the selected tracks at either the top or bottom of the Tracks window, depending on whether you choose descending (top) or ascending (bottom) in the Order list.
Size	If you choose this attribute, SONAR puts the tracks in order by size, either in descending or ascending order.
Output	If you choose this attribute, SONAR sorts the tracks by output number, either in descending or ascending order. SONAR considers non-numbered outputs to have lower numbers than numbered outputs.
Channel	If you choose this attribute, SONAR sorts the tracks by channel number, either in descending or ascending order: • If you choose ascending order, SONAR puts all MIDI tracks at the bottom of the Tracks window, with the lower channel numbers first. • If you choose descending order, SONAR puts all MIDI tracks at the top of the Tracks window, with the higher channel numbers first.

3. Choose the order in which to sort from the Order list.
4. Click OK.

SONAR sorts the tracks according to the settings you chose.

To Insert a Blank Track

1. Right-click in the Track pane at the place where you want to insert a track, and select ***Insert Audio Track*** to add an audio track or ***Insert MIDI Track*** to add a MIDI track.

   OR

1. Press Insert to add a track of the same type (audio or MIDI) as the current track.

SONAR shifts the current track and all tracks below it down by one, and inserts a blank, new track at the location of the highlight.

Configuring the Display of Tracks in the Track View

There are several commands in SONAR that allow you to configure the appearance of your tracks in the track view. You can use these commands to zoom in or out, show or hide any combination of tracks, and revert back to previous display settings. The following table lists each of these commands and provides an explanation of each:

Command...	Description...	Shortcut...
Show and Fit Selection	This command hides all tracks which are not selected. The remaining tracks are adjusted in size vertically and horizontally to fit in the Track view, without scrolling if possible. All track selections are lost after this command is executed.	Shift+S
Fit Tracks to Window	All currently displayed tracks are adjusted in size vertically to fit in the Track view, without scrolling if possible.	F
Fit Project to Window	This command resizes all tracks both vertically and horizontally to fit in the Tracks view.	Shift+F
Show Only Selected Tracks	This command hides all tracks which are not selected. The remaining tracks are adjusted in size vertically.	H
Hide Selected Tracks	Hides all selected tracks.	Shift+H
Show All Tracks	Shows all tracks in your project, including these hidden using the Track Manager.	A
Track Manager	Opens the Track manager dialog. For more information about the Track Manager dialog, see Track Manager dialog.	M
Undo View Change	This command restores the view to its previous state. There are up to 16 levels of undo.	U
Redo View Change	This command restores the view to the state prior to the Undo View Change command.	Shift+U

Copying Tracks

When you copy a track using the *Track-Clone* command, you can choose any of the following options:

- Events
- Properties
- Effects
- Link to Original Clip(s)

By default, SONAR copies the entire track to the next blank track, which is usually below the last track in the Track view. For more information on linked clips, see "Working with Linked Clips" on page 228.

To Copy a Track

1. Select a track. You can only clone one track at a time.
2. Choose *Track-Clone* to display the Clone dialog box.
3. Check the Events, Properties, and/or Effects boxes to indicate which items you want to copy.
4. Click OK.

SONAR copies the entire track to the next blank track, which is usually below the last track in the Track view.

Erasing Tracks

You can easily delete an entire track, including all of the track properties and all of its clips and events. Sometimes, you only want to erase, or **wipe**, the contents of a track, leaving the track properties as they are. If you delete or wipe a track by mistake, you can use *Edit-Undo* to restore the deleted material.

When you delete or wipe a track, the track information is not placed on the SONAR clipboard. To remove material from a track and place it on the clipboard, use the *Edit-Cut* command instead.

To Delete Tracks

1. Select the tracks you want to delete.
2. Choose *Track-Delete*.

SONAR deletes the selected tracks. You can also right-click individual tracks and choose *Delete Track* from the popup menu.

To Wipe Tracks

1. Select the tracks you want to wipe.
2. Choose *Track-Wipe*.

SONAR deletes all clips and events from the selected tracks, but leaves the track properties intact.

Arranging Clips

The Track view provides many ways for you to rearrange, copy, and paste clips to arrange your music the way you want. The easiest is to select the clips or portions of clips you want to arrange and then drag and drop them wherever you want. You can drag and drop clips in the Track view even while playback is in progress. You can also arrange clips via the clipboard using the **Edit-Cut**, **Edit-Copy**, and **Edit-Paste** commands, which work like those in almost all Windows programs.

The **Snap Grid** enables you to move clips to or by an exact amount of time, such as a quarter note or whole measure. See "To Change the Snap Options" on page 223.

Displaying Clips

Clips are displayed as rectangles in the Clips pane. Their position and length show you at a glance their starting times and lengths. You can control four aspects of their appearance:

- Color—By default, each track's clips are drawn in a different color. The clip colors restart at the tenth track. You can customize the default colors of clips in the Colors dialog or change the color of any individual clip in the Clip Properties dialog.

    Note: In audio clips, the waveform changes color, unless no clip contents are displayed. In MIDI clips, the clip background changes color.

- Name—You can also assign each clip a descriptive name, which is displayed in the upper-left corner of the clip.

- Contents—At your option, clips can be displayed with a graphical representation of the events in the clip. The effect is slightly different for MIDI and audio information as shown below:

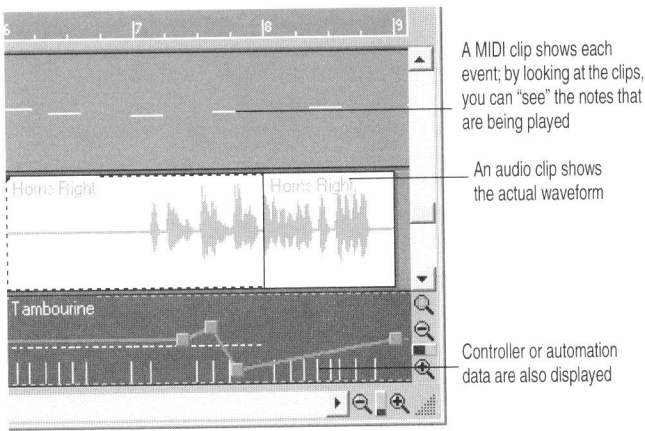

To inspect the clip contents more closely, use the zoom tools to increase the size in which clips are displayed. Note that displaying the contents of each clip makes your computer work a little harder. As a result, if your computer has an older, slower CPU you may want to turn off the display of clip contents.

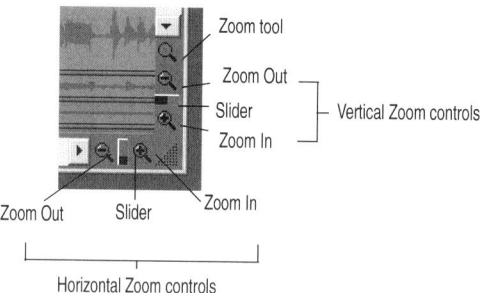

To Zoom Horizontally
- Click the horizontal zoom buttons to zoom in or out by a fixed percentage each time you click.

    Or

- Drag the horizontal zoom slider to zoom in or out by the amount you drag.

    Or

- Hold down the Ctrl key and press the right arrow key (to zoom in) or the left arrow key (to zoom out).

To Zoom Vertically
- Click the vertical zoom buttons to zoom in or out by a fixed percentage each time you click.

    Or

- Drag the vertical zoom slider to zoom in or out by the amount you drag.

    Or

- Hold down the Ctrl key and press the up arrow key (to zoom out) or the down arrow key (to zoom in).

To Zoom into a Selected Area
- Use the Zoom tool to drag-select an area of a clip or clips that you want to zoom to. When you release the mouse, the area you selected expands to fill the Clips pane window.

Zoom command keyboard shortcuts:

To do this...	Use this shortcut...
Zoom in vertically	Ctrl+down arrow
Zoom in horizontally	Ctrl+right arrow
Zoom out vertically	Ctrl+up arrow
Zoom out horizontally	Ctrl+left arrow
Undo Zoom	U
Redo Zoom	Shift+U
Turn On Zoom tool (use the Zoom tool to select the area to zoom to)	Z
Turn Off Zoom tool	Z
Display Now Time in Center of Clips Pane	G

To Display Clip Names and Contents

1. Right-click in the Clips pane, and choose *View Options* from the menu.
2. Check the Display Clip Names option to show clip names, or leave it unchecked to hide them.
3. Check the Display Clip Contents option to show clip contents, or leave it unchecked to hide them.
4. Click OK.

SONAR modifies the clips pane to show the information you want.

To Change Clip Names

1. Select the clips you want to rename.

2. Right-click on one of the selected clips and choose **Clip Properties**. SONAR opens the Clip Properties dialog box.

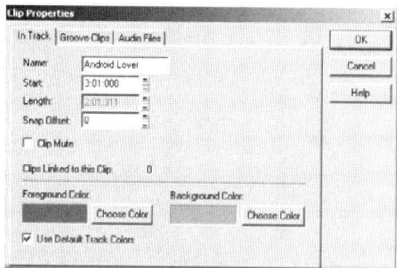

3. Enter a name for the selected clips, and click OK.

SONAR renames the selected clips.

To Change Clip Colors

1. Select the clips whose color you want to change.

2. Right-click on one of the selected clips and choose **Clip Properties**. SONAR opens the Clip Properties dialog box.

3. Choose a color as follows:

To do this...	Do this...
Use the default color	Check the Default Color box
Use a custom color	Click the Choose Color button and pick a color from the Color dialog box

4. Click OK.

SONAR changes the color of the selected clips.

Using the Navigator View

The Navigator view displays a large part of your project so you can see an overview of your song. The Navigator view is a floating version of the Navigator pane found at the top of the Track view.

Track Rectangle

The Track Rectangle appears as a green rectangle within the Navigator view. The Track Rectangle indicates the section of your project which appears in the Clips pane of the Track view. You can move the Track Rectangle or change its size.

To Move the Track Rectangle

1. Position your cursor inside the Track Rectangle until the icon changes to look like this: ⊕.
2. Click and drag the rectangle where you want and release.

To Change the Size of the Track Rectangle

1. Click one of the nodes on the rectangle border.
2. Drag to change the rectangle size.

To Change the Now Time in the Navigator view

1. Hold down the Ctrl key.
2. Click where you want the Now Time to be.

Double-clicking Clips

By default, double-clicking a MIDI clip in the Clips pane opens a Piano Roll view for that track, and double-clicking an Audio clip opens the Loop Construction view for that track. You can set the type of view opened when a clip is double-clicked. For example, you may want to open MIDI tracks in a Staff view rather than in a Piano Roll view.

To Set the View Opened by Double-clicking

1. Right-click in the Clips pane and choose *View Options*.
2. Select the types of view opened by double-clicking MIDI and audio clips.
3. Click OK.

Selecting Clips

Before you move, copy, edit, or delete clips you need to select them. There are several ways to select whole clips, as shown in the table:

To do this...	Do this...
Select a single clip	Click on the clip in the Clips pane.
Select several clips at once	Drag a rectangle around the clips.
Select all the clips in a track	Click on the track number in the Track view.
Select a portion of one or more clips	Press and hold the Alt key and drag across the clips. The Snap to Grid setting determines the size portion you can select.
Add clips to the selection	Hold the Shift key and either click on the clips or drag a rectangle around the clips.
Add or remove clips from the selection	Hold the Ctrl key and either click on the clips or drag a rectangle around the clips.
Add or remove all clips in a track from the selection	Hold the Ctrl key and click on the track number.

Moving and Copying Clips

You can copy or move clips using drag-and-drop editing or the *Cut*, *Copy*, and *Paste* commands. If you copy or move clips into tracks that contain existing material, you need to let SONAR know how to combine the two.

You have these options:

Option...	How it works...
Blend Old and New	Events in the copied or moved clip are placed into a new clip that overlaps with the existing clip. This is the same effect as sound-on-sound recording.
Replace Old with New	Events in the copied or moved clip are placed into a new clip, and any overlapping events in the existing clip are erased. This is the same effect as overwrite recording.
Slide Over to Make Room	The existing clips are shifted in time to make room for the new clips, so they will not overlap. If you check the Align to Measures option, shifted clips are always aligned to measure boundaries; otherwise, the clips are placed end to end.

When you use the **Edit-Paste** command to add information to a track that contains existing material, there is one final option you can choose.

Option...	What it means...
Paste as New Clips	New clips are created containing the events on the clipboard, exactly as described in the preceding table.
Paste into Existing Clips (MIDI clips only)	The events on the clipboard are merged into any existing clips that occupy the same region of time. This means you will never end up with clips that overlap.

Note that if you copy or move clips to new, empty tracks, you don't have to worry about these settings. In this case, the track properties that go with the clips are automatically applied to the new track.

When you use drag-and-drop editing:

- You can set the above options every time you perform an edit, or you can set them once and have the same settings carry over automatically. Check or uncheck the Ask This Every Time box in the Drag and Drop Options dialog to indicate your preference. Open the Drag and Drop Options dialog by right-clicking in the Clips pane and choosing **Drag and Drop Options** from the popup menu.

- If you drag to the edge of the Clips pane, it will scroll automatically in the direction you drag.

- If you change your mind while dragging clips, press the Escape key to cancel the operation.

SONAR also lets you move and copy clips between projects.

To Move Clips Using Drag and Drop

1. Select the clips you want to move.

2. If you want to move the clips by an exact amount of time, enable the Snap Grid (see "To Change the Snap Options" on page 223).

3. Position the mouse over one of the selected clips.

4. Press and hold down the left mouse button. A rectangle is displayed around the selected clips.

5. Drag the clips to their new location, and release the mouse button.

6. If necessary, choose the options you want from the Drag and Drop Options dialog box (use **Options-Global** and open the Editing tab, or right-click in the

Clips Pane and select **Drag & Drop Options** from the menu that appears), and click OK.

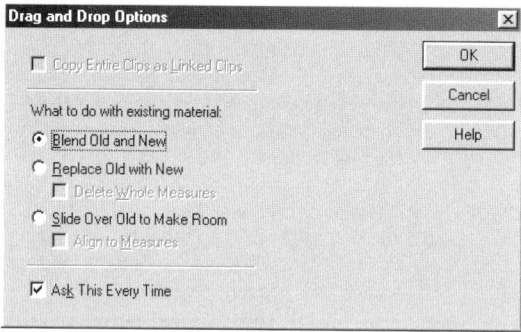

SONAR moves the clips to their new location.

Note:

Moving an audio clip (other than a Groove clip) to a part of your project that has a different tempo changes the size of the clip.

To Move Clips Using Cut and Paste

1. Select the clips you want to move.

2. Choose **Edit-Cut** to display the Cut dialog box.

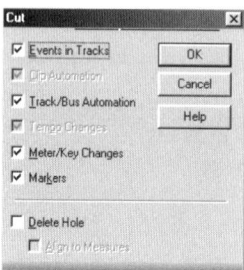

3. Choose the options you want and click OK. SONAR cuts the clips from the project and places them on the Windows clipboard.

4. Click in the Track pane to set the current track to be the one where clips should be pasted.

5. Set the Now time to be the time at which the clips should be pasted.

6. Choose *Edit-Paste* to display the Paste dialog box.

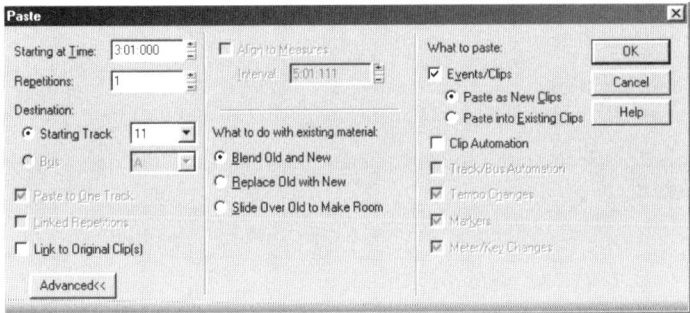

7. Choose the options you want and click OK.

SONAR places the clips in their new location.

To Move a Clip to a Specific Start Time

1. Select the clip you want to move.

2. Right-click on the selected clip and choose *Clip Properties*. SONAR opens the Clip Properties dialog box.

3. Enter a new start time, or use the spinners or keyboard to change the start time.

4. Click OK when you are done.

SONAR moves the clip to the start time you chose.

To Copy Clips Using Drag and Drop

1. Select the clips you want to copy.

2. Enable the Snap Grid, if desired.

3. Position the mouse over one of the selected clips.

4. Press and hold down the left mouse button. A rectangle is displayed around the selected clips.

5. Drag the clips to the new location, and release the mouse button.

6. If necessary, choose the options you want from the Drag and Drop Options dialog box, and click OK.

SONAR copies the clips to their new location.

To Copy Clips Using Copy and Paste

1. Select the clips you want to copy.
2. Choose **Edit-Copy** to display the Copy dialog box.
3. Choose the options you want and click OK. SONAR copies the clips to the Windows clipboard.
4. Click in the Track pane to set the current track to be the one where clips should be pasted.
5. Set the Now time to be the time the clips should be pasted.
6. Choose **Edit-Paste** to display the Paste dialog box.
7. Choose the options you want and click OK.

SONAR copies the clips to their new location.

To Delete Clips

1. Select the clips you want to delete.
2. Do one of the following:
   - Choose **Edit-Delete**, which brings up a dialog box—choose options and click OK.
   - Press the Delete key.

SONAR deletes the selected clips.

Nudge

Nudging is moving a clip or a MIDI note by a small amount to the left or right or up and down. There are three customizable settings for the Nudge feature. You can also nudge clips (in the Track view) or notes (in the Piano Roll view) up or down, and you can use keyboard shortcuts (see "To Nudge a Clip Using Keyboard Shortcuts" on page 220).

Nudge Settings

The Nudge tab in the Global Options dialog allows you to set the three Nudge settings.

To Nudge a Clip Left or Right

Use the following procedure to nudge a clip.

1. Select the clip you want to nudge.
2. Select **Process-Nudge Left(1-3)** from the menu to move the clip left or **Process-Nudge Right(1-3)** to move the clip right.

The amount the clip or note moves is determined by the settings in the Nudge tab of the Global Options dialog.

To Nudge a Clip Up and Down

Use the following procedure to nudge a clip (in the Track view) or MIDI note (in the Piano Roll view) up or down.

1. Select the clip or note you want to nudge.

2. Select **Process-Nudge-Up** to move the clip or note up or **Process-Nudge-Down** to move a clip or note down.

Clips move up or down one track at a time. Notes move up or down one pitch at a time.

To Change Nudge Settings

1. Select **Process-Nudge-Settings** to open the Nudge tab in the Global Options dialog box.

2. In one of the three Nudge groups, select one of the following:

   - Musical Time—Select a note length setting.

   - Absolute Time—Select one of the following absolute time options and a number in the first field

Absolute time setting...	Description...
Seconds	Whole seconds.
Milliseconds	Thousands of a second.
Frames	Number of frames. The default frame count is 30 frames per second. The number of frames varies depending on the setting in the Project Options dialog's clock tab.
Samples	A very small amount of time. For CD-quality audio there are 44,100 samples per second, so a value of 1 here would not move a clip by a perceptible amount.
Ticks	The number of ticks per quarter note varies depending on the setting in the Project Options dialog's clock tab. The default setting is 960.

   - Follow Snap Settings—Moves the clip or note by the current snap setting.

To Nudge a Clip Using Keyboard Shortcuts
1. Select the clip you want to nudge.
2. If necessary, turn on Num Lock (press the Num Lock key on your keyboard).
3. Press the appropriate Num Key.
    - Left 1—NumPad 1
    - Right 1—NumPad 3
    - Left 2—NumPad 4
    - Right 2—NumPad 6
    - Left 3—NumPad 7
    - Right 3—NumPad 9
    - Up—NumPad 8
    - Down—NumPad 2

Working with Partial Clips

SONAR lets you select, copy, move, and delete portions of a project even if they do not match clip boundaries. There are two ways to do this:

- Directly select portions of one or more clips.
- Select a range of times and one or more tracks. SONAR automatically selects the portions of clips that are in both the selected time range and the selected tracks.

You can then copy, move, or delete the material the same way you do with whole clips.

When you select portions of a clip, SONAR may round off the start and end times of your selection based on the Snap Grid. For more information, see "Defining and Using the Snap Grid" on page 222.

To Select a Portion of a Clip
1. Press and hold the Alt key.
2. Drag the mouse across part of a clip.

SONAR highlights the selected portion of the clip. You can edit this portion of the clip using all the normal editing commands.

To Select a Portion of Several Clips
1. Press and hold the Alt key.
2. Drag the mouse across part of several clips in adjacent tracks.

SONAR highlights the selected portions of all the clips. You can edit these portions of clips using all the normal editing commands.

To Select Partial Clips Using Time Ranges and Tracks
1. Select a range of time in one of the following ways:
   - Drag the mouse in the Time Ruler.
   - Click between two markers to select the time between the markers.
   - Use the F9 and F10 keys to set the beginning and end selection times.
   - Select a clip (SONAR selects the range of time covered by the clip).
   - Choose ***Edit-Select-By Time***, enter the start and end time, and click OK.
2. Select one or more tracks by clicking, Shift-clicking, or Ctrl-clicking on the track numbers in the Track view.
3. To adjust the start and end time of the selection, hold the Shift key while clicking on the Time Ruler.

The relevant portions of clips in the selected tracks are highlighted. You can edit these portions of clips using all the normal editing commands.

To Clear the Partial Clip Selection
You can clear the time-restricted selection in any of the following ways:

- Click in an empty area of the Clips pane to completely clear the selection.
- Choose ***Edit-Select-None*** or press Ctrl+Shift+A to completely clear the selection.
- Click on a single clip in the Clips pane to clear the time selection and select the clip.

Markers and the Snap Grid

SONAR has a collection of features you can use to simplify and speed the work you do arranging your projects. Here are a few of the most important things you can do:

- Show gridlines on measure boundaries in the Track view.
- Define and use the Snap Grid to make drag-and-drop editing more accurate.
- Create markers to identify and work with key time points in your project.

Showing Gridlines

Displaying gridlines, or vertical rules, in the Clips pane of the Track view makes it easy to see at a glance how clips align with each other, how they align with measure boundaries, and when they start and end.

To Show or Hide Gridlines

1. Right-click in the Clips pane and choose *View-Options* from the popup menu.

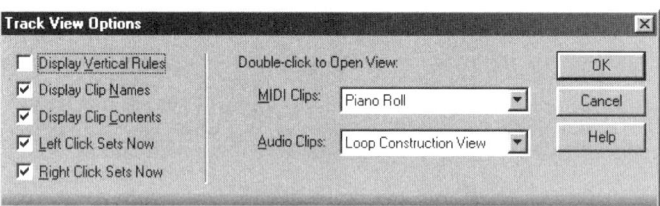

2. To show gridlines, check the Display Vertical Rules box. To hide gridlines, make sure the Display Vertical Rules box is not checked.
3. Click OK.

SONAR displays the Track view as you requested.

Defining and Using the Snap Grid

SONAR lets you define a snap grid that makes it easier to arrange clips and select time ranges. To use the Snap Grid, enable the snap feature and set an interval, such as a whole note, half note, or quarter note; a marker; an event; the start or end of a clip; or a user-defined number of frames, seconds or samples. From then on, when you move or copy clips or markers, items will be snapped to the nearest point on the Snap Grid. The Musical Time and Absolute Time options also apply when you perform a selection using the Time Ruler,

You can also use the Snap Grid to move clips **by** a certain interval, rather than snap them **to** the interval. Moving **by** an interval can be useful during drag-and-drop operations, if your events are not exactly aligned with measure or note boundaries.

The Snap Grid in each view is independent. For example, you can enable the Snap Grid in the Track view without enabling it in the Piano Roll or Staff views. You can also enable the Snap Grid in several different views, with different grid intervals in each one.

To Enable or Disable the Snap Grid

1. Press N to toggle the Snap to Grid button on or off.

    OR

1. To enable the Snap to Grid, click the Snap to Grid combo button in the Track view toolbar.

2. To disable the Snap to Grid, click the Snap to Grid combo button once again.

To Change the Snap Options

1. Click the down arrow in the Snap to Grid combo button or right-click on the Time Ruler and select *Snap Properties* from the popup menu to display the Snap to Grid dialog box.

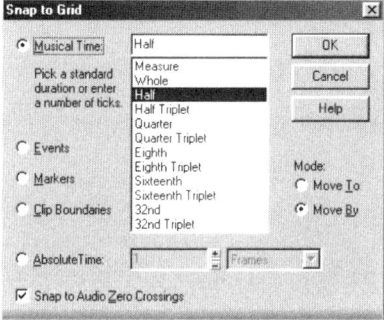

2. Select one of the following options:

    - Musical Time—note intervals (whole, half, etc.)
    - Events—any data in a clip
    - Markers—any marker in a project
    - Clip Boundaries—the start or end of any clip
    - Absolute Time—a number of samples, frames, or seconds set by you

3. If you selected Musical Time or Absolute Time, select Move To to align selections and clips to the grid, or Move By to move clips by the grid interval.

4. Click OK.

All time selections and drag-and-drop editing operations use the new Snap Grid interval.

Snap Offsets

Snap offsets allow you to set a point other than the beginning of a clip as the "snap" point used by the Snap to Grid. A snap offset is the number of samples from the beginning of the clip. Snap offsets affect all edits that obey the Snap to Grid setting. Once the snap offset is added, you can set the Timer Ruler to SMPTE or MBT time.

Note: You cannot set a snap offset for a Groove clip.

Creating a Snap Offset
Use the following to add a snap offset to a clip:

1. Locate the place in the clip where you want to put the snap offset, and set the Now Time to that location. Use the Scrub tool if necessary.

2. Right-click on the clip and select ***Set Snap Offset to Now Time*** from the menu that appears.

Edits to that clip, when the Snap to Grid button is depressed, now snap to the snap offset rather than the beginning of the clip.

Deleting a Snap Offset
1. Right-click on the clip and select Clip Properties from the menu that appears.

2. In the Snap Offset field enter 0 (zero) and click OK.

Creating and Using Markers

Markers are a way of associating a name with a time point in your project. You use markers to name sections of a project, to mark hit points in a film score, or simply to provide a shortcut for working with any time point in a project. Markers make it easy to:

- Jump to a specific time point in a project

- Select a portion of a project

- Enter a time in any dialog box, by pressing F5 and choosing the marker you want

You can see and work with markers in four ways:

- They are displayed in the Time Ruler at the top of the Track, Staff, and Piano Roll view.

- The Markers toolbar lets you add markers and jump to specific marker locations.

- The Markers view displays all markers and lets you add, edit, and delete markers.

- You can press F11 while playback is in progress to add a marker on the fly.

The time associated with a marker can be expressed in musical time or as a locked SMPTE time. If a marker has a musical time (measures, beats, and ticks), the marker stays at that musical time regardless of changes in tempo. If a marker has a locked SMPTE time (hours, minutes, seconds, and frames), the marker stays at the same time even when the tempo is changed. Locked markers are useful for projects that require you to sync the music or sound with film scores or multimedia presentations. See "To Add a Marker" on page 225.

SONAR takes the current Snap Grid settings into account when you move or copy markers. For example, if the Snap Grid is set to even measure boundaries, any time you move or copy a marker, the marker will be snapped to the beginning of the nearest measure. You are allowed to have any number of markers at a single time point.

To display the Markers view, choose **View-Markers** or click [icon] on the Views toolbar. From the Markers view, you can use the **File-Print** and **File-Print Preview** commands to print a listing of markers.

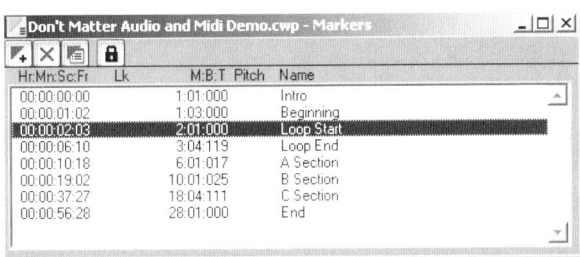

You can add markers while playback is stopped or while playback is in progress (on the fly). When you add a marker while playback is stopped, you can enter a name for the marker and either use the Now time or enter a different time. When you add a marker on the fly, the marker is named automatically and assigned the Now time. Using the Markers view, you can edit the names and times whenever you want.

To Add a Marker

1. Open the Markers dialog in one of the following ways:

    - Click [icon] in the Markers toolbar.

    - Press F11.

    - Choose **Insert-Marker**.

    - Click [icon] in the Markers view.

    - Ctrl-click in the marker section of the Time Ruler.

    - Right-click in the Time Ruler and select **Insert Marker**.

SONAR displays the Marker dialog box.

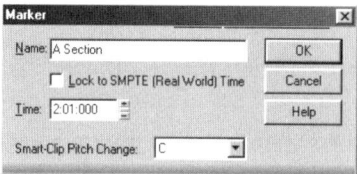

2. Enter a name for the marker in the Name box.
3. The time is set to the Now time. If you want, use the spinners to change the time or type in a new marker time.
4. Check the Locked to SMPTE box if you want to lock the marker to the SMPTE time.
5. Click OK.

SONAR adds the marker and displays it in the Time Ruler, the Markers view, and the Markers toolbar.

To Add a Marker on the Fly
- Click [icon] in the Markers toolbar, or Press F11.

SONAR adds a marker at the Now time and displays it in the Time Ruler, the Markers view, and the Markers toolbar.

To Edit a Marker
1. Either right-click on the marker in the Time Ruler, or choose a marker in the Markers view and click [icon]. SONAR displays the Marker dialog box.
2. Change the marker name, time, or other settings as desired.
3. Click OK.

SONAR updates the marker in the Time Ruler and the Markers view.

To Copy a Marker
1. Press and hold the Ctrl key.
2. Drag a marker in the Time Ruler of the Track view, Staff view, Tempo view, or Piano Roll view. SONAR displays the Marker dialog box.
3. Enter the desired marker settings and click OK.

SONAR copies the marker and displays it in the Time Ruler and the Markers view. You can also cut and paste markers directly from the Markers view.

To Lock or Unlock Several Markers

1. In the Markers view, select one or more markers. Use the Ctrl and Shift keys if necessary to modify the selection.

2. Select or deselect 🔒.

SONAR updates the markers.

To Move a Marker

- Drag the marker in the Time Ruler.

SONAR updates the marker time and shows it at the new location.

To Delete a Marker

1. Press and hold the left mouse button while pointing to a marker in the Time Ruler.

2. Press Delete, and release the mouse button.

SONAR deletes the marker. You can use ***Edit-Undo*** if you make a mistake.

To Delete Markers from the Markers View

1. In the Markers view, select one or more markers. Use the Ctrl and Shift keys if necessary to modify the selection.

2. Click ✕ or press Delete.

SONAR deletes the selected markers. You can use ***Undo*** if you make a mistake.

To Jump to a Marker

There are many different ways to jump to a specific marker:

- Choose a marker from the dropdown list in the Markers toolbar to jump to that marker.

- Click the Now time in the Position toolbar, press F5 to display a list of markers, choose the marker you want, and click OK.

- Press F5 twice to display a list of markers, choose the marker you want, and click OK.

- Click on a marker in the Markers view to set the Now time to that marker.

- Click ▶ or ◀ in the Markers toolbar to jump to the next or previous marker.

- Choose ***Go-Next Marker*** or ***Go-Previous Marker*** to jump to the next or previous marker.

To Select a Time Range Using Markers

You can select a range of times by clicking in the marker section of the Time Ruler:

- Click to the left of the first marker to select the time between the start of the project and the first marker.

- Click to the right of the last marker to select the time between the marker and the end of the project.

- Click between two markers to select the time between the markers.

- If looping is enabled, click to the right of the Loop Start marker to select the loop region

- If punch recording is enabled, click to the right of the Punch In marker to select the punch region

Working with Linked Clips

SONAR makes it easy to repeat a pattern over and over using a feature called **linked clips**. Linked clips always have the same contents, name, and display color. Any change you make to the internal contents of one of the clips, such as adding or editing notes or effects, automatically applies to all of them. Any number of clips may be linked with each other.

To create linked clips, copy the clips and when pasting, check the linked clips option in the Paste dialog box or the Drag and Drop Options dialog box. Linked clips are displayed with a dotted border, so they are easy to spot. You can also identify linked clips using the Clip Properties dialog box or the ***Select All Siblings*** (available in the Clips pane popup menu) command. You can easily unlink linked clips, and then edit them individually. You have two options when unlinking linked clips:

Option...	How it works...
New linked group	The clips you selected will still be linked to each other, but won't be linked to any clips that are not selected
Independent	Every selected clip will be completely independent

Once you have unlinked linked clips, you cannot re-link them except by using ***Edit-Undo***.

If you attempt to copy only a portion of a linked clip, the copy will not be linked to the original. Copies of a clip can be linked to the original only when you select and copy the entire clip.

To Make Linked Copies of a Clip Using Drag and Drop

1. Right-click in the Clips pane and choose **Drag & Drop Options** to display the Drag and Drop Options dialog box.

2. Check the option labeled Copy Entire Clips as Linked Clips.

3. Click OK.

4. Select the clips you want to copy.

5. Position the mouse over one of the selected clips.

6. Press and hold down the Ctrl key.

7. Press and hold down the left mouse button. A rectangle is displayed around the selected clips.

8. Drag the clips to their new location, and release the mouse button.

9. If necessary, confirm the options in the Drag and Drop Options dialog box, and click OK.

SONAR creates copies of the selected clips that are linked to the originals. Any change you make to one of the clips is applied to all linked clips, including the original clip.

To Make Linked Copies of a Clip Using Copy and Paste

1. Select the clips you want to copy.

2. Choose **Edit-Copy** to display the Copy dialog box.

3. Choose options as desired and click OK. SONAR copies the clips to the Windows clipboard.

4. Click in the Track pane to set the current track to be the one where clips should be pasted.

5. Set the Now time to be the time at which the clips should be pasted.

6. Choose **Edit-Paste** to display the Paste dialog box.

7. In the Paste dialog, choose one of two options:

    - Linked Repetitions—If you choose this option, only the new copies of the original clip are linked together. Edits you make to the new copies do not affect the original, and vice versa.

    - Link to Original Clip(s)—If you choose this option, the new copies and the original clip are linked together. Edits you make to any of the linked clips, including the original, affect all other linked clips in the group.

8. Choose the other options you want and click OK.

SONAR creates copies of the selected clips that are linked in the way you chose.

To Unlink Linked Clips
1. In the Clips pane, select the clips you want to unlink.
2. Right-click on any selected clip and choose **Unlink** from the popup menu. SONAR displays the Unlink Clips dialog box.
3. Choose the unlink option you want, and click OK.

SONAR unlinks the clips and updates the Clips pane accordingly. From now on, any changes you make to one of the clips are applied only to remaining linked clips, if any.

To Select the Clips That Are Linked to Another Clip
1. Select one or more clips in the Track view.
2. Right-click on any selected clip and choose **Select All Siblings** from the popup menu.

SONAR selects any clip that is linked to one of the currently selected clips.

Splitting and Combining Clips

SONAR provides several commands that are used to split and combine clips. Specifically, you can:

- Split a clip into several smaller clips
- Create a new clip from a selected portion of an existing clip
- Combine adjacent or overlapping clips into a single, longer clip

The following table summarizes the commands you can use:

To do this...	Use this command...	Notes...
Split clips into parts	*Edit-Split*	Works on all selected clips. You can also press the **s** key to split all selected clips at the Now Time.
Combine several clips into one	*Edit-Bounce to Clip(s)*	If the selected clips are in separate tracks, one clip is created for each track. All clip automation is applied destructively to the new clip.

Note:
Combining a stereo and mono clip always produces a stereo clip.

The **Split** command lets you split clips four different ways:

Option...	How it works...
Split at Time	Splits selected clips at a specific point in time. By default, the split occurs at the Now time, but you can choose any time you want.
Split Repeatedly	Splits selected clips at regular intervals, beginning at a specified time, with a specified duration. For example, you could split a long clip into 4-bar clips starting at measure 5.
Split at Markers	Splits selected clips at any marker location. This option is available only if your project has markers.
Split when Silent	Removes "silent" stretches of one measure or more from selected clips. The presence in a measure of any event—including those that make no sound, such as a patch change or lyric event—will cause that measure to be retained.

While the **Split** command works for both MIDI and audio clips, for audio clips, the **Split** command provides sample accurate editing and snap-to-zero capability.

Note that the **Edit-Undo** and **Edit-Redo** commands work with all three of these editing commands.

231

To Split Clips into Smaller Clips
1. Select the clips you want to split.
2. Right-click on any selected clip, and choose **Split** from the popup menu. SONAR shows the Split dialog box or press the S key to split the clip(s) at the Now Time.
3. Choose the Split option you want to use, and enter the settings you want to use.
4. Click OK.

Or

1. Select the clips you want to split.
2. Set the Now Time to the time you want to split the clips.
3. Press the *s* key.

SONAR splits the selected clips according to your instructions.

To Combine Clips
1. Select the clips you want to combine (the clips must be on the same track).
2. Right-click on of the clips and select **Bounce to Clip(s)** from the popup menu.

SONAR combines the selected clips into a single, new clip.

Take Management and Comping Takes

By default, SONAR stacks any overlapping clips on top of each other, but you can choose to display them in separate lanes in the same track. When you store clips in separate lanes, it's easy to mute and solo them individually and eventually come up with a composite take, with only the best clips playing back.

When you use loop recording, you can store all your takes in the same track, and then use the Mute tool or Audition (Selection Playback) to hear only the ones you want.

If you enable a track's **Track-Show Layers** menu option, SONAR stores the track's clips in separate lanes whenever any of the following happens:

- You use loop recording in Sound on Sound mode, and choose to store takes in a single track.
- You drag a clip onto another clip while the Blend Old and New option in the Drag and Drop Options dialog is enabled.
- You record over some pre-existing data while in Sound on Sound mode.
- You enable the **Track-Show Layers** menu option for a track that contains at least one overlapping clip.

Note 1: you can create as many lanes as you want.

Note 2: a multi-lane track has only one set of automation envelopes.

To enhance multi-lane editing, SONAR has a cropping tool (see procedure below), which automatically crops two overlapping clips that are in adjacent lanes so that they don't overlap.

For step-by-step instructions, see the following procedures:

To Enable or Disable the Multi-lane Option
1. Select the track or tracks you want to configure by Ctrl-clicking the track number of each track you want to configure.
2. Click the *Track-Show Layers* menu option. When the option is enabled, SONAR displays a checkmark next to the menu command.

When the option is enabled, SONAR displays overlapping clips in separate lanes in a track.

To Loop Record Multiple Takes into Separate Track Lanes
1. Use the *Transport-Record Options* command to open the Record Options dialog.
2. Under the Recording Mode options, choose Sound on Sound (Blend).
3. Under Loop Recording, choose Store Takes in a Single Track, and click OK.
4. Set your loop boundaries and start recording multiple passes through the looped area.
5. Stop recording.

When you finish recording, SONAR displays all your takes in separate lanes in the recording track.

To Move Clips to Different Lanes
- Set the Snap to Grid menu to the desired setting, and drag one or more clips to different lanes. If you drag a clip onto another clip, and you have Blend Old and New enabled in the Drag and Drop Options dialog (*Options-Global* command), SONAR displays the two clips in separate lanes.

Note 1: if you want to move a clip to the exact same time placement in an adjacent lane, hold the Shift key down while you drag.

Note 2: if the Automatic Crossfades button is enabled, SONAR adds a crossfade between any newly overlapped clips.

To Crop Overlapping Clips to Eliminate Overlap

1. In a multi-lane track, move either the Select tool or the Mute tool between two overlapping clips until the cursor turns into the overlap cropping tool.

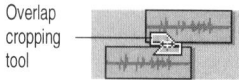
Overlap cropping tool

2. In the space between the clips, hold down the left mouse button and drag to the spot where you want the first clip to end and the second one to begin, and release the mouse. SONAR crops both clips so that they no longer overlap.

Clip Muting and Isolating (Clip Soloing)

Together with multi-lane tracks, clip muting and isolating (clip soloing) make it easy to build a composite take from multiple takes.

With the new Mute tool , that's in the Track view toolbar, SONAR offers two styles of clip muting:

- Default style—after you activate the Mute tool, you can drag through time ranges to mute all or part of a clip: dragging through the bottom half of a clip mutes the time range you drag through; dragging through the top half of a clip unmutes the range you drag through. The default setting in the Mute tool dropdown menu produces this behavior (you'll see a checkmark next to *Mute Time Ranges* under *Click+Drag Behavior*). If you want to temporarily switch to the Alternate style (see below), hold down the Alt key while you click.

- Alternate style—use the Mute tool to mute or unmute entire clips by clicking clips instead of dragging through time regions. A clip that is completely muted displays the Mute icon in its upper left corner. You can choose this behavior by choosing *Mute Entire Clips* under *Click+Drag Behavior* in the Mute tool dropdown menu. If you decide you want to temporarily switch to the Default style, hold down the Alt key while you drag.

In addition, you can also play back only selected data if you want by pressing the Shift key and the Spacebar at the same time.

Clip Muting with the Default Style

When you choose *Mute Time Ranges* under *Click+Drag Behavior* in the Mute tool dropdown menu, you can use the following procedures to mute all or parts of clips. This is the default behavior.

To Enable or Disable the Mute Tool
- Click the tool or press K on your keyboard. The Mute tool turns blue when it is enabled.

To Mute a Time Range Using Default Style
1. Make sure that *Mute Time Ranges* under *Click+Drag Behavior* in the Mute tool dropdown menu has a check mark.
2. If you want to mute a precise amount of time, enable the Snap to Grid button and set its menu to an appropriate value.
3. Using the Mute tool, drag inside the lower half of a clip.

SONAR mutes the area you dragged through and displays the muted waveform or MIDI data as a dotted line.

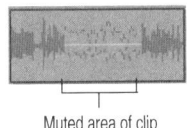

Muted area of clip

To Unmute a Time Range Using Default Style
1. Make sure that *Mute Time Ranges* under *Click+Drag Behavior* in the Mute tool dropdown menu has a check mark.
2. Using the Mute tool, click inside the upper half of a clip in the muted area.

To Mute or Unumute an Entire Clip Using Default Style
1. Make sure that *Mute Time Ranges* under *Click+Drag Behavior* in the Mute tool dropdown menu has a check mark.
2. Using the Mute tool, Alt-click anywhere in the clip (hold down the Alt key while you click).

When a clip is currently muted, SONAR displays the Mute icon in the upper left corner of the clip.

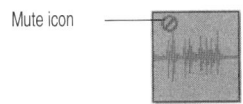

Mute icon

Note: if the clip you're muting or unmuting with this method already has one or more muted time ranges, these time ranges remain muted while you Alt-click the clip, so you don't lose any precise mute edits you've performed. To **completely** unmute the clip in the picture below, first Alt-click the clip to remove the Mute icon, and then drag through the upper half of the clip in the muted area(s).

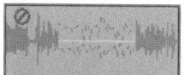

Clip Muting with the Alternate Style

When you choose *Mute Entire Clips* under *Click+Drag Behavior* in the Mute tool dropdown menu, you can use the following procedures to mute all or parts of clips. This is the alternate style.

To Enable or Disable the Mute Tool
- Click the Mute tool or press K on your keyboard. The Mute tool turns blue when it is enabled.

To Mute or Unumute an Entire Clip Using Alternate Style
1. Make sure that *Mute Entire Clips* under *Click+Drag Behavior* in the Mute tool dropdown menu has a check mark.
2. Using the Mute tool, click anywhere in the clip.

SONAR displays the Mute icon in the upper left corner of a muted clip.

Note: if the clip you're muting or unmuting with this method already has one or more muted time ranges, these time ranges remain muted while you Alt-click the clip, so you don't lose any precise mute edits you've performed.

To Mute a Time Range Using Alternate Style
1. Make sure that *Mute Entire Clips* under *Click+Drag Behavior* in the Mute tool dropdown menu has a check mark.
2. If you want to mute a precise amount of time, enable the Snap to Grid button and set its menu to an appropriate value.
3. Using the Mute tool, Alt-drag inside the lower half of a clip.

SONAR mutes the area you dragged through and displays the muted waveform or MIDI data as a dotted line.

To Unmute a Time Range Using Alternate Style
1. Make sure that **Mute Entire Clips** under **Click+Drag Behavior** in the Mute tool dropdown menu has a check mark.
2. Using the Mute tool, Alt-click inside the upper half of a clip in the muted area.

You can mute or unmute a clip without using the Mute tool if you want. Pressing Q on your keyboard toggles the mute status of all selected clips. Any muted time ranges remain muted.

Audition (Selection Playback)

The **Transport-Audition** command plays back only selected clips and/or time ranges.

To use the command, hold down the Shift key and then press the Spacebar. Only the selected data plays back.

Isolating (Clip Soloing)

Isolating clips mutes all the overlapping areas in a track except for the areas that you Ctrl-drag the Mute tool through (this is the Default style of isolating). With the Alternate style of isolating, you can Ctrl-click with the Mute tool to solo whole clips instead of regions. If you have a lot of clips to work with, you might find it quicker to isolate a few clips or regions rather than mute large numbers of clips or regions.

To Isolate a Region with the Default Style
1. Make sure that **Mute Time Ranges** under **Click+Drag Behavior** in the Mute tool dropdown menu has a check mark.
2. Using the Mute tool, hold down the Ctrl key and drag through the region of a clip or clips that you want isolated (soloed).

Any overlapping regions become muted. To de-isolate the isolated region, release the Ctrl key, and drag through the upper half of any muted regions.

If you want to temporarily switch to the Alternate style of isolating (see procedure below), hold down the Alt key along with the Ctrl key, and click whole clips instead of dragging through regions.

To Isolate Clips with the Alternate Style
1. Choose **Mute Entire Clips** under **Click+Drag Behavior** in the Mute tool dropdown menu.
2. Using the Mute tool, hold down the Ctrl key and click the clips that you want isolated.

Any overlapping clips become muted. To de-isolate the isolated clips, release the Ctrl key, and click any muted clips.

If you want to temporarily switch to the Default style of isolating, hold down the Alt key along with the Ctrl key, and drag through the regions you want isolated.

Track Folders

A track folder contains tracks in the Track pane of the Track view. The main characteristics of a track folder are:

- You can edit all the tracks in the folder as if you were editing a single track—the track folder displays a composite clip in the Clips pane. Selecting a time range in the composite clip selects data in all the enclosed tracks in the same time range; now you can edit the selected area of the composite clip.

- You can hide tracks in a folder, freeing up space on your screen.

- A folder can contain any type of track—you can put MIDI, audio, and synth tracks in the same folder.

- You can archive, mute, solo, arm, or input monitor all the tracks in a folder with one click—just click the A, M, S, R, or Input Echo button on the track folder.

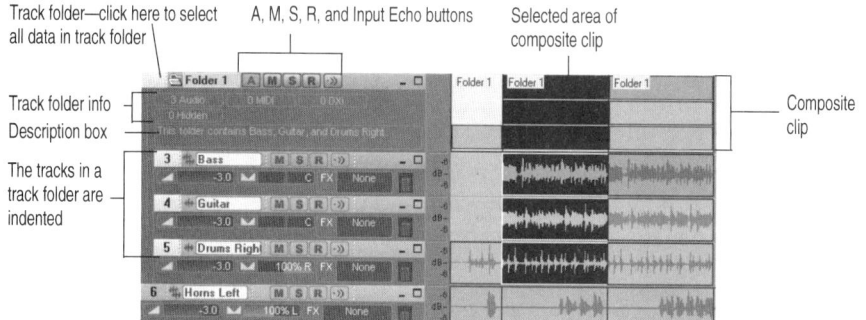

To Create a Track Folder

- Right-click in the Track pane of the Track view, and choose *Insert Track Folder* from the popup menu.

    Or

- Use the *Insert-Track Folder* menu command.

    Or

- Right-click a track that's not in a track folder and select *Move to Folder-New Track Folder* from the popup menu.

A new track folder appears in the Track pane.

To Add a Track to a Track Folder
- In the Track view, move the mouse cursor just to the right of the track number of a pre-existing track until the cursor turns into a black, double-ended arrow, and then click and drag the track's titlebar onto the track folder. Release the mouse.

Or

- Insert a track when a track within a track folder has focus.

Or

- Right-click a track that's not in a track folder and select **Move to Folder-Track Folder "n"** from the popup menu.

Or

- Select the tracks you want to add to the folder, right-click on the folder and select **Add Track(s) to Folder** from the menu that appears.

The added track appears in the track folder, and is indented a little to show that it's inside the track folder.

To Remove a Track from a Track Folder
- In the Track view, move the cursor just to the right of the track number of a track until the cursor turns into a black, double-ended arrow, and then click and drag the track's titlebar out of the Track Folder. Release the mouse.

Or

- Right-click the track and select **Remove From Folder** from the popup menu.

To Add Multiple Tracks to a Track Folder
1. Select the tracks you want to add.
2. Right-click a selected track and choose **Move to Folder-Track Folder "n"** from the popup menu.

To Remove Multiple Tracks from a Track Folder
1. Select the tracks you want to remove.
2. Right-click a selected track and choose **Remove From Folder** from the popup menu.

To Delete a Track Folder
1. In the Track view, right-click and select **Delete Track Folder** from the menu that appears.
2. SONAR asks you if you want to delete all the tracks in the folder along with the track folder—click **Yes** or **No**.

SONAR deletes the track folder. If you didn't choose to delete the tracks in the track folders, SONAR moves these tracks to the top level.

To Hide or Show the Tracks in a Track Folder
- Click the folder icon that's just left of the track folder's name.

To Select or Deselect all the Tracks in a Track Folder
- Click just to the left of the folder icon.

To Rename a Track Folder
- Double-click the track folder's name, type a new name, and press Enter.

    Or

- Right-click the track folder, choose **Folder Properties** from the popup menu, type a name in the Name field of the Folder Properties dialog, and click OK.

To Add a Description to a Track Folder
- Double-click the Description box, type a description, and press Enter.

    Or

- Right-click the track folder, choose **Folder Properties** from the popup menu, type a description in the Description field of the Folder Properties dialog, and click OK.

To Select all Clips in a Time Range
- Hold down the Alt key while dragging a selection on the composite clip.

Now you can edit, move, cut and paste all the selected clips by editing the selected part of the composite clip.

Adding Effects in the Track View

You can add both MIDI and audio effects directly from the Track view. SONAR adds these effects in real-time, preserving your track's original data.

To Add Effects in the Track View
1. Right-click in the FX bin of the track you want to add effects to. You may have to click the FX tab or the All tab that's at the bottom of the Track pane to display the FX bin, and also expand the track pane a little.

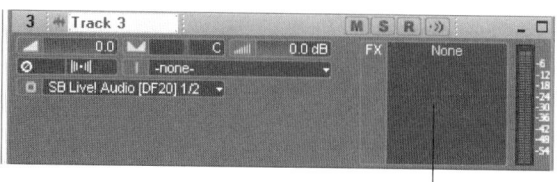

Right-click here to add an effect.

An effects popup menu appears. SONAR displays MIDI effects if you are editing a MIDI track, and audio effects for an audio track.

2. Select an effect from the menu.

   The name of the effect appears in the Effects bin and the effect's property page appears. To delete the effect, right-click the effect name and choose **Delete** from the popup menu.

3. Set the effects parameters or choose a preset.

Play your track and listen to the effect(s).

Note:

If you use the same effects for more than one track, it's more efficient to add the effects to a bus. See "To Patch a Track Through a Bus" on page 435

Changing Tempos

Your project can incorporate all kinds of tempo changes, including step changes from one tempo to another, gradual increases (accelerandos) or decreases (ritardandos), and almost any other type of change you can imagine. The tempo changes you add to your project become part of the project and are saved with the project file.

You can add tempo changes to your project in the following ways:

- Using the Tempo toolbar
- Using the **Insert-Tempo Change** and **Insert-Series of Tempos** commands
- By drawing tempo changes graphically in the Tempo view
- Inserting tempo changes in the Tempo view's Tempo List pane

The **Process-Fit to Time** and **Process-Fit Improvisation** commands can also be used to introduce tempo changes into your work file. For more information, see "Stretching and Shrinking Events" on page 288 and "Fit Improvisation" on page 304.

When you change the tempo of a project that contains audio, SONAR allows you to stretch or shrink audio clips when you have converted them to Groove clips and have enabled the Follow Project Pitch option in the Loop Construction view. Otherwise, the MIDI tracks will speed up or slow down while the audio tracks will play at the same speed. For more information about Groove clips, see "Working with Groove Clips" on page 260. Audio clips that are not Groove clips change in size when moved to a part of your project that has a different tempo.

Sometimes you don't want to adjust the speed of your audio. Here are some examples:

- If your project contains background music and a voice-over, you might want to change the tempo of the background music without altering the voice-over.

- If you're trying to modify the speed of some MIDI tracks to match a sampled drum groove, you want to leave the audio unchanged.

When you change the tempo of your project, clips having stretching enabled change tempo along with the project, while those that do not have stretching enabled do not. For more information on stretch-enabling clips, see "Enable Stretching" on page 252.

Tempos set when the clock source is set to MIDI Sync do not have any effect, because SONAR follows the external tempo. For more information, see Chapter 18, *Synchronizing Your Gear*.

Using the Tempo Toolbar

The Tempo toolbar displays the current tempo and lets you change the tempo as shown below:

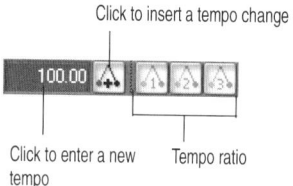

Click to insert a tempo change

Click to enter a new tempo   Tempo ratio

When you enter a new tempo directly in the toolbar, you change the most recent tempo setting in the project.

The tempo ratio buttons temporarily change the speed of playback, without affecting the actual tempo that is stored with your project (see Note, below). During playback, the tempo is multiplied by the current tempo ratio. By default, the three tempo ratios are 0.50 (half speed), 1.00 (normal speed), and 2.00 (double speed). You can change the tempo ratios that are associated with each button.

Note: Tempo ratios can only be used in projects that contain no audio tracks and cannot be used when using any form of synchronization. For more information, see Chapter 18, *Synchronizing Your Gear*.

To Change the Current Tempo in the Tempo Toolbar

1. Enable Groove clip Looping on any audio clips that you want to follow the tempo changes. Do this by selecting one or more clips, right-clicking a selected clip, and choosing **Groove-Clip Looping** from the popup menu. Each clip that has Groove clip Looping enabled has beveled edges instead of sharp corners. The same command disables Groove clip Looping on any selected clip that has Groove clip Looping enabled.
2. Click the current tempo in the Tempo toolbar.
3. Type a new value and press Enter, or use the spinners to change the tempo value.

SONAR changes the current tempo to the desired value.

To Set the Tempo Ratio

You can set the tempo ratio in several ways (remember, this function is not available if you have audio clips in your project):

- Click one of the tempo ratio buttons.
- Choose **Transport-Tempo Ratio 1**, **2**, or **3**.
- Press Ctrl+1, Ctrl+2, or Ctrl+3.

SONAR changes the speed of playback.

To Change the Tempo Ratio

1. Shift-click one of the tempo ratio buttons to display the Tempo Ratio dialog box.

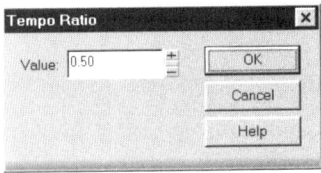

2. Enter a new value for the tempo ratio.
3. Click OK.

From now on, that tempo ratio button uses the ratio you entered.

Using the Tempo Commands

The *Insert-Tempo Change* and *Insert-Series of Tempos* commands can be used to change the existing tempo of a project or to introduce one or more tempo changes at various points in a project. You can enter tempo values directly, introduce smooth increase or decreases in tempo, or even use your mouse to tap out the tempo you want for some portion of a project.

To Insert a Tempo Change

1. Enable Groove clip Looping on any audio clips that you want to follow the tempo changes. Do this by selecting one or more clips, right-clicking a selected clip, and choosing *Groove-Clip Looping* from the popup menu. Each clip that has Groove clip Looping enabled has beveled edges instead of sharp corners. The same command disables Groove clip Looping on any selected clip that has Groove clip Looping enabled.

2. Click 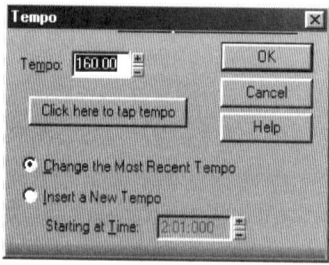 in the toolbar or choose *Insert-Tempo Change* to display the Tempo dialog box.

3. Check the Insert a New Tempo box.

4. Enter a new tempo in one of the following ways:
   - Type a value in the Tempo field.
   - Click the arrows to change the value.
   - Tap a new tempo in the space indicated in the dialog box.

5. Enter a starting time for the new tempo.

6. Click OK.

SONAR inserts a tempo change at the designated time.

To Insert a Series of Tempos

1. Enable Groove Clip Looping on any audio clips that you want to follow the tempo changes. Do this by selecting one or more clips, right-clicking a selected clip, and choosing **Groove-Clip Looping** from the popup menu. Each clip that has Groove clip looping enabled has beveled edges instead of sharp corners. The same command disables Groove Clip Looping on any selected clip that has Groove Clip Looping enabled.

2. Choose **Insert-Series of Tempos** to display the Insert Series of Tempos dialog box.

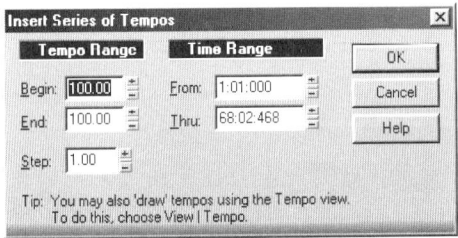

3. Enter a starting tempo, ending tempo, and step size.
4. Enter a starting and ending time for the series of tempo changes.
5. Click OK.

SONAR erases any existing tempo changes between the starting and ending time, and inserts a series of tempo changes that change smoothly between the starting and ending time. This command never inserts more than one tempo change on the same clock tick. Audio clips which you want to follow tempo changes can also be converted to Groove clips in the Loop Construction view.

To Modify the Most Recent Tempo Change

1. Enable Groove Clip Looping on any audio clips that you want to follow the tempo changes. Do this by selecting one or more clips, right-clicking a selected clip, and choosing **Groove-Clip Looping** from the popup menu. Each clip that has Groove Clip Looping enabled has beveled edges instead of sharp corners. The same command disables Groove Clip Looping on any selected clip that has Groove Clip Looping enabled.

2. Choose **Insert-Tempo Change** to display the Tempo dialog box.
3. Check the Change the Most Recent Tempo box.
4. Enter a new tempo in one of the following ways:
   - Type a value in the Tempo field.
   - Click the arrows to change the value.
   - Tap a new tempo in the space indicated in the dialog box.
5. Click OK.

SONAR changes the most recent tempo to the new value.

Using the Tempo View

The Tempo view provides a graphic display of the tempo. In the Tempo view you can use your mouse to draw tempo changes directly onto the graph. Choose ***View-Tempo*** or click 🔺 on the toolbar to display the Tempo view

The Tempo view provides both a graphic display of the tempo and a list of all tempo changes in your project. In the graphical display you can use your mouse to draw tempo changes directly onto the graph. In the tempo list, you can insert, edit, and delete individual tempo changes. Choose ***View-Tempo*** or click 🔺 on the toolbar to display the Tempo view. Click the Tempo List button 🔲 to display or hide the tempo list.

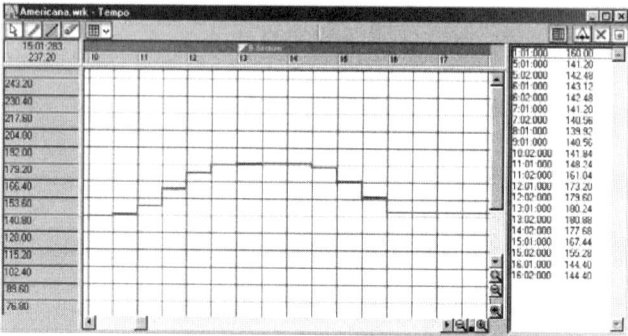

If an entire project has a single tempo, the graph shows a straight horizontal line, and a single tempo in the list.

The graph has several tools you can use to add or modify tempo changes:

Tool...	Name...	What it's for...
▢	Select	Drat the Select tool in either the Tempo list or graphic display to select tempos to edit
✏	Draw	Draw a custom curve indicating changes in tempo
✏	Line	Draw a straight line indicating a steady increase or decrease in tempo
✏	Erase	Eliminate tempo changes already in place for some portion of a project
🔲	Snap Grid	Controls how often you can insert tempo changes—for example, every measure, every eighth note, every 3 samples, etc.

If you make a mistake using any of these tools, you can use **Edit-Undo** to correct the error. When you use the Draw tool, the speed with which you drag the mouse determines the density of tempo events. To insert a larger number of relatively small tempo changes, move the mouse slowly. To insert a smaller number of relatively large tempo changes, drag the mouse quickly.

The Tempo List Pane has its own tools for editing tempo changes:

Tool...	Name...	What it's for...
	Insert Tempo	Insert a new tempo change
	Delete Tempo	Delete a tempo change
	Tempo Properties	Edit a tempo change

To Insert a Tempo Change in the Tempo View

1. Enable Groove Clip Looping on any audio clips that you want to follow the tempo changes. Do this by selecting one or more clips, right-clicking a selected clip, and choosing **Groove-Clip Looping** from the popup menu. Each clip that has Groove Clip Looping enabled has beveled edges instead of sharp corners. The same command disables Groove Clip Looping on any selected clip that has Groove Clip Looping enabled.

2. Select the ✏ or the ✏ tool.

3. Click in the Tempo view at any desired time point and tempo level.

SONAR introduces a tempo change at the indicated point.

To Steadily Increase or Decrease the Tempo in the Tempo View

1. Enable Groove Clip Looping on any audio clips that you want to follow the tempo changes. Do this by selecting one or more clips, right-clicking a selected clip, and choosing **Groove-Clip Looping** from the popup menu. Each clip that has Groove Clip Looping enabled has beveled edges instead of sharp corners. The same command disables Groove Clip Looping on any selected clip that has Groove Clip Looping enabled.

2. Select the ✏ tool.

3. Drag a line in the graph from the starting time and tempo to the ending time and tempo.

SONAR introduces a linear series of tempo changes.

To Draw a Series of Tempo Changes in the Tempo View

1. Enable Groove Clip Looping on any audio clips that you want to follow the tempo changes. Do this by selecting one or more clips, right-clicking a selected clip, and choosing **Groove-Clip Looping** from the popup menu. Each clip that has Groove Clip Looping enabled has beveled edges instead of sharp corners. The same command disables Groove Clip Looping on any selected clip that has Groove Clip Looping enabled.

2. Select the tool.

3. Drag the cursor across the graph, adjusting the tempo level as you move left to right.

SONAR introduces a series of tempo changes.

To Erase Tempo Changes in the Tempo View

1. Enable Groove Clip Looping on any audio clips that you want to follow the tempo changes. Do this by selecting one or more clips, right-clicking a selected clip, and choosing **Groove-Clip Looping** from the popup menu. Each clip that has Groove Clip Looping enabled has beveled edges instead of sharp corners. The same command disables Groove Clip Looping on any selected clip that has Groove Clip Looping enabled.

2. Select the tool.

3. Drag the mouse over the graph to highlight the region you want to erase.

4. Release the mouse button.

SONAR deletes all tempo changes in the area you marked. The last tempo setting prior to the erased region is now in effect in that region.

To Insert a Tempo Change in the Tempo List in the Tempo View

1. Enable Groove Clip Looping on any audio clips that you want to follow the tempo changes. Do this by selecting one or more clips, right-clicking a selected clip, and choosing **Groove-Clip Looping** from the popup menu. Each clip that has Groove Clip Looping enabled has beveled edges instead of sharp corners. The same command disables Groove Clip Looping on any selected clip that has Groove Clip Looping enabled.

2. Click the Tempo List button to display or hide the tempo list.

3. Select any tempo change in the list.

4. Click Insert Tempo to open the Tempo dialog box.

5. Set the tempo, time, and other properties.

6. Click OK.

SONAR inserts the new tempo into the list.

To Edit a Tempo Change in the Tempo View

1. Enable Groove Clip Looping on any audio clips that you want to follow the tempo changes. Do this by selecting one or more clips, right-clicking a selected clip, and choosing ***Groove-Clip Looping*** from the popup menu. Each clip that has Groove Clip Looping enabled has beveled edges instead of sharp corners. The same command disables Groove Clip Looping on any selected clip that has Groove Clip Looping enabled.
2. Click the Tempo List button to display or hide the tempo list.
3. In the tempo list, select the tempo change to be edited.
4. Click Tempo Properties or double-click the tempo change to open the Tempo dialog box.
5. Edit the tempo properties as desired.
6. Click OK.

To Delete a Tempo Change from the Tempo List in the Tempo View

1. Enable Groove Clip Looping on any audio clips that you want to follow the tempo changes. Do this by selecting one or more clips, right-clicking a selected clip, and choosing ***Groove-Clip Looping*** from the popup menu. Each clip that has Groove Clip Looping enabled has beveled edges instead of sharp corners. The same command disables Groove Clip Looping on any selected clip that has Groove Clip Looping enabled.
2. Click the Tempo List button to display or hide the tempo list.
3. In the tempo list, select the tempo change to be deleted.
4. Click Delete Tempo, or press Delete.

SONAR deletes the selected tempo change. You cannot delete the first tempo in the list.

Undo, Redo, and the Undo History

SONAR provides very powerful ***Undo*** and ***Redo*** commands that let you move forward or backward through any portion of an editing session. Every project has its own independent undo history. This means you can return to any open project and use the ***Undo*** and ***Redo*** commands, even if you've spent the last hour working on a different project. The undo history of a project is lost when you close the project.

Remembering everything that is necessary to undo the changes you have made can use a lot of memory. If a change you are about to make requires too much memory and cannot be undone, you will be advised that the operation is too big to undo later and asked if you want to go ahead anyway. If you do choose to perform the operation, you will not be able to undo it. Therefore, you may want to save your project first.

The **Edit-History** command displays a complete history of the commands and actions you can undo for the current project. The Undo History dialog box looks like this:

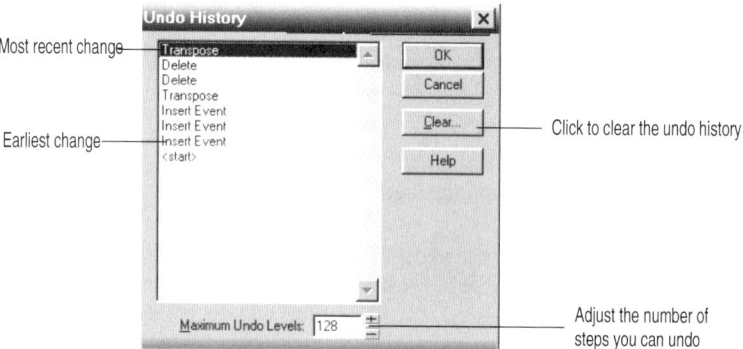

The **History** command is grayed out until you make a change to the current project that can be undone.

The History list is updated every time you make a change to a project. For example, if you insert a new note into a project using the Piano Roll view, that action is added to the History list. This entry remains on the list—even if you undo the change—so that you can redo the change later on. If you use the Erase tool to delete the note, this change is added to the History list.

You can click the Clear button in the Undo History dialog box to erase the undo history for the current project and free up some memory. If SONAR is low on memory, it may offer to erase the History list.

To revert to an earlier version of a project, highlight the entry in the History list that represents the point to which you'd like to return, and click OK. SONAR performs the necessary undo or redo actions to take you to that point. Once you edit the project (for example, by inserting a note), the History list is truncated at that point. Then, as you do further work, the History list grows again. Any events occurring before the event you highlighted remain on the list.

By default, SONAR keeps a history of up to 128 editing actions for each open project. Once that limit is reached, each new action pushes out the oldest item from the History list. You can raise or lower that number in the Undo History dialog box.

6

Using Loops

Loops are short digital audio clips which are often designed to be repeated over and over or "looped," although some loops, called one-shots, are intended to play just once. Groove clips, often used as loops, are digital audio clips that "know" their tempo and pitch information. Groove clips automatically respond to changes in a project's tempo and can have their root note pitch adjusted using pitch markers. In SONAR, you can import ACID™ loops, or digital audio clips and convert them to Groove clips. You can also record your own audio and create Groove clips. To download more Groove clips and loops, visit www.cakewalk.com.

Note:
Groove clips and ACIDized loops are loaded into RAM, and can take up a lot of memory. Once they're loaded though, copying them does not increase the amount of memory they take up.

In This Chapter

The Loop Construction View	252
The Loop Explorer View	256
Working with Loops	259
Working with Groove Clips	260
MIDI Groove Clips	267
Importing Project5 Patterns	271

The Loop Construction View

The Loop Construction view is where you create and edit Groove clips.

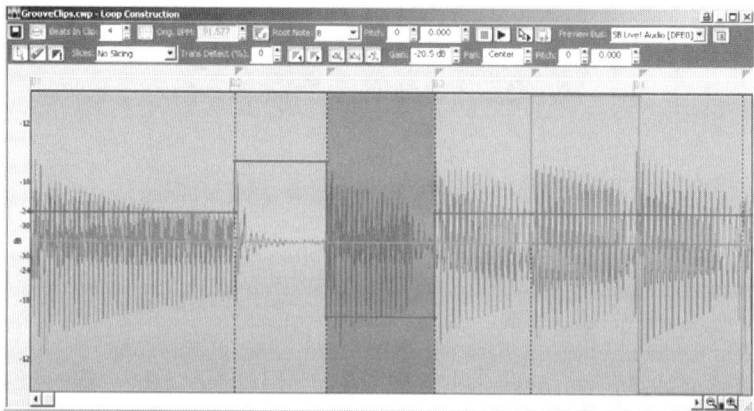

The Loop Construction view toolbar has tools for editing slicing markers and controls for previewing loops.

Loop Construction Controls

The following is a list of the tools and controls in the Loop Construction view, followed by a description:

Save Loop as WAV

This button opens the Save As dialog. The clip in the Loop Construction view is saved as a Groove Clip/Wave file that has tempo and pitch information stored in it, and can be opened in SONAR or ACID™. For more information, see "Saving Groove Clips as Wave Files/ACIDized Wave Files" on page 266.

Enable Looping

The Enable Looping button allows a clip to be looped by dragging in the Track view. Loop-enabled clips follow changes in the project tempo. Click the Enable Looping button to loop clips in the Track view by dragging the left or right side of a clip with your mouse. When you loop-enable a clip it automatically snaps to the nearest beat boundary (at 1, 2, 4, 8, 16 etc. beats). SONAR calculates the appropriate beat number. Change the number in the Beats in Clip field if you want to change the total number of beats in the clip.

Enable Stretching

The Enable Stretching button allows a clip to follow a project's tempo as it changes. It instructs SONAR to stretch or shrink the clip to fit the project's tempo. SONAR uses the Original BPM parameters to make the change.

Beats in Clip
The number of beats in the clip.

Original BPM
The tempo at which the clip was recorded.

Follow Project Pitch
The Follow Project Pitch option transposes the loop, if necessary, to the project pitch which you can set in the Markers toolbar. A loop recorded in the key of C, used in a project with a default project pitch of A, would be transposed down three semitones if the Follow Project Pitch checkbox was checked. You can also insert markers in the Time Ruler which change the project pitch. These markers, called pitch markers affect only Groove clips with Follow Project Pitch enabled.

Root Note
The Root Note represents the key in which the loop was originally recorded. The Follow Project Pitch feature uses this information, when checked, to transpose the loop to match the project's default project pitch and pitch markers.

Pitch (coarse)
You can set the transposition of a clip, independent from the project pitch, using the Pitch (Coarse) field. A positive number transposes the clip up by that number of semitones. A negative number transposes the clip down by that number of semitones. Remember that, if the Follow Project Pitch option is checked, the clip follows the project's pitch. Any transposition changes to the pitch with this option checked are changes to the project pitch, not the clip pitch.

An example: The project key is C. The clip key is D. If the Follow Project Pitch is enabled, the clip is transposed down by two semitones. A value entered into the Pitch (coarse) field adjusts the pitch from C. If you enter "-1" the pitch would be transposed down by one additional semi tone to B.

Another example: The clip pitch is E. The desired clip pitch is D. If the Follow Project Pitch option is not enabled, and a value of "-2" is entered in the Pitch (coarse) field, the clip is transposed down two semitones to D from the original pitch of E.

Pitch (fine)
The Pitch (fine) field allows you to make tuning adjustments or to transpose the pitch of a clip up to 50 cents. There are 100 cents in one semi tone. A Pitch (fine) setting of "1" adjusts the pitch up one hundredth of a semi tone. The Pitch (fine) option can "fine tune" a slightly out of tune clip so that it is in pitch with the remaining clips in a project.

Slices Menu

The Slices menu sets the resolution for the creation of markers, or the "slicing" of the looped clip. This menu uses note lengths, so the settings are:

- Whole notes
- Half notes
- Quarter notes
- Eighth notes
- Sixteenth notes
- Thirty-second notes

The automatic markers appear at the note resolutions according to the slider setting. At the eighth note setting, there are eight markers per measure.

This control works well for slicing audio that has more subtle changes in volume with few dramatic transients.

The markers in a loop clip preserve the timing of the audio at that moment. Too few or too many markers can cause unwanted "artifacts" when a loop clip is stretched.

Trans Detect (%)

The Trans Detect control senses transients in your audio clip and assigns a marker at the beginning and end of each one it finds. As the you increase the sensitivity (by using larger numbers) smaller transients are detected and the number of markers increases.

Stop Preview

Stops loop preview playback.

Preview Loops

Plays the current loop repeatedly. Use the Stop Preview control to stop playback.

Enable Slice Auto-Preview

Plays a slice when you click on it.

Click Auto-Preview Loop

Repeatedly plays a selected slice.

Preview Bus

Select the main out through which you want to listen to the clip.

Properties

The Properties button opens the Clip Properties dialog.

Select

Use the Select tool to move markers in the Markers bar.

Erase
Use the Erase tool to delete markers in the Markers bar.

Default All Markers
The Default All Markers tool restores all automatically generated markers to the original position and enables all those that were disabled. Manually created markers remain as is.

Previous Slice
Moves slice selection to the previous slice. Click on a slice to select it.

Next Slice
Moves slice selection to the next slice. Click on a slice to select it.

Show/Hide Gain Envelope
Clicking this button shows or hides the clip's gain envelope. Each slice of the clip has its own segment of the envelope, which you can adjust by dragging the segment up or down.

Show/Hide Pan Envelope
Clicking this button shows or hides the clip's pan envelope. Each slice of the clip has its own segment of the envelope, which you can adjust by dragging the segment up or down.

Show/Hide Pitch Envelope
Clicking this button shows or hides the clip's pitch envelope. Each slice of the clip has its own segment of the envelope, which you can adjust by dragging the segment up or down.

Slice Gain
Changes the selected slice's gain.

Slice Pan
Adjusts the selected slice's pan. Negative is left and positive is right.

Slice Pitch
Adjusts the selected slice's pitch. The first field is in half steps, the second field is in cents.

Slicing Markers
There are two types of slicing markers in the Loop Construction view: automatic and manual. Automatic markers appear in red and are automatically generated by SONAR when you loop enable a clip. The one exception to this is if you import an ACIDized wave file into SONAR. ACIDized files always appear with manual slicing markers. Manual markers appear in purple. If you add a marker or move an automatic marker, it turns purple to show you that it has been edited. For information on editing slicing markers, see "To Edit the Slicing Markers in a Groove Clip" on page 264.

Audio Scaling

Audio scaling is the increase or decrease in the size (scale) of the waveform in clip. Audio scaling allows you to make detailed edits by zooming in on the parts of the waveform closest to the zero crossing (silence) while preserving the track size. By showing just the quietest parts of a clip, you can make very precise edits.

The Audio Scale Ruler is located on the far left of the Loop Construction view.

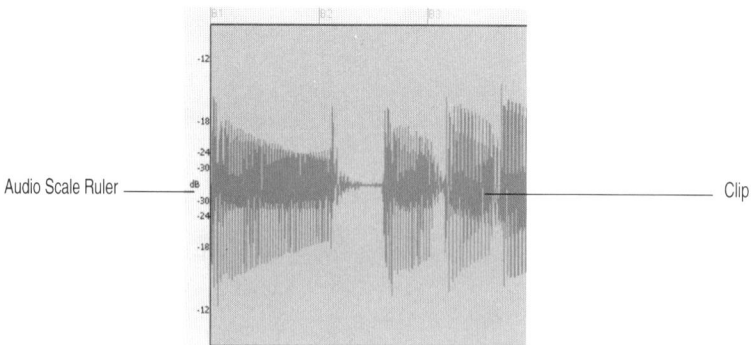

There are three display options in the Audio Scale Ruler:

- Percentage—shows audio scaling by percentage. For example, if the highest percentage in the Audio Scale Ruler reads 2.0%, then only the parts of the waveform which are within 2% of the zero crossing appear in the clip.

- dB—shows audio scaling by dB. For example, if the highest dB in the Audio Scaling Ruler reads -36, then only the parts of the waveform which are 36 dB below 0 dB appear in the clip.

- Zoom Factor—shows audio scaling by a factor. For example, if the Zoom Factor reads 10, then the waveform is zoomed in by a factor of 10.

The Loop Explorer View

SONAR's Loop Explorer view allows you to preview your Wave files before you drag and drop them into the Track view. If you preview a Groove clip, it plays back at tempo and in the key of your current project.

You can open the Loop Explorer view in any of the following methods:

- Select **View-Loop Explorer** from the menu.

- Click the Loop Explorer icon on the Views toolbar.

- Press Alt+1

The Loop Explorer view toolbar has the following controls:

Tool...	Name...	What It Does...
	Move Up	Opens the folder one level above the active folder.
	Refresh	Refreshes the active folder.
	Windows Explorer	Opens Windows Explorer at the same directory being viewed in the Loop Explorer view.
	Play	Plays the selected media file.
	Stop	Stops the playback of the selected file.
	Auto Preview	Automatically preview files when you click on them in the Loop Explorer view. If the selected file is a Groove clip, it plays back in the project tempo and key.
	Views	Allows you to change the way the files are viewed in the list view: • Large icons • Small icons • List • Details—displays the file size, date and when the file was created and last modified
	Preview Bus	Select the main out through which you want to listen to the loop.

Folders Pane

The Folders pane shows all of the available files and folders in the selected drive.

Contents List Pane

The Contents List pane displays the folders and files contained in the active folder.

To Preview a Groove Clip

1. Click the Auto-preview button in the Loop Explorer toolbar.
2. Click on a Wave file in the Content List pane.

   Each successive Wave file you select is previewed. You can also select multiple files and play them simultaneously.

   Or

1. Select a Wave file in the Content List pane.
2. Click the Play button in the Loop Explorer toolbar.
3. Click the Stop button to stop playing the selected Wave file.

When you preview a Groove clip in the Loop Explorer view, the clip plays in the project key and at the project tempo.

To Drag a Loop into a Project

1. Click and drag the Wave file from the Loop Explorer view to the Track view.
2. Drop the Wave file in the track and at the time in which you want it in your project. If you drop the file after the last track in your project, a new track is created for the file.

To Drag Multiple Loops into a Project

1. Select a Wave file and select additional by holding down the Ctrl key and selecting them.
2. Drag the Wave files from the Loop Explorer view to the Track view.
3. Drop the Wave files into the Track view at the time in which you want them in your project.

The Wave files appear on consecutive tracks in the Track view at the time selected.

Working with Loops

You can make any audio clip into a loop by checking the Enable Looping checkbox in the Clip Properties dialog. Once looping is enabled, you can drag out loops to create multiple repetitions. There are several other ways to enable looping:

To Enable or Disable a Clip for Looping
1. Double-click on the clip you want to loop.

    The Loop Construction view appears.

2. In the Loop Construction view, click the Enable Looping button .

    Or

    In the Track view, select a clip and press Ctrl+L or select ***Edit-Groove Clip Looping***.

To Create Repetitions of a Loop
1. Set the Snap value if you want the loop to repeat at precise time boundaries.
2. Move the cursor over the end of the loop-enabled clip until the cursor looks like this .
3. When the cursor changes, click the end or beginning of the clip and drag it to the right (if you are dragging out from the end) or left (if you are dragging from the beginning).

The clip repeats itself until you stop dragging.

To Create Partial Repetitions of a Loop
1. Move the cursor over the end of the loop-enabled clip until the cursor looks like this .
2. When the cursor changes, click the end or beginning of the clip and drag it to the right (if you are dragging out from the end) or left (if you are dragging from the beginning).

If the Snap to Grid button is on, you can create a partial loop as small as the Snap to Grid setting allows. For example, if your Snap to Grid setting is set to quarter notes, you can create partial repetitions as small as a quarter of a measure.

Working with Groove Clips

Groove clips are .WAV files that behave similarly to Sonic Foundry's ACIDized loops (SONAR also has MIDI Groove clips—see "MIDI Groove Clips" on page 267). Groove clips contain information about the audio content, including the original tempo, original reference pitch, number of beats in the loop, and audio transient information.

How Groove Clips Work in SONAR

Groove clips have information saved within them which allow them to adjust to changes in tempo and pitch. Groove clips can read a project's tempo and tempo changes, and can adjust their root note pitch when they read pitch markers. You can add pitch markers in the Track view's Time Ruler to transpose the Groove clip. As your project passes over a pitch marker, SONAR transposes your Groove clips based on the clip's root note reference pitch. If you insert no pitch markers in your project, there are no pitch changes in your Groove clips. The default project pitch is C.

Note:

When working with Groove clips, it is important to know the difference between *key* and *pitch*. Your project's key signature has no effect on Groove clips. The pitch of your Follow Project Pitch-enabled Groove clips is dictated by pitch markers in the Time Ruler. If there are no pitch markers in your project, these Groove clips play at the pitch set in the Markers toolbar (the default is C).

Note:

Groove clips must be at least one beat in length. If you try to loop-enable a clip of a shorter duration you may experience distortion or artifacts.

Using Groove Clips

Groove clips are easy to use because they automatically adjust to your project's pitch markers and tempo. You can import existing loops or create your own, using the Loop Construction view.

To Import a Groove Clip into Your Project

1. Select a Track in the Track view.
2. Set the Now Time to the place you want the clip to begin.
3. Select *File-Import-Audio* from the menu.

   The Open dialog appears.
4. Navigate to a directory that contains Groove clips and select one.
5. Click Open.

   Or

1. Open the Loop Explorer view.
2. Navigate to a directory that contains Groove clips.
3. Drag and drop a clip into the Track view, or double-click it to insert it at the Now Time.
4. The clip appears on the track and at the time in your project where you drop it, so if you want the clip on a new track, drop it after the last track in your project.

By default, Groove clips are loop-enabled and transposed to match the project's pitch.

Setting the Default Project Pitch

1. If necessary display the Markers toolbar by selecting *View-Toolbars* to open the Toolbars dialog. In the toolbar dialog click Markers and OK.
2. In the Markers toolbar, click the Default Groove Clip Pitch dropdown menu and select a pitch.

Your project now uses the root note of your clips to transpose to the project pitch. Use Pitch markers at different points in your project to change the pitch. For more information on Pitch markers, see "Using Pitch Markers in the Track View" on page 266.

Creating and Editing Groove Clips

Any audio clip can be converted to a Groove clip. Groove clips contain tempo, beat, and pitch information which SONAR uses to stretch and transpose the clips to match the project. Most Groove clips are loop-enabled, meaning that you can use the mouse to drag clip repetitions in the Track view. Groove clips can be either loop-enabled or not, although they usually are. When a Groove clip is loop-enabled, its edges appear beveled. It is sometimes desirable to create clips that follow the project's tempo and key, but are not intended to loop. The following is a list of the attributes contained in a Groove clip:

- Beats in clip—The number of quarter notes in a clip. A four measure clip in 4/4 time should have 16 beats. When you enable looping for a clip, SONAR calculates the number of beats in the clip using an algorithm. This calculation is very often accurate, but in some cases, for instance when the clip has a very slow or very fast tempo or if the clip has an unusual number of beats, then the number of beats in a clip may have to be edited manually in the Beats in clip field.

- Original tempo—The original tempo of the recording. SONAR uses the original tempo to adjust to your project's tempo. The original tempo must be specified for stretching clips.

    Note: When you loop-enable a clip, SONAR calculates the original tempo of the clip, and unless the clip's length is in exact beat or measure increments, the original tempo that SONAR calculates may vary from the recorded tempo. These fluctuations are usually quite small and do not affect the quality of the Groove clip you create.

- Reference note—The original key of the recorded clip. SONAR uses the Reference note when it transposes Groove clips to match your project's pitch.

These attributes can be edited in the Loop Construction view.

To Set the Number of Beats in a Groove Clip

When you open a clip in the Loop Construction view, SONAR determines the number of beats in the clip. In some cases the beat value may not be correct. The beats in clip value can only be changed if the clip is loop enabled.

Do the following to change value in the Beats in Clip field.

- Click the plus or minus button to the right of the Beats in clip field until the correct value is displayed.

To Change the Loop Construction View Time Ruler Display

You can display the Loop Construction view Time Ruler in measures or in samples. To toggle between the two modes, double click the Time Ruler.

To Set the Tempo of a Groove Clip

When creating a new Groove clip, SONAR sets the clip's tempo to the current project tempo. To ensure proper stretching behavior you must set the value in the Original BPM field to the tempo at which you recorded the clip. The tempo value of a clip can only be changed if the clip is stretch-enabled.

Do the following to change the value in the Original BPM field.

- Click the plus or minus button to the right of the Original BPM field until the correct value is displayed. For more precise tempos you can double-click in the Original BPM field and enter a tempo.

To Slice a Clip

1. Double-click on a clip in the Clips pane.

   The clip appears in the Loop Construction view.

2. Slice the clip using one or all of the following methods:

To do this...	Do this...
Slice the clip on note divisions	Move the Basic Slicing slider to the note resolution you want. The Basic Slicing slider's settings range from whole notes to 64th notes. Selecting quarter notes, for example, would create four markers per measure.
Slice the clip at transient peaks	Move the Transient Detection slider to the right until the larger transients in the clip are flanked by markers.
Slice the clip manually	Move your mouse to the space above the Time Ruler and double-click to add a marker. Click and drag the marker, if necessary, so it aligns with the beginning or end of a transient.

3. Play your project and adjust the slicing of your clip as necessary.

Note: You can use any or all of these methods to slice a clip. If you adjust both the Slices and Trans Detect menus, two markers may be placed right next to each other. If these markers are too close, the markers will automatically merge. Manual markers will not automatically merge.

263

To Transpose a Groove Clip to Match Your Project's Pitch

Follow this procedure to force the Groove clip to follow the project's default pitch.

1. Double-click the clip you want to transpose to the project's pitch.

   The clip appears in the Loop Construction view.

2. Click the Follow Project Pitch button.

To Transpose a Groove Clip by Semitones

Follow this procedure to transpose a Groove clip by any number of semitones.

1. Double-click the clip you want to transpose to the project's pitch.

   The clip appears in the Loop Construction view.

2. If the Follow Project Pitch button is enabled, click it to disable it.

3. In the Pitch (semitones) field, enter the number of semitones you want to transpose the clip by. A negative number in the Pitch (semitones) field transposes a clip down. A positive number in the Pitch (semitones) field transposes the clip up.

To "Fine Tune" a Groove Clip

Follow this procedure to make slight pitch changes to a clip.

1. Double-click the clip you want to transpose to the project's pitch.

   The clip appears in the Loop Construction view.

2. In the Fine Pitch (cents) field, enter the number of cents you want to adjust the pitch. You can enter a number from -50 (transpose the pitch down by a quarter tone) to 50 (transpose the pitch up by a quarter tone).

To Edit the Slicing Markers in a Groove Clip

The table below describes how to create and edit the slicing markers in the Loop Construction view.

To do this...	Do this...
Add a slicing marker	Move the mouse cursor to the Markers bar, at the beginning of a transient and double-click.
Delete a slicing marker	Select the Eraser tool and click on a marker.
Move a slicing marker	Click and drag a marker
Reset slicing markers to original positions	Click the Default All Markers button.

For more information on slicing markers, see "Slicing Markers" on page 255.

Editing Slices

Each slice (space between the slicing markers) can be adjusted in the Loop Construction view. You can adjust the following slice attributes:

- Gain
- Pan
- Pitch

To Preview a Groove Clip Slice

1. Double-click on a clip to open the Loop Construction view.
2. Click the Enable Slice Auto-preview button.
3. Click a slice to hear it.

To Adjust a Groove Clip Slice Gain

1. In the Loop Construction view, select the slice on which you want to adjust the gain.
2. In the Slice Gain field, click the plus or minus buttons to change the gain value.

    Or

    Click between the plus and minus keys until the cursor becomes a double arrow and drag up to increase the value or down to decrease the value.

To Adjust a Groove Clip Slice Pan

1. In the Loop Construction view, select the slice on which you want to adjust the pan.
2. In the Slice Pan field, click the plus or minus buttons to change the pan value. Negative is Left pan and positive is right pan.

To Adjust a Groove Clip Slice Pitch (Half Steps)

1. In the Loop Construction view, select the slice on which you want to adjust the pitch.
2. In the first Slice Pitch field, click the plus or minus buttons to change the pitch value.

To Adjust a Groove Clip Slice Pitch (Cents)

1. In the Loop Construction view, select the slice on which you want to adjust the pitch.
2. In the second Slice Pitch field, click the plus or minus buttons to change the pitch value.

To Adjust Slice Gain, Pan and Pitch Using Slice Envelopes

You can change an envelope's gain, pan and/or pitch settings by dragging the envelope up or down in that slice.

Saving Groove Clips as Wave Files/ACIDized Wave Files

Once you have created a Groove clip in SONAR, you can save the clip as a Groove Clip/Wave file, compatible with ACIDized wave files.

To Save a Groove Clip as a Riff Wave File/ACIDized Wave File

1. If you have not already done so, create a Groove clip. In the Loop Construction view, click the Save icon.

   The Save As dialog appears.

2. Use the toolbar in the Save As dialog to navigate to the location where you want to save the file.

3. In the File name field, enter a name for the file.

4. Click the Save button.

To Drag and Drop a Groove Clip Into Another Application

You can drag and drop clips from SONAR to another application or to a directory in Windows. When you drag a file from SONAR, the source file is copied and the copy is placed in the new directory or application.

Using Pitch Markers in the Track View

Pitch markers change the pitch at which Groove clips sound. All Groove clips in SONAR that have the Follow Project Pitch option enabled adjust their pitch as they encounter pitch markers in SONAR. If there are no pitch markers, all Groove clips play at the default project pitch, unless the Follow Project Pitch parameter is disabled.

Pitch marker: Groove clips with Follow Project Pitch enabled play with the Root Note transposed to C

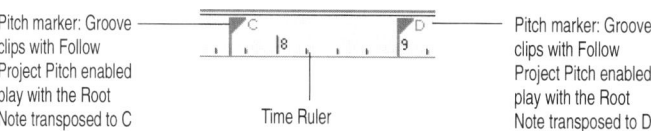

Time Ruler

Pitch marker: Groove clips with Follow Project Pitch enabled play with the Root Note transposed to D

To Enable a Clip's Follow Project Pitch Option

1. Right-click the clip and choose Clip Properties from the popup menu.

   The Clip Properties dialog appears.

2. On the Groove Clips tab, check the Follow Project Pitch checkbox.

3. Make sure that the Reference Note field is correct. When your project reaches a pitch marker, SONAR transposes each groove clip that has the Follow Project Pitch option enabled by the difference between the clip's Reference Note and the current Project Pitch.

4. Click OK to close the dialog.

To Change Your Project's Default Pitch

1. Display the Markers toolbar, if it's not already displayed, by using the *View-Toolbars-Markers* command.

2. In the Default Groove-Clip Pitch dropdown menu at the right end of the toolbar, choose your project's default pitch.

SONAR transposes each groove clip that has the Follow Project Pitch option enabled by the difference between the clip's Reference Note and the current Project Pitch. Your project's pitch changes wherever you insert a pitch marker. If you don't insert any pitch markers, your project stays at its default pitch.

To Create a Pitch Marker

1. In the Track view, right-click in the Time Ruler.

2. Select Create a Marker from the menu that appears.

3. The Marker dialog appears.

4. In the Groove Clip Pitch dropdown, select a pitch.

5. Click OK.

To Move a Pitch Marker

- Click and drag a pitch marker to a new location on the Time Ruler.

MIDI Groove Clips

MIDI Groove clips are MIDI clips that you can roll out like audio Groove clips, and you can also choose to have SONAR transpose MIDI Groove clips when your project reaches a pitch marker.

You can change any MIDI clip into a MIDI Groove clip (or back into a regular MIDI clip) by selecting the clip and using the *Edit-Groove Clip Looping* command. A MIDI clip that has its Groove clip feature activated appears with *beveled edges* in the Clips pane.

Here are some other features of MIDI Groove clips:

- You can roll out copies in either direction (just like audio Groove clips). The Snap-to-Grid setting determines what beat boundaries (if any) you can roll to.

- You can edit individual repetitions without altering any other copies (*unlike* audio Groove clips). **Note**: If you then roll the edge of your MIDI Groove clip back over the area you edited, you will lose your edits.

- All new repetitions are based on the first clip (just like audio Groove clips). However, if you split a repetition from its original source clip, the repetition becomes independent: if you copy this clip, SONAR treats it as an original clip.

- You can import MIDI Groove clips from the Import MIDI dialog, the Loop Explorer view, and by dragging and dropping from the Windows Explorer.
- You can preview MIDI Groove clips in the Import MIDI dialog.
- You can edit MIDI Groove clips wherever you can edit regular MIDI clips.

For step-by-step information, see the following procedures, and also "Exporting, and Importing MIDI Groove Clips" on page 269.

To Enable or Disable a MIDI Clip's Groove Clip Function
- Select the clip and press Ctrl+L.

    Or

- Select the clip and use the *Edit-Groove Clip Looping* command.

    Or

- Right-click the clip and choose *Groove Clip Looping* from the popup menu.

A MIDI clip that has its Groove clip feature activated appears with *beveled edges* in the Clips pane.

To Create Repetitions of a MIDI Groove Clip
1. Set the Snap value if you want the clip to repeat at precise time boundaries.
2. Move the cursor over the end or beginning of the clip until the cursor looks like this .When the cursor changes, click the end or beginning of the clip and drag it to the right (if you are dragging out from the end) or left (if you are dragging from the beginning).

The clip repeats itself until you stop dragging.

To Transpose a MIDI Groove Clip
1. Select the MIDI Groove clip.
2. Hold down the Alt key, and press the + or - key on your computer keyboard to raise or lower the clip's pitches a half-step at a time. You don't have to stop playback.

    Or

1. Right-click the clip and choose *Clip Properties* from the popup menu.

    The Clip Properties dialog appears.

2. On the Groove Clips tab, in the Pitch (semitones) field, choose the number of half-steps you want to transpose the clip by: choose negative numbers to transpose down, or positive numbers to transpose up.

Either method transposes the original clip and all repetitions. The original clip displays a positive or negative number in parentheses showing any transposition value you've added to the clip.

If you use pitch markers to transpose a clip, any transposition value you add to the clip by the above two methods changes the final pitch by whatever transposition value you've added.

To Transpose a MIDI Groove Clip with Pitch Markers

Use the same method you use for audio Groove clips: see "Using Pitch Markers in the Track View" on page 266.

Exporting, and Importing MIDI Groove Clips

You can not export MIDI Groove clips by saving your project as a Standard MIDI File—Standard MIDI Files do not contain MIDI Groove clip data, such as transposition value, etc. When you import MIDI Groove clips, you can preview them in the Import MIDI dialog.

There are two methods for exporting MIDI Groove clips:

- Using the *File-Export-MIDI Groove Clip* command
- Dragging a MIDI Groove clip from SONAR to the Windows Explorer

There are three methods for importing MIDI Groove clips:

- Using the *File-Import-MIDI* command
- Using the Loop Explorer view
- Dragging a MIDI Groove clip from the Windows Explorer to a MIDI track in SONAR

For step-by-step information, see the following procedures:

To Export MIDI Groove Clips with the File Command

1. Highlight the MIDI Groove clip that you want to export.
2. Use the *File-Export-MIDI Groove Clip* command.

   The Export MIDI dialog appears.
3. Navigate to a folder where you store MIDI Groove clips.
4. Type a name for the clip in the File Name field.
5. Click the Save button.

SONAR exports the MIDI Groove clip, which contains the information displayed in the Clip Properties dialog, on the Groove-Clips tab, except for the Pitch (semitones) field, which does not get exported.

To Export a MIDI Groove Clip with Drag and Drop

- Drag the MIDI Groove clip that you want to export to the folder in the Windows Explorer where you want to keep it.

To Import MIDI Groove Clips with the File Command
1. Move the Now Time to the place where you want to import the clip.
2. Highlight the track you want to import the clip into.
3. Use the *File-Import-MIDI* command.

   The Import MIDI dialog appears,
4. Navigate to a folder where you store MIDI Groove clips. Make sure that the Files of Type field is set to MIDI File.
5. Highlight the file you want to import—the File Info field displays the file's MIDI Groove clip data, if any.
6. If you want to preview (listen to) the highlighted file, click the Play button in the Import MIDI dialog. When you decide to import the highlighted file, click the Open button.

To Import MIDI Groove Clips from the Loop Explorer View
1. Make sure that the Snap-to-Grid setting is appropriate for what you want to do.
2. If the Loop Explorer view is not open, use the *View-Loop Explorer* command to display it.
3. Navigate to a folder where you store MIDI Groove clips.
4. Do either of the following:
   - Drag the file you want to the track and time where you want it.
   - Move the Now Time to the place where you want to import the file, highlight the track you want to import the file into, and double-click the file.

To Import a MIDI Groove Clip with Drag and Drop
1. Make sure that the Snap-to-Grid setting is appropriate for what you want to do.
2. In the Windows Explorer, navigate to a folder where you store MIDI Groove clips.
3. Drag the MIDI Groove clip to the track and time where you want it to go.

Importing Project5 Patterns

Project5 is Cakewalk's pattern-based soft synth work station that has its own library (pattern bin) full of MIDI and audio patterns, stored on disk. If you have Project5 MIDI patterns on your hard disk, you can import them directly into SONAR.

To Import a Project5 Pattern
1. Move the Now Time to the place where you want to import the pattern.
2. Highlight the track you want to import the pattern into.
3. Use the *File-Import-MIDI* command.

   The Import MIDI dialog appears,
4. Change the Files of Type field to P5 Pattern.
5. Navigate to a folder where you store Project5 MIDI patterns.
6. Highlight the file you want to import.
7. To import the highlighted file, click the Open button.

SONAR imports the pattern to the selected track at the Now Time.

Editing MIDI Events and Controllers

SONAR lets you edit the events in your projects in dozens of different ways. The Piano Roll view lets you add and edit notes, controllers, and automation data interactively, using a graphic display. SONAR's many editing commands can improve the quality of recorded performances, filter out certain types of events, and modify the tempos and dynamics of your projects. The Event List view lets you see and modify every detail of your project. Finally, you can apply a variety of effects and filters to enhance your MIDI data.

SONAR has many additional commands and features for working with audio. For more information, see "Editing Audio" on page 349.

In This Chapter

Event Inspector Toolbar 274
The Piano Roll View 275
Selecting and Editing Events 283
Slip Editing MIDI (Non-destructive Editing) 291
Changing the Timing of a Recording 294
Searching for Events 305
Controllers, RPNs, NRPNs, and Automation Data 311
The Event List View 318
MIDI Effects (MIDI Plug-ins) 325

Event Inspector Toolbar

The Event Inspector toolbar is available from the View menu by selecting **View-Toolbars** and checking Event Inspector in the Toolbars dialog. The Event Inspector has the following:

- Time
- Pitch
- Velocity
- Duration
- Channel

To Display a Note's Properties in the Event Inspector Toolbar
- Select a note.

If you select multiple notes, the Event Inspector toolbar displays the note value if all selected note values are the same. If the note values are different, the Event Inspector does not display anything.

To Change a Note's Properties Using the Event Inspector Toolbar
1. Select a note.
2. In the appropriate Event Inspector toolbar field, change the value. See the table below for a description of valid value entries for each field in the Event Inspector toolbar.

Event Inspector Field...	Valid Values...
Time	Any valid M:B:T time value. Separate values with a colon or a space. For example, measure 2, Beat 3, Tick 720 would be written as 2:3:720.
Pitch	Note names (C0 through G10) and note numbers (0 through 127) are valid in this field. Also, you can use a modifier to raise or lower the value by a number of half-steps. To raise the pitch by 2 half-steps, type +2 and press enter. To lower the pitch by 2 half-steps, type -2 and press enter.
Velocity	A velocity value or modifier value are valid in this field. Valid velocity values are 0 through 127. Valid modifier values are +/- 0 through 127.
Duration	A PPQ value.
Channel	1 through 16.

The Piano Roll View

The Piano Roll view displays all notes and other events from one or more MIDI tracks in a grid format that looks much like a player piano roll. Notes are displayed as horizontal bars, and drum notes as diamonds. Pitch runs from bottom to top, with the left vertical margin indicating the pitches as piano keys or note names. Time is displayed running left to right with vertical measure and beat boundaries. The Piano Roll view makes it easy to add, edit, and delete notes from a track.

The Piano Roll view consists of the Note Map pane, the Drum Grid pane, the Note pane, the Controllers pane, and the Track List pane.

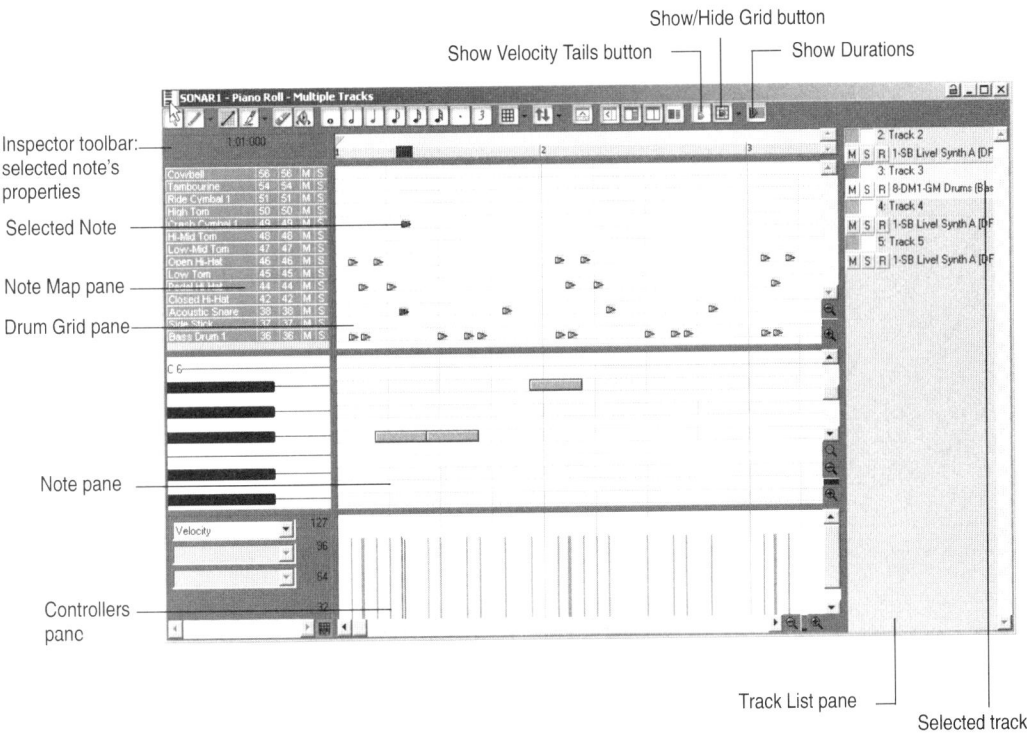

Note Map Pane

In this pane displays your drum map settings, mute or solo an individual pitch, and preview individual pitch sounds. For more information about the Note Map Pane, see "The Note Map Pane" on page 342.

275

Drum Grid Pane

In the Drum Grid pane you can add, delete and edit notes and note properties in any MIDI track(s) assigned to a drum map. For more information, see "The Drum Grid Pane" on page 344.

Note Pane

In this pane you can add, edit, and delete notes in any MIDI track(s) not assigned to a drum map.

Controllers Pane

In this pane you can edit controllers, RPNs, NRPNs, velocity, pitch wheel, and aftertouch data, during playback or recording, in real time. Select the controller you want to edit from the Controller dropdown list at the top of the Piano Roll view. For more information, see "Controllers, RPNs, NRPNs, and Automation Data" on page 311.

Track List Pane

The Track List pane is home to a list of all tracks currently displayed in the Piano Roll view. In this pane you can enable and disable editing of a track's data; mute, solo and arm a track; and show or hide the track's data in the Note pane or Drum Grid pane. Track numbers, names and output ports appear in the Track List pane. You can show or hide the Track List pane by clicking the Show/hide track pane button ▣ in the Piano Roll view toolbar.

Opening the View

There are several ways to open the Piano Roll view:

- In the Track view, select the track you want to see, then choose *View-Piano Roll* or press Alt+5

- In the Track view, right-click on a track and choose *View-Piano Roll* from the popup menu

- Double-click on a MIDI clip in the Clips pane

Each selected track is displayed. You can always switch to a different track or tracks—simply click the ▣ button (or press T) and choose the track you want.

The Piano Roll view lets you edit notes and controllers during playback or recording, in real time. This means you can loop over a portion of your project and hear any change you make on the next loop. The Piano Roll view also shows notes on-screen as you record them.

Like the Track view, the Piano Roll view includes zoom tools that let you change the vertical and horizontal scale of the view. The Piano Roll view also has a Snap to Grid ▣ button. For more information on this feature, see "Defining and Using the Snap Grid" on page 222.

Selecting and Editing Notes

The Piano Roll view is a very convenient place to select, edit, and copy notes within a track or tracks. You must make the track you want to edit the current track. The current track appears with a dotted line around it in the Track List pane. To display the Track List pane in the Piano Roll view, click the Show/Hide Track List pane button ⌘. The following shows three tracks in the Track List pane:

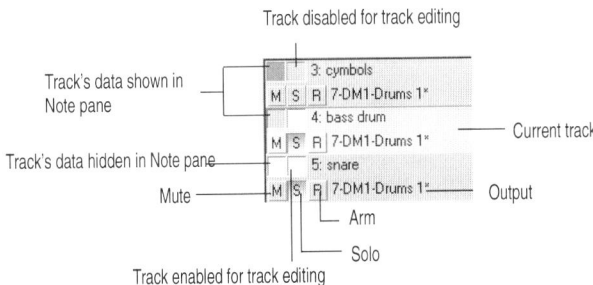

To make the a track the current track in the Track List pane, click on the track. When a thin dotted line surrounds the track, it is the current track.

There are several ways to select notes in the Piano Roll view:

- Click and drag in the Time Ruler to select notes (and other MIDI events) that start playing within the time range
- Use the Select tool ▧ to select notes
- Click or drag the piano keys to the left of the Note pane or the drum map rows in Note Map pane to select all notes of the given pitch(es)

You can use Shift-click to add notes to the selection and Ctrl-click to toggle between adding to or removing from the selection.

You can add notes to a clip simply by clicking in the Note pane or Drum Grid pane with the pencil tool. You can use the Resolution buttons to set the duration for new notes you enter. You can edit notes freely, using the mouse to change the start time, pitch, or duration. You can also right-click any note to edit the start time, pitch, duration, velocity, and channel of that note. You can move and copy notes beyond the boundary of the clip in which they are located. When you move the notes, the clip will be extended as needed, unless the notes are moved to a section that includes a slip-edited clip, in which case a new clip may be created.

The Piano Roll view also lets you **scrub** the tracks that are currently displayed. The Scrub command lets you drag a vertical bar over the view so that you can hear the notes in the track(s). You can scrub forward or backward at any speed. Scrubbing can be handy when you want to locate a bad note or listen to the effects of changes you have made without playing back at normal speed.

To Select Notes with the Selection Tool

1. Click [cursor icon] to select the Select tool.
2. Select notes as shown in the table:

To do this...	Do this...
Select a single note	Click on the note
Select several notes at once	Drag a rectangle around the notes you want to select
Add to the selection	Hold the Shift key while selecting notes
Toggle the selection	Hold the Ctrl key while selecting notes

Selected notes are highlighted (50% gray mask) in the Piano Roll view, and the time selection is set to the range of note start times.

To Select All Notes of Certain Pitches

- Click the piano keys on the left side of the Note pane or the drum map rows in the Note Map pane as shown in the table:

To do this...	Do this...
Select all notes of a single pitch	Click on the piano key or map row
Select all notes of several pitches	Drag across the keys or map rows
Add to the selection	Hold the Shift key while clicking on a piano key or map row
Toggle the selection	Hold the Ctrl key while clicking on a piano key or map row

To Edit a Note

1. Click ![icon] to select the Draw Line tool (or the Draw tool ![icon], if you have do not have Auto Erase enabled).

2. Edit notes as described in the table:

To do this...	Do this...
Change the start time, but not the duration	Drag the left edge of the note in either direction. The start time of the note is moved to the new location.
Change the pitch	Drag the middle of the note up or down.
Change the duration	Drag the right edge of the note in either direction.

If the snap grid is enabled and set to Snap To, the start time of each note is restricted to points on the snap grid, and the length of each note is restricted to an even multiple of the snap increment. For example, if the snap resolution is set to a quarter note, you can move notes only to quarter-note boundaries, and you can increase or decrease the duration only by quarter notes. If the snap grid is set to Move By, notes can only be moved by multiples of the snap resolution.

To Change Note Velocity or Channel

1. Right-click a single note to display the Note Properties dialog box.

2. Edit the desired start time, pitch, duration, velocity, or channel.

3. Click OK when you are done.

SONAR updates the note event accordingly. Note that you can also edit note velocity in the Controllers pane and the Note Properties toolbar. For information on changing note velocities in the Drum Grid Editor, see "Editing Note Velocities" on page 341. For more information, see "Velocity, Pitch Wheel, and Aftertouch" on page 313.

To Move Notes

1. Click ![select] or press S to select the Select tool.
2. Select one or more notes.
3. Drag the selected notes to a new location.

   The Drag and Drop Options dialog appears. If you have unchecked the Ask This Every Time checkbox in the Drag and Drop Options dialog, SONAR uses that last option you set in that dialog. To change the option, right-click in the Clips pane of the Track view and select **Drag and Drop Options** from the popup menu.

4. Select an option and click OK.

SONAR moves the selected notes.

To Copy Notes

1. Click ![select] or press S to select the Select tool.
2. Select one or more notes.
3. Press Ctrl+C.

   The Copy dialog appears.

4. Click OK in the Copy dialog.
5. Change the Now time to the place you want to paste the note(s).
6. Press Ctrl+V.

   The Drag and Drop Options dialog appears.

7. Select an option in the Drag and Drop Options dialog and click OK.

SONAR copies the selected notes.

To Add a Note

1. Click the Draw tool button ![draw] or press D to select the Draw tool.
2. Select a note duration by clicking one of the note icons in the Piano Roll view toolbar.
3. Press and hold the left mouse button in the Piano Roll view. SONAR adds a new note.
4. Drag the note to the desired pitch and time.
5. Release the left mouse button.

To Erase a Note

1. Click the Erase button ![erase] or press E to select the Erase tool.
2. Click on any note to delete it.

To Erase Several Notes

1. Click the Erase button or press E to select the Erase tool.
2. Drag the cursor across notes to delete them.
3. Release the mouse button when you are done.

To Select and Erase Notes

1. Click the Select button or press S to select the Select tool.
2. Select one or more notes.
3. Press Delete to delete the notes.

To Erase Notes Using Auto Erase

The Auto-Erase feature makes the Draw tool into an eraser as well as a drawing tool. When the Auto-Erase feature is on, the Draw tool creates a note if used where there are no existing notes, but deletes notes that you click on.

1. Click the arrow on the right side of the Draw tool and select Auto Erase if it is not already checked.
2. Click on the note you want to erase.

   When the Auto Erase option is enabled, clicking in the Note pane or the Drum Grid pane creates a note if there is no note present and deletes any note you click on.

To Temporarily Turn off Auto-Erase

If you want to edit a note's start time or duration, you must turn off Auto-Erase. You can do so by unchecking the menu item in the Draw tool menu. You can also temporarily turn off Auto-Erase.

1. Hold down the Alt key.
2. Make edits in the Drum Grid Editor or the Note pane.
3. Release the Alt key.

To Scrub the Project

1. Click or press B to select the Scrub tool.
2. Press and hold the left mouse button in the Piano Roll view. SONAR displays a vertical line and plays any notes that are underneath the line.
3. Drag the line to the left or right, at any desired speed.

Note that the Mute, Solo and Arm buttons do not affect Scrub. If the track is hidden, however, you do not hear notes in that track.

Working with Multiple Tracks in the Piano Roll View

You can simultaneously edit as many tracks as you want in the Piano Roll view. When you display several tracks at the same time in the Piano Roll view, you control which track(s) you can see and/or edit by using the buttons in the Track List pane. You can show or hide the Track List pane by clicking the Show/hide track pane button in the Piano Roll view toolbar.

The following is a list of ways to optimize the multiple track functionality in the Piano Roll view.

Selecting Tracks
Use the Pick Tracks combo button to assign tracks to the Track List pane. Click on the left side of the Pick Tracks combo button to open the Pick Tracks dialog box. Click on a track name to select it. Hold down the Ctrl key and click more track names to select additional tracks. Click on the right side of the Pick Tracks combo button to show the Down/Up popup menu. Selecting Down moves the track or range of tracks down by one. Selecting Up moves the track or range of tracks up by one. For example, if you have tracks 2, 3 and 7 displayed in the Track List pane and you select Down, the Track List pane displays tracks 1, 2, and 6.

Display
If the notes of two tracks overlap, the notes of the topmost track in the Track List pane appear over the notes of the other track. You can move a track up or down by in the Track List pane by clicking and holding on the track and moving the track to the desired position.

All tracks ending in the same digit (2, 12, 22, etc.) share the same color. The default colors can be changed using *Options-Colors*.

The Enable/Disable Track Editing Button
The Enable/Disable Track Editing button sets whether or not you can edit the notes of a track in the Piano Roll view. When the button appears white, editing is enabled and the track appears in color. When the button appears gray, editing is disabled and the track appears in gray.

Note: The Enable/Disable Track Editing button only disables the Piano Roll view tools; other editing commands are still operational.

The Show/Hide Track Button
The Show/Hide Track button controls whether or not a track appears in the Note pane. The button appears in color when toggled on, white when off.

The Invert Tracks Button
If you use the Show/Hide Track button to hide any tracks in the Track List pane, you can show all these tracks and hide the ones that are currently displayed by clicking the Invert Tracks button.

Note Names

You can change the instrument definition for the active track in the Piano Roll view. Right-click the piano keys in the Note pane to open the Note Names dialog where you can use note names that are defined as part of any instrument definition. For more information about instrument definitions, see Chapter 16, *Using Instrument Definitions*.

To Change the Active Track's Instrument Definition

1. Right-click the left side of the Note pane (where the piano keys or note names are displayed) to display the Note Names dialog box.

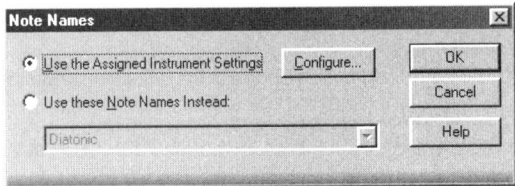

2. To use the note names from the assigned instrument (the default), click Use the Assigned Instrument Settings. Click Configure to change the instrument definitions.

3. To override the default setting, click Use These Settings Instead, and choose the note names and mode you want to work with.

4. Click OK when you are done

The Piano Roll view is updated with the settings you request.

Selecting and Editing Events

SONAR has many other editing commands that you can use to modify the events that make up your project. Here are some of the things you can do:

- Transpose events, clips, tracks, or an entire project to a different key
- Shift events to an earlier or later time
- Stretch or shrink material to a different length
- Reverse the notes in a clip to create new arrangements
- Modify the note velocities

The following sections describe these editing commands and how to use them. SONAR also has some special commands you can use to modify or clean up a performance or to search for or select events that meet certain criteria. For more information, see the following sections of this chapter.

Transposing

The *Process-Transpose* command transposes the pitches of selected note events up or down by a fixed number of steps. It does so by changing the MIDI key numbers of note events. Simply enter the number of half-steps—a negative number to transpose down, a positive number to transpose up.

SONAR can also perform diatonic transposition, which shifts all the notes up and down the major scale of the current signature by the designated number of steps. For instance, if you specify an amount of +1 and the key signature is C-major, a C becomes a D (up a whole step), an E becomes an F (up a half step), and so on. Diatonic transposition assures you that the transposed notes fit with the original key signature.

As an option, you can choose to transpose selected audio clips along with any selected MIDI clips. SONAR uses pitch-shifting (a plug in for changing audio pitch) to perform the transposition. You can transpose audio only a single octave in either direction (-12 to +12), and you cannot transpose audio when you are using diatonic transposition.

To Transpose Selected Events

1. Select the tracks, clips, or events you want to transpose.

2. Choose *Process-Transpose* to display the Transpose dialog box.

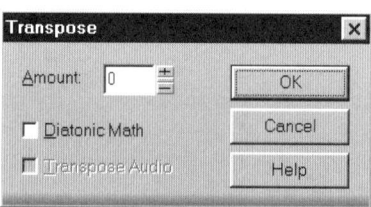

3. Use the spinners or enter the number of semi-tones to transpose.

    Or

    Use the + and - keys on your keypad to go up or down by one or [and] to go up or down by octaves.

4. Check Diatonic Math if you want to transpose along the major scale of the current key.

5. Choose *Transpose Audio* if you want to pitch-shift selected audio clips.

6. Click OK when you are done.

SONAR transposes the selected events.

Shifting Events in Time

The Track view lets you move entire clips forward or backward in time by using drag and drop editing or by changing the start time of selected clips. The ***Process-Slide*** command is slightly more flexible—you can use it to shift individual events and markers (or selected events and markers) either forward or backward in time. This has an effect that is similar to the Time+ parameter in the Track view. However, the ***Process-Slide*** command modifies the time stored with each event, while the Time+ parameter simply applies a temporary change during playback.

You can also use the ***Process-Slide*** command to move markers located within the selection. If you have selected any locked markers, SONAR will ask whether they should slide, too.

To Shift Events in Time

1. Select the events and/or markers you want to shift.
2. Choose ***Process-Slide*** to display the Slide dialog box.
3. Check the types of event you want to slide (events and/or markers).
4. Enter the number of measures, ticks, seconds, frames or samples to slide. Enter a negative number to shift material earlier. Note that you cannot slide any event earlier than 1:01:000. For example, if the current selection starts at 2:01:000, you cannot slide events earlier by more than one measure.
5. Click OK when you are done.

SONAR shifts the selected events and/or markers.

Inserting Time or Measures into a Project

The ***Insert-Time/Measures*** command lets you insert any number of blank measures, ticks, seconds, or frames into a project. You can insert the blank measures (or other period of time) into all tracks or into one or more selected tracks. If you insert the blank time into the entire project, all events in each track—markers, meter and key settings, and tempo changes—are shifted automatically by default. If you insert the blank time into one or more selected tracks, only the events in those tracks are shifted by default. You can always choose which types of events should be shifted.

To Insert a Single Blank Measure into a Project

1. Press Ctrl+Shift+A or select ***Edit-Select-None*** to make sure that no track or time range is selected.
2. Set the Now time to the place where you want to insert the measure.

3. Choose *Insert-Time/Measures* to display the Insert Time/Measures dialog box.

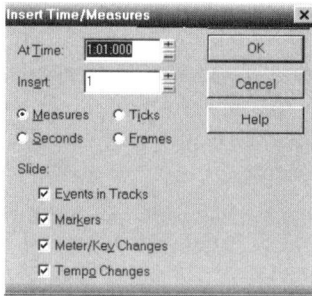

4. Verify that the settings are correct and click OK.

SONAR inserts a blank measure at the Now time.

To Insert Blank Time or Measures into a Project

1. Press the 5 key on the numeric keypad (Num Lock must be off) or select *Edit-Select-None* to make sure that no track or time range is selected.

2. Select the range of time you want to insert by dragging in the Time Ruler.

3. Choose *Insert-Time/Measures* to display the Insert Time/Measures dialog box.

4. If necessary, adjust the time at which blank space will be inserted.

5. If necessary, change the length of time to insert by entering a number and choosing the units you want from the list.

6. Choose the types of events that should be shifted automatically from the Slide list.

7. Click OK when you are done.

SONAR inserts the desired amount of blank time into the project.

To Insert Blank Time or Measures into Selected Tracks

1. Select the range of time you want to insert by dragging in the Time Ruler.

2. Select one or more tracks by Ctrl-clicking on the track numbers.

3. Choose *Insert-Time/Measures* to display the Insert Time/Measures dialog box.

4. If necessary, adjust the time at which blank space will be inserted.

5. If necessary, change the length of time to insert by entering a number and choosing the units you want from the list.

6. Choose the types of events that should be shifted automatically from the Slide list.

7. Click OK when you are done.

SONAR inserts the desired amount of blank time into the project.

Deleting Measures or Time from One or More Tracks

There are two methods for deleting time or measures:

- If there is any audio or MIDI data in the area you want to delete, you can use the ***Edit-Delete*** command to delete the area that you select. Portions of MIDI clips may have no data in them: they have boundaries but no dark lines inside—if that's the case, use the following method.

- If there is no data in the area you want to delete, you can simply drag any clips that come after the empty area to their proper destinations. You can also use this method if there is data in the area you want to delete—you just have to choose whether you want to replace the data in the deleted area, blend it with the data you're moving, or slide it over to make room.

To delete time when there **is** audio or MIDI data in the area you want to delete:

1. In the Track view, select the track(s) you want to delete measures or time from by doing one of the following:

    - Select a single track by clicking the track number.
    - Select multiple tracks by Ctrl-clicking the track numbers.

2. Set the Snap to Grid value to the unit of time you want to delete. For example, if you want to delete whole measures, set the Snap to Grid value to a whole measure.

3. In the Clips pane, select the measures or time you want to delete by dragging in the Time Ruler located just above the first track.

4. Select ***Edit-Delete***.

    The Delete dialog box appears.

5. Click the following checkboxes:

    - Events in Tracks
    - Delete Hole—if you want the data that comes after the hole to retain its same placement in a measure, check the **Shift by Whole Measures** option.

6. Click any of the other options you want to delete.

7. Click OK.

SONAR deletes the time or measures you selected.

To delete time when there **is no** audio or MIDI data in the area you want to delete (or if there is data, but you like to drag and drop):

1. Set the Snap to Grid value to the unit of time you want to delete. For example, if you want to delete whole measures, set the Snap to Grid value to a whole measure.

2. In the Track view, select the clips you want to move.

3. Drag one of the selected clips to its proper destination—the Drag and Drop Options dialog box appears.

4. Choose options and click OK.

All the selected clips move by the amount that you dragged the mouse.

Stretching and Shrinking Events

The ***Process-Length*** and ***Process-Fit to Time*** commands can be used to stretch or shrink a portion of a project. ***Process-Length*** lets you stretch or shrink the selection by a fixed percentage and makes the adjustment by altering the individual events. A value of 200 percent, for example, stretches the selection to twice its original length, while a value of 50 percent shrinks the selection to half its original length.

Process-Fit to Time stretches or shrinks the selection so that it ends at a specific time, expressed in either measure:beat:tick (MBT) or hours:minutes:seconds:frames (SMPTE) format. This command gives you a choice of modifying the events or modifying the underlying tempo. This is useful when you want a portion of a project to have an exact length. The start time of the selection does not change, but the end time is altered as necessary to fit the required time interval.

Both of these commands offer the option to stretch audio clips along with the MIDI information. Sometimes you don't want to adjust the speed of your audio.

Here are some examples:

- If your project contains background music and a voice-over, you might want to change the tempo of the background music without altering the voice-over

- If you're trying to modify the speed of some MIDI tracks to match a sampled drum groove, you want to leave the audio unchanged

- If your audio consists solely of sound effects, you most likely do not want to adjust them

Audio can be stretched or condensed up to a factor of 4 (e.g., it can be shrunk to as little as 25 percent of its original length, or expanded to as much as 400 percent of its original length).

You can also use the *Process-Length* command to alter only the start times or the durations of notes. For example, changing the durations of notes to 50 percent of their original length can create a staccato effect.

To Stretch or Shrink Using Percentages

1. Select the events you want to change.
2. Choose *Process-Length* to display the Length dialog box.

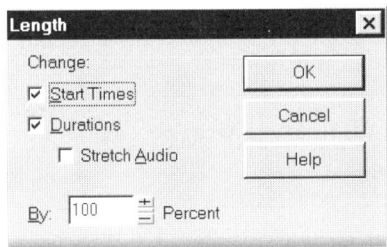

3. Choose to change the Start Times and/or Durations of selected notes by checking the boxes.
4. If you want to stretch selected audio clips, check the Stretch Audio box.
5. Use the spinners or type in the desired percent change in length.
6. Click OK when you are done.

SONAR modifies the length of selected events.

To Stretch or Shrink to a Specific Length

1. Select the events you want to change.
2. Choose *Process-Fit to Time* to display the Fit to Time dialog box.

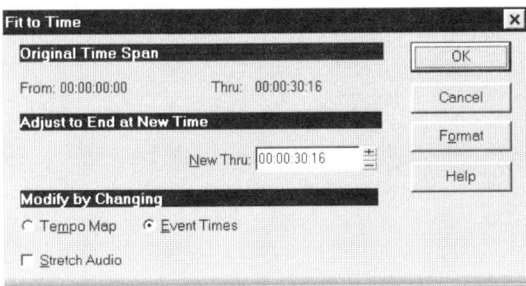

3. Enter the desired end time in the New Thru box. Click Format to switch between MBT and SMPTE format.

289

4. Choose one of the following:

- Tempo Map—Choose this option if you want the tempo to change but not the duration of notes and events. For example, if your clip contains quarter notes, and you want those notes to stay quarter notes even though the elapsed time of the clip changes, choose Tempo Map. SONAR alters the tempo but not the events in the track.

- Event Times—Choose this option if you want the tempo(s) to remain unchanged while note durations and event start times change.

    Important note: This option is unavailable if your selected data includes any Groove clips.

5. If you want to stretch selected audio clips, check the Stretch Audio box.
6. Click OK when you are done.

SONAR modifies the length of selected events or changes the tempo map, as you requested.

Reversing Notes in a Clip

The ***Process-Retrograde*** command reverses the order of events in a selection. If one or more clips are selected, then the events within each clip are reversed. If several clips are selected from the same track, then the order of the clips is also reversed. You could use this command, for example, to take a scale or other long run of notes and reverse the order in which they are played. The ***Process-Retrograde*** command does not reverse the contents of audio clips. It only changes their start times. You can use the ***Process-Audio-Reverse*** command to reverse audio clips.

To Reverse the Sequence of Notes or Other Events

1. Select the notes you want to reverse.
2. Choose ***Process-Retrograde***.

SONAR reverses the order of the selected events.

Adding Crescendos and Decrescendos

The ***Process-Scale Velocity*** command lets you create crescendos and decrescendos on those instruments that respond to MIDI velocity. Most such instruments map changes in velocity to changes in note loudness. Many synthesizer patches alter the timbre of the sound as well, so that higher velocities produce brighter, as well as louder, sounds. Changes in velocity also affect the playback of audio clips.

This command lets you set a starting and ending velocity for the entire time range of the selection. SONAR scales the velocity of each event to create a smooth linear change in velocity. As an option, you can enter a starting and ending percentage; existing velocity values are modified by the designated percentage.

You can also edit note velocities in the Controllers pane of the Piano Roll view, which lets you draw shapes other than straight line changes. For more information, see "Using the Controllers Pane" on page 313.

To Scale Velocities
1. Select the events whose velocity data you want to change.
2. Choose **Process-Scale Velocity** to display the Scale Velocity dialog box.

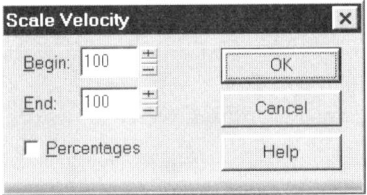

3. Enter the starting and ending velocity values.
4. Check the Percentages box if the values are percentages.
5. Click OK when you are done.

SONAR alters the velocity of selected events.

Slip Editing MIDI (Non-destructive Editing)

Slip editing allows you to non-destructively hide or reveal the beginning of a clip, the end of a clip, or both. The hidden material in a clip is not heard during playback. All hidden material remains intact and can be restored. All Slip Editing movements correspond to the current snap to resolution. For more information about the snap to grid, see "Defining and Using the Snap Grid" on page 222.

Slip Editing Modes
Slip editing has three modes:

Trimming
As a default, when slip editing a clip, the clip's contents always remains fixed in time. If the first measure of a clip is hidden using slip editing, the remaining material does not shift forward in time by a measure. The first measure of the clip is simply muted during playback. Playback of the clip resumes at the second measure.

Slide-trimming
If you want the clip's contents to shift in time, you can move the material in a slip edited clip by using modifier keys, clicking on the middle of the clip and moving it either right or left.

Scroll-trimming

You can also shift the clip's contents in time, in relation to either the beginning or end of the clip itself, by scroll-trimming.

Using Slip Editing for MIDI Clips

When Slip Editing the beginning of a MIDI clip, if you drag the start of the clip past the beginning of a note (Note On), the entire note is lost even if it extends into the part of the clip which remains visible. Only notes completely contained in the slip edited clip remain.

When Slip Editing the end of a MIDI clip, if you drag the end of the clip so it covers part of a note, the note's duration is trimmed accordingly.

If you insert a new MIDI event which does not fall within the boundary of a slip-edited clip, a new MIDI clip, which contains the new MIDI events, is created.

Important:

Adding controller data beyond the slip-edited boundaries of a slip-edited clip in the Piano Roll view results in the slip-edited data being displayed in the Piano Roll view. To avoid this, you can use the *Apply Trimming* command to destructively edit the clip before adding the controller data.

To Slip-edit a MIDI Clip

1. Make edits according to the following table:

To do this...	Do this...
Trim the beginning of a clip	Move the cursor over the beginning of a clip. When the cursor changes in appearance to look like this , click and drag the clip to the right until you have removed the unwanted information.
Trim the end of a clip	Move the cursor over the beginning of a clip. When the cursor changes in appearance to look like this , click and drag the clip to the left until you have removed the unwanted information.

Scroll-trimming a clip (Moving the clip contents in time while maintaining the clips start and end time)	Press the Alt+Shift keys while moving the cursor over the middle of the clip. When the cursor changes to look like this ▣, click and drag the clip to the left or right as desired. The contents (MIDI data) in the clip follow the Snap to Grid resolution, i.e. if your resolution is set to half note, the contents of your clip moves in half-note intervals.
Slide-trimming the beginning of a clip (Moving the start time of the clip and the clip's contents while preserving the end time)	Press the Alt+Shift keys and move the cursor over the beginning of the clip. When the cursor changes to look like this ⇨, click and drag the beginning to the desired start time.
Slide-trimming the end of a clip (Moving the end time of the clip and the clip's contents while preserving the clip's start time)	Press the Alt+Shift keys and move the cursor over the end of the clip. When the cursor changes to look like this ⇦, click and drag the end to the desired location.

The hidden information in the slip-edited clips remains intact but is not heard during playback

To Permanently Delete Slip-edited MIDI Data
1. Select the clips that contain the slip-edited data you want to delete.
2. Select the *Edit-Apply Trimming* command.

SONAR permanently deletes the slip-edited data from the clips you selected.

Slip-editing Multiple MIDI Clips
You can slip-edit multiple clips at the same time.

To Slip-edit Multiple MIDI Clips at Once
1. Select the clips you want to slip-edit.
2. Move your cursor over the beginning or end range of the selected clips until your cursor changes too look like this: ⇦.
3. Drag the boundary to the desired location and release.

293

Changing the Timing of a Recording

When you record a performance, there may be problems you'd like to correct. For example, the note timing may not have been as accurate as you would like. Or, you may have recorded without using a metronome and strayed from the tempo in one direction or another.

SONAR has two types of commands that you can use to modify the timing of a clip. The **Quantize** commands alter the timing of the notes in your recording so that they fit a time grid.

The grid can have fixed time intervals or intervals that are based on some existing note pattern. The **Fit to Improvisation** command, on the other hand, sets up a series of tempos that fit the material you have recorded. Here's a summary of when to use each type of command:

Use this command...	To do this...
Quantize	Change the timing of the notes you've recorded to fit with the tempo of a project
Fit to Improvisation	Change the tempos of a project to fit with the performance you've recorded

These two types of commands are discussed in the following sections.

Quantizing

Quantizing is one of the most important editing functions in SONAR. You use this feature to correct timing errors you make when recording from a MIDI instrument or to adjust the timing of audio clips.

Very few musicians are capable of performing in perfect time. As you play, you are likely to strike some notes slightly before or after the beat or to hold some notes slightly longer than you intended. The **Quantize** commands can help to correct these types of timing mistakes.

SONAR has two different quantize commands:

Command...	How it works...
Process-Quantize	Adjusts the start time and duration of selected notes so that they line up with a fixed size grid
Process-Groove Quantize	Lays a grid over an existing piece of music (the *groove pattern*), and then adjusts the start time, duration, and velocity of selected notes so that they line up with the grid

These commands have quite a few settings, making them very flexible and powerful. In addition, both of these commands lets you create, save, and re-use presets. This means that once you find the settings you like, you can save them and then apply them to other projects in a consistent way.

Resolution

The **resolution** indicates the spacing of the grid. You can use any value from a whole note down to a thirty-second note triplet. You can also specify resolution in clock ticks. A rule of thumb is to select a resolution that matches the smallest note in the region you are quantizing. If you are quantizing a run of sixteenth notes, use a sixteenth note as the resolution. If you are quantizing a mix of sixteenth and eighth notes, you should still use a sixteenth note. At the default timebase of 480 PPQ, 480 clock ticks is equal to quarter-note resolution.

When you use **Groove Quantize**, SONAR creates a grid at the desired resolution on top of the notes in the groove. For example, if the groove contains only quarter notes but you choose sixteenth-note resolution, SONAR builds the grid by dividing the space between each quarter note into four equal sections. In places where the groove file contains no notes, SONAR builds a fixed grid of the desired resolution.

Offset

Normally, the resolution grid is aligned evenly with the start of measures and beats. As an option, you can shift the grid earlier or later by any desired number of clock ticks. If the resolution is a quarter note and you've set the offset to +3 ticks, then a note that is originally near 1:01:000 would be moved to 1:01:003—three ticks beyond the beat boundary.

Duration

As an option, SONAR can adjust the duration of note events so that each note ends one clock tick before the start of the nearest resolution-sized note. This ensures that the notes do not overlap, which can cause problems on some synthesizers. The adjustment may lengthen the duration of some notes and shorten the duration of others.

When you use *Groove Quantize*, the duration adjustment compares the note length to the duration of the sample note in the groove. If no duration information is available, SONAR uses the distance to the start of the groove event closest to the end of the note.

Velocity

The velocity adjustment, which is only available with the *Groove Quantize* command, adjusts the note velocity to the velocity of the corresponding notes in the groove.

Strength

The human ear is tuned to the slight "imperfections" we hear from most musicians. If you quantize a project so that all notes are perfectly in position, it may end up sounding mechanical or rigid. To avoid this, SONAR lets you adjust the **strength** of the adjustment. A strength of 100 percent indicates that all notes are moved so that they are in perfect time, while a strength of 50 percent means that all notes are moved half-way towards the desired position. This lets you "tighten up" the timing as much as you want, without going too far.

The *Groove Quantize* command also lets you control the strength of duration and velocity adjustments. As you work with this command, you will notice that the note start time has a greater effect than the duration on the rhythmic feel of the track. For this reason, changing the starting times (time strength close to 100 percent) has a more noticeable effect than changing durations (duration strength close to 100 percent). However, there are situations in which you might want to change both to avoid ending up with notes that overlap or with unwanted rests.

Swing

Many projects do not have notes positioned on a perfectly even time grid. For example, projects with a swing feel, though they may be written entirely in eighth notes, are often played more like eighth-note triplets, with the first note extended and the second one shortened. The **swing** option lets you distort the timing grid so each pair of notes is spaced unevenly, giving the quantized material a swing feel.

A swing value of 50 percent (the default) means that the grid points are spaced evenly. A value of 66 percent means that the time between the first and second grid points is twice as long as the time between the second and third points. The figure below illustrates the effect of the swing setting on the timing grid:

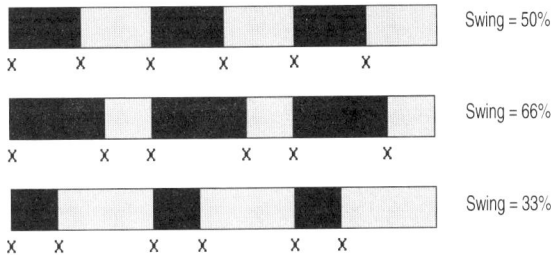

Window

When you quantize some portion of a project, you might not want to adjust notes that are very far from the grid. The **window**, or **sensitivity**, setting lets you choose how close to the resolution grid a note must be located for quantize to move it.

A window of 100 percent includes all notes and guarantees that all notes will be shifted to lie exactly on the grid. The window extends half the resolution distance before and after the quantization point. A window of 50 percent extends only a quarter of the way toward the adjacent quantization points.

When you use *Groove Quantize*, you can also perform adjustments on out-of-window events. There are four options:

Option...	How it works...
Do Not Change	Notes outside the window are not changed.
Quantize to Resolution	Notes outside the window are snapped to a regular grid of the specified resolution.
Move to Nearest	The window or sensitivity setting is ignored—all notes are moved toward the nearest reference event, regardless of how far off the grid they are located.
Scale Time	SONAR finds the two closest events before and after the event in question that are within the window sensitivity and adjusts any bracketed out-of-window events so that their relative timing is the same. This option can uniformly speed up, slow down, or shift out-of-window events.

Other Settings

If you want, you can restrict the types of events that are affected by the *Quantize* commands to only notes, lyrics, and audio clips. If you choose this option, SONAR will not modify other events, like controllers.

To Use the Quantize Command

1. Select the material you want to quantize using any of the selection tools and commands.

2. Choose *Process-Quantize* to display the Quantize dialog box.

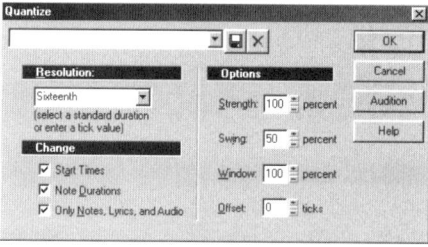

3. Choose one of your own presets from the list, or enter the settings you want according to the table:

Setting...	What to do...
Resolution	Choose a note size or enter the number of clock ticks
Change	Check the event types and characteristics you want to change
Options	Enter values for Strength, Swing, Window, and Offset

4. Click Audition if you want to hear how the quantization will sound; press Stop to stop auditioning the change.
5. Make adjustments as necessary.
6. Click OK when you are done.

SONAR quantizes the selected MIDI information and audio clips. You can use *Undo* to restore the material to its original state.

To Use the Groove Quantize Command

1. Select the track or clip you want to quantize, using any of the selection tools and commands.
2. Choose **Process-Groove Quantize** to display the Groove Quantize dialog box.

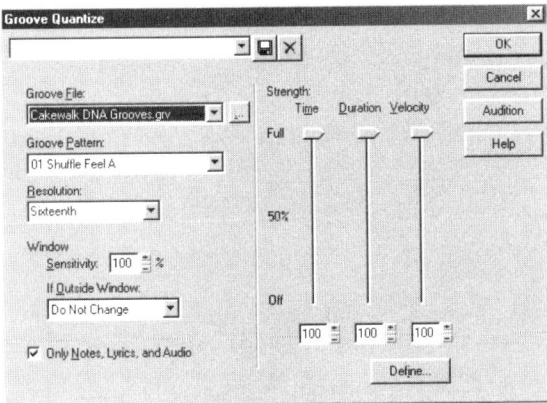

3. Choose a groove file from the Groove File field.
4. Choose a groove pattern from the Groove Pattern field.

5. Use the following fields to configure your pattern:

Setting...	What to do...
Resolution	Choose a note size or enter the number of clock ticks
Window Sensitivity	Enter the window sensitivity value (percentage)
If Outside Window	Choose what should happen to events outside the window
Only Notes, Lyrics and Audio	Check to prevent MIDI controller, aftertouch, and xRPN data from being adjusted
Stretch Audio	Check to stretch audio clips to adjust their duration
Strength	Use the sliders or enter values for Note strength, Duration strength, and Velocity strength

6. Click Audition if you want to hear how the quantization will sound; press Stop to stop auditioning the change.

7. Make adjustments as necessary.

8. Optionally, type a name in the preset field (located at the top of the dialog box) and click the Save button to save your settings.

9. Click OK when you are done.

SONAR quantizes the selected MIDI information and audio clips. You can use **Undo** to restore the material to its original state. If you saved your settings, you can apply them to any pattern you want by selecting the pattern and choosing a preset from the preset field. To delete a group of settings, select the group from the preset field and click the Delete button.

Defining a Groove

To use the groove quantize feature, you must create or choose a small snippet of music—the groove pattern—for SONAR to use as the timing and accent reference. You can use either of the following:

- A track, clip, or portion of a clip stored on the Windows clipboard
- A groove stored in a SONAR groove file

Any MIDI data that you place onto the Windows clipboard can be used as a groove pattern. With a carefully defined groove pattern, you can give an old project an entirely new feel. If you like the groove pattern you have created, you can save it to a groove file.

Groove files can store one or more groove patterns. SONAR supports two types of groove files:

- DNA™ grooves, which contain only timing information but are compatible with some other MIDI sequencer software products
- SONAR's native groove format, which stores timing, duration, and velocity information and can handle longer patterns and longer gaps between quantization points

You can add groove patterns to these files from the Windows clipboard, edit existing patterns, or delete patterns you do not want to keep. There is no limit to the number of groove patterns that can be stored in a single file. You can organize your grooves into several files or keep them all together in a single file. Groove files have an extension of .GRV.

A groove pattern can be as short or long as you like. If the groove pattern is shorter than the material to be quantized, the pattern will be repeated as many times as necessary.

To Define a New Groove
1. Select the music that defines the groove using any of the selection tools and commands.
2. Choose **Edit-Copy** to place the music onto the Windows clipboard.

You can now use the **Groove Quantize** command with the clipboard as the "Groove File."

To Save a Groove Pattern
1. Select the music that defines the groove using any of the selection tools and commands.
2. Choose **Edit-Copy** to place the music onto the Windows clipboard.
3. Choose **Process-Groove Quantize** to display the Groove Quantize dialog box.
4. Choose the Clipboard as the groove "Groove File."

5. Click the Define button to display the Define Groove dialog box.

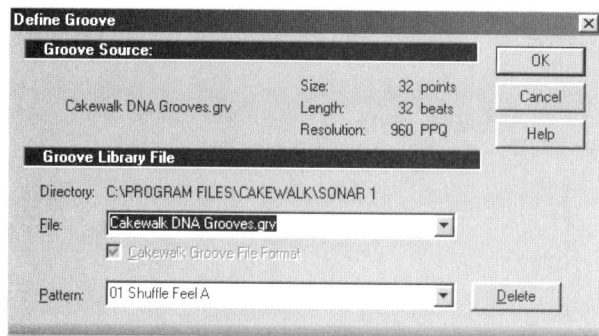

6. Select an existing groove file, or enter the name for a new groove file.

7. Enter a pattern name, or choose an existing pattern to replace.

8. Click OK.

9. If you are replacing a groove, verify that you want to delete the existing version.

10. Click Close when you are done to return to the Groove Quantize dialog box.

SONAR stores the groove in the file and chooses the new groove as the current groove source.

To Copy an Existing Groove

1. Choose **Process-Groove Quantize** to display the Groove Quantize dialog box.

2. Choose the groove file and groove pattern you want to copy.

3. Click the Define button to display the Define Groove dialog box.

4. Select an existing groove file, or enter the name for a new groove file.

5. Enter a pattern name, or choose an existing pattern to replace.

6. Click OK.

7. If you are replacing a groove, verify that you want to delete the existing version.

8. Click Close when you are done to return to the Groove Quantize dialog box.

SONAR stores the groove on the Windows clipboard and chooses the new groove as the current groove source.

To Delete a Groove

1. Choose ***Process-Groove Quantize*** to display the Groove Quantize dialog box.
2. Click the Define button to display the Define Groove dialog box.
3. Select the file containing the groove to delete.
4. Select the pattern name of the groove.
5. Click the Delete button, and confirm that you want to delete the groove pattern.
6. Repeat steps 3 to 5 for each groove you wish to delete.
7. Click Close when you are done to return to the Groove Quantize dialog box.

Groove Quantize Tips

Here are some tips to help you with groove quantizing:

Aligning sloppy tracks with a good one. Select the portion of the "good" track that you want to apply to the "sloppy" tracks and copy it to the Clipboard. Select the portion of the sloppy tracks you want to modify. Choose ***Process-Groove Quantize***, choose the Clipboard as the groove source, and click OK.

Accenting beats in each measure. Create a sample measure containing note events at the desired accent points. Give the notes on the accented beats a greater velocity and the others a lesser velocity. Select the measure, copy it to the Clipboard, and then choose ***Process-Groove Quantize***. Set the velocity strength as high as necessary so that the notes get accented the way you want.

Stealing that feeling. Suppose you have a dry piece that was composed and entered into SONAR with a rigid sense of timing (for example, using step recording). You've recorded a bass line that has exactly the off-beat rhythmic dynamic you want for the dry piece. You'd like to force your other tracks to share that feel. Copy the bass track to the Clipboard; from the Groove Quantize dialog box, select the Clipboard as the groove source; choose a resolution value roughly on the order of the duration of the bass notes and a window of 100 percent. SONAR aligns the melody note events with the nearest bass notes.

Synchronizing rhythm and solo tracks. If you want to preserve the unique rhythm of each track but want to synchronize them together in time, try a larger resolution value and a smaller window. For example, suppose you have one track with a highly stylized drum beat and another track containing a jazz solo with some very nice runs in it. The drum beats fall primarily on quarter notes, but the solo consists of runs of fast notes that aren't quite sixteenth triplets. Copy the drum track to the Clipboard, and groove quantize using a quarter-note resolution and a window of perhaps 10 percent. SONAR aligns the solo notes near the quarter-note drum beats but maintains the feel of the solo during the fast runs of notes in between.

Correcting off-tempo tracks. Suppose you have both rhythm and melody tracks recorded, but the melody was played erratically. First, copy the rhythm track to the Windows clipboard. Then use groove quantize with a whole-note resolution, a window of 25 percent or less, and with the Scale Time option selected. The *Groove Quantize* command will synchronize the melody track with the groove source at roughly measure boundaries, while maintaining the relative timing of the notes in each measure.

Fixing a bad verse. Copy a good verse to the Clipboard. Then change the selected range to cover only the bad verse. Perform a groove quantize using the Clipboard contents as the groove source. The rhythms of the two verses then match.

Fit Improvisation

SONAR lets you record music from a MIDI controller without requiring that you use a fixed tempo. In fact, if you record without using a metronome, you are very likely to end up with a recording that does not fit onto a fixed tempo grid.

The *Process-Fit Improvisation* command lets you take a recording and create a tempo map (with measure and beat boundaries) that fits what you played. Your performance is not changed in any way, even though the note start times and durations are adjusted to fit the new tempo map. This is important if you later want to use any of SONAR's editing features that depend on a proper tempo map for best results.

To use this command, you must record a reference track containing a single clip that matches your original track or tracks but has only a single note on each beat boundary. You should make sure that the reference track has one event for every single beat, with no extra beats or missing beats. The first beat of the reference track should be at 1:01:000. You can use any editing command to adjust the reference track.

If you want, you can use other types of events as markers on the reference track, such as a sustain pedal. Remember, however, that MIDI sustain pedals generate one event when the pedal is pressed and another when it is released. So if you want to use the sustain pedal for the reference track, keep this in mind. Click down, up, down, up, for one, two, three, four.

Remember that the better the quality of your reference track, the better job the *Fit Improvisation* command can do. You want each of your reference track events to be as close as possible to the beat of the music. Note that some keyboards transmit aftertouch events when you record your reference track. These extra events will prevent *Process-Fit Improvisation* from working properly. Therefore, you should delete these events before using this command, or filter them out when recording the reference track (using *Options-Global-MIDI*).

To Fit Tempos to an Improvisation

1. Record the reference track.
2. Select the reference track.
3. If necessary, combine all clips in the reference track into a single clip using the *Edit-Bounce to Clip(s)* command.
4. Choose *Process-Fit Improvisation*.

SONAR adds tempo changes as necessary to fit the tempo grid to the reference track. When you're done, you should mute the reference track, since the reference track events are not rescaled.

Note:

If the resulting tempo grid exceeds 250 beats per minute, you will see an error message. If this happens, you can shorten the start times of each event using the *Edit-Length* command, decrease the tempo to compensate for the change, and then try again.

Searching for Events

The events in a project have many different parameters. For example, all MIDI notes have a channel, starting time, pitch, velocity, and duration. Controllers have a controller number and value. SONAR makes it simple to find, select, and modify events that have certain values for specific attributes.

Here are some of the things you can do and the commands that you would use to do them:

Action...	Command...
Search through a project to find the first event that has specific attributes, and then search again to find the next such event	*Go-Search, Go-Search Next*
Select all the events in a project that have the specified attributes	*Edit-Select-By Filter*
Modify an existing selection to keep only those events that have the specified attributes	*Edit-Select-By Filter*
Replace all events that meet specified attributes with modified versions of the events	*Edit-Interpolate*

These capabilities can help you find problem spots or errors in a project or make systematic changes to events that have particular attributes. All of these capabilities rely on the use of an **event filter**, which lets you choose the types of events you want to work with and the range of values in which you are interested.

Event Filters

When you select individual clips, or select portions of clips by dragging the Time Ruler, you automatically select all the events that fall within the designated time range. Sometimes you need finer control over which events are selected. For example, you might want to:

- Select the notes that are played in a certain octave, so you can copy them to another track

- Select and boost the velocity of notes that have a velocity below a certain threshold

- Find the first patch change event on a particular track

- Select and change the duration of all notes that occur on the third beat of any measure

The Event Filter dialog box looks like this:

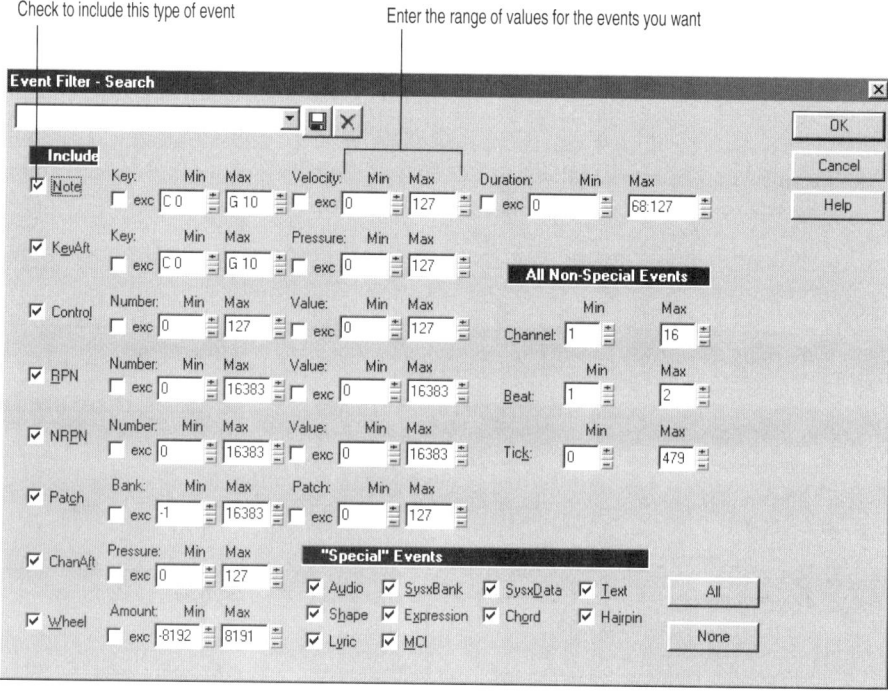

Different types of events have different parameters, as shown in the table:

This event type...	Has these parameters...
Note	Pitch, velocity, and duration
Key Aftertouch	Pitch and pressure value
Controller	Controller number and value
RPN/NRPN	RPN/NRPN number and value
Patch Change	Bank and patch numbers
Channel Aftertouch	Pressure value
Pitch Wheel	Value

The event filter only accepts events that meet all the specified ranges. This means that a note event must fall within the pitch range, the velocity range, and the duration range in order to be included. The event filter can also be used to accept events that occur in a range of channel numbers, beats, and clock ticks.

You can choose either to *include* or *exclude* the events that meet the specified criteria. To exclude events within the designated range and select the ones outside the designated range, check the **exc** checkbox for that value range.

The event filter can also be used to identify several special event types: audio, System Exclusive events, Lyrics, MCI commands, envelope shades, and a few others. You do not enter a range of values for these special events; SONAR finds all events of the types you choose.

The All and None buttons help you set up the event filter the way you want:

Click this button...	To do this...
All	Set the event filter to include all events. You can then modify the value ranges to narrow down your search or uncheck the types of events you want to exclude.
None	Set the event filter to *not* include any events. Starting from a blank slate, you can check off the types of events you want to find or select and enter the desired ranges of values.

In any place in the event filter where you would normally enter a pitch string, you can also enter the pitch by pressing a key on your MIDI keyboard. Also, you can use the question mark in place of the octave number as a wild card. This lets the event filter accept a single note, regardless of the octave. For example, the pitch string C? will match a C in any octave.

Searching for an Event

The *Go-Search* command is used to find the next event (searching forward from the Now time) that meets the criteria you lay out in an event filter. Once you have found the first such event, you can find the next event that meets the criteria using the *Go-Search Again* command (or by pressing F3).

To Search for an Event

1. Choose *Go-Search* to display the Event Filter dialog box.
2. Set up the event filter to find the events you want.
3. Click OK.

SONAR finds the next event that meets the criteria and sets the Now time to the start time of that event. To find the next occurrence, press F3 or choose *Go-Search Again*.

Selecting Events

The *Edit-Select-By Filter* command is used to refine a selection by applying an event filter to an initial selection. You can use this command any number of times to refine the selection even further. Before using this command, use any of the selection commands and tools to create an initial set of selected event. You can use the *Edit-Select-All* command to select all events in the current view.

The Track view cannot display individual selected events. As a result, the *Edit-Select-By Filter* command will not necessarily change the appearance of the Track view. SONAR applies the event filter rule, but the change is not visible. However, once you change the selection in any way (for example, by clicking on a track number or by clicking in the Time Ruler), the effects of the event filter are erased. If you want to use the filter, you must choose *Edit-Select-By Filter* again and click OK to use the same filter values.

Note:

The shading of a clip in the Track view indicates how many of the events in the clip are selected. If the clip is shown in solid black, all events in the clip are selected. If a portion of a clip is shown in medium gray, all the events in that time range are selected. If the clip is shown in light gray, only some of the events in the shaded time range are selected.

To Select Events Using the Event Filter

1. First, select an initial set of tracks, clips, or events.
2. Choose **Edit-Select-By Filter** to display the Event Filter dialog box.
3. Set up the event filter to find the events you want.
4. Click OK.

SONAR searches the currently selected events and weeds out those that do not meet the requirements of the event filter.

Example: Splitting Left-Hand and Right-Hand Parts

Suppose you recorded a keyboard riff on Track 1 but want to split the left and right hands apart into separate tracks so you can edit them separately. Suppose that all the right-hand notes are above C4. Here's how to proceed:

1. Select all of Track 1 by clicking on the track number in the Track view.
2. Choose **Edit-Select-By Filter** to display the Event Filter dialog box.
3. Click the None button to clear the dialog box.
4. Check the Note checkbox, and enter a minimum value of C4. The maximum should already be set to C9.
5. Click OK. SONAR selects all the notes from C4 up.
6. Choose **Edit-Cut** to move the selected notes to the clipboard.
7. Choose **Edit-Paste** and paste the events to a different track.

Process-Interpolate

The **Process-Interpolate** command is an extremely flexible way of manipulating the data parameters of events. It works something like the search-and-replace function in a word processor but with scaling rather than simple replacement.

This command uses two event filters. The first event filter lets you set up your search criteria. The second event filter is used to define the replacement value ranges. When an event satisfies the search criteria, its parameters are scaled between the search ranges and the replacement ranges. This permits transposition, inversion, key signature changes, and other operations to be accomplished with this one simple command.

In the second Event Filter dialog box, the checkboxes and value ranges for beats and ticks are ignored. Only the replacement value ranges for the selected event types are used.

The **Process-Interpolate** command understands a wild card octave number in the second event filter to mean, "replace the original note with a different note in the original octave." Using octave wild cards for both the search and replacement event filters lets you, for instance, change all E-flats to E-naturals, preserving the octave of each note.

A few examples will illustrate some of the many uses of the *Process-Interpolate* command. These examples apply to the note event type, though the command can be used on any type of event.

Parameter...	Search range...	Replacement range...	Effect...
Pitch (key)	From C2 to C4	From C4 to C6	Transposes all notes in the search range up two octaves
Pitch	From E2 to E2	From Eb2 to Eb2	Converts all Es in octave 2 to Eb in the same octave
Pitch	From E? to E?	From Eb? to Eb?	Converts all Es in all octaves to Eb in the same octave
Pitch	From E? to E?	From E? to Eb5	Converts all Es to Eb in octave 5
Pitch	From C1 to C8	From C8 to C1	Inverts all the notes in the specified range
Velocity	From 0 to 127	From 80 to 127	Compresses the velocity values into a narrower range
Velocity	From 0 to 127	From 127 to 0	Inverts the velocity values (makes loud notes soft, and soft notes loud)
Duration	From 0:01:00 to 0:02:000	From 0:01:000 to 0:01:000	Converts all notes that are between a quarter note and half note in length, and makes them all quarter notes
Channel	From 1 to 1	From 2 to 2	Changes all events on MIDI channel 1 to MIDI channel 2
Channel	From 1 to 16	From 4 to 4	Reassigns all events to MIDI channel 4

Controllers, RPNs, NRPNs, and Automation Data

SONAR projects contain a lot more information than the notes and digital audio files that are at the heart of your work. Controllers, RPNs, and NRPNs (xRPNs, for short) are special types of events used by MIDI software and hardware to control the details of how MIDI music is played. Automation data are used to adjust volume, pan, and other parameters of MIDI and audio tracks on the fly while playback is in progress.

SONAR lets you enter or edit controller, xRPN, and automation data in several ways:

- Using envelopes in the Track view (see Chapter 13, *Using Automation*)
- Using the Controllers pane in the Piano Roll view
- Using the **Insert-Series of Controllers** command
- Using the automation features of the Track view and Console view
- Event by event in the Event List view

Editing data in the Track view's Clips pane or the Piano Roll view's Controllers pane gives you great flexibility. You can examine the controllers in graphical form and edit them even while recording or playback is in progress. This means you can loop over a portion of your project and hear any change you make on the next loop.

Note: MIDI envelopes you create in the Piano Roll Controllers pane and MIDI envelopes you create in the Track view Clips pane are actually separate envelopes, even if they control the same parameter. Both kinds of envelopes are visible in the Clips pane, and should generally not be used to control the same parameter. You can convert Piano Roll view envelopes to Track view envelopes by selecting the time range and tracks that the Piano Roll envelopes occupy, and using the **Edit-Convert MIDI To Shapes** command.

For more information on automation, see Chapter 13, *Using Automation*, and Chapter 11, *Mixing and Effects Patching*. For more information about the Event List view, see "The Event List View" on page 318.

Controllers

Controllers are the MIDI events such as volume, sustain pedal, and pan that you use to change the sound while you're playing. You can enter controller data from within SONAR, or record them from external devices such as MIDI keyboards.

Controllers let you control the detail and character of your music. Say you're playing a guitar sound on your synthesizer, but it sounds lifeless and dull. That's partly because a guitar player doesn't just play notes one after another—he often bends or slides on the strings to put emotion into his playing. You can use controllers in the same way, creating bends, volume swells, and other effects that make sounds more realistic and more fun to listen to.

Your computer can work the controllers on your electronic instrument by sending MIDI Controller messages. The MIDI specification allows for 128 different types of controllers, many of which are used for standard purposes. For example, controller 7 is normally used for volume events, and controller 10 is normally used for pan. Every controller can take on a value ranging from 0 to 127.

The Piano Roll toolbar contains several dropdown lists that let you choose the controller you want to see and edit. The contents of these lists depend on the output and channel settings and on the instrument assigned to that output and channel. Different instruments use controllers in different ways. See Chapter 16, *Using Instrument Definitions*.

Note:

SONAR has automatic searchback for all continuous controller data to ensure that the correct controller values are in effect regardless of where you start playback. Suppose you start playback halfway through a project. SONAR searches back from that point to find any earlier controller values that should still apply.

RPNs and NRPNs

RPNs (Registered Parameter Numbers) and NRPNs (Non-Registered Parameter Numbers) are similar to controllers, except that both the parameter number and data value can be any number between 0 and 16,383.

When RPNs and NRPNs are transmitted via MIDI or stored in a standard MIDI file, they are converted into four separate controller messages. SONAR detects incoming xRPN messages from MIDI inputs or files and reassembles them into a single RPN or NRPN event. This provides the convenience of single RPN or NRPN events in SONAR plus compatibility with existing files, equipment, and software. The following table shows the controller numbers SONAR uses for RPN and NRPN events:

Message...	Parameter number MSB Controller...	Parameter number LSB Controller...	Data value MSB Controller...	Data value LSB Controller...
RPN	101	100	6	38
NRPN	99	98	6	38

Automation Data

The Track and Console views allow you to record automation data that define changes in volume, pan and many other parameters throughout a project. The automation data can include step changes recorded using the snapshot button or continuous changes recorded while using the knobs, faders, and buttons.

The Track view allows you to create envelopes to adjust several parameters. For more about automation, see Chapter 13, *Using Automation*.

Velocity, Pitch Wheel, and Aftertouch

SONAR lets you display and edit several other types of data the same way you do controller data. These data include:

- MIDI note velocities
- MIDI pitch wheel or pitch-bend messages
- MIDI channel aftertouch (ChanAft) values
- MIDI key aftertouch (KeyAft) values

Remember that note velocity is an attribute of each note and not a completely separate event. You cannot add or remove velocity events in the Controllers pane, but you can use the line and draw tools to adjust the velocity values for existing notes. You can also edit velocities with the ***Edit-Scale Velocities*** command. For more information, see "Adding Crescendos and Decrescendos" on page 290. You can edit individual note velocities in the Note Properties dialog box, described in "Changing Note Properties" on page 536.

Using the Controllers Pane

The Controllers pane is the lower half of the Piano Roll view.

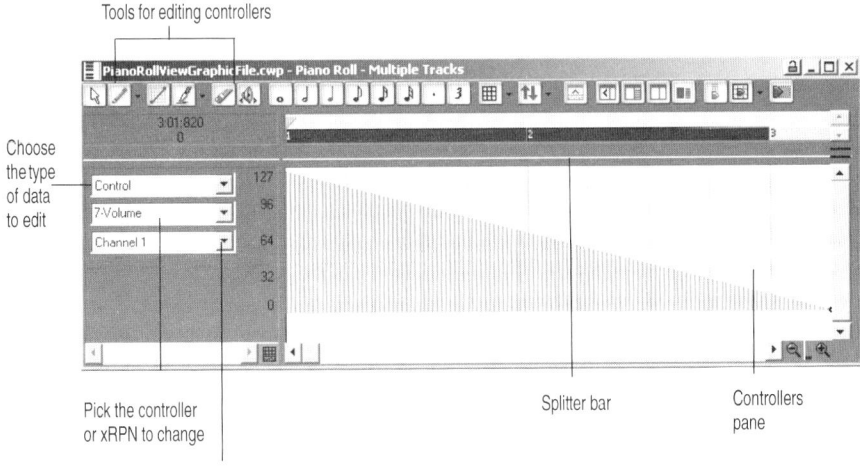

The Controllers pane looks like a graph; the horizontal axis represents time, and the vertical axis represents the event values. Each event appears as a single vertical line, and the height of this line shows the value of the event. The Controllers pane shows events for all the clips in a track or multiple tracks. You can only see one type of controller at a time, and you must select All Channels from the Channel dropdown list to view more than a single MIDI channel. The exception is velocity data, which are not channel specific. You can zoom in and out on the Controllers pane using the zoom and unzoom buttons on the toolbar. To zoom all the way in or out in a single step, hold the Shift key while you click on the tool.

Selection methods in the Controllers pane are similar to those in other views. Here is a summary:

- Click on a controller to select it
- Shift-click to add other controllers to the selection
- Ctrl-click to toggle the selection state of a controller
- Drag a rectangle around several controllers to select them
- Click and drag in the Time Ruler to select all controllers in a time range
- Click between two markers to select the controllers that lie between the markers

The Controllers pane has several tools you can use to add or modify events. The following tools apply only to the track that is selected in the Track List pane:

Tool...	Name...	What it's for...
	Select	Select controller events, so you can delete them
	Draw Line	Draw a straight line indicating a steady increase or decrease in controller value
	Draw	Draw a custom curve indicating changes in controller value. Draw a straight line by holding down the Shift key while using the Draw tool.
	Erase	Erase controller changes already in place

Note that you can also add controllers using the *Insert-Series of Controllers* command. If you make a mistake using any of these tools or commands, you can use *Undo* to correct the error.

When you use the Draw tool, the speed with which you drag the mouse determines the density of controller events. To insert a larger number of controller events with relatively small changes in value, move the mouse slowly. To insert a smaller number of controller events with relatively large changes in value, drag the mouse quickly.

Creating a change that sounds smooth does not always require making the value change by one on each tick. Bigger jumps may sound very gradual if the tempo is fast. Also, many devices round off the controller values. For example, many instruments respond to volume controller values of 100 and 101 with exactly the same loudness. Using too high a density of controller events can backfire by making the computer work so hard during playback that it is unable to keep up. This will usually cause hiccups or poor timing during playback.

To Display Controller, RPN, NRPN, Velocity, Pitch-Bend, or Aftertouch Data

1. Select the track whose controller or xRPN data you want to see by clicking on the track number in the Track view.
2. Choose *View-Piano Roll* to display the Piano Roll view.
3. Click the Show/Hide Controller Pane button .
4. Choose the data you want to see according to the table:

To see this...	Do this...
Controller data	Choose Control from the first dropdown list in the toolbar, and then choose the controller and channel from the second and third dropdown lists
RPN or NRPN data	Choose RPN or NRPN from the first dropdown list in the toolbar, choose which RPN or NRPN you want from the second dropdown list, and choose the channel from the third dropdown list
Velocity data	Choose Velocity from the first dropdown list
Pitch-bend data	Choose Wheel from the first dropdown list, and the MIDI channel from the third dropdown list
Aftertouch data	Choose ChanAft from the first dropdown list, and the MIDI channel from the third dropdown list

SONAR displays the data in the controllers pane.

To Insert a Controller Value

1. In the Controllers pane, choose the data type, controller or xRPN number, and channel (if applicable) from the lists in the toolbar.
2. Select the Draw tool or the Draw Line tool .
3. Click in the Controllers pane view at any desired time point and value.

SONAR adds a controller at the indicated point.

To Draw a Linear Series of Controllers
1. Choose the data type, controller or xRPN number, and channel (if applicable) from the lists in the toolbar.
2. Select the ✎ tool.
3. Drag a line in the Controllers pane from the starting time and value to the ending time and value.

SONAR adds a series of controllers and erases any existing controller values in the same time interval.

To Draw a Series of Controller Value Changes
1. Choose the data type, controller or xRPN number, and channel (if applicable) from the lists in the toolbar.
2. Select the Draw tool ✎.
3. Drag the cursor across the Controllers pane, adjusting the value as you move left to right.

SONAR adds a series of controllers and erases any existing controller values in the same time interval.

Tip:
When using the Draw tool ✎, you can press and hold the Shift key to draw a straight line.

To Insert a Series of Controllers
1. Choose *Insert-Series of Controllers* to display the Insert Series of Controllers dialog box.
2. Choose the controller type from the Insert list.
3. Choose the controller number or type from the Number list.
4. Use the spinners or enter the desired MIDI channel.
5. Enter a starting and ending value in the Begin and End boxes.
6. Enter a starting and ending time in the From and Thru boxes.
7. Click OK when you are done.

SONAR inserts a series of controller events with values that change smoothly over time from the starting to the ending value indicated in the dialog box. This command never inserts more than one event on the same clock tick. If any controllers of the type you have selected already exist in the time region, SONAR deletes these before inserting the new ones.

To Remove or Erase Controllers

1. Choose the data type, controller or xRPN number, and channel (if applicable) from the lists in the toolbar.
2. Select the Eraser tool .
3. Drag the mouse over the desired region to highlight the region you want to erase.
4. Release the mouse button when you have highlighted the desired region.

SONAR deletes all controllers of the selected type. (Note that you cannot delete velocity events in the Controllers pane. You must delete the notes that have those velocities.)

To Convert MIDI Controller Envelopes to Shapes

1. In the Clips pane, select the time range and track(s) that contain the controller data you want to convert.
2. Use the **Edit-Convert MIDI To Shapes** command.

   The Convert MIDI To Shapes dialog box appears.
3. In the Type field, select the type of controller you want to convert.
4. In the Value field, select the controller number of the controller you want to convert. For example, if you're converting a volume envelope to a shape, select 7.
5. In the Channel field, select the channel of the controller you want to convert, and click OK.

SONAR converts the Piano Roll view controller envelope you selected to a Track view shape that controls the same parameter.

Note: If two clips overlap, the **Edit-Convert MIDI To Shapes** command converts the controller envelopes in both clips, in whatever parts of the clips lie in the selected time range.

The Event List View

The Event List view shows events in a list format. You can insert, delete, or modify any kind of event, including notes, pitch-wheel data, velocity, MIDI controllers, patch changes, Wave files, lyrics, text strings, MCI commands, System Exclusive meta-events, and more.

There are three ways to open the Event List view:

- Select one or more tracks and choose **View-Event List**
- Select one or more tracks and click [icon] in the Views toolbar
- Right-click a clip in the Clips pane and choose **View-Event List** from the popup menu

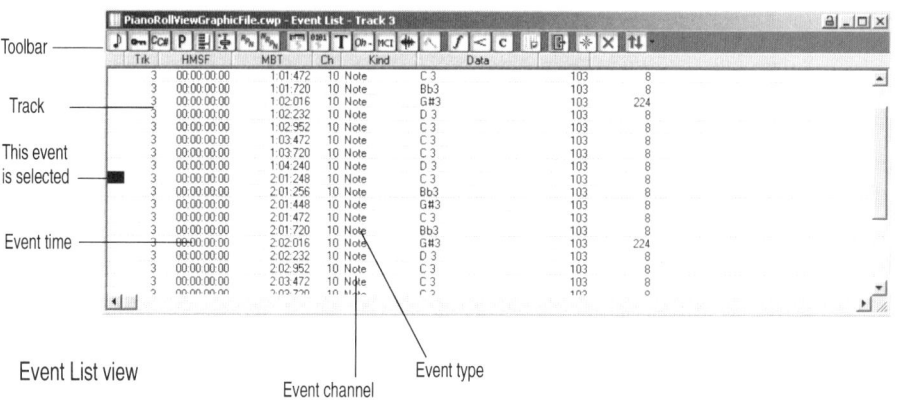

Event List view

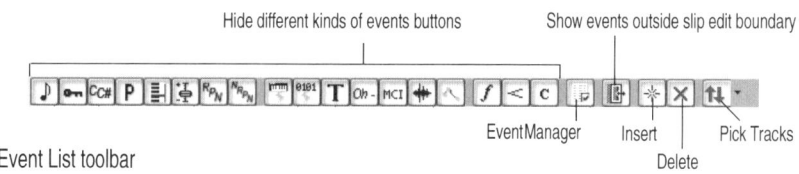

Event List toolbar

The events in the selected tracks are listed one per line, from top to bottom. As you move the highlight through the event list, SONAR updates the Now marker (time display). During playback, the event list scrolls to display the events at the current time. The current event is centered in the Event List during playback, and the highlight is on the correct event when playback stops. Any time you change the Now time, the event list is updated and the highlight is moved to the event that will be played next.

When the Event List view includes more than one track, events are mixed together in chronological order. For example, if you select tracks 1 and 3 when you open the Event List view, you see a single list of intermingled events from tracks 1 and 3. You can have any number of Event List views, each containing any number of tracks, open at the same time. You can change the tracks shown in the Event List view by clicking the ⇅▼ button and choosing the tracks you want.

Event List Buttons and Overview

Each line of the Event List view shows a single event along with all of its parameters. There are many different types of events. All share the following parameters:

- The time of the event, displayed in SMPTE (hours:minutes:seconds:frames) format
- The time of the event, displayed in MBT (measures:beats:ticks) format
- The event type, or **kind** of event

The remaining parameters vary by event type. You can hide or show each kind of event by clicking its button in the Event List toolbar or by checking its checkbox in the Event Manager dialog box. Here is a summary listing of the parameters that apply to each type of event.

Short name and display button...	Type of event...	Parameters...
Note ♪	MIDI note	Pitch (MIDI key number), velocity (0-127), duration (beats:ticks or simply ticks), MIDI channel (1-16)
KeyAft	MIDI key aftertouch	Pitch (MIDI key number), pressure amount (0-127), MIDI channel (1-16)
Control CC#	MIDI controller change	Controller number (0-127), controller value (0-127), MIDI channel (1-16)
Patch P	MIDI patch change	Bank select method, bank number, number or name of the patch, MIDI channel (1-16)
ChanAft	MIDI channel aftertouch	Pressure amount (0-127), MIDI channel (1-16)
Wheel	MIDI pitch wheel position	Wheel position (-8192 to 8191, where the center is 0)
RPN	Registered Parameter Number	Parameter number (0-16383), parameter value (0-16383), MIDI channel (1-16)

319

NRPN	Non-registered Parameter Number	Parameter number (0-16383), parameter value (0-16383), MIDI channel (1-16)
Sysx Bank	System Exclusive data bank	Sysx bank number (0-8191)
Sysx Data	System Exclusive data message	Sysx message up to 255 bytes long
Text	Text	Text
Lyric	Lyric	Text (a single word or syllable)
MCIcmd	Windows Media Control Interface (MCI) command	MCI command text
Wave Audio	Digital audio wave	Name, velocity (0-127), and number of samples
Shape Events	Automation graph segments made up of a solid line between two nodes	Change in values, kind of shape, and length in MBT format. Note: Shape events cannot be edited, only deleted.
Expression	Staff view expression marking	Text of expression mark
Hairpin	Staff view dynamics marking	Direction (crescendo or diminuendo) and duration
Chord	Staff view chord symbol	The name of the chord
Event List Manager	Opens Event Manager dialog box	Shows or hides various kinds of events
Events Out of Slip Edit Boundaries	Events that are outside of slip-edited boundaries	Note, audio, or controller data
Insert Event	Inserts a copy of highlighted event—double-click the event's Kind parameter to change it to the kind of event you want	Whatever the highlighted event's parameters are
Delete Event	Deletes the highlighted event	Whatever the highlighted event's parameters are

Pick Tracks and Show Next/Previous Track	Left side of button opens Pick Tracks dialog; right side of button opens Next Track/Previous Track dropdown menu	Allows you to pick what tracks the Event List shows events for

Here are some notes about events and their parameters:

- The Channel parameter in the Track view can force an event to play on a different MIDI channel from the one shown in the event list.
- Pedal marks entered in the Staff view are displayed in the Event List view as controller events (64).
- Many keyboards do not support key aftertouch and channel aftertouch. Consult the *User's Guide* for your keyboard for more information.
- When you double-click the value of a patch event, SONAR displays the Bank/Patch Change dialog box. For more information about bank and patch changes, "To Insert a Bank/Patch Change" on page 138.
- See Chapter 17, *Using System Exclusive Data*, for more information about System Exclusive banks.
- See Chapter 9, *Editing Audio*, for more information about audio clips.

Selecting Events in the Event List View

The following table describes how to select events in the Event List view:

To do this...	Do this...
Select a single event	Click on the event.
Select multiple, contiguous events	Select the first event, hold the Shift key down and click the last event.
Select multiple, contiguous events using the arrow keys	Hold down the Ctrl and Shift keys while pressing the up or down arrows.
Select multiple, non-contiguous events	Select an event, hold the Ctrl key while selecting additional events

Additional information about note events and MCIcmd events appears later in this chapter.

Event List Display Filter

You can configure the Event List view to display different event types, as described in the following table:

To do this...	Do this...
Hide events of a certain type	Select the event type in the toolbar, in the Event List view popup menu, or in the Event Manager. To display a type of event, deselect it.
Open the Event Manager	Choose **Event Manager** from the popup menu, or click .
Show or hide slip-edited events	As a default, if you slip edit the boundaries of a clip, all events outside those boundaries are hidden in the Event List view. If you want to see these events, click this button . **Note:** You can not edit slip-edited material in the Event List view.

Editing Events and Event Parameters

The Event List view lets you add, delete, or change events one by one. You can also print the list of events or audition the events one at a time to see how they sound.

You can change the parameters of any event by moving the rectangular highlight to the cell you want to change and doing one of the following:

- Type a new value and then press Enter

- Press the - and + keys on the numeric keypad to decrease or increase values by a small amount

- Press the [and] keys to decrease or increase values by a larger amount

- Click and hold the mouse button, and then drag the mouse up or down to change the value by a small amount

- Click and hold both mouse buttons, and then drag the mouse up or down to change the value by a larger amount

- Double-click a cell, and then enter or choose a new value

If you change the time of an event, it may also change its position in the event list. The Event List view follows that event to its new location.

If you try to change the event type (kind of event), SONAR lets you choose the kind of event you want from a dialog box. When you change one kind of MIDI event into another kind of MIDI event, SONAR preserves the parameters as fully as possible.

Note: Shape events cannot be edited, only deleted.

To Insert a New Event
1. Move the highlight (use the mouse or arrow keys) to the point at which you want to insert an event.
2. Press Insert, or click ⁕. SONAR makes a copy of the highlighted event.
3. Change the event to the kind of event you need by double-clicking the name of the event that's listed in the Kind column. The Kind of Event dialog box appears.
4. Choose what kind of event you want and click OK. SONAR changes the highlighted event to the kind you chose.
5. Edit the event time and other parameter values as required.

If the Event List is initially empty, pressing the Insert key creates a default note event.

To Delete an Event
1. Move the highlight (use the mouse or arrow keys) to the event you want to delete.
2. Press Delete, or click ✗.

SONAR deletes the event.

To Delete Several Events
1. Select the events you want to delete by clicking, dragging, or Ctrl or Shift-clicking in the first column of the Event List view.
2. Choose *Edit-Cut*.

SONAR deletes the selected events.

To Print the Event List
1. Choose *File-Print Preview* to display a preview of the printed event listing.
2. Click the Zoom button (or just click the page) to zoom in and out, and use the Page Up and Page Down keys to review the pages.
3. Click Print to print the event list, or click Close to close the Preview window without printing.

To Play Events Step by Step

1. Using the keyboard, hold the Shift key and press the Spacebar to play the currently highlighted event. If the event is a note event, it plays until you release the Spacebar.

2. When you release the Spacebar, the highlight moves to the next event.

3. Continue pressing the Spacebar to play events one by one.

4. To edit the last event you heard, release the Shift key.

The highlight moves back to the last event you heard, so you can make changes. You can also audition a single event using the mouse. Ctrl-click on an event to play the event. If the event is a note or Wave event, it plays until you release the mouse button.

Additional Event Information

Note Events—There are three values parameters for note events:

- A pitch, which represents the MIDI key number as a note and an octave.

- A velocity (0–127), which is how fast the key is struck. Some keyboards don't transmit or receive velocity messages.

- A duration, which is how long the note lasts. This amount is shown in beats:ticks format. (If the note lasts less then one beat, then only the number of ticks is shown.)

Note names may also represent percussion instruments, and lists of such note names are sometimes associated with a particular percussion patch. The note C3, for example, may really be "kick drum." If a patch is associated with a percussion note name list, the name of the percussion instrument appears in Event List view rather than a note and an octave from the piano keyboard.

SONAR uses the following notation to display flats and sharps in this and other views:

Character...	Meaning...
b	flat
#	sharp
"	double flat
x	double sharp

MCIcmd Events

Media Control Interface (MCI) commands are special events that let you control other multimedia hardware and software (e.g., CD-ROM drives, laserdiscs, sound cards, animations, video) during playback. MCI commands are part of the multimedia extensions in Windows. MCIcmd events have one parameter—the command line text of the MCI command. Here are some examples:

This command...	Does this...
PLAY C:\TRAIN.WAV	Plays the Wave file TRAIN.WAV
PLAY C:\VIDEOS\VACATION.AVI	Plays the video file VACATION.AVI from the VIDEOS folder
SET CDAUDIO TIME FORMAT TMSF PLAY CDAUDIO 3	Plays a specific track from the CD drive
STOP CDAUDIO	Stops the CD from playing

While MCI commands can be used to play Wave files, these files are played at their normal speed and are not necessarily synchronized with MIDI or other audio data. By contrast, Wave audio clips are played in lock-step synchronization with MIDI and other audio data.

For complete documentation of Windows MCI commands, search for MCI on the Microsoft World Wide Web site (www.microsoft.com).

MIDI Effects (MIDI Plug-ins)

SONAR provides the ability to use plug-in MIDI effects. Using plug-in effects is similar to using the MIDI processing commands off-line. The overall procedure is as follows:

- Select the MIDI data to be affected.
- Choose the effect you want from the **Process-MIDI Effects** menu or from the popup menu's **MIDI Effects** menu.
- Set effect parameters (or select a preset if you've made one for this purpose).
- Click Audition to preview the music with the effect applied.
- Click OK to apply the effect to the selected MIDI data.

If you're not happy with the result, choose **Edit-Undo** before doing any additional work.

MIDI effects can be applied to whole or partial clips. For example, you can apply an echo to just one note.

MIDI effects can also be applied to MIDI tracks in real time (during playback) in the Track and Console views. Unlike any of the processing described so far, using effects in real time is non-destructive. This means that the MIDI data itself is not modified. See "Mixing and Effects Patching" on page 419 for more information on real-time effects.

Note:
Offline effects may cause your MIDI events to grow in size. For example, when you apply echo, the clip may need to grow to accommodate the tail end of the echo.

Presets

The MIDI effects dialog boxes support the use of presets. Presets are a way to store dialog box settings so that you can apply the exact same processing or effect again in the future. The following table tells you how to use presets:

To do this...	Do this...
Save the current settings as a preset	Enter a preset name and click the Save button 💾
Use a preset	Select the preset from the dropdown list
Delete a preset	Select the preset, then click the Delete button ❌

Quantizing

The ***Quantize*** command moves events to (or towards) an evenly-spaced timing grid. The Quantize effect is similar to the ***Process-MIDI Effects-Cakewalk FX-Quantize*** command. For more information, see "Other Settings" on page 298.

The quantize effect parameters are as follows:

Parameter/ Option...	Meaning...
Start Times	Quantize event start times.
Durations	Quantize event durations.
Resolution	The spacing of the grid used for quantization.
Tuplet	Specify the resolution as a tuplet note, for example 5 notes in the time of 4.
Strength (%)	The strength of the adjustments. 100% indicates perfect quantization; otherwise, the command moves the notes only part way towards the desired position.
Swing (%)	The distortion of timing used to produce a swing feel. A value of 50% indicates a straight rendition; negative and positive values produce distortion of the timing grid. For more information about swing, see "Swing" on page 297.
Window (%)	The sensitivity of quantization. A value of 100% causes all notes to be quantized. Lower values cause the effect not to quantize notes that are far from the timing grid.
Offset (Ticks)	The offset of the quantization grid from the start of measure boundaries. A value of 0 indicates perfect alignment. Values less than 0 shift the grid points earlier; values greater than 0 shift the grid later.
Randomize	Causes a random time offset to be added to or subtracted from each new event time. You must also specify the maximum offset, as a percentage of the quantization resolution.

To Quantize MIDI Data

1. Select the data to be affected.
2. Choose ***MIDI Effects-Quantize*** from the ***Process*** menu or from the popup menu to open the Quantize dialog box.
3. Set the quantization parameters, as described in the table above.
4. Click OK.

SONAR applies the specified quantization to the selected data.

Adding Echo/Delay

The *Echo Delay* command creates a series of repeating echoes of each note. The echo notes can decrease or increase in velocity, and can be transposed from the original by regular intervals.

The parameters used to specify the echo/delay effect are as follows:

Parameter/ Option...	Meaning...
Decay (%)	The reduction in velocity with each echo. A value greater than 100% indicates an increase in velocity.
No. Echoes	The number of echo notes for each original note. If the velocity reaches 0 before the specified number of echoes, the effect generates no more echo notes.
Delay	The delay between successive echo notes.
Delay Units	The units used to specify the delay. You may specify delay in ticks, in milliseconds, or as a note duration.
Tap	The delay you specify by tapping the control with the mouse.
Swing (%)	The distortion of timing used to produce a swing feel to the echo. A value of 0% indicates a straight rendition; negative and positive values produce distortion of the timing grid. For more information about swing, see "Swing" on page 297.
Transpose (Steps)	The number of steps to transpose each echo note from the previous. You can specify a Diatonic or Chromatic scale.

To Apply Echo/Delay to MIDI Data

1. Select the data to be affected.
2. Choose **MIDI Effects-Cakewalk FX-Echo Delay** from the **Process** menu or from the popup menu to open the Echo Delay dialog box.
3. Set the echo/delay parameters, as described in the table above.
4. Click OK.

SONAR applies the specified echo effect to the selected data.

Filtering Events

The *Event Filter* command lets you remove events from the MIDI data, keeping or passing through only those events that you specify. The Event Filter effect works almost identically to the event filter used by the *Edit-Select-By Filter* command. For more information, see "Event Filters" on page 306.

To Apply an Event Filter to MIDI Data

1. Select the data to be affected.
2. Choose *MIDI Effects-Cakewalk FX-Event Filter* from the *Process* menu or from the popup menu to open the Event Filter dialog box.
3. Set the event filter parameters.
4. Click OK.

SONAR applies the specified event filter to the selected data, removing all those events that do not meet the filter criteria.

Adding Arpeggio

The *Arpeggiator* command applies an arpeggio to its input and plays it back in real time. You can make it arpeggiate with a swing feel, or straight and staccato or legato, vary its speed and direction, and specify its range.

The parameters used to specify the arpeggiator effect are as follows:

Parameter/Option...	Meaning...
Swing (%)	The distortion of timing used to produce a swing feel. A value of 0% indicates a straight rendition; negative and positive values produce distortion of the timing grid. For more information on swing, see "Swing" on page 297.
Rate	The delay between successive notes.
Units	The units used to specify the delay. You may specify delay in ticks, in milliseconds, or as a note duration.
Legato (%)	The smoothness of the notes of the arpeggio. 1 percent plays each notes and releases it instantly. 99 percent plays each note up to the start of the next note.
Path	The direction of the arpeggio. Options are *Up, Up* (arpeggios go up), *Up, Down* (arpeggios go up, then down), *Down, Down* (arpeggios go down), *Down, Up* (arpeggios go down, then up).
Play thru	The disposition of the notes you play to specify the arpeggio. Checked plays the original notes. Unchecked filters out the original notes.

Specify output range	The range over which the arpeggio plays. Checked specifies that the arpeggiator repeats notes at each octave over the entire specified range. Unchecked specifies that the arpeggiator includes only the notes you actually play.
Lowest note	The MIDI number of the lowest note of the arpeggio. Numbers run from 0 to 127.
Span (Notes)	The number of half-steps in the range. Numbers run from 12 to 127.
Use chord control	The chord you specify. Checked specifies that the arpeggiator infers the chord from the notes played in the range. It identifies the chord in the Chord recognized box and uses it to play arpeggios for notes outside the range.
Lowest note	The MIDI number of the lowest note the arpeggiator uses for chord recognition (0 to 126).
Span (Notes)	The number of half-steps in the range. Numbers run from 1 to 127.
Chord recognized	The chord the Arpeggiator recognizes and plays.

To Apply the Arpeggiator to MIDI Data

1. Select the data to be affected.
2. Choose **MIDI Effects-Cakewalk FX-Arpeggiator** from the **Process** menu or from the popup menu to open the Arpeggiator dialog box.
3. Set the arpeggiator parameters, as described in the table above.
4. Click OK.

SONAR applies the specified arpeggio effect to the selected data.

Analyzing Chords

The **Chord Analyzer** command analyzes chords. You select the notes to be analyzed in one of SONAR's windows, then open the Chord analyzer and press the Audition button. The chord appears on the MIDI display and the staff, and its name with possible alternatives appears in the Chords recognized box.

You can play the notes on your MIDI input device and have the Chord Analyzer identify the chords in real time. You do not have to set to playback.

You can open the Chord Analyzer in the Track and Console views, press Playback and have the Chord Analyzer identify the chords in real time

The Chord Analyzer has a single parameter:

Parameter/ Option...	Meaning...
Examine every x (MIDI ticks)	The frequency with which the Chord Analyzer samples the chord. Lower numbers (smaller intervals) are more accurate, but require more computation.

To Analyze a Chord
1. Select the notes to be analyzed.
2. Choose **MIDI Effects-Cakewalk FX-Chord Analyzer** from the **Process** menu or from the popup menu to open the Transpose dialog box.
3. Click the Audition key.

SONAR displays the chord and its name.

To clear the display, press the Clear button.

Note: When analyzing chords you may see chords being displayed before you hear them. You can reduce the amount of time these chords appear ahead of playback. To do so, open the MIDI tab in the Global Options dialog (**Options-Global**) and enter a lower value in the Prepare Using "N" Milliseconds Buffer option. Excessively low values may cause glitches during playback, so it is best to gradually reduce the value in this option until the desired result is achieved.

Changing Velocities

The **Velocity** command lets you adjust velocities of MIDI notes. You can set velocity values, set scale values, add specific or random offsets, create smooth transitions, and limit the velocity range.

The velocity effect options are as follows:

Parameter/ Option...	Meaning...
Set all velocities to X	Sets all velocities to the specified value.
Change velocities by X	Adds a specified increment to all velocities.
Scale velocities to X% of their current value	Multiplies all velocities by a constant factor.
Change gradually from X to Y	Creates a smooth velocity change across the selection.

Change gradually from X% to Y%	Scales velocities by a gradually changing factor.
Limit range from X to Y	Brings all velocities into the specified range.
Randomize by +/- X	Adds or subtracts a random offset from each velocity. You must also specify the maximum offset. You can select this option in addition to one of the previous options.
Tendency	The tendency of the random offset to be lower or higher, on a scale from -10 to 10.

To Change Note Velocities

1. Select the data to be affected.
2. Choose **MIDI Effects-Cakewalk FX-Velocity** from the **Process** menu or from the popup menu to open the Velocity dialog box.
3. Select options as described in the table above.
4. Click OK.

SONAR changes note velocities according to the specified options.

Transposing MIDI Notes

The **Process-MIDI Effects-Cakewalk FX-Transpose** command is a flexible transposition feature. You can perform simple chromatic or diatonic transpositions, transpose from one key to another, or define your own custom transposition.

The transpose options are as follows:

Parameter/ Option...	Meaning...
Interval	Specifies chromatic transposition. Transposes notes by the specified number of steps.
Diatonic	Specifies diatonic transposition. Transposes notes by the specified number of scale steps within the specified scale.
Key/Scale	Specifies transposition from one scale and key to another.
Custom Map	Specifies custom transposition as defined by the map.

Offset	For Interval transposition, the number of steps for the transposition. For Diatonic Transposition, the number of scale degrees for the transposition. For Key/Scale transposition, a number of octaves added to each note after transposition.
Key	For Diatonic transposition, the key in which the transposition is made.
From, To	For Key/Scale transposition, the starting and ending key and scale.
Transposition Map	A table of pitch mappings for the specified transposition. You can select to show the pitches as note names or as note numbers. For Diatonic and Key/Scale transpositions, pitches not in the starting (from) key are indented. To Change a pitch mapping, click on a From pitch and select a To pitch with the popup slider. If you change a pitch mapping, the transposition type is automatically set to Custom Map.
Constrain to Scale	For Diatonic and Key/Scale transpositions, forces all non-scale notes to be transposed to the nearest appropriate scale tone.

To Transpose MIDI Data

1. Select the data to be affected.

2. Choose **MIDI Effects-Cakewalk FX-Transpose** from the **Process** menu or from the popup menu to open the Transpose dialog box.

3. Set the transposition options as described in the table above.

4. Click OK.

SONAR transposes the selected data according to the options you specified.

8 Drum Maps and the Drum Grid Pane

There are several panes in the Piano Roll view designed for use with MIDI drum tracks: the Note Map pane which lists the original pitch values and the mapped values for each note, and the Drum Grid pane which displays your drum tracks (any track assigned to a drum map) and where you can edit your drum tracks.

In This Chapter

The Basics.	336
Creating and Editing a Drum Map	336
Using Drum Maps	340
The Note Map Pane.	342
The Drum Grid Pane	344
The Pattern Brush Tool	345

The Basics

Drum maps are virtual MIDI ports that you create and edit. Drum maps give you total control over all the MIDI drum sounds you have access to either in the form of software (DXi synths) or hardware (external MIDI sound modules).

Drum maps in SONAR allow you to do the following:

- Re-map note events, for example, map a General MIDI drum kit to a non-General MIDI drum kit.
- Create a custom drum kit from several MIDI devices (DXi synths, hardware synths) and play it from a single MIDI track if desired.
- Use the Drum Grid Editor to show only the drum sounds you want to see.
- Sort drum sounds to suit your needs.
- Mute and solo individual drum sounds

Creating and Editing a Drum Map

You can create a drum map by either modifying an existing drum map or by creating a new drum map.

The Drum Map Manager

In the Drum Map Manager dialog you can create and save drum maps for use with hardware or software synths and samplers. You can customize drum maps to select specific sounds on any of your available sound sources.

To Open the Drum Map Manager Dialog

You can open the Drum Map manager in one of the following ways:

- Select *Options-Drum Map Manager* from the menu

  Or

- Click on the Output field of your MIDI drum track and select *Drum Map Manager*

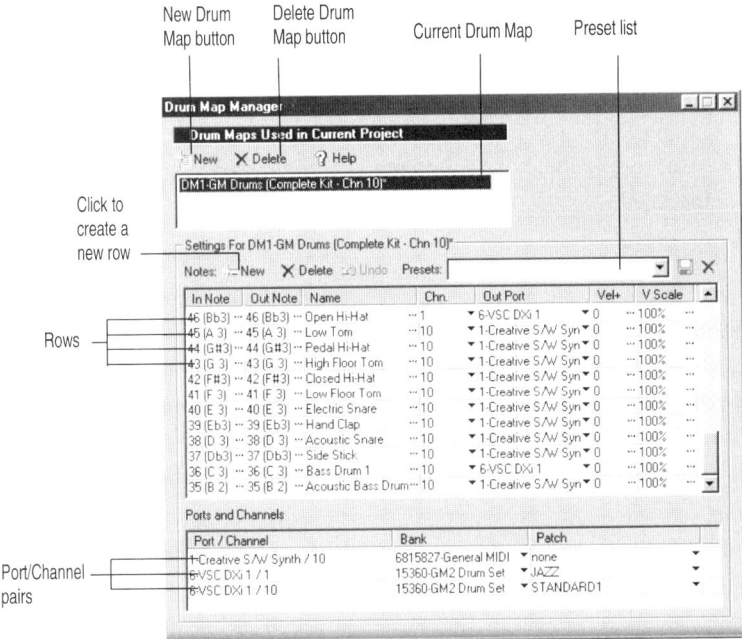

Drum Maps Used in Current Project

This field displays all the currently available drum maps. click the New button to create a new drum map and Delete to delete a drum map. Select a drum map to display the drum mappings in the Drum Map Manager. All drum maps in this field are saved with the current project.

Presets

Presets can be used to populate the fields in the Drum Map Manager. This field is also used to save new drum maps by entering a name in the field and clicking the save button.

Settings

The Settings section is where you map the following for each In Note (source):

- In Note—The source MIDI note value.
- Out Note—The MIDI note value that plays on the destination sound source.
- Name—The user-defined name for the row.
- Chn—The channel on which the note is transmitted.
- Out Port—The hardware output port or software virtual output port to which you are sending the note.
- Vel+—Apply a velocity offset setting to an individual mapped pitch.
- V Scale—The V Scale value sets a level of compression or expansion. A value below 100% is compression. A value above 100% is expansion. The Vel+ setting allows for gain make-up.

Ports and Channels

This section lists each unique Port and Channel pairing. This allows you to make quick global changes that Port and Channel pairing's bank and patch settings.

Working in the Drum Map Manager

The following table lists several ways of editing settings in the Drum Map Manager.

To do this...	Do this...
Audition a row	Select the row and press Shift+Spacebar
Sort rows	Drag and drop a row to a new location
Select multiple rows	Click a row, hold down the Ctrl key while selecting additional rows
Change the Output Port for all rows with the same Channel/Port	Press Ctrl+Shift while changing the port.
Undo an edit	Press the Undo button ↶ Undo

The Map Properties Dialog

The Map Properties dialog lets you change all the settings for an individual mapped note in your drum map. The settings in the Map Properties dialog are the same as a single row in the Drum Map Manager. If you want to edit more than one drum note pitch mapping, click the Map Mgr button to open the Drum Map Manager dialog.

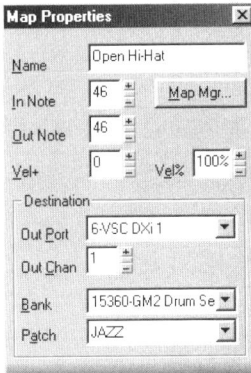

To Open the Map Properties Dialog
- Double-click on a row in the Note Map pane.

   Or

- Right-click on a row in the Note Map pane and select **Map Properties** from the menu that appears.

Saving a Drum Map

Use the following procedure to save a new or modified drum map.

1. In the Drum Map Manager, enter a name for the new drum map in the Preset field.

2. Click the Save button 💾.

Drum map presets are saved and available for all projects. Drum maps are saved on a per-project basis.

Using Drum Maps

The following topics cover using drum-mapped tracks, including how to display drum tracks in the Drum Grid pane and how to edit note velocities.

Assigning a MIDI Track to a Drum Map

Use the following procedure to assign a MIDI track to a drum map:

To Assign a MIDI Track to a Drum Map
1. Display the Track view if it is minimized.
2. In the track you want to assign to a drum map, click the Output dropdown and select a drum map from the options in the menu that appears.

Opening a Drum Map

Use the following procedure to open a drum map in the Drum pane:

To Open a Drum Map
1. In the Track view, assign the drum map you want to open to a MIDI track. See "Assigning a MIDI Track to a Drum Map" on page 340.
2. Select the MIDI track you just assigned the drum map to and select *View-Piano Roll*.

To Open All Tracks Assigned to a Drum Map
1. Select a single track assigned to the drum map.
2. Hold down Ctrl+Shift while selecting *View-Piano Roll*.

Displaying Tracks in the Drum Grid Pane

Use the following procedure to display a drum track or tracks in the Drum Grid pane.

To Display Tracks in the Drum Grid
1. Create a drum map if you have not already done so. See Creating and Editing a Drum Map"Creating and Editing a Drum Map" on page 336.
2. Change the focus to the Track view.
3. In the track(s) you want to view in the Drum Grid Editor, select a drum map from the Output dropdown menu.
4. Select the tracks you want to view in the Drum Grid Editor and select *View-Piano Roll*.

The Piano Roll view appears with the selected track's data appearing in the Drum Grid Editor.

Velocity Tails

In the Drum Grid pane, you have the option of showing the velocity of each note as a series of bars. The higher the bars, the higher the velocity value.

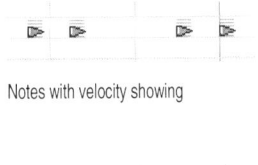

Notes with velocity showing

Notes without velocity showing

To Display Velocity Tails in the Drum Grid Pane

- Click the Show/Hide Velocity Tails button [image] in the Piano Roll view toolbar.

  Or

- Press the Y key.

Editing Note Velocities

In the Drum Map Editor you can display note velocities as a series of horizontal bars behind the note. Click the Show/Hide Velocity Tails button [image] to display note velocities.

To Edit a Note Velocity in the Drum Grid Pane

1. Click the Draw tool button [image].

2. Move your cursor over the velocity tail you want to edit until the cursor changes to look like this: [image]

3. Click and drag the velocity tail. Drag it up to increase the velocity. Drag it down to decrease the velocity.

341

To Edit Multiple Note Velocities in the Drum Grid Editor

When you edit multiple notes that have different initial velocities, the velocities are adjusted on a relative basis, so if you reduce a velocity by 50%, all other selected notes have their velocities reduced by the same percentage. For example: you select three notes. The first has a velocity of 100, the second a velocity of 50, and the third a velocity of 30. You click and drag the velocity of the first note down to 50. The second note's velocity changes from 50 to 25 and the third note's velocity changes from 30 to 15.

1. Select the notes you want to change the velocity of.

2. Click the Draw tool button .

3. Move your cursor over the velocity tail you want to edit until the cursor changes to look like this:

4. Click and drag the velocity tail. Drag it up to increase the velocity. Drag it down to decrease the velocity.

Previewing a Mapped Sound

Use the following procedure to hear the drum sound you have mapped a note to.

To Preview a Mapped Sound

- In the Note Map pane, click on the name of the sound you want to hear.

The Note Map Pane

The Note Map pane displays the current drum map. In the Note Map pane each row represents a pitch. The Note In pitch is the recorded pitch. You map the recorded pitch to whatever pitch you want using the Note Out pitch setting. You can also change the name of the mapped note and mute or solo the mapped note.

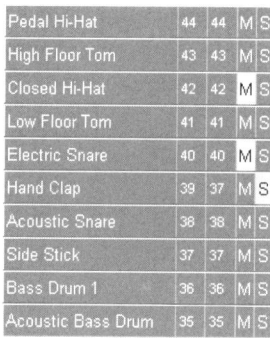

Changing Mapped-note Settings
You can change the following settings in the Note Map pane:

- Mapped-note name
- Note Out
- Mute
- Solo

To Change the Name Setting
The name of a mapped note in the Note Map pane is a user-assigned variable. Make it descriptive for easy reference. To change the Name setting, use the following procedure:

1. In the Note Map pane, double-click on the appropriate row.

   The Map Properties dialog appears.

2. In the Map Properties dialog, enter a new name in the Name field and press the Enter key.

To Change the Note Out Setting
The Note Out setting is the actual note you hear when the Note In value is played. To change the Note Out setting, use the following procedure:

1. In the Note Map pane, double-click on the appropriate row.

   The Map Properties dialog appears.

2. In the Map Properties dialog, enter a new value in the Note Out field and press the Enter key, or use the +/- buttons to change the value and press the Enter key.

To Change Multiple Note Out Settings
1. Open the Drum Map Manager.
2. In the Drum Map Manager, select a contiguous range of rows by selecting the first in the range, and holding down the Shift key while selecting the last in the range.

   Or

   Select a non-contiguous range by selecting one row and holding down the Ctrl key while selecting additional rows.

3. Hold down both the Ctrl and Shift keys while selecting a new Output in the Output column.

To Mute or Solo a Mapped Note

The Mute and Solo controls in the Note Map pane allow you to mute or solo an individual mapped note. To mute or solo a mapped note, use the following procedure:

- In the Note Map pane, click the Mute M or Solo S button in the appropriate row.

    Or

- Right-click on the row you want to mute or solo and select **Mute** or **Solo** from the menu that appears.

To Display the Note In and Note Out Values By Their Pitch Name

You have the option of showing the Note In and Note Out values by their pitch names. To do so, use the following procedure:

- Right-click on any row in the Note Map pane and select the **Display Pitch Names** command from the menu that appears.

To Change the Order of Mapped Notes in the Drum Map Pane

Use the following procedure to change the order of mapped notes in the Note Map pane.

1. Move your cursor over the row you want to move in the Note Map pane.

2. When your cursor changes to look like this , click and drag the row to the place you want it to be and release the mouse button.

The Drum Grid Pane

The Drum Grid pane is where you edit your drum tracks. The Drum Grid pane is the top pane in the Piano Roll view and opens automatically when you open a MIDI drum track.

Grid Lines

The Drum Grid pane is divided into a time grid. You can set the resolution of the grid lines from 1/4 note to 1/64 note, or to follow the current snap grid setting.

The Show/Hide Grid Lines combo button toggles on and off the grid lines in the Drum Grid pane and sets the grid line resolution.

To Turn on Grid Lines in the Drum Map Pane

- Click the Show/Hide Grid Lines combo button 📊 in the Piano Roll view toolbar.

    Or

- Press the I key.

To Set the Drum Map Pane Grid Line Resolution

- Click the down arrow on the Show/Hide Grid Lines combo button 📊 and select an option from the menu that appears.

The Pattern Brush Tool

The Pattern Brush tool 🖊, on the Piano Roll View toolbar, allows you to insert multiple notes using your mouse, either following a pattern used in an existing MIDI file or at the current note duration setting.

How the Pattern Brush Tool Works

When you select the Pattern Brush tool you can click and drag in the Drum Grid pane (also works in the Note pane) to produce a series of notes. Which notes appear in the Drum Grid depends on the settings you make in the Pattern Brush tool's dropdown menu. To open the Pattern Brush tool's dropdown menu, click the right side of the Pattern Brush tool.

The following table covers the options found in the Pattern Brush tool's dropdown menu:

Option...	Description...
Velocity	Select this option to open the Pattern Velocity dialog. The value you enter in this dialog sets the default velocity for all notes entered using the Pattern Brush tool unless you select Use Pattern Velocities.
Use Pattern Velocities	Select this option to use the note velocities used in the custom pattern file you are using. If you are using the Note Duration option, this option is not available.
Use Pattern Polyphony	Select this option to use the pitch values from the custom pattern file you are using. If you are using the Note Duration option, this option is not available. When using this option, the vertical position of your mouse does not affect the note pitches draw; that information is read from the pattern.
Note Duration	This option uses the current note duration setting in the Piano Roll View toolbar as the interval between notes.

To Paint Notes Using the Pattern Brush Tool

1. Open a track in the Drum Grid pane or the Note pane.
2. In the Pattern Brush tool's dropdown menu, select **Note Duration**.
3. In the Piano Roll View toolbar, select a note duration. This value is the interval between notes when using the Pattern Brush tool.
4. Click the Pattern Brush tool to select it.

   Your cursor should appear like this when in the Drum Grid pane.

5. Click where you want to begin placing notes and drag until you have inserted all the notes you want.
6. Release the mouse button.

SONAR creates a series of notes, at equal intervals.

To Paint a Custom Pattern of Notes Using the Pattern Brush Tool

1. Open a track in the Drum Grid pane.
2. In the Pattern Brush tool's dropdown menu, select the custom pattern you want to use. If you need to create a custom pattern, see "Creating Custom Patterns" on page 347.
3. Click the Pattern Brush tool to select it.

   Your cursor should appear like this when in the Drum Grid pane.

4. Click where you want to begin placing notes and drag until you have inserted all the notes you want.
5. Release the mouse button.

To Use a Custom Pattern's Note Velocities

1. Open a track in the Drum Grid pane.
2. In the Pattern Brush tool's dropdown menu, select the custom pattern you want to use. In the Pattern Brush tool's dropdown menu, select **Use Pattern Velocities**.
3. Click the Pattern Brush tool to select it.

   Your cursor should appear like this when in the Drum Grid pane.

4. Click where you want to begin placing notes and drag until you have inserted all the notes you want.
5. Release the mouse button.

To Use a Custom Pattern's Pitch Values

1. Open a track in the Drum Grid pane.

2. In the Pattern Brush tool's dropdown menu, select the custom pattern you want to use. In the Pattern Brush tool's dropdown menu, select **Use Pattern Polyphony**.

3. Click the Pattern Brush tool to select it.

   Your cursor should appear like this when in the Drum Grid pane.

4. Click where you want to begin placing notes and drag until you have inserted all the notes you want.

5. Release the mouse button.

Creating Custom Patterns

You can create custom patterns and use the Pattern Brush tool to quickly paint them into the Drum Grid pane. Use the following procedure to create a custom pattern.

To Create a Custom Pattern

1. Create a new file, or open an existing MIDI file or pattern file that you want to edit.

2. Right-click in the Time Ruler where you want the pattern to start and select **Insert Marker** from the menu that appears.

   The Marker dialog appears.

3. Enter the name you want to use for the first pattern and click OK.

4. In a MIDI track, enter a pattern of notes.

5. If you want to create a second pattern, repeat steps 2 through 4.

6. Create as many patterns as you want, ending the last pattern with a marker called "end".

7. Save the file as a MIDI file (.MID) in the Pattern Brush Patterns folder in the directory where you installed SONAR.

   Note: You can change the default directory where SONAR looks for patterns in the Folders tab of the Global Options dialog.

You may need to re-start SONAR to see the new patterns in the dropdown menu next to the Pattern Brush. The name you gave the file appears with an arrow next to it. Move your mouse over it to see a subdirectory which contains each of the patterns you created.

347

9 Editing Audio

The Track view lets you edit and arrange audio clips. You can perform basic tasks such as cut, copy, paste, and move; apply simple audio processing such as gain change, fades, and equalization; and use sophisticated audio effects such as stereo chorus and reverb. The Track view lets you see your audio clips on a timeline, arranged by track, to help you visualize the organization of your project's audio data.

Most audio processing commands and audio effects can be used from the Event List view as well, by selecting one or more audio clips, then choosing the desired command from the ***Process-Audio*** or ***Process-Audio Effects*** menu. Plug-in effects can also be applied to audio data non-destructively, in real time, in both the Console and Track views. For more information, see Chapter 11, *Mixing and Effects Patching*.

In This Chapter

Digital Audio Fundamentals	350
Basic Audio Editing	357
Basic Audio Processing	365
Advanced Audio Processing	369
Slip-editing Audio (Non-destructive Editing)	375
Fades and Crossfades	380
Audio Effects (Audio Plug-ins)	386

Digital Audio Fundamentals

Digital audio is a numeric representation of sound; it is sound stored as numbers. In order to understand what the numbers mean, you need to start with the basic principles of **acoustics**, the science of sound.

Basic Acoustics

Sound is produced when molecules in the air are disturbed by some type of motion produced by a vibrating object. This object, which might be a guitar string, human vocal cord, or a garbage can, is set into motion because energy is applied to it. The guitar string is struck by a pick or finger, while the garbage can is hit perhaps by a hammer, but the basic result is the same: they both begin to vibrate. The rate and amount of vibration is critical to our perception of the sound. If it is not fast enough or strong enough, we won't hear it. But if the vibration occurs at least twenty times a second and the molecules in the air are moved enough, then we will hear sound.

Example—A Guitar String

To understand the process better, let's take a closer look at a guitar string.

When a finger picks a guitar string, the entire string starts to move back and forth at a certain rate. This rate is called the **frequency** of the vibration. Because a single back and forth motion is called a **cycle**, we use a measure of frequency called **cycles per second**, or **cps**. This measure is also known as **Hertz**, abbreviated **Hz**. Often the frequency of vibration of an object is very fast, so we can also express the frequency in thousands of cycles per second, or **kilohertz** (abbreviated **kHz**).

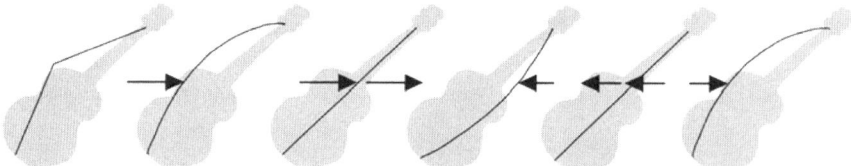

The actual distance the string moves is called its **displacement**. This is proportional to how hard the string is plucked. A greater displacement results in a louder sound.

The displacement of the string changes as the string vibrates, as shown here:

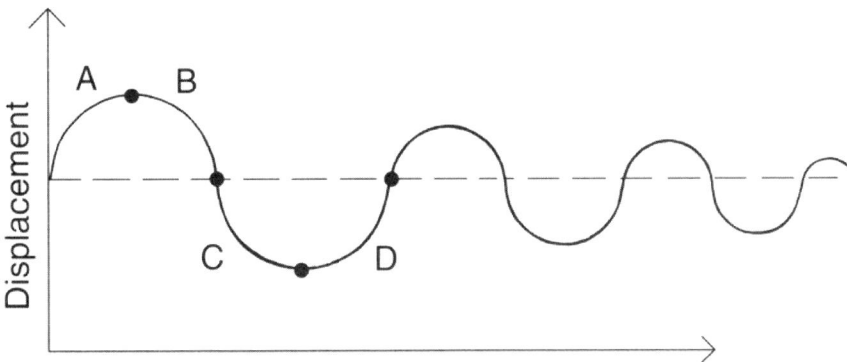

The segment marked "A" represents the string as it is pulled back by the pick; "B" shows it moving back towards its resting point, "C" represents the string moving through the resting point and onward to its outer limit; then "D" has it moving back towards the point of rest. This pattern repeats continuously until the friction of the molecules in the air gradually slows the string to a stop. As the string vibrates, it causes the molecules of air around it to vibrate as well. The vibrations are passed along through the air as **sound waves**. When the vibrations enter your ear, they make your eardrum vibrate, and you hear a sound. Likewise, if the vibrating air hits a microphone, it causes the microphone to vibrate and send out electrical signals.

In order for us humans to hear the sound, the frequency of the vibration must be at least 20 Hz. The highest frequency sound we can hear is theoretically 20 kHz, but, in reality, it's probably closer to 15 or 17 kHz. Other animals, and microphones, have different hearing ranges.

If the simple back-and-forth motion of the string was the only phenomenon involved in creating a sound, then all stringed instruments would probably sound much the same. We know this is not true, of course; the laws of physics are not quite so simple. In fact, the string vibrates not only at its entire length, but at one-half its length, one-third, one-fourth, one-fifth, and so on. These additional vibrations (**overtones**) occur at a rate faster than the rate of the original vibration (the **fundamental frequency**), but are usually weaker in strength. Our ear doesn't hear each frequency of vibration individually, however. If it if did, we would hear a multinote chord every time a single string were played. Rather, all these vibrations are added together to form a complex or composite sound that our ear perceives as a single tone.

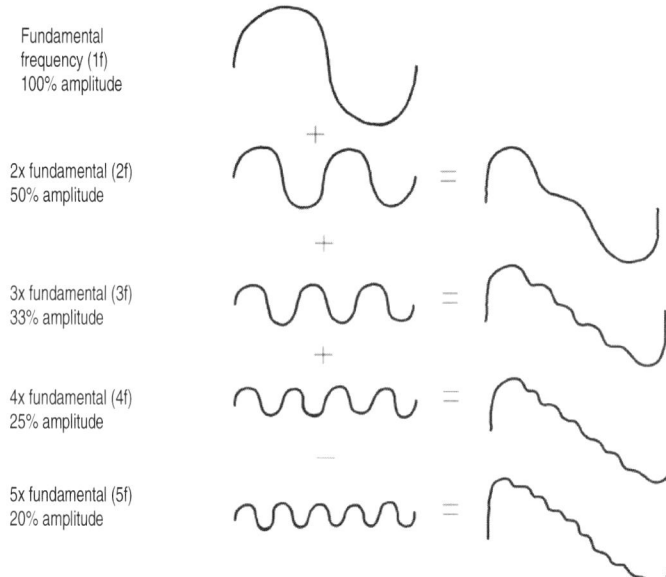

This composite waveform still doesn't account for the uniqueness of the sound of different instruments. For example, stringed instruments usually have a resonator. In the case of the guitar, the resonator is the big block of hollow wood to which the string is attached (the guitar body). This has a major impact on the sound we perceive when a guitar is played because it enhances or amplifies some of the vibrations produced by the string and diminishes or attenuates others. The ultimate effect of all the vibrations occurring simultaneously, being altered by the resonator, adds up to the sound we know as guitar.

Waveforms

A sound wave can be represented in many different ways: as a mathematical formula, as a series of numbers, or graphically as a **waveform**. A waveform displays the size, or **amplitude**, of the vibration as a function of time. For example, the waveform of the sound of the plucked guitar string might look like this:

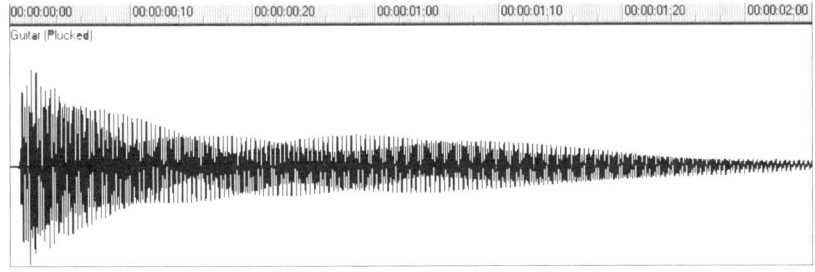

The waveform of a trumpet blast might look like this:

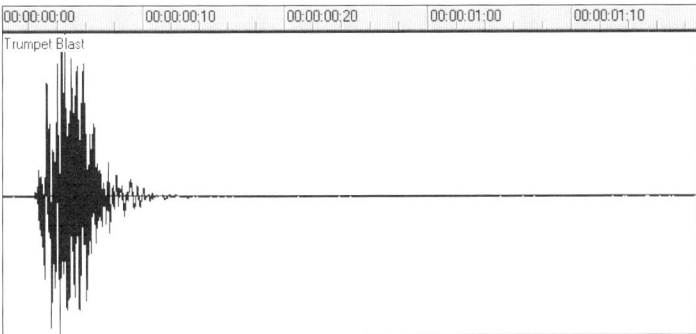

And the waveform of a spoken word might look like this:

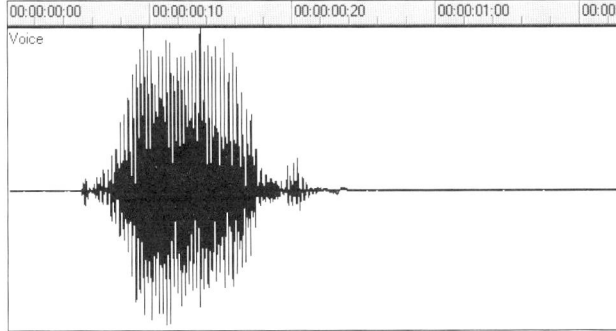

The three waveforms shown above are quite different from one another, both in appearance and sound. Each has its own characteristic shape, or envelope, and

353

each has its own complex combination of frequency components, which can change across the duration of the sound.

The center line of a waveform is the zero line; it corresponds to the rest position (displacement of 0) of the original vibrating object. (A waveform for perfect silence would be a horizontal line at zero.) Back and forth motions of the vibrating object translate to upward (positive) and downward (negative) excursions of waveform amplitude. For example, a close-up of a portion of the guitar waveform might look like this:

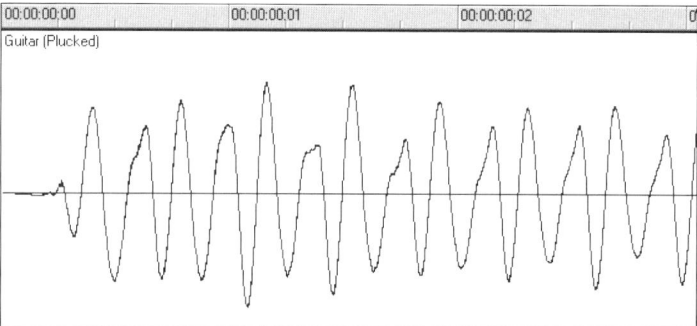

The waveform crosses the zero line twice during each complete vibration. These **zero-crossings** are important in digital audio processing; they are good places to cut waveforms apart and splice them together. If waveforms are cut or spliced at other locations, clicks and pops can occur. The maximum amplitude of the waveform in each vibration is also important: it determines the strength of the vibration, and thus the loudness of the sound.

Recording a Sound

To record digital audio, your computer monitors the electrical signal generated by a microphone (or some other electroacoustical device). Because the signal is caused by a sound, the signal strength varies in direct proportion to the sound's waveform. The computer measures and saves the strength of the electrical signal from the microphone, thus recording the waveform.

There are two important aspects of this measuring process. First is the **sampling rate**, the rate at which the computer saves measurements of the signal strength. It is a known fact of physics that you must measure, or **sample**, the signal at a rate at least twice that of the highest frequency you wish to capture. For example, suppose you want to record a moderately high note on a violin—say the A whose fundamental frequency is 440 Hz and all overtones up to five times the fundamental. The highest frequency you want to capture is 2,200 Hz, so you need to measure the electrical signal from the microphone at least 4,400 times per second.

Since humans can hear frequencies well above 10 kHz, most sound cards and digital recording systems are capable of sampling at much higher rates than that. Typical sampling rates used by modern musicians and audio engineers are 22 kHz, 44.1 kHz, and 48 kHz. The 44.1 kHz rate is called **CD-quality**, since it is the rate used by audio compact discs.

The other important aspect of the measuring process is the **sampling resolution**. The sampling resolution determines how accurately the amplitude of each sample is measured. At present, the music industry has settled on a system that provides 65,536 different values to assign to the amplitude of a waveform at any given instant. Thus, each sample saved by your computer requires 2 bytes (16 bits) to store, since it takes 2 bytes to store a number from –32,768 to 32,767. The scaling of the electrical input signal level to amplitude value is determined by your audio hardware and by the position of your input level control.

What if the amplitude of the sampled signal gets too high, such that a 16-bit number is not large enough to represent it? What typically happens is that the signal is **clipped**, cut off at the maximum value.

Here is what a clipped waveform might look like:

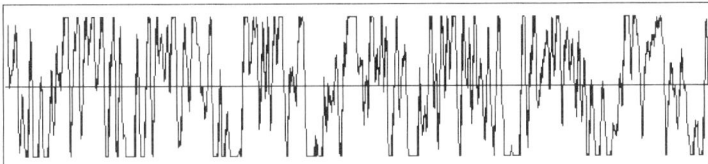

Clipping is not usually desirable and may have unpleasant audible effects. Sudden irregularities in the waveform of any type can cause clicks, pops, and distortion of the original sound.

The Decibel Scale

In acoustics, the decibel (dB) scale is a scale for measuring the relative loudness of two sounds. For example, environmental noise is often measured as follows:

$L = 20 \log (p/p0)$

where L is the sound pressure level (in dB), p is the sound pressure amplitude, and p0 is a reference amplitude of 20 micropascals (less than one billionth of atmospheric pressure). On this scale, a barely audible sound (p = p0) has a sound pressure level of 0 dB, normal conversation (p = 1,000*p0) is at a level of around 60 dB, and a jet engine at close range (p = 1,000,000*p0) is at a level of around 120 dB.

Similar decibel scales are used in other branches of science and engineering to measure electrical power levels and other signal levels, always with respect to some reference level.

In SONAR, decibels are used in several places:

- To scale the amplitude of the waveform (***3dB Louder*** and ***3dB Quieter*** commands)
- To indicate volume levels of audio tracks in the Track view and Console view
- To indicate the effects of filters and equalizers

The reference level (0 dB) usually corresponds to the current loudness of the sound. A positive change in decibels makes the sound louder; a negative change makes the sound quieter.

Audio Clips

If you have read from the beginning of the chapter, you should have a good idea of what is contained in a SONAR audio clip. An audio clip contains a long series of numbers, or samples, representing the fluctuating amplitude of a waveform. Audio clips are typically quite large, hundreds of kilobytes to many megabytes in size. By comparison, a MIDI event takes only a few bytes to store.

The Track view lets you see your audio waveforms in great detail; you can zoom in until you see the individual samples.

You should also now be aware of some things to watch out for when editing your audio data. First, if you cut audio clips apart or splice them together, you should do so at zero-crossings in the waveform (places where the amplitude is zero), in order to avoid sudden changes in amplitude that may cause clicks and pops. Second, you should beware of clipping. Clipping of the audio waveform can occur if you record a signal at too high a record level, or if you apply audio processing or effects that increase the waveform amplitude too much. If you accidentally cause the waveform to clip, you should undo the command and try again with different parameters.

Clipping can also occur in other situations, for example, if you try to play or mix several loud audio tracks together, the aggregate signal strength may at times exceed the clipping limit, and the output signal will be distorted. To correct the problem, you can create a volume envelope to reduce the level in loud audio clips or reduce the track volume in the Console or Track views.

Managing Audio Data

Because of the great size of audio data, SONAR uses an intelligent scheme for storing audio clips on disk to conserve disk space and minimize the time it takes to load and save data. Audio data is not stored directly in your project file, but rather in separate files in a special directory. For more information, see "System Configuration" on page 628.

You can export your project as RealAudio, MP3, WMA, or a Wave file. You can also convert your project's MIDI data to audio and export it to any of the above formats. For more information, see "Preparing Audio for Distribution" on page 459.

Basic Audio Editing

The Track view lets you perform basic editing tasks such as cut, copy, paste, delete, drag-and-drop, split, and bounce. You can drag fade-ins and fade-outs onto a clip using your mouse or you can set complex envelopes on both clips and tracks. You can use envelopes to change settings for gain (volume), pan, mute, bus send level and bus send pan. The Scrub tool lets you audition portions of audio by dragging the mouse.

Use the Select tool to make selections.

Here is a summary of the ways in which you can select audio clips:

To do this...	Do this...
Select a single clip	Click the clip
Select several clips at once	Drag a rectangle around them
Select part of an clip	Press Alt and drag over a portion of the clips
Add clips to the selection	Press Shift and either click the clips or drag a rectangle around the clips
Add or remove clips from the selection	Press Ctrl and either click the clips or drag a rectangle around the clips
Add or remove clips in a track from the selection	Click the track number
Select clips in a time range	Drag in the Time Ruler
Select clips between two markers	Click between the markers
Remove all selections	Click in an empty area outside of any clip

Editing Clip Properties

Audio clips have several properties that you can change:

Property...	Description...
Name	The name of a clip is used in the Track view and Event List view. You can assign any name to help you remember the contents of the clip.
Start	The start determines when the sample is played.
Length	The length indicates the size of the clip.
Snap Offset	A value that represents the number of samples into the clip at which the clip snaps to.
Display Color	The clips color in the Track view.

To Change an Audio Clip's Name
1. Right-click the audio clip and choose *Clip Properties*.

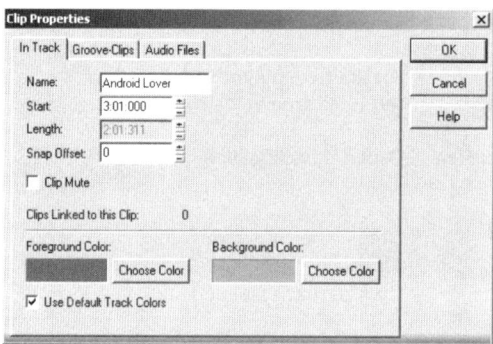

2. Type a new name in the Name box.
3. Click OK.

The new clip name appears in the upper left corner of the clip.

To Change a Clip's Start
1. Right-click an audio clip and choose *Clip Properties*.
2. Enter a new starting time in the Start field.
3. Click OK.

The Track view displays the clip at the new starting time.

Moving, Copying, Pasting and Deleting Audio Clips

Clips can be cut, copied, pasted, and deleted with *Edit* menu commands, or moved and copied with drag-and-drop techniques. For more information, see "Arranging" on page 203 for details.

Audio Scaling

Audio scaling is the increase or decrease in the size (scale) of the waveform in a track. Audio scaling allows you to make detailed edits by zooming in on the parts of the waveform closest to the zero crossing (silence) while preserving the track size. By showing just the quietest parts of a clip, you can make very precise edits.

You can change the audio scale using keyboard shortcuts or the Audio Scale Ruler.

The Audio Scale Ruler is located in the vertical splitter bar between the Clips pane and the Track pane.

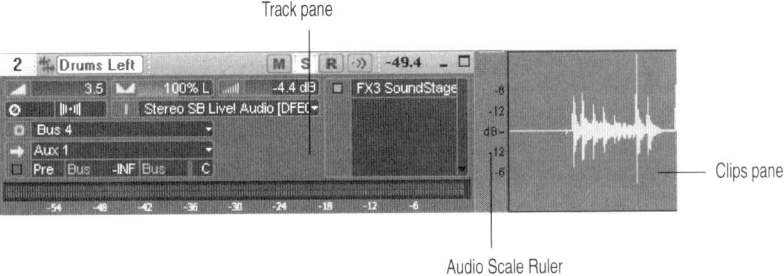

There are three display options in the Audio Scale Ruler:

- Percentage—shows audio scaling by percentage. For example, if the highest percentage in the Audio Scale Ruler reads 2.0%, then only the parts of the waveform which are within 2% of the zero crossing appear in the clip.

- dB—shows audio scaling by dB. For example, if the highest dB in the Audio Scaling Ruler reads -36, then only the parts of the waveform which are 36 dB below 0 dB appear in the clip.

- Zoom Factor—shows audio scaling by a factor. For example, if the Zoom Factor reads 10, then the waveform is zoomed in by a factor of 10.

Note: The Audio Scale Ruler display reflects the type of audio clip directly beneath it. If it is a stereo clip, the Audio Scale Ruler appears in stereo (one for each channel). If it is a mono clip it appears in mono. Also, the Audio Scale Ruler only displays numbers when it is of above a certain height. If you cannot see the Audio Scale Ruler, increase the size of your track or tracks.

To Change the Audio Scale Display Option

1. Right-click on the Audio Scale Ruler in any track.

   A menu appears. The current display option is checked.

2. Select an option from the menu.

To Scale All Audio Tracks Together

To scale all audio tracks together, follow the instructions in the table below:

To do this...	Do this...
Increase the scale for all tracks	Press Alt+Up Arrow. Or Hold down the Ctrl key and click the Vertical Zoom In button. When you hold down the Ctrl key and position your cursor over the Vertical Zoom In button, your cursor looks like this:
Decrease the scale for all tracks	Press Alt+Down Arrow. Or Hold down the Ctrl key and click the Vertical Zoom Out button. When you hold down the Ctrl key and position your cursor over the Vertical Zoom Out button, your cursor looks like this:
Increase/Decrease the scale for all tracks using your mouse	Hold down the Ctrl key, click the Vertical Zoom Fader and drag the fader up or down. When you hold down the Ctrl key and position your cursor over the Vertical Zoom fader, your cursor looks like this:

To do this...	Do this...
Increase to maximum scale	Hold down the Ctrl and Shift keys and click the Vertical Zoom In button. When you hold down the Shift and Ctrl keys and position your cursor over the Vertical Zoom In button, your cursor looks like this:
Decrease to minimum scale	Hold down the Ctrl and Shift keys and click the Vertical Zoom Out button. When you hold down the Shift and Ctrl keys and position your cursor over the Vertical Zoom Out button, your cursor looks like this:

To Scale a Single Track

To scale a single audio track, follow the instructions in the table below:

To do this...	Do this...
Increase/decrease the scale of individual stereo or mono tracks	There are several ways to increase or decrease the size of an individual audio track's or clip's waveform: • Press Ctrl+Alt+Up/Down arrows • Click and drag vertically in the track's Audio Scale Ruler. When you click and drag in the Audio Scale ruler of a track, your cursor looks like this: • Select the Zoom tool, hold the Shift key and drag around the clip you want to zoom in on. When you have the Zoom tool selected in the Track view toolbar and you drag over a section of audio, your cursor looks like this: • Select the Select tool, hold down the Shift key and *z* keys, and drag around the clip you want to zoom in on. When you have the Select tool selected and the Shift and z keys held down, your cursor looks like this:
Restore a track to minimum scale	Double-click in the track's Audio Scale Ruler.

To Undo Audio Scaling
- Press the U key.

To Scale a Single Track Using the Audio Scale Ruler
- In the track in which you want to change the audio scale, click in the Audio Scale Ruler and drag. Drag up to increase the audio scaling. Drag down to decrease the audio scaling.

To Hide the Audio Scale Ruler
1. Right-click in the Clips pane.
2. Select *View Options* from the menu that appears.

   The Track View Options dialog appears.

3. In the Track View Options dialog, uncheck the Show Audio Scale checkbox and click OK.

Splitting Audio Clips
You can split long audio clips into shorter ones. This lets you extract and rearrange individual sounds, adjust timing and alignment, and apply effects selectively. Audio clips can be split using the Scissors tool in the Track view or with the *Split* command.

To Split Clips with the Scissors Tool
1. If necessary, zoom-in in the Track view and use the Scrub tool to determine where you want to make a split.
2. If you want the split to be made on a note or measure boundary, a marker, or by an event, open the Snap to Grid dialog, make the appropriate settings and click the Snap to Grid button to turn on the Snap to Grid.
3. Click the Scissors tool button on the Track view toolbar.
4. Click once to make a single split, or to make two splits, click where you want the first split, drag within a clip and release to make a second split.

To Split Clips with the Split Command
1. Select the clip you want to split.
2. Right-click the selected clip and select *Split* from the menu.

   The Split Clips dialog appears.

3. In the Split Clips dialog, select from the following options.

Option...	Description...
Split At Time	Specify the time at which you want to split the clip and the time format.
Split Repeatedly	Specify the first measure at which you want to split the clip in the Starting At Measure field and the intervals at which you want to split the clip in the And Again Every field.
Split At Each Marker	Creates a split in the clip at every marker.
Split When Silent For At Least	Creates a split after each period of silence which exceeds the number of measures specified.

SONAR splits the audio clip according to your specifications. Each new clip has the same name as the original clip.

Note: A shortcut to split a selected clip is to move the Now time to where you want to split it, and press *s* on your computer keyboard.

Bouncing to Clips

Individual audio clips in the same track can be combined into a single clip with the ***Bounce to Clip(s)*** command.

Note:

Like any clips, slip-edited clips can be combined with other clips using the ***Bounce to Clip(s)*** command. When a slip-edited clip is combined with another clip, any slip-edited data (audio clips or MIDI events that are cropped from view) is overwritten.

To Bounce to Clips

1. Select the clips to be combined in the Track view.
2. Choose ***Edit-Bounce to Clip(s)***.

The clips are combined into a single clip. Empty space between clips is filled with silence in the new clip. All clip automation from the source clips is applied to the new clip.

To Bounce Multiple Audio Clips to a New Track

1. Select the clips to be combined in the Track view.
2. Choose ***Edit-Bounce to Track(s)***.

    The Bounce to Track(s) dialog appears.

3. Select the track you want to bounce to in the Destination field.
4. Select other options in the Mixdown Audio/Bounce to Track(s) dialog and click OK.

The clips are combined into a single clip on the destination track. Empty space between clips is filled with silence in the new clip.

Scrubbing

You can use the Scrub tool to locate or audition a particular sound or passage as you drag the mouse. You can scrub a single audio track by dragging over that track or all tracks by dragging in the Time Ruler.

Note: The Scrub tool is not affected by current Mute and Solo settings of a track.

To Audition Audio with the Scrub Tool

1. Click the Scrub tool.
2. Click and drag the pointer over an audio track.

Tip:
To hear the clips in all audio tracks, drag with the Scrub tool in the horizontal ruler.

Basic Audio Processing

Audio processing commands let you modify audio data according to some rule or algorithm. The rule can be as simple as reversing the audio data or multiplying it by a certain factor, or as complex as performing a Fourier analysis and selectively amplifying or attenuating sounds at certain frequencies. Among the basic audio processing commands are ones to increase and decrease volume, to reverse the data, and to perform equalization.

Audio processing commands can work on whole, partial and non-contiguous clips. For example, suppose you want to make certain words in a vocal passage softer. You can create a volume envelope and use it to lower the volume, non-destructively in just the section of the track containing those words. You could also use the *3dB Quieter* command to lower the volume destructively.

You should listen to the results of your work after each audio processing command. If you don't like what you hear, you can use *Edit-Undo* to restore your audio data to its previous state.

Many of the dialog boxes associated with SONAR's audio processing and effects commands have two important features: Audition and Presets.

The Audition button is used to audition the processed audio data. When you click Audition, SONAR processes the first few seconds of your data, then plays it repeatedly until you click Stop. This helps you to get an idea of whether the settings in the dialog box are producing the desired effect.

The audition duration is three seconds by default. You can change this value by choosing **Options-Global**, selecting the **General** tab and changing Audition Commands for ( ) Seconds.

Presets are a way to store dialog box settings so that you can apply the exact same processing or effect again in the future. The following table tells you how to use presets in the effects dialog boxes.

To do this...	Do this...
Save the current settings as a preset	Enter a preset name and click the Save button 💾
Use a preset	Select the preset from the dropdown list
Delete a preset	Select the preset, then click the Delete button ❌

Many audio processing and effects presets are supplied with SONAR.

Increasing or Decreasing Volume

SONAR provides three commands to boost or cut the volume of audio data. The *3dB Louder* and *3dB Quieter* commands are used to increase or decrease the volume by three decibels, respectively. For more information on the decibel scale, see "The Decibel Scale" on page 355. You can apply these commands several times in succession to get a larger boost or decrease. The *Normalize* command "normalizes" the audio data: it boosts the volume until the maximum amplitude is reached somewhere in the data. By normalizing the data, you achieve the maximum possible volume without distortion or clipping.

Like all the audio processing commands, these commands work by modifying the waveform data. You can achieve volume changes non-destructively using automation. For more information, see Chapter 13, *Using Automation*.

When increasing or decreasing the volume of audio clips, you should consider the following points:

- *Normalize* and *3dB Louder* raise the noise floor; that is, while they increase the volume of the signal, they also amplify the noise it contains. (This is true when you raise the volume by other means, too.)

- *3dB Louder*, if applied to a signal that is already fairly loud, may cause the waveform to exceed the maximum amplitude and clip.

- *Normalize*, by raising the waveform amplitude to the maximum, puts the signal in danger of being clipped if you subsequently apply a command or effect that boosts the signal slightly. If this occurs, you may have to back up and apply *3dB Quieter* to the normalized signal before the other processing.

- Each application of *3dB Quieter* erodes the signal structure slightly; you cannot repeatedly apply *3dB Quieter*, then use *3dB Louder* to return to the original waveform.

- Due to the nature and limitations of digital audio, the sum of all audio signals played together cannot exceed the waveform amplitude limit. Even though no individual clip is clipped, the combination may cause distortion.

If the selection contains any loud signals, *Normalize* may not seem to have any effect. This is because the volume increase is determined by the loudest audio in the selection. If an audio clip contains segments that are too quiet and others that are loud, you should probably split off the quiet segments into separate clips and then normalize those.

To Boost Audio Volume by Three Decibels
1. Select the audio data to be affected.
2. Choose *Process-Audio-3dB Louder* from the menu.

SONAR increases the volume of the selected audio by 3dB.

To Decrease Audio Volume by Three Decibels
1. Select the audio data to be affected.
2. Choose *Process-Audio-3dB Quieter* from the menu.

SONAR decreases the volume of the selected audio by 3dB.

To Normalize Audio Data
1. Select the audio data to be affected.
2. Choose *Process-Audio-Normalize* from the menu.

SONAR increases the volume of the selected audio to the maximum it can reach without clipping.

Reversing Audio Data

By reversing audio data, you can make it play backwards. You may wish to do this to obtain unusual sounds for special effects.

The *Reverse* command does not reverse the musical position of audio data. Use the *Process-Retrograde* command to invert the order of clips in time.

To Reverse Audio Data
1. Select the audio data to be affected.
2. Choose *Process-Audio-Reverse* from the menu.

SONAR reverses the selected audio data.

Equalizing Audio Data

Equalization lets you boost or decrease the volume of sounds at different frequencies. For example, you can boost the bass, cut high-frequency hiss, or brighten mid-range vocals.

SONAR provides a graphic equalizer that lets you boost or decrease the volume of audio clips in ten frequency bands. The width of each band doubles as you go from low to high frequencies; thus, the centers of the bands are each an octave apart.

Boosting the audio signal too much may result in clipping or distortion. If this occurs, you may need to undo the command, then decrease the volume one or more times with the *3dB Quieter* command, or insert a volume envelope, before equalization.

To Equalize Audio Data
1. Select the audio data to be modified.
2. Choose *Process-Audio-Graphic EQ* from the menu, to open the Graphic EQ dialog box.
3. Choose a preset, or adjust the sliders to the desired equalization.

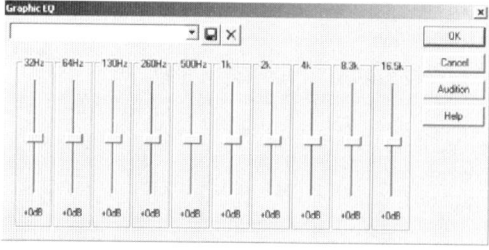

4. Click Audition to hear a preview of the first three seconds of the selected audio with the equalization applied.

5. Click OK when the settings are the way you want.

SONAR applies the specified equalization to the selected audio.

Advanced Audio Processing

SONAR provides a number of advanced audio processing commands for power users. Among these are commands to remove silent sections of audio from the data and to apply parametric equalization, fades, and crossfades.

Removing Silence

The **Remove Silence** command detects sections of audio that fall below a given loudness threshold, and replaces those sections with absolute silence. **Remove Silence** gives you the option of actually deleting the silent sections from the selected audio clips, splitting long audio clips into a greater number of shorter audio clips.

SONAR treats passages of absolute silence intelligently. It doesn't store stretches of silence on disk, and thereby conserves disk space. During a passage of absolute silence, SONAR sends no signal to the digital output port; this results in cleaner audio playback. **Remove Silence** is great for cleaning up your final audio mix, because it can mute all audio tracks in which the live performers were "laying out."

Using **Remove Silence** to split long audio clips into smaller ones opens a variety of creative possibilities.

The parameters in the Remove Silence dialog box are used to specify exactly what you mean by silence. More precisely, **Remove Silence** employs what is called a digital noise gate. The gate is a type of filter, it passes data through, or stops it from passing through, according to certain criteria. Parameters in the dialog box specify the conditions under which the gate is opened and under which it closes again.

The digital noise gate parameters are described in the following table.

Parameter...	Meaning...
Open Level (dB)	The loudness threshold for opening the noise gate. The gate officially opens when loudness rises above this level, although it can open earlier because of the Attack Time.
Close Level (dB)	The loudness threshold for closing the noise gate. The gate officially closes when loudness falls below this level, although it can stay open later because of the Release Time.
Attack Time (ms)	The value in this field is the interval of time after the volume reaches the Open Level for the gate to fully open. Opening the gate gradually produces a fade-in effect instead of an instant on-off sound.
Hold Time (ms)	The minimum time for the gate to stay open. Hold Time is useful when you've set high open and close levels, for example, when your source signal is very loud. Noise gates set this way tend to react to repeated percussive passages (such as drum rolls) by repeatedly opening and closing; this can sound unpleasant. By setting a hold time, you can ensure that the gate stays open long enough during percussive passages.
Release Time (ms)	The amount of time after the Close Level is reached that the gate actually closes. This lets the tail end of sounds pass through without being clipped.
Look Ahead (ms)	The value in this field causes the gate to open slightly before the sound reaches the Open Level so you don't lose the sound's attack.

To Remove Silence
1. Select the audio data to be affected.
2. Choose **Process-Audio-Remove Silence** to open the Remove Silence dialog box.

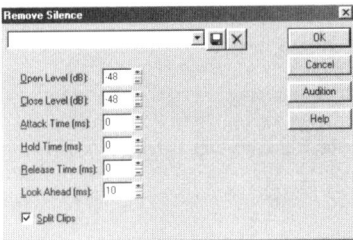

3. Set the digital noise gate parameters as described in the table above.
4. Check the Split Clips box to delete the silent sections of audio.
5. Click OK to remove silence from the selected data.

SONAR processes the audio as directed.

Extracting Timing
The Extract Timing command creates MIDI notes and (optionally) tempo changes based on rhythmic peaks in audio.

The Extract Timing command first analyzes the audio for pulses-sudden percussive changes in volume. Then, from each pulse's position and intensity, Extract Timing synthesizes new timing information, in the form of note events or tempo changes.

This command offers exciting ways to get your MIDI data to "groove" along with audio rhythm tracks. For example, using Extract Timing you can:

- Generate MIDI notes that play along with a rhythm, retaining all the accents in the rhythm track
- Create templates for the **Process-Groove Quantize** command, so that your MIDI tracks play with the same feel as your audio rhythm track
- Adjust the tempo and feel of an existing sequence to match that of a new rhythm track
- Record a new MIDI sequence on top of an audio rhythm track, letting the audio track determine the tempo map for the song

Extract Timing works in two steps: Pulse Analysis and Timing Synthesis. In the first step, the selected audio is scanned for sudden percussive attacks. You must adjust the Pulse Analysis parameters, then click Audition to see the results and decide if the pulses are satisfactory. The Pulse Analysis parameters are as follows:

Parameter/Option	Meaning
Preset field	Use this field to choose and enter presets. Click the Save button to save any group of new settings after you enter a name in the Preset field. Click the Delete button to delete any selected group from the Preset field.
Trigger Level (db)	The loudness of audio needed to trigger a new pulse.
Minimum Length (ms)	The minimum allowable amount of time between pulses. If you are working with dynamic source material, and Extract Timing seems to generate clusters of pulses that seem incorrect, you should experiment with increasing the value of this parameter.
Find a Steady Rhythm	Tells SONAR to look for a steady rhythm among all the pulses it finds. For example, if you're analyzing a drum track that consists of a steady beat on the snare and kick-drum, but which also has some syncopated accents, you can use this option to ignore the syncopation and retain only the backbeat.

In the second step, you set the Timing Synthesis parameters to determine how the pulses are converted to musically meaningful data. The Timing Synthesis parameters are as follows:

Parameter/Option	Meaning
Insert Tempo Changes	Tells SONAR to insert tempo changes in the appropriate places in your song to ensure that the sequence plays in time with the rhythm track. Remember to also set the Expected Pulse Duration, because it defines the metronome markings for all tempo changes.
Expected Pulse Duration	The musical time value for each pulse that was found. For example, if you're analyzing a drum beat that has steady eighth notes on the high-hat, you should set this value to Eighth for the correct tempo changes to be inserted.

Convert Pulses to MIDI Note	Tells SONAR to create a MIDI note event for each pulse that was found. The Note Velocities parameter lets you select which velocity will be used
Note Velocities	The velocity of generated MIDI notes. You can either select Vary With Pulse Level to adjust velocity to the dynamic structure of the original source material, or select Set All To Same Value to assign each inserted MIDI note a specified velocity.

When using Extract Timing, keep in mind the following:

- It knows nothing about the musical context of the audio.
- It does not know, and cannot figure out, the approximate tempo of the audio, the feel, or the time signature.

It only knows how to listen for sudden changes in volume. You must guide it with your own knowledge about the music.

To Extract Timing from Audio Data

1. Select the audio data to be analyzed.
2. Choose **Process-Audio-Extract Timing** to open the Extract Timing dialog box.
3. Set the Pulse Analysis parameters as described in the table above, or choose a preset from the preset field.
4. Click Audition to get visual feedback in the Clips pane, so you can be sure the pulses are aligned to your liking. If not, readjust the parameters and try again.
5. Set the Timing Synthesis parameters as described in the table above.
6. Click OK.

The generated events are automatically placed on the Clipboard. You can paste them to a new track, or use them directly in another command (such as Groove Quantize).

Parametric Equalization

The *Parametric EQ* command lets you apply a high-pass, low-pass, band-pass, or band-stop filter to your audio data. You must specify the filter type and parameters as follows:

Parameter...	Meaning...
High pass	Removes frequencies that are below the cutoff F1.
Low pass	Removes frequencies that are above the cutoff F1.
Band pass (Peak)	Removes frequencies that lie outside the range F1-F2.
Band stop (Notch)	Removes frequencies that lie within the range F1-F2.
F1 (Hz)	First frequency cutoff.
F2 (Hz)	Second frequency cutoff.
Quality	The sharpness the frequency cutoff, that is, how far outside the cutoff range a frequency must be for its gain to be fully reduced. Higher Quality values are sharper.
Cut (dB)	The maximum amount of gain reduction to apply to stopped frequencies.
Gain (dB)	The overall level for the filtered audio. Setting the gain too high may result in clipping or distortion.

Note:

For band filters, setting F1 and F2 close together may cause distortion or ringing.

To Apply the Parametric Equalizer to Audio Data
1. Select the audio data to be affected.
2. Choose *Process-Audio-Parametric EQ*, or right-click and choose *Parametric EQ* from the menu, to open the Parametric EQ dialog box.

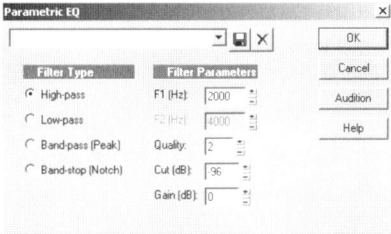

3. Set the filter type and parameters as described in the table above.
4. Click OK.

SONAR applies the specified filter to the selected data.

Slip-editing Audio (Non-destructive Editing)

Slip editing allows you to non-destructively hide or reveal the beginning of a clip, the end of a clip, or both. The hidden material in a clip is not heard during playback. All hidden material remains intact and can be restored. All slip editing movements correspond to the current snap to resolution. For more information about the snap to grid, see "Defining and Using the Snap Grid" on page 222.

Important:
Like any clips, slip-edited clips can be combined with other clips using the *Bounce to Clip(s)* command and slip-edited clips in a track can be mixed down to another track. When a slip-edited clip is combined with another clip or an effect is applied to a clip using the *Edit-Apply Audio Effects* command, any slip-edited data (audio clips or MIDI events that are cropped from view) is **overwritten**.

Slip-editing Modes

Slip-editing has three modes:

Trimming

As a default, when Slip-editing a clip, the clip's contents always remains fixed in time. If the first measure of a clip is hidden using slip editing, the remaining material does not shift forward in time by a measure. The first measure of the clip is simply muted during playback. Playback of the clip resumes at the second measure.

Slide-trimming

If you want the clip's contents to shift in time, you can move the material in a slip edited clip by using modifier keys, clicking on the middle of the clip and moving it either right or left.

Scroll-trimming

You can also shift the clip's contents in time, in relation to either the beginning or end of the clip itself, by scroll-trimming.

Using Slip-editing

Use the following procedures to slip-edit clips.

To Slip-edit an Audio Clip

1. Right-click on the clip you want to slip-edit.
2. Select *Clip-Properties* from the menu.

   The Clip Properties dialog appears.
3. Select the Action tab.
4. Make sure the Enable Looping checkbox is unchecked.
5. Click OK.

6. Make edits according to the following table:

To do this...	Do this...
Trim the beginning of a clip	Move the cursor over the beginning of a clip. When the cursor changes in appearance to look like this , click and drag the clip to the right until you have removed the unwanted information.

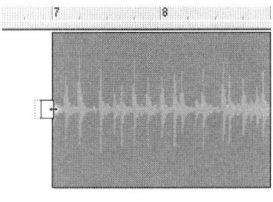

Clip before slip-editing

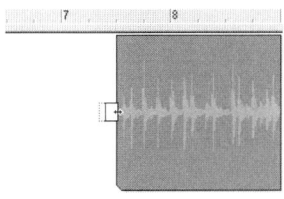

The same clip with the first two beats of the measure slip-edited

Trim the end of a clip	Move the cursor over the beginning of a clip. When the cursor changes in appearance to look like this , click and drag the clip to the left until you have removed the unwanted information.

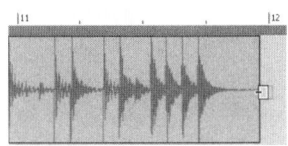

Clip before slip editing

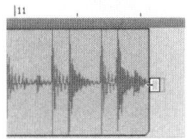

The same clip with the last quarter measure slip-edited

Scroll-trimming a clip (Moving the clip contents in time while maintaining the clips start and end time)	Press the Alt+Shift keys while moving the cursor over the middle of the clip. When the cursor changes to look like this , click and drag the clip to the left or right as desired. The contents (audio data) in the clip follow the Snap to Grid resolution, i.e. if your resolution is set to half note, the contents of your clip moves in half-note intervals.

Clip before scroll-trimming

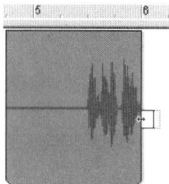

The same clip with the clip shifted by 3 beats

Slide-trimming the beginning of a clip (Moving the start time of the clip and the clip's contents while preserving the end time)	Press the Alt+Shift keys and move the cursor over the beginning of the clip. When the cursor changes to look like this 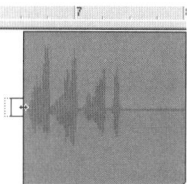, click and drag the beginning to the desired start time.

Clip before slide-trimming

The same clip with the clip slide-trimmed by 2 beats

Slide-trimming the end of a clip (Moving the end time of the clip and the clip's contents while preserving the clip's start time)	Press the Alt+Shift keys and move the cursor over the end of the clip. When the cursor changes to look like this 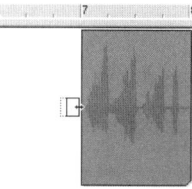, click and drag the end to the desired location.

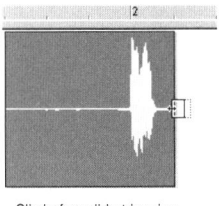
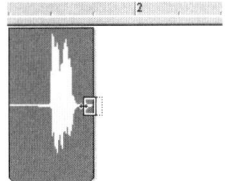

Clip before slide-trimming

The same clip with the clip shift-cropped by 2 beats

The hidden information in the slip edited clips remains intact but is not heard during playback

To Permanently Delete Slip-edited Data
1. Select the clips that contain the slip-edited data you want to delete.
2. Select the *Edit-Apply Trimming* command.

SONAR permanently deletes the slip-edited data from the clips you selected.

Slip-editing Multiple Audio Clips
You can slip-edit multiple clips at the same time.

To Slip-edit Multiple Clips at Once
1. Make sure all clips are not loop-enabled.
2. Select the clips you want to slip-edit.
3. Move your cursor over the beginning or end range of the selected clips until your cursor changes to look like this: .
4. Drag the boundary to the desired location and release.

Fades and Crossfades

Fades are a gradual increase or decrease in volume at the beginning (fade-in) or end (fade-out) of a clip. A crossfade is when one clip fades out while another fades in. There are two ways to create fades and crossfades in SONAR: offline (destructive) and real-time (non-destructive).

Using Fades and Crossfades in Real Time

You can create real-time fades and crossfades in the Track view's Clips pane. Real-time fades and crossfades do not change the data in the clip. SONAR reads the fade-in, fade-out or crossfade in the clip and adjusts the gain accordingly. You can edit he crossfade's start time and end times.

You can set the type of fade-in or fade-out you want to use as a default:

- Linear—A straight line, raising or lowering the volume at a steady rate.

- Slow Curve—A curved fade which starts to change the volume slowly at first and then rapidly increasing (fade-in) or decreasing (fade-out) the volume.

- Fast Curve—A curved fade which starts to change the volume quickly at first and then rapidly decreasing (fade-out) or increasing (fade-in) the volume.

The following crossfade combinations are possible:

Crossfade combination...	Looks like this...
Linear out/Linear in	
Linear out/Slow Curve in	
Linear out/Fast Curve in	

Slow Curve out/Linear in

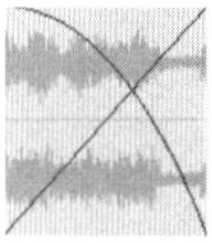

Slow Curve out/Slow Curve in

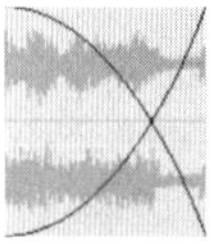

Slow Curve out/Fast Curve in

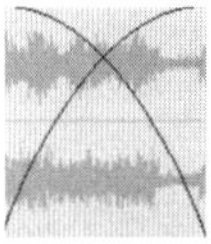

Fast Curve out/Linear in

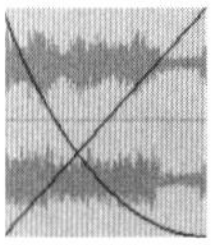

Fast Curve out/Slow Curve in

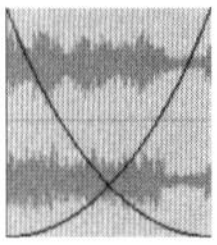

Fast Curve out/Fast Curve in

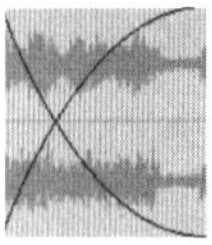

To Create a Real-time Fade-in in an Audio Clip

Use the following procedure to create a fade-in in an audio clip:

1. In the Track view's Clips pane, move your mouse over the top part of the beginning of a clip until the cursor looks like this: .

2. When your cursor changes, click and drag to the right until you reach your desired fade-in length.

As you drag your mouse a fade-in appears on your clip.

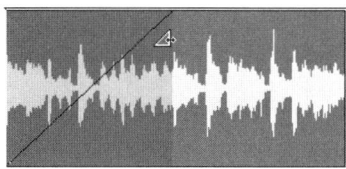

To Create a Real-time Fade-out in an Audio Clip
Use the following procedure to create a fade-out in an audio clip:

1. In the Track view's Clips pane, move your mouse over the top part of the end of a clip until the cursor looks like this: ▧ .

2. When your cursor changes, click and drag to the left until you reach your desired fade-out length.

   As you drag your mouse a fade-out appears on your clip.

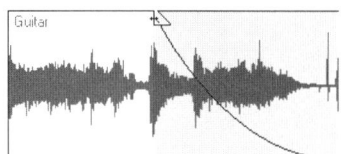

To Create an Automatic Crossfade (Real-time)
Use the following procedure to create a crossfade between two audio clips:

1. In the Track view, click the Enable/Disable Automatic Crossfades combo button located next to the Snap to Grid button or press the *x* key.

2. Click the down arrow on the Enable/Disable Automatic Crossfades combo button, select **Default Crossfade Curves** and select a crossfade curve.

3. Select and drag an audio clip so that it overlaps another audio clip. You should overlap the clips by the length you want the crossfade.

4. When you have the clip positioned where you want it, release the mouse button to drop the clip.

   The Drag and Drop Options dialog appears.

5. In the Drag and Drop Options dialog, check the Blend Old With New checkbox and click OK.

6. The two clips now overlap with a crossfade, looking something like this:

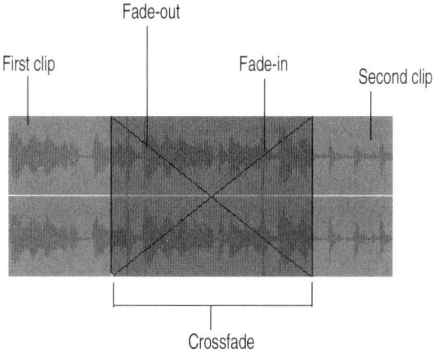

You can edit fade-ins and fade-outs. You can change the start, end and position of a fade. The following procedures all demonstrate edits to a fade-in, but fade-outs work exactly the same.

To Edit the Start Time of a Fade While Maintaining the End Time of the Fade

Changing the start time of a fade-in is essentially slip editing the beginning of the clip. The beginning of the fade-in can not be separated from the beginning of the clip. Use this procedure to change the start time of the fade-in while maintaining the current end time of the fade:

1. In the Clips pane, move your cursor over the bottom part of the beginning of a clip which has a fade-in.

2. When your cursor looks like this ⌐⌐ , click and drag the beginning of the fade-in (and the clip) to the desired location and release.

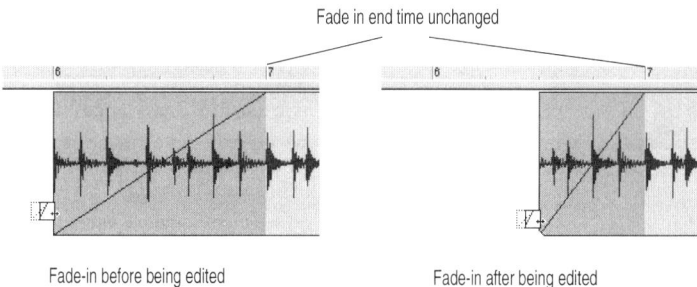

To Edit the Start Time of a Fade While Maintaining the Length of the Fade

Use this procedure to change the start time of the fade-in while maintaining the current end time of the fade:

1. In the Clips pane, move your cursor over the middle part of the beginning of a clip which has a fade-in.

2. When your cursor looks like this ⌁ , click and drag the beginning of the fade-in (and the clip) to the desired location and release.

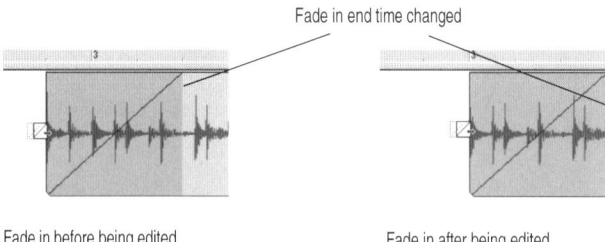

Fade in before being edited   Fade in after being edited

To Change an Existing Fade

Use the following procedure to change an existing fade on a clip:

1. Move your cursor over the beginning of a fade-out or the end of a fade-in, until your cursor looks like this: ⌁ .

2. Right-click to and select the desired fade type from the menu that appears.

To Change an Existing Crossfade

Use the following procedure to change an existing crossfade:

1. Move your cursor over the region where the crossfade is.

2. Right-click and select the desired crossfade from the menu that appears.

Applying Fades and Crossfades Offline

SONAR provides several commands for applying gradual volume changes to audio data. The first command, **Fade/Envelope**, lets you fade in or fade-out, and lets you choose an envelope, a curve that governs the rate of the fade. The starting envelope can be linear (straight line), exponential, or inverse exponential. You can change the shape of the envelope before applying the fade.

The envelope in the Fade/Envelope dialog box is made of one or more connected line segments (the linear curves are a single segment, the exponential curves consist of nine segments each). Although the endpoints of the curve are fixed, you can move the intermediate points, and create new intermediate points, to change the shape of the curve.

To do this...	Do this...
Move a point	Click and drag it to a new location
Insert a new point	Click on the line between existing points
Remove a point	Drag it onto the next point
Restart from the original curve	Click Reset

The second command, *Crossfade*, lets you create a smooth transition from one audio clip to another, by fading two overlapping audio clips simultaneously (one fades out, the other fades in). As with *Fade/Envelope*, you can choose from three different starting curves and change the shape of the curve.

To Apply a Fade to Audio Data

1. Select the audio data to be affected.
2. Choose *Process-Audio-Fade/Envelope* to open the Fade/Envelope dialog box.
3. Select an envelope from the dropdown list.

4. If desired, manipulate the curve as described in the table above.
5. Click OK.

SONAR applies the fade to the selected audio data.

385

To Crossfade Two Overlapping Clips

1. Select two overlapping audio clips. They need not be on the same track, but they must overlap in time for the command to have any effect.

2. Choose **Process-Audio-Crossfade** to open the Crossfade dialog box.

3. Select an envelope from the dropdown list.

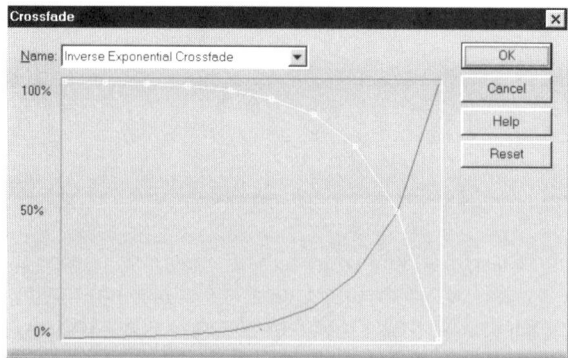

4. If desired, manipulate the curve as described in the table above. You can manipulate only the curve pertaining to the first of the two overlapping clips; the second curve is automatically adjusted so that the two curves constantly add up to 100%.

5. Click OK.

SONAR applies the two fades to the selected data.

Audio Effects (Audio Plug-ins)

SONAR provides the ability to use plug-in audio effects using Microsoft's DirectX technology. Some audio plug-in effects are supplied with SONAR. Others can be purchased from third-party software manufacturers, and appear automatically in SONAR's menus once they are installed on your system. If you need help when using a plug-in, press the F1 key on your computer keyboard to open the plug-in's help file. Please note that third-party plug-ins may not have a help file.

This section describes the effects that are included with SONAR.

Using plug-in effects is similar to using the audio processing commands off-line. The overall procedure is as follows:

- In the Track view, right-click the Fx field and select an effect from the popup menu.

- Set effect parameters (or select a preset).

- Listen to the track and adjust parameters based on what you hear.

You can add audio effects, like MIDI effects, to audio tracks in real time (during playback) in the Console and Track views. Unlike any of the audio processing discussed so far, using effects in real time is non-destructive. This means that the audio clip data itself is not modified, and no new audio files are created. See "Mixing and Effects Patching" on page 419, for more information on real-time effects.

Note:

Offline effects may cause your audio clips to grow in size. For example, when you apply reverb, your clip may need to grow to accommodate the tail end of an echo.

Applying Audio Effects

From the Console and Track views you can destructively apply audio effects for one or more tracks. When you are pleased with the audio effects you have patched into a track, you can apply the effects to the track. Destructively applying effects to a track saves resources, allowing you to include additional tracks and/or effects.

To Apply Audio Effects

Add one or more audio effects to one or more tracks in either the Track view or the Console view, and then:

1. In the Track view, select the tracks you want to be affected.
2. Select ***Process-Apply Audio Effects*** from the menu.
3. If desired, select the option to delete the effects after applying them.
4. Click OK.

If you do not delete the effects from each track after applying them, they remain active.

Note:

Applying effects can be undone, but the effects are not then re-patched in the Effects bin.

Mixing Audio Effects

The dialog box for each plug-in effect has a Mixing tab that provides three options for processing the data.

Option...	Meaning...
Process In-Place, Mono to Mono	Audio is processed clip-by-clip, in mono format. The processed output of the plug-in replaces the original clip's data, in-place. (If the plug-in produces only stereo output, SONAR automatically converts the audio to mono.)
	This option is best for effects like Time/Pitch Stretching and Parametric Equalization.
Process In-Place, Creating Stereo Output Tracks	Audio is fed into the plug-in, clip-by-clip, in mono format. A new stereo track is inserted beneath the selected track, and the stereo output of the plug-in is placed into this stereo track. (If the plug-in produces only mono output, SONAR automatically converts it to stereo.)
	If you check Keep Original Data, SONAR won't delete the original audio data. This lets you create stereo wet-only tracks for finer mixing control. If you leave Keep Original Data unchecked, the processed data will replace the original audio clips.
Create a Send Submix	All selected audio tracks are mixed down into a stereo submix. This stereo submix is fed into the plug-in, in stereo. The stereo output of the plug-in is placed into a new stereo track at the destination you choose.
	If you check Keep Original Data, SONAR won't delete the original audio data. If you leave it unchecked, the processed data will replace the original audio clips.

Adding Parametric Equalization

The *Cakewalk-FxEQ* command lets you apply a complex filter to your audio data. The complex filter is a combination of up to eight simple filters or bands, each defined individually.

Parameters for each filter are described in the following table:

Parameter/Option...	Meaning...
Voice	The voice field lists the band which the other parameters are affecting.
Center Frequency—coarse	The center frequency of the current band (the band listed in the Voice field). The range is from 20 Hz to 20,000 Hz.
Center Frequency—fine	A fine tuning of the center frequency.
Bandwidth (Q)—coarse	The bandwidth of the selected voice.
Bandwidth (Q)—fine	A fine tuning of the bandwidth of the selected voice.
Active Channel L + R	When selected the EQ affects both the left and right channels.
Active Channel L	When selected the EQ affects the left channel only.
Active Channel R	When selected the EQ affects the right channel only.
Bypass	The plug-in is bypassed in the chain.
Band (1-8)	Each band can be set to a different frequency and bandwidth or bypassed by clicking its bypass button immediately above the band's selection button.
Lo Shelf	A low frequency gain or cut. Lo Shelf can be set from between 20 and 200 Hz
Hi Shelf	A high frequency gain or cut. Hi Shelf can be set as low as 4000 Hz
Trim	The trim setting for the plug-in.

The horizontal axis shows increasing frequency; the vertical axis shows the gain or attenuation at each frequency. If the curve is above the horizontal center line, parts of the signal at that frequency will be boosted; if the curve is below the center line, the signal will be attenuated.

Parametric equalization is useful in many different circumstances. For example, you can use it to boost low frequencies or high frequencies, to attenuate 60-cycle hum or high-frequency noise, or to boost a particular instrument sound for use in other SONAR commands.

To Apply the Parametric Equalizer to Audio Data

1. Select the audio data to be affected.
2. Choose **Audio Effects-Cakewalk-FxEq** from the **Process** menu or from the popup menu to open the Cakewalk FxEq dialog box.
3. Click band number 1 to set options for the Band 1, as described in the table above.
4. Click band number 2 to set it as current and set parameters for the second band. Repeat for as many bands as you need.
5. Click OK.

SONAR applies the composite filter to the selected data.

Adding Chorus

The **Cakewalk-FxChorus** command fattens the audio to make one instrument sound like many. When many people sing together, for example, each of their voices is slightly out of tune and off the beat. Therefore, detuning and delaying the signal makes many instruments sound richer, including guitars, vocals, and strings.

The Chorus effect has the ability to act on a stereo track or a stereo pair, a pair of consecutive tracks, one of which is panned hard left (0), the other of which is panned hard right (127). The feedback signal can be crossed between the tracks to create a richer stereo effect.

The parameters used to specify the chorus effect are as follows:

Parameter/Option...	Meaning...
Voice Settings—delay(ms)	The amount of delay in milliseconds for the selected voice.
Voice Settings—mod depth	The modulation depth setting determines the amount of range the Chorus sweeps.
Voice Settings—pan	Left/Right pan. 0 is center. -1 is hard left. 1 is hard right.
Voice Settings—mod freq.	The modulation frequency sets the speed of the Chorus's sweep.
Voice 1-4	Four separate choruses. Bypass a voice by clicking the on button above the voice's selection button.
Global	Controls all four voices.
Mix Level	The Wet/Dry mix of the output. If set all the way to the left, the chorus has no effect on output. If set all the way to the right eliminates all dry signal.
Output Level	Output volume level.
Bypass	The plug-in's bypass button.

To Apply Chorusing to Audio Data

1. Select the audio data to be affected. Select a stereo pair for stereo chorusing.
2. Choose **Audio Effects-Cakewalk-FxChorus** from the **Process** menu or from the popup menu to open the Cakewalk FxChorus dialog box.
3. Set the chorus parameters, as described in the table above.
4. Click OK.

SONAR applies the specified chorus effect to the selected data.

Applying Delay

The **Cakewalk-FxDelay** command creates a series of repeating signals from the original signal. You can create a single echo on the original signal, or a series of echoes up to five seconds apart.

Parameters for the Delay effect are identical to those for the Chorus effect. The difference is that with Chorus the delay parameters can range from 0 to 80 ms, whereas with Delay the delay parameters can range from 0 to 5000 ms. As with Chorus, Delay can act on a stereo pair of tracks

The parameters used to specify the chorus effect are as follows:

Parameter/Option...	Meaning...
Delay(ms)—coarse	The delay time in milliseconds.
Delay(ms)—fine	A fine tuning of the delay time.
Feedback	The regeneration of the delay.
Pan	Left/Right pan. 0 is center. -1 is hard left. 1 is hard right.
Voice 1-4	Four separate delays. Bypass a voice by clicking the on button above the voice's selection button.
Global	Controls all voices.
Mix Level	The Wet/Dry mix of the output. If set all the way to the left, the chorus has no effect on output. If set all the way to the right eliminates all dry signal.
Output Level	The output volume level.
Bypass	The plug-ins bypass button.

To Apply Delay to Audio Data

1. Select the audio data to be affected. Select a stereo pair for stereo delay.
2. Choose **Audio Effects-Cakewalk-FxDelay** from the **Process** menu or from the popup menu to open the Cakewalk FxDelay dialog box.
3. Set the parameters in the dialog, as described in the table above.
4. Click OK.

SONAR applies the specified delay effect to the selected data.

Adding Flanging

The *Cakewalk-FxFlange* command mixes the original signal with a slightly delayed version of the signal, so that the two are out of phase. This creates a spacey, ethereal sound.

The parameters used to specify the chorus effect are as follows:

Parameter/Option...	Meaning...
Delay(ms)—factor	The delay time for
Feedback—factor	The amount of output signal that is fed back through the flanger.
Pan—factor	Left/Right pan. 0 is center. -1 is hard left. 1 is hard right.
Mod. Freq.—factor	The speed at which the pitch modulates
Voice 1-2	Two separate flangers. Bypass a voice by clicking the on button above the voice's selection button.
Global	Controls both voices.
Mix Level	The Wet/Dry mix of the output. If set all the way to the left, the chorus has no effect on output. If set all the way to the right eliminates all dry signal.
Output Level	Plug-ins output volume.
Bypass	The plug-ins bypass button.

To Apply Flanging to Audio Data

1. Select the audio data to be affected. Select a stereo pair for stereo flanging.
2. Choose *Audio Effects-Cakewalk-FxFlange* from the *Process* menu or from the popup menu to open the Cakewalk FxFlange dialog box.
3. Set the parameters in the dialog, as described in the table above.
4. Click OK.

SONAR applies the specified flanging effect to the selected data.

Applying Reverb

The *Cakewalk-FxReverb* command adds many small echoes to a signal to create the illusion of spaciousness. By changing the parameters, you can simulate a stage, a hall, an arena, or a variety of other room types. The reverb parameters are as follows:

Parameter/Option...	Meaning...
Room Size	Set the size of the room. **Note**: Automation changes in this parameter should be made only during periods of silence in a track to prevent artifacts from being introduced to the signal.
Decay Time	The time after which the reverberation of a signal stops.
High Frequency Rolloff	Removes high frequencies from the output.
High Frequency Decay	How much faster the high frequencies rolloff
Density	The number of reflections in the reverb.
Pre Delay	Time before the reverb starts.
Motion Rate	The motion rate is measured in Hz and is designed to simulate movement in a room.
Motion Depth	This setting sets the amount of motion for the Motion Rate parameter.
Level	The plug-in's output volume.
Mix	The Wet/Dry mix of the output. If set all the way down, the chorus has no effect on output. If set all the way up eliminates all dry signal.

To Apply Reverb to Audio Data

1. Select the audio data to be affected. Select a stereo pair for stereo reverb.
2. Choose *Audio Effects-Cakewalk-FxReverb* from the *Process* menu or from the popup menu to open the Cakewalk FxReverb dialog box.
3. Set the reverb parameters, as described in the table above.
4. Click OK.

SONAR applies the reverb effect to the selected data.

Shifting Pitch

The *Cakewalk-Pitch Shifter* raises or lowers the pitch of an audio signal, while leaving the duration of the audio clip unchanged. The pitch shift parameters are as follows:

Parameter/Option...	Meaning...
Pitch	The amount by which the pitch is changed, in semitones
Dry Mix (%)	The volume of the original, unprocessed signal passed to the output
Wet Mix (%)	The volume of the processed signal passed to the output
Feedback Mix (%)	The amount of pitch-shifted signal that is fed into a delay line
Delay Time (ms)	The length of the delay in milliseconds
Mod. Depth (ms)	The amount the delay time will vary

To Apply Pitch Shift to Audio Data

1. Select the audio data to be affected.
2. Choose **Process-Audio Effects-Cakewalk-Pitch Shifter** to open the Cakewalk FX Pitch Shifter dialog box.
3. Set the pitch shift parameters, as described in the table above.
4. Click OK.

SONAR applies the pitch shift to the selected data.

This is a fast pitch shifter that uses minimal computation time. The *Cakewalk Time/Pitch Stretch* command, described below, can produce higher quality output, but requires a lot more computational time.

Stretching Time and Pitch

The *Cakewalk-Time/Pitch Stretch* command lengthens or shortens audio data, and raises or lowers pitch. Time and pitch can be stretched independently. You can use this effect to stretch or compress audio while preserving pitch, or to change pitch while preserving duration, or both. Time/Pitch Stretch is not available in real-time. For real-time time and pitch stretching, use Groove clips. For more information, see Chapter 6, *Using Loops*.

The time/pitch stretch parameters are as follows:

Parameter/Option...	Meaning...
Time (%)	The new length of the audio clip, as a percentage of the length of the original clip.
Pitch	The amount by which the pitch is changed, in semitones.
Source Material	The type of audio data. Selecting an option sets recommended values for the Block Rate, Overlap Ratio, Crossfade Ratio, Accuracy, and Algorithm parameters.
Block Rate (Hz)	Used to calculate the size of the data "blocks" processed by Time/Pitch Stretch. Lower values lead to larger block sizes. If the material to be processed is generally less percussive or lower in pitch, using a lower block rate will make the algorithm operate more efficiently.
Overlap Ratio	The amount of overlap between consecutive blocks.
Crossfade Ratio	The crossfade amount for the blocks.
Accuracy	The accuracy of the calculations. Normal is good for most sounds. High accuracy gives slightly better quality, but takes longer to process.
Algorithm	The algorithm used for pitch stretching. The MPEX algorithm is the default. Select Normal if you want to use the same algorithm used by previous versions of SONAR.

The Time and Pitch parameters can be set by typing numbers in the appropriate boxes, or by dragging the sliders or the crosshair in the graph. Holding Shift while dragging the crosshair snaps the crosshair to the nearest axis: X (time), Y (pitch), or the diagonal (equal time and pitch). Diagonal values on the graph can be processed very quickly and with very high quality, but have the trade-off that changing pitch does not preserve duration, and vice versa.

For the most natural-sounding results, choose low settings; transpose by no more than a third or a fourth. Higher values, though, can be used for special effects.

Note:
This is a fast pitch shifter that uses minimal computation time.

To Apply Time/Pitch Stretch to Audio Data
1. Select the audio data to be affected.
2. Choose *Audio Effects-Cakewalk-Time/Pitch Stretch* from the *Process* menu or from the popup menu to open the Cakewalk FX Time/Pitch Stretch dialog box.
3. Set the time/pitch stretch parameters, as described in the table above.
4. Click OK.

SONAR applies the time/pitch stretch to the selected data.

10 Working with Software Synthesizer

You can use a variety of software synthesizer formats with SONAR™, including DXi's, VSTi's, ReWire instruments, SoundFonts, and stand-alone soft synths. SONAR includes the Cyclone DXi, which allows you to stack up to 16 ACIDized loop tracks side-by-side for editing with automatic tempo synchronization (see the Cyclone topics in the online help). A software synthesizer is a software program that produces various sounds through your sound card when the soft synth program receives MIDI data from a MIDI controller or sequencer program. **DX Instruments**, or **DXi's**, are a plug-in form of software synthesizer designed for responsive, low-latency performance on the Windows platform. Some DXi's can be programmed to generate rhythmic patterns and do not require MIDI input from SONAR. You can control and play DXi's in real time using their internal interface or external MIDI devices like keyboards, guitar synths, or wind controllers. You can automate the controls of some DXi's. Some DXi's are used as MIDI-controlled audio processors, such as vocoders, intelligent pitch shifters, or tempo-based delays. You can patch plug-in effects to DXi tracks.

You can now use **VST Instruments** and effects with SONAR, using the included VST Adapter, which runs when you install SONAR. You can run it manually when you get new VST plug-ins (see "Using VST Synths and Plug-ins" on page 417).

SONAR has a **Synth Rack view** to make inserting a DXi or ReWire instrument into a one-step process, and to make viewing and configuring these instruments simple. SONAR also supports **multi-port DXi's**, which allow you to use different audio tracks and effects for each patch or group of patches in a multi-timbral, multi-port DXi.

In This Chapter

Kinds of Soft Synths. 400
Synth Rack View 400
DX Instruments (DXi's) 401
ReWire Instruments. 410
Stand-alone Synths 415
Using VST Synths and Plug-ins. 417

Kinds of Soft Synths

There are several basic kinds of soft synths:

- DXi (plug-in synths built with DirectX technology)—These programs appear as plug-ins for audio tracks or buses, just like plug-in effects. They can also be inserted in SONAR's Synth Rack view.

- ReWire instruments—These instruments can function as stand-alone devices that you play with a MIDI controller or through the ReWire instrument's internal sequencer, or with recorded MIDI data from SONAR.

- Stand-alone synths—These programs work like external MIDI modules. You select the stand-alone synth's MIDI driver as an output for a MIDI track in your sequencer program (SONAR), and the track plays the stand-alone synth as if it were an external MIDI module.

- SoundFonts—The SoundFont format is a product of Creative, which makes the SoundBlaster sound cards. You need either a SoundBlaster sound card or the LiveSynth Pro DXi software to use SoundFonts.

Note: If you play DXi's in real time from a MIDI controller, you'll get noticeably better performance if you use WDM or ASIO sound card drivers instead of the older MME type. The lower latency of WDM and ASIO drivers provides quicker real-time response to note on/off and other commands. Playback of recorded MIDI data is not affected by your audio driver.

Synth Rack View

Open the Synth Rack view with the ***View-Synth Rack*** command. The Synth Rack view lets you view, insert, delete, and configure your DXi, VSTi, and ReWire soft synths. You can also mute and solo any or all of them from this view. Each time you insert a soft synth into your project, a new row appears in the Synth Rack view with the name of the soft synth and its current preset. You can select different presets from the view. You can insert as many copies of the same DXi soft synth as you like; each new copy appears in a new row and has the same name, but has a higher number after the name (ReWire soft synths can only have one copy open). The new higher-numbered name also appears on the menus of audio track inputs and MIDI track outputs.

Insert button — Currently inserted synths

There is much more information about the Synth Rack view in the online help. Press F1 when the Synth Rack view is open and on top to display the appropriate help topic.

DX Instruments (DXi's)

In order to play a DXi from a MIDI controller or with recorded MIDI data, you need to have at least one audio track that lists the DXi in its Input field, and at least one MIDI track that lists the DXi in its Output field. The data from the MIDI track feeds the audio track and plays the DXi. If you're playing the DXi with a MIDI controller, the MIDI track that's feeding the audio track must have the focus (gold or tan color). You can also patch the DXi into an audio track's Fx field instead of an audio track's Input field.

To add a DXi to the audio tracks' In menus (drop-downs) and the MIDI tracks' Out menus, you have to insert each DXi that you want to use into each project. There are two basic ways to insert DXi's in SONAR:

- You can insert DXi's from the Synth Rack view or with the ***Insert-DX Instruments*** command. If you use this method, you can choose to have SONAR create the necessary audio and MIDI tracks, and patch them together correctly. If you want to use multiple audio tracks to take advantage of SONAR's support for the multi-output DXi 2 format, you need to create and patch additional MIDI tracks manually to feed the additional audio tracks.

- You can insert DXi's into Fx bins of individual audio tracks. If you use this method, you need to set a MIDI track's Output field to the name of the DXi you inserted. Then you can record MIDI data in the MIDI track to play the DXi with.

401

Multi-port DXi's

A multi-port DXi allows you the option of using a different audio track for every output that the DXi has. This allows you to use different plug-in effects for each sound (or in some cases, group of sounds) that a DXi produces. For example, if a DXi can produce 16 sounds at the same time, and has 4 outputs, you can send any of the 16 sounds out through any of 4 different outputs, giving you a choice of 4 different plug-in configurations for that DXi. You would use 4 different audio tracks: one for each output. If a DXi can produce 8 sounds at the same time, and has 8 outputs, you could use 8 audio tracks and 8 plug-in configurations. If you need more plug-in configurations or just more sounds, you can insert more copies of the same DXi, using new audio tracks for all of the new copy's outputs. You can also send all the MIDI tracks out the same output and audio track if you don't need separate plug-ins for each sound, or just want to use the DXi's internal effects.

The Insert DXi Synth Options dialog gives you the option of automatically creating a separate audio track for each output that the DXi has, or creating just one audio track for Output 1 of that particular DXi. Each new copy (also called an *instance*) of a DXi is considered to be a separate instrument, and appears in a separate row in the Synth Rack view, with a number after its name representing which copy it is.

Inserting a DXi

The procedure for inserting multi-output and single-output DXi's is basically the same. There are just more tracks possibly involved when you insert a multi-output DXi.

There are several places where you can insert a DXi into your project:

- Preferred method 1—You can insert the DXi into the project from the Synth Rack view. This method lets you use all of a multi-port DXi's outputs, if you want to. This method gives you the options of automatically creating a matched combination of an audio and MIDI track, creating just an audio track with the DXi patched as a track input, creating no new tracks, and creating separate audio tracks for each of the DXi's outputs.

- Preferred method 2—You can insert the DXi by using the ***Insert-DX Instruments*** command, which gives you the same insertion and output options as the Synth Rack view.

- Alternate method—You can insert the DXi into the Fx field of an audio track or bus. You must then change the Output field of a MIDI track to the name of the DXi you inserted in order to play the audio track or bus with data from the MIDI track. If you insert a multi-output DXi with this method, you can only use the first output of the DXi.

You can insert more than one copy (also called an *instance*) of the same DXi. Each new copy has the same name as the previous copy except for having a higher number after the name. Every copy appears in a separate row in the Synth Rack view, and in the drop-down menus of audio track inputs and MIDI track outputs.

To Insert a DXi from the Synth Rack View or Menu

1. If you want to use the Synth Rack view, open the Synth Rack view with the *View-Synth Rack* command, and click the Insert button ⊞ to display the popup menu of installed DXi's.

2. If you want to use the menu command, use the *Insert-DXi Synth* command to display the popup menu of installed DXi's.

3. In the popup menu, click the name of the DXi you want to insert.

   The Insert DXi Synth Preferences dialog appears, unless you've previously unchecked the Ask This Every Time checkbox that's in the dialog. If you have, SONAR inserts the DXi according to the preferences you set the last time you used the Insert DXi Synth Preferences dialog. If you need to open the Insert DXi Synth Preferences dialog when it's hidden, click the Insert DXi Synth Options button ▦ in the Synth Rack view toolbar.

4. Choose options from the Insert DXi Synth Preferences dialog according to the following:

   - If you want to create a MIDI track that uses the DXi as an output, check the Create These Tracks: MIDI Source Track checkbox.

   - If you want to create a single audio track that acts as an output for Output 1 of the DXi, check the Create These Tracks: First Synth Output (Audio) checkbox.

   - If you want to create separate audio tracks for each of the DXi's outputs, check the Create These Tracks: All Synth Outputs (Audio) checkbox.

   - If you want to use existing MIDI and audio tracks to play the DXi, uncheck all of the Create These Tracks options. SONAR adds the DXi to the audio track input and MIDI track output menus. You need to set an existing audio track's Input field to the DXi, and set an existing MIDI track's Output field to the DXi.

   - If you want to open the DXi's interface from this dialog, check the Open These Windows: Synth Property Page checkbox.

   - If you opened this dialog from the Insert menu and want to open the Synth Rack view, check the Open These Windows: Synth Rack View checkbox.

   - If you want to open this dialog every time you use the *Insert-DXi Synth* command, or click the Insert button in the Synth Rack view and choose a synth from the popup menu, check the Ask This Every Time option. If you always insert DXi's in the same way, you can uncheck this option so you don't have to deal with the dialog each time. To open the dialog when the option is unchecked, click the Insert DXi Synth Options button ▦ in the Synth Rack view toolbar.

5. Click OK, if you haven't already.

SONAR adds the DXi to the audio track input and MIDI track output menus, and creates any new tracks that you requested. The new tracks already have the correct inputs and outputs patched. Now you can record MIDI data in the DXi MIDI tracks, and/or play the DXi from a MIDI keyboard or controller.

To Insert a DXi in an Fx field

1. In either the Track or Console view, right-click the Fx field of an unused audio track or bus.

   Note: If you patch a DXi into a bus that has no audio track assigned to it, the DXi does not sound. Always use a bus that has at least one audio track sending data to it.

   The plug-in menu appears.

2. Under ***DXi Synth***, choose the name of a DXi.

   Two things happen: the DXi's interface appears, and the DXi's name appears in the track's or bus's Fx field, with a bypass button next to the name.

3. Set the DXi's parameters (choose sounds, effects, etc.), and drag its interface out of the way.

4. Click the Output field of a MIDI track to display the output menu.

5. Select the name of the DXi that you patched into the audio track or bus.

6. If the DXi is multi-timbral, choose a MIDI channel for the MIDI track.

7. Also in the MIDI track, select a bank and patch.

Now you can record some MIDI data into the MIDI track to play the DXi with. See "To Play a DXi with Recorded MIDI Data" on page 405.

You can also play the DXi in real-time from a MIDI controller. See "To Play a DXi from a MIDI Controller" on page 406.

Opening a DXi's Property Page

There are several different methods to open a DXi's property page (interface):

- When you insert the DXi from the Insert menu or Synth Rack view, check the Open These Windows: Synth Property Page checkbox in the Insert DXi Synth Options dialog.

- Double-click the name of the DXi in either a MIDI track's Output field or an audio track's Input field.

- Double-click the row in the Synth Rack view that displays the DXi.

- Double-click the name of the DXi in an Fx bin.

- Click one of the rows in the Synth Rack view to select it, and then click the Properties button in the Synth Rack toolbar (or press *c*).

Playing a DXi

There are several ways to play a DXi:

- You can record MIDI data and use the DXi as a playback device.

  Note: WDM or ASIO drivers do not improve performance when you play back recorded MIDI data—the improvement comes only when you play a DXi in real time from an external MIDI controller or keyboard.

- You can play the DXi in real time from a MIDI controller or keyboard. To avoid excessive latency, your sound card must be using a WDM or ASIO driver. Also, you must set mixing latency to the lowest achievable level (probably less than 10 msec.), which you do by using the *Options-Audio* command to open the Audio Options dialog box, and dragging the Buffer Size slider on the General tab.

- Some DXi's that use the DXi 2 format can send MIDI data, sometimes including MIDI notes, from their interfaces to SONAR. For example, some DXi's have MIDI keyboards built into their interfaces that you can click to send note on/off messages.

  Note: By default, SONAR does not echo any MIDI input or automation data that a DXi sends to any track, but can record this data in any armed MIDI track whose Output field is set to that particular DXi. If you do want to echo DXi input to any MIDI track that has the focus, open the Global Options dialog (*Options-Global* command), and on the MIDI tab, check the Echo DXi Input to All MIDI Tracks option. This option also makes it possible to move the controls in one DXi's interface and change the settings in some other DXi's interface, if the focus is on the MIDI track that's patched to the second DXi. It also makes it possible to record notes or automation data from the DXi to any armed MIDI track.

To Play a DXi with Recorded MIDI Data

1. Insert a DXi into the project (see "Inserting a DXi" on page 402, if necessary).
2. In the MIDI track that sends its output to the DXi, choose a MIDI channel.
3. Open the DXi's interface (if it's not open already) by clicking the Properties button in the Synth Rack view, or by double-clicking the name of the DXi if it's patched into the Fx field of an audio track.
4. Set the DXi's parameters (choose sounds, effects, etc.), and drag its interface out of the way (the DXi's interface does not have to be open for the DXi to sound).
5. If you want to save your DXi settings, type a name in the Presets field, and click the Disk icon that's next to the Presets field.
6. Record some MIDI data into the MIDI track.

When you play back the recorded MIDI data, you should hear the DXi through your sound card's outputs. If you don't, make sure your data is in the right range; a bank, patch, and Channel are selected; your monitor speakers or headphones are turned up; and that none of the relevant tracks are muted.

You can add effects to each of the DXi audio tracks. You can also add MIDI effects to your DXi MIDI tracks.

To Play a DXi from a MIDI Controller

1. Make sure your controller is set to local off.

2. Make sure that the Audio Engine button in the Transport toolbar is depressed.

3. Insert a DXi into your project (see "Inserting a DXi" on page 402, if necessary).

   Note: If you patch a DXi into a bus that has no audio track assigned to it, the DXi does not sound. Always use a bus that has at least one audio track sending data to it.

4. In the MIDI track that sends its output to the DXi, choose a MIDI channel.

5. Open the DXi's interface (if it's not open already) by clicking the Properties button in the Synth Rack view, or by double-clicking the name of the DXi if it's patched into the Fx field of an audio track.

   Note: You can also open a DXi's interface by double-clicking its name where it appears in a MIDI track's Out menu or an audio track's In menu.

6. Set the DXi's parameters (choose sounds, effects, etc.), and drag its interface out of the way.

7. If you want to save your DXi settings, type a name in the Presets field, and click the Disk icon that's next to the Presets field.

8. Make sure that the MIDI track has the focus (its titlebar is gold), and play your MIDI controller.

When you play your MIDI controller you should hear the DXi through your sound card's outputs. If you don't, make sure you're playing in the right range; a bank, patch, and Channel are selected; your monitor speakers or headphones are turned up; your controller is attached to your MIDI interface; and that none of the relevant tracks are muted.

To Remove A DXi from a Track or Bus

- If your DXi is patched into the Fx field of an audio track or bus, right-click the name of the DXi, and choose ***Delete*** from the popup menu.

  Or

- In the audio track that uses the DXi as an input, choose another input for the track.

To Remove a DXi from a Project

- If your DXi is patched into the Fx field of an audio track or bus, right-click the name of the DXi, and choose ***Delete*** from the popup menu.

- If your DXi is patched into the Input field of an audio track, go to the Synth Rack view, click the name of the DXi to select it, and then click the Delete button. SONAR deletes the DXi strip from the Synth Rack view and sets the audio inputs and MIDI outputs of all affected tracks to the next lower-numbered option. SONAR does not delete the affected tracks.

    Note: If you're using a ReWire instrument and not a DXi, always close the ReWire instrument's interface before you delete the instrument from SONAR, or close SONAR.

Muting and Soloing DXi Tracks

SONAR automatically places any audio and MIDI tracks that use DXi's into a group that makes muting and soloing the tracks easy:

- To mute or solo a MIDI track that is patched to a DXi audio track, simply mute or solo the MIDI track—SONAR automatically mutes or solos the correct audio track. If another MIDI track uses the audio track as an output, SONAR leaves the audio track unmuted.

- To mute or solo all the MIDI tracks that are patched to a specific DXi, simply mute or solo the audio track that the MIDI tracks are patched into.—SONAR automatically mutes or solos all the correct MIDI tracks.

    Or

- Click the M or S buttons (mute and solo, respectively) next to the DXi's name in the Synth Rack view. This mutes or solos all the tracks associated with this instance of the DXi.

You can use the mute and solo buttons in the Track view, Synth Rack view, or Console view.

Converting Your DXi Tracks to Audio

Once your project sounds the way you want it to, it's extremely easy to convert your DXi MIDI tracks to either new audio tracks, or Wave, MP3, or other exported files.

To Convert Your DXi Tracks to New Audio Tracks

1. Mute all tracks that you don't want to convert.

2. Use the ***Edit-Bounce to Track(s)*** command.

    The Bounce to Track(s) dialog box appears.

3. In the Source Category field, choose Tracks.

4. In the Channel Format field, choose mono if you want mono tracks, and stereo if you want stereo tracks.

5. In the Source/Buses field, make sure all 4 outputs are selected. This will create a separate audio track for each selected output.

6. In the Mix Enables field, make sure all choices are selected.

7. Click OK.

SONAR creates new audio tracks from the outputs you selected. When you're through converting, don't forget to mute your MIDI tracks so you won't hear them and the new audio track(s) at the same time.

To Export Your DXi Tracks as Wave, MP3, or Other Type Files

1. Mute all tracks that you don't want to export; make sure you don't mute the audio track that the DXi is patched into, or the MIDI track(s) that you are using as a source.

2. Use the *File-Export-Audio* command.

   The Export Audio dialog box appears.

3. In the Look in field, choose the location where you want the new, exported file to be.

4. Type a file name in the File name field.

5. Choose the type of file, the format, and the bit depth of the new file you're creating—for MP3 use 16 bits.

6. In the Mix Enables field, make sure all choices are selected.

7. Click OK.

SONAR creates a new audio file of the type you specified. Find the file in the folder you specified, and double-click it to listen to it.

Automating a DXi's Controls

Some DXi's have controls that you can automate by drawing envelopes in either the Track view or Piano Roll view. Some DXi's allow you to record the movements of their faders and other control knobs. Your DXi's manufacturer determines which controls (if any) you can automate.

Note: By default, you can only record MIDI or automation data sent by a DXi into a MIDI track whose Output field is set to that particular DXi. If you do want to record DXi input to any MIDI track that is armed, check the Echo DXi Input to All MIDI Tracks option on the MIDI tab of the Global Options dialog (*Options-Global* command).

To Record MIDI Input from a DXi's Interface

1. If you want to be able to record on any armed MIDI track, make sure that the Echo DXi Input to All MIDI Tracks option on the MIDI tab of the Global Options dialog (***Options-Global*** command) is enabled. Otherwise, you can only record on a MIDI track whose Output field is set to the DXi you're recording from.

2. Arm one or more MIDI tracks.

3. Set the record mode (***Transport-Record Options*** command). If you want to record different knobs on different takes, use Sound on Sound mode.

4. Open the DXi's interface and, if necessary, use its setup menu to enable recording the DXi's fader movements.

5. Move the Now time to the place where you want to record.

6. Click the Record button to start recording.

7. Move the DXi's controls in the way you want them to move. Some or all of the controls may not be capable of sending MIDI data to be recorded (only some DXi's of the DXi 2 format can do this).

8. Click the Stop button.

SONAR records the fader or knob movements. Check the Output fields of the MIDI tracks you recorded into and play back the track.

To Automate a DXi's Controls in the Track View

1. In a MIDI track that uses the DXi as an output, right-click in the Clips pane and choose ***Envelopes-Create-MIDI*** from the popup menu.

    The MIDI Envelope dialog box appears.

2. In the Type field, select Control, RPN, or NRPN.

3. In the Value field, click the drop-down arrow to see the menu of automatable controls, RPN's, or NRPN's that this DXi has, and select the one you want to automate.

4. In the Channel field, select the channel of the patch in your DXi that you want to control.

5. Click OK.

SONAR draws an envelope for the parameter that you chose. You can edit the envelope to make the parameter behave as you want it to. See "Drawing MIDI Envelopes in the Track View" on page 499.

To Automate a DXi's Controls in the Piano Roll View

1. Select a MIDI track that uses the DXi as an output and open the Piano Roll view.

2. In the Controller pane in the Piano Roll, select Control, RPN, or NRPN.

3. In the Value menu below the Controller menu, click the drop-down arrow to see the menu of automatable controls, RPN's, or NRPN's that this DXi has, and select the one you want to automate.

4. In the Controller pane at the bottom of the Piano Roll view, use the Draw tool to draw a graph of the desired controller values.

Note: MIDI envelopes in the Piano Roll Controllers pane and the Track view Clips pane are actually separate envelopes, even if they control the same parameter. Both kinds of envelopes are visible in the Clips pane, and should generally not be used to control the same parameter. You can convert Piano Roll view envelopes to Track view envelopes by selecting the time range and tracks that the Piano Roll envelopes occupy, and using the *Edit-Convert MIDI To Shapes* command.

ReWire Instruments

ReWire is a technology for transferring audio data between software applications in real time—the software equivalent of a multi-channel audio cable. ReWire is built on the following cornerstones:

- Real-time audio streaming between applications
- Sample accurate synchronization
- Common transport functionality

SONAR supports the ReWire 2.0 format, but with some differences. SONAR interacts with ReWire applications in the following ways:

- You can insert one instance of a ReWire application into each SONAR project. You can insert as many different ReWire applications into a project as your computer can handle.

- You can use a maximum of 16 devices or instruments for each ReWire application.

- To use a MIDI controller with both SONAR and your ReWire application, you need to enable separate MIDI In ports in both applications. If your MIDI interface only has one input, decide which application you want to use your controller in, enable the MIDI In port in that application, and disable it in the other application.

- You can insert ReWire devices into SONAR projects from the Synth Rack view or Insert menu, and you can tell SONAR to create the necessary audio tracks and one MIDI track at that time. You can also tell SONAR to open the ReWire application's property page, because, unlike DXi's, ReWire applications must have their property pages (interfaces) open in order to function.

- SONAR's tempo, transport, and loop points are linked to the ReWire application. Activating or changing any of these settings in the ReWire application(s) changes the same setting in SONAR. and vice versa. If you have several applications open and you make a change in one of them, it may be necessary to put the focus on the other application(s) to update their interfaces.

- You cannot send patch or bank changes from SONAR to the ReWire application. All other track property controls in SONAR control the ReWire device, except the pan controls on MIDI tracks. The pan controls on SONAR's audio tracks control the ReWire device's panning.

- You can mix down or bounce ReWire tracks in SONAR the same way you mix down or bounce DXi tracks (see "Converting Your DXi Tracks to Audio" on page 407).

- You can use SONAR's automation functions on both audio and MIDI tracks that the ReWire application uses.

- Muting or soloing an audio track that a ReWire device uses automatically mutes or solos the MIDI track that feeds that audio track. Muting or soloing a MIDI track that a ReWire device uses will mute or solo the corresponding audio track only if there is only one MIDI track feeding that audio track.

- You must always close your ReWire application(s) before you close SONAR. Some ReWire applications prevent SONAR from closing properly if the ReWire applications are still open.

Inserting a ReWire Instrument

After you install your ReWire applications and reboot your computer, the names of the ReWire applications appear in SONAR's Insert menu under ReWire Devices, and also in the Synth Rack view's Insert button popup menu.

To Insert a ReWire Instrument

1. Open a SONAR project. Do not launch your ReWire application.

2. In the SONAR's Synth Rack view, click the Insert button, and click ***ReWire Devices*** to display the submenu of installed ReWire devices.

    OR

    Use the ***Insert-ReWire Devices*** command to display the submenu of installed ReWire devices.

3. Click the name of the ReWire device you want to insert.

    The Insert DXi Synth Preferences dialog appears.

4. Choose options from the Insert DXi Synth Preferences dialog according to the following:

    - If you want to create a MIDI track that uses the ReWire Instrument as an output, check the Create These Tracks: MIDI Source Track checkbox.

    - If you want to create a single audio track that acts as an output for Output 1 of the ReWire Instrument, check the Create These Tracks: First Synth Output (Audio) checkbox.

    - If you want to create separate audio tracks for each of the ReWire Instrument's outputs, check the Create These Tracks: All Synth Outputs (Audio) checkbox.

    - If you want to use existing MIDI and audio tracks to play the ReWire Instrument, uncheck all of the Create These Tracks options. SONAR adds the ReWire Instrument to the audio track input and MIDI track output menus. You need to set an existing audio track's Input field to the ReWire Instrument, and set an existing MIDI track's Output field to the ReWire Instrument.

    - If you want to open the ReWire Instrument's interface from this dialog, check the Open These Windows: Synth Property Page checkbox (**always check this option**: ReWire Instruments do not sound unless their property pages are open).

    - If you opened this dialog from the Insert menu and want to open the Synth Rack view, check the Open These Windows: Synth Rack View checkbox.

    - If you want to open this dialog every time you use the ***Insert-ReWire Instrument*** command, or click the Insert button in the Synth Rack view and choose a synth from the popup menu, check the Ask This Every Time option. If you always insert ReWire Instruments in the same way, you can uncheck this option so you don't have to deal with the dialog each time. To open the dialog when the option is unchecked, click the Insert DXi Synth Options button 🔳 in the Synth Rack view toolbar.

5. Click OK to close the dialog.

   SONAR adds your ReWire devices to the audio track In menus and the MIDI track Out and Ch menus, creates any tracks you requested, adds the ReWire instrument to the Synth Rack view, and opens the ReWire application's interface.

6. If you get an error message about a MIDI Input problem from your ReWire application, click OK and then use SONAR's ***Options-MIDI Devices*** command to open the MIDI Devices dialog and select the MIDI In port to want to use to record into SONAR. Use your ReWire application's menus to choose a different MIDI In port for your ReWire application. If your MIDI interface only has one input, you have to decide whether you want to use your MIDI controller in SONAR or in your ReWire application. If you want to use your controller in your ReWire application, deselect your MIDI In port in SONAR's MIDI Devices dialog, and select that input in your ReWire application.

7. In the MIDI track whose output is the ReWire audio track, click the drop-down arrow in the Ch field to display the names of the available ReWire devices in your ReWire instrument.

8. Click the name of the device you want to use.

9. Make sure that the audio track you want to hear the ReWire instrument through has the appropriate ReWire channel listed in its Input field.

Now you can record MIDI data in the MIDI track and hear it through the audio track. If you want to use different audio tracks for each ReWire device, see the following procedure.

Note: Always close your ReWire applications before closing a SONAR project.

To Use Separate Audio Tracks for Each ReWire Device

1. Open SONAR, insert a ReWire instrument, and choose All Synth Outputs (Audio) in the Create These Tracks field of the Insert DXi Synth Preferences dialog. Make sure you choose to open the Synth window, and click OK.

   SONAR inserts the ReWire instrument and creates multiple audio tracks.

2. In your ReWire application, assign the devices you want to use to the outputs or channels you want to use. For example, in Propellerheads Reason, you use the back panel of the mixer to drag cables from a device to the output channel you want to use for that instrument.

3. In SONAR, set the Output field of a MIDI track to the name of your ReWire application, and set the Ch. field to the name of the ReWire device you want to play with this track.

4. Record some MIDI data in the track and play it. Find the audio track whose Input field lists the output channel you patched your device into—the playback meter lights up as you play the MIDI track that plays your device.

Now you can use separate effects for each of your ReWire devices.

Note: Always close your ReWire applications before closing SONAR or a SONAR project.

Mixing Down ReWire Instruments

To either mix down or bounce ReWire instruments to new audio tracks, use the same procedures as for DXi's.

For more information, see "Converting Your DXi Tracks to Audio" on page 407

Automating ReWire Instruments

You can automate audio and MIDI tracks that are patched to ReWire instruments the same ways you can automate any of SONAR's audio and MIDI tracks.

For more information, see Chapter 13, *Using Automation*.

ReWire Troubleshooting Guide

The following lists some common issues when you use ReWire with SONAR:

- **SONAR Won't Close Properly**—Always close your ReWire applications before closing SONAR or a SONAR project.

- **Rebirth Won't Play After I Open Its Property Page**—Make sure that the Loop switch in Rebirth is enabled.

- **My ReWire Project Plays at a Different Tempo when Opened from SONAR**—When you open a ReWire project from SONAR, the ReWire project assumes SONAR's default tempo, which is 100. Change SONAR's tempo to match your ReWire project.

- **My MIDI Controller Works in SONAR or my ReWire Application, but not Both**—Choose different MIDI In ports for both SONAR and your ReWire application. Do this in SONAR by using the *Options-MIDI Devices* command, and highlighting the MIDI In port you want to use in SONAR. If you only have one MIDI In port on your MIDI interface or sound card, enable that input in either SONAR or your ReWire application, and disable that input in the other application.

- **I Get a MIDI Input Error Message When I Open a ReWire Application**—If you only have one MIDI Input port on your MIDI interface, you probably have that one reserved for SONAR, leaving none for your ReWire application. If you would rather use your MIDI controller in the ReWire application instead of SONAR, you can deselect your MIDI input port in SONAR's MIDI Devices dialog (*Options-MIDI Devices* command), and then select that MIDI Input from whatever menu your ReWire application has for that purpose. If you have multiple inputs on your MIDI interface, simply select different ones for SONAR and your ReWire application.

Stand-alone Synths

After you install this kind of synth and restart your computer, the name of the synth's MIDI driver appears in SONAR's MIDI Devices dialog box under Outputs.

Playing a Stand-alone Synth

SONAR plays this kind of synth by seeing it as additional MIDI outputs in both the MIDI Devices dialog box and in MIDI tracks' output fields.

To Play a Stand-alone Synth

1. Use the *Options-MIDI Devices* command to open the MIDI Devices dialog box.
2. In the Outputs field, make sure the name of your stand-alone synth's MIDI driver is highlighted, and click OK.
3. Click the Output field of an unused MIDI track to display the output menu.
4. Select the name of the stand-alone synth's MIDI driver.
5. If your stand-alone synth is multi-timbral, change the track's MIDI channel to the same one that the synth uses for the sound you want to hear.
6. Select a bank and patch on your stand-alone synth, if you haven't already.
7. Record some MIDI data in the MIDI track, or play any MIDI controller that's an input for the MIDI track.

When you play your MIDI controller or play back the recorded MIDI data, you should hear the stand-alone synth through your sound card's outputs. If you don't, make sure you're playing in the right range and that your monitor speakers or headphones are turned up, and that none of the relevant tracks are muted.

Recording a Stand-alone Synth

There are several ways to record a stand-alone synth:

- You can use the synth's wave capture function, if it has one. See your synth's documentation for a procedure. Make a note of where the resulting captured Wave file is stored, and then you can import the file into SONAR by using the ***File-Import-Audio*** command.

- You can connect your sound card's outputs to your sound card's inputs, either internally or externally, depending on your sound card's design. After you do this, you need to arm an audio track in SONAR and select one of your sound card's wave drivers as an input. Start recording, and make sure the MIDI track that is routed to the synth is playing back.

- You can use your sound card's wave capture or "what-you-hear" option, if it has one. See the following procedure.

To Record A Stand-alone Synth with your Sound Card's Wave Capture Function

1. Pick a destination audio track and set the Input field to Stereo.

   Note: If you have more than one sound card installed, select the one that your stand-alone synth uses as an output.

2. Arm the destination track.

3. Mute or archive any tracks that you don't want to record to the destination track.

4. If SONAR's metronome is set to use any software synth to produce a click, disable the metronome during recording option in the Project Options dialog box. To do this, select ***Options-Project*** to open the Project Options dialog box, select the Metronome tab and uncheck Recording in the General section.

5. Open your sound card's mixer device. This is normally done by double-clicking the speaker icon on the Windows taskbar, or by choosing ***Start-Programs-Accessories- Multimedia-Volume Control-Options-Properties***.

   Note: Some sound cards, such as the SoundBlaster Live, have their own proprietary mixer. If yours has one, please use it instead.

6. Click Adjust Volume For Recording, and make sure all boxes below are checked.

7. Click OK, and locate the slider marked MIDI, Synth, Mixed Input, or What You Hear. Check the Select box at the bottom, then close the window.

8. In SONAR, click the Record button.

SONAR records all the MIDI tracks that are assigned to the stand-alone synth as a stereo audio track.

After you finish recording, mute the MIDI tracks that you just recorded so you don't hear them and the new audio track at the same time.

Using VST Synths and Plug-ins

You can use VST synths and plug-in effects the same way you use DXi synths and plug-in effects. The Cakewalk VST Adapter program runs automatically when you install SONAR, and adapts your VST plug-ins to use as DX plug-ins. Each time you install new VST synths and/or plug-in effects, you can run the program manually to adapt your new plug-ins.

To Register VST Plug-ins and Instruments to Use as DXi Plug-ins

1. Use the Windows Start menu: *Programs-Cakewalk-Cakewalk VST Adapter 4-Cakewalk VST Adapter 4*. This opens the VST Configuration Wizard.

2. Follow the instructions in the Wizard, and when the VST Plug-in Search Paths dialog appears, click the Add button to browse for the folders where you installed your new VST plug-in(s).

3. After your folders are displayed in the VST Plug-in Search Path dialog, choose from these options to decide how configuration will proceed:

   - Re-scan failed plug-ins—choose this option if there was an error when you originally scanned a plug-in.

   - Re-scan existing plug-ins—choose this option if you're having trouble with an existing plug-in, or if you want to change how plug-ins are displayed in your plug-ins menu.

   - Subdivide menu—choose this option if you want to add breaks between plug-ins in your plug-in menu, to make it easier to read.

   - Don't add VST prefix—choose this option if you don't want the plug-ins you're about to scan to be labeled VST (name of plug-in) in your plug-ins menu.

4. Click Next to have the adapter scan all the displayed folders for VST plug-ins.

   The adapter finds your plug-ins and lists them in the VST Plug-in Configuration dialog.

5. Select a plug-in you want to configure, and click Properties. The VST Plug-In dialog appears, with the selected plug-in listed, and some Plug-in Options:

   - Details—clicking this button opens a Properties dialog that lists the pathname and a few other details about the plug-in.

   - Enable as DXi plug-in—enable this option if you want to use the plug-in as an audio effect.

   - Configure as DXi synth—enable this option if you want to use the plug-in as a soft synth.

   - Do not intercept NRPNs—the adapter uses NRPNs to run automation of your VST plug-ins. However, some instruments have their own implementation of this process, so checking this box passes the NRPNs directly to the instrument, allowing it to manage its own automation.

   - Force stereo operation—some host applications assign a single, mono track to carry a VST plug-in's output. Checking this option forces the host to use two mono tracks or a single stereo track.

   - Editor size—the X field lets you choose the width of the plug-in's property page (in pixels), and the Y field lets you choose the height of the page.

6. Choose the options you want for this plug-in, and click OK.

   The adapter configures the plug-in and returns to the VST Plug-In Configuration dialog.

7. If you want to finish, select no more plug-ins and click Next; otherwise, repeat steps 5 and 6 for additional plug-ins.

Mixing and Effects Patching

This chapter describes SONAR™ as a live digital mixer that gives you full track-by-track control over recording and playback of your project. You can mix in either the Track view or the Console view.

The Console view now has a 4-band EQ patched to every audio track (Producer Edition only). The Console view and the Track view support automation, which lets you record and play back volume and pan changes, and other track parameters. For more information on automation, see Chapter 13, *Using Automation*.

In This Chapter

Preparing to Mix	*420*
Mixing MIDI	*428*
Routing and Mixing Digital Audio	*430*
Metering	*436*
Freeze Tracks and Synths	*441*
Using Real-Time Effects	*444*
Using Control Groups	*449*
Using Remote Control	*454*
Bouncing Tracks	*456*
Preparing Audio for Distribution	*459*

SONAR lets you mix together the digital audio portions of a project, including all real-time effects and control movements, to a stereo track or stereo pair of audio tracks. You can use the mixed-down tracks to create a CD master or to put your work on the World Wide Web.

Preparing to Mix

The Console and Track views contain all the controls you need to mix your project. To open the Console view click the Console view button or choose *View-Console*. The Track view is always open.

The Console View

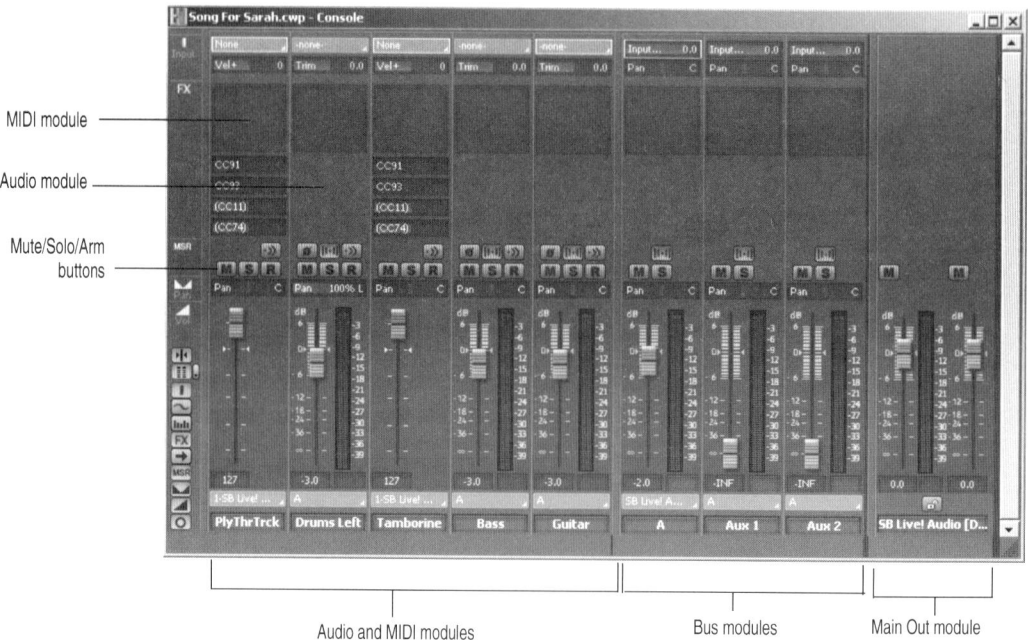

Sound controls in the Console view are grouped in **modules**. There are four types of modules:

Module type...	What you can do...
MIDI track	Set the track's output, channel, bank, and patch; set the input; mute, solo, and arm the track; set channel volume, panning, chorus, and reverb levels; add real-time effects
Audio track	Set the track's output (bus or Main out destination); choose an input; monitor input levels; mute, solo, and arm the track; set track volume and panning; add real-time effects; send audio data to buses or main outs.
Bus	Receive input from one or more audio tracks, add real-time effects, and send the results to a main out or another bus
Main outs	Monitor output levels using meters and control the stereo volume of audio to an output on your audio interface. To adjust both the left and right volume levels at the same time, use the Link button 🔒 for that module.

One module's name is always outlined with a white line. This corresponds to the track with the focus. You can change the focus by clicking to the right of the module's volume fader.

The Console view contains several different types of controls. Here's how they are used:

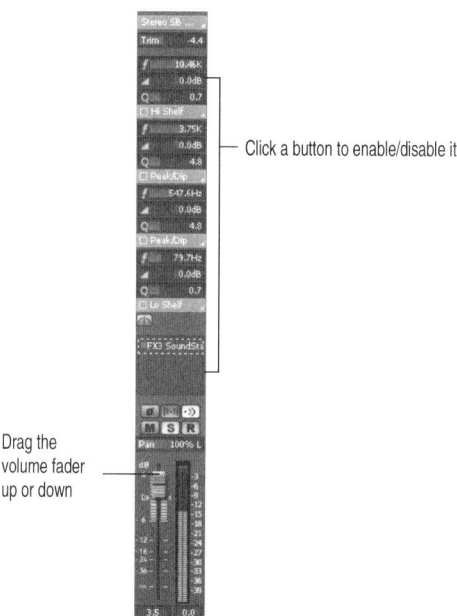

You can adjust Console view controls in the following ways:

- Click on the center of the knob and drag the mouse up or down to adjust the knob
- Click and drag a fader up or down
- Double-click the center of the knob to return it to its snap-to position

Volume and pan faders also have snap-to positions; double-click a fader's knob to return the fader to its snap-to value.

The controls and effects patch points all have tool tips associated with them. To see a description of a particular control or effect, simply rest the cursor over the item for a few seconds.

The Track View

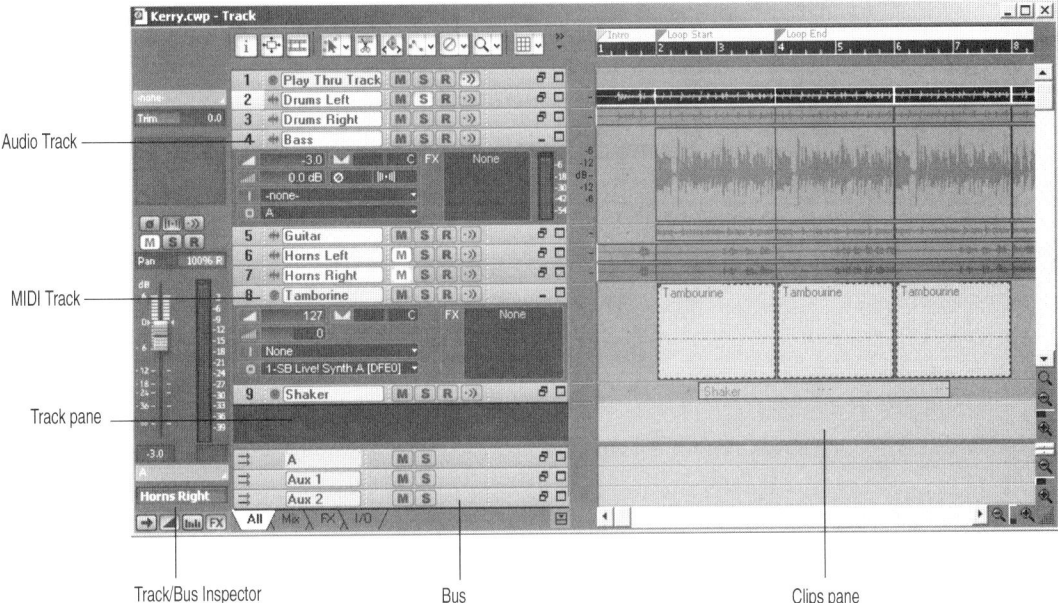

There are three types of modules in the Track view:

Track type...	What you can do...
MIDI track	Set the track's output, channel, bank, and patch; set the input; mute, solo, and arm the track; set channel volume, panning, chorus, and reverb levels; add real-time effects.
Audio track	Set the track's output; set the input and monitor input levels; mute, solo, and arm the track; set track volume and panning; add real-time effects; send audio data to buses or main outs.
Bus	Receive input from one or more audio tracks, add real-time effects, and send the results to a main out or another bus.

423

The Track view contains several different types of controls. Here's how they are used:

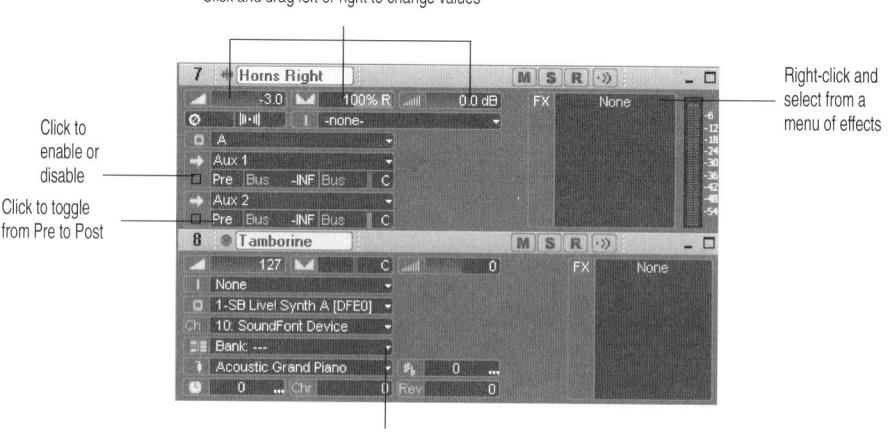

For information on using the controls in the Track view, see Chapter 3, *Changing Track Settings*.

Volume, pan, bus send level and bus send pan also have snap-to positions; double-click the control to return it to its snap-to value.

The controls and effects patch points all have tool tips associated with them. To see a description of a particular control or effect, simply rest the cursor over the item for a few seconds.

Configuring the Console and Track Views

The Console and Track view can be reconfigured in a variety of ways. You can:

- Choose the tracks that you want to see
- Adjust the display of audio meters and clip indicators
- Change the number of buses
- Set control snap-to positions
- Insert new tracks
- Name tracks and buses

Meters are helpful in determining the relative volumes of your audio tracks and in detecting and preventing overload. By default, the Console view displays output level meters in main out modules at all times, and displays record level meters in individual tracks whenever they are armed and have an audio input. The display of meters, however, can place a considerable load on your computer. Showing only the peak indicators, or hiding the meters entirely, can reduce the load on your computer. This may increase the number of audio tracks and real-time effects you can play back at one time.

In the Track view there are several ways to configure which tracks are displayed.

To Display All the Tracks in a Project
- Click the View tool's down arrow and select Show all tracks from the View tool menu.

To Hide Selected Tracks
1. Select the tracks you want to hide.
2. Click the View tool's down arrow and select Hide tracks from the View tool menu.

To Display Only Selected Tracks
1. Select the tracks you want to display.
2. Click the View tool's down arrow and select Show selected tracks from the View tool menu.

To Choose the Tracks that are Displayed Using the Track Manager
1. Click the down arrow next to the View tool and select Track Manager to open the Track Manager dialog box.

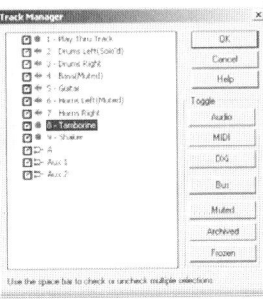

2. In the list, check those tracks you would like displayed in the view in which you are working, and uncheck the rest. You can use Shift-click, Control-click, or the quick select buttons to select multiple modules; press the Spacebar to check or uncheck all the selected modules at once. Please note that the track display selections you make in the Track view do not affect those in the Console view and vice versa.

3. Click OK.

To Hide a Bus or Track
- Right-click on the module and choose *Hide Track* or *Hide Bus*.

To Narrow a Module (Console view only)
1. Right-click in the space next to the module's volume fader.
2. Select *Narrow Strip* from the menu that appears.

To Narrow or Widen all Modules in the Console View
- Click the Narrow/Widen Modules button .

To Display Meters in the Console View
- Click the Show Meters button .

To Customize the Meter Display in the Console View
You can choose which meters you want to display in the Console view. Hiding meters helps to conserve CPU cycles, potentially giving you more power for real-time plug-ins or simultaneous tracks.

1. Click the down arrow next to the Show Meters button .
2. Select *Track Record Meters*, *Track Playback Meters*, *Bus Meters* or *Mains Meters* from the menu that appears.

To Show or Hide Meters in the Track View
- Click the Show/Hide Meters button to display all meters or click on the arrow to the right of the Show/Hide Meters button to display only the meters you want to see or to customize the appearance of your meters.

Option...	What it does...
Record meters	Displays record meters for any armed track.
Playback meters	Displays playback meters.
Output bus meters	Displays meters in buses

For more information about metering options, see "Changing the Meters' Display" on page 438.

To Change a Meter's Range
- Right-click on the meter and choose a new range.

To Add a Bus
1. Right-click in the Bus pane (to add a bus at the end of the current buses) or over an existing bus (to add a bus before it).
2. Select Insert Bus from the menu that appears.

A bus appears in the Bus pane.

To Delete a Bus
1. Right-click in the Bus pane over an existing bus.
2. Select Delete Bus from the menu that appears.

The bus is deleted from the Bus pane.

Note: If you have any track or bus routed through the bus you delete, the signal will be rerouted to the bus's output.

To Create a Bus Send in a Track
1. Right-click in an empty part of the Track pane (Track view) or a track module (Console view).
2. Select *Insert Send* for a list of buses available.
3. Select a bus from the list.

To Set the Snap-to Position of a Knob or Fader
1. Set the control to the desired position.
2. Right-click on the control and choose *Set Snap-To=Current*.

From now on, the control returns to this position when double-clicked.

To Insert a New Track
1. Right-click on an empty area in the Console view or on the title bar of a track in the Track view.
2. Choose *Insert Audio Track* or *Insert MIDI Track*.

SONAR adds a new track to the project.

To Rename a Track or Bus
1. In the Console view, click on the module name. In the Track view double-click on the Track name.
2. Type a new name.
3. Press Enter.

If you rename a track, the new name is copied to the Track view. If no name has been assigned to a track, the Console view and Track view display the track's number.

To Link Left/Right Faders in a Console View Module
1. In the module whose faders you want to link, adjust the volume of each fader to the appropriate level.
2. Click the Link button.

427

Mixing MIDI

SONAR gives you many tools to control your MIDI mix. When your MIDI tracks sound the way you want them to, there are several ways to convert them to audio (see "Converting MIDI to Audio" on page 429).

Mixing a MIDI Track

You can control the mixing and playback of a MIDI track as follows:

To do this...	Do this...
Add a real-time MIDI effect to the track	Right-click in the Effects patch point and select an effect from the list (for more information, "Using Real-Time Effects" later in the chapter)
Remove an effect	Select the effect and press **Delete** or right-click and select **Delete**.
Select the output	Click the Output control and choose one from the list
Select the channel	Click the Channel button and choose one from the list
Select the bank	Click the Bank button and choose one from the list
Select the patch	Click the Patch button and choose one from the list
Set the Chorus level	Adjust the Chorus slider
Set the Reverb level	Adjust the Reverb slider
Mute the track	Click the Mute button
Solo the track	Click the Solo button
Arm the track for recording	Click the Arm button
Set the Pan level	Adjust the Pan fader
Set the Volume level	Adjust the Volume fader
Select the input	Click the input button and choose one from the list

When moving the Volume fader, the Value box in the toolbar displays the level from a scale of 0 (minimum) to 127 (maximum). When you move the Pan slider, the Value box displays the pan value on a scale that ranges from 100% Left to 100% Right with center represented by a C.

Converting MIDI to Audio

The following options cover three basic MIDI setups:

- If your MIDI tracks play back through a DXi soft synth, use either the ***File-Export-Audio*** or ***Edit-Bounce to Track(s)*** commands (see the procedures in "To Export Your DXi Tracks as Wave, MP3, or Other Type Files" on page 408, and "To Convert Your DXi Tracks to New Audio Tracks" on page 407).

- If your MIDI tracks play back through your sound card's synthesizer, see the procedure below.

- If your MIDI tracks play back through external MIDI modules, simply connect their analog outputs to the inputs on your sound card, and record to new audio tracks.

To Convert a Sound Card's Synth Tracks to a Stereo Audio Track

1. Pick a destination audio track and set the Input field to Stereo-(name of your sound card).

   Note: If you have more than one sound card installed, select the one that your synth uses as an output.

2. Arm the destination track.

3. Mute or archive any tracks that you don't want to record to the destination track.

4. If SONAR's metronome is set to use any software synth to produce a click, disable the metronome during recording option in the Project Options dialog box. To do this, select ***Options-Project*** to open the Project Options dialog box, select the Metronome tab and uncheck Recording in the General section.

5. Open your sound card's mixer device. This is normally done by double-clicking the speaker icon on the Windows taskbar, or by choosing ***Start-Programs-Accessories- Multimedia-Volume Control-Options-Properties***.

6. Open the sound card's recording control window (the command is probably ***Options-Properties-Adjust Volume For Recording***) and make sure all boxes below ***Adjust Volume For Recording*** are checked.

7. Click OK, and locate the slider marked MIDI, Synth, Mixed Input, or What You Hear. Check the Select box at the bottom, then close the window.

8. In SONAR, click the Record button.

SONAR records all the MIDI tracks that are assigned to the sound card synth as a stereo audio track.

After you finish recording, mute the MIDI tracks that you just recorded so you don't hear them and the new audio track at the same time.

Routing and Mixing Digital Audio

This section covers mixing your project's digital audio.

Audio clips in each track are processed by any real-time audio effects you have patched in place, passed through the track pan control and volume fader, and then sent to the designated bus or main out, in stereo.

This is shown in the picture below:

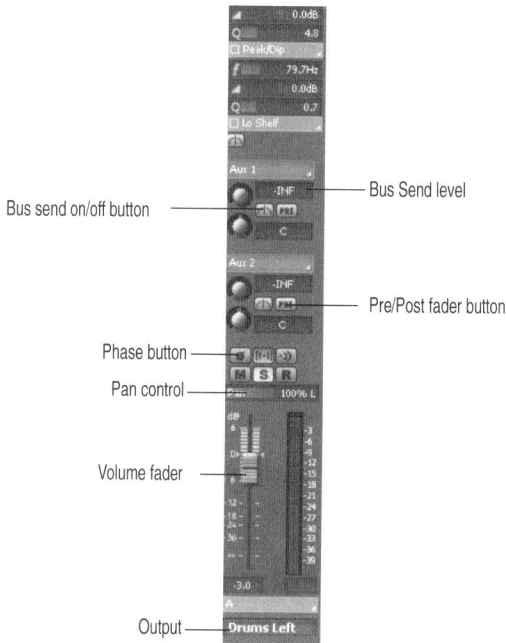

Any audio track can be tapped, before or after the track volume control, and sent to one or more buses. A bus can tap any number of audio tracks. Each track's data passes through the track's send level knob on its way to the bus. This is shown in the diagram below:

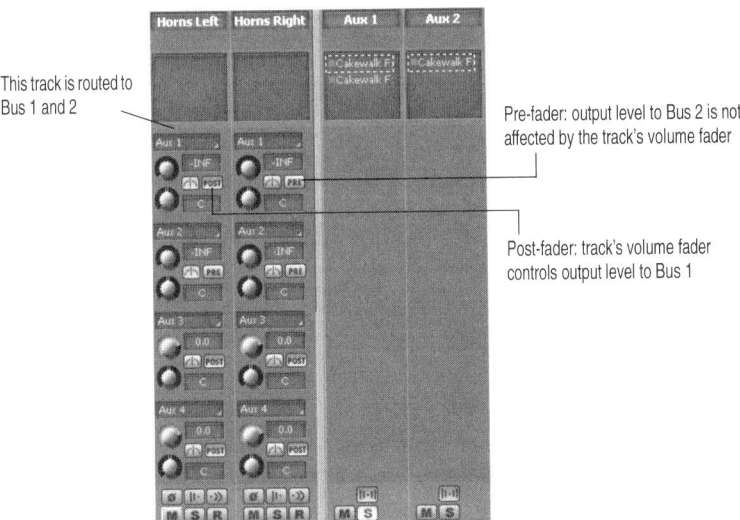

The audio in each bus passes through the send level and pan controls, is processed by any real-time effects you have patched, sent through the output level and pan controls, and then sent to the designated main out, in stereo.

At each main out, all audio data from audio tracks and buses that were routed to that main are mixed together. Finally, the data passes through each main's master volume fader

Audio Tracks

The following graphic shows an audio track's signal flow:

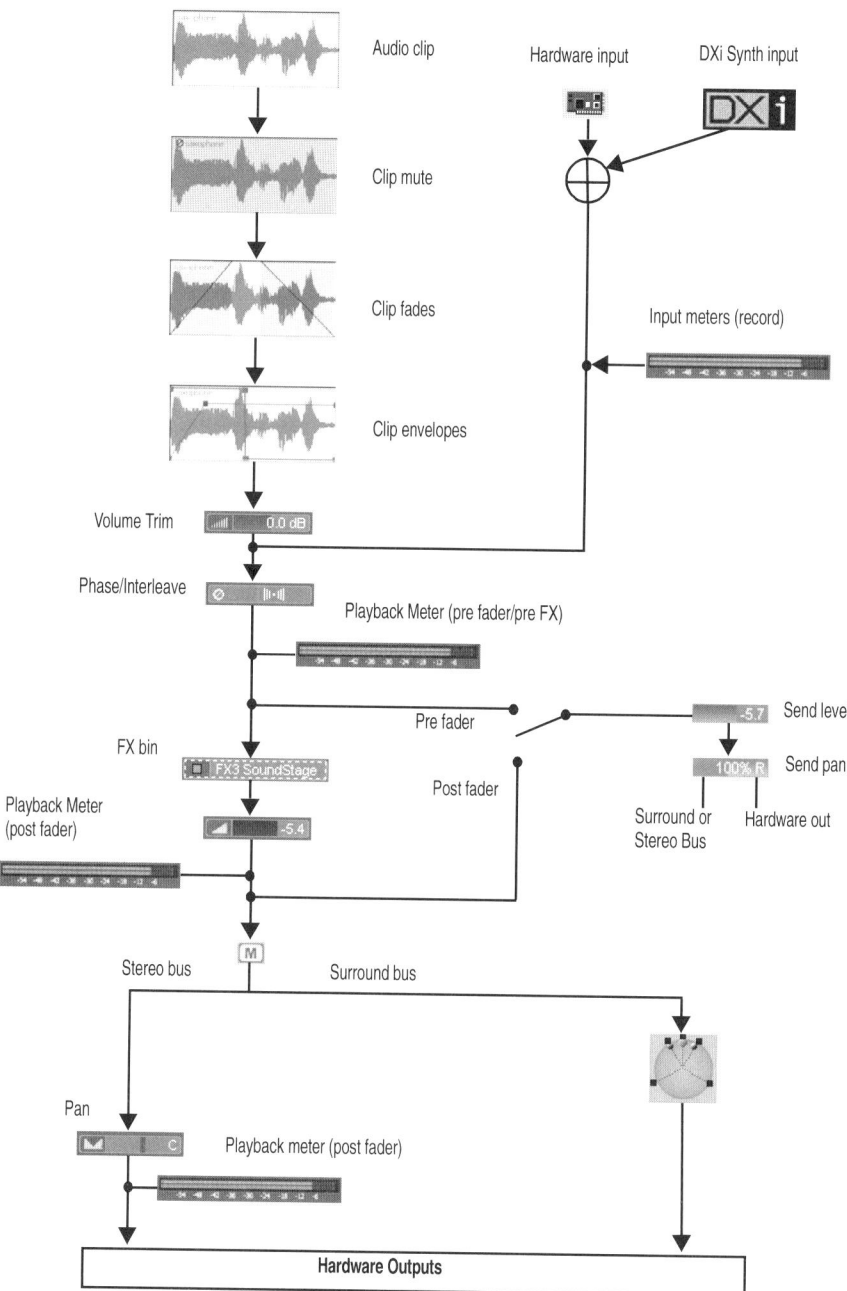

You control the mixing and playback of an audio track as follows:

To do this...	Do this...
Add a real-time audio effect to the track	Right-click in the Effects patch point and select an effect from the list (for more information, see "Using Real-Time Effects" later in the chapter)
Remove an effect	Select the effect and press **Delete** or right-click and select **Delete**.
Send audio data from the track to a bus	Select the corresponding Bus Send Enable and set the Bus Send Level (for more information, see "Stereo Buses" on page 434")
Mute the track	Click the Mute button
Solo the track	Click the Solo button
Arm the track for recording	Click the Arm button
Set the Pan level	Adjust the Pan control
Set the Volume level	Adjust the Volume fader
Select the output	Click the dropdown arrow in the Output field and choose one from the list
Select the input	Click the dropdown arrow in the Input field and choose one from the list

SONAR displays volume in dB (decibels). When adjusting the volume or bus send level controls, a value of 0 dB indicates full signal strength; positive values, up to 6 dB, indicate a signal gain; negative values indicate an attenuated signal. When you move the Pan control, the Value box displays the pan value on a scale that ranges from 100%L (hard left) 100%R (hard right).

Stereo Buses

Buses are useful for mixing together different audio tracks (in stereo) and applying effects to the mix. You can mix the tracks at different volume levels by adjusting each track's bus send level. Buses output to either other buses or to a main out.

You control the bus as follows:

To do this...	Do this...
Send audio data from an audio track to the bus	In an audio track, press the Bus Send Enable button corresponding to the bus, or choose the bus as an output for the track
Set the level of the audio data sent to the bus	In an audio track, set the Bus Send Level corresponding to the bus, or volume fader if the output is to the bus
Set the pan of the audio data sent to the bus	Adjust the Bus Send Pan knob
Set the input level to the bus	Adjust the Input gain on the bus itself
Set the input panning to the bus	Adjust the Input pan on the bus itself
Add a real-time audio effect to the bus	Right-click in the FX patch point and select an effect from the list (for more information, see "Using Real-Time Effects" on page 444)
Remove an effect	Select the effect and press **Delete**, or right-click and choose **Delete**
Set the output level	Adjust the Output volume
Set the output panning	Adjust the Pan setting
Select the output	Click the Output button and choose one from the list

Surround Buses (Producer Edition Only)

Surround buses are useful for mixing and adding effects to create a surround mix.

As with Audio strips, the Value box in the toolbar displays the send and return levels in decibels and the send and return balance values on a scale of 100%L to 100%R.

To Patch a Track Through a Bus

1. Open the Console view (*View-Console*) or the Track view (*View-Track*).

2. If you want to add effects to the bus, right-click in the FX bin of a bus (if it is not in use already) and choose an effect from the effects popup menu. (If you are working in the Track view, you may first need to display the Bus pane by clicking the Show/Hide Mains and Buses button ▣ located at the bottom of the Track view.)

   The name of the effect you have chosen appears in the bus FX bin.

3. Set the effect's parameters and close it.

4. Repeat steps 2 and 3 for any additional effects you want to use.

5. In a track module that you want to patch through the bus, do the following:

   - Drag the Bus Send Level control for the bus to the approximate level you want.
   - Drag the Bus Send pan to the approximate setting you want.
   - Click the Bus Enable button for the appropriate bus.

6. Repeat step 5 for all the tracks you want to patch through the bus.

7. In the bus, adjust the Input Gain and Output volume controls to the approximate level you want.

8. In the bus, drag the Input pan and Output pan controls to the approximate positions you want.

9. Play your tracks and adjust the Send Level controls, the pan controls, etc.

To Mute or Solo a Bus

Each bus has a Mute button and a Solo button. These controls act like the Mute and Solo buttons in a track, but they affect all the signal routed through the bus.

1. Open the Track view or the Console view.

2. Click the Mute or Solo button in the bus you want to mute or solo.

Main Outs

Each enabled hardware channel has a main out channel strip in the Console view. Main outs are the final destination for all of your audio in SONAR. Main outs accept input from both tracks and buses.

Main outs contains a left channel and a right channel, but only one volume fader. You control the left/right balance of each main out with the balance slider.

Here's what you can do in a main out module:

To do this...	Do this...
Set the output volume	Adjust the Volume control
Adjust the left/right balance	Adjust the pan slider that's on that output module

Metering

The Console and Track views both have meters to measure playback level, record level, bus output level, and main output level. The Track view also has bus return meters. You can configure the meters differently in each view, if you want.

The responsiveness of your record meters (which also measure input monitoring) is dependent upon the latency setting in the Audio Options dialog and the settings in the Audio Meter Ballistics dialog. With higher latency settings the meters may appear sluggish.

There are three basic things you should know about meters:

- What the meters measure
- How to show or hide different kinds of meters
- How to choose display options for each kind of meter

Note: Metering uses significant amounts of your computer's processing power, especially RMS metering. If you need to free up resources, turning off metering where you don't absolutely need it helps. Using peak metering on tracks and peak plus RMS metering on the main out is a good option. To **disable all metering**, turn off metering in **both** the Track view and Console view.

What the Meters Measure

The following table summarizes what each kind of meter measures:

Kind of meter...	What it measures...
Record	The level of the instrument listed as an input for the track you are monitoring—the track must be armed to enable the meter
Playback	A playback meter measures the playback level of any pre-existing data in the track you are monitoring, either before or after the track faders, depending on what display options you choose
Main outs	The level of the signal output by each main out.
Buses	The level of the output signal the bus is sending back from the effects.

Hiding and Showing Meters

The display and configuration of the meters in the Track view is independent of the meters in the Console view, and vice versa. Buttons in the Track view and Console view toolbars hide or show all the meters of each kind in each view. To show or hide meters on individual tracks or buses, use the right-click popup menu that's available from the title bar of each track or bus.

Note: If you want to conserve the maximum amount of your CPU's resources, turn off all metering in **both** the Track and Console views.

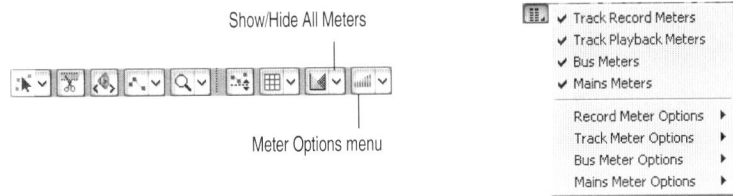

Track view toolbar   Console view Show Meters button and menu

To Show or Hide all Record Meters

- In the Console view, click the Show Meters button. This button hides or shows all the meters in the Console view.

- In the Track view, click the arrow to the right of the Show/Hide Meters button and select Record Meters from the menu that appears.

437

To Show or Hide Individual Record Meters in the Track View
- Right-click the title bar of a track to display the track popup menu and click the **Show Record Meter** option to show or hide the record meter for that track.

To Show or Hide All Playback Meters
- In the Console view, click the dropdown menu to the right of the Show Meters button and select **Track Playback Meters** from the menu that appears.

- In the Track view, click the arrow to the right of the Show/Hide Meters button and select Playback Meters from the menu that appears.

To Show or Hide Individual Playback Meters in the Track View
- Right-click the title bar of a track to display the track popup menu and click the **Show Playback Meter** option to show or hide the playback meter for that track.

To Show or Hide All Main and Bus Meters in the Track View
- In the Track view, click the arrow to the right of the Show/Hide Meters button and select Output Bus Meters from the menu that appears.

To Show or Hide All Bus Meters in the Console View
- In the Console view, click the dropdown menu to the right of the Show Meters button and select **Bus Meters** from the menu that appears.

To Show or Hide All Main Meters in the Console View
- In the Console view, click the dropdown menu to the right of the Show Meters button and select **Main Meters** from the menu that appears.

To Show or Hide Individual Bus Meters in the Track View
- In the Track view, right-click the title bar of a main or bus to display the popup menu and click the **Show Meter** option to show or hide the meter for that bus.

Changing the Meters' Display

You control the range and kind of units that the various meters display in the Track and Console views. The display of meters in each of the two views is independent of the display in the other view. In the Track view, you can access all meter options from the Show/Hide Meters button. In the Console view, you can access all meter options from the Show Meters button.

The dropdown menus give you the following display options:

Menu option...	What it does...
Peak	Choosing this option causes the meter to display the highest amplitude in the signal that occurs in a complete cycle of a frequency.
RMS	Choosing this option causes the meter to display more of an average of the amplitudes that occur in a complete cycle of a frequency. RMS, or Root-Mean-Square, is a little over seventy per cent of peak level.
Peak + RMS	Choosing this option causes the meter to display both the RMS and peak levels. The RMS level is displayed by the solid bar on the left side of the meter, and the peak level is displayed as a small line that follows the RMS level just to the right of it.
Pre Fader/Post Fader (This option is for playback and bus meters only)	Choose Pre Fader or Post Fader to measure the playback level either before or after the track's or bus' volume fader.
Pre Fader/Post FX (This option is for the buses only)	Choose Pre Fader/Post FX to measure the bus volume before the fader, but after any real-time effects.
-12 dB....-90 dB	Choosing one of these numbers sets the scale of the meter to a certain range of dB. For example, choosing -90 dB sets the range of measurement of that meter to 90 dB. **Note:** You can also change the scale of a meter by right-clicking the meter to display a popup menu and choosing a new dB range.
Show Labels	Clicking this option hides or shows the dB markings on the meter. Hiding the markings shrinks the meter significantly, saving space.
Hold Peaks	Choosing this option causes the meter to display a small vertical line (the peak marker) that shows the peak level and then decays until a new peak is reached.
Lock Peaks	Choosing this option causes the meter to lock the peak marker at the highest level, until a higher level occurs.

Changing the Meters' Performance

There are two major factors that determine the performance of meters in SONAR. One is audio latency which you can adjust, within the limits of your audio hardware drivers, in the General tab of the Audio Options dialog. The second is the settings in the Audio Meter Ballistics dialog.

SONAR 4 now has configurable meter ballistics that allow you to adjust the rise and fall times of both the RMS and Peak Meters. Out of the box, SONAR 4 ships with industry-standard settings that mimic meter ballistics for common hardware consoles.

The following table covers how to adjust your meter settings to meet your needs.

To do this...	Do this...
Increase or decrease meter refresh rates	In the Audio Meter Ballistics dialog (select **Options-Audio Meter Settings** to open), adjust the Refresh rate field. Valid values are from 25 to 250 milliseconds.
Change the decay rate (the amount of time the meter display stays at its peak)	In the Audio Meter Ballistics dialog, adjust the Decay Rate value. Valid values are from 1 to 150 milliseconds.
Increase or decrease the amount of time the meter displays a peak value	In the Audio Meter Ballistics dialog, adjust the Hold Time value. Valid values are from 0 to 5000 milliseconds.
Adjust rise and fall times	In the Audio Meter Ballistics dialog, adjust the Rise or Fall settings for RMS or Peak. Valid Rise values are from 0 to 1000 milliseconds. Valid Fall values are from 0 to 2500 milliseconds.

Here are the default values for the various settings:

- Refresh Rate = 40 msec
- Peak Hold – Decay Rate = 50 msec
- Peak Hold – Hold Time = 750 msec
- RMS Rise = 300 msec
- RMS Fall = 300 msec
- Peak Rise = 0 msec
- Peak Fall = 1000 msec

Freeze Tracks and Synths

The Freeze feature allows you to temporarily bounce your track, including soft synths and effects, to reduce the amount of CPU power needed. The Freeze feature also works for synths patched in the Synth Rack.

Note: if you delete or replace any part of the bounced track, and then unfreeze the track or synth, you'll create a gap in the spot where the deleted or replaced data was.

The following are the available commands for track freezing:

- Freeze Track—bounces the audio in the track to a new audio clip or clips, applies any effects, and disables the FX bin.
- Unfreeze Track—discards the bounced audio, restores the original audio, and enables the FX bin. Audio will be re-bounced if you choose Freeze again.
- Quick Unfreeze Track—hides and mutes the bounced audio, restores the original audio, and enables the FX bin. Bounced audio is retained, however, and toggling between Quick Freeze and Quick Unfreeze should be instantaneous.
- Quick Freeze Track—only available after a Quick Unfreeze, the Quick Freeze function redisplays and unmutes the bounced audio instantaneously.

The following are the available commands for synth freezing:

- Freeze Synth—audio from a DXi is bounced and placed on the DXi's audio track. Output from the DXi is disabled, as is the FX bin on the audio track.
- Unfreeze Synth—discards bounced audio, enables the DXi and track FX bin. Bounced audio is discarded, and will be re-bounced if you choose Freeze again.
- Quick Unfreeze Synth—hides and mutes the bounced audio, enables the DXi and track FX bin. Bounced audio is retained, and toggling between Quick Freeze and Quick Unfreeze should be instantaneous.
- Quick Freeze Synth—only available after a Quick Unfreeze, the Quick Freeze function redisplays and unmutes the bounced audio instantaneously, disables the DXi, and any effects on the DXi audio track.

There is also a Freeze option in **Options-Global-General**:

- Unload Synth After Freeze—When enabled, DXi's are unloaded from memory when frozen, saving resources. This can free up a lot of memory if your synth uses samples, but it can take a long time to reload the synth if you decide to do so.

Note: Similar to the "Unload Synth After Freeze" behavior, when a DXi is manually disabled in the Synth Rack, it is also unloaded from memory. Keep in mind that Windows does not necessarily release freed memory until it is needed, so you may not see an immediate drop in usage when a synth is frozen or disabled.

To Freeze a Track
1. Right-click on a track.
2. Select *Freeze Track* from the menu that appears.

SONAR bounces the audio in the track to a new audio clip or clips, applies any effects, and disables the FX bin.

To Unfreeze a Track
1. Right-click on a track.
2. Select *Unfreeze Track* from the menu that appears.

SONAR discards the bounced audio, restores the original audio, and enables the FX bin. Audio will be re-bounced if Freeze is chosen again.

To Do a Quick Unfreeze of a Track
1. Right-click on a frozen track.
2. Select *Quick Unfreeze Track* from the menu that appears.

SONAR hides and mutes the bounced audio, restores the original audio, and enables the FX bin. Bounced audio is retained, however, and toggling between Quick Freeze and Quick Unfreeze should be instantaneous.

To Quick Freeze a Track
1. Right-click on a track that you did a Quick Unfreeze on.
2. Select *Quick Freeze Track* from the menu that appears.

Only available after a Quick Unfreeze, the Quick Freeze function redisplays and unmutes the bounced audio instantaneously

To Freeze a Synth (DXi)
- Right-click a DXi MIDI or audio track, and choose *Freeze Synth* from the menu that appears.

    Or

- In the Synth Rack view, click the Freeze/Unfreeze button [*].

SONAR bounces the DXi's audio data to the DXi's audio track. SONAR disables the DXi's output, and disables the FX bin on the DXi's audio track.

To Unfreeze a Synth (DXi)
- Right-click a DXi MIDI or audio track, and choose *Unfreeze Synth* from the menu that appears.

    Or

- In the Synth Rack view, click the Freeze/Unfreeze button [*], and choose *Unfreeze Synth* from the menu that appears.

SONAR discards bounced audio, enables the DXi and the DXi audio track's FX bin. SONAR will be re-bounce the audio if you choose Freeze again.

To Do a Quick Unfreeze of a Synth (DXi)

- Right-click a frozen DXi MIDI or audio track, and choose **Quick Unfreeze Synth** from the menu that appears.

    Or

- In the Synth Rack view, click the Freeze/Unfreeze button ![], and choose **Quick Unfreeze Synth** from the menu that appears.

SONAR hides and mutes the bounced audio, enables the DXi and track FX bin. Bounced audio is retained, and toggling between Quick Freeze and Quick Unfreeze should be instantaneous.

To Quick Freeze a Synth (DXi)

- Right-click a quick frozen DXi MIDI or audio track, and choose **Quick Freeze Synth** from the menu that appears.

    Or

- In the Synth Rack view, click the Freeze/Unfreeze button ![], and choose **Quick Freeze Synth** from the menu that appears.

Only available after a Quick Unfreeze, the Quick Freeze command redisplays and unmutes the bounced audio instantaneously, disables the DXi, and any effects on the DXi audio track.

To Set Freeze Options

1. Right-click an audio or DXi track, and choose **Freeze Options** from the menu that appears.

    Or

1. In the Synth Rack view, click the Freeze/Unfreeze button ![], and choose **Freeze Options** from the menu that appears.

2. Choose options in the Freeze Options dialog. For help choosing options, click the Help button in the dialog.

Using Real-Time Effects

In the Console view and Track view, you can use plug-in effects non-destructively, in real time. You can also hear your plug-in effects in real time on any live instruments you are recording—just make sure Input Monitoring is enabled (see "Input Monitoring" on page 180).

For example, suppose you want to add a reverb effect to an audio track containing a recorded violin solo. You could do it in two different ways:

- Destructive—The digital audio data itself is modified. Although this may be exactly what you want, it does limit your options. If you want to modify the effect parameters slightly or to remove the effect and try a different effect, you must use the *Undo* command, or revert to a saved copy of the original data.

- Non-destructive (real-time)—The digital audio data in your track is not changed but simply altered on the fly during playback. This means you can experiment with effects parameters, bypass effects, or remove them entirely at any time. Since most effects require complex numeric calculations, real-time effects processing puts a heavy load on your computer's CPU. If you use too many effects, the CPU will not be able to keep up and playback will sound choppy and disconnected.

You can also apply real-time audio effects to a submix in a bus. For example, rather than patching separate reverb effects in each of several guitar tracks, you can mix the guitar tracks together in a bus and apply a single reverb effect to the submix. This makes much more efficient use of CPU time. Patching effects on a bus also opens up new creative possibilities.

There are several reasons why you might want to apply effects offline (destructively):

- If you want to apply more effects than your CPU can handle, applying some of the effects offline will reduce CPU usage during playback.

- If you want to apply effects to an individual audio clip, rather than the whole track, it is simpler to do so using offline effects.

The *File-Export-Audio* command, allows you to apply real-time effects when you export, so you do not need to apply your effects destructively or use the *Edit-Bounce to Track(s)* command to prepare the tracks beforehand. For information about exporting audio, see "Preparing Audio for Distribution" on page 459.

Effects Parameters

Each effect in an effects patch point has its own independent set of parameter values. For example, you can apply a short reverb in one track and a long reverb in another track. The dialog boxes for real-time effects contain the same parameters as the offline effects, though there are a few differences:

- You can adjust the parameters while playback is in progress, so there is no need for an Audition button.
- For Audio effects, because mixing is handled through the Track view or Console view, there is no Mixing tab.
- You do not need to click OK for the effect to be applied.

Refer to the sections "MIDI Effects (MIDI Plug-ins)" on page 325 and "Audio Effects (Audio Plug-ins)" on page 386 for descriptions of the effects and their parameters.

How to Use Real-Time Effects

It is very easy to use the real-time effects in the Track view and Console view. Here's what to do:

To do this...	Do this...
Add a real-time effect to a MIDI track, audio track or bus	Right-click in the effects bin of the track or bus you want to add the effect to, and select an effect from the popup menu.
Change the order in which effects are used	In the Track view, drag an effect left or right in the effects bin. In the Console view, drag an effect up or down in the effects bin.
Edit an effect's parameters	Double-click on the effect to open the effect's dialog box.
Move an effect to a different bin	Drag the effect to another effects bin.
Copy an effect to a different bin	Hold down the Ctrl key and drag the effect to another effects bin.

When you place an effect in the patch point, an abbreviated name is used to describe the effect. Sometimes the limited space makes it impossible to identify the effect. If this occurs, simply rest the cursor over the effect for a second or two, and a tooltip will pop up to display the full name of the effect.

Using the Per-track EQ (Producer Edition Only)

Each audio track in the Console view in the Producer version of SONAR has a 4-band EQ patched into it by default. You can hide the EQ, hide its graph (plot), display only one band, or display all four bands

Here's a graphic of the EQ and its controls:

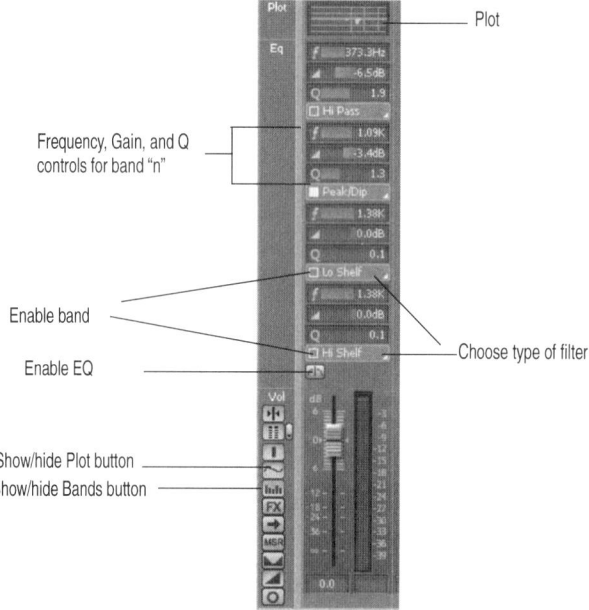

Here's how to use it:

To Hide the EQ in all Audio Tracks
- In the Console view, click the EQ button so that it's not lit: ![icon].

To Show One Band's Controls
- In the Console view, click the EQ button so that it's yellow: ![icon].

To Show All Four Bands' Controls
- In the Console view, click the EQ button so that it's blue: ![icon].

To Choose What Band You're Controlling When Only One Band is Showing
- Click the Band menu that's at the bottom of the EQ display, and choose the band number you want to control.

To Enable or Disable the EQ
- Click the Enable/Disable button that's next to the Band menu: .

To Choose the Filter Type for Each Band
- Click the filter type menu that's just above the Band menu, and choose a filter type.

To Enable or Disable a Band
- Click the Enable/Disable button that's on the left side of the band type menu.

To Set Frequency, Gain, and Q for Each Band
- In the band that you want to configure, drag the frequency slider (f icon), gain slider (triangle icon), or Q slider (Q icon), respectively, to the left or right. The value is displayed just to the right of each icon, and the plot (graph) changes as you drag.

To Hide or Show the Plot (Graph)
- Click the Plot button.

To Open the EQ Interface
- Double-click the Plot.

Applying Audio Effects

You can destructively apply audio effects for one or more tracks. When you are pleased with the audio effects you have patched into a track, you can apply the effects to the track. Applying effects to a track saves resources, allowing you to include additional tracks and/or effects.

Note:
When applied effects are undone, they are not re-patched in the Effects bin(s).

To Apply Multiple Audio Effects Offline

1. Add one or more audio effects to one or more tracks in either the Track view or the Console view.
2. In the Track view, select the tracks or clips you want to be affected.
3. Select *Process-Apply Audio Effects*.

   The Apply Audio Effects dialog appears.
4. If desired, select the option to delete the effects after applying them.
5. Click OK.

If you do not delete the effects after applying them, they remain active.

Applying MIDI Effects

You can destructively apply the MIDI effects in a track's patch point. This makes it easy for you to experiment with MIDI effects before you commit to them on a more permanent basis.

To Apply MIDI Effects Destructively

1. In the Track view, select the tracks or clips to be affected.
2. Select *Process-Apply MIDI Effects*.
3. If desired, select the option to delete the effects after applying them.
4. Click OK.

If you don't delete effects after applying them, they continue to be active during playback, even though they have already been applied.

CPU Usage of Audio Effects

The number of real-time audio effects that your computer can handle depends on the number of audio tracks in your project, the number and type of effects you want to use, and the type and speed of your CPU. Certain effects are more CPU-intensive than others, and enabling certain settings (such as using equalization within the Stereo Reverb) increases CPU usage for those effects.

Using Control Groups

SONAR lets you link faders, knobs, or buttons in the Track and Console views into **groups**. Groups are collections of controls whose movements are linked together. For example:

- Two volume faders or controls can be grouped so that when you increase or decrease the volume of one track, the volume of the other track changes in exactly the same way.

- Four mute buttons can be grouped so that when you click on the mute button to mute track 1, tracks 1 and 2 are muted and tracks 3 and 4 are un-muted.

The Console view and Track view identify controls, knobs and faders that are grouped using a colored group indicator that is displayed on the controls in each group. The controls in group A are displayed with a red indicator, the controls in group B with a green indicator, and so on. Controls, faders and knobs can be grouped together.

When you group buttons together, the way they work is based on their position when you create the group:

- Buttons that are in the same position when grouped will turn on and off together at all times.

- Buttons that are in opposite positions when grouped will always remain in opposite positions.

When you group buttons with knobs or faders, the button turns on/off when the knob or fader reaches its halfway point.

You have several additional options. There are there general types of groups: absolute, relative, and custom. Here's how they work.

Absolute

The range of motion in all controls in the group is identical. When you move one control in the group, all other controls in the group move the same amount in the same direction. The controls do not necessarily need to start at the same level. Here are two examples:

Example 1

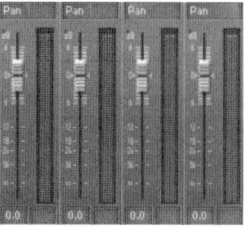

The controls are grouped in this position

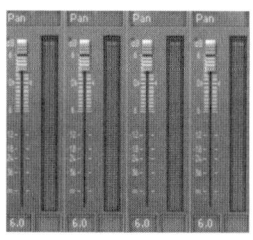

The first control's raised to maximum

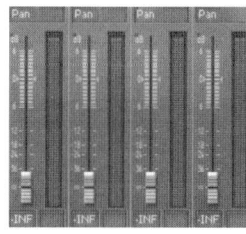

The first control is lowered to minimum

Example 2

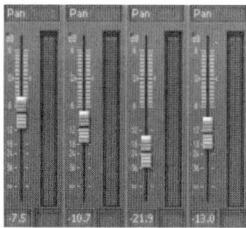

The controls are grouped in this position

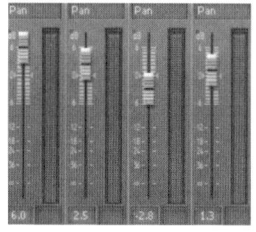

The first control is raised to maximum

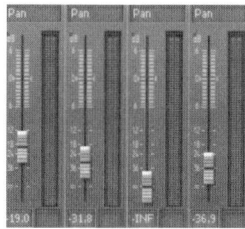

The fourth control is lowered to minimum

Relative

The range of motion for controls in the group is not the same. All controls in the group have the same value at one point—the lowest level for send, return, and volume levels, and zero for pan controls. Here are two examples:

Example 1

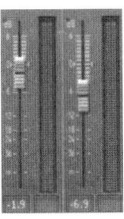

The volume controls are grouped in this position

The first control is raised to maximum volume

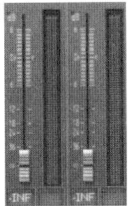

The first control is lowered to zero volume

Example 2

The pan controls are grouped in this position

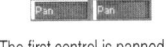

The first control is panned to center

The first control is panned to the right

Custom

Sometimes you want to define a more complex relationship between the controls in a group. For example:

- You want two controls two operate in reverse—when one fader drops, the other increases (cross fade).

- You want two volume faders grouped so that they are locked together at maximum level, but drop at different rates.

- You want two faders to be locked together with the same range of motion, but a third fader grouped with them to have a different range of motion.

Custom groups let you set the range of motion for each control in the group by entering a starting and ending value. As any one control in the group is moved from is starting position to its ending position, the other controls in the group exercise their full range of motion.

When you have defined a custom group, you can adjust the starting and ending position of each control using the Group Settings dialog box or using popup menus on the controls in the group.

To Add a Control to a Group
1. Right-click on the control.

2. Choose a group from the *Group* submenu.

SONAR adds the control to the group. Controls, knobs and faders are highlighted with the group's color indicator.

To Remove a Control from Its Group
1. Right-click on the control.

2. Choose *Ungroup* from the menu.

SONAR removes the control from the group and displays the control with the neutral color indicator.

To Override a Control's Grouping
- Hold down the Ctrl key while moving the control.

The control remains part of the group and functions as such once the Ctrl key is lifted.

To Set the Group Type to Relative or Absolute
1. Right-click on any control in the group and choose *Group Properties* to display the Group Properties dialog box.

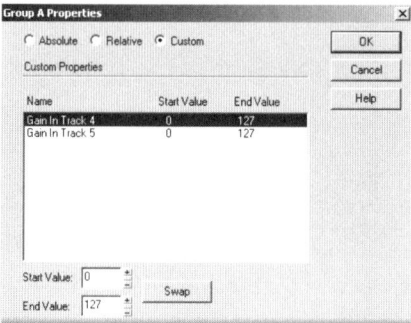

2. Choose Absolute or Relative as the group type and click OK.

SONAR uses the type to determine the range of motion for the group's controls.

To Create a Custom Group

1. Right-click on any control in the group and choose **Group Properties** to display the Group Properties dialog box.

2. Choose Custom as the group type. The starting and ending values for each control are displayed.

3. To change the starting or ending value for a control, click on the control in the list and enter new values in the Start and End box.

4. To swap the starting and ending value, click the Swap button.

5. Click Close when you are done.

SONAR uses the type to determine the range of motion for the group's controls.

To Adjust the Start Value of a Control

1. Set the control to the desired starting value.

2. Right-click on the control.

3. Choose **Set Start = Current**.

SONAR sets the start value of the control.

The **Set Start = Current** and **Set End = Current** commands set the range of motion that a grouped control moves through as the other members of the group move through their starting and ending values. You don't have to designate a group as a custom group to create a custom group—just group some controls and set their starting and ending values.

To Adjust the End Value of a Control

1. Set the control to the desired ending value.

2. Right click on the control.

3. Choose **Set End = Current**.

SONAR sets the end value of the control.

The **Set Start = Current** and **Set End = Current** commands set the range of motion that a grouped control moves through as the other members of the group move through their starting and ending values. You don't have to designate a group as a custom group to create a custom group—just group some controls and set their starting and ending values.

Using Remote Control

This section explains how to assign knobs or sliders on a MIDI controller to control specific parameters on specific tracks. If you have a control surface with groups of faders such as a Tascam US-428 or CM Labs MotorMix, see the online help topic "Working with External Devices."

SONAR's Remote Control function lets you use a MIDI device to remotely control knobs, buttons, and sliders in the Track and Console views. For example, you can:

- Use a key on your keyboard to temporarily mute a track
- Work the send level in a bus with your pitch bend wheel
- Set the main volume levels with NRPN messages
- Prevent SONAR from sending any controller messages to your MIDI device.
- Record automation from an external controller

If you set up remote control for a grouped control, the remote control works all controls in the group.

The type of MIDI message used to work a control is selected in the Remote Control dialog box. The options are as follows:

Message option...	Message effect on buttons...	Message effect on sliders and knobs...
None	No remote control	No remote control
Note On	The button state is toggled	The slider/knob is alternately maximized and minimized
Note On/Off	The button state is toggled when Note On is received, and toggled again when Note Off is received	The slider/knob is maximized when Note On is received, and minimized when Note Off is received
Controller	Not applicable	The slider/knob value is set to the controller value
Wheel	Not applicable	The slider/knob value is set to the wheel value, with the values mapped from their original range of –8,192 to 8,191 to a range of 0 to 127
RPN	Not applicable	The slider/knob value is set to the RPN value, with the values mapped from their original range of 0 to 16,383 to a range of 0 to 127
NRPN	Not applicable	The slider/knob value is set to the NRPN value, with the values mapped from their original range of 0 to 16,383 to a range of 0 to 127

To Set Up Remote Control for a Knob, Button, or Fader

1. Right-click on the control and choose **Remote Control** from the popup menu.
2. Choose the remote control type, as described in the table above.
3. Set the note or controller number if applicable.
4. Set the MIDI Channel field to the channel that your controller sends out.
5. Click OK.

You can now work the control from your MIDI device. If you arm the control for automation and click the Record Automation button in the SONAR Transport, you can record your external controller's knob or fader movements.

To Disable Remote Control
- Right-click on the control and choose **Disable Remote Control** from the popup menu.

To Prevent SONAR from Sending Controller Data to Your MIDI Device
- Right-click each knob or fader in SONAR that is sending unwanted controller data to your MIDI device and choose **Disable Control** from the popup menu.

Using the Learn Option
The Learn option in the Remote Control dialog allows you to bind a parameter in SONAR to a knob or fader on your controller.

To Bind a Control Using the Learn Option
1. Right-click on the parameter you want to arm in either the Track view or Console view and select **Remote Control** from the popup menu.
2. Move a knob or fader on your controller.
3. Click the Learn button in the Remote Control dialog and click OK.

The control in SONAR is now bound to the knob or fader on your controller.

Bouncing Tracks

The **Edit-Bounce to Track(s)** command lets you combine one or more audio tracks into a submix. A submix can be a mono track, a stereo track or several mono tracks that contain the mixture of the original tracks, preserving the volume, pan, and effects for each track. If you're bouncing tracks that are routed to a surround bus (SONAR Producer only), you can bounce them to as many mono tracks as you have surround channels, by choosing the Split Mono option in the Channel Format field of the Bounce to Tracks dialog, and also choosing a surround bus in the Source Category field. After their creation, the submix tracks are just like any other tracks—you can edit them, add effects, copy them to another project, etc. The original, unmixed audio tracks are not deleted, so you can archive them and recover them later, or continue using them as before.

The **Edit-Bounce to Track(s)** command operates completely offline, meaning you can mix down tracks that may be too complex for your machine to actually play in real time.

Here are some reasons to use **Edit-Bounce to Track(s)**:

- Your mix is so complex that real-time playback is impossible. **Edit-Bounce to Track(s)** produces the correct mix, and store the result in a new track or tracks.

- You require more CPU time for your real-time effects. With **Edit-Bounce to Track(s)**, you can premix some of your tracks with real-time effects applied, saving CPU time during playback.

If you mix down to tracks that already have data, the new events are placed in the track, but do not overwrite existing material.

To Mix Down (Bounce) Audio Tracks

1. Set all volume, pan, effects, and automation settings just as you want them.
2. Select the tracks or clips you want to mix down.
3. If you are using effects on the tracks and want to mix the effects down at this time, select the whole length of the longest track or clip plus an extra measure for the reverb or effects "tail."
4. Choose **Edit-Bounce to Track(s)** to open the Bounce to Track(s) dialog.

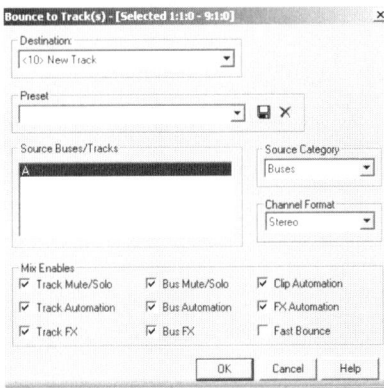

5. Select the first destination track for the mixdown.
6. If you've saved a preset configuration for the Bounce to Tracks dialog, select it now in the Preset window.

7. In the Source Category field, select the source you want to use for your bounced track(s) from the following options:

- Tracks—choosing this option creates new separate tracks for each track you highlight in the Source Buses/Tracks field. Each track you highlight will produce a new mono track, stereo track, or two new mono tracks (the Split Mono option), depending on what you choose in the Channel Format field.

- Buses—choosing this option creates new separate tracks for each bus you highlight in the Source Buses/Tracks field. Each bus you highlight will produce a new mono track, stereo track, or two to eight new mono tracks (the Split Mono option), depending on whether the bus is a stereo or surround bus, and depending on what you choose in the Channel Format field.

- Main Outputs—choosing this option creates new separate tracks for each main output you highlight in the Source Buses/Tracks field. Each main output you highlight will produce a new mono track, stereo track, or two to eight new mono tracks (the Split Mono option), depending on whether the output is a stereo output or the Surround Main, and depending on what you choose in the Channel Format field.

- Entire Mix—choosing this option bounces your entire mix down to a new mono track, stereo track, or two to eight new mono tracks (the Split Mono option), depending on whether the output is a stereo output or the Surround Main, and depending on what you choose in the Channel Format field.

8. Select a channel format: the kind of track(s) you want to create with your bounce.

9. Select source buses or tracks.

10. In the Mix Enables field, choose the elements you want to include in the mixdown. If you want to exclude muted tracks and/or include only soloed tracks, make sure Track Mute/Solo is checked. Make sure **Fast Bounce** is checked, otherwise the bounce process will take as long as it takes to play your selected track data in real time.

    Note: If you have patched a DXi (plug-in synth) into a track or bus, make sure you check Track FX to include DXi's that are patched into tracks, and check Bus FX to include DXi's that are patched into buses.

    Note: If you don't check Track Automation, any initial volume and pan settings in an exported track are ignored and the track's audio data will be exported at the level that exists in the track, with pan set to center. If you don't check Clip Automation, any trim settings are ignored during export.

11. If you want to save your settings as a preset, type a name for them in the Preset window, and then click the floppy disk icon that's next to the Preset window.

12. Click OK.

SONAR mixes the audio data and a new track or tracks appear in your project.

Preparing to Create an Audio CD

You can create an audio CD from any wave file or files (extension .WAV) of up to either 74 or 80 minutes (depending on the recordable CD media you have). If your projects are audio only, you can simply mix down to a stereo wave file. If your projects contain MIDI, you must first convert the MIDI tracks to audio tracks. Once you have all the stereo wave files you want to include on your CD, you are ready to burn a CD. Most CD burners come with CD burning software, if yours did not, you will need to buy CD burning software, like Cakewalk's Pyro. To download a free demo of Pyro, visit the Cakewalk website.

Preparing Audio for Distribution

The *File-Export Audio* command exports your project as a new file or files that you can burn to a CD, or distribute via the Web or e-mail. In addition, SONAR Producer allows you to export surround-encoded files (see "Exporting Surround Mixes" on page 492). The following export formats are supported:

Format...	Definition...
Wave (surround files in Wave format are supported by SONAR Producer only)	The standard digital audio format used under Windows for burning CDs, with a file extension of .WAV
RealAudio	Digital audio encoded and compacted for streaming over the Internet, with a file extension of .RA
Windows Media Advanced Streaming Format (includes Windows Media Pro; surround files are supported by SONAR Producer only)	Compressed digital audio for streaming over the Internet, with the file extension .WMA.
MP3	Highly compressed digital audio designed for quick downloads via the Internet, with the file extension .MP3. The MP3 encoder that comes with SONAR is a trial version which will time-out. The full version is available for download at www.cakewalk.com.
OMF	The Open Media Format, created by AVID Technology, is designed to port a project to other applications or platforms. OMF files preserve tracks, clip positions, slip edits and some other project attributes depending on which application is writing or reading the OMF file.

If your audio hardware is configured for stereo playback, Wave files are created in stereo; if your audio hardware is configured for monophonic playback, the Wave file is created in mono.

To Export Audio to RealAudio Format

1. Set all volume, pan, effects, and automation settings just as you want them.
2. If you only want to mix down parts of tracks, select those clips now.
3. If you are using effects in your project and want to mix the effects down at this time, select the whole length of the longest track or clip plus an extra measure for the reverb or effects "tail."
4. Choose **File-Export-Audio** to open the Export Audio dialog box.
5. Select a destination folder using the Look In field.
6. Enter a file name.
7. Choose Real Audio from the Files of Type dropdown list.
8. In the Source Category field, select one of the following options:
   - Tracks—choosing this option creates a separate file for each track that you select in the Source Buses/Tracks field.
   - Buses—choosing this option creates a separate file for each bus that you select in the Source Buses/Tracks field.
   - Main Outputs—choosing this option creates a separate file for each main output that you select in the Source Buses/Tracks field.
   - Entire Mix—choosing this option creates one file for your entire mix.
9. In the Source Buses/Tracks field, choose the buses or tracks you want to use as a source to create your mix. If you chose Tracks in the Source Category field, only tracks will show up as choices in this field.
10. In the Channel Format field, select one of the following options:
    - Stereo—All exported tracks and clips are mixed down to a stereo file or files.
    - Mono—All exported tracks and clips are mixed down to a mono file or files.
    - Split Mono—All exported tracks and clips are mixed down to separate mono files.
11. Choose the sample rate that you want your exported file to be.
12. Select the bit depth that you want the exported file to use. If your source file is 16 and you export to 24, you get more precision for any audio effects in the mix (and a larger file). If your source file is 24 and you export to 16, you lose some sound definition, but you get some of it back if the Dithering option is on in the Audio Options dialog box (see "Dithering" on page 468 for more information).

13. In the Mix Enables field, choose the elements you want to include in the mixdown. If you want to exclude muted tracks and/or include only soloed tracks, make sure Track Mute/Solo is checked.

    Note: If you have patched a DXi (plug-in synth) into a track or bus, make sure you check Track FX to include DXi's that are patched into tracks, and check Bus Returns to include DXi's that are patched into buses.

    Note: If you don't check Track Automation. any initial volume and pan settings in an exported track are ignored and the track's audio data will be exported at the level that exists in the track, with pan set to center. If you don't check Clip Automation, any trim settings are ignored during export. If you don't check Master Automation, any volume and balance settings at the main outs are ignored.

14. If you want to save the settings you created in the Export Audio dialog, type a name for them in the Preset window and then click the floppy disk icon that's next to the window.

15. Click Export.

    The RealAudio settings dialog box appears.

16. Select options as described in the table below and click OK.

The audio is compacted and exported to the RealAudio file or files.

The RealAudio Settings dialog box lets you define the settings for the RealAudio data in an exported file, as follows:

Option...	Meaning...
Title	Title of the file
Author	Author of the file
Copyright	Copyright statement
Enable Perfect Play	Lets people with low-bandwidth connections download a higher resolution version of the audio, at the expense of download time
Enable Mobile Play	Lets people download file to a local drive for playback later
Target Connection Rate	Choose as many different connection rates as your listeners may need. Then your listeners can choose the rate that's best for them when they play your project.
Include RA 5.0 Compatible Stream	Ensures compatibility with older versions of RealAudio
Content Type	Optimizes the data for specific content

You may choose several formats if you wish. The RealAudio 2.0 formats are good for backwards compatibility with older players and for 14.4 Kb capability. The remaining formats let you choose Mono or Stereo playback. Stereo formats trade bandwidth for stereo, so use these only when the stereo aspect is important.

To Export Audio to Wave File Format

1. Set all volume, pan, effects, and automation settings just as you want them.
2. If you only want to mix down parts of tracks, select those clips now. If you don't select anything, everything's selected.
3. If you are using effects on the tracks and want to mix the effects down at this time, select the whole length of the longest track or clip plus extra time for the reverb or effects "tail."
4. Choose **File-Export-Audio** to open the Export Audio dialog box.
5. Select a destination folder using the Look In field.
6. Enter a file name.
7. Choose one of the following from the Files of type dropdown list:
   - Riff Wave—choose this if you want to export a standard wave file, or if you're exporting a surround project in wave format.
   - Broadcast Wave—choose this if you want to create a Broadcast Wave file (see description below).
8. In the Source Category field, select one of the following options:
   - Tracks—Choosing this option creates a separate file for each track that you select in the Source Buses/Tracks field.
   - Buses—Choosing this option creates a separate file for each bus that you select in the Source Buses/Tracks field.
   - Main Outputs—Choosing this option creates a separate file for each main output that you select in the Source Buses/Tracks field.
   - Entire Mix—Choosing this option creates one file for your entire mix, unless you're exporting a surround mix with Split Mono selected in the Channel Format field.
9. In the Source Buses/Tracks field, choose the buses or tracks you want to use as a source to create your mix. If you chose Tracks in the Source Category field, only tracks will show up as choices in this field.

10. In the Channel Format field, select one of the following options:
    - Stereo—All exported tracks and clips are mixed down to a stereo file or files.
    - Mono—All exported tracks and clips are mixed down to a mono file or files.
    - Split Mono—All exported tracks and clips are mixed down to separate mono files.
    - Multichannel—All exported tracks are mixed down to a multichannel wave file or files.
11. Choose the sample rate that you want your exported file to be.
12. Select the bit depth that you want the exported file to use. If your source file is 16 and you export to 24, you get more precision for any audio effects in the mix (and a larger file). If your source file is 24 and you export to 16, you lose some sound definition, but you get some of it back if the Dithering option is on in the Audio Options dialog box (see "Dithering" on page 468 for more information).
13. In the Mix Enables field, choose the elements you want to include in the mixdown. If you want to exclude muted tracks and/or include only soloed tracks, make sure Track Mute/Solo is checked.

    Note: If you have patched a DXi (plug-in synth) into a track or bus, make sure you check Track FX to include DXi's that are patched into tracks, and check Bus Returns to include DXi's that are patched into buses.

    Note: If you don't check Track Automation. any initial volume and pan settings in an exported track are ignored and the track's audio data will be exported at the level that exists in the track, with pan set to center. If you don't check Clip Automation, any trim settings are ignored during export. If you don't check Master Automation, any volume and balance settings at the main outs are ignored.
14. If you want to save the settings you created in the Export Audio dialog, type a name for them in the Preset window and then click the floppy disk icon that's next to the window.
15. Click Export.

The audio is exported to the Wave file or files.

If you chose Broadcast Wave as the export format, the following information is stored in the file(s):

- Description—A brief description of the contents of the Broadcast wave. Limited to 256 characters.

- Originator—The author of the Broadcast wave. This information is taken from the Author field in the File Info dialog.

- Originator Reference—A unique reference identifier created by SONAR.

- Origination Date—The date the file was created.

- Origination Time—The time the file was created.

- Time Reference—The SMPTE time stamp for the beginning of broadcast wave.

To Export a Project in Windows Media Format

1. Set all volume, pan, effects, and automation settings just as you want them.

2. If you only want to mix down parts of tracks, select those clips now.

3. If you are using effects on the tracks and want to mix the effects down at this time, select the whole length of the longest track or clip plus extra time for the reverb or effects "tail."

4. Choose **File-Export-Audio** to open the Export Audio dialog box.

5. Select a destination folder using the Look In field.

6. Enter a file name.

7. Choose Windows Media Advanced Streaming Format from the Files of type dropdown list.

8. In the Source Category field, select one of the following options:

    - Tracks—choosing this option creates a separate file for each track that you select in the Source Buses/Tracks field.

    - Buses—choosing this option creates a separate file for each bus that you select in the Source Buses/Tracks field.

    - Main Outputs—choosing this option creates a separate file for each main output that you select in the Source Buses/Tracks field.

    - Entire Mix—choosing this option creates one file for your entire mix, unless you're exporting a surround mix with Split Mono selected in the Channel Format field.

9. In the Source Buses/Tracks field, choose the buses or tracks you want to use as a source to create your mix. If you chose Tracks in the Source Category field, only tracks will show up as choices in this field.

10. In the Channel Format field, select one of the following options:
    - Stereo—All exported tracks and clips are mixed down to a stereo file or files.
    - Mono—All exported tracks and clips are mixed down to a mono file or files.
    - Split Mono—All exported tracks and clips are mixed down to separate mono files.
    - Multichannel—All exported tracks are mixed down to a multichannel WMA file or files.
11. Choose the sample rate that you want your exported file to be.
12. Select the bit depth that you want the exported file to use. If your source file is 16 and you export to 24, you get more precision for any audio effects in the mix (and a larger file). If your source file is 24 and you export to 16, you lose some sound definition, but you get some of it back if the Dithering option is on in the Audio Options dialog box (see "Dithering" on page 468 for more information).
13. In the Mix Enables field, choose the elements you want to include in the mixdown. If you want to exclude muted tracks and/or include only soloed tracks, make sure Track Mute/Solo is checked.

    Note: If you have patched a DXi (plug-in synth) into a track or bus, make sure you check Track FX to include DXi's that are patched into tracks, and check Bus Returns to include DXi's that are patched into buses.

    Note: If you don't check Track Automation. any initial volume and pan settings in an exported track are ignored and the track's audio data will be exported at the level that exists in the track, with pan set to center. If you don't check Clip Automation, any trim settings are ignored during export. If you don't check Master Automation, any volume and balance settings at the main outs are ignored.

14. If you want to save the settings you created in the Export Audio dialog, type a name for them in the Preset window and then click the floppy disk icon that's next to the window.
15. Click Export.

    The Windows Media Format Encode Options dialog appears.
16. Select options and click OK.

The audio is compacted and exported to a file or files with the extension .wma.

To Export a Project in MP3 Format

1. Set all volume, pan, effects, and automation settings just as you want them.

2. If you only want to mix down parts of tracks, select those clips now.

3. If you are using effects on the tracks and want to mix the effects down at this time, select the whole length of the longest track or clip plus an extra measure for the reverb or effects "tail."

4. Choose **File-Export-Audio** to open the Export Audio dialog box.

5. Select a destination folder using the Look In field.

6. Enter a file name.

7. Choose MP3 from the Files of type dropdown list.

8. In the Source Category field, select one of the following options:

    - Tracks—choosing this option creates a separate file for each track that you select in the Source Buses/Tracks field.

    - Buses—choosing this option creates a separate file for each bus that you select in the Source Buses/Tracks field.

    - Main Outputs—choosing this option creates a separate file for each main output that you select in the Source Buses/Tracks field.

    - Entire Mix—choosing this option creates one file for your entire mix.

9. In the Source Buses/Tracks field, choose the buses or tracks you want to use as a source to create your mix. If you chose Tracks in the Source Category field, only tracks will show up as choices in this field.

10. In the Channel Format field, select one of the following options:

    - Stereo—All exported tracks and clips are mixed down to a stereo file or files.

    - Mono—All exported tracks and clips are mixed down to a mono file or files.

    - Split Mono—All exported tracks and clips are mixed down to separate mono files.

11. Choose the sample rate that you want your exported file to be.

12. In the Bit Depth field, select 16. If your source file is 24 and you export to 16, you lose some sound definition, but you get some of it back if the Dithering option is on in the Audio Options dialog box (see "Dithering" on page 468 for more information).

13. In the Mix Enables field, choose the elements you want to include in the mixdown. If you want to exclude muted tracks and/or include only soloed tracks, make sure Track Mute/Solo is checked.

    Note: If you have patched a DXi (plug-in synth) into a track or bus, make sure you check Track FX to include DXi's that are patched into tracks, and check Bus Returns to include DXi's that are patched into buses.

    Note: If you don't check Track Automation. any initial volume and pan settings in an exported track are ignored and the track's audio data will be exported at the level that exists in the track, with pan set to center. If you don't check Clip Automation, any trim settings are ignored during export. If you don't check Master Automation, any volume and balance settings at the main outs are ignored.

14. If you want to save the settings you created in the Export Audio dialog, type a name for them in the Preset window and then click the floppy disk icon that's next to the window.

15. Click Export.

    The Cakewalk MP3 Encoder dialog appears.

16. Choose options and click OK.

The audio is compacted and exported to a file or files with the extension .MP3.

To Export a Project as an OMF File

OMF (Open Media Format) files are designed for cross-platform compatibility.

1. Select *File-Export-OMF*.

   The Export OMF dialog appears.

2. In the File Name field, enter a name for the file.

3. In the Save as Type field, select the OMF version you want to save the project as. Version 1 is compatible with older applications. See your target applications documentation for information on which version it supports.

4. In the Audio Packaging section, select Embed Audio Within OMF if you want to save the audio in the OMF file, or Reference Audio Externally if you want to store the audio in a subdirectory.

5. In the Audio Format section, select what file format you want your audio saved in.

6. Check the Split Stereo Tracks into Dual Mono option if you want to save stereo interleaved tracks as a pair of mono tracks.

7. Check the Include Archived Tracks option if you want to export the tracks in your project that are currently archived.

8. Check Mix Each Groove Clip as a Separate Clip option if you want to save Groove clips (ACIDized files) as separate clips. This may increase significantly the amount of time it takes to export your project, if there are many Groove clips in your project.

9. Click Save.

Note: OMF files save the following:

- Tracks
- Clip positions
- Slip edits
- Fades and crossfades (as destructive edits)

The following information is discarded:

- Volume
- Pan
- Automation
- Effects

Dithering

Dithering is a process you can use when you convert a 24-bit file to 16 bits. SONAR offers the new Pow-r dithering process, short for Psycho-acoustically Optimized Wordlength Reduction, which can produce 16-bit files that sound indistinguishable from their 24-bit source files. Dithering adds a small amount of noise to the 16-bit file to approximate the sounds that were lost when the other 8 bits were removed. When this option is turned on, SONAR uses dithering when you import a 24-bit file into a 16-bit project. Also, because many SONAR features such as effects use 32-bit processing, SONAR applies dithering when you bounce or freeze tracks with dither turned on. Doing lots of bouncing and/or freezing with dither turned on can build up noise in your project, however turning it off produces a small amount of distortion during bounces and freezes instead. Dithering is not applied or needed if you work in 24-bit mode, until you decide to export a 16-bit file, at which time you can turn it on if you want.

SONAR offers four kinds of dithering:

- Rectangular—basically white noise, and the least CPU-intensive, this type of dither is more audible than the Pow-r dither types, but works well with loud projects, or ones that use distortion.

- Pow-r 1—adds a fairly consistent amount of noise below 10k, then quickly increases. Good for compressed music with few quiet sections.

- Pow-r 2—adds a little less noise than Pow-r 1 until around 9k, then increases fairly rapidly. More CPU-intensive than Pow-r 1.

- Pow-r 3—adds the least amount of noise in the most audible range, then jumps up at about 8k and again above 10k. Good for classical music or any music that has a wide range of volume. Most CPU-intensive and transparent of all choices.

12 Surround Mixing

SONAR Producer fully supports surround mixing (SONAR Studio can open surround projects created in Producer, converting them to stereo). SONAR (Producer) can create finished surround mixes in all popular surround formats, including Windows Media 9 Pro. You can use a joystick to control surround panning if you want.

Note: it's always advisable to know the required sampling rate and audio driver bit depth for the target medium that your surround project will be used in. That way you can work in the correct format from the start, without having to convert later. You can set these parameters in the Audio Options dialog (***Options-Audio*** command).

To get a complete understanding of SONAR's surround functions, start with the "Surround Basics" on page 472.

In This Chapter

Surround Basics 472
Configuring SONAR for Surround Mixing 473
Panning in Surround 479
Joystick Support 485
Surround Metering 486
Bass Management 487
Surround Effects 488
Importing Surround Mixes 491
Exporting Surround Mixes 492

Surround Basics

Surround sound is a common name for various techniques for positioning audio in reference to the listener. Whereas regular stereo is limited to left/right positioning, within a relatively narrow field, surround sound opens possibilities of positioning an audio source anywhere around the listener. Surround sound comes in many formats. The differences between the formats are in three areas:

- The number of speakers—this varies from 3/2 all the way to 10.2 and beyond.
- The angles of the speakers.
- The intended final coding format—this depends on the media the audio will be "stored" on: film, broadcast video or DVD, for example.

The most common format is 5.1, which consists of five full-range channels and a low-frequency effects (LFE) channel (the ".1" in 5.1 is the LFE or sub channel). The five full-range channels are reproduced by left, right, and center speakers positioned in front of the listener (L, R, and C for short), and left and right surround speakers positioned behind the listener (Ls and Rs for short). The LFE channel can be routed to the main speakers or to a subwoofer that can be positioned almost anywhere.

The center channel is typically used to lock dialog or sounds to a video screen. The LFE channel is generally routed to a subwoofer to enhance low audio frequencies for effects such as explosions or crashes. Audio in this channel is limited to a range of approximately 25 Hz to 120 Hz.

Configuring SONAR for Surround Mixing

This section covers setting up SONAR for surround sound.

Using Surround Format Templates

A Surround Format template specifies the number of speakers and the order in which the speakers are arranged.

There are several different surround formats, including LCRS, 5.1, 6.1, and 7.1, with 5.1 being most common. The number after the decimal point refers to the number of Low Frequency Effect (LFE) speakers. However, there are even different flavors of 5.1. The different flavors specify in which order the speakers are arranged, and the speaker angles. For example:

Surround Format	Speaker Order
5.1 SMPTE/ITU	L, R, C, LFE, Ls, Rs
5.1 Music Alternative	L, R, Ls, Rs, C, LFE
5.1 Film Alternative	L, C, R, Ls, Rs, LFE

The speaker positions, moving clockwise from center, are identified as:

Label	Speaker
C	Center (directly in front of listener)
Rc	Right of Center
R	Right (standard Stereo placement)
Sr	Side right—directly to the right of the listener
Rs	Right Surround
Cs	Surround (rear center)
Ls	Left Surround
Sl	Side Left—directly to the left of the listener
L	Left (standard Stereo placement)
Lc	Left of center
LFE	Low Frequency Effect speaker(s)—placed according to room acoustics

To mix in surround sound in SONAR, you must insert at least one surround bus.

A project can include multiple surround buses, but all surround buses in a project use the same surround format (5.1, 7.1, etc.).

The project's surround format is based on one of the following Surround Format templates:

- 2.0
- 2.1
- LCR
- LRC+LFE
- LRS
- LFS+LFE
- Matrix UHJ
- QUAD
- 4.1 (SMPTE/ITU)
- Quad+LFE
- PanAmbio 4.1
- LCRS
- Surround (SMPTE/ITU)
- Surround Media
- LCRS+LFE
- 5.1 (Standard 3/2)
- 5.1 (Film/Alternative)
- 5.1 (Music/Alternative)
- 5.1 (SMPTE/ITU)
- 6.0 (Hexagon)
- 6.0 (Film/Alternative)
- 6.0 (Music/Alternative)
- 6.1 (Film/Alternative)
- 6.1 (Music/Alternative)
- 6.1 (SMPTE/ITU)
- 7.0 (Heptagon)

- 7.0 (Film/Alternative)
- 7.0 (Music/Alternative)
- 7.1 (Film/Alternative)
- 7.1 (Music/Alternative)
- 7.1 (SMPTE/ITU)
- 8.0 (Octagon)
- 8.0 (Film/Alternative)
- 8.0 (Music/Alternative)
- 8.1 (Film/Alternative)
- 8.1 (Music/Alternative)
- 8.1 (SMPTE/ITU)

5.1 (SMPTE/ITU) is the default template.

The Surround Format templates are hard-coded, and cannot be deleted. However, you can freely assign any enabled audio output port to any surround channel, and save the configuration as a preset.

Surround settings are per project. Surround speaker assignments default to unique audio output channels when you choose a new template.

You configure your surround settings in the Project Options dialog on the Surround tab (use the ***Options-Project*** command and click the Surround tab).

Choosing a Surround Format

Using the ***Options-Project*** command and clicking the Surround tab displays several fields of surround options. Choosing a surround format sets the number of speakers your project is using, and lets you choose a specific sound card output for each speaker. Here you can also choose parameters for bass management, and for downmixing, which means converting a surround mix into a stereo mix.

The group of sound card outputs that you choose on the Surround tab of the Project Options dialog make up the "Surround Main." The Surround Main becomes a choice on the Outputs menus of tracks and buses as soon as you insert a surround bus into your project. You won't see a "Surround Main" output module in the output modules section of the Console view, because it's just a term for the group of sound card outputs you choose for surround mixing. The pan control on any track or bus that outputs to the "Surround Main" controls which hardware outputs receive the signal that the track or bus sends to the "Surround Main."

SONAR saves the surround settings you choose on the Surround tab of the Project-Options dialog with your project, including your downmixing parameters. If you have some particular settings you might use again, you can save a group of settings as a preset (except for downmixing parameters—you can change these, but they aren't saved in presets). To save a group of settings as a preset, type a name in the Presets field and then click the Disk icon that's to the right of the field. When you want to use this preset in a project, just choose it from the Presets dropdown menu.

To Choose a Surround Format and Set Sound Card Outputs

1. Use the **Options-Project** command.

   The Project Options dialog appears.

2. Click the Surround tab.

3. Select a format from the Surround Format dropdown.

   The diagram to the right of the Surround Format menu changes to illustrate the speaker placement of the format that you chose.

4. In the Output column, assign each channel to a sound card output.

   Note: Consumer-grade sound cards, such as Audigy or SoundBlaster, typically reserve output 4 for the LFE channel. Check your sound card manual for details.

5. Click OK.

Note: Take a moment to make sure your speakers are correctly hooked up to the corresponding outputs before you attempt any playback. See the diagram in the Project Options dialog for the speaker setup. If you are not sure what the abbreviations for the speaker names are, see "Surround Basics" on page 472.

Surround Buses

You have to have at least one surround bus in your project to use surround sound. A surround bus differs from a stereo bus in that it simply has more channels. For example, if a project is set to 7.1, then the bus has 8 channels: 7 directional channels and one LFE channel.

To Insert a Surround Bus

1. In the Bus Pane of the Track view or the Console view, right-click to display a popup menu of bus options.

2. Select **Insert Surround Bus** from the popup menu.

   Or

- Use the **Insert-Surround Bus** menu command.

Routing in Surround

Tracks can send output to a surround bus, the Surround Main, or a hardware output. If a track is routed to a surround bus or the Surround Main, it has surround meters and a surround panner. You can route any track or bus to another bus, the Surround Main or a hardware out. However, you are prevented from creating a signal loop by routing the signal back into a bus that is already in the signal flow. The following table lists how each of these routing options affects the signal:

Signal Flow	Result
Track to stereo bus	No change
Mono track to surround bus	Mono signal is routed to both Left and Right channels of surround format. You can change the routing to other surround channels by using the surround panner on the track.
Stereo track to surround bus	Stereo left channel is routed to Left channel of surround format; stereo right channel is routed to Right channel of surround format. You can change the routing to other surround channels by using the surround panner on the track.
Track to hardware output	No change
Stereo bus to stereo bus	No change
Stereo bus to surround bus or the Surround Main	Stereo left channel is routed to Left channel of surround format; stereo right channel is routed to Right channel of surround format. You can change the routing to other surround channels by using the surround panner on the stereo bus.
Stereo bus to hardware output	No change
Surround bus to stereo bus	Surround channels are downmixed to stereo
Surround bus to surround bus or the Surround Main	No change

To Assign a Track to a Surround Bus or Surround Main
- Click in the track's output field and select a surround bus, the Surround Main, or New Surround Bus as an output.

Downmixing

Downmixing is a way of previewing your surround project in stereo only. There are various cases where surround is not available and it may be that someone plays your project in stereo only. A radio broadcast is a good example. Downmixing is a valuable tool for determining if your project will sound good in stereo. However, you can export your project in stereo, and SONAR uses your downmix settings to create your exported file.

The following table lists the downmixing settings in the Surround tab of the Project Options dialog and gives a brief description of what the setting does. You can also manually enter other values besides these preset ones:

Downmixing Setting	Options
Center Downmix Level (dB)	These options determine how much of the center is mixed to the left and right. • -3 dB—Maintains the same level of center channel sound when you listen in a typically reverberant room • -4.5 dB—a compromise level between -3dB and -6 dB • -6 dB—Maintains the same level of center channel sound when you listen to direct sound without typical room reverberations • -INF—Eliminates all of the Center channel signal
Surround Downmix Level (dB)	The amount of Left Surround and Right Surround mixed into the Left and Right channels respectively. • -3 dB—Maintains the same level of surround • -6 dB—Reduces the level of surround so that it doesn't compete with center channel sound such as dialog • -INF—Eliminates all of the Surround channel signal
LFE Level (dB)	The amount of the LFE channel mixed into the Left and Right channels respectively. • -12 (or type in a value)—lets you choose the level of LFE in the stereo mix • -INF—Eliminates all LFE

To Downmix a Project

1. If you do not have a stereo bus in your project, create one by right-clicking in the Bus pane in the Track view or Console view and selecting **Insert Stereo Bus** from the menu that appears.

2. Open the Project Options dialog (**Options-Project** command), select a center downmix level and a surround downmix level in the Surround tab, and click OK.

3. In each of the surround buses, assign the output to a stereo bus.

4. Listen to your project through the stereo bus, and make any final adjustments to the stereo mix by changing the values in the Surround tab of the Project Options dialog.

5. If you want to export your stereo mix, use the **File-Export Audio** command. This command obeys your downmix settings.

Panning in Surround

Unlike stereo panning which sends sound to left and right speakers, surround panning means sending sound to multiple speakers at points along a circle.

When a track/bus/send is assigned to a surround bus, the Pan control turns into a multi-dimensional surround panner. The surround panner comes in four sizes:

- Micro—this is found in the Track view.

- Small—this is found on sends.

- Medium—this is the surround panner which is displayed in the Track Inspector and Console view.

- Large—this is a large surround panner (see "Controlling Surround Panning" on page 480) which has additional controls, and appears when you right-click a surround panner and choose **Open Surround Panner** from the popup menu, or double-click outside the surround panner circle, or press Enter when the panner has focus.

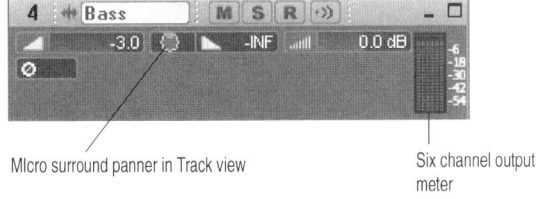

Micro surround panner in Track view

Six channel output meter

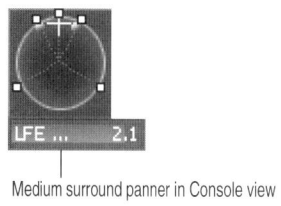

Medium surround panner in Console view

The small and large panners are always synchronized; the large panner simply provides increased resolution when you adjust the surround pan position. The large surround panner can be resized like any other floating window.

Note 1: Surround panning is not available for tracks/sends that are routed to non-surround buses.

Note 2: If the track/bus/send is reassigned to a stereo bus, any surround automation will be orphaned, but will automatically reconnect if the track/bus/send is later assigned back to a surround bus.

Controlling Surround Panning

Here are pictures of the large surround panner and medium surround panner:

Large Surround Panner

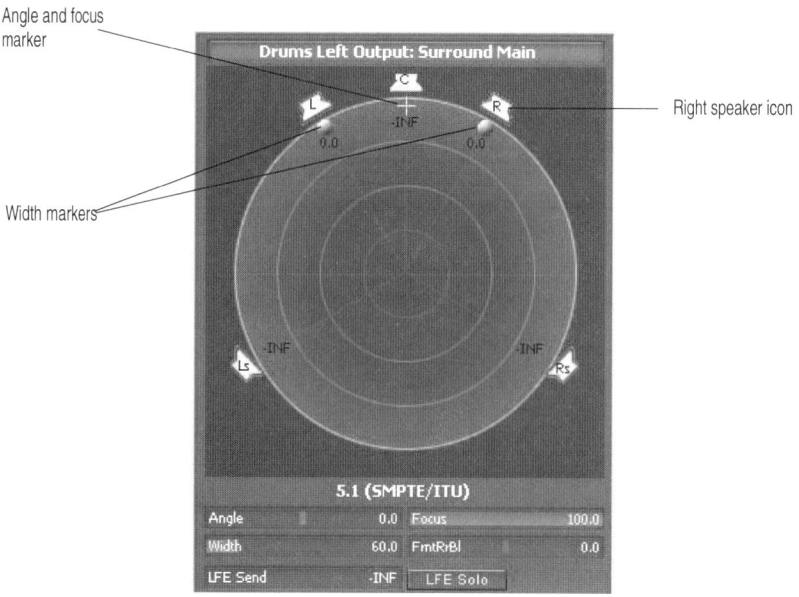

Medium Surround Panner

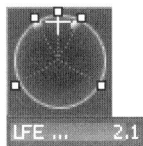

The large surround panner has some sliders at the bottom that the medium surround panner doesn't have, except for the LFE Send slider, which the medium panner has. Except for the sliders, the large and medium surround panners have the following controls:

- Angle and Focus marker—a small sphere that you can drag in any direction to both control and display the following two parameters:

  - **Angle**—this is the perceived angle of the sound source as it differs from the position directly in front of the listener. The scale is 0 to 180 degrees on the listener's right, and 0 to -180 degrees on the listener's left. 0 means the sound is coming from directly in front of the listener, and plus or minus 180 degrees means that the sound is coming from directly behind the listener.

  - **Focus**—this is the perceived distance of the sound source from the center of the circle on a scale of 0 to 100, 0 meaning the center of the circle, and 100 meaning the perimeter.

- Width markers—these are two smaller spheres equidistant from the Angle and Focus marker. Their distance from each other and from the front of the circle shows the Width value (see definition below). You can also drag the Width markers to control Angle and Focus.

- Speaker icons/squares—each surround channel is represented by a speaker icon in the large panner, and a white square in the small panner. The large panner also has a corresponding volume level in dB directly in front of each icon. The position of each speaker icon shows you each speaker's position in the surround mix. Clicking a speaker icon or square **mutes** the corresponding channel, causing the icon or square to become grey. Double-clicking the icon **solos** its channel, turning the icon green.

- Angle slider (large panner only)—this slider both displays and controls the angle value.

- Focus slider (large panner only)—this slider both displays and controls the focus value.

- **Width** slider (large panner only)—this slider both displays and controls the width value. *Width* is a measure of how wide an area the sound seems to be coming from on a scale of 0 to 360 degrees. At 0 and 360 degrees, the sound seems to all come from a single speaker. At 180 degrees the sound seems to come from directly opposite sides. The default angle matches the project's left and right channel angle. For example, in 5.1 SMPTE/ITU surround, the default width is 60 degrees.

- Front/Rear Balance slider (large panner only)—abbreviated as FrntRrBl, this slider adjusts the front and rear balance. Drag it to the left to reduce the level from the front speakers, or drag it to the right to reduce rear level.

- LFE slider—this slider both displays and controls the level of sound sent to the LFE channel.

- LFE Only button (large panner only)—this button mutes all channels except the LFE channel.

To Open the Large Surround Panner
- Right-click the small surround panner or the pan control in a track, and choose **Open Surround Panner** from the popup menu.

  Or

- Select a track, and either use the ***View-Surround Panner*** command, or click the Surround Panner button in the Views toolbar.

  Or

- Double-click outside the Surround Panner circle.

  Or

- Press Enter when the panner has focus.

To Change the Angle
- In either the large or small surround panner, drag the Angle and Focus marker to the left or right.

  Or

- In the large surround panner, drag the Angle slider.

To Change the Focus
- In either the large or small surround panner, drag the Angle and Focus marker toward or away from the center.

  Or

- In the large surround panner, drag the Focus slider.

To Mute a Surround Speaker
- In the large surround panner, click a speaker icon to mute its output. The speaker icon turns grey when the speaker is muted.

    Or

- In the small surround panner, click a white square to mute a speaker's output. The square turns grey when the speaker is muted.

To Solo a Surround Speaker
- In the large surround panner, double-click a speaker icon to solo its output. The speaker icon turns green when the speaker is soloed.

    Or

- In the small surround panner, double-click a white square to solo a speaker's output. The square turns green when the speaker is soloed.

To Change the Width
- In the large surround panner, drag the Width slider.

To Change the Front/Rear Balance
- In the large surround panner, drag the FrntRrBl slider left to reduce front level, or right to reduce rear level.

To Change the LFE Send Level
- In either the large or small surround panner, drag the LFE slider.

Note: double-clicking any surround panner control will reset the control to its default value, which for the LFE control is -INF.

To Solo or Unsolo the LFE Channel
- In the large surround panner, click the LFE Solo button.

To Isolate a Signal in One Speaker
- In the large surround panner, drag the Width slider to 0, the Focus slider to 100, and then drag the Angle slider until the sphere icon is directly in front of the correct speaker.

    Or

- Press the desired Numeric Keypad key that represents the speaker position (7=L, 8=C, 9=R, see "Keyboard Shortcuts" on page 484).

To Group Panner Controls
- In the large surround panner, right-click each slider that you want to add to the group, and choose *Group-"n"* from the popup menu.

Now you can move a single slider, and all sliders in that same group move synchronously.

Note: if you group sliders that are in the same surround panner, you can no longer move the markers that represent those sliders' values. You can only move a grouped marker by moving its associated slider.

Keyboard Shortcuts

The following shortcuts allow you to control a surround panner from the keyboard:

Shortcut...	Function...
Alt+drag	Constrains to angle
Alt+Shift+drag	Constrains to angle at 100% focus
Ctrl+Shift+drag	Constrains to focus only
Shift+click	Sets panner point to the point that you click (large and medium panners only)
Shift+drag controls (Angle, Width, etc.)	Fine resolution
Up/Down cursor keys	Move to next/previous widget in surround panner
Left/Right cursor keys	Move to next/previous panner in same track
Ctrl+up/down	Move to surround panner in another track
Ctrl+NumPad 0-9	Speaker mutes
NumPad 0-9	Jump to speaker angle at 100% focus

NumPad assignments:

- 0 = n/a
- 1 = Ls
- 2 = Cs
- 3 = Rs
- 4 = Sl
- 5 = n/a
- 6 = Sr
- 7 = L
- 8 = C

- 9 = R
- / = Lc,
- * = Rc

Automating Surround Panning

You can arm or disarm for automation all the controls in a surround panner by clicking any control in the surround panner (except LFE Solo), and choosing *Arm for Automation* from the popup menu.

Joystick Support

SONAR Producer allows you to use a joystick to control surround panning. A force-feedback joystick such as the Microsoft® SideWinder® Force Feedback 2 joystick can add a tactile element to mixing sessions, and add button control to some SONAR transport and/or menu commands with the extra buttons on the joystick module.

The joystick will grab the current pan position/sphere anytime you pull the trigger button (the "firing" button under your index finger). When recording automation, you write new automation every time you pull the trigger button.

Various joystick buttons can be used to:

- Control SONAR's transport
- Switch focus to adjacent tracks/sends
- Solo/unsolo current channel
- Open/close the large surround panner window

To Connect the Joystick to SONAR Producer

1. Use the *Options-Control Surfaces* command.

2. In the Control Surfaces dialog, click the Add button, and choose Joystick Panner in the Control Surfaces field of the Control Surface Settings dialog; click OK.

3. Close the Control Surfaces dialog, and display the Control Surfaces toolbar (*View-Toolbars-Control Surfaces* command).

4. On the left side of the toolbar, choose Joystick Panner in the dropdown menu, and then click the Properties button that's on the right side of the toolbar.

5. In the Joystick Panner dialog, select button 1 in the Buttons field, and then select Engage Pan Mode in the Button Actions field.

6. Now select Button 2, and select Engage Pan Nav Mode in the Button Actions field.

7. Select any other buttons your joystick has (one at a time), and connect them to any transport or menu commands you want in the Button Actions field; close the Joystick Panner dialog.

Now when you hold down button 1 (the "trigger button"), the joystick controls the surround panner on the current track or send. When the pan/sphere is in the desired position, let button 1 up to hold the position. When you hold down button 2, move the joystick vertically to change the current track, and horizontally to change to a different send control. The window on the right side of the Control Surfaces toolbar displays the names of the current track and send. Use any other buttons you configured to control other SONAR Producer functions.

You can save your button assignments as a preset by typing a name for the current group of settings in the Presets window in the Joystick Panner dialog, and then clicking the floppy disk icon that's next to the Presets window. Whenever you want to load a preset, just select it in the Presets window.

Surround Metering

Meters in tracks routed to surround buses or the Surround Main, and meters in surround buses work the same as stereo meters (see "Metering" on page 436), however, surround meters display more channels. For example, a project in 5.1 would have a six-channel meter.

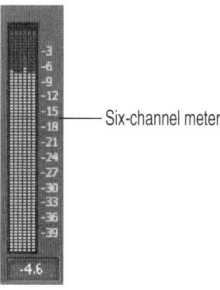
Six-channel meter

Bass Management

A bass management system takes all the frequencies below a certain frequency (normally 80Hz) from the main channels, and the signal from the LFE channel, and mixes them together into the speaker that is best equipped to handle them. This is usually a subwoofer, but sometimes the left and right front speakers are used if a subwoofer isn't available. The reason why this is done is to make use of the subwoofer for more than the occasional low frequency effect, since the subwoofer is there anyway, and to lower the effective response of the system to about 25 Hz.

When you encode to Dolby Digital, the LFE channel gets a +10dB gain on playback from Dolby's decoder. This gives you the option of delivering some really powerful deep bass during playback, such as in that earthquake sound effect in your recording. Consider also that this +10 dB of low bass can also be added to any low bass that came out of the other 5 channels from redirection, so you realistically can deliver a sound from the subwoofer that is more than +20dB above the sound from any other speaker.

What this means during mixing is that you would have to turn the analog gain to your subwoofer up 10 dB relative to the other 5 speakers, so that you hear the sound as it will be played back in home theater systems that use bass management, and you will get your levels set right in the mix.

SONAR's bass management system allows you to monitor how a surround project will sound with bass management, so you don't have to change the gain to your subwoofer during mixing. SONAR's bass management system only applies to monitoring, and is ignored when you export your file.

To Monitor With Bass Management
1. If necessary open the project you want to use bass management in.
2. Select **Options-Project** from the SONAR menu.

   The Project Options dialog appears.
3. Click the Surround tab.
4. Check the Monitor with Bass Management option.
5. Select an option in the Low Pass Cutoff (Hz) dropdown, and click OK.

Surround Effects

SONAR lets you use your existing stereo or mono effects as surround effects. SONAR does this through the SurroundBridge, which automatically sets up your existing mono & stereo plug-ins so you can patch them into surround buses (buses, **not tracks**).

The SurroundBridge

The SurroundBridge automatically loads enough instances of a plug-in to handle all your surround channels. For example, if you patch a *stereo* effect into a surround bus that uses 5.1 SMPTE/ITU panning, the SurroundBridge automatically assigns the Left and Right channels of the bus to instance 1 of the plug-in, assigns the Left Surround and Right Surround channels to instance 2, the Center channel to instance 3, and the LFE channel to instance 4. If you patch a mono effect into a surround bus, the SurroundBridge assigns each channel to a single instance of the mono effect, which would create six instances of the effect on a 5.1 surround bus. You can view and edit these assignments on the SurroundBridge tab that's in the property page of every effect that's patched into a surround bus. For example, if you want a certain effect on the Left Surround channel of a surround bus, but not on the Right Surround channel, you can assign these two channels to different instances of the effect you're patching by choosing options on the SurroundBridge tab of the effect's property page.

The SurroundBridge also links the automatable parameters of each instance so that when you change a parameter in one instance, you automatically change the same parameter in all the other instances. You can unlink parameters individually, or per-instance (see "How to Patch and Configure Surround Effects" on page 489).

Effect Property Pages

A single property page controls all instances of an effect that is patched into a surround bus. The effect's property page displays a different tab for each instance of the effect. By default, when you change an automatable parameter on one tab of the property page, that change is duplicated on all the tabs of the property page. However, you can "unlink" individual parameters from the other tabs by clicking the Unlink Controls button in the effect property page, and while the button is enabled (red), move the parameter you want to unlink, and then click the Unlink Controls button again to disable it. Now you can change that parameter on one tab without changing the same parameter on the other tabs. You can also link or unlink all of an instance's parameters by using the controls on the SurroundBridge tab.

Effect Presets

You can use existing (non-surround) effects presets when you patch an effect to a surround bus—selecting a non-surround preset sets all of a plug-in's instances to the settings of the preset; selecting a surround preset sets each instance's parameters individually, according to the information stored in the preset.

How to Patch and Configure Surround Effects

For step-by-step instructions, see the following procedures.

To Patch an Effect Into a Surround Bus

- Right-click the FX bin of a surround bus and choose a mono or stereo effect from the popup menu.

The SurroundBridge patches multiple instances of the effect you chose into the bus's FX bin (however, only one effect appears in the bin), with default assignments of surround channels to plug-in instances.

To Change Channel Assignments for a Patched Effect

1. If the effect's property page is not open, display it by double-clicking the name of the effect in the surround bus's FX bin.
2. On the SurroundBridge tab of the effect's property page, use the dropdown menus in the Left Input and Right Input columns to assign individual surround channels to instances of the effect.

Your assignments take effect immediately, and the names of the tabs in the property page change to reflect the new assignments.

To Unlink Individual Effect Parameters from Other Effect Instances

1. In the property page of an effect that's patched into a surround bus, click the Unlink Controls button so that it turns red.
2. Make some adjustments to the automatable parameters you want to unlink (non-automatable parameters are not linked together). You can select parameters on any tab.
3. When you're finished adjusting parameters, click the Unlink Controls button again so that it's not red.

Now you can adjust the parameters you adjusted, without automatically adjusting the same parameters that are on other tabs of the effect's property page.

A list of the parameters that you unlinked appears in the Unlinked Controls field on the SurroundBridge tab, with the instance number listed in the Plug-in # column of the Unlinked Controls field.

If you unlinked some but not all of an instance's parameters, the instance's checkbox in the Controls Linked to Group column appears **grey**, with a check.

To view a list of the automatable parameters in a particular effect, uncheck one of the Controls Linked to Group checkboxes on the SurroundBridge tab, and read the list in the Unlinked Controls field.

To Relink Individual Effect Parameters to Other Effect Instances

1. In the Unlinked Controls field on the SurroundBridge tab, select the parameters you want to relink—if the parameters you want to select are adjacent, you can Shift-click the first and last ones in the group. If they're not adjacent, you can Ctrl-click them individually.

2. Click the Relink Controls button.

The parameters you relinked are removed from the list.

To Unlink All of an Instance's Parameters from Other Instances

1. In the property page of an effect that's patched into a surround bus, click the SurroundBridge tab.

2. Find the instance you want to unlink in the Plug-in # column, and uncheck its Controls Linked to Group checkbox.

The parameters you unlinked appear in the Unlinked Controls field, with the instance number listed in the Plug-in # column of the Unlinked Controls field.

Note: to relink all of an instance's parameters, recheck its Controls Linked to Group checkbox.

To Disable an Instance

- On the SurroundBridge tab of the effect's property page, uncheck the Enable checkbox of the plug-in you want to disable. The instance's tab becomes greyed-out when you do this. You can re-enable the instance by rechecking the checkbox.

The Enable checkbox is a separate bypass system from the Bypass button that is on the instance's individual property tab. Disabling an instance by using the Enable checkbox lightens the CPU load by taking the instance out of the processing path. The Bypass button on the instance's property tab does not change color when you click the Enable checkbox, because it is a separate system. The Bypass button is automatable in some plug-ins.

To Save a Preset

1. Set the effect's parameters the way you want them.

2. In the Presets field of the effect's property page, type a name for the preset, and click the floppy disk icon that's just right of the Presets field.

Saving a preset of an effect that's patched into a surround bus creates a surround preset, which includes channel assignments and parameter linkage settings.

Importing Surround Mixes

SONAR imports multi-channel (surround) files as a group of mono files. If the files contain information that labels the speaker location of each channel in the file, SONAR copies these labels to the clips in your audio tracks, but does not pan the tracks according to these labels. This is because you may not have your SONAR project set to the same multi-channel format as the imported project.

You can import the following types of multi-channel files:

- Multi-channel PCM wave files (.WAV)

- Dolby AC3 encoded files. (.AC3)—these are encoded for Dolby surround. You will need to install an AC3 decoder filter such as this one: http://ac3filter.sourceforge.net in order to be able to decode these files in SONAR. **Important**: After installing the above AC3 codec, go to Control Panel and launch the "AC3 Filter" control panel applet. From there you can set up the default speaker output for this filter to 5.1 channels. Until you do this it will only stream in stereo. Also check the sample rate of the imported file. It's recommended that you set your project sample rate to whatever the file uses before importing. Otherwise the import process will go through a time consuming resampling pass for each channel.

- Windows Media Pro

To Import a Surround Multi-channel File
1. Use the *File-Import-Audio* command to open the Import Audio dialog.
2. Select a file of a supported file type.
3. Check Import As Mono Tracks.
4. Click Open.

SONAR imports each channel to a separate mono track.

Tip: You can also rip the soundtrack from a video file by opening the video file directly from the Import Audio dialog.

Exporting Surround Mixes

You can export your surround mixes as multi-channel PCM wave files, or as Windows Media Pro files.

To Export a Surround Multi-channel File

1. Use the *File-Export-Audio* command to open the Export Audio dialog.
2. Type a name for your file.
3. In the Files of Type field, choose one of the following:
   - If you want to create a multi-channel wave file, choose RIFF Wave.
   - If you want to create a multi-channel Windows Media file, choose Windows Media Advanced Streaming Format.
4. In the Source Category field, choose Buses, Main Outputs, or Entire Mix.
5. Choose the bus or buses in the Source Buses/Tracks field that you want to export your mix from.
6. Choose Multichannel in the Channel Format field.
7. Choose any other options you want such as Sample Rate and Bit Depth.
8. If you want to save the settings you created in the Export Audio dialog, type a name for them in the Preset window and then click the floppy disk icon that's next to the window.
9. Click Export.

SONAR exports your project in the file format you selected.

13 Using Automation

Automation means to record the movement of a fader, knob, or other control so that the next time you play your project, that control moves automatically. SONAR allows you to graphically automate much more than just volume and pan controls—you can automate individual controls, faders, and knobs that control the main outs, individual tracks, buses, individual effects' parameters (including some plug-in synths), and even individual clips. You can also group several controls together and automate them all by recording only a single control's movements. All automatable controls are in the Console view and the Track view (including the Clips pane), however, you can also graphically automate MIDI controllers from the Piano Roll view in addition to the Console and Track views. You can enable or disable all automation by clicking the **Enable Automation Playback** button in the Automation toolbar. Display the Automation toolbar by using the *View-Toolbars* command and making sure that the Automation checkbox is checked in the Toolbars dialog box.

In This Chapter

Quick Automation Guide	494
The Automation Toolbar	495
Automation Methods	495
Automating Effects	507
Reassigning Envelopes	510
The Envelope Editing and Node Editing Menus	511

Quick Automation Guide

The following table summarizes Console and Track view automation:

What you can automate...	Parameters you can automate...	How you can automate them...
Individual tracks	Gain, pan, mute, bus send gain, bus send balance, MIDI controllers, MIDI chorus and reverb, pitch wheel, channel aftertouch, RPN and NRPN	Draw envelopes in the Clips pane, record the fader movements, or take a snapshot
Buses	Input gain and pan, output gain and pan	Draw envelopes in the Clips pane, record the fader movements, or take a snapshot
Individual effects (DirectX 8 plug-ins)	Varies with the effect	Draw envelopes in the Clips pane, record the fader movements, or take a snapshot
Soft Synth controls	Varies with the synth	See "Automating a DXi's Controls" on page 408
Groups of faders or other controls	Whatever the faders or other controls in the group control	Record fader movements
Individual clips	Gain and pan for audio clips, velocity for MIDI clips	Draw envelopes in the Clips pane

In addition, SONAR allows you to copy and paste envelopes between tracks. The **only** controls that you **can't automate** are the Arm, Solo, Pre/Post, Interleave (Mono/Stereo selector), Bus Enable, and Phase buttons; and the Trim fader.

The Automation Toolbar

Display the Automation toolbar by using the ***View-Toolbars*** command to open the Toolbars dialog box, and making sure that the Automation checkbox is checked. If you slide the cursor over each button or field in the toolbar, tool tips pop up to tell you each function. The Automation toolbar gives you quick access to some powerful automation controls:

- **Snapshot button**—Click this button to take a snapshot of all controls at a particular Now time. When you play back your project, when your project reaches the Now time where you took the snapshot, all controls snap to the positions they held when you took the snapshot.

- **Disarm All Automation Controls button**—Click this button to disarm every control that is armed for automation recording.

- **Enable Automation Playback button**—Click this button to either enable or disable any automation data the project contains.

- **Envelope/Offset mode button**—Click this button to toggle between Envelope mode and Offset mode.

Automation Methods

There are several ways to automate controls in the Track and Console views:

- Recording the movements of individual faders, knobs, or controls—this method includes any knob, slider, or control except the Solo, Arm, Phase, Interleave, Vol Trim, Bus Enable, Pre/Post buttons, bank, patch, channel, key+, time+, input and output.

- Drawing envelopes in the Clips pane for audio and/or MIDI data

- Recording automation data from an external controller

- Snapshots

Recording Individual Fader or Knob Movements

This method works in both the Track view and Console view. Arming a parameter for automation and clicking the Record Automation button ![icon] starts automation recording and plays your project while you record automation. You can only record or erase automation data when you click the Record Automation button. SONAR does not record any automation data until you depress the mouse over the control that you armed. SONAR stops recording when you release the mouse.

To Record Individual Fader or Knob Movements

1. Right-click the fader or control you want to automate.

    The Automation popup menu appears (if the control is automatable).

2. Choose **Arm for Automation** from the popup menu.

    SONAR highlights the control with a red outline and turns on the red Auto label in the Status bar at the bottom of the SONAR window.

3. Click the Record Automation button ![icon] that's in the Transport toolbar to start recording, and move the armed control the way you want it to move.

4. Stop recording by clicking the Stop button, or by pressing the Spacebar.

5. Make sure that the Enable Automation Playback button ![icon] in the Automation toolbar is depressed; rewind the project, play it, and listen to the results.

6. Do one of the following:

    - Rewind the project and re-record the automation data.

        OR

    - If you are happy with the result, right-click the armed control and deselect **Arm for Automation** from the menu.

After you record the automation data, SONAR draws a graph of it (an envelope) in the Clips pane, which you can edit with the mouse (see the rest of this chapter).

You can also group controls, so that automating one control automates all the controls in the group.

Drawing Audio Envelopes in the Track View

This method is only available in the Clips pane and Bus pane, and works for both tracks and buses. Drawing an automation envelope for audio data overwrites any preexisting envelope for the same parameter that occurs at the same time in the same track or bus.

To Draw Audio Envelopes in the Track View

1. Right-click in the Clips pane in the track (or bus) you want to automate.

   The Clips pane popup menu appears.

2. From the menu, choose **Envelopes-Create Track Envelope-(name of the control you want to automate)**. Notice the envelope's color at the right side of the menu.

   The envelope appears in the Clips pane as a straight, dotted line in the envelope's individual color, with a node (very small rectangle) at the beginning. When you move the cursor over the envelope, a vertical, double-ended arrow appears under it with the name and current value of the envelope in a box next to the cursor. The envelope's vertical position reflects the current value of the parameter you are editing.

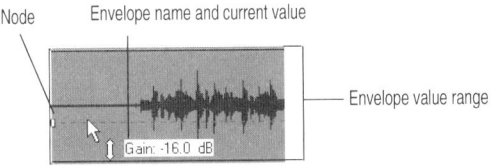

   Note: An automated mute envelope changes the track's mute status whenever the envelope crosses the middle of its value range.

3. Using either the Select or Envelope tools, move the cursor over the envelope until a vertical, double-ended arrow appears under it (notice that the name and current value of the envelope appear in a box next to the cursor), and right-click the envelope. If you use the Envelope tool, you can't accidentally edit any other data besides the envelope.

   The Envelope Editing menu appears.

4. Choose **Add Node** from the menu.

   A node appears on the envelope.

   Note: A shortcut to add a node is to double-click the envelope.

5. Move the cursor over the node until a cross appears under it, and drag the node in any direction you want.

6. Double-click the envelope to add another node.

7. Drag the new node in any direction you want and release the mouse.

8. Move the cursor over the segment of the envelope that lies between the two nodes until the double-ended arrow appears, and right-click the envelope to open the Envelope Editing menu.

9. Choose one of the following **shapes** from the Envelope Editing menu:

   - Jump—This choice causes the envelope to make a ninety degree jump where the envelope reaches the second node. SONAR displays jumps with a dotted line, meaning that there is automation data at the nodes where the dotted line begins and ends, but not where the line itself is.

   - Linear—This choice draws a straight line between the two nodes.

   - Fast Curve—This choice draws a curve between the two nodes that changes value rapidly at first, but more slowly toward the end of the curve.

   - Slow Curve—This choice draws a curve between the two nodes that changes value slowly at first, but more rapidly toward the end of the curve.

   SONAR adds a shape between the nodes. You can drag any shape except a jump up or down and it maintains its curve or angle. To edit a jump, drag the node that's at either end of the jump.

Play the project and listen to the results. You can undo any step by using the **Edit-Undo** command (Ctrl+Z) directly after that step. You can drag the nodes in any direction you want. You can play back your project with or without the automation data by clicking the Enable Automation Playback button in the Automation toolbar.

Note: When you add a "gain" envelope to a track in SONAR, you increase the track's level post-effects, or after the effects processors. Some hardware mixers call this level "volume," because it is post-effects, but other mixers refer to this as "gain." Either way, SONAR's gain envelopes increase a track's level after the effects processors in the signal chain.

When you add multiple envelopes to a track or bus, you can choose which envelopes you want to display. See "Showing or Hiding Envelopes" on page 502.

You can also draw envelopes on MIDI tracks. See "Drawing MIDI Envelopes in the Track View" on page 499.

Drawing MIDI Envelopes in the Track View

This method is only available in the Clips pane. You can also draw MIDI controller data in the Piano Roll view, but the technique is different (see "Using the Controllers Pane" on page 313).

Note: MIDI envelopes you create in the Piano Roll Controllers pane and MIDI envelopes you create in the Track view Clips pane are actually separate envelopes, even if they control the same parameter. Both kinds of envelopes are visible in the Clips pane, and should generally not be used to control the same parameter. You can convert Piano Roll view envelopes to Track view envelopes by selecting the time range and tracks that the Piano Roll envelopes occupy, and using the ***Edit-Convert MIDI To Shapes*** command.

To Draw MIDI Envelopes in the Track View

1. Right-click in the Clips pane in the track you want to automate.

    The Clips pane popup menu appears.

2. If you want to create an envelope to control volume, pan, chorus, reverb, or automated mute, choose ***Envelopes-Create Track Envelope*** and choose one of those items from the menu.

    The envelope appears in the Clips pane as a straight, dotted line in the envelope's individual color, with a node (very small rectangle) at the beginning. When you move the cursor over the envelope, a vertical, double-ended arrow appears under it with the name and current value of the envelope in a box next to the cursor. The envelope's vertical position reflects the current value of the parameter you are editing.

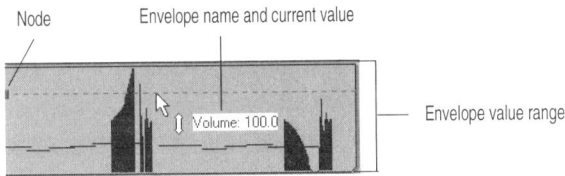

Note: An automated mute envelope changes the track's mute status whenever the envelope crosses the middle of its value range.

3. If you want to create an envelope to control any other MIDI controller, choose ***Envelopes-Create Track Envelope-MIDI...***.

   The MIDI Envelope dialog box appears:

   - In the Type field, choose what kind of MIDI event you want to control with your envelope.
   - In the Value field, choose the name of the controller you want to edit.
   - In the Channel field, choose the MIDI channel that you want the envelope to send data on, and click OK.

   SONAR creates the envelope you chose.

4. Move the cursor over the envelope until a vertical, double-ended arrow appears under it, and right-click the envelope.

   The Envelope Editing menu appears.

5. Choose ***Add Node*** from the menu.

   A node (very small rectangle) appears on the envelope.

   Note: A shortcut to create a node is to double-click the envelope.

6. Move the cursor over the node until a cross appears under it, and drag the node in any direction you want.

   When you release the mouse, the envelope changes to follow the node's new position.

7. Double-click the envelope to add another node.

8. Drag the new node in any direction you want and release the mouse.

9. Move the cursor over the segment of the envelope that lies between the two nodes until the double-ended arrow appears, and right-click the envelope to open the Envelope Editing menu.

10. Choose one of the following **shapes** from the envelope editing menu:

    - Jump—This choice causes the envelope to make a ninety degree jump when the envelope reaches the second node. SONAR displays jumps with a dotted line, meaning that there is automation data at the nodes where the dotted line begins and ends, but not where the line itself is.
    - Linear—This choice draws a straight line between the two nodes.
    - Fast Curve—This choice draws a curve between the two nodes that changes value rapidly at first, but more slowly toward the end of the curve.
    - Slow Curve—This choice draws a curve between the two nodes that changes value slowly at first, but more rapidly toward the end of the curve.

SONAR adds a shape between the nodes. You can drag any shape except a jump up or down and it maintains its curve or angle. To edit a jump, drag the node that's at either end of the jump.

Play your track and listen to the results. You can undo any step by using the ***Edit-Undo*** command (Ctrl+Z) directly after that step. You can play back your project with or without the automation data by clicking the Enable Automation Playback button in the Automation toolbar.

When you add multiple envelopes to a track, you can choose which envelopes you want to display. See "Showing or Hiding Envelopes" on page 502.

You can also draw envelopes on audio tracks. See "Drawing Audio Envelopes in the Track View" on page 497.

Dotted Lines

The dotted line in an envelope shows two things:

- There is no automation data at the time in a track where the dotted line is.

- The value of the last piece of automation data that exists before the dotted line is represented by the vertical level of the dotted line.

You can move an automated control while your project plays, and if you move it during a time where that control has a dotted line in its envelope, the control will stay where you move it. As soon as the Now time reaches a node or solid line, the control snaps to the value of the node or solid line.

Drawing Envelopes on Clips

You can also draw envelopes on audio clips, but only for gain and pan. On MIDI clips, you can draw velocity envelopes. If there is already a track-level envelope on the clip, the clip envelope data merges with the track envelope data.

Note: The Trim value of a track is actually a clip parameter, not a track parameter. SONAR applies clip volume settings, including Trim, to a clip before the clip's audio data reaches any plug-in effects. Effects can sound very different when their incoming data changes volume, even if the final volume is unchanged.

To Draw Envelopes on Clips

1. Right-click the clip that you want to draw the envelope on.

   The Clips pane popup menu appears.

2. Choose ***Envelopes-Clip-(Gain or Pan or Velocity)*** from the menu.

   An envelope appears on the clip with a node at each end.

Edit the envelope just as you would a track envelope.

Showing or Hiding Envelopes

You can choose to show or hide any or all envelopes in a track or bus.

To Show or Hide All Envelopes

1. In the Track view toolbar, click the drop-down arrow that's next to the Envelope tool to display the Envelope Options menu.

2. Choose either *Show All Envelopes* or *Hide All Envelopes*.

To Show All of One Kind of Envelope

1. In the Track view toolbar, click the drop-down arrow that's next to the Envelope tool to display the Envelope Options menu.

2. Choose the kind of envelope that you want to show.

To Show or Hide Individual Envelopes

1. Right-click the Clips pane in the track that contains the envelope(s) that you want to show or hide.

   The Clips pane popup menu appears.

2. Choose *Envelopes-Show Track Envelopes*.

   A menu of all the envelopes in the track appears. A checkmark appears to the left of each envelope that is currently showing.

3. Click the name of one envelope that you want to show (if it's currently hidden), or hide (if it's currently showing).

   SONAR hides or displays the envelope.

4. Repeat steps 1 to 3 for each envelope that you want to show or hide.

You can also hide, but not show, individual envelopes by right-clicking an envelope and choosing *Hide Envelope* from the Envelope Editing menu.

Deleting Envelopes

To Delete a Single Envelope

1. Move the cursor over the envelope until a vertical, double-ended arrow appears under it, and right-click the envelope.

   The Envelope Editing menu appears.

2. Choose *Delete Envelope* from the menu.

SONAR deletes the envelope.

To Delete Several or All Envelopes

1. Select the data that contains the envelopes you want to delete—you can select parts of tracks, one or more whole tracks, or all tracks.

2. Use the *Edit-Cut* command to open the Cut dialog box.

3. Select Track/Bus Automation if it's listed.

4. Select Clip Automation if it's listed.

5. Click OK.

SONAR deletes any track and clip envelopes that are in the data you selected.

Copying and Pasting Envelopes

You can copy and paste envelopes or parts of envelopes between tracks and clips. You can not, however, copy and paste a clip envelope without also copying and pasting the audio or MIDI data that is in that clip. If you paste a clip envelope into a track without the clip that it came from, the clip envelope becomes a track envelope.

To Copy an Envelope

1. In the Track view or the Clips pane, select the track or clip that has the envelope you want to copy. If you want to copy all the automation data in the track, select the whole track. If you want to select only a clip, but want to select any track envelopes in that track, click the dropdown arrow next to the Select tool , and make sure that the *Select Track Envelopes With Selected Clips* option has a checkmark next to it.

2. Press Ctrl+C or use the *Edit-Copy* command.

   The Copy dialog box appears.

3. Choose Clip Automation and/or Track/Bus Automation.

   Note: If the Track/Bus Automation field is greyed-out, you must re-select a part of the clip that contains either a node or a solid line (shape). A dotted line by itself is not an envelope and can not be copied.

4. Choose any other kinds of data you want to copy—if you only want to copy the automation data, choose only Track/Bus Automation and/or Clip Automation.

5. Click OK.

SONAR copies the data you selected to the clipboard.

To Paste an Envelope

1. Select the track(s) and location (Now Time) you want to paste the data to.
2. Press Ctrl+V or use the *Edit-Paste* command.

   The Paste dialog box appears.
3. Choose a track and location to paste to, if you haven't already.
4. Click OK.

SONAR pastes the automation data and any other types of data you chose in the Copy dialog box into the track and location you selected.

Resetting Envelopes and Nodes to Current or Neutral Values

You can reset an envelope so that it becomes a horizontal line at the current value of the parameter it controls, which eliminates any curves or jumps from the envelope. You can reset a node so that it jumps to the neutral value of the parameter it controls. For example, the neutral value of the pan parameter is C, or 0%.

To Reset an Envelope to the Current Value

1. Move the Now time to where the envelope's value is to your liking.
2. Right-click the envelope to display the Envelope Editing menu.
3. Choose *Clear All* from the menu.

SONAR resets the envelope to the current value.

To Reset a Node to a Neutral Value

Do either of the following:

- Double-click the node.
- Move the cursor over the node until it a cross appears under it, right-click the node, and choose *Reset Node* from the popup menu.

The node jumps to the neutral value for the parameter it controls.

Envelope Mode and Offset Mode

There are two modes which control how your volume faders, pan faders, bus send faders, and bus send pan faders behave during playback. The two modes are **Envelope mode** and **Offset mode**.

Envelope mode—In envelope mode, volume and pan faders follow the project's automation and do not respond to changes you make in real-time.

Offset mode—In Offset mode, you "offset" the current automation in a track using a parameter's controls. For example, if a pan envelope is set to hard left (100% left) and you adjust the pan in offset mode to 100% right, then the pan parameter is now set to hard right. Setting the pan in offset mode to 50% right would set the pan to the center.

Note: Any position that you set a fader to in Offset mode remains in effect when you switch back to Envelope mode. For example, if you set a volume fader to -INF while in Offset mode, switch to Envelope mode and drag the fader to its maximum level, you will not hear anything.

To Turn On Offset Mode

There are several ways to turn on Offset mode in SONAR:

- In the Track view toolbar or Console view toolbar, click the Offset button.
- In the Automation toolbar, click the Offset button.
- Press the *o* key.

In Offset mode, all controls that can be offset appear with a plus sign. For example Vol+.

The following audio controls support both Envelope and Offset modes:

Control	Envelope Mode Range	Offset Mode Range
Volume	-Infinity to +6dB, default is 0dB	-Infinity to +6dB, default is 0dB
Pan	100% L to 100% R, default is C	100% L to 100% R, default is C
Bus Send Level	-Infinity to +6dB, default is 0 dB	-Infinity to +6dB, default is 0dB
Bus Send Pan	100% L to 100% R, default is C	100% L to 100% R, default is C
Bus Return Level	-Infinity to +6dB, default is 0dB	-Infinity to +6dB, default is 0dB
Bus Return Balance	100% L to 100% R, default is C	100% L to 100% R, default is C
Main Out Volume	-Infinity to +6dB, default is 0dB	-Infinity to +6dB, default is 0dB
Main Out Balance	100% L to 100% R, default is C	100% L to 100% R, default is C

The following MIDI controls support both Envelope and Offset modes:

Control	Envelope Mode Range	Offset Mode Range
Volume	0 to 127, default is 101	0 to 127, default is 101
Pan	100% L to 100% R, default is C	100% L to 100% R, default is C
Chorus	0 to 127, default is 0	-127 to 127, default is 100
Reverb	0 to 127, default is 0	-127 to 127, default is 100

To Open Non-SONAR Envelope Display on a Percentage Scale

You can globally configure the placement of 0 dB for your envelopes in the Clips pane. The default placement in the Clips pane of 0 dB is roughly 1/3 from the top of the clip. You can change the position of 0 dB in all envelopes to the middle of the clip.

There are several advantages when using the Envelope Display on a Percentage Scale option:

- It makes it easier to tell if there have been any changes.
- There is a finer resolution around 0 dB.

Note: In Envelope mode, newly created volume clips appear at the same dB value as the current Vol setting. For example, if the Vol setting is +3 dB, a newly created volume envelope appears above the middle of the clip.

To Display Envelopes on a Percentage Scale

1. Select *Options-Global* to open the Global Options dialog.
2. In the General tab, click the Display Envelopes on Percentage Scale checkbox.
3. Click OK.

Snapshots

A snapshot is a group of settings that SONAR's controls snap to when your project reaches a certain Now Time. You set all the controls to the values you want, and then create a snapshot of these settings at a particular Now Time. This approach is useful, for example, when your project contains a variety of distinct sections and you want to make a sudden change in one or more settings between the sections.

To Create a Snapshot

1. Move the Now Time to the location where you want to create the snapshot.

2. Make sure that the Automation toolbar is visible—use the *View-Toolbars* command and make sure that the Automation checkbox is checked.

3. Set all controls the way you want them to be at this particular location in the project.

4. Arm the controls whose positions you want to record by right-clicking each one and making sure the *Arm for Automation* command has a checkmark next to it in the automation popup menu.

5. Click the Snapshot button [icon] in the Automation toolbar.

   SONAR records the positions of all armed controls.

6. Play your project and listen to the results. You can undo the snapshot by using the *Undo* command, or by taking another snapshot at the same Now Time.

7. Disarm all controls by clicking the Disarm All Automation Controls button [icon] in the Automation toolbar, or by clicking the red Aut indicator in the Status bar.

You can play back your project with or without the automation data by clicking the Enable Automation Playback button [icon] in the Automation toolbar.

Automating Effects

SONAR allows you to automate compatible DirectX plug-ins, giving you real-time control over dozens of effects parameters.

Note: When using automatable effects, the CPU meter may fluctuate rapidly within a few percentage points. This is normal behavior.

Automating Individual Effects Parameters

You can automate the parameters of some of SONAR's effects by drawing envelopes, or recording fader movements, or creating snapshots.

To Record Fader or Knob Movements for an Individual Effect's Parameters

1. Patch an automatable effect into the track or bus where you want to use it, and close the effect's dialog box when it appears.

2. In the track or bus where you patched the effect, right-click the name of the effect and select **Arm Parameter** from the popup menu (if the effect is not automatable, that choice is greyed-out on the menu).

   The effect's envelope dialog box appears, listing all the parameters you can arm in the Param Armed list.

3. Check all the parameters you want to automate at this time (caution: it's difficult to move more than one control when you are recording) and click OK.

4. Double-click the effect's name to open its dialog box; make sure that the dialog box does not block SONAR's transport controls.

5. Start recording by clicking the Record Automation button that's in the Transport toolbar, and move the knobs or faders that control the relevant parameters.

6. When you finish moving the knobs and faders, click the Stop button in the Transport toolbar.

Play back the track and listen to the result. Then you can either re-record the automation or disarm the parameters. You can disarm all armed parameters at once by clicking the red Aut indicator that's in the Status bar at the bottom of the SONAR window, or by clicking the Disarm All Automation Controls button that's in the Automation toolbar.

To Draw Envelopes for an Individual Effect's Parameters

1. Patch an automatable effect into the track or bus where you want to use it, and close the effect's dialog box when it appears.

2. Right-click in the Clips pane in the track (or bus) where you patched the effect.

   The Clips pane or Bus pane popup menu appears.

3. If you opened the Clips pane popup menu, choose **Envelopes-Create Track Envelope-(name of the effect you patched)**. If you opened the Bus pane popup menu, choose **Create Bus Envelope-(name of the effect you patched)**.

   The effect's envelope dialog box appears, listing all the parameters you can automate in the Envelope Exists list.

4. Check all the parameters you want to create envelopes for; as you check each envelope choice, you can choose a color for the envelope by clicking the Choose Color button that's in the lower right corner of the dialog box.

   Note: You can change a plug-in envelope's color whenever you want by highlighting its name in the effect's envelope dialog box and clicking the Choose Color button.

5. Click OK.

All the envelopes that you checked appear in the track or bus you were working in. You can edit them just like any other envelopes.

Recording Groups of Faders and/or Knobs

You can group various faders, knobs, and other controls together so that when you record the movements of one fader or knob, all the controls in the group move.

To Record Groups of Faders and/or Knobs

1. Group the controls (faders, knobs, etc.) that you want to record by right-clicking each control and choosing ***Group-(letter name of the group)*** from the popup menu—make sure you add them to the same group.
2. Arm each control in the group by right-clicking each one and choosing ***Arm for Automation*** from the popup menu.
3. Click the Record Automation button and move one of the controls in the group.
4. When you're through recording your automation data, click the Stop button in the Transport toolbar.

Listen to your project and either re-record the automation, or disarm each armed control by right-clicking each one and choosing ***Arm for Automation*** from the popup menu, or by clicking the Disarm All Automation Controls button in the Automation toolbar.

Recording Automation Data from an External Controller

You can record automation data from an external controller or a MIDI keyboard.

To Record Automation Data from an External Controller

1. In either the Track view or Console view, right-click the control or knob that you want to control externally, and choose **Remote Control** from the popup menu.

    The Remote Control dialog box appears.

2. If your controller sends standard MIDI messages, RPN's, or NRPN's, choose a controller (such as Wheel) with which to control your knob or control. Also choose the MIDI channel your controller will be sending the automation data on (it doesn't have to be the same channel that the knob or control's track plays back on), and click OK.

3. If your controller works by sending SysX information instead, choose options in the SysX fields, and click OK.

4. In either the Track or Console view, arm the knob or control for automation that you just configured for remote control.

5. Click the Record Automation button and move the slider or wheel that you selected on your external controller.

6. When you finish recording the automation, click the Stop button in the Transport toolbar.

Listen to your project and either re-record the automation, or disarm each armed control by clicking the Disarm All Automation Controls button in the Automation toolbar. You can disable remote control by right-clicking the relevant knob or fader and choosing **Disable Remote Control** from the popup menu.

Reassigning Envelopes

You can reassign an envelope to control a different parameter from the one it originally controlled. For example, you can reassign a volume envelope to control pan.

To Reassign an Envelope

1. Move the cursor over the envelope until the cursor changes to a double-ended arrow, and right-click the envelope.

    The Envelope Editing menu appears.

2. Choose **Assign Envelope-(*name of the parameter you want the envelope to control*)**.

The envelope changes color to reflect its new parameter assignment.

The Envelope Editing and Node Editing Menus

The Envelope Editing menu appears when you move the cursor over an envelope until a **double-ended arrow** appears under it, and right-click the envelope. The Node Editing menu is almost identical, and appears when you move the cursor over a node until a **cross** appears under it and right-click. The menus contain the following options:

Menu Option...	What it Does...
Jump (Envelope Editing menu only)	This choice causes the envelope to make a ninety degree jump between two nodes. SONAR displays jumps with a dotted line, meaning that there is automation data at the nodes where the dotted line begins and ends, but not where the dotted line itself is.
Linear (Envelope Editing menu only)	This choice draws a straight line between two nodes.
Fast Curve (Envelope Editing menu only)	This choice draws a curve between the two nodes that changes value rapidly at first, but more slowly toward the end of the curve.
Slow Curve (Envelope Editing menu only)	This choice draws a curve between two nodes that changes value slowly at first, but more rapidly toward the end of the curve
Add Node (Envelope Editing menu only)	This choice adds a node, which is a point on the line that you can drag, to the place on the envelope where you right-clicked.
Hide Envelope	This choice hides the envelope that you right-clicked. You can re-display the envelope by right-clicking in the same track and choosing **Envelopes-Show Track Envelopes-(name of the envelope you want to show)** from the Clips pane popup menu.
Assign Envelope-(name of the parameter you want to control)	This choice reassigns the envelope to control the parameter that you choose.
Delete Envelope	This choice deletes the envelope.
Clear All	This choice deletes everything from the envelope except the first node.

Reset Node (Node Editing menu only)	This choice resets the node to the parameter's neutral value.
Delete Node (Node Editing menu only)	This choice deletes the node.
Properties (Node Editing menu only)	This choice opens the Edit Node dialog box, which allows you to edit the node's value and location.

Automated Muting

The Mute buttons in the Track view and Console view work in two ways:

- You can record or draw automation for each Mute button, and the automation data controls the buttons.

- You can click a Mute button while playback is in progress and manually override any automation data for that button.

A track's Mute button can display the muted or unmuted status of either the automation envelope or of manual muting. The **Track-Show Automated Mute** command causes the Mute button on a selected track to show whether the track's mute envelope (if any) is in the muted or unmuted position (the *automated mute status*). When the command is disabled, the track's Mute button shows whether you have depressed the Mute button manually or not (the *manual mute status*). When the command is enabled, the Mute button displays an envelope icon through the M: . Besides the **Track-Show Automated Mute** command, you can also right-click a Mute button and choose **Switch to Automated Mute** from the popup menu.

To Draw a Mute Envelope

1. In the Clips pane, right-click in the track you want to mute, and choose **Envelopes-Create Track Envelope-Automated Mute** from the Clips pane popup menu.

   An envelope appears at the bottom of the track.

2. Add nodes to the envelope and edit it so that the envelope is more than 50% of its maximum height wherever you want the track muted.

To Record a Mute Button's Movement

1. Right-click the Mute button you want to automate and choose **Arm for Automation** from the popup menu.

2. Click the Automation Record button, click the Mute button on and off where appropriate, and stop recording.

SONAR draws an automated mute envelope in the track you recorded on.

Layouts, Templates and Key Bindings

A **layout** is the current arrangement of all the views that pertain to a particular project. The layout of each project is stored automatically as part of every project file. In addition, you can save the current layout or load any saved layout and apply it to the current project. You might want to create a layout so you can easily arrange the views in a convenient size and position on the screen.

A **template** is a special file that is used as a pattern to create other, similar files. You might create a template file that defines a particular musical ensemble (say, a string quartet) or a particular studio configuration (MIDI instruments, audio outputs, and so on). Templates make it fast and easy to create and configure new projects.

Note that toolbars are not part of a file layout or template. The toolbar arrangement you choose is stored automatically from session to session.

A **key binding** lets you associate SONAR commands with keys on your MIDI or computer keyboard. This makes it easy for you to access specific features more quickly and efficiently. You can even assign saved layouts to key bindings for quick access.

In This Chapter

Layouts 514
Templates 517
Key Bindings 520

Layouts

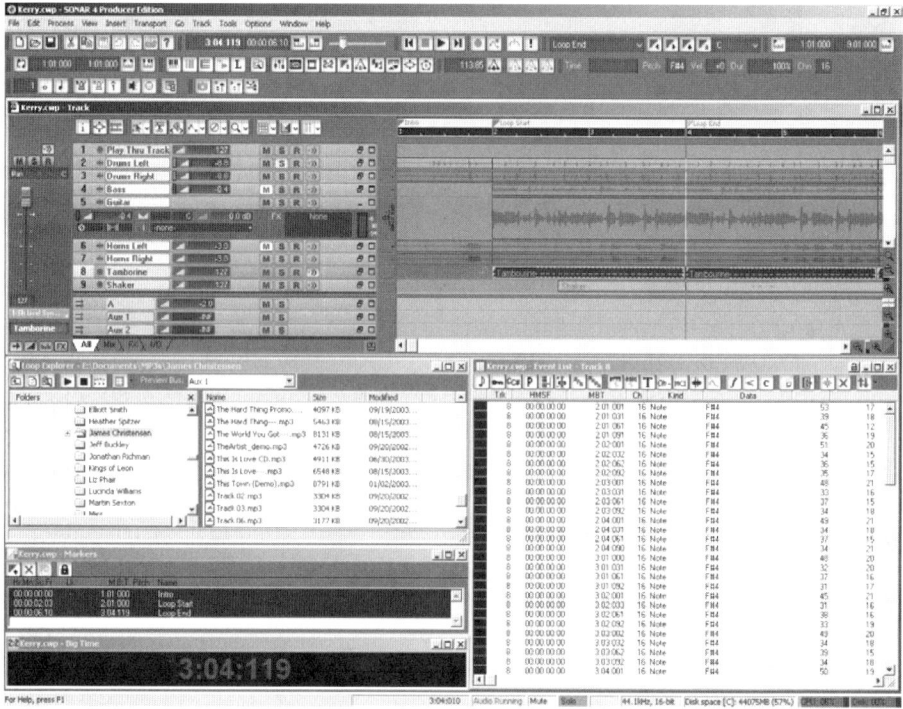

The layout of the views that are displayed for a project is stored automatically in the project file when you save the project. By default, the layout of all the views is restored when the file is opened. You can automatically arrange all open views so that they are all visible by using the **Window-Tile in Rows** command.

In addition, you can save the current layout in a separate list—the global layout list. Once you have saved the layout in this list, you can apply it to any open project. The global layout list can contain as many layouts as you want. Layouts in the list can be updated, renamed, and deleted.

Layouts are stored in a folder on your hard disk. To change the default folder for layouts, choose **Options-Global**, click the Folders tab, and type the name of a different folder in the Window Layouts field (or click the browse button that's at the right end of the Window Layouts field, and select a new folder).

There are two options in Windows Layouts dialog (select *View-Layouts* to open) that control how layouts are used, as described in the following table:

Option...	Meaning...
Close Old Windows Before Loading New Ones	If checked, SONAR™ will close all the views of the current project before applying the layout. If you leave this option unchecked, existing views remain open and additional views are created according to the settings in the layout.
When Opening a File, Load Its Layout	If checked, the views of a project are automatically arranged according to the stored layout when the project file is opened. If this option is not checked, only the Track view (and File Info view, if applicable) are displayed when the project file is opened.

To Create or Save a Layout

1. Arrange the views for the current project the way you want.
2. Choose *View-Layouts* to display the Window Layouts dialog box.
3. Click Add to display the New Global Layout dialog box.
4. Enter a name for the layout, and click OK. The layout is added to the list.
5. Click Close to exit the Window Layouts dialog box.

To Update a Layout

1. Arrange the views for the current project the way you want.
2. Choose *View-Layouts* to display the Window Layouts dialog box.
3. Choose the layout you want to update from the list.
4. Click Add to display the New Global Layout dialog box.
5. Leave the layout name unchanged, and click OK.
6. Click OK to confirm that you want to update the layout.
7. Click Close to exit the Window Layouts dialog box.

To Load a Layout

1. Choose *View-Layouts* to display the Window Layouts dialog box.
2. Choose the layout you want from the list.
3. Click Load.

Views of the current project are arranged according to the layout settings.

To Delete a Layout
1. Choose *View-Layouts* to display the Window Layouts dialog box.
2. Choose the layout you want to delete from the list.
3. Click Delete.
4. Click OK to confirm that you want to delete the layout. The layout is removed from the list.
5. Click Close to exit the Window Layouts dialog box.

To Rename a Layout
1. Choose *View-Layouts* to display the Window Layouts dialog box.
2. Choose the layout you want to rename from the list.
3. Click Rename to display the Rename Existing Layout dialog box.
4. Enter a new name for the layout, and click OK. The layout is renamed in the list.
5. Click Close to exit the Window Layouts dialog box.

To Set Layout Options
1. Choose *View-Layouts* to display the Window Layouts dialog box.
2. Check the options you want.
3. Click Close.

To Load a Layout with a Keyboard Command
1. Use the *Options-Key Bindings* command to open the Key Bindings dialog box.
2. In the Type of Keys field, click either Computer or MIDI. If you click MIDI, also make sure the Enabled checkbox is checked.
3. If you selected MIDI in the Type of Keys field, under MIDI Shift Options select either Key or Controller, and select a value for whichever one you pick.
4. Under Bindings, scroll through the Key field and select the key that you want to trigger the layout command with.
5. In the Function field, scroll down towards the end of the list, and under Global Layouts, click the name of the layout you want to assign to the key you selected.
6. When both the Key and the Function are highlighted in their respective fields, click the Bind button to bind them together.
7. Click OK.

Now you can load the layout you selected by pressing the MIDI keys or computer keys that you bound to that particular layout. You can bind as many layouts as you have available key combinations.

Floating Views and Dual Monitor Support

SONAR supports dual monitors and allows you to float most of your views to a second monitor giving you more options when working and increasing the number of views that you can have open at one time.

Important: Dual monitor support requires that you have a video card that supports dual monitors. Follow your hardware manufacturers instructions for using dual monitors.

You can float views in SONAR without having a second monitor. Floating a view allows you to move it out of SONAR, over the SONAR toolbars and menus for example, giving you added flexibility when using SONAR with other applications. All views except the Track view can be floated.

To Float a View
1. Open the view you want to float.
2. Click the view's icon located in the upper left corner of the view.

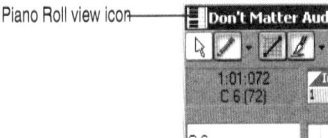

3. In the menu that appears, click *Enable Floating*.
4. Move the view wherever you want.

Templates

Template files make it easy to create new projects with certain predefined settings. To create a template file, create a new project file and arrange the project settings the way you want, then save the project as a template file. Template files have a file extension of .CWT. When you create a new project, you can use the template as the basis for the new project. SONAR looks for template files in a particular folder on your hard disk. By default, this folder is the program folder. To change the template directory, choose *Options-Global* and click the Folders tab.

Every time you start SONAR, a new, empty project is displayed. If you want, you can determine the settings for this default project by creating and saving a special template file, called NORMAL.CWT. If you create or update the NORMAL.CWT file, SONAR will display this template automatically when the program is started.

As a rule, any parameter that is saved in a project file is also saved in a template file. Following are some useful parameters that are saved in template files:

- Track configuration and track parameters
- Timebase
- Sysx banks
- File information and comments
- Tempo settings
- Meter and key settings
- Clock and synchronization information
- MIDI data
- MIDI In/Out/Thru settings
- MIDI metronome settings
- Selection start and end times
- Record mode and punch-in times
- Drum maps
- Audio data
- Automation

The following parameters are saved globally and are not stored in template or project files:

- Initialization file parameters
- Big Time font settings
- MIDI device settings
- Instrument definitions
- Autosave options
- Key bindings
- Color settings

To Create a Template
1. Create a new file using the *File-New* command.
2. Add tracks.
3. Set one or more parameters to be the way you want.
4. Choose *File-Save As* to display the Save As dialog box.
5. Choose Template from the Save as Type list.
6. Enter a template file name and click Save.

SONAR saves the template file.

To Create a New Project from a Template
1. Choose *File-New* to display the New Project File dialog box. The list contains the names of all existing templates.
2. Choose a template from the list.
3. Click OK.

SONAR creates the new project and displays it in the Track view.

Template Example: Three MIDI Instruments

Suppose that your system has only a single MIDI output but you own three different synthesizers:

- One synthesizer set to receive on channels 1 through 8
- A general MIDI synthesizer module set to receive data on all 16 channels
- A drum machine set to receive on MIDI channel 10

Here's how you can use a template to make it easy to create new projects that are already configured for the instruments you own.

To Create the Example Template File
1. Choose *File-New* to create a new project file.
2. Insert 16 MIDI tracks.
3. In the Ch dropdown menu of track 10, enter 10. The drum machine responds to channel 10. For consistency, the drums can be placed on track 10.
4. The second synthesizer responds to channels 1 through 8. These can be placed on tracks 1 through 8. For each track, enter the corresponding channel number using the Ch dropdown menu for each track. You should now have tracks 1 through 8 set to channels 1 through 8.
5. The third synthesizer can respond to 16 MIDI channels, but the only channels left are 9 and 11 through 16. Enter these numbers in the corresponding tracks. You will need to mute the unused channels on the third synthesizer (1 through 8 and 10) so they won't play. These are assigned to the drum machine and the second synthesizer.

6. Name each track and set any track parameters, such as starting patch, volumes, panning, reverb, chorus, and transposition.

7. If you like, configure other parameters needed in your projects, such as auto-send Sysx banks, tempo settings, window positions, and comments.

8. Choose *File-Save*, and save the file as a template named MY3SYNTHS.

Now, each time you want to start working on a new project, you can simply load your template and start recording.

Key Bindings

Key bindings let you associate SONAR commands with keys on both your MIDI keyboard and your computer keyboard. This makes it easy for you to access specific features more quickly and efficiently.

In addition, SONAR supports:

- Importing key bindings from other popular sequencer programs (see "Importing Key Bindings" on page 523)

- Exporting key bindings from SONAR (see "Exporting Key Bindings" on page 523)

- Use of any single key as a key binding (number keys on the number pad are separate keys from the other number keys)

- Changing the key bindings for commands that were previously hardwired, including hotkey commands in the various views

Any one or two of the Ctrl, Alt, and Shift keys can be used in combination with other keys. Preset key combinations appear in bold, with the command that they're currently assigned to listed at the bottom of the Key Bindings dialog.

Rather than tie up all the notes on your MIDI keyboard with key bindings, SONAR lets you define a key binding shift key on your MIDI keyboard that indicates when you want to use a key binding. For example, you could designate the lowest note on your MIDI keyboard as the key binding shift key, and then assign different notes to specific commands (for example, C4 to *Process-Quantize*, C5 to *Process-Groove Quantize*, and so on). If you press the C4 key by itself, the note plays normally. If you press the C4 key in combination with the lowest key on your keyboard (the key binding shift key), then it's just as if you had chosen the *Process-Quantize* command from the menu.

You can choose one of two options to define the key binding shift key:

- MIDI key (typically, the very lowest or highest key on your MIDI keyboard)
- Controller event (typically, one of the pedals)

If you use a MIDI key as the key binding shift key, then you lose the ability to play that note by itself. When you play the note, SONAR assumes you are about to choose one of the key bindings you have created and ignores the note. If this is ever a problem, you can disable MIDI key bindings without canceling the key assignments and then re-enable the MIDI key bindings later on.

You can use a key binding to execute a command only when that command is possible. For example, the *File-Save* command is disabled when no projects are open. If you have assigned the Ctrl+F2 key combination to the *File-Save* command, it won't do anything when no projects are open.

You can use MIDI key bindings and computer keyboard key bindings at the same time.

You use the *Options-Key Bindings* command to set up and manage your key bindings. Here's how:

To Create a Key Binding Using the Computer Keyboard

1. Choose *Options-Key Bindings* to display the Key Bindings dialog.
2. Check Computer in the Type of Keys list.
3. To quickly scroll to the key or key combination you want, click the Locate Key button, and then press the key or keys you want to use.
4. Highlight the key combination you want to use in the Key list. Keys on the number pad appear as Num "n." If a key or combination is already bound to a command by default, the name of the key appears in bold text, and the command it is bound to appears at the bottom of the dialog under Current Key Assignment. Binding a key or combination to a command and clicking OK overwrites any default binding for that key or combination.
5. In the Bind Context menu, select the context in which you want to use the key binding.
6. Highlight the command you want to assign from the Function list.
7. Click Bind to bind the key combination to the command.

    SONAR places an asterisk next to the key(s) that you chose, and draws a line from the highlighted key(s) to the command that the key(s) will trigger. Any keys that are assigned to commands have asterisks next to them. Any commands that have keys assigned to them list the keys in the Computer column and/or the MIDI column.
8. Repeat steps 3 through 7 for all the keys you want to bind.

9. If you want to save these key bindings for other sessions, make sure that the Save Changes for Next Session checkbox is checked.

10. Click OK when you are done.

SONAR assigns the key(s) you chose.

To Create a Key Binding Using a MIDI Keyboard

1. Choose *Options-Key Bindings* to display the Key Bindings dialog.

2. Check MIDI in the Type of Keys list.

3. Check the Enable box to make sure MIDI key bindings are enabled.

4. If you haven't already done so, create a key binding shift key by doing one of the following:

    - Check Key under MIDI Shift Options, and enter the name of the key you want to use.

    - Check Controller under MIDI Shift Options, and choose the controller you want from the list.

5. Highlight the key you want to bind from the Key list (if you click inside the Key window to put the focus on it, you can then play a note on your MIDI keyboard, and the note automatically becomes highlighted in the Key window).

6. Select the command you want to bind from the Function list.

7. Click the Bind button.

    SONAR places an asterisk next to the Key that you chose, and draws a line from the highlighted key to the command that it's bound to. Any keys that are assigned to commands have asterisks next to them. Any commands that have keys assigned to them list the keys in the Computer column and/or the MIDI column.

8. Repeat steps 5 through 7 for all the keys you want to bind.

9. If you want to save these key bindings for other sessions, make sure that the Save Changes for Next Session checkbox is checked.

10. Click OK when you are done.

SONAR assigns the key(s) you chose.

To **disable** MIDI key bindings, uncheck the Enable box in the Key Bindings dialog.

Importing Key Bindings

SONAR can use key bindings from other sequencer applications. Clicking the Import button in the Key Bindings dialog allows you to choose a new set of key bindings. After you import new key bindings, you can edit and save them the way you do with the default key bindings.

To Import Key Bindings

1. Choose *Options-Key Bindings* to display the Key Bindings dialog.
2. Click the Import button to open the Import Key Bindings dialog.
3. Navigate to the SONAR program folder (you don't have to store them there).
4. Choose a key bindings file from the choices in the program folder. Key bindings files use the file extension .KBN.
5. Click Open.

SONAR loads the key bindings you chose.

Exporting Key Bindings

Clicking the Export button in the Key Bindings dialog allows you to export the current set of key bindings, so that they are available when you want to switch key bindings.

To Export Key Bindings

1. Choose *Options-Key Bindings* to display the Key Bindings dialog.
2. Click the Export button to open the Export Key Bindings dialog.
3. Navigate to the folder where you want to save the key bindings.
4. Type a name for the key bindings.
5. Click Save.

SONAR saves the key bindings, and adds the file extension .KBN to the filename.

15 Working with Notation and Lyrics

This chapter describes three SONAR™ views that are used to edit the music notation and lyrics of your project.

- SONAR's Staff view lets you work with your composition in a standard musical staff, guitar tablature and a virtual guitar fretboard. You can add, move, and delete notes with your mouse or with your computer keyboard. You can add chord names, guitar chord grids, expression marks, hairpin symbols, pedal marks, and lyrics. And you can print professional-quality notation of a complete arrangement or individual parts, with up to 24 staves per page.
- The Meter/Key view lets you view, insert, and edit meter and key changes at any measure boundary in the project.
- The Lyrics view lets you edit a track's lyrics, and can be used to cue you with the lyrics during playback or recording.

In This Chapter

The Staff View	526
Basic Musical Editing	531
Chords and Marks	543
Tablature	550
Printing	559
The Meter/Key View	560
Working with Lyrics	565

The Staff View

The Staff view is composed of a Staff pane and a Fretboard.

When you first open the Staff view, you may see only the Staff and not the Fretboard. Resize the Staff view by dragging its edges until you can see everything easily. When you save your file, whatever size the Staff view is will be the way it appears the next time you open the file.

The Staff pane displays MIDI note events as musical notation. For some musicians, this may be the most familiar and comfortable view in which to work. The Staff pane provides many features that make it easy for you to compose, edit, and print music.

For guitar players who are new to musical notation, the Fretboard represents the notes in the Staff pane as they would appear on a six-string guitar neck in standard tuning. The number of strings and the tuning are configurable. All notes that appear in the Staff pane at the Now time are shown in the Fretboard. If you enter notes in the Staff at the Now time, they appear on the Fretboard. Likewise, you can enter notes into the Staff at the Now time by clicking the guitar strings on the fretboard. Notes and chords shown in the Fretboard can be easily edited by dragging them up and down the guitar strings.

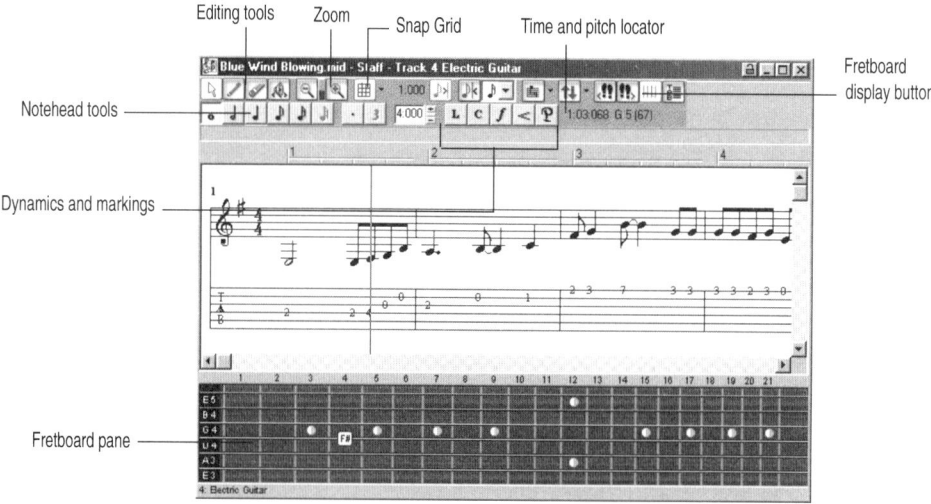

Opening the Staff View

There are three ways to open the Staff view:

- In the Track view, select the MIDI tracks you want to see, then click the Staff View button 🗐.
- In the Track view, select the MIDI tracks you want to see, then choose **View-Staff**.
- Right-click on a track in the Clips pane and choose **Views-Staff** from the menu.

You can always change the tracks that are displayed: click the Pick Tracks button and select the tracks you want. You can display one or more tracks.

The Staff view lets you edit, delete, copy, and move notes during playback or recording, in real time. This means you can loop over a portion of your project and hear any change you make on the next loop. You can freeze the Staff view from automatic scrolling during playback by pressing the Scroll Lock key.

Like many other views, the Staff view includes zoom tools that let you change the vertical and horizontal scale of the view. The Staff view also has a Snap to Grid button. For more information on this feature, see "Defining and Using the Snap Grid" on page 222.

Staff Pane Layout

The Staff pane can display up to 24 staves of standard and percussion notation. When you open the Staff pane, SONAR automatically picks a clef for each track—bass or treble—by looking at the range of pitches in the track. If a track has notes that fall into both clefs, or no notes at all, SONAR automatically splits the track into two staves, treble and bass. You can change the assignment of clefs with the Staff View Layout dialog box.

When you split a track into treble and bass staves, you must select a split point. Notes at or above the split are placed into a treble staff, notes below the split are placed into a bass staff.

A wide variety of editing options for notes, layout, and MIDI effects are available from the Staff Pane Right-Click menu.

Percussion settings are discussed in the section "Setting Up a Percussion Track" on page 556.

The Staff Pane Right-Click Menu

The Staff pane Right-Click menu offers the following editing options:

Menu command	Result
MIDI Effects	Opens the MIDI Effects submenu. See "MIDI Effects (MIDI Plug-ins)" on page 325 for more information.
Layout	Opens the Staff View Layout dialog box.
Regenerate Tablature	Opens the Regenerate Tablature dialog box. "Regenerate TAB" on page 553 for more information.
Export to ASCII TAB	Saves the track in TAB format with the extension .TXT.
Quantize	Opens the Quantize dialog box. See "Quantizing" on page 327 for more information.
Groove Quantize	Opens the Groove Quantize dialog box. See "Quantizing" on page 327 for more information.
Transpose	Opens the Transpose dialog box. See "Transposing" on page 284 for more information.
Slide	Opens the Slide dialog box.
Interpolate	Opens the Event Filter Search dialog box. See "Process-Interpolate" on page 309 for more information.
Length	Opens the Length dialog box. See "Stretching and Shrinking Events" on page 288 for more information.
Scale Velocity	Opens the Scale Velocity dialog box. See "Adding Crescendos and Decrescendos" on page 290 for more information.
Retrograde	Reverses the order of selected events and clips.
Deglitch	Opens the Deglitch dialog box. See "Deglitch Dialog" on page 537 for more information.
Fit to Time	Opens the Fit to time dialog box. See "Stretching and Shrinking Events" on page 288 for more information.
Fit Improvisation	See "Fit Improvisation" on page 304.

To Change the Staff Pane Layout

1. Click the Staff View Layout button ![icon] to open the Staff View Layout dialog box.
2. Select a track from the list (if the track you want to edit is not in the list, click the Pick Tracks button in the Staff view toolbar and select it). The Clef option shows the track's clef.
3. Select a new clef from the list.
4. If you select Treble/Bass, select a Split point.
5. If you select one of the Percussion options, click Percussion Settings to set up the appearance of percussion notes.
6. Repeat steps 2-5 for other tracks.
7. Click Close when you are done.

SONAR displays tracks using the new staff settings.

Tip:
If a piano part's left-hand and right-hand parts overlap, a split point will not correctly separate the two parts into treble and bass staves. You may prefer to put the two parts into two separate tracks.

The Fretboard

The Fretboard shows you the notes located at the Now time in the Staff pane, laid out on a virtual guitar fretboard. For example, if the Staff pane shows you this:

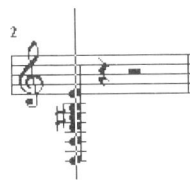

The Fretboard pane shows you this:

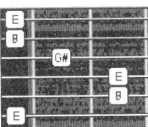

The Fretboard stays in sync with the Now Time during playback and recording, and stays in sync with the scrub time during scrubbing. The color of each note on the Fretboard is the same as the color of the corresponding clip in the Track view. (See "Arranging Clips" on page 209 for information about setting clip properties.)

To turn the display of the Fretboard on or off, click ▥.

Fretboard Popup Menu

When you right-click the Fretboard in the Staff view, the Fretboard popup menu appears, giving you choices for note editing, Staff view layout, and Fretboard appearance.

Menu command	Result
Select	Changes your cursor to the Select tool.
Draw	Changes your cursor to the Draw tool.
Erase	Changes your cursor to the Erase tool.
Scrub	Changes your cursor to the Scrub tool.
Layout	Opens the Staff View Layout dialog box.
Select Fretboard Track	Controls which of the displayed tracks receive the notes you enter on the Fretboard.
Export to ASCII TAB	Saves the track in ASCII TAB format with the extension .TXT.
Mirror Fretboard	Inverts Fretboard so highest-sounding string appears at the bottom.
Rosewood Hi	Fretboard appears in rosewood with high screen resolution.
Rosewood Lo	Fretboard appears in rosewood with low screen resolution.
Ebony Hi	Fretboard appears in ebony with high screen resolution.
Ebony Lo	Fretboard appears in ebony with low screen resolution.
Maple Hi	Fretboard appears in maple with high screen resolution.
Maple Lo	Fretboard appears in maple with low screen resolution.

Basic Musical Editing

The Staff view's tools let you edit a project by manipulating the elements of standard music notation. Using these tools, you can create and edit notes, pedal marks, expression marks, hairpins, and lyrics.

Inserting Notes on the Staff

You can add notes to your composition with simple point-and-click techniques. To help with your composing, SONAR gives you audio feedback as you place each note.

You can insert notes anywhere in the Staff pane, but inserting them at the Now time gives you control over the exact time you want to insert to. The Shift-Right/Left Arrow command moves the Now Time forward or backward by the amount of the note duration you choose. Six buttons let you select a note duration ranging from a whole note to a 32nd note. Buttons to the right of the notehead buttons let you select dotted note or triplet modifiers. The Ctrl+Right Arrow/Ctrl+Left Arrow commands pages you through the track, sounding each note as the cursor passes over it. You can also page through the track by clicking the Play-Next button or the Play-Previous button that are in the Staff view toolbar.

Note: You cannot insert notes whose durations are less than the value in the Display Resolution field, which is located in the top level of the Staff view toolbar.

You may want to pick a different snap-to grid value for a particular note. For example, if you want to insert a half note in the last quarter note position in a measure (in order to get two tied quarter notes), you must set the snap resolution to a quarter note. SONAR will automatically convert the half note to two tied quarter notes. The same method can be used to insert a syncopated note, such as a quarter note at an eighth note position.

You may also wish to disable the Fill Durations and Trim Durations options before you enter notes on the staff. This will allow you to see the true durations of all the notes you enter. These options are discussed in "Changing the Way Notes Are Displayed" on page 539.

To Insert a Note on the Staff

1. Disable the Fill Durations and Trim Durations buttons in the Staff view toolbar, if desired (this is usually the best way when you're entering notes).

2. Click the Display Resolution button in the Staff view toolbar and choose a resolution that's as small or slightly smaller than the smallest note you plan to enter.

3. Click the Draw tool.

4. In the second row of the Staff view toolbar, select a note duration, and a modifier (dot or triplet) if desired. You cannot insert a note that's shorter in length than the note in the Display Resolution field.

5. Move the Now time to the location where you want the new note by pressing Shift-Right arrow or Shift-Left arrow. Notice the vertical line that marks the Now time in the Staff pane. The line moves by the duration of the note you selected to enter.

6. Click the cursor on the vertical line at the pitch that you want.

7. To add a sharp or flat, right-click the note to open the Note Properties dialog box—in the Pitch field, use the + or - buttons to raise or lower the pitch, and click OK. You can type enharmonic spellings into the Pitch field, such as C#5, E"4. and Fx6. The double quotation mark produces a double flat, and the x produces a double sharp.

SONAR places the new note in the staff. If desired, drag the note horizontally or vertically to a new time or pitch.

Inserting Notes with the Fretboard

You can also enter notes onto the staff from the fretboard using the mouse. You always enter notes into the staff at the Now time.

To Insert Notes on the Fretboard with the Mouse

1. Click in the Time Ruler to set the Now time.

2. Click to select the Draw tool.

3. Select a note duration, and a modifier (dot or triplet) if desired.

4. Click on the guitar strings in the fretboard to enter notes. You can enter up to six simultaneous notes (one per string).

5. Advance the Now Time by the current note duration using the right arrow key while holding down the shift key. This allows you to quickly enter a series of notes.

Selecting Notes

Use the Selection tool to make selections. Selection methods in the Staff view are similar to those in other views. Here is a summary:

To do this...	Do this...
Select a note or other symbol	Click it
Select several symbols at once	Click and drag a rectangle around them
Add symbols to the selection	Press Shift and either click on the symbols or drag a rectangle around the events
Add or remove symbols from the selection	Press Ctrl and either click on the symbols or drag a rectangle around the events
Select symbols in a time range	Click and drag in the Time Ruler
Select symbols between two markers	Click between the markers
Remove all selections	Click in an empty area

Note:

Tied notes must be selected together, since the series is really just a single MIDI note. To select tied notes, you must click or drag a rectangle around the first note of the series.

Moving, Copying, and Deleting Notes on the Staff

Selections can be cut, copied, pasted, and deleted with *Edit* menu commands. The techniques are similar to those used in other views. Selections can also be dragged and dropped to copy or move them. To keep track of your current position while dragging, you can keep an eye on the time and pitch locator in the upper-right corner of the Staff view.

Notes can be dragged horizontally, to a new time, or vertically, to a new pitch or staff. When you drag a note up or down to a new pitch, the note normally snaps to the notes in the current key signature (diatonic scale). This makes it easy to drag notes quickly among pitches that are in the current key.

If you need to transpose more than a few notes, use the *Process-Transpose* command. For more information, see "Transposing" on page 284.

To Move a Single Note in the Staff View

1. Click the Select tool or the Draw tool.
2. Click the note to be moved.
3. Drag the note to a new time, pitch, or staff.

SONAR moves the note to the new location.

To Move Several Notes in the Staff View

1. Click the Select tool.
2. Select the notes to be moved.
3. Click one of the selected notes.
4. Drag the notes to a new time, pitch, or staff.

SONAR moves the notes to the new location.

To Copy One or More Notes in the Staff View

1. Click the Select tool.
2. Select the notes to be copied.
3. Press and hold the Ctrl key.
4. Drag the notes to a new time, pitch, or staff.

SONAR inserts copies of the notes at the new location.

To Erase Notes with the Eraser

1. Click the Erase tool.
2. Click any notehead to erase the note.
3. To erase several notes, click and drag the eraser.

Any notes whose notehead is touched by the eraser will be deleted.

Moving Notes from within the Fretboard

You can drag notes displayed in the fretboard horizontally along each string to change their pitch. They always change in the chromatic scale. You can not drag notes from one string to another.

To Change the Pitch of a Single Note in the Fretboard

1. Click in the Time Ruler to set the Now time to the time of the note you want to change.

2. Click the Select tool or the Draw tool.

3. Drag the note along the string to a new fret.

SONAR moves the note to the new pitch.

To Change the Pitch of a Chord in the Fretboard

1. Click in the Time Ruler to set the Now time to the time of the chord you want to change.

2. Click the Select tool.

3. While pressing Shift, click each of the notes you would like to change.

4. While continuing to press Shift, drag the notes along the strings.

SONAR moves the notes you selected to the new pitches.

Tip:

You can also move the Now time pointer to the exact note by using the Step Play buttons.

Auditioning

Sometimes it is useful to listen to your music slowly, note-by-note, rather than at full speed. For example, you may need to locate a bad note, or you may be trying to learn the correct fingering for a difficult passage.

The Staff view has two features that let you audition your composition at reduced speed: Scrub and Step Play. The Scrub tool lets you drag a vertical bar over the staff, playing the notes as it goes. You can scrub backward or forward at any speed. Step Play lets you step through the project note by note, in either direction.

To Audition with the Scrub Tool

1. Click the Scrub tool.

2. Drag the mouse horizontally through the Staff pane to play the notes.

SONAR plays any notes the scrub line passes over.

To Play Notes with Step Play

1. Set the Now time by clicking in the Time Ruler.
2. Step through the music as follows:

To do this...	Do this...
Step forward	Click 👣, or press Ctrl+right arrow
Step backward	Click 👣, or press Ctrl+left arrow

Changing Note Properties

The Staff view lets you edit all the MIDI parameters for a note, including those not normally portrayed by standard musical notation. Note properties are as follows:

Property...	Meaning...
Time	The starting time of the note
Pitch	The note's pitch
Velocity	The note's velocity (0 to 127)
Duration	The note's duration, in ticks or in beats and ticks
Channel	The MIDI channel on which the note is played
Fret	The fret at which the note is played on the neck
String	The string on which the note is played

To Edit a Note's Properties
1. Right-click the note to open the Note Properties dialog box.

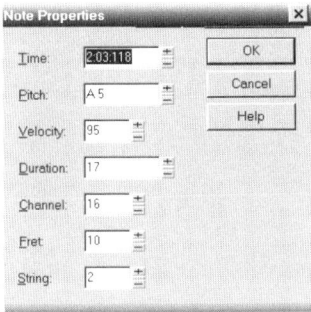

2. Edit the note's properties, as described in the table.
3. Click OK.

SONAR changes the note's parameters and redraws the note if necessary.

Deglitch Dialog
When recording MIDI guitar, even the best players occasionally play unintended notes. The Deglitch feature allows you to filter out the softest, shortest, and highest notes in the file.

There are three filters in the Deglitch dialog:

Pitch
With the Pitch filter you can set the maximum pitch allowed in the track. If a MIDI event has a higher pitch than the maximum you set, it is removed.

Velocity
With the Velocity filter you can set a minimum velocity allowed in the track. If a MIDI event has a lower velocity than the one you set, it is removed.

Duration
With the Duration filter you can set a minimum note duration for the track in either ticks or milliseconds. If a MIDI event has a shorter duration than the one you set, it is removed.

To Use the Deglitch Filter
1. Select a track or a section of track.
2. Select *Process-Deglitch* from the menu.

   The Deglitch dialog box appears.
3. Check each of the filters you want to use.
4. Enter the parameters (maximum or minimum values) you want for each of the filters you are using.
5. Click OK.

If you are not happy with the result, select Edit/Undo from the menu to restore the original MIDI track.

Working with Triplets
The Staff view places certain limitations on the use of triplets. The limitations are:

- Triplets must occur in full sets of three.
- All three steps in a triplet must be notes (no rests) of the same basic duration.
- There can be no ties in or out of, or within the triplet.

In most cases, the Staff view can recognize triplets in MIDI data. However, the slight timing inaccuracies inherent in live performances can complicate the detection of triplets. If working from performance data, you may find it useful to quantize the notes closer to exact triplet positions using the *Process-Quantize* command. See "Quantizing" on page 327 for details.

To Enter a Triplet
1. Turn on the Snap to Time option.
2. Click the Draw tool ✏.
3. Click the appropriate notehead button.
4. Select the Triplet option ③.
5. Enter the first note at the desired location in the staff.

SONAR inserts all three triplet notes at the same pitch. You can then drag the second and third notes to their correct pitch locations.

Beaming of Rests
The Staff view supports beaming of rests, a practice that is popular with rhythmically complex music. Beam lengths are extended to include rests that are integral parts of the beamed group of notes. Short stems, called stemlets, extend from the beam toward the rest. This makes the rhythms easier to read, because the beat boundaries are made clear.

To Enable Beaming of Rests

1. Click Layout button [icon] to open the Staff View Layout dialog box.
2. Select the Beam Rests option.
3. Click OK.

Thereafter, the Staff view beams rests as though they were notes.

Changing the Way Notes Are Displayed

Unlike musical notation programs, SONAR uses the MIDI events themselves as the permanent representation of the music; thus, the Staff view is only an interpretation of a MIDI performance.

MIDI notes do not always correspond exactly to notes on a staff. Whereas a staff defines precise grid-like starting times and durations for notes, a MIDI note can start at any arbitrary time during the project, and last for any length of time. If you record a performance from a MIDI keyboard, for example, you'll find that some notes may start slightly before the beat, and some a little after, and that the notes end a little late or a little early. Although these slight imperfections are what gives a performance its "human" quality, you don't necessarily want to see all these imperfections notated with excruciating precision.

The Staff view has two options you can select to affect the way MIDI notes are displayed on the staff:

Option...	Purpose...
Fill Durations	Visually rounds up note durations to the next beat or the next note, whichever comes first.
Trim Durations	Visually rounds down note durations if they extend a little way past the start of the next note.

Here's what the Staff view looks like with and without these options:

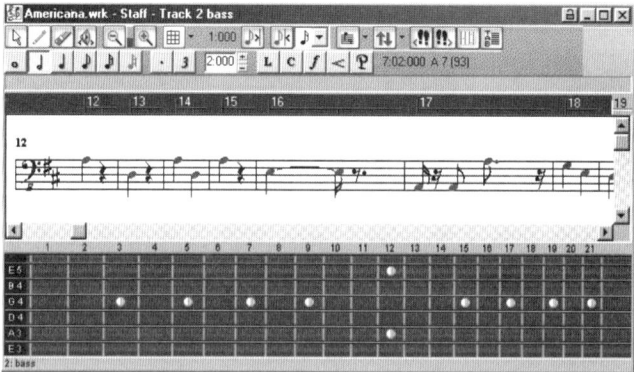

Fill and Trim off

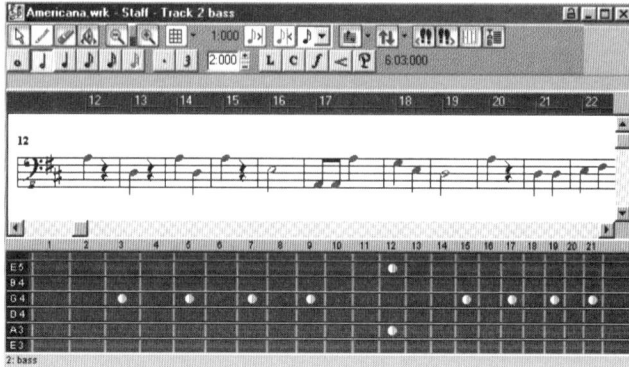

Fill and Trim on

On the other hand, if you are entering notes into the Staff view with the mouse, Fill and Trim Durations may produce confusing results. For example, with Fill Durations, an inserted eighth note in 4/4 time would look like a quarter note until you insert another eighth note immediately following it. It is recommended that you turn off the Fill Durations and Trim Durations options when entering notes; these options are more appropriate for looking at notes you recorded via a performance.

Using Enharmonic Spellings

Any musical note can be referred to by several different names. For example, C#3 and Db3 identify the same pitch, as do G#4 and Ab4. The most appropriate name depends upon the current key signature, but can also depend on musical context.

SONAR uses a set of rules to automatically add accidentals (sharps, flats and naturals) to notes based on the current key signature. These rules cover the most common musical situations and usually lead to pleasing results. However, there is no guaranteed right way to resolve accidentals. Doing so ultimately requires knowledge regarding what key or scale is being evoked—knowledge that only the composer possesses. For example, if a modulation is being prepared, then the new key signature has not yet been completely established, and the harmony has already begun to shift. In fact, there may not even be a scale in a diatonic sense: chromatic scales, for instance, are supposed to sharp on the way up and flat on the way down. Because no set of rules will suffice for all situations, the composer needs the ability to override any default choice.

Notes in SONAR normally do not have a forced enharmonic spelling. This means that they will automatically change to match the default for a new key signature. If you specify spelling that matches the default choice, SONAR will drop any forced spelling and switch back to default behavior. Otherwise, the forced spelling is remembered for that note, and will not change to follow the key signature. If you change the pitch of a note by some other means (for instance, by dragging it up or down), it will lose any forced spelling, because it very likely no longer applies to the new pitch. Enharmonic spelling overrides for each note are saved in the project file.

When you type a note's enharmonic spelling, use the following table as a guide:

Accidental...	Character...	Example...	Displays as...
Flat	b	Cb5	
Sharp	#	C#5	

Double flat	"	C"5	
Double sharp	x	Cx5	

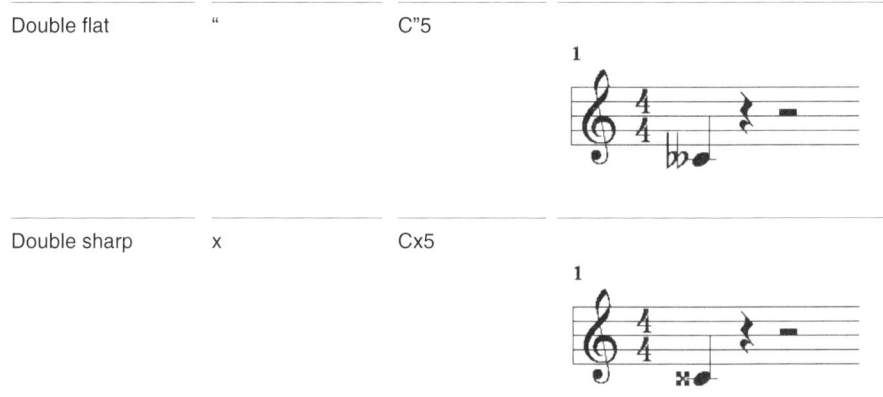

To Change a Note's Enharmonic Spelling
1. Right-click the note to open the Note Properties dialog box.
2. In the Pitch textbox, type a new spelling for the note.
3. Click OK.

SONAR displays the note with the new enharmonic spelling.

You can change enharmonic spellings in other views, such as the Event List view, by similarly typing a new spelling wherever the note pitch is displayed as a text string.

You can also use the ***Process-Interpolate*** command to change enharmonic spellings—for example, to change multiple occurrences of Eb5 to D#5, or even all Ebs to D#s. See "Process-Interpolate" on page 309 for more information.

MIDI Channels and the Fretboard
You can display notes on the fretboard based on the note event's MIDI channel. (Do not confuse this with the Track MIDI channel.) A single track can hold events on many different MIDI channels. See "Assigning a MIDI Channel (Chn)" on page 141 for more information. Displaying notes using this method is 100% accurate because each string is represented by an individual MIDI channel. For example, String 1 = MIDI channel 11, String 2 = MIDI channel 12, etc.

To Display Notes on the Fretboard Using their MIDI Channels
1. Set your MIDI Guitar to transmit on 6 consecutive channels. This is often referred to as "MONO" mode. Refer to your MIDI Guitar device documentation for more information.
2. Select and Arm a track.
3. If you want the data from all 6 strings to be recorded to a single track, set the Input to OMNI. If you want each string on a separate track, you need to set up

each individual track to record on the corresponding MIDI channel. The GR-30 Guitar Synthesizer template is designed to do this, so you may want to open that from the Quick Start Menu or from the File menu. To use the File menu method, choose **File-Open** and choose Cakewalk Template from the Files of type field. Then choose the Roland GR-30 template.

4. Open the Staff view.
5. Click the Staff View Layout button.
6. Click Define.
7. In the Method field, click MIDI Channel.
8. In the 1st Channel field, set SONAR to transmit on the same series of MIDI channels that you chose in step 1. Select 1 for 1-6, 2 for 2-7, etc.

   MIDI guitar devices can transmit in MONO using a different series of MIDI channels, but SONAR needs to be listening to the same channels in order to properly display the MIDI guitar input.

9. Click Close.
10. Click OK.

SONAR displays notes on the Fretboard based on their MIDI channels.

If you are planning to record or input notes from a MIDI guitar synth or MIDI converter, you need to set this up on the instrument. In the case of the Roland GR-30, for example, you set it to send on MIDI Channel 11, MONO. This sends out each corresponding string on channels 11-16.

Chords and Marks

The Staff view lets you add and edit chord symbols, dynamic markings, hairpin symbols, and pedal events. Like notes, these symbols are placed in the score with the Draw tool. They can be selected, cut, copied, pasted, deleted, and dragged and dropped. With the exception of pedal marks, though, these symbols have no audible effect; they serve only to enhance and clarify the printed score.

Adding Chord Symbols

The Staff view lets you enter chord symbols above the staff. You can enter both ordinary chord names and guitar chord symbols, which display both the chord name and fingering. SONAR has a large number of predefined chords from which you can choose. You can also define and save your own chords.

If a track is split into treble/bass staves, chords are allowed only above the upper (treble) staff.

SONAR stores its library of chords in the file *chords.liw*. The chords in the library are sorted into groups. You can add and remove chords from the library, create new groups (i.e., for alternative guitar tunings), and add chords from a different library file.

You edit chords in the Chord Properties dialog box. Chord properties are shown in the following table:

Property...	Meaning...
Time	The time of the chord, in measure, beat, and tick (MBT) format
Name	The name of the chord
Group	The chord group

The Chord Properties dialog box also lets you draw guitar chord grids and manage the chord library.

You can suppress the display of all guitar chord diagrams by deselecting the Show Chord Grids option in the Staff view's Layout dialog box. With this option disabled, only chord text appears.

To Add a Chord Symbol

1. Click the Draw tool .
2. Select the Chord tool c .
3. Position the pointer above the staff (the pointer changes to a pencil when you are in a legal position).
4. Click to place a chord symbol.

SONAR inserts a copy of the most recently added chord (by default, C). You can then edit the symbol to display the chord you want.

To Move a Chord Symbol

1. Click the Draw tool .
2. Drag the chord symbol to a new location.

To Edit a Chord Symbol

1. Right-click the symbol to open the Chord Properties dialog box.

2. Edit information about the chord according to the table:

To do this...	Do this...
Move a chord in time	Change the Time property.
Give the chord a new name	Select a chord from the dropdown list, or type a new name. Use # for sharp and b for flat.
Add descriptive text to the chord name	Type the text in square brackets after the chord name. The text does not appear in the Staff view.
See a different set of chords	Select a group from the list. This option only applies if you have created a custom chord library.

3. If desired, select a group from the list and/or create a guitar chord grid.

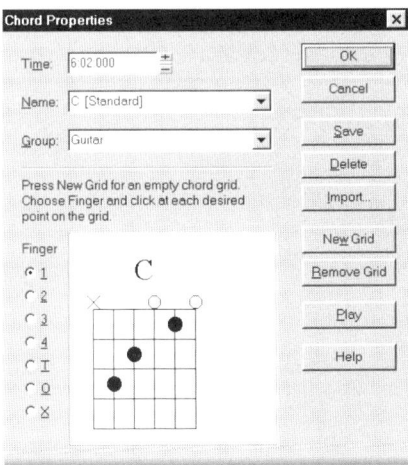

4. Click OK.

The Staff view displays the chord with the new properties, moving it to a new time if necessary.

545

To Add a Guitar Chord Grid

1. Right-click the chord symbol to open the Chord Properties dialog box.
2. Follow the instructions in the table:

To do this...	Do this...
Display a blank chord grid	Click New Grid
Place a dot on the grid	Select the finger number (1-4, or T for Thumb), then click the grid at the appropriate string and fret location
Assign an open string	Select O, then click on the string
Assign a muted string	Select X, then click on the string
Change the finger assigned to a dot	Click the dot repeatedly to cycle through the fingers
Insert a fret designation	Click to the right of the grid and enter the number of the index finger fret in the Chord Fret Number dialog box
Play the chord (Audition)	Click Play
Remove the chord grid	Click Remove Grid

3. Click OK.

The Staff view displays the chord with the new guitar chord grid.

To Manage the Chord Library

1. Right-click the chord symbol to open the Chord Properties dialog box.
2. Follow the instructions in the table:

To do this...	Do this...
Add a chord to the library	Select a group, enter a name in the Name box, enter a guitar grid (if desired), and click Save.
Delete a chord from the current group	Select the chord from the list and click Delete.
Add a new group	Type a name for the group in the Group textbox and click Save.
Delete a group	Select a group from the list and click Delete.
Merge chords from an external chord library	Click the Import button and select a file. Chord libraries have the extension .liw.

3. Click OK.

SONAR saves the chord library with the changes you made.

Adding Expression Marks

Expression marks tell a performer how to interpret the notes and durations on the page. They provide a necessary supplement to simple notation, in which notes have only pitch and duration, but no hint of how loudly, softly, or smoothly, they are to be played. Dynamic marks—from *ppp* (pianississimo) for "very, very softly" through *fff* (fortissimo) for "very, very forcefully"—allow notation to convey volume instructions. Expression marks are also needed to specify other aspects of performance, such as whether a passage is to be played legato or staccato. Finally, expression marks can be used to convey to the performer the composer's suggestions or requirements as to how a passage should be interpreted. In such cases the language used can leave much to the imagination, as in *with majesty* or *abrasively*.

Expression marks do not change the underlying MIDI data. They only provide information to the reader on how a piece should be performed.

If the track is split into treble/bass staves, expression marks are allowed only below the treble staff.

When entering an expression mark, you can leave a dangling hyphen at the end of an expression mark to insert automatic spaced hyphens until the next expression mark. For example:

cresc.   -   -   -   *ff*

It is often desirable to terminate such a series of hyphens with a blank expression mark. For example:

accel.   -   -   -

Expression text is italicized in the Staff view. Standard dynamic markings also appear bold.

To Add an Expression Mark

1. Click the Draw tool.
2. Select the Expression tool.
3. Position the pointer below the lowest note in the staff. (The pointer changes to a pencil when you are in a legal position.)
4. Click to open an insertion box.
5. Type the expression mark text. Press Esc to abort the operation.
6. Press Enter, or press Tab or Shift-Tab to move to the next or previous mark, respectively.

SONAR inserts the new expression mark below the staff.

To Edit an Expression Mark

1. Right-click the expression mark to open the Expression Text Properties dialog box.

2. Edit the time and text of the expression mark as desired.
3. Click OK.

The Staff view displays the expression mark with the new text, including moving it to a new time if necessary. You can also use the Draw tool and click on an expression mark directly to change its text.

Adding Hairpin Symbols

Some musical phrases vary dynamically, increasing or decreasing in loudness for dramatic effect. SONAR lets you insert traditional crescendo and diminuendo hairpin symbols that convey this information to a performer, as shown here:

If the track is split into treble/bass staves, hairpin symbols are allowed only below the treble staff.

To Add a Hairpin Symbol

1. Click the Draw tool.

2. Select the Hairpin tool.

3. Position the pointer below the staff (the pointer changes to a pencil when you are in a legal position).

4. Click to place a hairpin symbol.

SONAR inserts a copy of the most recently added hairpin symbol, which you can edit as desired.

To Edit a Hairpin Symbol

1. Right-click on the hairpin symbol you want to edit.

    The Hairpin Properties dialog appears.

2. Change any of the following parameters:

    - Time—The beginning time of the hairpin symbol
    - Crescendo or Diminuendo
    - Duration—Enter the number of beats followed by a colon (for example 4: for one measure in 4/4 time) or a PPQ number value.

Adding Pedal Marks

Pedal marks traditionally indicate where the sustain pedal of a piano is to be pressed and for how long. With SONAR, you can achieve the same effect by inserting a pair of symbols indicating when the sustain pedal controller is to be turned on (down) and when it is to be turned off (up). Unlike chord symbols, expression marks, and hairpin symbols, each pedal symbol corresponds to a MIDI event. The other symbols are purely ornamental, intended to provide a composer with a way to communicate suggestions or requirements to performers.

Pedal event parameters are as follows:

Parameters...	Meaning...
Time	The time of the event, in measures, beats, and ticks (MBT).
Channel	The MIDI channel on which the event will be sent.
Value	The event value. A value of 127 depresses the pedal, a value of 0 raises it. (Some advanced synthesizers support values between 0 and 127 for "partial pedaling.")

If the track is split into treble/bass staves, pedal marks are allowed only below the bass staff.

You can suppress the display of all pedal marks by deselecting the Show Pedal Events option in the Staff view's Layout dialog box.

To Add a Pedal Mark

1. Click the Draw tool.
2. Select the Pedal tool.
3. Position the pointer below the staff (the pointer changes to a pencil when you are in a legal position).
4. Click to place a pedal mark.

SONAR inserts a pair of pedal symbols (a pedal down and a pedal up). You can click and drag either symbol to a new time.

To Edit a Pedal Event

1. Right-click the pedal symbol (pedal down or pedal up) to open the Pedal Event Parameters dialog box.

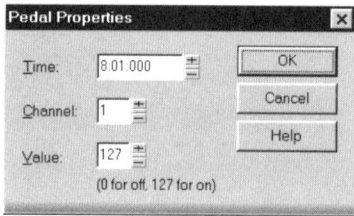

2. Edit the pedal event parameters, as described in the table above.
3. Click OK.

SONAR changes the pedal event parameters, including moving the symbol to a new time if necessary.

Tablature

The Staff view can display guitar or bass MIDI tracks as tablature. You can generate and edit tablature or enter notes on either the fretboard or on the tablature staff to create a new track. You can export tablature to an ASCII file for printing or distribution on the Web.

Tablature Settings

Both the Staff View Layout dialog box and the Tablature Settings dialog box create tablature settings for a whole track at a time. To modify tablature for selected parts of a track, select part of a track and use the Regenerate command.

In the Staff View Layout dialog box you can choose a preset style of tablature by choosing from the Preset popup menu, or you can define your own style by clicking the Define button in the Staff View Layout dialog box to open the Tablature Settings dialog box.

To Define a Tablature Style

1. In the Staff View Layout dialog box, click the name of the track you want to define tablature for.

2. Click the Define button (lower right corner).

    The Tablature Settings dialog box appears.

3. Click the Tablature tab and choose a tablature method from the Method dropdown list. There are three methods to determine how the TAB is displayed:

    - **Floating** - which allows the notes to spread over the entire fretboard

    - **Fixed** - This specifies where on the neck these notes should be played. When Fixed is selected the Finger span and Lowest fret fields are used together to define the "box" where the notes are displayed. The Finger span parameter determines how many consecutive frets will be used to display the note. For example, if Finger span is set to 4, then SONAR will attempt to place all the notes within those 4 frets. The Lowest Fret then determines where on the fretboard the notes will be displayed within the Finger span. The red box in the fretboard display changes to reflect the settings in these two parameters.

    - **MIDI Channel** - This uses the event's MIDI channel to determine which string the note should be displayed on. When MIDI Channel is selected, the user chooses which series of MIDI Channels should be considered. This is useful for MIDI Guitarists that record parts in MONO mode, where each string transmits on a different MIDI channel. (Values: 1 - 11). Selecting "1" in the 1st Channel field will cause it to use MIDI channels 1 - 6, selecting 2, 2 - 7, and so on.)

    Note: Select the Skip Channel 10 option if you are using a Yamaha G50 or other device which reserves channel 10.

4. Type a number into the Number of Frets field. This determines how many frets the guitar has that the tab is based on.

5. In the String Tuning fields, choose the instrument from the dropdown list and number of strings from the Number of Strings field.

    The open string pitches for the instrument you choose automatically appear in the string number fields below the dropdown list.

6. Customize any of the open string pitches by using the "+" or "-" buttons on the string number fields.

7. Save your settings by typing a name into the Preset field at the top of the dialog box and clicking the disk icon next to it. You can remove presets from the list by clicking the X button next to the disk icon.

The next time you want to use these settings for a track, choose your Preset in the Staff View Layout dialog box from the Presets dropdown list.

Changing Fretboard Texture and Orientation

You can change fretboard texture and orientation (high string on top or bottom of neck) in the Staff View Layout dialog box, or by right-clicking the Fretboard.

To Change the Fretboard Texture and Orientation

1. Open the Staff View Layout dialog box.
2. Click the Define button (lower right corner).

   The Tablature Settings dialog box appears.

3. Click the Fretboard tab.
4. In the Texture field, choose a texture from the dropdown list.
5. If you want to reverse the standard string orientation, in the Orientation field click Low String on Top (Mirror).
6. Click OK.

The Fretboard changes to reflect your choices.

Quick TAB

SONAR quickly creates a tablature based on standard fingering patterns. After you try the quick version, you can customize the tablature to your liking.

To Create a Quick TAB

1. Open a file that contains a MIDI guitar track.
2. In the Track view, select the track number of the track you want to display tablature for.
3. Select *View-Staff*.

   The Staff view appears, displaying a fretboard and the notation of your MIDI track. To see everything, you may need to resize the Staff view by dragging the top border upward a few inches.

4. From the Staff view toolbar, click the dropdown arrow on the Staff View Layout button to display the tablature dropdown list.
5. Choose Quick TAB from the dropdown list.

   A tablature grid appears, displaying the fret numbers for all the notes in the track.

6. From the File menu, choose Save. Saving your file saves TAB settings for each track you generated TABs for.

Press the Spacebar to play your file. Notice that the Fretboard displays the name of each note above the string and fret you would play it on as the note plays.

Regenerate TAB

The *Regenerate TAB* command works on selected regions in a track to modify the fingering according to the method you choose. The TAB display by default uses the 'floating' algorithm which allows the notes to spread over the entire fretboard. By choosing the "fixed" algorithm instead, you can designate a specific finger span and lowest fret which causes the TAB of a selected region to be displayed within this range. This usually creates a more compact fingering system.

The *Regenerate TAB* command gives you a third choice for displaying tablature MIDI channel. This uses the event's MIDI channel to determine which string the note should be displayed on. When MIDI Channel is selected, the user chooses which series of MIDI Channels should be considered. This is useful for MIDI Guitarists that record parts in MONO mode, where each string transmits on a different MIDI channel.

To Regenerate TAB
1. In the Staff view, use the Select tool to drag a rectangle around the notes or TAB numbers you want to change.
2. In the Staff view toolbar, click the dropdown arrow on the Staff View Layout button to display the tablature dropdown list.
3. Choose **Regenerate TAB** to open the Regenerate Tablature dialog box.
4. Select Fixed from the Method field and fill in values for Finger Span (usually 4), Lowest Fret, and Number of Frets (usually 21).
5. Click OK.

SONAR regenerates a TAB based on your specifications. If notes are out of the range you specified, SONAR displays them as close to that range as possible.

Entering Notes from the TAB Staff

You can enter notes or chords directly from the TAB staff.

To Enter Notes from the TAB Staff
1. Open the Staff View, and choose Quick TAB from the tablature dropdown menu.
2. Press Ctrl+Home to move the Now Time to the start of the project. You may want to display the Now Time by choosing **View-Big Time**.
3. Choose the desired note duration (keyboard shortcut: press 1 for whole note, 2 for half, 3 for a 32nd note, 4 for quarter, 6 for a 16th note, 8 for an 8th note).

4. Click the Draw tool.

5. Enter a note by clicking a line in the TAB staff.

6. Without letting go of the mouse, click and drag the cursor up to set the fret number.

Tip:
You can move ahead in the track by pressing Shift-Right Arrow, and move back in the track using the Shift-Left Arrow. The Now Time moves by the amount of the note duration you choose in the Staff toolbar.

Single Note Editing from the TAB Staff
SONAR enables you to edit single notes from the TAB staff in several ways:

- With the Draw tool selected, drag fret numbers up or down. When you reach the desired fret number, release the mouse.

- With the Draw tool selected, move a note to a different string by holding down the Alt key while you drag the fret number to a different line. If the note you are moving won't play on the string you are dragging it to, you won't be able to move it.

- Right-click the fret you want to edit. A list of fret numbers appears. Select the one you want, and the fret you right-clicked changes to the fret number you selected.

Editing Chords or Groups of Notes from the TAB Staff
To edit chords or groups of notes in the TAB staff, first select which notes you want to edit, and then drag them to new pitches or strings.

To Edit Chords or Groups of Notes from the TAB Staff
1. Click the Select tool in the Staff view toolbar.

2. In the TAB staff, drag a rectangle around the chord or group of notes you want to edit, and release the mouse.

3. Drag the fret numbers you selected up or down by the amount you want.

4. You can drag the notes to different strings by holding down the Alt button while you drag. If the notes you are moving won't play on the strings you are dragging it to, you won't be able to move it.

To Export to an ASCII TAB File

1. Select the track you want to export.
2. Open the Staff view.
3. In the Staff view, click the Export to ASCII TAB button.

   The Save As dialog appears.
4. Enter a file name in the File name field.
5. Click OK.

SONAR saves the track with the file extension .TXT.

Editing Notes and Chords from the Fretboard

You can transpose single notes or chords from the Fretboard.

To Transpose Single Notes

1. Move the Now Time to the note you want to edit by pressing Shift-Right/Left Arrow. You may need to change the note duration by clicking one of the note icons in the Staff view toolbar.
2. Use the Select tool to drag the note left or right on the fretboard.

To Transpose Chords

1. Move the Now Time to display the chord you want to transpose.
2. Shift-select all the notes in the chord.
3. Shift-drag the chord to a new position and release the mouse.

Entering Notes from the Fretboard

If you prefer to work with the Fretboard instead of a musical staff, Cakewalk makes it easy to enter notes from the Fretboard. You can enter single notes or chords by clicking the string and fret of the note you want to enter at the Now Time position.

1. Display the track you want to add notes to in the Staff view.
2. In the Staff view toolbar, click the Draw tool.

   Now the cursor appears as a pencil when you move it over the Staff or Fretboard.
3. Move the Now Time to where you want to start entering notes by pressing Shift-Right Arrow or Shift-Left Arrow. Each press of the arrow moves the Now Time by the amount of the note duration, which you select by clicking the note icons in the Staff view toolbar. You may want to display the Now Time by choosing *View-Big Time*.

4. Enter a note by clicking the string and fret where you would play the note.

   The note appears on the Fretboard, in the Staff, and in the TAB if you have generated one (you can generate a Quick TAB by choosing **Quick TAB** from the tablature dropdown menu that you open by clicking the dropdown arrow on the Staff View Layout button).

5. If you are entering a chord, continue clicking notes at the same Now Time. To move ahead, press Shift-Right Arrow and click a new note duration, if desired.

You can delete a note right after you enter it by pressing Ctrl+Z, or at any time by clicking the Eraser tool and clicking the note in the notation or TAB staffs.

Cakewalk gives you several options to play and hear the notes in your track:

- Scrubbing enables you to click each note in the Fretboard and hear it play. Select the Scrub tool and click the note.

- Scrub strumming enables you to "strum" chords by dragging the Scrub tool through a chord. With the Scrub tool selected, drag through a chord on the Fretboard from below it or above it and back and forth.

- Ctrl+Right Arrow/Ctrl+Left Arrow moves the cursor through the track, playing each note as it reaches it.

Working with Percussion

The Staff view can display percussion tracks on a five-line percussion staff or on a single percussion line. The staff usually displays notes for a drum set or multiple percussion instruments; the line is used to display notes for a single instrument (although it need not be so).

SONAR lets you control the appearance of percussion staffs in considerable detail. You can display percussion notes using several different types of noteheads and articulation symbols, and you can map any percussion sound to any position on the percussion staff (in a percussion track, each MIDI note value designates a different percussion instrument; mapping lets you display any instrument in any position on the staff, regardless of the underlying MIDI note value). You can save your settings as a preset, and use them again on other tracks and in other projects. SONAR supplies a standard preset based on the General MIDI percussion standard and popularly accepted percussion staff positions and noteheads.

Setting Up a Percussion Track

Before you use the percussion capabilities of the Staff view, your percussion track should be set up correctly. This will allow you to hear the proper sounds when placing notes and during playback, and will allow you to see the correct percussion instrument names rather than generic note names in the Piano Roll view, Event List view, and Percussion Notation dialog box.

To Set Up a Percussion Track

1. Right-click on the track in the Track pane and choose **Track Properties** to open the Track Properties dialog box.
2. Assign the output and channel for your percussion instrument. For example, if the output is assigned to a sound card that supports General MIDI, use channel 10.
3. Click Instruments to open the Assign Instruments dialog box.
4. Make sure that the output/channel combination used by your track is assigned to a percussion instrument definition. For example, channel 10 of a General MIDI output should be assigned to the General MIDI Drums instrument definition.
5. Click OK in both dialog boxes.

SONAR shows the new track output and channel in the Track view, and will use the proper percussion instrument names in the Piano Roll view, Event List view, and Percussion Notation dialog box.

For more information about instrument definitions, see Chapter 16, *Using Instrument Definitions*.

Setting Up a Percussion Staff or Line

The first time you display a percussion track in the Staff view, SONAR picks a default percussion clef for the track. Tracks with only one note value are assigned the Percussion Line clef. Tracks with multiple note values are assigned the Percussion Staff clef.

If you want to change a Percussion Staff to a Percussion Line or vice versa, or if you want to change another type of staff to a percussion staff, you can do so in the Staff View Layout dialog box. If you change a track's clef to a non-percussion clef, the percussion notation settings will be lost.

The lowest and highest lines on the Percussion clef are E5 and F6, respectively. The Percussion Line represents E5.

By default, percussion staffs are given SONAR's default note bindings and notehead assignments. If you want to use your own notation, or if you want to set up the appearance of a percussion line, you need to use the Percussion Notation Key dialog box. In this dialog box, the percussion sounds and staff positions that are bound have an asterisk near their names. When you select a bound percussion sound, a line joins the sound to its staff position. Each percussion sound can be bound only to a single position, but each position may be bound to several sounds. You can use different notehead types and articulation symbols to visually distinguish the sounds.

To Assign a Percussion Staff or Line to a Track

1. Click the Staff View Layout button to open the Staff View Layout dialog box.
2. Select your percussion track from the list.
3. Select *Percussion Staff* or *Percussion Line* from the Clef dropdown list.
4. Click Percussion Settings to set up the appearance of percussion notes (see below).
5. Click Close.

SONAR changes the track's clef to the selected percussion clef.

To Set Up a Track's Percussion Notation Key

1. Click the Staff View Layout button to open the Staff View Layout dialog box.
2. Select your percussion track from the list.
3. Click Percussion Settings to open the Percussion Notation Key dialog box.
4. Set up the percussion notation key according to the following table:

To do this...	Do this...
Map (bind) a percussion sound to a line or space on the staff	Select the sound (or corresponding MIDI note) in the MIDI Note list, select the intended position in the percussion staff in the Display As list, then click Bind.
Set the notehead and articulation mark for a percussion sound	Select the sound in the MIDI Note list, then select a Notehead Type and Articulation Symbol. (Only bound sounds can be assigned a notehead type and articulation symbol other than the default.)
Control how unbound percussion sounds display	In the Display As list, click the pitch that you want all unbound notes to display as. Then select a Notehead Type and Articulation Symbol, then click the Default note button to apply your changes.
Remove a binding	Select the percussion sound in the MIDI Note list, then click Unbind. Unbound notes are displayed in the default position.
Load a preset	Select the preset from the Preset list.
Save your settings as a preset	Click the Save button and enter a preset name.
Clear all bindings	Click Zap All.
Select notes in the note lists with a MIDI keyboard	Click in the MIDI Note or Display As list, then strike a key on your keyboard.

5. Click OK to close the Percussion Notation Key dialog box.
6. Click Close to close the Staff View Layout dialog box.

The Staff view shows the percussion clef with the note bindings and noteheads you assigned.

Ghost Strokes

In percussion notation, parentheses around a note mean that it is a ghost stroke, played very lightly and barely heard. SONAR supports ghost strokes by displaying parentheses around any percussion note event with velocity less than 32 (a fixed, arbitrary threshold). If necessary, you can adjust the Vel+ parameter of the track and the velocities of the individual notes to effectively move this threshold without changing the way the note sounds.

Printing

The Staff view provides printing support of standard musical notation in nine staff sizes. The Staff view prints general project information from the File Info dialog box (see "Labeling Your Projects" on page 199) at the beginning of the score, including the song's title (or file name), subtitle (dedication), playing instructions, author/composer, and copyright. In addition, SONAR identifies the tracks by number and name, and numbers each measure and each page.

To Print a Score

1. Make sure the Staff view is the current window.
2. Choose **File-Print Preview**.
3. If you want, click Zoom, or click in the music, to zoom the view in and out.
4. Click the Configure button to select a rastral size.
5. When zoomed out, you can press Page Up and Page Down to navigate between pages.
6. Click Print.

SONAR displays the Windows Print dialog box, from which you can set up your printer and print the score.

Alternatively, you can choose **File-Print** and skip the print preview window.

The Meter/Key View

The Meter/Key view lets you enter meter and key changes at measure boundaries. Meter and key changes affect all tracks.

What Is Meter?

The meter—also known as the time signature—describes how to divide time into rhythmic pulses. When you set the meter, you are specifying the number of beats per measure and the note value of each beat. Common meters include:

- 2/4 (two beats per measure, quarter note gets a beat)
- 4/4 (four beats per measure, quarter note gets a beat)
- 3/4 (three beats per measure, quarter note gets a beat)
- 6/8 (six beats per measure, eighth note gets a beat)

The top number of a meter is the number of beats per measure, and can be from 1 through 99. The bottom number of a meter is the value of each beat; you can pick from a list of values ranging from a whole note to a thirty-second note.

The meter affects several things in SONAR:

- Metronome accents
- How measure, beat, and tick (MBT) times are calculated and displayed
- How the Staff view is drawn

While SONAR in general allows meters to have up to 99 beats per measure, the Staff view cannot display such measures. You will receive an error message if you try to use the Staff view with meters exceeding its limit.

Internally, SONAR stores times as "raw" ticks or clock pulses. The **timebase**—the number of pulses per quarter note (PPQ)—is adjustable, from 48 to 960 PPQ. If you are using a timebase of 120 PPQ and the project file is in 4/4 time, then a whole measure equals 480 ticks. See "Setting the MIDI Timing Resolution" on page 169 for more information about the timebase.

Usually the easiest approach to working with meter changes is to set all of them up before doing any recording. Use the Meter/Key view or the *Insert-Meter/Key Change* command to add meter changes at the desired measures.

What Is Key?

In musical terms, a key is a system of related notes based on the tonic (the base pitch) of a major or minor scale. A key signature is a group of sharps or flats placed immediately to the right of the clef sign. The key signature tells a performer that certain notes are to be systematically raised or lowered.

There are fifteen different key signatures—seven with sharps, seven with flats, and one without either. The fifteen key signatures correspond to fifteen different major scales, and to fifteen different minor scales (for example, the key signature for C major is the same as for A minor).

The key signature affects several things in SONAR:

- The key signature controls how SONAR displays notes. In the Event List view and some dialog boxes, SONAR converts the MIDI pitch number to labels like Db (D-flat in the key of C).
- The Staff view uses the key signature to display notation correctly.
- How the notes are transposed when the Diatonic option is enabled.

The key signature affects only how SONAR displays pitches for you. Changing the key signature does not affect the MIDI key number (pitch) stored with each note. To actually transpose pitches, use the Transpose command or edit notes individually by using the Piano Roll, Event List, or Staff views.

Note: Groove clips are not affected by changes to your project's key. Groove clips follow the default project pitch value, located on the Markers toolbar, and Pitch markers in the Time Ruler. For more information, see "Using Pitch Markers in the Track View" on page 266.

Frequently you use only one key signature for an entire project, but SONAR supports multiple key signatures and multiple meter changes in a project. The default key is C. You can change these defaults by creating your own default template file. For more information, see "Templates" on page 517.

Opening the Meter/Key View

To open the Meter/Key view, click ▦ or choose *View-Meter/Key*.

The Meter/Key view displays a list of meter/key changes in the project. There is always an entry for measure 1, because there must always be a meter and key signature for the project. The default meter is 4/4 and the default key is C. You can change these defaults by creating your own default template file. For more information, see "Templates" on page 517.

Each meter/key change has the following properties:

Property...	Meaning...
At Measure	The measure where the meter/key change takes place.
Beats per Measure	The number of beats per measure, the upper number in the time signature.
Beat Value	The note length of a beat, the lower number in the time signature. 2 corresponds to a half note, 4 to a quarter note, 8 to an eighth note, etc.
Key Signature	The key signature.

Adding and Editing Meter/Key Changes

The Meter/Key view displays a list of all the meter/key changes in the project. You can add, delete, or edit meter/key changes by clicking the buttons at the top of the view. You can also insert meter/key changes into the project with the *Insert-Meter/Key Change* command.

To Add a Meter/Key Change

1. Open the Meter/Key view.

2. Click Add, or choose *Insert-Meter/Key Change*, to open the Meter/Key Signature dialog box.

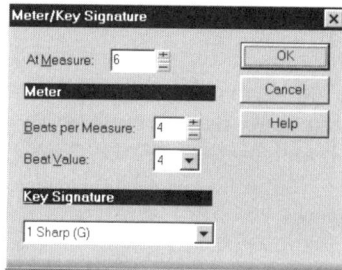

3. Enter information about the new meter/key change.
4. Click OK.

SONAR inserts the meter/key change into the project. The meter/key change will appear in the Staff view at the appropriate measure.

To Delete a Meter/Key Change
1. Select the meter/key change to be deleted from the list.
2. Select additional meter/key changes by using Shift-click and Ctrl-click.
3. Click Delete ☒.

SONAR removes the meter/key change from the project. You cannot delete the first meter/key change from measure 1 of a project.

To Move a Meter/Key Change
1. Select the meter/key change to be moved.
2. Click Add ✳.
3. Edit the Measure parameter to the meter/key change's new measure.
4. Click OK.
5. Select the original meter/key change again.
6. Click Delete ☒.

SONAR removes the original meter/key change and inserts a copy of it at the new measure.

To Edit a Meter/Key Change
1. Select the meter/key change to be edited.
2. Click Change 🗐 to open the Meter/Key Signature dialog box.
3. Edit the meter/key change properties.
4. Click OK.

SONAR changes the properties of the meter/key change.

Music Notation for Non-concert-key Instruments

For historical reasons, certain musical instruments are traditionally notated in a transposed key rather than the actual key. For example, a normal (Bb) trumpet part is written in the key one whole step higher than the actual concert key, and an Eb alto sax part is written a major sixth higher. Musicians have traditionally learned to read and refer to the notes they play using the proper transposition interval for their instrument.

SONAR supports these non-concert instrumental keys through use of the Key+ control in the Track view. Simply enter or record the notes into the instrument's track transposed as the musician would expect them, and then set the proper transposition interval in the Key+ control to make it play in the correct key. For example, a Bb trumpet track should have all its notes a whole note higher than concert pitch, and should have Key+ set to -2 to transpose it two chromatic steps back down. Remember, not all trumpets are Bb instruments!

To Notate a Bb Trumpet Part

1. Record or enter the notes using the pitches that the musician who will be reading the part needs to see. For example, if the non-transposing instruments are playing in the key of C, a Bb trumpet player needs to see the notes a whole step higher—the key of D. The instrument itself sounds a whole step lower than concert pitch, so when a Bb trumpet plays in the key of D, it sounds in the key of C.

   Now that the pitches appear the way that the trumpet player needs to see them, the problem is that when you play your project, the MIDI notes in the trumpet track sound a whole step too high.

2. In the Track view, force SONAR to play the trumpet track a whole step lower by entering -2 (negative 2) in the Key+ field and pressing Enter.

Now the trumpet part in the Staff view appears in the key of D—SONAR automatically adds two sharps to the trumpet track's key signature—but the track sounds in the key of C because you entered -2 in the Key+ field (you may need to close the Staff view and reopen it to see the new key signature). The Staff view automatically transposes the key signature for each track according to the track's Key+ value. Multiple tracks appear and can be printed as an orchestral score, with the proper different key signatures for each track.

Note that this Key+ information is saved in SONAR .CWP files, but not in standard MIDI files. If you save a file as a MIDI file, the Key+ transposition will be applied to each note event, so that the file will sound the same, but the Key+ information will be lost. If you're reading in a MIDI file, you can easily set up the non-concert instrument tracks and then save the file as a normal project file. First set the Key+ offset to reflect the non-concert instrument's key signature. Then, use Transpose to compensate for the Key+ offset.

Working with Lyrics

SONAR lets you create, edit, and display lyrics, the words and syllables associated with notes in a track. Lyrics can be the words to a song, the text of a vocal passage, a narration to be read along with the music, cues of some type, or text totally unrelated to the music. Each word or syllable in the lyrics must be associated with a note in a MIDI track. Each MIDI track can have its own lyrics.

Although lyrics can logically be associated with digital audio data, you cannot actually place lyrics in an audio track. If you want to create lyrics for an audio track, you must create an auxiliary MIDI track to hold the lyrics.

You can enter and edit lyrics in two ways:

- Using the Lyrics tool in the Staff view
- Using the Lyrics view
- Inserting lyric events in the Event List view.

The Staff view is usually the preferred location for entering lyrics, since you can see the notes with which the lyrics are associated. The Lyrics view can also be used for entering or editing lyrics, but its main strength is that it can display lyrics in a larger, more readable format. You might use the Lyrics view to display song lyrics during recording and playback, so performers can see the words and sing along. You can make the font size in the Lyrics view as large as desired, so that the lyrics can be read at a distance from the monitor. During playback, the current line in the lyrics is enclosed in a box and the current word is highlighted.

Lyric events are similar to text events. Like any other event, they occur at a particular time. They contain text, just like general-purpose text events, but generally they contain only a single word (or syllable of a word). As events, Lyrics can be edited in the Event List view (see "The Event List View" on page 318).

Adding and Editing Lyrics in the Staff View

The Staff view displays lyrics below their associated track. If the track is split into treble/bass staves, lyrics are aligned with notes in both staves, but are displayed below the treble staff.

When a lyric word or syllable spans multiple notes, a trailing underline or series of regularly spaced hyphens is automatically drawn, following conventional lyric notation practice.

To Add Lyrics to a Track

1. Click the Draw tool.

2. Select the Lyrics tool.

3. Position the pointer below the staff, under the first note to be assigned lyrics. (The pointer changes to a pencil when you are in a legal position.)

4. Click to open an insertion box.

5. Follow the instructions in the table:

To do this...	Do this...
Enter a word or syllable	Type it in the insertion box
End the word or syllable and move to the next note	Type a space, tab, or hyphen
Skip over a note	Type a space or hyphen
Move back to the previous note	Press Shift-Tab

6. Press Enter when you are done.

SONAR displays the new lyrics below the staff.

To Edit Lyrics

1. Click the Draw tool.

2. Click the word you want to change.

3. Edit the word as desired.

4. Press Enter.

SONAR replaces the old word with the new one.

Opening the Lyrics View

There are three ways to open the Lyrics view:

- In the Track view, select the track whose lyrics you want to see, then click L.

- In the Track view, select the track whose lyrics you want to see, then choose **View-Lyrics**.

- Right-click a clip in the Clips pane and choose **Lyrics** from the menu

The Pick Track button opens a dialog box where you can select the track whose lyrics you want to see. Select the desired track, then click OK.

To select a font for the display, use one of the following:

Option/Button...	Purpose...
f_a	Selects the first font. By default, this is a small font useful for editing.
f_b	Selects the second font. By default, this is a larger font useful for reading lyrics at a distance.
Font...	Opens a dialog where you can select a font. The selected font is then assigned as Font A or B (depending on which is currently selected).

Adding and Editing Lyrics in the Lyrics View

Lyrics appear in the Lyrics view as a stream of syllables, each one associated with a note in the track. In this context, a **syllable** is any continuous string of characters, without a hyphen. For example, "love," "desire," and "infatuation" are all syllables; each one would be associated with a single note. If you want to break a word into multiple syllables, you must hyphenate the word. For example, "de-sire" would map onto two notes, since it is now two syllables long.

When you enter the lyrics, you can mark the syllables the way you want, or you can simply type the text in normally and use automatic hyphenation to break the text into syllables. This means that you can add lyrics to a project by copying and pasting them from another application (such as a word processor), and then hyphenate them automatically.

To extend a single syllable over more than one note, you can use extra hyphens, separated by spaces. For example, in "Oh-say can you see…", the "Oh" is extended over two notes. If a track contains no lyrics yet, the display will show only a series of hyphens (one for each note in the track).

If you enter more syllables than there are notes in the track, SONAR assigns the extra lyrics times at quarter note intervals.

To Enter Lyrics in the Lyrics View

1. Click in the upper left corner of the view to position the cursor at the start of the text.

2. Follow the instructions in the table:

To do this...	Do this...
Enter a word or syllable	Type it
End a word or syllable and move to the next note	Type a space or hyphen
Break a line for easier viewing	Press Enter

To Edit Lyrics in the Lyrics View

Editing in the Lyrics view follows standard Windows conventions for cursor movement, selection, cut (Ctrl+X), copy (Ctrl+C), paste (Ctrl+V), and delete (Delete). When you pause, SONAR will update all lyric events in the track.

To Hyphenate the Lyrics

1. If you want, select a portion of the lyric text. If you do not select any text, all the lyrics will be hyphenated.

2. Click the Hyphenate button.

SONAR hyphenates the lyrics.

16 Using Instrument Definitions

Instrument definitions are a powerful feature of SONAR™ that makes it easier for you to find the banks, patches, and controllers of your MIDI instruments. An instrument definition is a file that contains the names of the banks, patches, note names, bank select method, and controllers of an instrument. Instrument definitions for many popular MIDI instruments are included with SONAR or are available on the Cakewalk web site (www.cakewalk.com). If an instrument definition is not available for your instrument, and you are familiar with MIDI and how it works, you can use SONAR to create your own instrument definition.

Most MIDI instruments available today are General MIDI (GM) compatible, which means that they come with the standard set of sounds or patches defined by the GM standard. SONAR initially assumes that your MIDI instruments are GM compatible. The names of patches and controllers that you initially see displayed throughout SONAR are drawn from the GM specification.

At the same time, many MIDI instruments provide additional sounds and controllers beyond those required by the GM standard. In addition, some older MIDI instruments are not GM compatible. If you are using one of these instruments with SONAR, you can use instrument definitions to make sure that the names of banks, patches, and controllers that you see in SONAR are the same ones you see on the display screens of your MIDI keyboards and modules.

In This Chapter

Assigning Instruments 570
Importing Instrument Definitions 572
Creating Instrument Definitions 573
Instrument Definition Tutorial 582

Assigning Instruments

SONAR lets you assign a MIDI instrument definition to each available MIDI output and channel. The assignments you make determine the MIDI bank names, patch names, note names, and controller names that you see during your SONAR session.

Suppose that you have a Roland GS-compatible synthesizer attached to MIDI output 1. By assigning all 16 channels of MIDI output 1 to the Roland GS instrument definition, you ensure that the bank, patch, note, and controller name lists you see displayed in SONAR are the same ones that you see on the display screen of your synthesizer.

Often, you want to assign a different instrument to channel 10, which is usually used for percussion. For example, you might assign the Roland GS instrument definition to channels 1 through 9 and 11 through 16, but you would most likely want to assign the Roland GS Drumsets instrument definition to channel 10. That way, any SONAR tracks you assign to channel 10 on that output use the names of drum sets for patch names, and drum notation in the Piano Roll view. If you have several MIDI outputs, with a different MIDI module attached to each one, you would normally assign a different instrument definition to each MIDI output.

For convenience, you can assign a block of channels to one instrument and then change the assignment of one or more of those channels without changing the others. For example, you can highlight all 16 channels of the first MIDI output and assign them to the Roland GS instrument definition. Then, you can highlight channel 10 of that same MIDI output and assign it to the Roland GS Drumset instrument definition. Channels 1 through 9 and 11 through 16 on the first MIDI output will stay assigned to Roland GS.

If you only have one MIDI output, but have several MIDI modules attached to it, you can assign a few channels to each module. For example, you might have a Roland synth receiving on MIDI channels 1 through 9, a Roland drum machine receiving on channel 10, and a basic GM-compatible synth receiving on channels 11 through 16. In this case, you'd use three different instrument definitions for your one and only MIDI output.

To Assign Instrument Definitions to MIDI Outputs and Channels

1. Choose *Options-Instruments* to display the Assign Instruments dialog box.

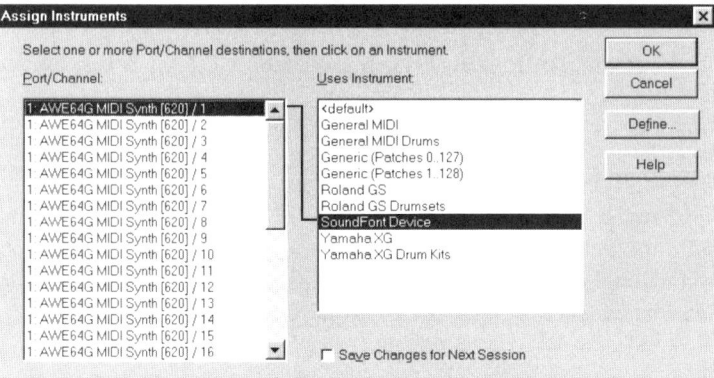

2. Select one or more MIDI outputs and channels from the Output/Channel list (use Shift-click and Ctrl-click to select multiple outputs and channels). You can also drag through a bunch of channels to select them. For example, if you want to assign the first 16 MIDI channels on output 1 to a certain MIDI module, drag through the first 16 items in the Output/Channel list to select them.

3. Choose the instrument definition to which the selected outputs and channels should be assigned from the Uses Instrument list. A black line connects the two lists. If your MIDI module's name doesn't appear in the list and you don't want to use General MIDI bank and patch names for it, see "Importing Instrument Definitions" on page 572.

4. To save these changes permanently, check the Save Changes for Next Session box.

5. Click OK to apply your changes.

From now on, the bank, patch, controller, and note names from the assigned instrument definition are used throughout SONAR on any track that uses one of the output/channel combinations you selected in the Output/Channel list.

To Clear Instrument Assignments

1. Choose *Options-Instruments* to display the Assign Instruments dialog box.

2. Select the MIDI outputs and channels whose assignments you want to remove from the Output/Channel list.

3. Choose <default> from the Uses Instrument list. A black line connects the two lists.

4. Click OK when you are done.

You don't really clear instrument assignments—you reassign them to use the default (General MIDI) instrument definition. After you reassign the output/channel combinations, the default (GM) bank, patch, controller, and note names are used throughout SONAR. on any track that uses one of the output/channel combinations you reassigned in the Output/Channel list.

Importing Instrument Definitions

When you install SONAR, a few common instrument definitions are already set up for you and ready to use. SONAR also includes several hundred additional instrument definitions that you can import.

These instrument definitions are stored in text files in your SONAR folder, organized largely by manufacturer. For example, all the instrument definitions for Roland gear are stored in the ROLAND.INS file; all the instrument definitions for Yamaha gear are stored in the YAMAHA.INS file. The Misc.ins file contains miscellaneous instrument definitions.

If SONAR does not include an instrument definition for your MIDI instrument, you can find additional and updated instrument definitions on the Downloads section of the Cakewalk World Wide Web site (www.cakewalk.com). Simply download the files to your SONAR folder, unzip if necessary, and import the instrument definitions as described below.

When you import an instrument definition, it is added to the master instrument definition file MASTER.INS. The contents of this file determines the list of instruments that appear in the Assign Instruments dialog box.

To Import Instrument Definitions
1. Choose *Options-Instruments* to display the Assign Instruments dialog box.
2. Click Define to display the Define Instruments and Names dialog box.
3. Click Import to display the Import Instrument Definitions dialog box.
4. Choose the file that contains instrument definitions for your manufacturer, and click Open. SONAR displays a list of all the instrument definitions in the file.
5. Choose one or more instruments from the list, and click OK.
6. Click Close to close the Define Instruments and Names dialog box.

The instrument definitions you imported should now appear in the Uses Instrument list in the Assign Instruments dialog box.

Creating Instrument Definitions

SONAR lets you create and edit instrument definitions. To create an instrument definition, you must answer these types of questions:

- What are the names of the patches in each bank?
- Which note names should be used for each patch?
- What are the names of the MIDI Controllers for this instrument?
- Which RPN and NRPNs are available on the instrument?
- Which Bank Select method does the instrument use?

To collect this information, you need the MIDI documentation for your instrument.

Here's a general outline of the steps you must follow to create an instrument definition:

- Create a new instrument in the Instrument tree.
- Create any new name lists in the Names tree that are required for the instrument.
- Drag name lists and possibly a bank select method to the new instrument from the Names tree.
- Close the Define Instruments and Names dialog box.

For detailed instructions, see "To Create a New Instrument" on page 575.

You define instruments in the Define Instruments and Names dialog box, shown below:

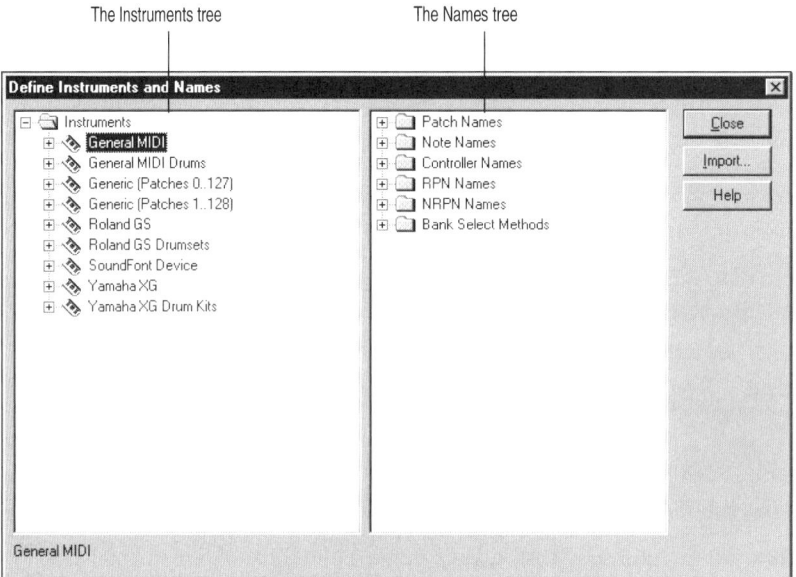

The Define Instruments and Names dialog box contains two trees:

- The Instruments tree in the left half of the dialog box lists all defined instruments and their characteristics
- The Names tree in the right half of the dialog box shows all the resources you use to define an instrument

You expand or collapse the folders and lists in each tree by clicking on the + or – key shown to the left of each item. You can also right-click on an item and choose **Expand** or **Collapse** from the menu, or double-click on an item to expand or collapse it.

To define an instrument, you drag resources from the Names tree to the name of an instrument on the Instruments tree. Each resource is color-coded—you can only drag a Names list to an Instrument tree branch of the same color. For example, you can only drag a list from the Patch Names folder in the Names tree to a Patch Names for Banks folder in the Instruments tree.

There are six components to an instrument definition:

- Method for bank selection
- Patch names, such as Piano and Bass
- Note names, which are most frequently used to name drum notes, such as kick or snare
- Controller names, like volume and pan
- Names for Registered Parameter Numbers (RPNs)
- Names for Non-Registered Parameter Numbers (NRPNs)

The instrument definitions organize all names (patches, notes, controllers, RPNs, and NRPNs) into lists. You may be able to define a new instrument using existing name lists. For example, two models of synthesizers made by a particular manufacturer may have identical patch name lists but use different NRPNs. In this case, you can use the same patch name lists for both instruments, but you would need to use a different NRPN list (or perhaps create a new NRPN list) for the second synth.

If you want your changes to be remembered the next time you run SONAR, make sure the Save Changes For Next Session option in the Assign Instruments dialog box is checked before clicking OK. Otherwise, to make only temporary changes, be sure to remove the check from that option.

To Create a New Instrument
1. In the Define Instruments and Names dialog box, right-click the word Instruments at the top of the Instrument tree, and choose **Add Instrument** from the popup menu.
2. Type a name for the new instrument and press Enter.

The new instrument is provided with default settings for all of its characteristics.

To Rename an Instrument
1. In the Define Instruments and Names dialog box, right-click an Instrument name in the Instrument tree and choose **Edit** from the popup menu.
2. Type the new name and press Enter.

To Delete an Instrument
1. In the Define Instruments and Names dialog box, right-click an Instrument name in the Instrument tree and choose **Delete** from the menu.
2. Confirm that you want to delete the instrument.

To Save an Instrument Definition
1. Click Close to close the Define Instruments and Names dialog box.
2. Click OK.

SONAR saves the instrument definition in the MASTER.INS file.

To Export an Instrument Definition
1. In the Define Instruments and Names dialog box, right-click an Instrument name in the Instrument tree and choose Export from the menu to display the Export Instrument Definition dialog box.
2. If you don't want to save the file in the folder that's listed in the Save In field, navigate to the folder in which you do want to save the file.
3. Enter a file name and click Save.

SONAR saves the file, with the filename extension .INS.

Note: Exporting instrument definitions allows you to share them with other SONAR users.

Creating and Editing Patch Name and Other Lists
You can create and edit the various lists in the Names tree that make up each instrument definition. Patch name, note name, and controller name lists can contain up to 128 entries, numbered 0 through 127. RPN and NRPN name lists can contain up to 16,384 entries, numbered 0 through 16,383.

To Create and Edit Name Lists
- To create, edit, or work with name lists, go to the Names tree of the Define Instruments and Names dialog box, and follow the directions in the following table:

To do this...	Do this...
Create a new name list	Duplicate an existing Patch Names or other list by doing one of the following: expand the folder that contains the name list, highlight the name list and press the Ins (Insert) key; highlight the folder and press Shift-Insert; or right-click any folder or name list and choose **Add Names List** from the menu. Then type a name for the list and press Enter.
Delete a name list	Highlight the names list and press the Del (Delete) key; or right-click on the name list and choose **Delete** from the menu. You will see a warning if the list is used by any instrument definition. If you delete the list anyway, the instrument definition will change automatically.
Add the next item in a name list	Highlight a name and press the Ins key, or right-click on a name and choose **Add Name** from the menu. Then enter the name.

Add a name anywhere in a list	Highlight the name of a list and press Shift-Insert, or right-click on the name of a list and choose **Add Name** from the menu. Then enter the name.
Delete names from a list	Highlight the Names List or Name, and press Del. You can also right-click, then choose **Delete**.
Edit a name in a list	Highlight the name or name list and press F2, or right-click and choose **Edit** from the menu. Then enter the new name.

Copying Name Lists

You can easily create new lists that are similar to other lists. For example, suppose you want to create a new patch name list called NewList that is almost identical to the General MIDI patch list, but with one or two small changes. Here's how you proceed:

- Create a new patch name list in the Patch Names folder of the Names tree called, for example, NewList.

- Drag the new list onto the General MIDI list in the Names tree. You will be asked if you want to base NewList on the General MIDI list.

- Click OK. NewList will now be listed under the General MIDI branch. Any patch names that exist in the General MIDI list apply to NewList, too.

- Add new patch names to NewList. These names will override those in the list on which NewList is based.

If you change your mind about NewList and want to make it a stand-alone, separate list, simply drag it to the Patch Names root folder.

Assigning the Bank Select Method

Your synthesizer uses one of four bank select methods to switch back and forth between banks of sounds. To find the method used for your instrument, check the instrument's *User's Guide* or the manufacturer's web site. The four methods are as follows:

Method...	Used for...
Normal	Instruments that respond to Controller 0 or Controller 32 bank select messages
Controller 0 only	Instruments that only respond to Controller 0 bank select messages
Controller 32 only	Instruments that only respond to Controller 32 bank select messages
Patch 100..127	Instruments that let you change banks by sending patch changes between 100 and 127

The bank select method you choose affects the bank numbers that you assign to each patch list, as described in the following section. Here's how you compute the bank numbers:

Bank select method...	To compute the bank number...
Normal	Take the value of Controller 0, multiply it by 128, and add the value of Controller 32 to derive the bank number.
	Note: A synthesizer manufacturer may refer to Controller 0 as the MSB (Most Significant Byte) and to Controller 32 as the LSB (Least Significant Byte).
Controller 0 only	The value of Controller 0 is the bank number.
Controller 32 only	The value of Controller 32 is the bank number.
Patch 100..127	Take the patch number and subtract 100 to derive the bank number.

Here is an example of the Normal bank select method. According to the documentation for the Roland JV-1080 synthesizer, the PR-A Bank has a Controller 0 value of 81 and a Controller 32 value of 0. You compute the bank number that you enter in the instrument definition as follows: (81 x 128) + 0 = 10,368.

To Change the Bank Select Method

1. Highlight and expand the instrument in the Instrument tree.

2. Expand the Bank Select Method branch in the Names tree.

3. Drag the desired bank select method from the Names tree to the Instrument tree.

Assigning Patch Names

A MIDI instrument can have up to 16,384 banks of 128 patches each. Patches can have names, like "Piano" for patch number 0, "Bass" for patch number 1, and so on. Normally, each bank contains a different set of patches, so each bank needs a separate patch name list. Most synthesizers start with a patch number of 0.

You can assign a patch name list to each bank. You can also assign a default patch name list to the instrument, which is used for all banks for which you haven't assigned a specific list. The previous section describes how to compute the bank numbers to which each patch name list is assigned.

Each bank can also be assigned a special Drum flag, which indicates that all patches in that bank contain drum sounds. If you set this flag, the Piano Roll view will display drum notes as diamonds, and the Staff view will use percussion notation.

To See the Assignment of Patch Name Lists to Banks

1. Expand the instrument definition by clicking the + sign next to the instrument name.
2. Expand the Patch Names for Banks folder by clicking the + sign. The list expands to show the bank numbers and the patch name list that is assigned to each bank.

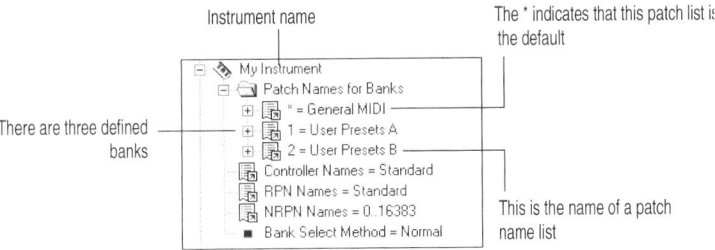

To Add a Bank or Change the Patch Names for a Bank

1. Drag a patch name list from the Names tree to the Patch Names for Banks folder of the instrument you're editing in the Instrument tree.
2. Enter a bank number, or enter –1 to indicate that this list of patch names should be used as the default.

SONAR displays the updated banks and patch name lists. If necessary, SONAR adds a new bank to the instrument definition.

To Remove a Bank or Patch Name List

1. In the Instrument tree in the Patch Names for Banks folder of the instrument you're editing, highlight the bank and patch names list.
2. Press the Del key, or right-click on the bank name and choose **Delete** from the popup menu.

To Set or Clear the Drum Flag

- Right-click on the bank in the Instrument tree, and choose **Drums** from the popup menu.

Assigning Note Names

Each patch may have a list of up to 128 names for notes. Usually, note names are labels for percussion instruments. For example, the pitch C3 may really be "Kick Drum," and D3 may be "Snare." Because a drum machine may provide different drum kits for each patch, SONAR lets you specify a different list of note names for each patch. The Piano Roll and Event List views show you these note names.

You can assign a note name list to each patch. You can also assign a default note name list to the instrument, which is used for all patches for which you haven't assigned a specific note name list.

Each patch can also be assigned a special Drum flag, which indicates that this patch contains drum sounds. If you set this flag, the Piano Roll view will display drum notes as diamonds, and the Staff view will use percussion notation.

There are several standard note name lists provided with SONAR:

Note name list...	Contents...
0..127	The numbers 0 through 127
Diatonic	The default MIDI note names (like C4, E5, and so on)
General MIDI Drums	The default instrument names for the General MIDI drum patch

To See the Assignment of Note Name Lists to Patches

1. Expand the instrument definition by clicking the + sign next to the instrument name.
2. Expand the Patch Names for Banks folder by clicking the + sign.
3. Continue expanding the tree by clicking the + sign, until the tree is fully expanded.

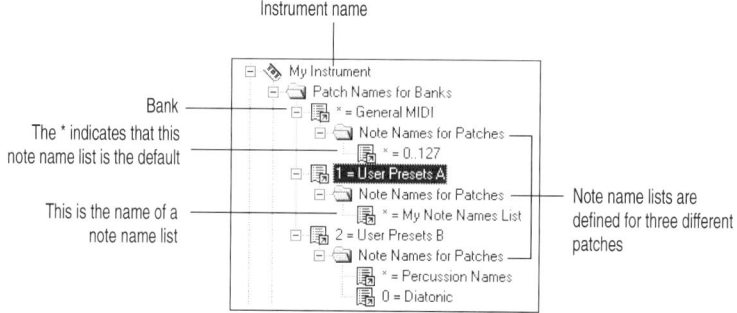

To Change the Note Names for a Patch

1. Drag a note name list from the Names tree onto the Note Names for Patches folder of the instrument and bank you're editing in the Instruments tree.

2. Enter the patch number that should use these note names, or enter –1 to indicate that this list of note names should be used as the default.

SONAR displays the updated patch and note name lists. If necessary, SONAR adds a new patch to the instrument definition.

To Remove a Note Name List

1. In the Instrument tree in the Note Names for Patches folder of the instrument you're editing, highlight the name of the note names list (for example, "diatonic").

2. Press the Del key, or right-click on the note name list and choose **Delete** from the popup menu.

To Set or Clear the Drum Flag

- Right-click on the patch in the Instrument tree, and choose **Drums** from the menu.

Assigning Controller, RPN, and NRPN Names

SONAR lets each instrument have its own lists of controller names, RPN names, and NRPN names. There is always exactly one list of each type per instrument.

To See the Controller, RPN, and NRPN Name Lists

1. Expand the instrument definition by clicking the + sign next to the instrument name.

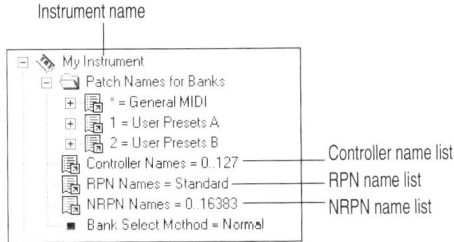

To Change the Controller, RPN, or NRPN Name List

1. In the Names tree, expand the branch containing the Controller name lists, RPN name lists, or NRPN name lists.

2. Drag the desired name list from the Names tree onto the corresponding branch of the Instrument tree.

SONAR displays the updated Controller, RPN, or NRPN name lists.

UsesNotesAsControllers=n

Some MIDI devices, certain mixers for example, use MIDI Note events instead of Continuous Controller events for automation. It is often desirable to treat the Note events as Controller events in order for them to obey the "Zero Controllers When Play Stops" and "Patch/Controller Searchback Before Play Starts" settings.

You can enter this variable in any instrument definition by using a text editor, such as Windows Notepad. The variable should be entered directly below an instrument definition. For example:

[Mackie OTTO-1604]

UsesNotesAsControllers=1

Control=Mackie OTTO-1604

Patch[*]=Mackie OTTO-1604

Key[*,*]=Mackie OTTO-1604

NoControllerReset=n

Any port/channel using an instrument definition that has a NoControllerReset flag set to 1 does not receive a "zero controller" message upon stop. You can enter this variable in any instrument definition by using a text editor, such as Windows Notepad. The variable should be entered directly below an instrument definition. For example:

[Yamaha Promix 01 Control Chan]

NoControllerReset=1

Control=Yamaha Promix 01 Control Chan

Patch[*]=Yamaha Pro Mix 01

This parameter should be used when it is undesirable to zero/reset controllers when playback stop, such as when using an external effects processor that uses MIDI controllers for real-time parameter control, or when using a digital mixer as a MIDI control surface (and not using the generic control surface plug-in).

Instrument Definition Tutorial

The following tutorial takes you through the process of setting up an instrument definition for a Roland keyboard so that the bank and patch names, including any self-created sounds, read the same in Sonar as they do on the display screen of your keyboard instrument.

Why Use Instrument Definitions?

The main reason to import or create an instrument definition is so you can use patch names that are specific to the MIDI module you're using, instead of using generic General MIDI patch names. It's much easier to find a particular sound on a MIDI module when the actual names of the patches in the current bank of sounds pop up on a list, instead of just the numbers 0 to 127, or General MIDI names like Trumpet. Of course, if you're only using General MIDI modules, General MIDI patch names might be all you need. You can also rename each MIDI output with the name of the MIDI module it's connected to. For example, it might be more meaningful to name a MIDI output Roland Sound Canvas instead of MOTU MIDI Express 5. That way, you won't have to remember that you connected the Sound Canvas to the MOTU MIDI Express output number 5—the name Sound Canvas shows up as an option in the Output field of each MIDI track in SONAR's track view. Also if you have an effects processor or module that's hard to get to in your studio, you may find it convenient to control it from SONAR.

What Can They Do and Not Do?

Instrument definitions don't increase the number of sounds or the capabilities of your modules, they just make it easier to find and remember the sounds and/or MIDI controllers you want to use, if they're not all generic General MIDI items. After you define an instrument, SONAR displays the names that you choose for the sounds in each of that instrument's banks, rather than displaying the same 128 General MIDI names over and over for each bank of sounds.

Where Do Instrument Definitions Come From?

The patch names and other characteristics of each particular MIDI module are supplied by the manufacturer, and are contained in an instrument definition file, which is a text file written in a format SONAR can read. Many of these files come with SONAR, and many more are available at Cakewalk's web site, and also at lilchips.com. Instrument definition files have the extension .INS and can contain a definition for only one instrument, or definitions for several instruments. For example, the file ROLAND.INS contains definitions for many Roland modules. The file MISC.INS contains miscellaneous definitions that might include your instrument if you don't see a specific file for it. You can find these files in your SONAR folder. The file MASTER.INS contains all the instrument definitions currently loaded into SONAR, and determines the list of instruments that appears in the Assign Instruments dialog box.

Start of Tutorial

Let's say you have a Roland XP-10 and you want SONAR to display all of its patch names from all of its banks, including any self-created sounds you add to it.

Let's start by importing the names of the built-in banks and patches that the XP-10 has.

To Import a Roland Instrument Definition

1. Choose **Options-Instruments** to display the Assign Instruments dialog box.
2. Click Define to display the Define Instruments and Names dialog box.
3. Click Import to display the Import Instrument Definitions dialog box.
4. Choose the file that contains instrument definitions for your manufacturer, which in this case is the ROLAND.INS file, and click Open. SONAR displays a list of all the instrument definitions in the file.
5. Scroll down the list, select the Roland XP-10, and click OK.
6. Click Close to close the Define Instruments and Names dialog box.

The instrument definition you imported should now appear in the Uses Instrument list in the Assign Instruments dialog box.

When you import an instrument definition, it is added to the master instrument definition file MASTER.INS. The contents of this file determines the list of instruments that appear in the Assign Instruments dialog box.

Now let's assign the XP-10 definition to some channels on a MIDI output:

To Assign the Roland XP-10 Bank and Patch Names to a MIDI Output

1. Choose **Options-Instruments** to display the Assign Instruments dialog box.
2. Let's assign all 16 MIDI channels on output 1 to use the XP-10 bank and patch names:

    - Drag through the first 16 items in the Port/Channel list to select them.
    - From the Uses Instrument list, click Roland XP-10. A black line connects the two lists.

3. To save these changes permanently, enable the Save Changes for Next Session option.
4. Click OK to apply your changes.

From now on, any track that uses any of channels 1 to 16 on output 1 displays bank and patch names from the XP-10.

To check this, assign a MIDI track in a project to Ch 1, assign the Output field to 1-Roland XP-10, and then examine the dropdown lists in the Bnk and Pch fields of the track. You should see bank and patch names that are specific to the Roland XP-10.

Let's check some of our bank and patch lists to see if they match up with what we see on the screen of the XP-10. On the XP-10, let's look at the Vari 1 bank: if we look at tone (tone means the same as patch) #005 in the Vari 1 bank on the XP-10, we see that it is called Detuned EP1. If we change the bank on a MIDI track to 128-Roland XP-10 Var #01, and look at the menu of patches in the Pch field, we see that there is no name listed for patch #004 (Roland numbers its patches from 1 to

128; SONAR numbers patches from 0 to 127, so patch #004 in SONAR is the same patch number as patch #005 on the Roland). Let's look at some of the other Roland XP-10 patch name lists in the right window of the Define Instruments and Names dialog box to see if another one has the right patch names in it, and rename it Var #01.

To Substitute and Rename a Patch List

1. Use the *Options-Instruments* command to open the Assign Instruments dialog box, and click the Define button to open the Define Instruments and Names dialog box.

2. In the Names Tree window on the right, click the + sign on the Patches folder to expand the tree of patch name lists.

3. Scroll down to the Roland XP-10 Var #08 list and click its + sign to expand it.

4. Compare the names on the Var #08 list with the patch names of the Vari 1 instruments on the Roland's display screen. You'll see they are the same.

5. Let's substitute the Var #08 list for the Var #01 list that SONAR currently lists as the XP-10's second bank, which has a bank change number of 128:

    - In the Instruments tree in the left window, click the Roland XP-10 entry to expand it, and then expand the Patch Names for Banks list that's directly under it.

    - Expand the Patch Names tree in the right window and find the Roland XP-10 Var #01 list (if there is one) and right-click it to display the popup menu.

    - Choose *Edit* from the popup menu, and change the name from Roland XP-10 Var #01 to Roland XP-10 Var #011.

    - In the same tree find the Roland XP-10 Var #08 list and change the name from Roland XP-10 Var #08 to Roland XP-10 Var #01.

    - Drag the newly renamed list from the Patch Names tree in the right window to the Patch Names for Banks tree in the left window.

    - In the Bank Number dialog box, enter 128, and click OK.

6. Click the Close button to close the Define Instruments and Names dialog box and click OK to close the Assign Instruments and Names dialog box.

Examine the new bank and patch data in a track that uses 1-Roland XP-10 as an output. In the Bnk field, select 128 Roland XP-10 Var #01, then look at the dropdown list of patches in the Pch field. The list should now have the same names that the Roland keyboard uses for its Vari 1 bank.

The Roland XP-10, like most MIDI keyboards, allows you to create your own sounds and store them in one or more User banks. You can create patch name lists in SONAR that are the same as the names you gave to each of your own sounds.

Checking Bank Numbers

You can calculate bank numbers by using the methods described in "Assigning the Bank Select Method" on page 577, but you might find it easier to use the following method:

To Check the Bank Numbers

1. Set up a MIDI track to record from your MIDI keyboard or module.

2. Click the Record button to start recording, and change banks on your keyboard.

3. Stop recording, and open the Event List view.

4. The bank change you recorded is displayed in the Event List view in this way: in the Data column you'll see what kind of bank change method your keyboard uses (probably Normal), and in the column to the right of that data is the number of the bank you changed to.

When we changed the Roland XP-10 to the User 1 bank, we recorded a bank number of 8192.

To Create a Patch Name List for Your Own Sounds

1. You could create a new list by copying and renaming an existing list (right-click a list and choose **New Patch Name List** from the popup menu), but since the instrument definition we imported for the XP-10 includes a list called Roland XP-10 User Tone 1, let's just edit that one: in the Names Tree window on the right, right-click the Roland XP-10 User Tone 1 list and choose **Add Patch Name** from the popup menu.

   A new patch field appears, with the text "0 = 0" inside.

2. Replace the first number in the patch field with the number of a patch you stored in User Bank 1 on the Roland.

3. Replace the second number in the patch field with the name you made up for the patch you just gave a number to, and press Enter.

4. Assign names to as many patch numbers as you want—the numbers between 0 and 127 that you don't assign any names to show up in the Track view Pch column just as patch numbers with no other names.

5. When you finish assigning names, drag your edited patch list to the Roland XP-10 Patch Names for Banks tree in the left window.

6. Enter 8192 as the bank number, which we know is the correct bank number from the previous procedure.

7. Click the Close button to close the Define Instruments and Names dialog box and click OK to close the Assign Instruments and Names dialog box.

Now you can select the 8192-Roland XP-10 User Tone 1 bank in the Bnk field of a MIDI track, and then examine the patch list in the Pch field: you should see the patch list that you just created.

Using System Exclusive Data

SONAR™'s System Exclusive (Sysx) librarian provides you with 8192 banks in which to hold MIDI System Exclusive messages. A **bank** is a storage area plus some associated parameters such as a destination output and an optional description. Each bank can hold any number of messages; the amount of data it can hold is limited only by available memory. The banks are saved in the SONAR project file. Each bank can also be saved as a .SYX file.

In This Chapter

What Is System Exclusive?	588
Using the System Exclusive View	588
Sending Sysx Banks at Startup	589
Importing, Creating, and Dumping Sysx Banks	590
Editing Sysx Banks	593
Sysx View Buttons	593
Transmitting Banks During Playback	595
Real-time Recording of System Exclusive Messages	596
Sysx Echo	596
Sysx .INI File Settings	597
Troubleshooting	598

What Is System Exclusive?

System Exclusive data is MIDI's way of letting each synthesizer manufacturer transmit private data about its products. A System Exclusive message has a manufacturer ID; the rest of the message is completely proprietary and varies for each manufacturer, even for each of its products. SONAR does not understand what this data means; it simply can hold onto it for you. You can take snapshots of your equipment's configuration and store them in SONAR's System Exclusive banks for transmitting back to the equipment. You may want to do this simply to back up your equipment's patches and/or settings, much like backing up your computer's hard drive in case something goes wrong. Or you may configure your equipment differently for each project's requirements, which is why storing System Exclusive banks with each SONAR project file can be useful. Of course, for merely backing up your equipment, you can have a project containing only System Exclusive data and no notes.

Sysx Events

SONAR provides two distinct kinds of Sysx events: **Sysx Bank** and **Sysx Data**.

- **Sysx Bank:** You can use Sysx Bank events to transmit one of the project's 8192 banks of System Exclusive data. These banks can be recorded, viewed, and edited in the Sysx view, and each bank can contain one or more very large System Exclusive messages. Sysx Banks may also be marked Auto, so that they are sent when the file is loaded rather than during the start of playback.

- **Sysx Data:** You can also use Sysx Data events, which can each contain a single System Exclusive message up to 255 bytes long. You can view the message bytes in the Event List view.

Sysx Data events can be recorded in real time. See "Real-time Recording of System Exclusive Messages" on page 596 for more information.

Using the System Exclusive View

The System Exclusive view has a list box for a maximum of 256 Sysx banks, plus a toolbar of buttons. Most of the buttons affect whatever bank you have selected in the list. Certain buttons will be disabled if the selected bank is empty. To open the System Exclusive view, choose the *Sysx* command from the *View* menu, or click the Sysx view icon in the Views toolbar.

SONAR stores Sysx messages as either Sysx banks or Sysx data. The main difference is in the number of bytes in the message, and also that Sysx data is only visible in the Event List view as SysxData events. A Sysx data message can have up to 255 bytes in it. You can send Sysx data to an instrument without interrupting playback (depending on the speed of your computer and the number of bytes in the message), however, sending a Sysx bank stops playback until all of the Sysx bank is transmitted. Sysx banks are usually sent to your instrument when you load your work file. SONAR asks you each time you load a project file if you want to send any existing Sysx banks the file contains that are marked for auto-sending. Clicking the Auto Send Bank button ⬆ in the Sysx view toolbar marks or unmarks a selected bank for auto-sending.

Sending Sysx Banks at Startup

You can tell SONAR to send certain Sysx banks to your instrument(s) each time you open the project file that the banks are in.

To Send Sysx Banks at Startup

1. In the Sysx view, select a bank that you want to send to an instrument when you open the current project.

   SONAR highlights the bank you select.

2. Click the Auto Send Bank button ⬆.

   A checkmark appears next to the bank name in the Auto column to show that the bank is marked for auto-sending.

3. While the bank is still highlighted, click the Output button to open the Sysx Bank Output dialog.

4. Enter the number of the output you want to send this bank out through, and click OK.

   The output number you entered appears next to the selected bank in the Output column.

5. Repeat steps 1-4 for each bank you want to send, and save your project.

The next time you open a project, SONAR asks you if you want to send any Sysx banks in the project that are marked for auto-sending. If you click OK, SONAR sends the bank(s).

If you want SONAR to send auto-send banks every time you open a project without asking you, uncheck the checkbox in the Auto-Send Sysx dialog that says Ask this question every time. If you decide later that you want to be asked, use the **Options-Global** command to open the Global Options dialog, click the General tab, and check the checkbox that says Ask Before Sending System Exclusive (When Opening Projects).

Importing, Creating, and Dumping Sysx Banks

There are several ways to get a sysx bank into SONAR:

- You can import (load) an external .SYX file.
- You can edit an empty bank to create a new bank from scratch.
- You can dump a bank into SONAR from the synthesizer itself.

To Import a Sysx Bank into a Project

1. In the Sysx view, select an empty bank to import the new bank into (unless you want to add to or overwrite an existing bank).
2. Click the Load Bank from File button .

    The Open dialog appears.

3. If necessary, navigate to the folder that contains your .SYX files, select the one you want to import, and click Open.

The file appears as a new bank in the row you selected in the Sysx view. If you want SONAR to send this bank every time you open this project, make sure the bank is selected (highlighted), and click the Auto Send Bank button . A checkmark appears in the Auto column next to all auto-send-enabled banks.

To Create a Sysx Bank

1. In the Sysx view, select an empty bank, and click the Edit Data button (or double-click the empty bank).

    The Edit System Exclusive Bytes window appears.

2. Type your message(s). Each message you add to the window must begin with F0 and end with F7 (that's F zero and F seven). See your instrument's manual for the messages you can create.
3. When you finish typing the message(s), click OK to close the window.

After you close the editing window, your new bank appears in the Sysx view. Use the buttons in the toolbar to name it, give it an output number, and mark it for auto-sending, if you want. Save your project when you're finished.

To Dump a Sysx Bank into SONAR

1. Choose **Options-Global** and click the MIDI tab, and make sure that the System Exclusive item is checked. If it isn't, SONAR won't receive System Exclusive messages.

2. In the Sysx view, select an empty bank to dump the new bank into (unless you want to add to or overwrite an existing bank).

3. Click the Receive Bank button ⬇ (or press *c* on your computer keyboard).

   The Receive System Exclusive dialog appears, which contains a list of Dump Request Macros (DRMs). Each DRM has a name that describes the synthesizer the DRM controls and the type of data that the DRM asks the synthesizer to send.

4. Do one of the following:

   - If the name of your instrument and the kind of data you want to store in SONAR appears in the list, select your choice and click OK.

   - If your instrument and the type of data you want to record are not in the list, select You start dump on instrument, click OK, and press whatever button on your synthesizer that starts a Sysx bank dump. The You start dump on instrument option is not really a Dump Request Macro. It tells SONAR that you will initiate a dump (or multiple dumps) from the front panel of the synthesizer.

5. The DRM may prompt you for additional information, which you should supply.

   - **Patch number:** DRMs that are written to request an individual patch or configuration give you this prompt, so you can specify the one you want to have dumped.

     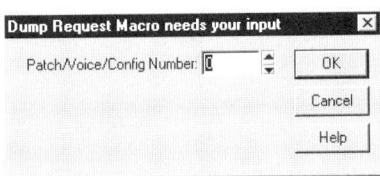

   - **Channel/unit number:** Most synthesizers have a Sysx channel or unit number. This covers the situation in which you own two of the exact same synthesizer, and want to do Sysx with each independently. Your synthesizer manual should describe the factory-set number.

     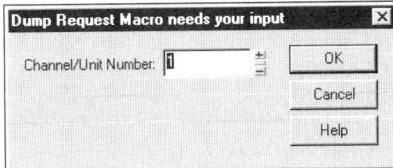

When your instrument starts sending the bank, the Sysx Receive window counts the bytes as SONAR receives them. If the count stays at zero for more than a couple of seconds, something is wrong. The synthesizer may not be hooked up to the MIDI interface in both directions, or you may have answered a DRM prompt incorrectly. Click Cancel. If any data were received, you will see the number of bytes in the bank list.

6. Once the bytes received count stops increasing, you can click Done to tell SONAR to stop receiving. However, if your synthesizer also displays a message when the instrument is finished sending a bank, wait until that message says the transmission is finished before you click Done.

The currently selected bank now holds the received Sysx data. At this point, you may want to give the bank a descriptive name by selecting it and clicking abc.

Note:

The SONAR librarian may not support synthesizers that require handshaking dump protocols. Some of these synthesizers have a backup protocol where they will do a normal dump if they don't get a handshake. Others do not.

More about Dump Request Macros

DRMs are defined in your DRM.INI file in the [Dump Request Macros] section. You may add your own DRMs or modify the ones that we have provided. Use the Windows Notepad to edit the file. Comments in the DRM.INI file itself describe how to write DRMs. The specific Sysx messages can be found in the instrument manual, or they can be obtained by contacting the manufacturer. Remember that a DRM must start with F0 and end with F7.

Sometimes you will find that the byte size is different when you use a DRM, as opposed to initiating the dump from the instrument. It is possible the instrument is dumping some additional information when you initiate the dump from the instrument, but you should be able to use either method without any problems.

When you press the Receive button in the Sysx window, you may pick from a list of Dump Request Macros. These are short System Exclusive messages sent to a synthesizer to make it dump (send back) System Exclusive data. DRMs are defined in your CAKEWALK.INI file in the [Dump Request Macros] section. You may add your own DRMs or modify the ones that we have provided. Use the Windows Notepad to edit the file.

Please note that many of the DRMs included with SONAR have been donated by customers who are using the particular equipment. In some cases, we have not been able to test those DRMs because we do not have access to that equipment. We redistribute such DRMs on an as-is basis. Additional user-supplied DRMs may be available on the Cakewalk web site (www.cakewalk.com).

Editing Sysx Banks

Editing a Sysx bank is very similar to creating one.

To Edit a Sysx Bank
1. In the Sysx view, select the bank you want to edit, and click the Edit Data button (or double-click the selected bank).

   The Edit System Exclusive Bytes window appears.

2. Edit your message(s). Each message in the window must begin with F0 and end with F7 (that's F zero and F seven). See your instrument's manual for the messages you can create.

3. When you finish editing the message(s), click OK to close the window.

Save your project when you're finished.

Sysx View Buttons

Here is a description of the buttons in the Sysx view.

Send
Send transmits the current bank's System Exclusive message. If nothing seems to happen, make sure you have correctly set the output (see later in this chapter). This button is disabled if the current bank is empty. The shortcut key is *s.*

Send All
Send All transmits all non-empty banks. The shortcut key is *l.*

Receive
Receive dumps data from a synthesizer into the bank. If the bank contains data, SONAR asks you whether you want the new data to overwrite the existing data or be appended to it. The shortcut key is *c.*

When receiving dumps, remember to connect both the MIDI In and Out ports of the synthesizer to the MIDI interface. Also, make sure that your instruments are set up to receive and/or transmit Sysx. Synthesizers that you normally use only to play sounds—for example, sound modules that don't have keyboards—don't need to be hooked up in both directions except for receiving dumps, so it is easy to forget this. (If you will only be *sending* Sysx messages to the device, the normal one-direction hookup is sufficient.)

Clear Bank ⊠
This deletes the selected bank. The shortcut key is *d*.

Name
You may enter a description for a bank by clicking this button. *Names are saved only in* .CWP *and* .CWB *files*. The shortcut key is *n*.

Auto
The Auto option tells SONAR to transmit that bank every time it loads the project file. You might use this option for banks that contain System Exclusive messages that load a set of sounds for a synthesizer at or before the start of a project.

Before transmitting, SONAR asks your permission. This is a safety feature for loading a file you have received from someone else; if it happens to contain data for your synthesizer(s), you might lose your patches and configuration information. However, if you don't want to be asked, choose **Options-Global**, click the General tab, and uncheck the box labeled Ask Before Sending Sysx. The shortcut key is *a*.

Output
Each bank is transmitted to a particular MIDI output, just as a track is. Click this button to change the output. The shortcut key is *p*.

Edit Bytes
Although SONAR**'s Sysx features are** designed mainly to store System Exclusive data for you, you can edit the bytes of shorter messages in hex format (many of the more popular synthesizers have special patch-editing programs available that let you edit data using sliders and other tools rather than raw hex data).

When you select a bank and click the Edit Bytes button, SONAR converts the binary data into a text representation and pops up the Edit System Exclusive Bytes dialog box, in which you can edit the text. If you make changes and click OK to keep them, SONAR tries to convert the text back into binary format. You'll get an error message if the text does not begin with an F0 and end with an F7, which are the System Exclusive begin and end bytes.

SONAR may not be able to convert the data to text format. The text representation requires three to four times more memory than the data itself, and the Edit System Exclusive Bytes dialog box can contain roughly as much text as *Notepad*. The shortcut key is *e*.

Load Bank and Save Bank
You can import banks from and save banks to files with the file extension .SYX. If you try to import to a bank that isn't empty, SONAR asks if you want to append or replace. The Load and Save buttons work only with .SYX, not SONAR project files or MIDI files.

You may also use this feature to copy a Sysx bank between two SONAR project files. Save the bank into a file, load the other SONAR project file, then load the bank again. This is also a good way to copy one bank to another in the *same* project file. The shortcut keys are *o* and *v* respectively.

To Export a Sysx Bank to Another Project

1. In the Sysx view, select the bank you want to export.
2. Click the Save Bank button .

    The Save As dialog appears.
3. Navigate to the folder in which you want to store the file.
4. Enter a file name and click OK.

    SONAR saves the file in the location you specified, with the extension .SYX.
5. Open the project to which you want to import the bank and select an empty bank in the Sysx view (unless you want to add the file to an existing bank).
6. Click the Load Bank from File button to open the Open dialog.
7. Navigate to the desired folder, select the .SYX file you want to import, and click Open.

    SONAR loads the selected bank into the current project.

Transmitting Banks During Playback

SONAR has a special meta-event, Sysx Bank, that lets you play a System Exclusive bank at a specified time in your project. You can use a Sysx meta-event to send any of the 8192 available Sysx banks at any time in a sequence. To do this, you have to insert a new event in the Event List using the Insert key on the PC keyboard. Next you have to double-click Event Kind and change it to System Exclusive. In the Values column, select the bank (0-8191) that you want to send.

MIDI is a serial data transmission, meaning it can do only one thing at a time. If you try to upload a huge sampler dump during a fast drum solo, playback will noticeably lurch. MIDI must complete the System Exclusive message before it can resume playback. The Sysx meta-event is appropriate only for very short System Exclusive messages. The exact length depends on various factors, such as the speed of your computer but as a rule of thumb, 100 bytes is a likely maximum, and even that may often be too large.

You don't need to use Sysx meta-events for sending System Exclusive information at the beginning of your project. Instead, use the Auto option for System Exclusive banks. Banks that are marked Auto are transmitted automatically by SONAR when it loads the project file they are stored in. Use the Sysx meta-event only when you need to send a Sysx Bank during the middle of the project.

Real-time Recording of System Exclusive Messages

You can record short System Exclusive messages in real time. These will end up in the track as the new Sysx Data types of events, which can hold System Exclusive messages up to 255 bytes long. Before you record any Sysx messages, choose **Options-Global**, click the MIDI tab, and make sure that System Exclusive is checked.

To Record Sysx Messages in Real Time
1. Arm a MIDI track for recording—use a track that's uses the output you want to send the Sysx data out through.
2. Press the Record button or press *r* to start recording.
3. Move the button or fader on your MIDI instrument that sends Sysx data.
4. Stop recording.

SONAR records your instrument's Sysx data as a Sysx Data event. Open up the Event List view for the track you recorded on to view the data. When you play back the MIDI track that the Sysx Data event is on, make sure that the Output field of the track is set to the output that the MIDI instrument you want to send Sysx data to is on.

Sysx Echo

You can configure SONAR to echo received System Exclusive messages to output devices.

To Echo Sysx Messages
1. Choose **Options-Global**.
2. Select the MIDI tab.
3. Check the Echo System Exclusive option.
4. Click OK.

SONAR echoes received Sysx data according to the echo settings on the MIDI Input tab of the Project Options dialog box.

Sysx .INI File Settings

The TTSSEQ.INI initialization file contains settings that govern the sending and receiving of System Exclusive information. If you are experiencing difficulties using Sysx, you will probably be able to correct the problem by adjusting these settings.

The options described below occur in the [Options] section of the TTSSEQ.INI file. You can edit this file using the Windows Notepad. Every time you add or change one or more lines in TTSSEQ.INI, you must restart SONAR in order for the change to take effect.

SysxSendDelayMsecs=n
This setting causes SONAR to delay n milliseconds if it encounters an F7 in a System Exclusive bank, but only if the line SysxDelayAfterF7=n is not zero. The line SysxDelayAfterF7=n enables a delay between Sysx messages, while the line SysxSendDelayMsecs=n sets the size of the delay.

n = 60 Default value (in milliseconds)

SysxDelayAfterF7=n
This setting causes SONAR to delay Sysx transmission for a certain amount of time if it encounters an F7 in a System Exclusive bank. This gives some instruments the required amount of "breathing" time necessary to process the Sysx transmission. The default delay is 1/18 of a second, but can be changed by also adding the SysxSendDelayMsecs=n line, where n is the number of milliseconds that the delay lasts.

The possible values of n in the line SysxDelayAfterF7=n are 0 and 1. Their significance is as follows:

n = 0 No delay

n = 1 Delay between each Sysx message

SysxSendPacketSize=n
System Exclusive bytes are transmitted in packets, with a 1/18-second default delay between each packet. Setting this value to a smaller number will help slower synthesizers avoid overflowing their internal buffers. This line sets the number of bytes between each Sysx transmit delay.

n = 1024 Default value (in bytes)

Troubleshooting

SONAR Is Not Receiving Sysx Messages
- Make sure all your devices are connected correctly.
- Make sure you have the right MIDI Input selected by using the **Options-MIDI Devices** command.
- Make sure that your instrument is set up to transmit System Exclusive data.

Sysx Bank Names Don't Show When I Open a File
Sysx bank names are only saved in .CWP and .CWB files (not in .MID files).

SONAR Doesn't Include a DRM for My Instrument
If there is no Dump Request Macro (DRM) for your instrument, you should select You start dump on instrument, then initiate the Sysx dump from the instrument. Once the bytes received count stops increasing, click Done to tell SONAR to stop receiving. The currently selected bank now holds the received Sysx data. You can rename the bank if you want by selecting the bank and clicking the Name button.

You can also add a DRM for any unlisted instrument. For more information on how to do this, read the section "More about Dump Request Macros" on page 592 earlier in this chapter.

Synthesizers Reporting MIDI Data Errors
Some synthesizers will report data errors when you try to send Sysx information to them. This usually happens when SONAR sends data at a rate too fast for the synthesizer to keep up. You can use the SysxSendPacketSize=number setting in TTSSEQ.INI to make SONAR transmit Sysx data more slowly, as described in Sysx .INI File Settings.

Try setting the number to 64. If that does not solve the problem, try successively smaller values. If 64 works, you may try larger values until it stops working; go back to the largest value that worked and you will have the fastest transmission rate that the problematic synthesizer can keep up with.

My Equipment Is Not receiving Sysx from SONAR
Make sure the instrument is set up to receive System Exclusive messages. In the Sysx View, make sure the right output is selected. Verify that the Sysx message originally transmitted from the same kind of instrument. An instrument will not recognize Sysx messages from a different make or model of instrument.

Finally, try adjusting the parameters in the TTSSEQ.INI file, as described earlier in this chapter.

Timing Requirements When Receiving Sysx

Some MIDI devices have special timing requirements when receiving System Exclusive transmissions. If your equipment has problems receiving System Exclusive data from SONAR, you might need to introduce some small delays to allow the equipment to digest the information it is receiving.

The line in TTSSEQ.INI that reads SysxDelayAfterF7=n enables SONAR to introduce a delay between each Sysx message so that the instrument has some time to respond to the message. Setting n to be 1 enables the delay. The line SysxSendDelayMsecs=n lets you control how many milliseconds the delay is, where n is the number of milliseconds that the delay lasts.

Roland Equipment

Some Roland equipment—notably, the GR-1 and GR-50 Guitar Synthesizers—have problems receiving Sysx packets in fast succession. You must use the setting SysxDelayAfterF7 = 1 with these devices.

Ensoniq Instruments

Successfully sending Sysx messages to most Ensoniq instruments requires that you add the following three lines to the [Options] section of TTSSEQ.INI:

SysxDelayAfterF7=1	Enables delay
SysxSendDelayMsecs=200	Sets delay time to 200 milliseconds
SysxSendPacketSize=65535	Increases packet size to 64k

600

18 Synchronizing Your Gear

Your computer is often used with other equipment: sound cards, MIDI equipment, and digital tape decks or other digital recording tools. All these devices can have their own built-in clocks or timing mechanisms.

When several pieces of equipment are used together, it's important that they operate in synchronization. For this to happen, all the equipment must rely on the same source of clock or timing information. SONAR™ lets you use many different types of synchronization so that you can get your work done quickly and efficiently.

In This Chapter

Synchronization Overview 602
Choosing Clock Sources When SONAR is the Master 603
MIDI Synchronization 604
SMPTE/MIDI Time Code Synchronization 608
MIDI Machine Control (MMC) 615

Synchronization Overview

SONAR supports several different types of synchronization, which rely on a variety of different clock sources:

Clock source...	Timing is determined by...
Internal	The clock on the computer motherboard
Audio	The clock on the computer's sound card
MIDI Sync	The clock on an external MIDI device
SMPTE/MIDI Time Code (MTC)	A time code signal (in SMPTE or some other format) recorded on some external medium **or generated and sent by SONAR**

When you use either the internal or audio clock, SONAR can control other MIDI devices using MIDI Sync. In this case, SONAR is the "master" device and the other MIDI devices are the "slaves."

When MIDI Sync is the clock source, SONAR operates either in response to incoming MIDI messages or as the sender. In this case, SONAR can be either the master or the slave. Note that audio playback is not supported when using MIDI Sync with SONAR as the slave.

When SMPTE/MIDI Time Code (SMPTE/MTC) is the source of timing information, SONAR operates in response to incoming MTC messages. These messages could be generated by:

- An external MIDI device that is capable of generating MIDI Time Code (like the Roland VS880)

- A MIDI interface that is converting other time code signals (like SMPTE, EBU, or film time code) into MIDI Time Code

When you use some of these synchronization options, some SONAR commands work differently. This chapter describes each of the synchronization options, how and why each is useful, and the effect each option has on other features and commands.

The Sync toolbar lets you change back and forth quickly between the different clock settings:

You can also choose the sync mode as follows:

1. Choose **Options-Project**, and click the Clock tab.
2. Choose the desired clock source from the Clock list.
3. Click OK.

The clock source and the type of synchronization that is used are options that are stored as part of your project files. For example, one of your projects might be set up to use the internal clock; a second might use the Audio clock and MIDI Sync with SONAR as the master timing source; and another might use SMPTE/MTC Sync as the clock source.

Many technical support requests concern synchronization problems, which are among the hardest to diagnose and duplicate over the phone. If you experience problems, before you call, perform as much experimentation and gather as much information as possible about what does and doesn't work. The more prepared you are, the more we can help.

Choosing Clock Sources When SONAR is the Master

When SONAR is used alone, or with an external device that does not have its own clock or timing signal, you use one of two clock sources: Internal or Audio.

When the clock source is set to Internal, SONAR uses the clock built into the computer or the computer's MIDI interface as its timing source. If your projects contain only MIDI (no audio), this is the most efficient method of playback.

If your projects contain MIDI and audio, or only audio, you should set the clock source to Audio. This lets the sound card clock determine the correct speed for audio playback and automatically synchronizes MIDI playback to match the audio. For more information, see "System Configuration" on page 628. You cannot use the tempo ratio controls when using the audio clock, because the audio playback speed is determined by the audio clock.

When either of these clock sources is used, you can also configure SONAR to drive other MIDI devices using MIDI Synchronization. For more information, see "MIDI

Synchronization" on page 604. If you need to send MIDI Time Code (MTC), SONAR will send this data regardless of the clock setting.

To Use the Internal Clock Source

1. Click ▣ on the Sync toolbar.

   OR

1. Choose **Options-Project**, and click the Clock tab.

2. Check the Internal box.

3. Click OK.

To Use the Audio Clock Source

1. Click ✦ on the Sync toolbar.

   OR

   Choose **Options-Project**, and click the Clock tab.

2. Check the Audio box.

3. Click OK.

MIDI Synchronization

MIDI Synchronization, or **MIDI Sync**, is usually used to synchronize SONAR with drum machines, stand-alone MIDI hardware sequencers, and sequencers built into MIDI keyboards. SONAR can slave to MIDI Sync, and can send MIDI Sync on multiple output ports.

When MIDI devices are synched, the master device sends messages to all other devices to start and stop playback and to keep all the devices in sync. To change the tempo of a project, you adjust the tempo on the master device. The playback tempo on all slave devices is then set automatically.

The following MIDI messages are sent by the master device to support MIDI Sync:

Message...	How it is used...
Start	This message tells slave devices to start playing from the beginning of the currently loaded sequence.
Stop	This message tells slave devices to stop playback.
Continue	This message tells slave devices to continue playing from the current location in the currently loaded sequence.
Song Position Pointer (SPP)	This message tells slave devices to change the current location to the designated point in the project. SONAR normally issues an SPP message immediately prior to any Start or Continue message.
Clock	The master sends clock messages to each slave device at the rate of 24 per quarter note. The slave devices use these messages to establish the tempo and stay in sync.

When you start playback on the master MIDI device, for example, it sends a Start message to all slave devices, announcing that playback has started. If the slave devices are set up correctly, they receive the message and start playing back with the master device. When SONAR is set up as the master device, you can enable or disable these messages.

SONAR as the Slave

When SONAR is slaved to an external MIDI device, the following changes occur:

- When you click the Play or Record button, a message (Waiting for MIDI Sync) is displayed in the status bar. When you start your external device, SONAR will follow.

- If you change the tempo using an external device, the SMPTE time code display in SONAR will be incorrect.

- SONAR will not transmit MIDI Start, Continue, Stop, and Clock messages.

- Digital audio will play back, but not necessarily in sync.

To Use MIDI Sync with SONAR as the Slave

1. Configure the external MIDI device you want to use as the master device to transmit MIDI Sync.
2. Configure external slave devices to receive MIDI Sync.
3. Choose **Options-MIDI Devices** to display the MIDI Devices dialog box.
4. Make sure that your MIDI interface is highlighted in the Inputs list, and click OK.
5. Click ![] on the Sync toolbar to use the MIDI Sync clock source.

From now on, SONAR starts playback and recording only after the appropriate message is received from the master device.

Tip:
Make sure the Status bar is displayed when using MIDI Sync. Otherwise, you will not be able to see the MIDI Sync status messages. To display the Status bar, choose **Options-Global** and click the General tab. Then check the Show Status Bar box.

SONAR as the Master

There are several options, found on the Sync tab of the Project Options dialog box, which you can use when SONAR is the MIDI Sync master device:

Option...	What it's for...
Transmit MIDI Start/Continue/Stop/Clock	Choosing this option causes SONAR to tell the slave when to start, when to continue, when to stop, and what timing data to go by (SONAR's).
Use Start, Never Continue (greyed out unless above option is checked)	If you are using an external drum machine to repeat a drum pattern or loop, you might always want playback on the drum machine to start at the beginning of the loop. When this option is chosen, SONAR sends a Start message to all slave devices when playback is started, even if you are in the middle of a project. (Normally, SONAR would send a Continue message if playback starts from the middle of a project.)
Transmit MIDI Song Position Pointer (SPP)	When this options is checked, SONAR sends an SPP message before starting or continuing playback. If you are using a drum machine as described previously, you might want to disable this option.

Option...	What it's for...
Locate Delay for SPP Recipient	Some older MIDI devices take a small amount of time to respond to SPP messages. This option causes SONAR to delay briefly after sending an SPP message, to give the slave device time to respond. The delay is in 1/18ths of a second. Enter 1 for a 1/18th second delay, 2 for 2/18ths of a second, or 18 for a full second delay.
MIDI Sync Output Ports	Choose the outputs that your slave devices are connected to

To Use MIDI Sync with SONAR as the Master

1. Configure your external MIDI devices to receive MIDI Sync.
2. Click ▢ or ✹ on the Sync toolbar to use the Internal or Audio clock source.
3. Choose **Options-Project**, and click the Sync tab.
4. Check the Transmit MIDI Start/Continue/Stop/Clock box.
5. For most applications, check the Transmit MIDI Song Position Pointer box.
6. If you are using a drum machine to play patterns or loops, check the Use Start, Never Continue option and disable the Transmit MIDI Song Position Pointer option.
7. In the MIDI Sync Output Ports field, check off the output ports that you want to send the sync signal out of.
8. Click OK.

From now on, the transport controls in SONAR control playback on the external MIDI devices.

Using MIDI Sync with Drum Machines

The most flexible way to use a MIDI drum machine is to record the notes it generates into SONAR, then use that machine as a MIDI playback device. This lets you edit, cut, paste, and copy your drum parts like any other clip. You can use MIDI Sync to record the notes from the drum machine into SONAR as follows:

1. Use the drum machine's pattern-composing facilities to compose your drum part.
2. Configure the drum machine to be a slave device that receives MIDI Sync messages.
3. Configure SONAR to send MIDI Stop/Start/Continue/SPP messages.
4. Record the drum part from SONAR. The drum machine starts automatically when recording begins and stops automatically when you press Stop.
5. Switch the drum machine out of MIDI Sync mode so that it acts simply as a sound-producing module.

Troubleshooting MIDI Sync

If you experience problems with MIDI Sync when SONAR is the master device, verify that your external devices are configured correctly to respond to MIDI Sync. Most devices have a Clock option that should be set to External or MIDI.

If SONAR does not respond to MIDI Sync as a slave device, verify that your external devices are configured correctly to transmit MIDI Sync. Remember that only one external device can be used as the master clock source.

SMPTE/MIDI Time Code Synchronization

SMPTE/MIDI Time Code Sync (SMPTE/MTC) is another method of synchronization that lets SONAR act as a master or slave to external devices. SONAR can send or receive SMPTE/MTC messages to or from external devices that can generate or receive MTC. SONAR can send MTC on multiple output ports simultaneously.

SMPTE/MTC is a position and timing reference that indicates the current location in the project and how quickly the project should be playing. Time code labels the position in a project in hours, minutes, seconds, and frames. The speed of playback is indicated by a **frame rate**.

Time code is recorded onto tape using a device called a time code generator. The process of recording a time code signal onto a track is called **striping**. Normally, the start of a tape stripe has a particular time, expressed in hours, minutes, seconds, and frames. For example, the tape stripe might start at 00:00:00:00, 01:00:00:00, or any other time. The material recorded on the tape usually starts anywhere from 10 seconds to several minutes after the start of the time code. Sometimes, the tape stripe starts at a time like 00:59:50:00, and the material starts 10 seconds later, at 01:00:00:00.

When you create a new SONAR project, by default the project is configured so that the beginning of bar 1 is synchronized with a time code of 00:00:00:00. If the starting point of the material on your tape or external project is not 0, you need to enter an offset to tell SONAR the time code that corresponds to the start of the project.

To Enter an Offset

1. Select *Options-Project*.

    The Project Options dialog appears.

2. Click on the Clock tab.

3. In the Clock tab, enter an offset in the SMPTE/MTC Offset field. To enter an offset of 15 seconds, type 0,0,15 and hit enter. The SMPTE/MTC Offset value should now be 00:00:15:00 or 15 seconds.

Frame Rates

Seven time code frame rates are supported in SONAR, which are normally used for the following types of applications:

External Timecodes...	Cakewalk Setting	Description...
24 frames per second	24 FPS	Used for theatrical film worldwide. Any film in North America or Japan uses this setting.
25 frames per second (EBU timecode)	25 FPS	Used for PAL/SECAM video, video and some film in countries that use 50 Hz wall electricity. This is the setting to use when synchronizing to any European video format.
29.97 frames per second non drop-frame	29.97 FPS NDF	NTSC non-broadcast and short length video in North America and Japan. Some music projects. This setting synchronizes the video perfectly with SONAR, but the sequencer position displayed in the Now Time and Big Time displays will gradually drift and become incorrect over long periods of time. The audio and MIDI synchronization to the external device will not be affected by this discrepancy.
29.97 frames per second drop-frame	29.97 FPS DF	NTSC broadcast and long format video in North America and Japan. This setting synchronizes the video perfectly with SONAR, but the sequencer position displayed in the Now Time and Big Time displays will gradually drift and become incorrect over long periods of time. The audio and MIDI synchronization to the external device will not be affected by this discrepancy.
30 frames per second non drop-frame	30 FPS NDF	Most music projects and some film in North America. This is the best choice for any music project and should be used unless the situation dictates otherwise.
30 frames per second drop-frame	30 FPS DF	Not a standard type of timecode, used rarely for speed correction and transfer problems in tape based systems.

For more information on frame rate time formats, see the documentation for your time code hardware.

Refer to the documentation for your MIDI interface or external MIDI device for additional information about SMPTE/MTC.

To Use SONAR as the Master MTC Generator

1. Configure the clocks on each external device that you want to synchronize to receive SMPTE/MTC. Make sure they're connected to MIDI outputs from your computer or MIDI interface.

2. Click 🖳 or 🔶 on SONAR's Sync toolbar to use the Internal or Audio clock source (to display the Sync toolbar, use the *View-Toolbars-Sync* command).

3. Use the *Options-Project* command to open the Project Options dialog.

4. On the Sync tab, check the Transmit MTC checkbox (you can also click the Transmit MTC button on the Sync toolbar).

5. In the Frame Rate field (it's just below the Transmit MTC checkbox), choose the frame rate that your project uses (see "Frame Rates" on page 609, if necessary).

6. In the MTC Output Ports field, check off the outputs that you want to send MTC on (the outputs your external devices are connected to).

7. Click OK.

SONAR saves your sync and MTC output port settings with your project. However, output ports are saved by their number only, not their name. Their number is determined by the order in which they appear in the MIDI Devices dialog under Outputs (*Options-MIDI Devices* command). If you change the order of devices in this dialog, the MTC output ports in your project will retain the same numbers, but those numbers will now refer to different outputs. Also, if you reduce the number of highlighted outputs in the MIDI Devices dialog, and the MTC ports you chose have higher numbers than what are currently highlighted in the MIDI Devices dialog, SONAR does not substitute new port numbers. Also, SONAR does not send MTC if SONAR's Tempo Ratio buttons are set to any value other than 1.

To Configure SONAR to Sync to SMPTE/MTC

1. Click the SMPTE/MTC mode button in the Sync toolbar.
2. Select *Options-Global* and click on the Timecode tab.
3. Select one of the following options:

    - Ask first, then switch to clock source and start—this option prompts SONAR to alert you when it detects a SMPTE/MTC signal, asks if you want to sync to the incoming signal, and if you respond that you do, switches the clock source and starts to receive the signal.

    - Always switch the clock source and start—SONAR automatically switches to the clock source of the incoming signal and begins to receive the signal.

    - Do not switch clock source, but start if in SMPTE/MTC mode—this option automatically syncs to the incoming signal if SONAR is in SMPTE/MTC mode.

    Note: The final option, Never switch clock source, never start, should never be used if you are attempting to sync to an external clock source.

4. Click OK.
5. Choose *Options-Project*, and click the Clock tab.
6. Choose the frame rate and time offset that are appropriate for your source material.
7. Click OK to close the dialog box.
8. Choose *Options-MIDI Devices* to display the MIDI Devices dialog box.
9. Make sure that your MIDI interface is highlighted in the Inputs list. If your interface also has a Sync driver, highlight that as well, then click OK.

When SONAR is the slave, here's how things work:

- SONAR monitors for a SMPTE/MTC signal. You are able to perform other action in SONAR while waiting for the signal.

- Start playback on the external device. It takes about two seconds for SONAR to lock from the time it receives time code input.

- If the time code is earlier than the start of the project (based on the time code offset), another message (Chasing...) is displayed in the status bar. When the time code reaches the start of the project, SONAR starts to play in sync.

- If the time code is at or after the start of the project, SONAR starts playback as soon as it locks to the time code.

- When the external device stops (or when the time code ends), SONAR will stop.

Note: If you want SONAR to switch its clock source to SMPTE/MTC automatically when SONAR receives a SMPTE/MTC signal, you can choose this option on the Timecode tab of the Global Options dialog.

Playing Digital Audio under SMPTE/MTC Sync

SONAR gives you two choices for controlling audio playback when using time SMPTE/MTC Sync:

Option...	How it works...
Trigger and freewheel	Audio event playback is started (or triggered) at the exact time code, but then the audio plays at its own internal rate (or freewheels). When audio freewheels, it can gradually drift from the time code due to variations in the time code signal.
Full chase lock	The speed of audio event playback is continually adjusted to stay in sync with the time code. If the external clock drifts or changes rate, SONAR adjusts the audio playback speed to stay in sync. This adjustment may introduce slight pitch changes, but those changes will be negligible if the external clock is reasonably steady.

Some digital sound cards (such as the Frontier Design Wavecenter or the Antex Studio Card) have external clock inputs. If you are using one of these cards, and an external clock source like a digital tape deck is the master timing source for the project, choose the Trigger and Freewheel option. The clock input on the audio card guarantees that there is no drift between the time code and audio playback.

To Set the Audio Playback Option

1. Choose *Options-Audio*, and click the Advanced tab.
2. Check the desired option from the Synchronization list.
3. Click OK.

Audio playback under time code sync is handled according to the setting you chose.

SMPTE/MTC Sync and Full Chase Lock

When using SMPTE/MTC Sync with full chase lock, the first time you play any audio the pitch may fluctuate wildly for up to 30 seconds. Also, you may occasionally note the pitch of the audio sounding consistently high or low pitch.

A simple analogy makes this behavior easy to understand: Synchronizing audio to SMPTE/MTC is a lot like trying to get even and stay neck-and-neck with another car on the freeway. If the car is ahead of you, you need to drive faster to catch up to it. If it's behind you, you have to slow until the car catches up to you. Once the two cars are neck-and-neck, you can simply keep going at the same speed, unless the other car changes its speed. If the other car speeds or slows, you must speed or slow too.

The first time you play audio under SMPTE/MTC Sync, the audio clock has to get even with the external clock. This could mean racing ahead, which raises the pitch of the audio, or stepping on the brakes, which lowers the pitch of the audio. These fluctuations continue until SONAR matches its playback speed to the external clock, which usually takes no more than 30 seconds. The stable playback speed, by the way, may be slightly faster or slower than the normal audio playback speed, resulting in a slight change in the pitch of the audio. Here's the best way to address this problem:

- Start each new SONAR session by playing some audio under SMPTE/MTC Sync.

- Let the audio play for 30 seconds or until all audio pitch fluctuations stop.

Once this procedure is complete, SONAR knows the difference in rates between the external time code and the audio clock on your sound card. For the rest of the session, SONAR will start playback closely in sync, without any drastic pitch changes.

If the external timing source were 100 percent stable, the audio would stay in sync with the external clock. Unfortunately, no timing source is perfect. Therefore, every once in a while after playback has started, SONAR may need to vary the playback speed by a tiny amount to stay even with the time code. If the time code signal is unstable (as might be the case from an analog source), these variations can cause noticeable changes in audio pitch, which can in turn cause audible audio distortion.

Troubleshooting SMPTE/MTC Sync

The most common problems with SMPTE/MTC Sync, and ways to correct or avoid them, are shown in the following table:

Problem...	What to do...
The tape is striped incorrectly	Check the tape stripe using your time code generator and, if necessary, restripe the tape.
The MIDI interface isn't producing MIDI Time Code	Use utility programs that come with your MIDI interface to make sure that the time code stripe is being received (sometimes you must enable a Time Code Sync option). Check the MIDI interface settings to make sure that MIDI Time Code is being generated.
The frame rate is set incorrectly	The frame rate on the stripe must match the frame rate you set in SONAR.
The offset is set incorrectly	The offset you enter in SONAR must match the start time of recorded material on the tape.
SONAR is not configured correctly	Verify and/or repeat the steps in "To Configure SONAR to Sync to SMPTE/MTC" on page 611.
Audio playback drifts out of sync with the tape	Enable the Full Chase Lock option, which keeps audio from freewheeling.
SONAR continues playing for up to one full second after the time code stops	Some time code readers tolerate dropouts of up to one second, without affecting playback. When you stop the tape deck, it takes a full second for the reader to realize that this isn't merely a dropout and to signal the end of the time code to SONAR. This does not indicate any problem with time code sync.

MIDI Machine Control (MMC)

MIDI Machine Control (MMC) is a protocol that controls an MMC-equipped remote device via MIDI. SONAR lets you use MMC to start and stop playback and recording on remote MIDI devices such as tape decks, video recorders, and even other software packages. If you have several MMC-controllable devices in your studio, assign each a unique Unit ID so that MMC commands can be addressed to a particular device.

MMC is very powerful when used with MIDI Time Code sync. For example, suppose you have an MMC-equipped digital tape deck that generates time code and want to use the tape deck as the timing master for a project. You can set up your equipment and software so that the transport controls in SONAR send MMC messages to the tape deck, which in turn starts and stops playback in SONAR via SMPTE/MTC Sync. In this configuration, SONAR's transport buttons (Play, Record, and Stop) are simply remote control substitutes for the buttons on your tape deck. In this type of configuration, you must choose one MMC-controllable device as the time code master.

When MMC is enabled, press Play to start playback on all connected MMC devices, and press Stop to stop all connected devices. If you press Record while playback is underway, all connected MMC devices (e.g., tape decks) begin recording on any armed tracks. If you stop recording (without stopping playback), SONAR instruct the tape decks to punch out. You must arm and disarm tracks on the tape deck; you cannot do this from SONAR.

If you have established punch-in/out points using the ***Transport-Record Options*** command, SONAR will attempt to preprogram the punch-in and punch-out times. However, your equipment must recognize the MMC event command for this feature to work. (Consult the owner's manual or contact the equipment manufacturer for more information.) If your equipment behaves erratically with automated punch-in, don't attempt to use it when those pieces of equipment are connected.

SONAR instructs MMC devices to locate the current project position only when playback or recording is started. This prevents excessive wear on the motors and tape heads of the devices.

To Configure MIDI Machine Control

1. Choose *Options-Project*, and click the Clock tab.
2. Select SMPTE/MTC as the clock source.
3. Click the MIDI Out tab.
4. Check the Transmit MMC box.
5. Enter the ID of the master timing device in the Time Code Master's Unit ID box.
6. Click OK.

MMC is now enabled.

To Disable MIDI Machine Control

1. Choose *Options-Project*, and click the MIDI Out tab.
2. Make sure the Transmit MMC box is not checked, and click OK.

MMC is disabled.

Audio File Management

Project files in SONAR do not contain the digital audio itself. A SONAR project file (.CWP) references the audio contained in the project, so care must be taken when backing up your digital audio projects. This chapter covers file management, including backing up your projects.

In This Chapter

The Project Files Dialog. 618
Project Files and Bundle Files 619
Audio Folders. 620
Backing Up Projects with Digital Audio 624
Deleting Unused Audio Files 625

The Project Files Dialog

SONAR projects, extension .CWP, contain all your project information with the exception of your digital audio data. This data is stored in a separate folder or folders. You can opt to save the data for all of your projects in a single audio folder, or create multiple folders.

The Project Files dialog lists all of your project's audio files and their location. This dialog is a valuable tool for managing your audio files.

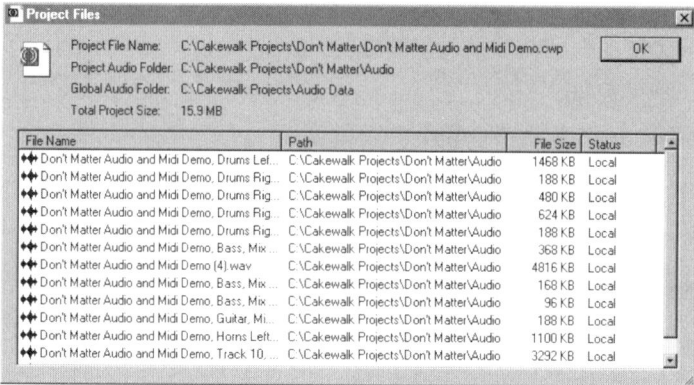

How to use the Project Files Dialog

The Project Files dialog has important information, including:

- Exactly which folders all of your audio files are saved in—know at a glance if you can backup your project by copying the audio folder and the .CWP file or if you need to do a Save As to round up files not in your project's audio folder.

- The filenames for each audio file your project is referencing

- The size of your project—important if you are going to backup your project

Project Files and Bundle Files

SONAR project files contain various project settings, any MIDI data, and references which "point" to audio clip data. The audio data (and video data) itself is not saved in a project file. To save audio as well, save your project as a Bundle file (extension .CWB). Bundle files contain everything that a project file contains in addition to the digital audio. Bundle files are useful for backing up projects and for transporting on removable media, like a Zip or Jaz disk.

The following are descriptions of both file types:

File Type...	Description...	When to Use...
.CWP	Contains MIDI data, project settings, and pointers to audio data in your Data directory. Project files contain no audio data, so they are small. Backing up a Project file does not back up the associated audio data.	Project files are good for routine projects. You can use Project files and back them up as Bundle files at various steps during a projects development.
.CWB	Contains all project data, including all audio data. Bundle files are large.	Bundle files are useful for backing up projects or for transporting a project to another computer (to bring it to a friend's house, for example).

Note: Due to Windows limitations, bundle files (.CWB) are limited to a size of 2 GB.

To Create a Bundle File

1. Choose ***File-Save As*** to display the Save As dialog box.
2. Choose Bundle from the Save as Type list.
3. Enter a file name and click OK.

SONAR compacts all the audio and merges it with the remaining project data in a bundle file.

To Unpack a Bundle File

1. Choose *File-Open* to display the Open dialog box.

2. Choose a file with a .CWB extension.

3. Click Open

   If you have the Per-project Audio Folders option enabled in the Global Options dialog, the Unpack Bundle dialog appears. If this option is not enabled, the bundle file opens and all audio data is stored in the Global Audio Folder.

4. If you want to store the project in its own folder do the following in the Unpack Bundle dialog:

   - Enter a project filename in the Project Name field.

   - Use the browse button to the right of the Location field to select a destination folder for the project, or to create a new folder, enter a new folder pathname in the Location field.

   - Use the browse button to the right of the Audio Path field to select a destination folder for the project's audio data, or to create a new folder, enter a new folder pathname in the Audio Path field.

   OR

   If you want to store the project in the Cakewalk Projects folder, and its audio in the Global Audio Folder, uncheck the Store Project Audio in its Own Folder option.

5. Click OK.

Audio Folders

By default, SONAR stores audio data separately from the rest of your projects, as wave files placed into a special folder called the **Global Audio Folder**, the location of which is listed in the Global Audio Folder field on the Audio Data tab in the Global Options dialog. You can also create audio folders on a per-project basis.

Important Note: Previous versions of Cakewalk used a folder called the WaveData, in the product directory.

Global Audio Folders

You can change the location of the Global Audio Folder. This may be necessary if, for example, your hard disk is full and you want to move all audio data storage to a different hard disk. We strongly recommend that you do not change the location of the Global Audio Folder unless absolutely necessary.

If your original Global Audio Folder contains any audio files with the extension .WAV, you must manually move these files to the new Global Audio Folder using the

Windows Explorer, or open the project and use the Missing Audio dialog to find and move the missing files.

To Change the Global Audio Folder

1. Choose *Options-Global* and click the Audio Data tab.

2. Enter the pathname of the new Global Audio Folder in the Global Audio Folder field, or click the browse button that's at the right end of the Global Audio Folder field to browse to the new directory.

3. Click OK when you are done.

4. Use the Windows Explorer or some other program to move all audio files from the old Global Audio Folder to the new Global Audio Folder.

All new audio files will be stored in the new Global Audio Folder, unless you decide to use per-project audio.

It is safer, but more time-consuming, to first save all projects as bundle files, change the Global Audio Folder, then open the bundle files. This ensures that all of the audio data is properly moved to the new Global Audio Folder.

Per-project Audio Folders

You have the option of using a single audio data folder or using different audio data folders for each project. By default SONAR stores audio data in the Global Audio Folder. If you want to use per-project audio folders, use the following procedure:

To Use Per-project Audio Folders

1. Select *Options-Global*.

   The Global Options dialog appears.

2. Select the Audio Data tab.

3. In the Per-Project Audio section, check the Use Per-Project Audio Folders option.

4. Click OK to apply the change.

Once you have enabled the per-project audio folders, the New Project File allows you to choose the directory where you want to store the new project and a subdirectory where you want to store the project's audio data.

To Create a New Project Using Per-project Audio

1. Select *File-New*.

   The New Project File dialog appears.

2. Enter a filename in the Name field

   The Location and Audio Path directories are automatically updated in the following format:

   - C:*default directory**project name*. The default directory for new projects is assigned in the Folders tab of the Global Options dialog. *project name* is the project's per-project folder name.

   - C:*default directory**project name*\Audio. The default directory for new projects is assigned in the Folders tab of the Global Options dialog. *project name* is the project's per-project folder name, and Audio is the subfolder where your audio data will be stored.

3. If you want, rename the Location and/or Audio Path directories.

4. Click OK.

To Save an Existing Project Using Per-project Audio

You may have older files that are not using per-project audio folders. If you want to save these files using a per-project audio folder, use the following procedure:

1. Make sure that per-project audio folders is enabled in the Global Options dialog.

2. Open the project whose audio you want to store using per-project audio.

3. Select *File-Save As*.

   The Save As dialog appears.

4. If you want, change the name of your project.

5. In the Project Path field, enter the new directory where you want to save the project, or use the Browse button to the right of the field to navigate to an existing directory.

6. Check the Copy all audio with project option.

7. Click Save.

8. SONAR copies the project to the directory specified in the Project Path field and stores all the project's audio in the directory specified in the Audio Path field.

   Note: After you use the above procedure, you have two versions of the same project.

Imported Audio Files

By default, SONAR will make a copy of any audio data imported using the *File-Import-Audio* command and place the imported audio into the project's audio folder. You can configure SONAR to simply reference audio from its current location if, for example, you want to import large quantities of audio data into a project and don't want to consume time and disk space by making copies of the files. Copies are always made if the imported audio does not match the current project's sampling and bit rates (and if you edit any of the imported audio data). Automatic handling of imported files is enabled by default. Do not disable this option unless you are prepared to manage the audio files individually. Creating backups of your projects is very easy if all your audio is stored in a single, per-project directory.

To Change Handling of Imported Files

Use the following procedure to allow or disallow file sharing between projects:

1. Choose *Options-Global* and click the Audio Data tab.

2. Check the Always Copy Imported Audio Files option to create copies of all imported audio clips as a default.

    OR

    Uncheck Always Copy Imported Audio Files option to reference imported audio from its current location.

    Note: You can override this setting when importing audio by checking or unchecking the Copy Audio to Project Folder option in the Import Audio dialog.

3. Click OK when you are done.

Imported files will be handled based on the settings you have chosen.

Backing Up Projects with Digital Audio

There are several ways to back up your projects in SONAR. You can use per-project audio folders to keep all a project's audio in its own folder, use the Consolidate Project Audio command to create a backup copy of all your project's audio, or you can save a project as a bundle file (.CWB).

The following table lists several backup methods:

Backup Method...	Advantages...
Per-project Audio Folders If you are using per-project audio folders you can create a copy of the project folder and its audio subfolder.	This method is an exact copy of your project, preserving all clips and pathname information.
Consolidate Project Audio If your project references audio from multiple folders, for example you have a library of loops that you share between several projects, you can gather all the audio for your project into a single folder using the *Consolidate Project Audio* command. The *Consolidate Project Audio* command copies every audio file your project references into a backup folder beneath the projects audio data folder. Creating a copy of all your project's audio may take a lot of disk space.	Allows you to create a complete backup of all project audio even if the audio is in multiple locations. Creates a new folder which you can move or delete without fear of losing the original audio files.
Bundle Files A **bundle file** is a single file that contains all the information—except video—used in a project. A bundle file includes everything that is stored in a normal project file, plus all the digital audio that is used in the project.	Creates a single file for ease of portability.

To Backup Projects Using Per-Project Audio Folders

Use this procedure to create a backup of a project that has its own project folder.

1. Open the project you want to backup.
2. Select *File-Project Audio Files*.

    The Project Files dialog appears.

3. In the Project Files dialog, check the Path column to make sure that every audio file is stored in the project's audio folder. If any files are stored in folders other than the project's audio folder, you should use the *Consolidate Project Audio* command to move all audio to the project's audio folder.
4. Close the Project Files dialog once you have confirmed that all audio files are in the project's audio folder.

5. Close the project.

6. Using Windows Explorer, copy the project folder and its contents, including the project's audio folder, to its backup location (CD-R, CD-RW, Zip or Jaz drive, another hard drive, network drive, etc.).

You have now created a copy of your project. It is a good idea to open the project once you have backed it up to confirm that all audio loads properly.

To Create a Backup Using Consolidate Project Audio

Use this procedure to backup a project that has multiple audio folders:

1. Open the project you want to backup.

2. Select *Tools-Consolidate Project Audio*.

3. A message box appears listing the destination folder for your audio backup.

4. Click OK to confirm.

5. Using Windows Explorer, copy the project, the backup folder and all its contents, including the project's audio folder, to its backup location (CD-R, CD-RW, Zip or Jaz drive, another hard drive, network drive, etc.). **The Consolidate Project Audio command only copies the audio in your project, so make sure you copy the project (.CWP) along with the backup folder.**

6. Once you have copied the backup folder you can delete it to free up disk space.

Deleting Unused Audio Files

The *Tools-Clean Audio Folder* command is used to delete digital audio files in an audio folder if they are no longer used by any of your projects. You should use this command from time to time to free up disk space.

This command searches your entire system for project files, and then compiles a list of all the audio files in a specified folder that are not in use by any of these projects. You can then choose to delete these audio files. Make sure that all of your important project (.CWP, .WRK) files are stored on your local hard disk(s) before using this command. If your project files are stored elsewhere (removable media, etc.), then you risk accidentally deleting important audio files that are associated with your projects.

If you are using another utility program that protects you from accidentally deleting important files (such as Norton Protect), you may need to disable that program. Otherwise, the next time you use the *Tools-Clean Audio Folder* command you may once again find these not-quite-deleted files.

To Delete Unused Audio Files

1. Make sure all project files that contain audio are immediately accessible on a hard disk.
2. Choose **Tools-Clean Audio Folder** to display the Clean Audio Folder dialog box.
3. Click the Browse button to the right of the Audio Path field and navigate to the folder you want to search for unused audio files.
4. If you want to search all subfolders of the folder you chose in the Audio Path field, click the Recursive option.
5. Click the Find button. SONAR searches the selected directory for audio files that appear to be unused by any existing projects, and displays the names of these files in the list.

    SONAR searches the entire system for project files. Audio files in the folder or folders you decide to search which do not belong to any of the projects on your system appear in the Clean Audio Folder dialog. If any corrupted or unreadable project files exist on your system, the Unreadable Files dialog appears. It is very important that you restore any unreadable files from a backup before continuing, otherwise you risk data loss.

6. Follow the instructions in the table:

To do this...	Do this...
Listen to a file	Highlight the file name in the list and click Play
Delete a file	Highlight the file name in the list and click Delete
Delete all files	Click Delete All, and click Yes to confirm

7. Click Close when you are done.

20 Improving Audio Performance

Digital audio presents several challenges: it is large, gobbling up enormous amounts of disk space, especially at higher sampling rates and bit-depths, and it is CPU-intensive. Added to this mix is the wide variety of audio hardware available today. This chapter covers some common problems with recording and playback and how to configure your computer and audio hardware for optimum performance.

Note: One of the quickest ways to improve audio performance is to use WDM or ASIO sound card drivers instead of the older MME type. See "WDM vs. MME Drivers" on page 638.

In This Chapter

System Configuration. 628
Improving Performance with Digital Audio 634

System Configuration

This section covers optimizing your system configuration to work with SONAR.

The Wave Profiler

The Wave Profiler is a utility that analyzes the sound cards in your computer and determines the best DMA (Direct Memory Access) settings for communicating with SONAR. These DMA settings are displayed in samples, at the sample rates and bit depths your sound card supports. The Wave Profiler also sets a value in milliseconds for the Buffer Slider, which controls mixing latency. The Wave Profiler is unnecessary if you are using an ASIO driver. One of the best ways to improve mixing latency is to use a sound card that uses a WDM or ASIO driver instead of MME (legacy) type. For a comparison of the two types of drivers, see "WDM vs. MME Drivers" on page 638.

The DMA settings are used to ensure that a project that contains both MIDI and digital audio plays back in tight synchronization. If SONAR is not configured properly with your audio device's DMA settings, MIDI and digital audio material may not play back correctly.

Note to users of previous Cakewalk products: The DMA settings in versions of Cakewalk prior to SONAR 1.0 were displayed in bytes rather than samples. Using your previous DMA settings in SONAR will not work. Try the settings that wave profiler displays, and if you are not satisfied, only then attempt to optimize your settings.

The Wave Profiler utility runs automatically the first time you run SONAR. If you have a sound card with a WDM driver installed, SONAR will detect this and run the wave profiler determining the best DMA settings for the supported bit depths and sample rates of your sound card. You can force the use of the MME interface by checking the option on the Advanced Tab in the Audio Options dialog box that says, "Always Use MME Interface Even When WDM Drivers are Available". This option forces any card that has WDM drivers to use the MME interface instead. After you restart SONAR you will be prompted to run the wave profiler, this time it will determine the DMA settings using MME instead of WDM. This is especially useful if you have multiple sound cards, one of which does not support WDM.

Note: SONAR does not support the use of WDM and MME simultaneously. To use a sound card with WDM drivers with a sound card using MME drivers, you must check the "Always Use MME Interface Even When WDM Drivers are Available" option in the Advanced tab of the Audio Options dialog. This forces the sound card using WDM drivers to use the MME interface.

Note: It is possible to load a 48 kHz project when you are using a sound card that does not support 48 kHz. SONAR does not warn you when you do this. Your project may crash, or it may appear to record audio when your project is not actually recording.

All of your audio settings are listed in the Audio Options dialog box, which you open with the **Options-Audio** command. The following list summarizes all the settings that the Wave Profiler sets. You can override all of them except what audio drivers are listed in the Drivers tab:

- Input and output drivers
- DMA buffer sizes (in samples)
- Mixing latency

If you experience MIDI and audio synchronization problems during playback, before contacting technical support, run the Wave Profiler and try the default setting.

To Manually Run the Wave Profiler

1. Choose **Options-Audio** to open the Audio Options dialog box, and click the General tab.
2. Click Wave Profiler.

    The Wave Profiler examines each of your sound cards in turn, and displays the name of the sound card it detected under the following possible headings:

Heading...	What it means...
16 Bit Wave API	No WDM drivers were detected. Profiling using MME under Win9x and WinME
32 Bit Wave API	You may have chosen to force MME even when WDM drivers are available. **Note:** Windows 2000 will use this API when profiling MME.
WDM Kernel Streaming	WDM drivers were detected.

629

Enabling and Disabling Audio Devices

Your computer may have several installed devices like FAX modems and software synthesizers that Windows recognizes as sound cards containing audio drivers. You do not want to use these devices for audio input or output. If they are listed as audio drivers in the Audio Options dialog box, you need to disable them.

To Enable or Disable an Audio Device

1. Choose *Options-Audio* to open the Audio Options dialog box and click the Drivers tab.

2. In the Input Drivers and Output Drivers fields, do one or both of the following:

    - To enable an audio device, click the name of the device so that it is highlighted.

    - To disable an audio device, click the name of the device so that it is not highlighted.

3. Click OK.

Disabling a device in the Audio Options dialog box usually prevents conflicts with other audio devices. Occasionally you may need to disable a device in the Windows Control Panel.

SONAR also allows you to choose the sound card whose clock should be used to control recording and playback timing (if you only have one sound card, SONAR automatically uses it). Every sound card's clock crystal is slightly different, which causes minor differences in the actual playback rate on each card. These differences may lead to slight synchronization problems if you use one card for recording and a different one for playback. Generally, you should choose your highest quality sound card for both recording and playback timing. Note that while some multichannel sound cards have multiple drivers, most sound cards have only a single audio driver.

To Select Playback and Record Timing Masters

1. Choose *Options-Audio* to open the Audio Options dialog box and click the General tab.

2. In the Playback Timing Master and Record Timing Master fields, select which sound cards you want to control playback and record timing, respectively.

3. Click OK.

While you must choose a playback timing master, you can route audio output through any number of devices at once. For example, suppose your computer has both a high-end audio card and a basic built-in sound card. You should choose the high-end sound card as the record and playback timing master. However, using the buses in the Console or Track views, you could create a headphone or monitor mix and route it through the built-in sound card.

Configuring SONAR for 18 bit-, 20-bit, and 24-bit

Operation

When first installed, SONAR is configured to create 16-bit audio sampled at 44.1kHz. Nearly all sound cards support this kind of audio data. A growing number of "professional" cards are capable of recording and playing back audio at higher bit depths (18-bit, 20-bit, and 24-bit) and sampling rates (48 kHz and 96 kHz). SONAR allows you to take advantage of these higher bit depths and sampling rates. In order to get the best results, do the following:

- Set the desired audio driver bit depth and sampling rate before recording or importing audio.

  It is important to set the audio driver bit depth and sampling rate before you import or record any audio. Lowering the audio driver bit depth from 24 bit to 16 bit degrades the quality of your project's existing audio. Also, a project's sampling rate can only be altered before you add any audio. To set the audio driver bit depth and sampling rate, open the Audio Options dialog box (*Options-Audio* command), click the General tab, and choose values from the Audio Driver Bit Depth and Sampling Rate fields.

- Choose a file bit depth of 24 if you intend to use your sound card at an audio driver bit depth of 18, 20 or 24.

  SONAR allocates memory in bytes (8-bits each). If you do not choose a 24-bit file depth (3 bytes), SONAR truncates your 18-, 20- or 24-bit data down to 16 bits (2 bytes), defeating the benefits of your sound card's higher bit depth capability. Set the file bit depth by opening the Audio Options dialog box (*Options-Audio* command), clicking the General tab, and choosing a value from the File Bit Depth field.

- Pick a bit format for your data on the Driver Profiles tab of the Audio Options dialog box in the Stream > 16 Bit Data As field. You may need to consult your sound card's documentation to find the optimum setting.

- **Check the Cakewalk Website for the latest information about sound cards**

- **Keep in mind that using 24-bit depth and/or a high sampling rate needs a lot of disk space and a fast CPU.**

  24-bit projects use 50% more disk space than 16-bit projects. If you have a large number of audio tracks, the amount of disk space needed for your project could become quite large. Also, a powerful CPU may be required to play back the large 24-bit tracks, particularly if you use real-time effects.

Note: Some audio devices, especially USB devices that use WDM drivers, can not operate in 24-bit mode unless a variable in SONAR's AUD.INI file is set to 1. The variable is Use24BitExtensible=<0 or 1>, which goes in the [*name of your audio device ('n' in, 'n' out)*] section or the AUD.INI file. For more information, see the initialization file topics in the online help.

For more information about working at 24-bit depth, see the online help topic "24-bit Tips."

Converting Sample Rates and Bit Depths

In general, it's better to keep the sample rate and audio bit depth of a project consistent from start to finish, but SONAR has tools and procedures to accomplish the following tasks:

- Preparing higher-quality audio (greater than 16-bit, 44.1 kHz) for CD burning (CD format is 16-bit, 44.1 kHz)
- Rewriting audio files at different bit depths
- Converting the sample rate of a project
- Importing 24-bit audio into a 16-bit project
- Importing 16-bit audio into a 24-bit project
- Importing audio that has a different sample rate into a project

Here are the steps involved:

To Prepare Higher-quality Audio for CD Burning

1. Use the *File-Export Audio* command to open the Export Audio dialog. Choose RIFF Wave in the Files of Type field, Export to Stereo File(s) in the Format field, and 16 in the Bit Depth field.

2. After exporting the audio, close SONAR and open up your sound card control panel (for Midiman cards, usually the Delta Control Panel, for Echo Audio, usually the Echo Console, for MOTU it's the 324 console, etc.) Once the control panel is open change the setting for your sample rate to 44.1 kHz.

3. Next launch SONAR and use the *Options-Audio* command to open the Audio Options dialog. In the General section change the Audio Driver Bit Depth to 16. Change Default Settings for New Projects to 44100 Hz for the Sampling Rate and 16 bits for the File Bit Depth.

4. After making these adjustments, click the Wave Profiler button in the Audio Options dialog. In some instances, with certain audio hardware configurations you may be prompted with an audio driver error dialog during this process. This is nothing to be concerned about. You will have to exit SONAR, re-launch, verify the settings you made in the Audio Options dialog, and click the Wave Profiler button again. When you can successfully run the Wave Profiler without an audio driver error, proceed to the next step.

5. Create a new project (*File-New* command). The Normal option is fine for this.

6. Import the mixed down audio by using the *File-Import Audio* command.

7. Confirm the bit depth and sample rate of the imported audio by using the *File-Info* command, and clicking File Stats. The File Stats dialog lists the correct sample rate and bit depth.

8. Final step: use the *File-Export Audio* command. Be sure to select 16 for the Bit Depth and uncheck all Mix Enables.

Now you can burn your exported audio file to CD, using Cakewalk MediaWorks, or other software.

To Rewrite Audio Files at Different Bit Depths
1. Use the *Tools-Change Audio Format* command to open the Change Audio Format dialog.

2. Choose a new bit depth in the New Bit Depth field.

3. If you're changing to 16 bits, you can check or uncheck the Apply Dither checkbox. Dithering means to add a certain audio signal to 16 bit audio to make it sound more like it did as a 24 bit signal.

4. Click OK.

SONAR rewrites the audio tracks in your project at the new bit depth.

To Convert the Sample Rate of a Project
1. Select an audio track and use the *File-Export Audio* command to open the Export Audio dialog.

2. Select the options you want, and click Export to export the track.

3. Repeat steps 1 and 2 for all the audio tracks you want to convert.

4. After you've exported all the tracks you want to convert, open the Audio Options dialog (*Options-Audio* command), and on the General tab, change the Sampling Rate field to the desired number.

5. Use the *File-New* command to open a new project.

6. Use the *File-Import Audio* command to open the Import Audio dialog.

7. Select the audio files you just exported (hold down the Ctrl key while you click each one), and click Open to import the files.

SONAR imports the selected files at the new sampling rate.

To Import 24-bit Audio into a 16-bit Project
1. Open the Audio Options dialog (*Options-Audio* command), and on the General tab, change the File Bit Depth field to 24.

2. Use the *File-New* command to open a new project.

3. Import the 24-bit audio into the new project.

4. Use the *Tools-Change Audio Format* command to open the Change Audio Format dialog.

5. Choose 16 in the New Bit Depth field.

6. You can check or uncheck the Apply Dither checkbox. Dithering means to add a certain audio signal to 16 bit audio to make it sound more like it did as a 24 bit signal.

7. Click OK. SONAR rewrites the audio clips at 16 bits.

8. Open the 16-bit project that you want to import the audio into.

9. Drag or paste the rewritten audio clips into the 16-bit project.

To Import 16-bit Audio into a 24-bit Project

- Just use the *File-Import Audio* command to import the 16-bit audio files.

To Import Audio That Has a Different Sample Rate

1. Use the *File-New* command to open a new project.

2. Open the Audio Options dialog (*Options-Audio* command), and on the General tab, change the Sampling Rate field to the same rate that your project uses.

3. Use the *File-Import Audio* command to import the audio file(s) (this converts them to the new sample rate).

4. Open the project that you want to import the audio into, and drag or paste the resampled audio clips into the target project.

Improving Performance with Digital Audio

When a project contains many tracks of digital audio or when many real-time effects are in use, your computer may have difficulty keeping up during playback. When this occurs, you'll hear portions of the audio drop out, stutter, or pop. Or maybe your project responds slowly to real-time effects and volume changes. In an extreme case audio playback may stop altogether. If you experience a dropout, a dialog appears with suggestions for fixing the problem. This section covers performance issues specific to digital audio, including how to get the more tracks of audio, more real-time effects, lower latency and how to fix audio dropouts.

Getting the Most Out of Your PC

The maximum number of audio tracks you can expect to play on your computer depends on the audio sample rate, the speed of your hard disk, and the speed of your computer's CPU.

The effect of your CPU on audio track throughput is much more difficult to quantify. Throughput is affected by the type of chip, clock speed, the number and type of real-time effects in use, cache size and settings, and many other factors.

There are a variety of things you can do to increase the number of audio tracks and effects you can play on your computer, as outlined in the following table:

Approach...	How it works...
Avoid compressed disks	If you use DoubleSpace, Stacker, or some other disk compression system, it will slow down playback of audio tremendously. Configure your system so that the Data directory is on a hard disk that is not compressed.
Exit other programs	The more programs you have open, the more CPU cycles you are taking away from your project. Exit any programs unnecessary to the task at hand.
Refrain from other activity during playback	If you open and close windows or do lots of editing while playback is in progress, you may steal CPU cycles that would otherwise be used for playback.
Apply some audio effects offline	If you are happy with your real-time effects, consider using the **Process-Apply Audio Effects** command to apply those effects offline. Then remove those effects from real-time use and free up lots of CPU power.
Archive unused audio tracks	Audio tracks that are muted continue to place a load on your processor. To lessen the burden and free up cycles to handle more audio, archive all unused audio tracks. See "To Archive or Unarchive Tracks" on page 126 for more information.
Mix down your audio tracks	If your project contains many different audio tracks or many real-time effects, you can use the **Edit-Bounce to Track(s)** command to reduce all of this content to a stereo track. Having done this, you can archive the original tracks (in case you need them later) and play only the new tracks, lessening the computational burden on your computer.
Change I/O Buffer Size on the Advanced tab of the Audio Options dialog box	The default setting is 64 KB. Yours may work better with 128, 32, or 16. If those values don't help, try 256, 512, or move on to another remedy.

Defragment your hard disk	If your hard disk is fragmented, playback of audio will be slower. Use the Disk Defragmenter to correct the situation.
Turn off the Clip Audio Mix Upon Overflow option on the Advanced tab of the Audio Options dialog box.	Unless your mix is really distorted, you won't usually need this option.
Turn off the Apply Dither option on the Advanced tab of the Audio Options dialog box.	Dithering subtly improves your mix, but most people can't hear it. Turn it back on for mastering.
Enable disk caching	By default, SONAR bypasses all disk caching, which typically results in better performance with audio data. If your computer has a very large amount of RAM (128 MB or more) and your audio tracks include many repeated sections, enabling caching may improve SONAR's audio performance. Choose **Options-Audio** and click the Advanced tab to change the disk cache settings.
Record audio at a lower sampling rate	If you don't require CD quality 44.1 kHz audio, then record your audio at a lower sampling rate of 22.05 kHz or 11.025 kHz. Choose **Options-Audio** to change the sampling rate. This method is useful only before you start work on a project. Once the audio sampling rate for a project has been set, it cannot be changed.
Disable the Display Clip Contents options	Drawing the contents of audio clips in the Clips pane uses some CPU cycles. If you are using a slow machine, you may want to disable this feature. To do so, right-click in the Clips pane, choose **View Options**, and disable the Display Clip Contents option.

Digital Audio Files and Storage

Digital audio requires a large amount of disk storage. The table below shows the disk space requirements in megabytes for a single minute of digital audio in mono and stereo at various sampling rates:

Sampling rate	16 bit	24 bit
11 kHZ Mono	1.3 MB per minute	1.9 MB per minute
11 kHZ Stereo	2.5 MB per minute	3.8 MB per minute
22 kHz Mono	2.8 MB per minute	3.8 MB per minute
22 kHz Stereo	5.0 MB per minute	7.6 MB per minute

44.1 kHZ Mono	5.0 MB per minute	7.6 MB per minute
44.1 kHZ Stereo	10.1 MB per minute	15.1 MB per minute
48 kHz Mono	5.5 MB per minute	7.6 MB per minute
48 kHz Stereo	11.0 MB per minute	16.5 MB per minute
96 kHz Mono	11.2 MB per minute	16.5 MB per minute
96 kHz Stereo	22.0 MB per minute	33.0 MB per minute

For more information, consult the online help topic, Dropouts and Other Audio Problems.

Mixing Latency

SONAR has a slider in the Audio Options dialog box, on the General tab, to set mixing latency. Mixing latency is the amount of time SONAR allocates to prepare a buffer full of audio data for playback. Lower latency settings add processing time because of the need to refill the smaller data buffers more often. You may need to use the slider to **increase** mixing latency under the following conditions:

- You use lots of real-time effects, and you hear dropouts. Check the CPU meter for high readings; try increasing the latency.

- Your sound card does not function well at lower latency. Some sound cards just do not function well at lower latency settings. Even though SONAR's CPU meter and Dropout indicator report no problems, if you hear dropouts try increasing the mixing latency.

Sound cards differ in the precision of their timing, what size audio buffers they require, and other characteristics. SONAR has a utility called the Wave Profiler that can usually automatically detect the type of sound card that you have installed and configure its settings for best performance. If your sound card is a well-known model, you can usually use SONAR without having to change many audio settings. However, if you experience synchronization problems between MIDI and digital audio, like to use different sample rates and bit depths, or want to experiment with mixing latency, you need to do some optimization yourself.

WDM vs. MME Drivers

In almost every situation, the newer WDM (Windows Driver Model) sound card drivers that most sound card vendors are creating are a much better choice than the older MME (Multi-Media Extensions) drivers. If your sound card vendor has a WDM driver, by all means use it. The following table compares their characteristics:

WDM...	MME...
Lower latency	Usually higher latency
Works with Windows XP, 2000, ME, 98 SE, but not 98 Gold	Works with Windows 98, and ME. Some MME drivers may work with Windows 2000.
Most sound card vendors have produced a WDM driver.	MME drivers are widely available.
	Note: If you use two or more sound cards at the same time, and not all of them have WDM drivers, you must force the WDM drivers to function as MME drivers. Do this in the Audio Options dialog box on the Advanced tab by checking the Always Use MME Interface Even When WDM Drivers Are Available checkbox.

ASIO Drivers

SONAR supports ASIO drivers. You are limited to a single sound card when using an ASIO driver.

To Use an ASIO Driver

Use the following procedure to enable SONAR for use with an ASIO driver.

1. Select ***Options-Audio*** to open the Audio Options dialog.

2. In the Audio Options dialog, click the Advanced tab.

3. In the Playback and Recording section, select ASIO from the Driver Mode dropdown menu.

4. Restart SONAR.

Queue Buffers

SONAR allows you to set the number of queue buffers in the Audio Options dialog box, in the General tab. A higher number of queue buffers will take longer to fill, and therefore cause an increase in latency. A lower number of queue buffers decreases latency, but may cause "dropouts." The default setting is 2. For more information, see the online help topics: "Mixing Latency", and "Dropouts and Other Audio Problems."

Status Bar/CPU Meter/Disk Meter

SONAR has several tools to help you identify and correct audio problems, including the CPU meter, the Disk meter, and the Dropout indicator. These tools are all located on the Status bar, which is at the bottom of the screen. The Status bar also contains a measurement of available hard disk space. If you do not see the Status bar, go to **Options-Global**, select the **General** tab, and make sure **Show Status Bar** is selected. The Status bar contains the following fields, reading from left to right:

- Now time—The left-most field on the Status bar shows the Now time.

- Audio Running—Whenever the Audio Engine button in the Transport toolbar is depressed, the Audio Running indicator lights up.

- Dropout indicator—The Dropout indicator is in the same field as the Audio Running indicator. The Dropout indicator displays the word **Dropout** whenever your project requires more resources than your CPU, main memory, and disk can supply.

- Mute—Whenever a track is muted, the Mute indicator lights up. You can click the Mute indicator to unmute all muted tracks.

- Solo—Whenever a track is soloed, the solo indicator lights up. You can click the Solo indicator to unsolo all soloed tracks.

- Arm—Whenever a track is armed for recording audio or MIDI data, the red Arm indicator lights up. This indicator is in the same field as the red Aut indicator. You can click the Arm indicator to disarm all armed tracks.

- Aut—Whenever any control is armed for automation recording, the red Aut indicator lights up. This indicator is in the same field as the red Arm indicator. You can click the Aut indicator to disarm all armed tracks

- Disk Space—This field shows how many megabytes of disk space you have left on the hard drive where your wave data directory is. It also shows this amount of space as a percentage of that drive's total space.

- CPU meter—The CPU meter displays the time it takes to process a buffer full of audio data as a percentage of the maximum time available to process that data and maintain uninterrupted playback. There is some tolerance built into the meter, so it's very possible that it will exceed 100% at times (more so during recording than playback). When the meter exceeds 100%, it displays the word "Overload."

- Disk meter—The Disk meter measures how much of the available time SONAR is using to perform input/output functions on your hard disk. The size of your setup's I/O buffer (listed in the Audio Options dialog box, in the Advanced tab) determines how much time is allowed to perform disk operations and maintain uninterrupted playback. When SONAR performs disk operations, the Disk meter jumps up in value and shows the percentage of the allowed time SONAR is taking to complete each cycle of disk Input/Output.

- If you experience a dropout or your CPU or Disk meters are reading high, there are steps you can take to improve your audio performance. For more information, see Dropouts and Other Audio Problems in the online help.Some plug-ins do not function well at a 96 kHz sampling rate:

    Using an audio bit depth of 24 can enhance the performance of some plug-ins, but raising the sampling rate to 96 kHz does not offer much improvement, and can cause some plug-ins to add unintended artifacts to the sound. Using a 24-bit, 44.1 kHz setup for your audio provides plenty of enhanced performance for plug-ins that can take advantage of it, without risking the problems that 96 kHz audio causes with some plug-ins.

Appendix A: Troubleshooting

If you're having a problem with SONAR™, don't panic. This appendix lists some common problems and how to solve them.

If you don't find an answer here, there are two other important places to look for help:

- Check the ReadMe file that came with your software. It contains additional information that wasn't available when this *User's Guide* was printed. To view the Readme file, select **Help-View README.RTF**.

- Visit our World Wide Web site at www.cakewalk.com, where you'll find answers to frequently asked questions, tech support documents, program patches and updates, and more.

When I Play a File, I Don't Hear Anything

Open a project (.CWP) and click the Play button. If you don't hear any music, try the following suggestions:

Possible problem...	What to do...
Your speakers aren't connected properly or the volume is turned down.	Make sure your speakers are on and the volume is turned up.
Your sound card isn't hooked up correctly.	See if other programs play sound correctly through your speakers. A good program to try is the Media Player (**Start-Programs-Accessories-Multimedia-Media Player**). If other programs do not work, check your sound card documentation to make sure the card is properly installed and configured.

You don't have Bank and Patch settings in your MIDI track	Check the Bank and Patch settings for each track. Make sure that each track has a Bank and Patch assigned to it.
You don't have an Output setting	Check Output settings for each track. Make sure that each MIDI track is assigned to a MIDI output which is connected to a MIDI device capable of playback. Make sure each audio track is assigned to an output that is connected to your speaker system.
No MIDI output device is selected.	Choose **Options-MIDI Devices**, and check the Output device list. Make sure that your computer sound card is highlighted and at the top of the list. If this doesn't work, try choosing different output devices, one at a time, to see if any of them produces sound.
Your sound card or MIDI interface is not set up correctly.	Make sure you have installed and tested each card according to the manufacturer's instructions.
You may have too many MIDI drivers.	Make sure you only install the drivers that you need, and remove any old or unused drivers. To access the driver list, choose **Start-Settings-Control Panel**, then double-click Multimedia and click on the Advanced tab.
Your MIDI driver is incorrect or outdated.	Make sure that the driver you have installed is the correct driver for your hardware. Also try downloading and installing the latest driver release from your hardware manufacturer.
Your MIDI driver is configured incorrectly.	Make sure the driver's IRQ and port address settings match the physical settings on the card.

If none of these suggestions works, check our web site for additional suggestions or contact technical support.

I Can't Record from My MIDI Instrument

If you are unable to record music from your electronic keyboard, synthesizer, or other MIDI instrument, first test to see if you are able to play back a project through the keyboard. Then try the following:

Possible problem...	What to do...
No MIDI input device is selected.	Choose **Options-MIDI Devices**, and check the Input device list. Make sure that the MIDI input on your computer sound card is highlighted.
Your MIDI cables are reversed.	Make sure that the MIDI Out plug is connected to the MIDI In jack on your keyboard and that the MIDI In plug is connected to the MIDI Out jack on your keyboard.
SONAR™ is not receiving MIDI data.	Check the MIDI Input/Output Activity monitor on the Windows Status bar. Check to see if the left LED is flashing red. If not, then SONAR™ is not receiving MIDI data. Check you connections and try again.
You have not set up SONAR™ to record.	Make sure that 1) you have chosen an input for the track; 2) you have armed the track for recording; and 3) you have pressed the Record button, and not the Play button.

If none of these suggestions works, check our web site for additional suggestions or contact technical support.

When I Play a File Containing Audio, the Audio Portion Doesn't Play

Open a bundle file (.CWB) and click the Play button. Do you hear the audio tracks in the project (there may be MIDI tracks in the bundle file, so you must mute them). If not, try the following:

Possible problem...	What to do...
Your speakers aren't connected properly, or the volume is turned down.	Make sure your speakers are connected properly and the volume is turned up.
Your sound card isn't hooked up correctly.	Run the Microsoft Sound Recorder (*Start-Programs-Accessories-Multimedia-Sound Recorder*). Open any wave file and see if it plays sound correctly through your speakers. If not, check your sound card documentation to make sure the card is properly installed and configured.
The volume setting is turned down on your software mixer.	Double-click on the yellow speaker icon in the Windows task bar to display the mixer, and make sure all the volume settings are turned up and that none are muted.
Your audio tracks are assigned to the wrong output.	Check the output assignment for your audio tracks in the Track pane.
SONAR doesn't recognize your sound card.	Choose **Options-Audio**, click the General tab, and then click the Wave Profiler button to test your audio hardware. Then, re-open the bundle file and try again.

If none of these suggestions works, check our web site for additional suggestions or contact technical support.

I Can't Record Any Audio

If you are unable to record audio through your sound card, try the following suggestions:

Possible problem...	What to do...
The track is not set up to receive audio input.	Make sure that the input for the track you are recording (in the Track view) is set to an Audio input before recording.
The software mixer is not set up properly.	Double-click on the speaker icon in the Windows task bar to display the mixer. Choose **Options-Properties**, select Adjust Volume for Recording, and click OK. Make sure the appropriate Select boxes have checkmarks and the input volume is turned up.
Your sound card isn't hooked up correctly.	Try recording audio using the Microsoft Sound Recorder (**Start-Programs-Accessories-Multimedia-Sound Recorder**). If it fails, check your sound card documentation to make sure it is properly installed and configured.
You have not set up SONAR to record.	Make sure that 1) you have chosen an input for the track; 2) you have armed the track for recording; and 3) you have pressed the Record button, and not the Play button.

If these suggestions don't work, check our web site for additional suggestions or contact technical support.

My Track or Bus Fader is Maximized, But There's No Sound or Level

SONAR has two modes that govern how fader levels function: Envelope Mode and Offset Mode. In Envelope Mode, any envelopes in the track or bus control the level, and ignore any movements you make to the fader. In Offset mode, any envelopes in the track or bus *add* their level to any level that the fader contributes. For example, the level you see in the Vol field of a track's properties combines with the levels that any volume envelope in that track produces as the track plays. When you switch back to Envelope mode, any level that the Vol field displays while in Offset mode continues to combine with any envelope in the track, but does not show in the Vol field while you're in Envelope mode. So, if you have a large negative value such as -INF in the Vol field, even though the volume envelope is at its maximum level, the sum of the two values is still inaudible because the negative value is so large.

Whenever you have mysterious levels in a track or bus, click the Envelope/Offset Mode button that is in the Track view toolbar to switch modes, and then look in the track or bus property fields to see what values show. Change the values to neutral ones if you don't want them to affect your levels.

The Music Is Playing Back with the Wrong Instrument Sounds

If the tracks in your project are assigned to the same MIDI output and channel, the same sound will be used for all of them. To fix this problem, simply assign each track to a different channel (using the Channel control in the Track view), and then choose the sound (or patch) you want to use for each one. If you are playing songs through your MIDI keyboard or synthesizer, you need to 1) check that your instrument is able to receive MIDI data on multiple channels, and 2) configure your instrument to play a different patch on each channel (this is called Multi Mode on many instruments). See the documentation for your instrument for more information.

Another possibility is that you are playing back a GM (General MIDI)-authored MIDI file on a non-GM compatible device.

How Do I Use SONAR to Access All the Sounds on My MIDI Instrument?

SONAR is normally set up to access the 128 sounds that are part of the General MIDI standard. SONAR also includes custom instrument definitions that match the sounds on many popular instruments. To use a custom instrument definition:

1. Choose **Options-Instruments** to display the Assign Instruments dialog box.
2. Click the Define button to display the Define Instruments and Names dialog box.
3. Click Import, and then choose the file for the manufacturer of your instrument.
4. Choose your instrument from the list and click OK.
5. Click Close to return to the Assign Instruments dialog box.
6. Select from the Output/Channel list all the outputs and channels that are being sent to that instrument.

7. Click on the instrument in the Uses Instrument list.
8. Click OK when you are done.

If your manufacturer or instrument doesn't appear, check our web site to see if an updated instrument definition is available. You can also create your own instrument definition. For more information on instrument definitions, see Chapter 16, *Using Instrument Definitions*.

My Keyboard Doubles Every Note I Play

When your keyboard doubles the notes, each note seems heavier or thicker than usual, as if two notes of the same pitch are emitted when you press the key. Also, you may find that you can play only half as many notes at one time before some of the held notes drop out.

This can occur when MIDI echo is enabled. The keyboard plays the note for the key you've pressed. At the same time, the note is sent through the MIDI interface and echoed back to the keyboard, where it is played a second time.

The best way to resolve the problem is to disable Local Control on the keyboard, following the instructions that came with the keyboard. This stops the keyboard from playing independently. The keys you play still produce sound on the keyboard because they are echoed back by the MIDI interface. In many cases, SONAR disables local control automatically when the program is started, but this is not always possible.

It's also possible that your keyboard is transmitting information on two channels at once. To see if this is so, create a new project and record two notes from the keyboard. Then look at what you've recorded in the Event list view. If you see four notes displayed instead of two, then your keyboard is transmitting on two channels. See the documentation for your keyboard to learn how to correct the problem.

I Don't See the Clips Pane in the Track View

The splitter bar may be so far to the right that the Track pane fills the entire Track view. Here's how to solve the problem:

1. Place your cursor over the splitter bar. It is located on the far right side of the Track view, just to the left of the vertical scroll bar. When you place the cursor over the splitter it changes to a double-headed arrow.
2. Click and drag the splitter bar to the left. You should be all set.

Why Can't SONAR Find My Audio Files?

SONAR looks for all audio data in a certain directory or folder, called the Data Directory, in Cakewalk Projects (or the WaveData Directory in previous versions of Cakewalk products). If you have renamed or moved either SONAR or the Data Directory, SONAR may not be able to find your audio files. If you know where the audio files are stored, choose **Options-Audio**, click Advanced and enter the full path name of the directory in the Data Directory box. If you don't know where the audio data are stored, choose **Start-Find-Files or Folders** and search for files named *.WAV.

For more information about the wavedata folder, see Chapter 19, *Audio File Management*.

I Get an a Error Message When I Change a Project to 24-bit Audio

Some audio devices, especially USB devices that use WDM drivers, can not operate in 24-bit mode unless a variable in SONAR's AUD.INI file is set to 1. The variable is Use24BitExtensible=<0 or 1>, which goes in the [*name of your audio device ('n' in, 'n' out)*] section.

For more information, see the initialization file topics in the online help.

Bouncing Tracks Takes a Long Time

By default, SONAR uses a buffer for bouncing tracks that is the same size as the Mixing Latency value that you set in the Audio Options dialog. But with some projects, especially ones that use certain soft synths, the bounce buffer needs to have its own value. You can set the value in the AUD.INI file with the BounceBufSizeMsec=0 line in the Wave section. At a value of 0, the bounce buffer is the same size as the Mixing Latency value that you set in the Audio Options dialog. You can set the bounce value to 100, or some value between 0 and 350 so that the bounce buffer will use a more efficient size for bouncing, which has different requirements from normal playback latency.

For more information, see the initialization file topics in the online help.

Why Do I Get Errors from the Wave Profiler?

Audio devices such as voice modems or speakerphone devices can cause an error message when running the Wave Profiler. Sometimes these errors are harmless; on other occasions you need to disable the voice modem or speaker-phone device before running the Wave Profiler. To do so:

1. Choose **Options-Audio** and click the Drivers tab.
2. Make sure that the voice modem or speaker-phone device is not selected in both the Input and Output device lists.
3. Click OK.
4. Choose **Options-Audio**, click the General tab, and run the Wave Profiler again.

I Hear an Echo When I Record

If you have input monitoring enabled, when you play an instrument that is plugged into your sound card, you hear the direct signal that goes straight through your sound card, and an instant later you hear the sound that is processed by SONAR, including any plug-in effects you may be using. Only the processed sound is recorded.

You can eliminate the echo in either of two ways:

- Mute the direct signal so you only hear the sound that is processed by SONAR. If you choose this method, you may hear too much of a lag between the time you play your instrument and the time you hear it, depending on the latency of your system (using WDM audio drivers is a great way to achieve lower latency).
- Disable input monitoring so you only hear the raw signal that's coming through your sound card. If you choose this method, you won't hear any plug-in effects you may be using.

To disable input monitoring:

- On the track where you want to disable input monitoring, click the track's Input Echo button so that it is in the off position:

To mute your sound card's direct sound:

1. Open the software mixer that controls your sound card. If your sound card uses the Windows mixer, open the mixer by using the **Start-Programs-Accessories-Entertainment-Volume Control** command, or by double-clicking the speaker icon on the Windows taskbar.

2. In the Play Control window of the mixer, check the Mute checkbox in the Line-In column, or in the column of whatever jack your instrument is plugged into, and close the mixer window.

Audio Distorts at Greater than 16 Bits

There are several settings in the Audio Options dialog box (***Options-Audio*** command) you need to set before using audio formats greater than 16. See "Configuring SONAR for 18 bit-, 20-bit, and 24-bit Operation" on page 630.

No Sound from My DXi

Use the following table to troubleshoot problems hearing a DXi in SONAR:

Possible problem...	What to do...
DXi doesn't sound when a recorded MIDI track is sent to it.	• Make sure you select a MIDI channel in the MIDI track's Output field; you may also need to select a Patch and Bank. • Make sure that neither the MIDI track nor the audio track that contains the DXi are muted. • Make sure the MIDI notes are in the right range for the DXi's patch.
DXi patched into a main out or bus doesn't sound.	• Make sure that at least one audio track is configured to send data to that bus. • Make sure that the Audio Engine button in the Transport toolbar is depressed.
DXi doesn't sound when you play a MIDI controller.	• Make sure that the Audio Engine button in the Transport toolbar is depressed. • Make sure that the MIDI track that has the focus lists the DXi in its Output field. • If you patched the DXi into an audio track, make sure that track is not muted. • If you patched the DXi into a bus, make sure that at least one audio track is configured to send data to that bus. • Make sure you're playing in the right range for the DXi's patch.

| I hear more than one sound when I play a DXi. | • Make sure your MIDI controller is set to local off. |

My Pro Audio 9 Files Sound Louder/Softer When I Open Them in SONAR

Pro Audio 9 has a setting in the Audio Options dialog box called MIDI Volume Mapping. This setting determines how many dB that a movement of a volume fader produces. This setting is not stored in each project file, so SONAR can't tell precisely what dB scale was used to produce the file you're opening. If the volume sounds incorrect:

1. Open SONAR's AUD.INI file (find it in your SONAR folder and double-click it).
2. Change the line that says VolMethod= "N." If N=1, change N to 0; if N=0, change N to 1.
3. Save the file and close it.
4. Reopen the Pro Audio file in SONAR. If the volume sounds correct, save the file in Sonar.
5. If other Pro Audio 9 files were opening correctly in SONAR, change the VoMethod=N line in SONAR's AUD.INI file back to what it originally was, and re-save the file.

I Can't Open My Project

Your project may have become corrupted, or SONAR is attempting to use a plug-in that is not longer on your system. You can attempt to open the project using Safe Mode.

To Use Safe Mode
- If you are opening a file from the Most Recently Used files list in the File menu, hold down the Shift key while selecting file name.
- If you are opening the file from the Open dialog, select the file in the dialog and hold down the Shift key while clicking the OK button.

  Safe Mode does the following:
  - Opens only the Track view.
  - Prompts you if you want to open the plug-ins saved with your project. Each plug-in gets a prompt, so you can open some and not open others.

SONAR Can't Find the Wavetable Synth or MPU401

Follow this procedure:

1. Open the Audio Options dialog (**Options-Audio** command), and on the Advanced tab, check the Always Use MME Interface, Even When WDM Drivers Are Available option.
2. Click OK to close the dialog.
3. Close SONAR and reopen it.
4. Use the **Options-MIDI Devices** command to open the MIDI Devices dialog.
5. Highlight the Wavetable synth and/or the MPU401 (or whatever synth your sound card contains).
6. Click OK to close the dialog.

Now your sound card synth and/or the MPU401 should appear in the drop-down menus of the Output fields of your MIDI tracks.

Appendix B: Hardware Setup

This appendix contains additional details on configuring your equipment for use with SONAR.

Connect Your MIDI Equipment

If you are using a MIDI interface (such as an MPU-401 or Sound Blaster MIDI option) with an external MIDI keyboard, you need to connect the equipment using MIDI cables.

It is possible to connect your equipment in some rather complex ways that may cause problems. If you call for technical support with a problem concerning equipment that doesn't seem to be responding, we'll probably suggest that you reconnect things in one of the ways listed below before we explore the problem further. Also be sure to check *Appendix A: Troubleshooting*, before calling us.

There are two methods that fit many circumstances. The one you choose depends on whether your keyboard has:

- All three types of MIDI jacks: In, Out, and Thru
- Only two types of MIDI jacks: In and Out

If you have only one keyboard, read the "If Your Keyboard Doesn't Have a MIDI Thru Jack" section (regardless of whether you have MIDI Thru or not).

If Your Keyboard Has a MIDI Thru Jack

If your keyboard has three MIDI jacks—In, Out, and Thru—then use the following diagram.

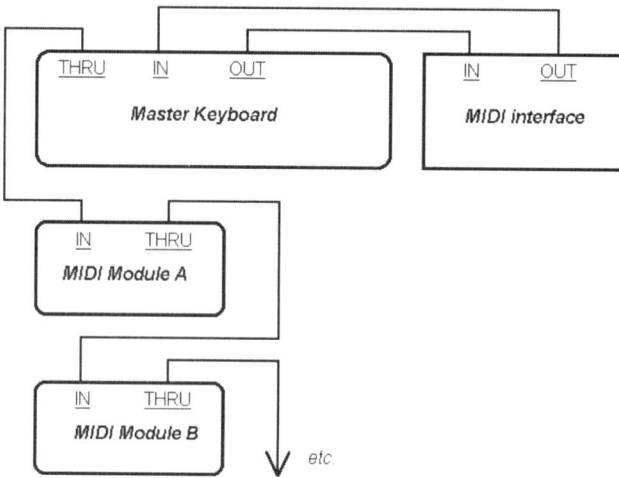

If you are using a 15-pin joystick adapter cable that splits into two MIDI cables:

- Connect the 15-pin jack to your computer's joystick port.
- Connect the In cable to your instrument's MIDI Out jack.
- Connect the Out cable to your instrument's MIDI In jack.

Here's a checklist:

Connect this...	To this...
Master keyboard Out	MIDI interface In
MIDI interface Out	Master keyboard In
Master keyboard Thru	Another MIDI module's In
That MIDI module's Thru	Yet another MIDI module's In

Continue the sequence, repeating the last connection for each of your sound modules.

Each MIDI device should be set to a unique MIDI channel or range of channels to avoid note-doubling. Refer to the manuals for your MIDI devices for information on how to set their MIDI channels.

Your MIDI interface may have a Thru jack as well as In and Out jacks. If your master keyboard lacks MIDI Thru, you can add more MIDI modules to your setup by connecting the MIDI interface's Thru to the first module's In. You can then chain subsequent modules onto the first module, as described earlier.

If your master keyboard now seems to double notes (they sound thicker), or if you can play only one half as many notes at once, first make sure that no MIDI channel is being used by more than one of your MIDI devices. If no MIDI channel is assigned to duplicate devices and you hear doubling or only half as many notes as you should, see "My Keyboard Doubles Every Note I Play" on page 647.

If Your Keyboard Doesn't Have a MIDI Thru Jack

If your keyboard has only two MIDI jacks—In and Out—or if you have only one keyboard, use the following diagrams instead:

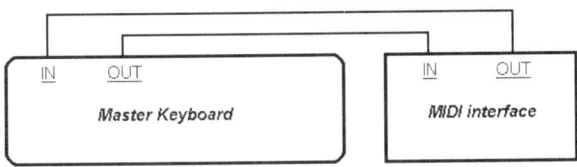

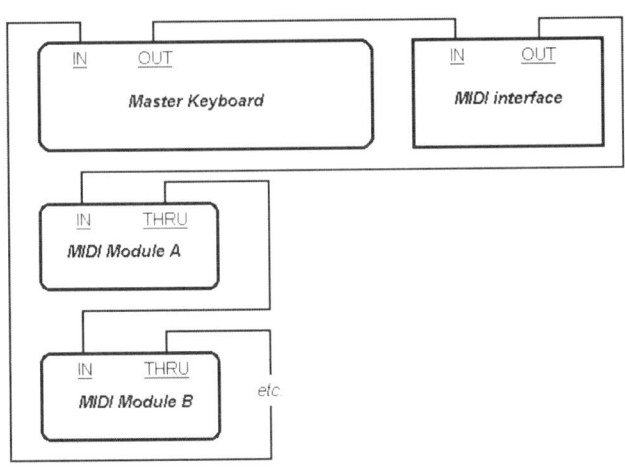

Each MIDI device should be set to a unique MIDI channel or range of channels to avoid note-doubling. Refer to the manuals for your MIDI devices for information on how to set their MIDI channels.

If your master keyboard now seems to double notes (they sound thicker), or if you can play only one half as many at once, first make sure that no MIDI channel is being used by more than one of your MIDI devices. If no MIDI channel is assigned to duplicate devices and you hear doubling or only half as many notes as you should, see "My Keyboard Doubles Every Note I Play" on page 647.

Set Up to Record Digital Audio

In general, the inputs of sound cards take 1/8" stereo mini-jacks. Sound cards usually have two inputs—one for line level inputs and the other for microphones (at mic level). The line level input is stereo; the mic input could be either stereo or mono. If your final output does not terminate in a 1/8" jack (and it probably doesn't), you will need an adapter to plug it into your sound card.

Most sound cards use the Windows Volume Control to adjust the master input and output volumes and to control which recording inputs are active. If you don't hear audio tracks, or if you can't easily control the audio volume in SONAR, go to **Start-Accessories-Volume Control** and check the settings there. See your sound card's documentation for more.

Electric Guitar Direct-In
You can connect an electric guitar directly to your sound card using a   1/4" mono to 1/8" stereo adapter. The following diagram shows this setup:

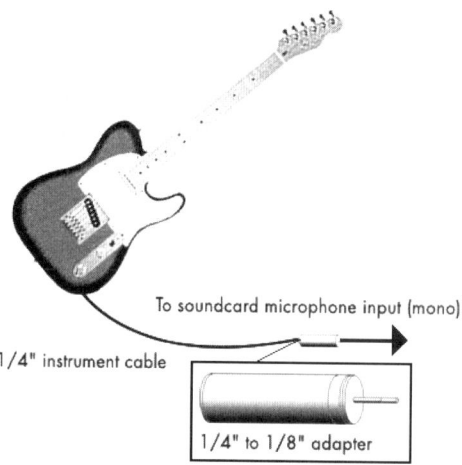

The 1/8" jack should be plugged into the sound card's mic input, although plugging into the line input may also work.

Electric Guitar Through Effects Rack

You can also plug an electric guitar into an effects rack, then send the output of the rack to the sound card's input, as shown in the following diagram:

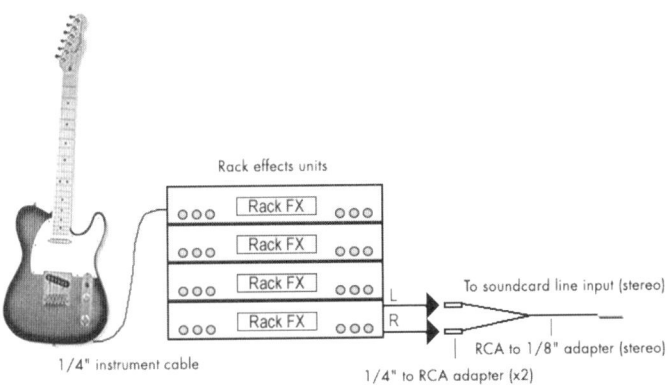

This diagram assumes that the output of the rack is at line level. If it is at pro level instead (+4 dB), and your card does not accept a +4 db input, you will need to attenuate (lower) the F/X rack's signal. To do this, use a mixer between the rack's output and the Y-adapter. If the rack has only a mono output, a 1/4" mono to 1/8" stereo adapter should be used instead of a Y-adapter.

If you want to connect a guitar amplifier's direct output to the sound card, you should base your setup on this example.

Microphone Direct-In

Microphones can be plugged into the sound card's mic input. Some inexpensive microphones are made especially for use with sound cards and come equipped with 1/8" jacks. However, better quality microphones take better quality cables, which do not terminate in 1/8" jacks. The diagram below illustrates how to connect a microphone that terminates in a 1/4" jack:

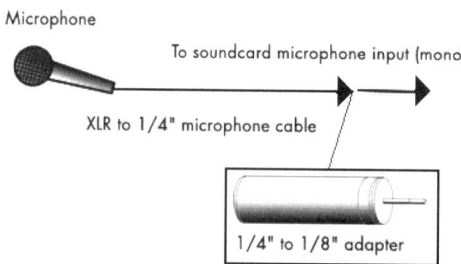

Home Stereo, CD Player, Radio Tuner, Preamp Output

The output of a stereo component can be connected to the sound card's line in, using a dual RCA to 1/8" stereo mini Y-adapter. Many portable cassette players come with this kind of adapter, or even with a single cable with all the necessary jacks. In the following diagram, a stereo component is connected to the Y-adapter using standard RCA cables:

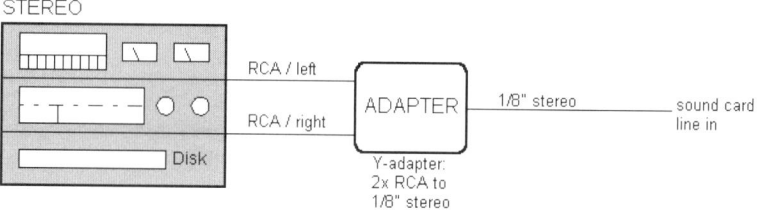

Internal CD Player

If you are using your computer's internal CD player, and it does not have its audio outs connected internally to the sound card, run a cable from the CD player's Headphone jack to the card's Line In jack. If there is no Headphone jack, you'll need to use an external CD player.

Mixer

You can connect a mixer to the sound card with a setup of the following kind:

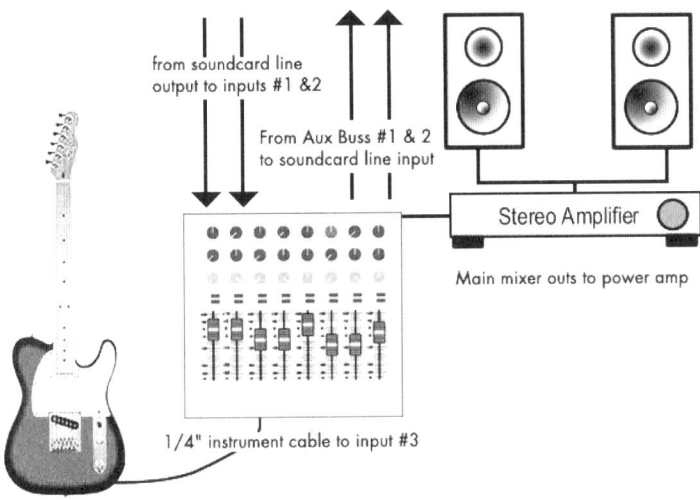

Note:

If your mixer has buses, use them! This helps avoid feedback.

Appendix C: Cyclone

Overview

The graphic below illustrates the Cyclone DXi views and controls.

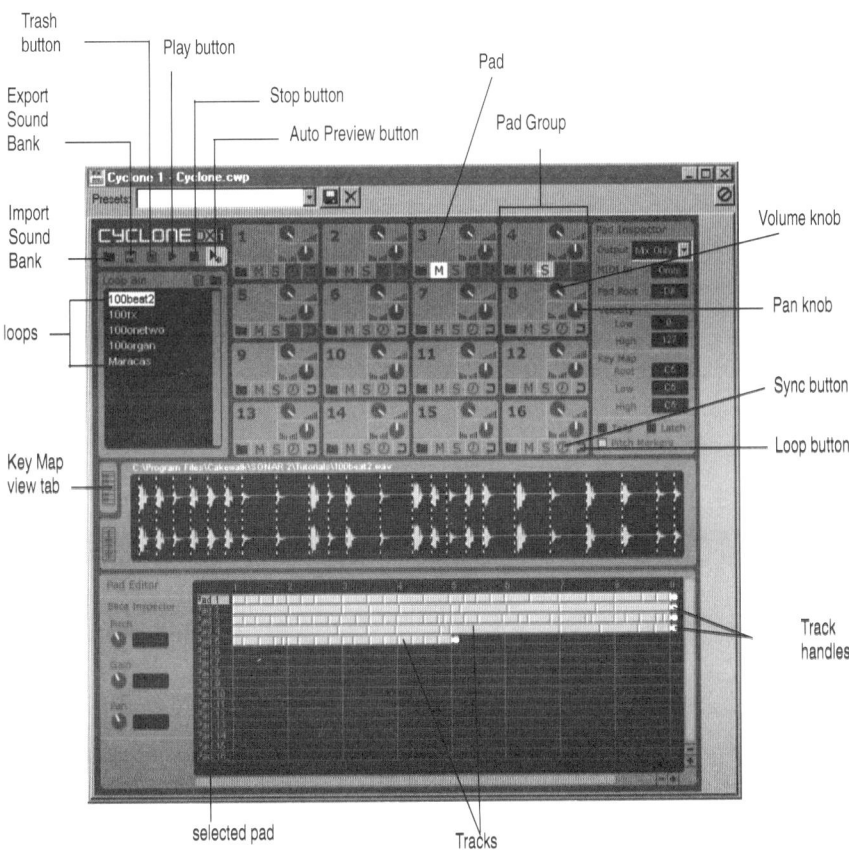

Cyclone DXi Toolbar

The following graphic shows each of Cyclone DXi's toolbar buttons:

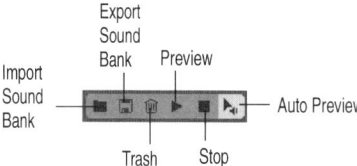

The following table describes each of Cyclone DXi's buttons:

Button...	Description...
Import Sound Bank	Opens the Open dialog so you can load an existing Sound Bank.
Export Sound Bank	Opens the Save As dialog to save the current settings as a Sound Bank (.CYC).
Trash	Clears the contents of the project.
Preview	Plays the selected pads or slices.
Stop	Stops playback.
Auto Preview	When Auto Preview is on, you can preview the sound of a slice by clicking a slice in the Loop view or an event by clicking an event in the Pad Editor. Also, you can click and drag a slice over events in the Pad Editor, releasing the mouse button when you hear the event you want to replace.

Pad Groups

The following graphic shows a close-up of a Cyclone DXi pad group:

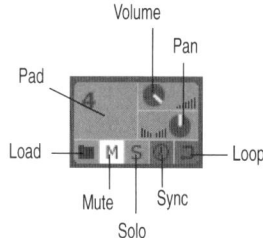

A Pad Group in Cyclone DXi has the following controls:

Control...	Description...
Pad	The trigger for playing a loop.
Volume knob	Adjusts the volume of the Pad Group. The volume value is displayed in the Pad Inspector.
Pan knob	Adjusts the pan of the Pad Group. The pan value is displayed in the Pad Inspector.
File Load button	Opens the Open dialog where you can navigate to the directory or directories where you store your files.
Mute button	Mutes the playback of the Pad Group.
Solo button	When selected, only that Pad Group plays.
Sync button	Synchronizes the playback of the Pad Group to SONAR. When selected, the Pad Group follows SONAR's tempo and pitch.
Loop button	When selected, the playback of the Pad Group repeats continuously.

Pad Inspector

The Pad Inspector has additional pad group controls:

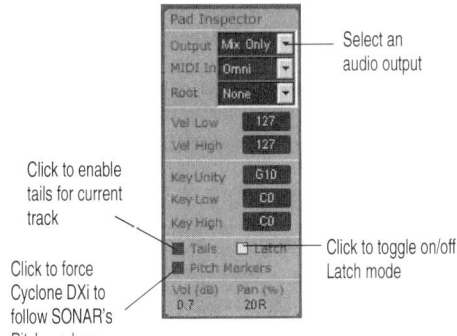

In the Pad Inspector there are the following controls:

Control...	Description...
Output	You can select from one of 16 audio outputs or use the Mix Only setting to use the Master out.
MIDI In	You can set which MIDI channel the pad group responds to. Each pad group could have a unique MIDI Input channel.
Pad Root	This setting is read from the file when it is imported. The first loop sets the Pad Root value for each additional loop.
Velocity—Low	The minimum velocity value that triggers the pad group.
Velocity—High	The maximum velocity value that triggers the pad group.
Key Map—Unity	The MIDI note value at which the loop plays at the Pad Root pitch. This value is assigned to a loop when it is imported. You can change the Unity value in the Pad Inspector or in the Key Map view.
Key Map—Low	The lowest MIDI note value that triggers the pad group. Both the Low and High not values transpose the pitch of the loop if they are different from the Unity note value. The transposition is relative to the Unity note. The played pitch of the loop is not same as the MIDI note that triggers it unless the Unity note and the Pad Root note are the same.
Key Map—High	The highest MIDI note value that triggers the pad group.
Tails	The tails feature extends the "tail" or decay of a slice which may otherwise have ended prematurely, drowned out by the next slice. This is particularly useful when you substitute a longer slice with a shorter one leaving room for a tail to sound.
Latch	The Latch option gives you a second mode for triggering pads. In Latch mode, a Groove Clip plays continuously when triggered until it is triggered again. With Latch mode disabled, a pad only plays as long as the key or mouse button is held and stops when you release. If you want to set all pads to the same Latch state, hold down the Shift key while setting the Latch for any one pad.
Pitch Markers	This option forces Cyclone DXi to follow SONAR's Pitch markers. When a Pitch marker is encountered, the loop is transposed by the same number of semi-tones as the pitch change in SONAR.

Loop Bin

The Loop bin, located right below the Cyclone DXi toolbar, is where you can place loops you want to use in Cyclone DXi. From the Loop bin you can drag and drop loops onto a Pad or into the Pad Editor.

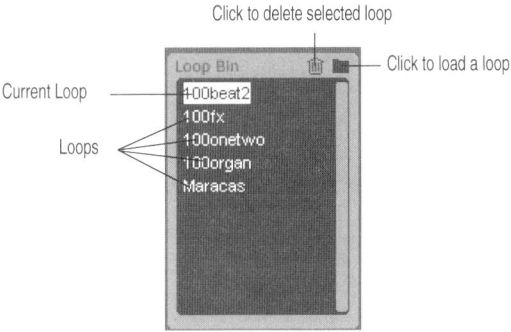

Loop View and Key Map View

The Loop view displays the content of the loop you have selected in the Loop bin. If the loop is an ACIDized loop, the loops transient markers separate the file's slices. From the Loop view, you can drag a slice onto an event in the Pad Editor.

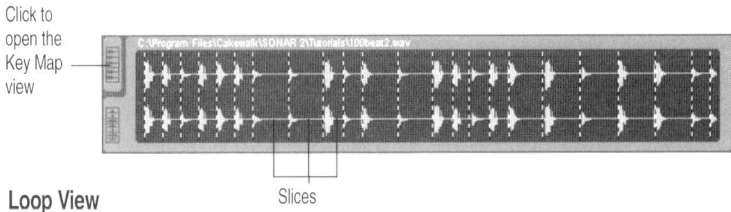

The Key Map view shares the same space in Cyclone DXi as the Loop view. You toggle between the two views by clicking on one of the tabs to the left of whichever view is displayed. The keyboard in the Key Map view shows the Unity note (in orange) and the range of notes that trigger the pad group (in blue). Drag the Unity

665

note to change its value. Drag the white triangles to extend the range of MIDI note values that trigger the pad group.

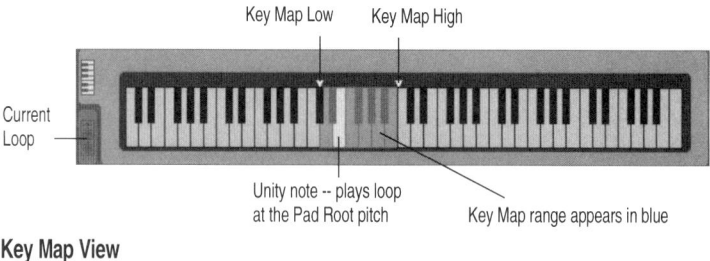

Key Map View

Pad Editor

The Pad Editor displays up to 16 "tracks," one for each pad in Cyclone DXi. Each track has the same number as the pad it represents. Each track is made up of events. An event represents a slice of a ACIDized loop, or in the case of standard wave files, it represents the entire file. Each track in the Pad Editor can be made up of slices from any number of different files. Each track in the Pad Editor terminates with a Track Handle. A Track Handle marks the point at which the track loops back to the beginning. You can move Track Handles using the mouse to any point in the Pad Editor, shortening or lengthening the length of the track.

Slice Inspector

The Slice Inspector has pitch, gain and pan offset controls. You can change the pitch of the slices in a loop to change the melody of the loop. If you want to edit multiple slices at the same time, select multiple slices by Shift-selecting them and adjust the controls you want.

Using Cyclone DXi

Cyclone DXi is a multi-output DXi, and you launch it the same way you launch other DXi's: by inserting it into a SONAR project. There are two basic ways to insert DXi's in SONAR:

- You can insert DXi's from the Synth Rack view or with the **Insert-DX Synth** command. If you use this method, you can choose to have SONAR create the necessary audio and MIDI tracks, and patch them together correctly. If you want to use multiple audio tracks to take advantage of SONAR's multi-output support, you need to create and patch additional MIDI tracks manually to feed the additional audio tracks.

- You can insert DXi's into Fx bins of individual audio tracks. If you use this method, you need to set a MIDI track's Output field to the name of the DXi you inserted. Then you can record MIDI data in the MIDI track to play the DXi with. This method does not allow you to use multiple outputs.

For step by step instructions, see "Inserting a DXi" on page 402, "Multi-port DXi's" on page 402, and "Converting Your DXi Tracks to Audio" on page 407.

Note: This documentation refers to any audio data that you can import into Cyclone DXi as **loops**, referring to ACIDized loops and standard Wave files.

To Load Loops into Cyclone DXi
- Click the folder icon that's on the Loop bin to display the Open dialog. Select a loop and click Open. Cyclone DXi loads the loop into the Loop bin.

  OR

- Click a folder icon that's on a particular Pad that you want to load a loop into. When the Open dialog appears, select a loop and click Open. Cyclone DXi loads the loop into both the Pad where you clicked the folder icon and the Loop bin.

  OR

- Drag a loop into Cyclone DXi from SONAR's Clips pane or Loop Explorer view.

  Note: ACIDized and Riff Wave files imported into Cyclone DXi can not be more than 64 beats long. Regular wave files are limited to 30 seconds. Cyclone DXi does not support 8-bit files.

To Audition Loops
- Select a loop in the Loop bin, and then click Cyclone DXi's Play button.

To Play Loops
1. Assign a loop to a pad or pads"To Assign a Loop to a Pad" on page 668.
2. Select the pad or pads you want to play by clicking on them.
3. Click the Preview button to play the selected pads.

   If the Loop button for that pad is depressed the loop plays indefinitely; you can stop it by clicking the Pad again.

   If the Loop button is not depressed, the loop stops when it reaches the end of its original length. You can stop it before then by clicking the Pad.

You can also trigger the Pads with a MIDI controller, or with recorded MIDI data.

To Play a Loop in Latch Mode
1. Assign a loop to a Pad"To Assign a Loop to a Pad" on page 668.
2. In the Pad Editor, select the track you want to loop in Latch mode.
3. In the Pad Inspector, click the Latch control to enable it. The Latch control indicator appears green when enabled.
4. Click the mouse on the pad to start the loop playing.
5. Click the mouse on the pad again to stop playing.

The loop stops playing as soon as you release the mouse button.

To Assign a Loop to a Pad
- Drag a loop from the Loop bin to a Pad.

  OR

- Click a folder icon that's on a particular Pad that you want to load a loop into. When the Open dialog appears, select a loop and click Open. Cyclone DXi loads the loop into both the Pad where you clicked the folder icon and the Loop bin.

  OR

- Drag a loop onto a Pad from SONAR's Clips pane or Loop Explorer view.

You can assign one loop per Pad.

To Synchronize a Loop to Cakewalk's Tempo
- Click the Sync button that's on the Pad that the loop is assigned to. The Sync button lights up when it's engaged.

To Set a Loop to Follow Cakewalk's Pitch Markers
1. In the Pad Editor, select the track you want to follow pitch markers.
2. In the Pad Inspector, click the Pitch Markers control. The Pitch Markers control appears green when enabled.

To Assign MIDI Keys to a Pad

1. Click the Pad that you want to trigger.
2. Click the Keyboard button in the Loop view to display the Key Map view.

    The blue keys between the Pitch Range markers show what MIDI keys trigger the Pad. The yellow key is the Root Note, which triggers the loop at its original pitch.

3. Drag the edge of the Pitch Range (the blue keys within the white triangle markers) to change the range of notes that trigger the loop. If the loop's pitch changing function is turned on, each MIDI key in the trigger range transposes the loop by the trigger note's distance from the Root Note.
4. Drag the yellow key to change the Root Note. The Root note does not have to be in the trigger range.
5. In the MIDI Chn field, choose the MIDI channel that the MIDI notes will use to trigger this pad with.

You can assign the same key ranges to all the Pads if you want. You can assign different velocity ranges to each pad, also.

To Assign a Velocity Range to a Pad

1. Click the Pad that you want to assign a velocity range to.
2. Click the Keyboard button in the Loop view to display the Key Map view.
3. In the Velocity Low field, fill in the lowest velocity that you want to trigger the Pad with.
4. In the Velocity High field, fill in the highest velocity that you want to trigger the Pad with.

Now the Pad only plays its loop when the Pad receives a MIDI note within its velocity range.

To Play a Pad with Recorded MIDI Data

1. Record some MIDI data into a SONAR MIDI track.
2. In the MIDI track's Output field, choose Cyclone DXi. Cyclone DXi must have been already inserted into the project in order for it to appear as a choice in the Output field.
3. In the MIDI track's Ch field, choose the number of the Cyclone DXi Pad that you want to trigger with this MIDI track.

Controlling Individual Pads—Volume, Pan, Mute, Solo, Sync, Looping, and Content

Each Pad has the following controls:

- Volume knob—turn to adjust.

- Pan knob—turn to adjust.

- Folder icon—click this to import a loop to an individual Pad.

- Mute button—click this to mute or unmute the loop that's assigned to an individual Pad.

- Solo button—click this to solo or un-solo the loop that's assigned to an individual Pad.

- Sync button—click this to synchronize (or unsynchronize) the Pad's loop to SONAR's pitch and tempo.

- Loop button—click this to cause or prevent the Pad's loop from repeating indefinitely between its track length markers that are in the Pad Editor.

To Export a Sound Bank

1. Click the Export Sound Bank button in the Cyclone toolbar.

    The Save As dialog appears.

2. Navigate to the directory where you want to save the Sound Bank.

3. Enter a name for the Sound Bank.

4. Click OK.

Cyclone DXi saves your Sound Bank. All wave files assigned to pads are saved. You can choose that Sound Bank in any Cyclone project SONAR automatically saves your current Cyclone settings, so you do not need to save a Sound Bank unless you want to use these settings in a different project.

To Import a Sound Bank

1. Click the Import Sound Bank button on the Cyclone toolbar.

    The Open dialog appears.

2. Navigate to the directory where you saved your Sound Bank, select it and click OK.

Cyclone DXi loads the loops and associated settings that make up the Sound Bank you loaded.

To Clear the Contents of a Project

- Click the Trash icon in the Cyclone DXi toolbar.

    Cyclone DXi deletes all loops from your project.

Mixing Down Cyclone DXi

You mix down a Cyclone DXi session the same ways you mix down any DXi.

For step-by-step instructions, see "Converting Your DXi Tracks to Audio" on page 407.

Loop Editing

Clicking a loop in the Loop bin displays that loop in the Loop view. The Loop view displays the selected loop as a series of slices that separate the transients in the loop. When the Auto-preview button is depressed, you can click each of the slices to hear it. If the loop is assigned to a Pad, the slices also appear in the Pad Editor as a series of **events**, which you can also click to hear. Clicking an event in the Pad Editor also highlights the corresponding slice in the Loop view.

You can drag slices from the Loop view to any position in any track in the Pad Editor in order to add data to a Pad, or replace an already-existing event If you can drag a slice along a series of events in the Pad Editor, if the Auto-preview button is depressed, each event sounds as you drag across it, enabling you to hear events before you decide to replace them.

To Add or Replace Parts of a Loop
1. In the Loop bin, click the loop that you want to use as source material.
2. Make sure that the Auto-preview button is on.
3. Drag the slice that you want to use from the Loop view to the slice or empty space in the Pad Editor that you want to place the slice.
4. If you dragged to an area that's to the right of the Track Length marker, drag the marker to the right until it's to the right of the new slice.

To Change the Length of a Track
- Drag the Track Length marker to the right or left to lengthen or shorten the track, respectively. You can include empty space in your track. If you depress the Loop button for that Pad (track), the track loops continuously between the beginning of the track and the Track Length marker.

To Set the Number of Divisions for a Slice
You can set the number of divisions in each slice. This controls how exact the placement of your slices is within the Pad Editor. Each division represents a place where a slice can "snap to" or begin.

1. In the Pad Editor, click the down arrow next to the Snap field.
2. From the dropdown menu that appears, select one of the following:
   - None
   - 1/beat
   - 2/beat

- 3/beat
- 4/beat
- 8/beat
- 12/beat
- 16/beat

The number of divisions per beat in Cyclone DXi is set.

Keyboard Shortcuts in Cyclone DXi

The following table lists the keyboard shortcuts in Cyclone DXi and explains what they do:

Keyboard Shortcut...	Description...
Shift selecting	Hold the Shift key to select multiple slices in the Pad Editor.
Shift drag	Hold the Shift key while dragging to maintain a slice's time.
Ctrl drag	Hold the Ctrl key while dragging to copy a slice.
Shift Ctrl drag	Hold the Shift and Ctrl keys simultaneously while dragging to copy the slice and maintain the slice's time.
Left and Right arrows	Turn on Auto Preview, select a slice in the Loop view or Pad Editor, and use the left and right arrow keys to listen to individual beats.

Undo and Redo

You can undo any edit you make in Cyclone DXi. If you decide, after you have used Undo, that you want the edit after all, you can Redo the edit. The number of edits you can Undo and Redo in Cyclone DXi is unlimited.

To Undo an Edit
Press the Ctrl+Z keys.

To Redo an Edit
Press the Shift+Ctrl+Z keys.

Appendix D: New Features in SONAR 4

SONAR 4 has several new features (some features are in SONAR Producer only). The following is a listing of each new feature, and a brief description.

Surround Mixing

SONAR Producer fully supports Surround Mixing. For more information, see Chapter 12, *Surround Mixing*.

SurroundBridge (Surround Effects Linker)

SONAR Producer has the new SurroundBridge that allows you to use any stereo or mono plug-in your surround mixes. For more information, see "Surround Effects" on page 488.

Track Folders

Track Folders contain other tracks, making editing much quicker, and freeing up screen space. For more information, see "Track Folders" on page 238.

Slip-editing Multiple Clips

You can now perform Slip Editing on multiple clips. For more information, see "Slip-editing Multiple MIDI Clips" on page 293, and "Slip-editing Multiple Audio Clips" on page 379.

Freeze Synths or Tracks

The Freeze feature allows synths and plug-ins you to temporarily bounce audio, saving on CPU usage. Freeze options can be found in the Synth Rack View and the Track menu. For more information, see "Freeze Synths or Tracks" on page 674.

Loop Construction View Enhancements

You can now edit the gain, pan and pitch of individual slices of a Groove clip. For more information, see "Editing Slices" on page 265.

Audio Metronome

SONAR now gives you the option of using audio for your metronome sounds. For more information, see "Setting the Metronome and Tempo Settings" on page 165.

Clip Muting and Isolating (Clip Soloing)

Now you can mute and solo individual clips or time regions. For more information, see "Clip Muting and Isolating (Clip Soloing)" on page 234.

Video Thumbnails

SONAR Producer has a new Video Thumbnails pane at the top of the Track view, which displays individual frames of a project's video at regular intervals in the project. For more information, see "Using the Video Thumbnails Pane" on page 154.

Enhanced Key Bindings

Now you can import key bindings from other popular sequencer programs, use single-key commands, and more. For more information, see "Key Bindings" on page 520.

Enhanced Import/Export/Bounce Features

SONAR now has preset controls for the Bounce to Tracks and Export Audio dialogs, allows you to export individual tracks to new files, and has friendly bounce-to-track names. SONAR Producer allows you to import and export surround-encoded files, including Windows Media Pro files.

For more information, see "Bouncing Tracks" on page 456, "Preparing Audio for Distribution" on page 459, "Importing Surround Mixes" on page 491, and "Exporting Surround Mixes" on page 492.

Navigator Pane in the Track View

The Navigator pane provides an overview for your whole project, allowing you to quickly move to any part or zoom in or out.

Take Management and Comping Takes

Composite tracks allow you to easily work with multiple takes in a single track. For more information, see "Take Management and Comping Takes" on page 232.

Audition (Selection Playback)

If you want, you can play back only selected clips and/or time regions. For more information, see "Audition (Selection Playback)" on page 237.

Nudge

You can now use keyboard or menu commands to "nudge" clips to the left or right by 3 different amounts that you can set. For more information, see "Nudge" on page 218.

Configurable Panning Laws

You can now choose different panning laws for different styles of mixing, and for greater compatibility with imported projects. For more information, see "Configurable Panning Laws" on page 140.

Joystick Support

SONAR allows you to use a joystick to control surround panning, and also many transport and menu commands. For more information, see "Joystick Support" on page 485.

PoW-r Dither

SONAR offers the new PoW-r dithering process, short for Psycho-acoustically Optimized Wordlength Reduction, which can produce 16-bit files that sound indistinguishable from their 24-bit source files. For more information, see "Dithering" on page 468.

Meter Ballistics

SONAR 4 has configurable meter ballistics. These allow you to adjust the rise and fall times of both the RMS and Peak Meters. Out of the box, SONAR 4 ships with industry-standard settings that mimic meter ballistics for common hardware consoles. For more information, see "Changing the Meters' Performance" on page 440.

Surround Plug-ins

SONAR 4 includes two new surround plug-ins: Pantheon Surround and Sonitus Surround Compressor.

Cakewalk TTS-1

The Cakewalk TTS-1 software synthesizer replaces the Edirol VSC.

Index

Symbols
.CWB files 198
    size limitation of 619
.CWP files 31
.CWT files 517
.MID files 198
.SYX files 587, 594
.TPL files 517

Numerics
16-bit audio
    importing into a 24-bit project 634
18 and 24 bit operation 630
24-bit audio
    importing into a 16-bit project 633
24-bit problems 648
3dB Louder 356, 366
3dB Quieter 356, 366
96 kHz audio and plug-ins 640

A
ACID files
    saving a loop as 266
ACIDized files
    tutorial 85
ACIDized loops 260
    saving a Groove clip as 266
Acidized loops
    memory usage 251
Acoustics 350
Add Node 497
Adjusting timing of notes *See* Quantizing
Aftertouch 313
    data display 315
    See also Channel Aftertouch
AIFF 195
Amplitude 352, 355
    waveform 356
Anchor points, see Snap offsets 224
Apply Trimming 293, 379
Archive 126
Archiving tracks 126
Arm 174
Arm for Automation 496
ASCII TAB
    exporting to 555
    saving as 555
ASIO drivers
    enabling 638
Audigy card
    LFE channel 476
Audio
    applying EQ to 368
    auditioning with scrub tool 365
    basic editing 357
    boosting volume by 3dB 367
    decreasing volume by 3dB 367
    digital 24, 350
    distortion 176

editing tutorial 81
effects 386
exporting 459
finding missing 157
importing 195
metronome 165
mixing 430
plug-ins 386
recording *See* Recording audio
routing 430
scrubbing 365
under SMPTE/MTC Sync 613
where it is stored 620
Audio 169, 629
Audio CD
how to create 459
Audio clips 356
Bounce to Clip(s) 364
changing name off 358
changing start time of 358
combining 364
copying 359
deleting 359
moving 359
pasting 359
properties of 358
splitting 363
to turn off automatic display of 179
Audio data
applying a fade to 385
backing up 624
deleting unused files of 625
distributing 459–467
equalizing 368–369
imported files 623
improving performance with 634
parametric equalization 375
playback problems 644
RealAudio settings 461
recording problems 645
reversing 368

stereo chorusing in 391
stereo delay in 392
time/pitch stretch in 397
Audio effects
chorus 390
controlling 433
CPU usage of 448
delay 391–392
DirectX technology 386
flanging 393
mixing 388
pitch stretching 388, 395–397
reverb 394
shifting pitch 395
time stretching 388, 395–397
See also Mixing; Reverb
Audio engine button 183
Audio events
editing 358
size of 387
Audio files
managing 617
Audio folders 620
per-project 621
Audio hardware
Wave Profiler 628
Audio performance
improving 627
Audio processing
playing backward 368
removing silence 369–371
See also Volume
Audio recording
tutorial 68
Audio scaling 359
Loop Construction view 256
Audio tracks
parameters 127
Audition 237
Auto arming 174
Auto punch 170
See also Punch recording

Auto save
　changing settings 199
Auto Send banks 594
Auto-Erase
　toggle off 281
　using 281
Automatic crossfades 380
Automatic MIDI echo
　turning off 146
Automating effects 507
Automation
　automated muting 512
　automating a DXi's controls 408
　automating groups of controls 509
　converting Piano Roll envelopes to Track view envelopes 311, 499
　copying and pasting envelopes 503
　deleting envelopes 502
　dotted lines 501
　drawing audio envelopes in the Track view 497
　drawing envelopes on clips 501
　drawing MIDI envelopes in the Track view 499
　drawing track envelopes for MIDI data 499
　Enable Automation Playback button 493
　Envelope tool 497
　faders and knobs in Console view 496
　jump 498
　methods 495
　quick guide 494
　reassigning envelopes to other parameters 510
　Record Automation button 496
　recording automation from an external controller 510
　recording individual fader or knob movements 496
　resetting envelopes to default values 504
　shapes 498
　showing or hiding envelopes 502
　snapshots 506
　surround panning 485
　the envelope and node editing menus 511
　toolbar 495
　using 493
Automation curves 498
Automation Data 311, 313
Automation toolbar 495
AVI files
　importing 150

B

Backing up your work
　audio data 624
　bundle files 198
　using per-project audio folders 624
Band filters 374
Banks 130, 136–138
　assigning a bank select method 577–578
　assigning patch names to 578–579
　assigning to a track 137
　load 594
　parameters 319
　save 594
　Sysx 587, 588
Bar lines
　adding to an improvised track *See* Fit Improvisation
Batch mode
　playing back files in 148
Beat Value 562
Beats per Measure 562
Beats, accenting 303
Beginning 118
Big Time view 42
　displaying 117
　font settings 117
Bit depth
　setting 169
Block Rate 396
Bounce to Clip(s) 364

Bounce to Track(s)
   combining tracks using 364
Bounce to tracks
   how to 457
Bouncing tracks 456
   takes too long 648
Broadcast wave files
   description of 463
   how to export 462
Bundle files
   creating 619
   opening 620
   size limit of 619
   unpacking 620
Burning a CD 459
Bus
   no level despite fader volume 645
Buses 38, 434, 435
   controlling 435
   sending audio data to 433

C

Cakewalk FX Parametric EQ 389–390
Cakewalk FX Stereo Chorus 390
Cakewalk FX Stereo Delay 391–392
Cakewalk FX Stereo Flange 393
Cakewalk FX Stereo Reverb 328, 394–395
Cakewalk Pitch Shifter 395
Cakewalk Time/Pitch Stretch 395–397
CD
   creating 459
   quality 355
   sampling rate 168
CD burning
   preparing audio with higher bit and/or sample rates 632
CD player
   connecting to 658
ChanAft event 319
Change audio format 633

Channel 130, 141, 279, 310
   assigning instruments to 570–572
   note property 536
   pedal event parameter 549
Chn parameter 141
Chord
   analyzing 331
Chord event 320
Chord Grid 546
Chord Library 546
Chord Symbols 543–547
Chords 320, 543–547
   editing from the fretboard 555
   properties of 544
Chorus 390–391
Clean Audio Folder 625, 626
Clear All 504
Clip muting 234
Clip muting with the alternate style 236
Clip muting with the default style 235
Clip properties 358
Clip soloing 234, 237
Clips 32
   arranging 209–218, 222
   arranging audio 349
   audio 356
   changing colors of 212
   combining 230–232, 364
   copying 214
   copying using copy and paste 218
   copying using drag and drop 217
   crossfading 386
   cutting and pasting 216
   deleting 218
   displaying 209, 211
   displaying contents 211
   displaying names 211
   drag and drop editing 215
   envelopes 501
   groove clips 251

linked 228–230
moving 214–217
moving to a specific start time 217
pasting as new 215
pasting into existing 215
performance effects of 636
properties 212, 217
renaming 212
reversing notes in 283, 290
selecting 35, 214
selecting partial 35
splitting 230
splitting options 231
trimming non-destructively 291, 375
not visible 647
Clock
sources 602–604
Clone 208
Clone 208
Cloning a track 208
Color
screen 45–46
Colors 45
Combining clips 230
Comping takes 232
Confidence recording 179
Connecting
electric guitar 26
microphone 26
Console view
adjusting knobs in 422
automating controls in 496
choosing inputs in 173
controls 422
linking controls in 449–453
modules 421
mute and solo in 125
overview 38
Consolidate Project Audio 625
Control event 319

Control groups 449
absolute 449, 452
custom 451, 453
editing 448, 452
relative 451–452
See also Automation Data
Controllers 307, 311, 319
adding series of 316
assigning, to instruments 581
data display 315
deleting 317
inserting a series 316
inserting values 315
numbers 312
pane 313–317
parameters 319
Controllers pane
description of 314
tools 314
Convert MIDI to shapes procedure 317
Converting bit depths 633
Converting DXi tracks to audio 407
Converting MIDI to audio 429
Converting sample rates and bit depths 632
Copyright 199
Count-in 165
CPS (cycles per second) 350
CPU meter 639
CPU performance 448, 634
Credits 199
Crescendos 290–291, 548
creating using *Process-Scale Velocity* 290
Cropping overlapping clips 234
Crossfade 380
changing the curve types in 384
curve types 380
Crossfade 385
Crossfade Ratio 396

681

Crossfades
   applying offline 384
   automatic 382
   non-destructive 380
Current track 144
Current track MIDI echo
   turning off 146
Curves
   types in fades and crossfades 380
Cut (dB) 374
Cycle 350
Cycles per second 350
Cyclone DXi
   editing loops in 671
   Key Map view 665
   keyboard shortcuts in 672
   loading loops in 667
   Loop bin 665
   Loop view 665
   overview 661
   Pad Editor 666
   pad groups 662
   Pad Inspector 663
   Slice Inspector 666
   toolbar 662
   using 667

D

Data
   sysx 587–599
Data directory 620
dB
   audio scaling by 256, 359
Decibel scale 355–356
Decrescendos 290
   creating using *Process-Scale Velocity* Velocity 290
Default pitch
   changing a project's 267
Defining instruments 31

Deglitch filter 537, 538
   using 538
Delay 391
   adding 328, 391
Delete 208
Digital audio recording *See* Recording audio
Digital audio *See* Audio
Digital distortion 176
Diminuendo 548
DirectX 386
Disk meter 639
Disks
   caching 636
   compressed 635
   fragmented 636
   storage requirements 636
Displacement 350
Distortion 374
Dithering 468, 633
DMA settings 29, 628
Dotted lines 501
Doubled notes 147
Downmixing 478
Drag and Drop 229
Drawing MIDI envelopes in the Track view 499
Drivers
   using ASIO 638
Drum editing 335
Drum Grid pane 344
   changing grid line display in 344
   displaying tracks in 340
   displaying velocity tails in 341
   editing note velocities in 341
Drum machines 607
Drum Map Manager
   opening 336
   working in 338
Drum Map Manager 336

Drum maps
  assigning a MIDI track to 340
  creating 336
  editing 336
  opening 340
  saving 339
  the basics 336
  tutorial 104
Dual monitor support 517
Dump Request Macros (DRM) 591, 592
Duration 189
  Fill 539
  note 296, 324
  note property 536
  parameter 319
  time 539
DX instruments 399
DXi 399, 405
  automating controls 408
  converting DXi tracks to audio 407
  inserting into a project 402
  multi-port 402
  muting and soloing 407
  recording output 407
  removing from a project 407
  removing from a track 406
DXi property pages (interfaces)
  how to open 404
DXi's
  overview 399

E

Echo
  adding 328, 391
  eliminating during recording 649
Echo/Delay
  adding 392
Edit-Apply Trimming
  deleting slip-edited data using 293, 379
Edit-Bounce to Clip(s)
  combining clips using 230, 364

Edit-Bounce to Track(s)
  mixing down tracks using 456
Edit-Convert MIDI To Shapes 311, 499
Edit-Copy
  arranging clips using 209
  copying envelopes using 503
  importing tracks from other projects with 196
Edit-Cut 208, 209, 216, 323, 503
Edit-Delete
  deleting clips using 218
  deleting measures using 287
  deleting time using 287
Edit-Groove Clip Looping
  enabling Groove clip looping using 259
Edit-History 249
Editing
  slip editing 291, 375
Editing audio
  tutorial 81
Editing MIDI
  tutorial 74
Edit-Paste
  arranging clips using 209
  importing tracks from a project using 196
  pasting envelopes using 504
Edit-Redo 170
Edit-Select-By Time 221
Edit-Select-None 221
Edit-Split
  splitting clips using 230
Edit-Undo 170, 208
Effects
  adding 139
  adding in the Track view 240
  audio 386
  automating 507
  chorus 390–391
  CPU usage of 448
  increasing number of 635
  MIDI 325
  real-time audio 444

relinking surround parameters 490
unlinking surround parameters 489
Effects with surround sound 488
Electric Guitar
   connecting 26
Enable Automation Playback button 493
End 118
Ensoniq instruments 599
Envelope Display on a Percentage Scale 506
Envelope mode 504
   troubleshooting 645
Envelope tool 497
Envelopes
   copying and pasting 503
   deleting 502
   drawing audio envelopes in the Track view 497
   drawing envelopes on clips 501
   drawing track envelopes for MIDI data 499
   resetting to default values 504
   showing or hiding envelopes 502
Envelopes-Track 497
EQ
   per-track 446
Equalization 368
   applying 368
   applying parametric 375, 390
   parametric 374, 389
Errors
   timing 294
   Wave Profiler 649
Event
   deleting 323
   inserting new 323
   searching for a 308
Event filters 306, 306–310
   selecting events using 309
   setting up 307
Event inspector toolbar 274

Event List view 41, 273, 318–325
   multiple tracks in 319
   note names in 580
   opening 318
   Pitch parameter 319
Event Parameters
   editing 322
Event types
   filtering 194
Events
   audio 326
   channel aftertouch 307
   controller 307
   editing 283, 322
   Key aftertouch 307
   MCIcmd 325
   note 307, 324
   out-of-window 298
   parameters 307, 310
   patch 321
   patch change 307
   pitch wheel 307
   searching a song for 305
   searching for 305
   selecting 308
   selecting controller 314
   shifting in time 285
   shifting the time of 143
   shrink using percentages 289
   step by step playback 324
   stretch using percentages 289
   stretching and shrinking 288
   transposing selected 284
   xRPN 307
Exporting
   audio 459, 462
   MP3s 466
   projects as OMF files 467
   RealAudio 460
   Windows Media Format files 464
Exporting key bindings 523
Exporting MIDI Groove clips 269

Exporting surround mixes 492
Exporting video 153
Expression event 320
Expression marks 320, 547–548
    editing 548
Extract Timing 371

F

Fade
    changing curve type of 384
Fade/Envelope 384–385
Faders 449
Fades 380
FAQs 641
FAX modems 630
Features, new 673
File
    opening 33
File extensions
    .CWB 198
    .CWP 31
    .CWT 517
    .MID 198
    .SYX 587, 594
File Info window 200
File menu
    Open 33
File-Close 198
File-Export-Audio 408, 429, 462, 464, 466
File-Export-OMF 467
File-Import-Audio 195, 261, 623
File-Info 199
File-New 162, 163, 519
File-Open 162
File-Print 200, 559
File-Print Preview 200, 559
File-Project Audio Files 624

Files
    .WAV 459
    audio 195
    bundle 148
    bundle, creating 619
    digital audio 627
    groove 300
    importing MIDI 197
    instrument definitions 572–584
    managing audio 617
    MIDI 148
    project 148
    RealMedia 459
    sequencing, for playback 148
    statistics 201
    StudioWare 32
    SYSX.INI 597
    using MCI commands to play 325
    Wave 459
File-Save 198, 199
File-Save As 198
Fill Durations 539
filters
    parameters for 389
Find Missing Audio dialog 157
Finding missing audio 157
Fit Improvisation 294
Fit to Time 241
Flanging 393
Floating a view 517
Floating views 517
    dual monitor support 44
Freezing tracks and synths 441
Frequency 350
    fundamental 351
Fretboard
    changing appearance 552
    displaying 530
    hiding 530
Fretboard pane *See* Fretboard
From 118

Front/rear balance slider 482
Full chase lock 612

G

Gain (dB) 374
Game sound 22
Ghost strokes 559
Global 162, 366
Global Audio Folder 620
Global Audio folder
   changing 621
Global Options
   autosave 199
   default folder 514, 517
   MIDI filter tab 194
Go menu
   Beginning 118
   End 118
   From 118
   Next Marker 227
   Next Measure 118
   Previous Marker 227
   Previous Measure 118
   Search 305, 308
   Search Next 305
   Thru 118
   Time 118
Gridlines, displaying 222
Groove clips 32, 251
   creating 262
   dragging into project 258
   editing 262
   editing slices 265
   following project pitch 264
   how they work 260
   importing into project 261
   MIDI 267
   previewing in Loop Explorer view 258
   tutorial 85
   using 261

   what they are 260
   working with 260
Groove Pattern 299
   copying 302
   defining 301
   deleting 303
   saving 301
Groove Quantize 295, 296
   using 299
Groove Quantize
   correcting a bad verse with 304
Grooves *See* Groove Pattern
Group 452
   chord property 544
Group Properties 453
Grouped controls
   automating 509
Grouping controls, faders, or knobs 449
Grouping surround panner controls 483
Guitar
   adding chord grid 546
   recording separate strings 192
Guitar, electric
   connecting 656–657

H

Hairpin event 320
Hairpin symbols 543, 548
   adding 549
Hardware setup 653
Help
   online xx
Help menu
   Quick Start 28
Help, online xx
Hertz 350
High Pass 374
Higher bit operation 630
History 250

Home Stereo
    connecting to 658
Hz 350

I

Importing
    audio files 195
    from a Cakewalk project 196–198
    music 195–200
Importing different sample rates 634
Importing key bindings 523
Importing MIDI Groove clips 269
Importing surround mixes 491
Input 130
Input Echo button 145
Input filtering 194
Input levels
    checking 177
Input Monitoring
    turning on or off for all tracks 147
Input monitoring 180
    disabling 649
    eliminating echo from 183
    enabling 183
Inputs
    choosing in Console view 173
    selecting 433
    setting source of 171
Insert menu
    Series of Controllers 316
    Series of Tempos 241, 245
    Tempo Change 241
    Time/Measures 285
Insert menuTempo Change 244
Insert-Bank/Patch Change 137, 138
Insert-Meter/Key Change 562
Insert-Meter/Key Changes 163
Insert-Time Measures 286
Instrument Definition Tutorial 582

Instrument definitions 569
    creating 573–581
    exporting 576
    importing 572–584
    name lists 576–577
    saving 576
Instrument sound
    choosing an 136
    parameter 130
    track settings 127
    wrong, on playback 646
    See also Instruments
Instruments
    accessing all sounds on 646
    assigning, to outputs 570–572
    bank assignments 577–578
    defining 573–576
    deleting 575
    non-concert key 142, 563–564
    patch names for 578–579
    problems recording from MIDI 643
    recording from MIDI 175
Instruments 571
Interpolate 142, 305, 309, 542
Interrupt request (IRQ) settings 29
Isolating 237

J

Joystick support 485
Jump 498

K

Key 561
    adjusting 141–142
    aftertouch 307
    signature 163–165, 561
Key Bindings 516

687

Key bindings 520
    creating using MIDI keyboard 522
    exporting 523
    importing 523
Key+ 130
KeyAft event 319
Keyboard
    connecting MIDI 25–26
    Local Control setting 147
    notes doubling on 647
    parameters 321
    patches 136–138
    recording accompaniments 192
Kilohertz 350

L

Large Transport toolbar 116
Latency 637
Layering synths
    live playback 146
Layouts 44, 513, 514–516
    creating 515
    deleting 516
    loading 515
    options 516
    renaming 516
    updating 515
Lead sheets *See* Notation and Lyrics
Length 289
LFE channel on consumer-grade sound
    cardsr 476
LFE Send level
    default value 483
Linked clips 228
    creating 228
    unlinking 228
Live MIDI playback
    controlling 144
Load Bank 594
Local Control 147
Locking views 43

Loop and Auto Shuttle 122
Loop Construction view 41, 252
Loop Explorer view 41, 256
Loop recording 184
    using 185
Loop/Auto Shuttle
    settings 122
    toolbar 122
Looping
    delays 144
    enabling loops for 259
    setting up 122–123
    using punch-in while 187
Loops 251
    ACIDized 260
    converting to Groove clips 262
    creating repetitions of 259
    dragging into project 258
    enabling looping of 259
    Groove clip tutorial 85
    previewing in Loop Explorer view 258
    working with 259
Low pass 374
Lyric event 320
Lyrics 565–568
    hyphenating 568
    in Lyrics View 567–568
    in Staff View 565–566
Lyrics view 42
    adding lyrics in 565
    editing lyrics in 565
    syllable 567

M

Mapped note
 changing the mapping of 343
 muting and soloing 344
Markers 44, 221
 adding 225
 adding on the fly 226
 copying 226
 creating 224–228
 deleting 227
 deleting from the Markers view 227
 editing 226
 jump to 227
 locking/unlocking 227
 moving 227
 pitch 266
 setting Now time with 118
 setting time range with 228
 snap-to grid 221
 using 224
Markers view 42
Marks 543
 expression 547–548
MBT (measure, beat and tick number) 114, 288, 549
MBT time
 entering 115
MCI (Media Control Interface) command 320, 325
MCIcmd event 320
Measure
 inserting a blank 285
Measures
 inserting 285
Meter 163, 560
Meter ballistics 440
Meter display 426
 changing 426

Meter/Key 163
 changes 163, 562–563
 view 42, 561
Meter/Key view 42
Metering
 changing the display of meters 436
 showing and hiding meters 436
 what the meters measure 436
Meters
 improving performance 440
 playback and record 425
Metronome 165
 audio 165
 changing settings 167
 setting for new project 166
 setting the 165–167
 using 165
Microphone
 connecting 26, 658
MIDI
 advantages of 24
 as remote control 454
 assigning a channel 141
 bank selection 137
 channel parameter 319
 channels 319
 choosing devices 136
 connecting keyboard 25–26
 converting MIDI to audio 429
 devices 134, 135, 611
 editing tutorial 74
 equipment connection 653–656
 how it works 24
 importing files 197–198
 input and echo controls 147
 key aftertouch 313
 machine control (MMC) 615–616
 messages
  controlling 121
  filtering 194
 mixing 428
 note parameters 536

689

note velocities 313
notes 539
Omni 171
output devices 134–136
outputs 134–136
pitch wheel 313
pitch-bend 313
playback settings 127–144
recording music from 175
routing data 134
setting up in and out devices 30
synchronization 604
synchronization status messages 606
time code 602
timing resolution 169
See also Controllers
MIDI controllers
  converting to shapes (track envelopes) 311, 499
MIDI data
  applying an event filter to 329
  applying echo/delay to 328
  applying the arpeggiator to 330
  quantizing 327
MIDI Devices 30, 135, 136, 606
MIDI Devices command 611
MIDI drivers
  changing 31
MIDI Echo
  turning on or off for all tracks 147
MIDI echo
  controlling 144
  Input Echo button 145
  multi-channels on one track 146
MIDI effects 325
  presets 326
MIDI equipment, connecting 653
MIDI files
  importing 197

MIDI Groove clips 267
  creating repetitions 268
  enabling groove function 268
  exporting and importing 269
  in Loop Explorer view 270
  previewing in the Import MIDI dialog 270
  transposing 268
  using pitch markers 269
MIDI In and Out devices
  driver changes 31
MIDI input filtering 194
MIDI input presets
  creating and editing 146, 194
MIDI keyboard
  multiple performers on multiple tracks 147
  playing multiple tracks from 146
MIDI notes
  editing using Note Inspector toolbar 274
MIDI playback
  live on multiple tracks 147
MIDI Sync 604
  status messages 606
  troubleshooting 608
  with drum machine 607
MIDI System Exclusive messages 587
MIDI THRU jack 654
MIDI Time Code
  sending and receiving 608
MIDI track parameters
  Input 128
  Outputs 128
  Pan 128
  track name 128
  track number 128
Mixer
  connecting to 659
Mixing
  controlling 433
  MIDI 428
  tracks 635
  tutorial 95

Mixing audio effects 388
    options 388
MME drivers
    compared to WDM drivers 638
Modules 421
Mono to Mono 388
Mono/Stereo buttons 127
MP3
    creating 98
MP3 files, creating and exporting 466
MPEG Video, importing 150
MPEX time/pitch stretch algorithm 396
MPU401
    can't find 652
MTC
    sending and receiving 608
Multi-channel MIDI recording 192
Multi-MIDI input 144
Multi-port DXi's 402
Musical Editing
    rests 538
Mute
    automating 512
Mute 125, 126
Mute 125
Mute button
    showing automated mute status 512
Mute buttons, grouping 449
Muting a DXi 407
Muting clips 234

N

Name, of a track 128, 130
Navigator view
    changing display of Clips pane using 213
    using 213
New features 673
New track
    adding 207
Newsgroups, Cakewalk xx
Next Marker 227

Next Marker 227
Next Measure 118
Non-destructive editing 291, 375
Normal template 163
Normalize 366, 367
Notation
    editing 531, 542
    non-concert key 563, 564
Notation and Lyrics 525
Note events 319
    transposing pitch of 284
Note Map pane 342
    previewing mapped sound in 342
Note names
    of patches 580–581
Note pane 276
Note velocities
    editing in the Drum Grid pane 341
Note velocity 283
    adjusting 142–143
    changing 332
    compressing 310
    displaying 313
    inverting 310
Notes 319
    changing display of 539–540
    changing properties of 279
    changing timing of 294
    doubling 647
    duration of 296
    editing 279, 533–535
    editing from the fretboard 555
    editing on the TAB staff 553
    editing, in real time 527
    erasing 280–281
    inserting 531
    inserting with the fretboard 532
    moving 280
    percussion 556
    properties of 536
    reversing 290

691

selecting 278, 533
selecting all of certain pitches 278
selecting and editing 277–281
size of 299
stuck 121, 144
transposing 141–142
using enharmonic spellings 541–542
Now Time
rewind on stop 117
Now time 44, 114, 118
changing 115
keyboard shortcuts 118
large print 117
NRPN (Non-Registered Parameter Number) 311, 312, 320
assigning, to instruments 581
data display 315
event 320
Nudge 218
moving clips left or right 218
moving clips up or down 219
settings 219
Number, of a track 130

O

Offset mode 504
OMF
exporting to 467
project data discarded when saved as 468
project data preserved in 468
saving projects as 467
Online Help xx
Options menu
Audio 169, 629
Colors 45
Colors 45
Drum Map Manager 336
Global 162, 366
Instruments 571
Key Bindings 516
MIDI Devices 30, 135, 136, 606

Project 167, 169
Outputs 130
assigning tracks to 136
MIDI 135
setting 134
Overlap Ratio 396
Overlapping clips
cropping to eliminate overlap 234
Overload 176
Overtones 351

P

Pan 130
adjusting 139
envelopes 501
setting 433
track settings 130
Pane 276
Pane, Staff 526
Panning in surround 479
Panning laws
changing 140
Parameters
chorus 390–391
effects 445
events 307, 310
filter 389
global 518
parametric equalization 374–375
pedal events 549
pitch 395
reverb 394
template file 518–519
Time/Pitch stretch 395–397
See also Events
Parametric EQ 374–375
parametric equalization 389–390
Partial clips
selecting 35

Patch 130, 136–138, 319
   assigning note names to 580–581
   assigning to a track 137
   event 319
   names 578–579
   numbers 307
Patch/Controller Searchback Before Play Starts 144
Patches
   downloading 641
Pattern Brush tool 345
   creating custom patterns for 347
   how it works 345
   painting a custom pattern with 346
   painting notes using 346
Pattern-based Step Recording 191
Patterns
   importing from Project5 271
Pedal events 543
   editing 550
   parameters 549
Pedal marks
   adding 549
Percentage
   audio scaling by 256, 359
Percussion
   channel 142
   ghost strokes 559
   line 557–559
   staff 557–559
   tracks 557
Percussion track
   setting up 557
Performance
   CPU, with FX effects 448
   improving audio 627
   maximizing disk and CPU 635
Per-project audio folders 621
Per-track EQ
   using 446
Phase
   inverting a track's 126

Piano Roll 315
Piano Roll envelopes
   converting to Track view envelopes 311, 499
Piano Roll toolbar 312
Piano Roll view 39, 273, 275
   Controllers pane 276, 315
   Drum Grid pane 276
   editing notes in 276–277
   editing notes in using Note Inspector toolbar 274
   Note Map pane 275
   note names in 578
   Note pane 276
   opening 276
   overview 39
   Track List pane 276
Piano Roll view envelopes
   converting to Track view shapes 317
Pitch
   changing a MIDI note's 279
   enabling Groove clips to follow 264
   fluctuating 613
   note property 536
   selecting 278
   shifting 395
   stretching 388, 395–397
Pitch markers
   creating 267
   MIDI Groove clips and 269
   moving 267
   transposing Groove clips with 266
   using 266
Pitch wheel 313
   parameters 319
Pitch-bend
   data display 315
Play 121
Play List 148
   to play files from 149

Playback 628–630
    audio drop-out during 634
    controlling 120, 428, 433, 612
    controlling using transport toolbar 44
    incorrect 628–630
    problems 630, 641–642
    settings, MIDI 127–144
    speed 608
    starting 121
    stopping 121
    track-by-track 124–126
    transmitting banks 595
Playback loop
    cancelling 123
    setting up 123
Playback State toolbar 125
playing 405
Plug-ins
    audio 386
    DXi 399
    MIDI 325
Plug-ins and 96 kHz audio 640
Polarity
    inverting a track's 126
Port Address settings 29
Ports
    assigning instruments to 571–572
Pow-r dithering 468
PPQ, see timebase 169
Preamp output
    connecting to 658
Preferences
    migrating from previous version of Cakewalk 28
Preferred interleave 127
Pressure value 307
Previewing MIDI Groove clips
    in Import MIDI dialog 270
Previous Marker 227
Previous Marker 227
Previous Measure 118
Printing

event list 323
    markers 225
    project information 200
    scores 559
Process-Apply Audio Effects
    applying realtime audio effects using 387
Process-Apply MIDI Effects
    apply realtime MIDI effects using 448
Process-Audio-3dB Louder
    boosting audio data volume using 367
Process-Audio-3dB Quieter
    reducing audio data volume using 367
Process-Audio-Apply Audio Effects
    apply multiple realtime effects using 448
Process-Audio-Crossfade
    creating a destructive crossfade using 386
Process-Audio-Extract Timing
    calculating tempo of audio using 373
Process-Audio-Fade/Envelope
    creating a destructive fade using 385
Process-Audio-Graphic EQ
    equalizing audio with 368
Process-Audio-Normalize 367
Process-Audio-Parametric EQ
    equalizing audio with 375
Process-Audio-Remove Silence 371
Process-Audio-Reverse
    playing audio backwards using 368
Process-Deglitch
    filtering MIDI data with 538
Process-Fit Improvisation 241, 304–305
Process-Fit to Time 288
Process-Fit to Time 241
Process-Groove Quantize
    using 299
Process-Interpolate 309
Process-Length
    shrinking events using 288
    stretching events using 288
Process-Quantize
    using 298
Process-Retrograde

694

reversing MIDI notes using 290
Process-Scale Velocity 290
Process-Slide
   shifting MIDI events in time using 285
Project
   creating a 161
   definition of 31
   importing material from another 196, 197–198
   information 199–200
   inserting measures into 285–287
   labeling 199–200
   opening 28, 33
   saving 199
   views 514
Project 167, 169
Project file 31
   creating new 162
Project Files dialog 618
   using 618
Project information
   diplaying 200
   editing 200
Project Options 603
   metronome 165
   MIDI out 144
   sync to SMPTE/MTC 611
   time base 169
Project pitch
   changing the default pitch 267
Project5
   importing patterns from 271
Project5 patterns
   importing 271
Projects
   working on 44
Property-Bank 138
Property-Channel 141
Property-Inputs 192, 193
Property-Key+ 142
Property-Pan 140

Property-Patch 138
Property-Time+ 143
Property-Vel+ 143
Property-Volume 139
Punch recording 185
   looping 187
   using 186

Q

Quantize
   effect 327
   offset option 299
   synchronizing rhythm and solo tracks with 303
   using 298
   Window setting 297
Quantize 294, 538
Queue buffers 638
Quick freeze 441
Quick TAB
   creating 552
Quick unfreeze 441
QuickTime video, importing 150

R

Radio tuner
   connecting to 658
Real Audio files, creating and exporting 460
Record 175, 178, 185, 188
Record
   audio 178
   MIDI 175
Record Mode 170, 615
Record Options 185, 187
Record Options 171

Recording
    Arming tracks for 174
    arming tracks for 174
    at low sampling rate 636
    audio 175
        choosing an input 171
        definition
        troubleshooting 644
    automation 496
    background noise in 175–176
    changing timing of 294, 304
    channel-by-channel 192
    checking input levels 177
    checking levels 175
    confidence 179
    controlling using Transport toolbar 44
    converting MIDI to audio 429
    digital audio *See* Recording audio
    eliminating echo 649
    erasing 178
    inputs 171
    loop 184–185, 186–188
    MIDI 175
    modes 170
    problems 643, 645
    punch-in 185–188
    specifying MIDI ports and channels to record by 192
    step 188–192
    step-pattern 191–192
    using confidence recording during 179
    volume 175
Recording a DXi 407
Recording Digital Audio
    tutorial 68
Recording fader movements 496
Recording MIDI
    tutorial 61
Recording modes
    Auto Punch 170
    Overwrite 170
    Sound on sound 170

Redo 249–250
Reject Loop Take 185, 188
Reject Loop Take 185
Relink surround effect 490
Remote control 454
Remove Silence
    Attack time 370
Remove Silence 369
    digital noise gate parameters 370
Reset 121
Resolution, quantizing parameter 295
Rests, beaming of 538
Retrograde 290
Reverb 394
Reverse 290, 368
Rewind 121
ReWire
    automating ReWire instruments 414
    inserting a ReWire instrument 412
    mixing down and bouncing ReWire instruments 414
    to use separate audio tracks 413
    troubleshooting guide 414
ReWire instruments 410
Riff Wave files
    saving a Groove clip as 266
RPN (Registered Parameter Numbers)
    event 319
RPNs (Registered Parameter Numbers) 311, 312, 319
    assigning, to instruments 581
    data display 315

S

Safe Mode 651
Sample rate
   definition 354
   setting 168, 169
Sample rates
   converting 633
   importing audio at different rates 634
Sampling rate
   setting 169
Sampling resolution 355
Save Bank 594
Save options 198
   bundle file 198
   Standard MIDI 198
Saving
   projects as OMF files 467
Saving a project 199
Scale Velocity 142, 291
Scissors tool
   splitting clips with 363
Scores, printing 559
Scoring
   film and video 23
Screen colors 45–46
Scrub tool 281, 365
   auditioning with 357
   locating bad note with 277
Search 305, 308
Search Again 308
Search Nex 305
Select All Siblings 228, 230
Select by Filter 305
Select by Filter 305, 308–309
Select by Time 221
Select None 221
Selection playback 237
Sensitivity setting
   quantizing parameter 297
Series of Controllers 314, 316

Series of Controllers
   inserting 316
Series of Tempos 244, 245
   inserting 241, 245
Set End=Current 453
Set Start=Current 453
Settings
   migrating from previous version of Cakewalk 28
Shapes 498
Show Automated Mute 512
Show layers 232
Silence
   removing 369–371
Silencing tracks 125–126
Slaving to SMPTE/MTC 611
Slide 285
Slip editing 291, 375
   modes 291, 376
      scroll-trimming 292, 376
      slide trimming 291, 376
      trimming 291, 376
   multiple clips 293, 379
   to permanently delete slip-edited data 293, 379
   using 292, 376
Slip-editing
   multiple clips 379
SMPTE 114, 288
SMPTE Synchronization
   frame rate 608
SMPTE/MTC Sync 608–614
   controlling audio with 612
   digital audio under 612
   troubleshooting 614
   with full chase lock 613
Snap Grid *See* Snap to Grid
Snap offsets 224
Snap to Grid 222–223
   enabling and disabling 223

Snapshots
  creating 506
Soft Synths
  tutorial 100
Soft synths
  kinds 400
Software synthesizers 399
  and WDM drivers 405
  DX instruments 399
  DXi 399
  playing a DXi 405
  recording a hardware-emulating synth 416
  removing from a track 406
Solo 126
Soloing a DXi 407
Soloing clips 234, 237
SONAR
  as master 606–607
  as slave 605–606
  basics 31
  features of 21–23
  installing 25, 26
  sync to SMPTE/MTC 611
  uninstalling 27
  using 46
Songs
  quantizing 297
  title 199
Sort 205
Sound card
  built-in 630
  high-end 630
Sound controls 421–423
Source Material 396
Split 232, 363
Splitting clips 230
  using Scissors tool 363
Staff pane 526
  changing layout of 529

Staff view 321, 525, 526
  changing layout of 527
  editing lyrics in 567–568
  opening 527
  overview 40
Staff, percussion 556–559
Start time 279
Status bar 639
Step Record 191
Step Record 189
Step Recording 188
  Auto Advance option 189
  Pattern option 191
  settings 189
  using 189
  using pattern-based 191
Step size 189
Stop 121, 175, 178, 185, 187, 188
Strength, quantizing parameter 296, 299
Striping 608
Stuck note, stopping 121
Surround effects 488
Surround front/rear balance slider 482
Surround Main 475
Surround mix parameters
  saving as presets 475
Surround mixes
  exporting 492
  importing 491
Surround mixing 471
Surround panner controls
  grouping 483
Surround panning 479
  automating 485
SurroundBridge 488
Swing 297, 299
Synchronization 601–616
  problems 629–630
  SMPTE/MTC sync 608
  status messages 606

698

types of 602–604
Synth Rack 402
Synth Rack view 400
Synthesizer
　DXi 399
　patches 136–138
　software 630
　with handshaking dump protocols 592
System Exclusive *See* Sysx
System sounds
　turning off 120
Sysx 587–599
　　　Dump Request Macros 592
　defined 588
　editing Sysx banks 593
　events 588
　importing, creating, and dumping sysx banks 590
　ini file settings 597
　Receive 593
　recording Sysx messages in real time 596
　sending sysx banks at startup 589
　Sysx echo 596
　Sysx view buttons 593
　to export a Sysx bank to another project 595
　transmitting banks during playback 595
　transmitting before playback 594
　transmitting during playback 595
　troubleshooting 598
　using the system exclusive view 588
Sysx Bank 588
Sysx Bank events 320, 588
Sysx Banks
　transmitting, during playback 595
Sysx banks
　auto send 594
　deleting 594
　Edit Bytes 594
　naming 594
　output 594

Receive 593
Send 593
Send All 593
Sysx Data 588
　in Event list 320
Sysx Data events 588
Sysx view 42, 587
　opening 588
　purpose of 42
　using 588–595

T

TAB
　saving as ASCII text 555
Tablature
　defining a style 551
　editing 554
　exporting as an ASCII text file 555
　generating 552
　Quick TAB 552
　regenerating 553
　saving as an ASCII text file 555
　settings 550
Take management 232
Taskbar indicators 45
Technical support xx
Templates 513, 517–520
　creating 519
Tempo
　changing 241, 243, 294
　correcting 304
　decreasing steadily 247
　drawing tempo changes 246
　editing a change 249
　erasing changes 248
　error 305
　increasing steadily 247
　inserting a change 244, 247
　inserting a series 245
　modifying the most recent change 245
　ratio 243

699

setting for new project 166
setting the 165–167
settings 165
view 246–248
Tempo Change 241, 244
Tempo commands
  using 244
Tempo view 42
Text 320
Text event 320
Thru 118
Time
  chord property 544
  event 288
  inserting blank 285–287
  MBT 114, 115
  note property 536
  pedal event parameter 549
  SMPTE 114, 116
  stretching 388, 395–397
  See also Markers; Now time
Time
  setting Now Time using 118
Time Display Format
  setting 152
Time offset (Time+) parameter 130, 143
Time ranges 222
  selecting 35
Time Ruler 119
  Loop Construction view 262
  setting to display SMPTE 119
Time ruler
  setting to display HMSF 119
Time signature 560
  setting 163, 164
Time+ 130
Time/Measures 285
Time/Pitch Stretch
  Pitch parameter 396
Time/Pitch Stretch 395

Timebase 169, 560
  setting 169
Timer Ruler
  setting to display MBT 119
Timing
  aligning 303
  errors 294
  extracting from audio 371
  resolution 169
Tools menu
  Clean Audio Folder 625, 626
  Consolidate Project Audio 625
Track
  current 144
  Show Automated Mute 512
Track folders 238
Track input 130
Track menu
  Archive 126
  Clone 208
  Delete 208
  Mute 125
  Property-Bank 138
  Property-Channel 141
  Property-Inputs 192, 193
  Property-Key+ 142
  Property-Pan 140
  Property-Patch 138
  Property-Time+ 143
  Property-Vel+ 143
  Property-Volume 139
  Solo 126
  Sort 205
  Wipe 208
Track name 128, 130
Track number 130
Track output 130
Track outputs 130
Track pane
  changing values in 133
  resizing 131

Track Properties
   channel 557
   Key+ 141
   output 134, 136, 557
   See also Tracks
Track *See* Tracks
Track status
   archive 124
   mute 124
   normal 124
   solo 124
Track view 33–35, 203
   adding effects in 139, 240
   bank settings in 136
   clips pane not visible in 647
   keyboard shortcuts in 34
   patch settings in 136
Track/Bus Inspector 35
Tracks 648
   adding lyrics to 565–566
   aligning 303
   archiving 126, 635
   arming 174, 433
   arranging 204
   assigning input channels and ports 193
   assigning to outputs 136
   bouncing 456
   changing the order of 205
   changing velocity of
   cloning 208
   copying 204, 208
   correcting off-tempo 304
   deleting 204
   deleting contents 208
   dragging to a new position 205
   editing properties of 134
   erasing 208
   increasing number of 425, 635
   inserting blank 207
   maximum number of audio 635
   mixing 635
   multi-lane 232
   muting 125, 433
   output devices of 134–136
   parameters of 128–134
   patch change in 137–138
   percussion 556–559
   recording in separate 192
   re-ordering 205–207
   selecting several adjacent 204
   selecting single 204
   setting channels for 141
   setting key offset of 142
   setting time offset of 143
   silencing 125–126
   soloing 126, 433
   sort by archived 205
   sort by channel 205
   sort by muted 205
   sort by name 205
   sort by port 205
   sort by selected 205
   sort by size 205
   sorting 205–207
   synchronizing 303
   time alignment of 143
   track folders 238
   transposing 141–142
   unarchiving 126
   unmuting 125
   viewing multiple in Piano Roll 282
   volume control of 139
   wiping 208
   See also Recording; Track Properties
Transport
   Record Options 171
   Reject Loop Take 185
Transport menu
   Loop and Auto Shuttle 122
   Play 121
   Record 175, 178
   Reset 121
   Rewind 121
   Step Record 189

Step Record 191
Stop 121
Transport toolbar 44
  Large 116
Transpose 141, 284, 533
Transposing 284
  notes 141–142
  parameter 130
Trigger and freewheel 612
Trim Durations 539
Triplets 538
Troubleshooting 641
  I can't open my project 651
  MIDI Sync 608
  no volume despite maximum envelope level 645
  SMPTE/MTC Sync 614
  Sysx 598–599
  Sysx data 598–599
  Wavetable synth and/or MPU401 missing 652
Tutorial
  Instrument Definition 582
Tutorial 1
  The Basics 48
Tutorial 10
  Cyclone DXi 108
Tutorial 2
  Recording MIDI 61
Tutorial 3
  Recording Digital Audio tutorial 68
Tutorial 4
  Editing MIDI 74
Tutorial 5
  Editing Audio 81
Tutorial 6
  Using Groove clips 85
Tutorial 7
  Mixing 95
Tutorial 8
  Drum maps 104

Tutorial 9
  Using Soft Synths 100

U

Unarchiving tracks 126
Undo 249
Undo History 249–250
Unfreeze 441
Uninstalling SONAR 27
Unlink surround effect 489
Updates 641
USB audio
  24 bit problems 648

V

Vel+ 130, 142–143
Velocity 307, 324, 536
  adjusting note 142–143
  compressing 310
  data display 313, 315
  inverting 310
  note 142–143, 296, 324
  note property 536
  parameter 130, 319
  setting 290–291
  See also Note velocity
Velocity tails
  displaying in the Drum Grid pane 341
Video
  deleting from a project 151
  disabling playback of 152
  enabling playback of 152
  exporting 153
  inserting in a project 151
  setting start time 153
  setting trim time 153
Video display format
  setting 152
Video playback
  stuttering problem 151
Video Playback, Import, and Export 150

Video thumbnails 154
Video view
    setting background color of 153
View options
    display clip names 211
Views 33–44
    allowing multiple instances of the same 43
    Event List 318
    floating 44, 517
    Fretboard 526
    Loop Construction 252
    Loop Explorer 256
    Lyrics 42, 525, 566–567
    Markers 42
    Meter/Key 42, 525, 560–563
    PianoRoll 275
    Play List 148, 150
    Staff 526
    Synth Rack 400
    Sysx 42, 588–595
    Tempo 42, 246
    Video 150
Volume
    adjusting 139
    changing audio data 386
    envelopes 501
    faders 449
    output 436
    recording 175–176
    setting 433
    track settings 130
VST instruments and plug-ins
    using 417

W

Wallpaper 45–46
Wave Audio event 320
Wave Device Profiler 628–630
    errors 649

Wave files
    creating and exporting 462
    how to export 462
    importing 195
Wave Profiler
    using 29
Waveform
    zooming in on 359
Waveform preview
    turning off 179
Waveforms 352–354
    clipped 355
    to not display while recording 179
Wavetable synth
    troubleshooting 652
WDM drivers
    compared to MME drivers 638
    improving audio performance 627, 628
    playing soft synths in real time 400
Wet Mix 395
Wheel event 319
Window
    Sensitivity 297, 298
Windows
    system sounds, turning off 120
Window-Tile in Rows 514
Wipe 208
Wipe 208
World Wide Web xx
    authoring 23
    Cakewalk site xx
    publishing audio on 459–467

703

Z

Zero Controllers When Play Stops 144
Zero-crossings 354
Zoom
    keyboard shortcuts 43
Zoom Controls 42
Zoom factor
    audio scaling by 256, 359
Zooming
    configuring the display of tracks in the Track view 207
    entire project 207

TWELVE TONE SYSTEMS, INC.
d/b/a CAKEWALK
LICENSE AGREEMENT

YOU SHOULD CAREFULLY READ ALL OF THE FOLLOWING TERMS AND CONDITIONS BEFORE USING THIS PRODUCT. INSTALLING AND USING THE PRODUCT INDICATES YOUR ACCEPTANCE OF THESE TERMS AND CONDITIONS. IF YOU DO NOT AGREE WITH THEM, YOU SHOULD PROMPTLY RETURN THE PRODUCT UNUSED AND YOUR MONEY WILL BE REFUNDED.

1. GRANT OF LICENSE. In consideration of payment of the license fee, Twelve Tone Systems, Inc., d/b/a Cakewalk ("Cakewalk" or the "Licensor") grants to you, the Licensee, a nonexclusive license to have one person use the enclosed Cakewalk software product (the "Product") on one personal computer at a time. If you want to use the Product on more than one personal computer at a time, or if you want to network the Product, you must obtain separate licenses from Cakewalk by calling (617) 423-9004. This license does not grant you any right to any enhancement or update to the Product. Enhancements and updates, if available, may be obtained by you at Cakewalk's then current standard pricing, terms and conditions.

2. OWNERSHIP OF THE PRODUCT. Portions of the Product incorporate certain material proprietary to third parties. Cakewalk and licensors of Cakewalk own and will retain all title, copyright, trademark and other proprietary rights in and to the Product. This License is NOT a sale of the Product or any copy of it. You, the Licensee, obtain only such rights as are provided in this Agreement. You understand and agree as follows:

2.1. You may NOT make any copies of all or any part of the Product except for archival copies of the computer software components of the Product as permitted by law;

2.2. You may NOT reverse compile, reverse assemble, reverse engineer, modify, incorporate in whole or in part in any other product or create derivative works based on all or any part of the Product.

2.3. You may NOT remove any copyright, trademark, proprietary rights, disclaimer or warning notice included on or embedded in any part of the Product.

2.4. You may NOT transfer the Product. If transferred, the original and subsequent owners forfeit all rights to use the software.

2.5 You may not use the documentation for any purpose other than to support your use of the SOFTWARE PRODUCT.

2.6 You may not perform engineering analyses of the SOFTWARE PRODUCT, including performance analyses, or benchmark analyses, without the written permission of Cakewalk.

3. CONTENT RESTRICTIONS. Unless specified elsewhere in your product package, the following restrictions apply to all digitally recorded sounds, MIDI or Cakewalk-format song files or rhythm patterns, and printed or digitally reproduced sheet music contained in the product package (the "content"):

> All content is protected by copyright and owned by Cakewalk or other parties that have licensed these works to Cakewalk.
>
> Any duplication, adaptation, or arrangement of the content without written consent of the owner is an infringement of U.S. or foreign copyright law and subject to the penalties and liabilities provided therein.
>
> You may not synchronize the content with any videotape or film, or print the content in the form of standard music notation, without the express written permission of the copyright owner.
>
> The content may not be used for broadcast or transmission of any kind.
>
> You may not resell or redistribute the content "as is" (i.e., stand alone) in any way, including for use in sampling or sample playback units, or in any sound library product, or in any radio or television broadcast, soundtrack, film or other commercial product in any media, whether the works remain in their original form or are reformatted, mixed, filtered, re-synthesized or otherwise edited.

4. LICENSEE'S RESPONSIBILITIES FOR SELECTION AND USE OF THE PRODUCT. Cakewalk hopes the Product will be useful to your business or personal endeavors. HOWEVER, CAKEWALK DOES NOT WARRANT THE OPERATION OF THE PRODUCT OR THE ACCURACY OR COMPLETENESS OF ANY INFORMATION CONTAINED IN THE PRODUCT. You, and not Cakewalk, are responsible for all uses of the Product.

5. WARRANTY.

5.1. Limited Warranty. Subject to the other provisions in Articles 4 and 5 of this Agreement, Cakewalk warrants to you, the original licensee, that the media on which the Product is recorded will be free of defects in material and workmanship under normal use for a period of thirty (30) days from purchase, and that the Product will perform substantially in accordance with the user guide for a period of thirty (30) days from purchase. Cakewalk's sole responsibility under this warranty will be, at its option, (1) to use reasonable efforts to correct any defects that are reported to it within the foregoing warranty period or (2) to refund the full purchase price. Cakewalk does not warrant that the Product will be error free, nor that all program errors will be corrected. In addition, Cakewalk makes no warranties if the failure of the Product results from accident, abuse or misapplication. Outside the United States, these remedies are not available without proof of purchase from an authorized international source. All requests for warranty assistance shall be directed to Cakewalk at the following address:

Cakewalk
268 Summer st.
Boston, MA 02210 U.S.A.
617 423-9004

5.2. Limitations on Warranties. THE EXPRESS WARRANTY SET FORTH IN THIS ARTICLE 4 IS THE ONLY WARRANTY GIVEN BY CAKEWALK WITH RESPECT TO THE ENTIRE PRODUCT; CAKEWALK MAKES NO OTHER WARRANTIES, EXPRESS, IMPLIED OR ARISING BY CUSTOM OR TRADE USAGE, AND SPECIFICALLY DISCLAIMS THE IMPLIED WARRANTIES OF NON-INFRINGEMENT, MERCHANTABILITY OR FITNESS FOR ANY PARTICULAR PURPOSE. CAKE-WALK SHALL NOT BE HELD RESPONSIBLE FOR THE PERFORMANCE OF THE PRODUCT NOR FOR ANY LIABILITY TO ANY OTHER PARTY ARISING OUT OF USE OF THE PRODUCT.

SOME STATES DO NOT ALLOW LIMITATIONS ON HOW LONG AN IMPLIED WARRANTY LASTS, SO THE ABOVE LIMITATION MAY NOT APPLY TO YOU. THIS WARRANTY GIVES YOU SPECIFIC LEGAL RIGHTS, AND YOU MAY ALSO HAVE OTHER RIGHTS WHICH VARY FROM STATE TO STATE.

6. LIMITATIONS ON REMEDIES. Cakewalk's liability in contract, tort or otherwise arising in connection with the Product shall not exceed the purchase price of the Product. IN NO EVENT SHALL CAKE-WALK BE LIABLE FOR SPECIAL, INCIDENTAL, TORT OR CONSEQUENTIAL DAMAGES (INCLUDING ANY DAMAGES RESULTING FROM LOSS OF USE, LOSS OF DATA, LOSS OF PROF-ITS OR LOSS OF BUSINESS) ARISING OUT OF OR IN CONNECTION WITH THE PERFORMANCE OF THE PRODUCT, EVEN IF CAKEWALK HAS BEEN ADVISED OF THE POSSIBILITY OF SUCH DAMAGES.

SOME STATES DO NOT ALLOW THE EXCLUSION OR LIMITATION OF INCIDENTAL OR CONSE-QUENTIAL DAMAGES SO THE ABOVE EXCLUSION OR LIMITATION MAY NOT APPLY TO YOU.

7. U.S. GOVERNMENT RESTRICTED RIGHTS. If you are a government agency, you acknowledge that the Product was developed at private expense and that the computer software component is provided to you subject to RESTRICTED RIGHTS. The rights of the government regarding its use, duplication, reproduction or disclosure by the Government is subject to the restrictions set forth in subparagraph (c)(1)(ii) of the rights in Technical Data and Computer Software clause at DFARS 252.227-7013, and (c)(1) and (2) of the Commercial Computer Software -- Restricted Rights clause at FAR 52.227-19. Con-tractor is Twelve Tone Systems, Inc., d/b/a Cakewalk.

8. TERMINATION. This License Agreement will terminate immediately if you breach any of its terms. Upon termination, you will be required promptly to return to Cakewalk or to destroy all copies of the Product covered by this License Agreement.

9. MISCELLANEOUS.

9.1. Governing Law. The terms of this License shall be construed in accordance with the substantive laws of the United States and/or Commonwealth of Massachusetts, U.S.A.

9.2. No Waiver. The failure of either party to enforce any rights granted hereunder or to take any action against the other party in the event of any breach hereunder shall not be deemed a waiver by that party as to subsequent enforcement of rights or subsequent actions in the event of future breaches.

9.3. Litigation Expenses. If any action is brought by either party to this Agreement against the other party regarding the subject matter hereof, the prevailing party shall be entitled to recover, in addition to any other relief granted, reasonable attorneys' fees and litigation expenses.

9.4. Unenforceable Terms. Should any term of this License Agreement be declared void or unenforceable by any court of competent jurisdiction, such declaration shall have no effect on the remaining terms hereof.

9.5. Certain components of this software are the property of Progressive Networks and its suppliers. You are not allowed to distribute these DLLs to others.

YOU ACKNOWLEDGE THAT YOU HAVE READ THIS LICENSE AGREEMENT, UNDERSTAND IT AND AGREE TO BE BOUND BY ITS TERMS AND CONDITIONS. YOU FURTHER AGREE THAT IT IS THE COMPLETE AND EXCLUSIVE STATEMENT OF THE LICENSE AGREEMENT BETWEEN YOU AND CAKEWALK WHICH SUPERSEDES ANY PROPOSALS, OR PRIOR AGREEMENT, ORAL OR WRITTEN, AND ANY OTHER COMMUNICATIONS BETWEEN YOU AND CAKEWALK RELAT-ING TO THE SUBJECT MATTER OF THIS LICENSE AGREEMENT.